(Continued on back endsheets)

Eighteenth-Century British Poets
First Series

Dictionary of Literary Biography • Volume Ninety-five

Eighteenth-Century British Poets
First Series

Edited by
John Sitter
Emory University

A Bruccoli Clark Layman Book
Gale Research Inc.
Detroit, New York, London

Manufactured by Edwards Brothers, Inc.
Ann Arbor, Michigan
Printed in the United States of America

Copyright © 1990
Gale Research Inc.
835 Penobscot Bldg.
Detroit, MI 48226-4094

ISBN 0-8103-4575-7
90-3500 CIP

Contents

Plan of the Series

The advisory board, the editors, and the publisher of the *Dictionary of Literary Biography* are joined in endorsing Mark Twain's declaration. The literature of a nation provides an inexhaustible resource of permanent worth. We intend to make literature and its creators better understood and more accessible to students and the reading public, while satisfying the standards of teachers and scholars.

To meet these requirements, *literary biography* has been construed in terms of the author's achievement. The most important thing about a writer is his writing. Accordingly, the entries in *DLB* are career biographies, tracing the development of the author's canon and the evolution of his reputation.

The purpose of *DLB* is not only to provide reliable information in a convenient format but also to place the figures in the larger perspective of literary history and to offer appraisals of their accomplishments by qualified scholars.

The publication plan for *DLB* resulted from two years of preparation. The project was proposed to Bruccoli Clark by Frederick G. Ruffner, president of the Gale Research Company, in November 1975. After specimen entries were prepared and typeset, an advisory board was formed to refine the entry format and develop the series rationale. In meetings held during 1976, the publisher, series editors, and advisory board approved the scheme for a comprehensive biographical dictionary of persons who contributed to North American literature. Editorial work on the first volume began in January 1977, and it was published in 1978. In order to make *DLB* more than a reference tool and to compile volumes that individually have claim to status as literary history, it was decided to organize volumes by topic, period, or genre. Each of these freestanding volumes provides a biographical-bibliographical guide and overview for a particular area of literature. We are convinced that this organization—as opposed to a single alphabet method—constitutes a valuable innovation in the presentation of reference material. The volume plan necessarily requires many decisions for the placement and treatment of authors who might properly be included in two or three volumes. In some instances a major figure will be included in separate volumes, but with different entries emphasizing the aspect of his career appropriate to each volume. Ernest Hemingway, for example, is represented in *American Writers in Paris, 1920-1939* by an entry focusing on his expatriate apprenticeship; he is also in *American Novelists, 1910-1945* with an entry surveying his entire career. Each volume includes a cumulative index of subject authors and articles. Comprehensive indexes to the entire series are planned.

With volume ten in 1982 it was decided to enlarge the scope of *DLB*. By the end of 1986 twenty-one volumes treating British literature had been published, and volumes for Commonwealth and Modern European literature were in progress. The series has been further augmented by the *DLB Yearbooks* (since 1981) which update published entries and add new entries to keep the *DLB* current with contemporary activity. There have also been *DLB Documentary Series* volumes which provide biographical and critical source materials for figures whose work is judged to have particular interest for students. One of these companion volumes is entirely devoted to Tennessee Williams.

We define literature as the *intellectual commerce of a nation:* not merely as belles lettres but as that ample and complex process by which ideas are generated, shaped, and transmitted. *DLB* entries are not limited to "creative writers" but extend to other figures who in their time and in their way influenced the mind of a people. Thus the series encompasses historians, journalists, publishers, and screenwriters. By this means readers of *DLB* may be aided to perceive litera-

---

ture not as cult scripture in the keeping of intellectual high priests but firmly positioned at the center of a nation's life.

DLB includes the major writers appropriate to each volume and those standing in the ranks immediately behind them. Scholarly and critical counsel has been sought in deciding which minor figures to include and how full their entries should be. Wherever possible, useful references are made to figures who do not warrant separate entries.

Each *DLB* volume has a volume editor responsible for planning the volume, selecting the figures for inclusion, and assigning the entries. Volume editors are also responsible for preparing, where appropriate, appendices surveying the major periodicals and literary and intellectual movements for their volumes, as well as lists of further readings. Work on the series as a whole is coordinated at the Bruccoli Clark Layman editorial center in Columbia, South Carolina, where the editorial staff is responsible for accuracy of the published volumes.

One feature that distinguishes *DLB* is the illustration policy–its concern with the iconography of literature. Just as an author is influenced by his surroundings, so is the reader's understanding of the author enhanced by a knowledge of his environment. Therefore *DLB* volumes include not only drawings, paintings, and photographs of authors, often depicting them at various stages in their careers, but also illustrations of their families and places where they lived. Title pages are regularly reproduced in facsimile along with dust jackets for modern authors. The dust jackets are a special feature of *DLB* because they often document better than anything else the way in which an author's work was perceived in its own time. Specimens of the writers' manuscripts are included when feasible.

Samuel Johnson rightly decreed that "The chief glory of every people arises from its authors." The purpose of the *Dictionary of Literary Biography* is to compile literary history in the surest way available to us–by accurate and comprehensive treatment of the lives and work of those who contributed to it.

The *DLB* Advisory Board

Foreword

The essays in this volume and its companion, *Eighteenth-Century British Poets, Second Series* (scheduled for publication in 1991), relate the works and lives of forty-nine poets who wrote and published in the eighteenth century. Since even this selection of the century's poets requires two volumes, the arbitrary if symbolic year of the death of Queen Anne forms a dividing line; thus, the eighteenth-century poets born by 1714 appear in the present volume, to be followed by those born under the Georges.

But if this chronological division is an invention whose parent is necessity, so too are the starting and stopping points for "eighteenth-century" poetry as a whole. While there are many arguments about the utility and identity of literary periods, one point of agreement is that such periods do not simplify life for historians by neatly beginning or ending at years such as 1700 or 1800. The adjective "eighteenth-century" is therefore to be understood as more convenient than conceptual. This neutrally chronological usage is becoming more common in criticism and scholarship of the period. One hears less now of terms such as "neoclassical" or "Augustan"–and certainly less of the "Age of Reason"–as labels implying common poetic principles for much or all of the eighteenth century or for the long period from 1660 to 1798. It has become increasingly difficult to assert that the writers of this period were conspicuously more committed to imitating and emulating Roman classicism than were most of the writers of earlier eras, that they idealized the Rome of Augustus Caesar, or that they agreed in believing "reason" either could or should predominate in poetry–or in life.

In place of the view that eighteenth-century poets were all preoccupied with reason, rules, and restraints, the emphasis in recent criticism has begun to fall with some regularity on the exuberance, the daring, and simply the diversity of the century's poetry. This last emphasis, at least, seems likely to strengthen as familiar figures are reconsidered and lesser-known writers are rediscovered or, in some cases, virtually discovered for the first time. The canon of eighteenth-

century poetry may not shift radically, but some changes are in view. For example, the *New Oxford Book of Eighteenth Century Verse* (1984), finely edited by Roger Lonsdale, does not merely give selections from the standard authors but also includes several writers who had not been reprinted since the eighteenth century, and its influence is already being felt. One impetus for resurveying the landscape comes from feminist criticism and more inclusive social history. Eleven of the authors discussed in these two volumes are women. Some of their names will be familiar to some readers, but perhaps within recent years just one–Anne Finch, Countess of Winchilsea–would have seemed an inevitable presence in such volumes. Lonsdale's more recent Oxford collection, *Eighteenth-Century Women Poets* (1989), will undoubtedly further discussion of many more women of the period.

The majority of the poets included here have appeared, of course, in standard collections from the late eighteenth century on. Alexander Pope remains the presiding genius of the century; and other familiar names remain at least that for readers of English poetry today: Jonathan Swift, John Gay, Matthew Prior, James Thomson, William Collins, Thomas Gray, Samuel Johnson, Thomas Chatterton, Christopher Smart, William Cowper, and Robert Burns. Parading side by side–"promiscuously," an eighteenth-century speaker would have said–in these volumes are also many unknown or barely known poets. If the omission of some minor writers disappoints some specialists, I hope they will be agreeably surprised by unexpected appearances here or there.

Reviewing this poetic parade, a reader may be struck by the sheer variety of eighteenth-century styles, forms, and themes. Politics, love, and religion readily come to mind in connection with satires, verse epistles, and odes, but a host of other topics or subtopics runs through the period's poetry. The contemporary American poet A. R. Ammons has expressed the wish for poetry capacious enough to "ingest" anything. The eighteenth century may have come closer to attaining that ambition than the twentieth. There is an irony in this situation, given our popular tendency to imagine these past writers as copyists dependent upon convention and decorum and ourselves as independent inventors; but it does seem to be the case that the range of subjects considered appropriate for poetry has narrowed since the eighteenth century. Not only the quiet landscape but also the trades and "industry" enacted upon it interested the poets; a seashore might prompt a pensive reflection, but it might as easily lead to subjects such as shipbuilding, naval prowess, and international commerce. The fact that some of the civic and technical exposition in the poetry seems perversely "unpoetic" to us points to decisive changes in the relation of poetry to political power from Romanticism onward.

Rightly or wrongly, eighteenth-century poets tended to feel that nearly any subject could be treated poetically. Few things were considered inescapably prosaic: significantly, that adjective was used almost exclusively to classify compositions, not experiences. If the subject were ordinary it might be elevated somewhat by careful diction, and if it were "low" it might be treated in mock-heroic fashion. General agreement about the existence of various poetic "kinds" or genres was in some important ways more liberating than confining; governed by several decorums rather than one, poetry had many mansions and could accommodate a multitude of voices. The twentieth-century theory that poetry tends to be univocal and authoritarian in contrast to the "dialogic" or multivocal novel really is better suited for describing literature after Romanticism than before the late eighteenth century. For many writers and for much of the eighteenth century, the novel and poetry were closer together than they have usually been since. From the mid-eighteenth century on, the more monolithic ideas of "pure poetry" and "genius" are heard more frequently, suggesting an increasing tendency to equate "poetic" with "lyric" expression and to depreciate narrative

and satire. But this development is strong only in relative terms. In *The Task* (1785), William Cowper is still eminently comfortable with a broad range of conversational voices and narrative digressions, where a later poet would probably feel the need to discard some of Cowper's material and to subsume the rest under a unifying personality, as William Wordsworth would soon begin to do in *The Prelude* (completed in 1805).

The same latitude that allowed eighteenth-century poetry to range over so many different scenes and subjects can place unfamiliar demands on its modern readers. While many of the century's poems are grounded in situations we still regard as perennially poetic, a great number are not. Where we might expect a letter to the editor, eighteenth-century readers and writers might have found a verse epistle just the proper response. In general, exposition and argument are now regarded as unpoetic, and didacticism is suspect even in literary prose; but for poets through much of the eighteenth century the "essay" was an attractive poetic possibility. Some parallels in our day to the subjects treated in Pope's *Epistle to Bathurst* (1732) might be insider trading in the stock market, government procurement scandals, and the strange new force of electronic credit; but it is difficult to imagine poetry being made of them now. Reading eighteenth-century poetry calls frequently on the reader's flexibility, therefore, and willingness to imagine many possible voices, sometimes within the same poem.

A general bibliography of works relating to the poets in both these *DLB* volumes will be published at the end of the Second Series.

The editor wishes to thank the contributors to these volumes not only for their good work but also for their good nature and patience in this many-voiced collaboration.

–John Sitter

Acknowledgments

This book was produced by Bruccoli Clark Layman, Inc. Karen L. Rood is senior editor for the *Dictionary of Literary Biography* series. Jack Turner was the in-house editor.

Production coordinator is James W. Hipp. Systems manager is Charles D. Brower. Photography editor is Susan Brennen Todd. Permissions editor is Jean W. Ross. Layout and graphics supervisor is Penney L. Haughton. Copyediting supervisor is Bill Adams. Typesetting supervisor is Kathleen M. Flanagan. Typography coordinator is Sheri Beckett Neal. Information systems analyst is George F. Dodge. Charles Lee Eggleston is editorial associate. The production staff includes Rowena Betts, Anne L. M. Bowman, Teresa Chaney, Patricia Coate, Sarah A. Estes, Mary L. Goodwin, Cynthia Hallman, Susan C. Heath, David Marshall James, Kathy S. Merlette, Laura Garren Moore, John Myrick, Cathy J. Reese, Laurrè Sinckler, Maxine K. Smalls, John C. Stone III, Jennifer Toth, and Betsy L. Weinberg.

Walter W. Ross and Parris Boyd did the library research with the assistance of the reference staff at the Thomas Cooper Library of the University of South Carolina: Gwen Baxter, Daniel Boice, Faye Chadwell, Cathy Eckman, Gary Geer, Cathie Gottlieb, David L. Haggard, Jens Holley, Jackie Kinder, Thomas Marcil, Marcia Martin, Laurie Preston, Jean Rhyne, Carol Tobin, and Virginia Weathers.

John Sitter, the editor, would like to express his gratitude to Kate Ravin and Annie Merrill for their editorial assistance.

ERRATA

279, col. 1, ll. 15-18 down; the Editor's Note should read: In a departure from normal *DLB* procedure, the author cites conjectural dates of composition, instead of dates of publication, after Swift's titles in the text.

287, col. 1, l. 15 up: sickness [sickness and

293, col. 2, l. 13 up: *On the Reverend Dean Swift* [*On the D—N, in the Person of a Lady in the North*

295, col. 1, l. 20 up: ends [Ends

295, col. 2, ll. 19-20 down: for Acheson [for Lady Acheson

295, col. 2, l. 13 up: *Caleb* [CALEB

295, col. 2, l. 12 up: *Alecto's* [ALECTO'S

296, col. 1, l. 4 down: cou'd. . . .) [cou'd:). . . .

Dictionary of Literary Biography • Volume Ninety-five

Eighteenth-Century British Poets
First Series

Dictionary of Literary Biography

Mary Collier

(1690 - after 1762)

Donna Landry
Wayne State University

BOOKS: *The Woman's Labour: An Epistle To Mr. Stephen Duck; In Answer to his late Poem, called The Thresher's Labour. To which are added, The Three Wise Sentences, Taken From The First Book of Esdras, Ch. III. and IV.* (London: Printed for the author & sold by J. Roberts, 1739); facsimile published in *The Thresher's Labour (Stephen Duck) and The Woman's Labour (Mary Collier)* (Los Angeles: Clark Memorial Library, 1985);

Poems, on Several Occasions, by Mary Collier . . . With Some Remarks on Her Life (Winchester: Printed by M. Ayres, 1762); republished as *The Poems of Mary Collier, the Washerwoman of Petersfield: To which is prefixed her Life, Drawn By Herself* (Petersfield: W. Minchin, n.d.).

Mary Collier appears to have been the first laboring-class woman to publish her poetry in England. So far as is known, the publication of her poems brought her little remuneration and no escape from her labors as a laundress, housekeeper, and farm worker in West Sussex and Hampshire. Her most important poem, *The Woman's Labour: An Epistle To Mr. Stephen Duck* (1739), is beginning to receive some scholarly attention, but until recently she was a poet almost entirely forgotten in literary history. *The Woman's Labour* is an important text for at least three reasons. First, the poem's appearance as early as 1739 suggests that English laboring-class feminism has a history that predates its usual association with the nineteenth century. Second, the poem demonstrates that a plebeian poet such as

Collier can take aesthetic advantage of her distance from the dominant literary culture by filling a familiar vessel–the georgic or the neoclassical epistle–with strong new content. And in so doing, she can challenge some of the sexual and sociopolitical assumptions of the very culture from which she has so skillfully appropriated her aesthetic materials. Finally, the poem combines an emergent working-class consciousness with an emergent feminist critique of the misogynist tendencies embedded in that consciousness.

In "Some Remarks of the Author's Life drawn by herself," her autobiographical preface to her collected poems of 1762, Collier says she was the child of "poor, but honest Parents" who taught her to read when she was very young. Her mother's death prevented Collier from ever going to school; as she grew up, she was of necessity "set to such labour as the Country afforded." She nursed her ailing father and, after his death, moved to Petersfield where she worked as a laundress, brewer, domestic servant, and field hand. At sixty-three Collier retired from her work as a washerwoman to take up the post of housekeeper at a farm near Alton; at seventy she retired to "a Garret (The Poor Poets Fate)" in that town, where she lived until her death, as she claimed, "in Piety, Purity, Peace, and an Old Maid." Throughout her life reading was her chief recreation, and at some point she learned to write to "assist" her memory. Her various employers seem to have regarded her as a curiosity, an example of that popular eighteenth-century phenomenon, a "natural genius." According to the "Advertisement" to the second edition of her collected poems, with proper education she "would have ranked with the greatest poets of [the] kingdom."

In 1739 she published, at her own expense, *The Woman's Labour*, in which she vindicated the women of her class in reply to Duck's accusations of their frivolity, laziness, and garrulity. She had learned his poems by heart, admiring his "unlettered" genius and his descriptions of the rigors of agrarian labor, but she thought he had been "too Severe" on the female sex. *The Woman's Labour* mounts a protofeminist critique of men's refusal to see women's work as productive, and in so doing, gives us vivid descriptions of what amounts to a triple shift of wage labor, housework, and caring for children. Laundering fine linen for the gentry becomes an epic contest, "Until with Heat and Work, 'tis often known, / Not only Sweat, but Blood runs trickling down / Our Wrists and Fingers; still our Work demands / The constant Action of our lab'ring Hands" (11. 184-187). Unlike Duck or James Thomson in *The Seasons* (1730), Collier gives us a powerful evocation of a winter of labor; to her, women's work is seasonless as well as ceaseless. And the empirical testimony that Collier offers—of wages of "Sixpence or Eight-pence" a day at best, so that women's projections of the future could only linger on the prospect of "*Old Age* and *Poverty*" (11. 199-201)—has been subsequently confirmed by social historians. *The Woman's Labour* appeared together with Collier's *The Three Wise Sentences, Taken From The First Book of Esdras, Ch. III. and IV.*, in which competing arguments as to what constitutes the greatest power on earth are offered. One of the contestants proposes "Woman," only to claim that divine truth, as the creator of all things including woman, is indisputably the greatest power. Collier often touches on feminist arguments, but only in *The Woman's Labour* does she pursue them vehemently and consistently. These poems went through three editions, the third of which includes a statement by nine respectable Petersfield residents testifying to Collier's authenticity.

In 1762 she published by subscription her collection *Poems, on Several Occasions*. Another edition of the same poems was also published, entitled *The Poems of Mary Collier, the Washerwoman of Petersfield*, with an "Advertisement" venerating her talents and indicating that she maintained a strong local following until her death. In addition to the 1739 poems, these volumes contain two elegies (one on Stephen Duck); a dialogue on marriage; versifications of Sam. 1:1-2 and the *Spectator*, no. 375; a celebration of the marriage of George III; and a reply to an exciseman "Who doubted her being the Author of the Washerwoman's Labour," in which she advocates female education as a means to gender equality. In this poem Collier asserts that women's inferior education is the basis of their social subordination and not merely an effect of it. This verse epistle represents her example of a genre that seems to have been obligatory for laboring-class poets and many female poets of the period from all classes, the poetical self-authentification statement, and as such it serves as a welcome autobiographical moment in an otherwise self-effacing oeuvre. Collier closes this text with a mock admission of female idiocy, from which she hopes the exciseman can protect himself, concluding: "Tho' if we Education had / Which Justly is our due, / I doubt not, many of our Sex / Might fairly vie with you." This challenge combines confidence in her sex with a plea for inclusion in the possessing of an unproblematized "education." It is a challenge that assumes education to be an unbiased equalizer between the sexes, something that women have been unjustly denied, and can safely possess; the question of misogyny within traditional erudition itself is not addressed.

Thus the radical potential of Collier's writing is limited. Her utopian impulses tend to manifest themselves in an assumed faith in a higher authority that will be capable of rectifying injustices sometime in the future. Here the savior is education, elsewhere in her work religion or the monarchy. Whether the topic be education, marriage, scriptural history, or royal dynasticism, Collier tends to couple moral reformism with a certain amiable accommodationism or compliance with the will of the fathers. Therefore, when men become kind and virtuous husbands, though not before, women will prefer marriage to spinsterhood. Kings should be militantly strong, if not explicitly expansionist, in the name of protestant liberty; royal couples should set the pattern of domestic virtue for their peoples. And women's interests can best be served by a humble commitment to fulfilling God's will, for which they will be rewarded.

In a sense, then, despite the fact that she speaks on behalf of women like herself, Collier usually writes in a way that is rhetorically "male-identified," written for a projected audience in which men predominate. This orientation is supported by the limited evidence we have of her rela-

THE

Woman's Labour:

AN

EPISTLE

TO

Mr. STEPHEN DUCK;

In ANSWER to his late Poem, called
THE THRESHER'S LABOUR.

To which are added,

The Three WISE SENTENCES,

TAKEN FROM

The Firſt Book of ESDRAS, Ch. III. and IV.

By *MARY COLLIER,*

Now a WASHER-WOMAN, at *Petersfield* in *Hampſhire.*

LONDON,

Printed for the AUTHOR ; and ſold by J. ROBERTS,
in *Warwick-lane* ; and at the Pamphlet-Shops near
the *Royal Exchange.* 1739.

Price Six-Pence.

Title page for Collier's first book, one of the earliest examples of English working-class feminism

tionships with patrons. The nine Petersfield residents attesting to her authenticity in the signed statement of 21 September 1739 are all men. The respective numbers of male (102) and female (62) subscribers listed in her *Poems, on Several Occasions* also support this sense of Collier's projected audience. It is as if Collier were permitted access to the public on the condition that radically different female desires and recommendations not be featured too prominently in her work.

A certain deferral of desire for radical social transformation can read much like a conservative resignation to the status quo, though such a reading would be neither historically accurate

nor responsive to the sexual and social nuances of Collier's texts–nor with Collier's aesthetic achievement. Her subtle innovations and breaks with convention, her skillful appropriation of stock neoclassicism and occasional verse forms, may not seem very daring to modern readers unless they have read widely in eighteenth-century literature and understand the near impossibility of Collier or any other plebeian writer without formal education managing to write anything recognizable as poetry in this period. *The Woman's Labour*, like Collier's other poems, if more dramatically than they, challenges institutionalized critical and aesthetic criteria as working-class poetry is likely to do. One runs up against some hard questions about how "literary value" is defined and allocated, about the importance of political criteria in evaluative judgments, and about whether or not the establishment of a female (or feminist) countercanon is a sufficient or even desirable project for revisionist literary historians to pursue. Currently, Mary Collier's work may be of more interest to historians than to literary critics, but like the neoclassical aesthetics of Collier's day, modern critical criteria are subject to change. Arguably, Collier's inclusion in this volume is evidence that such a change is already underway.

References:

Moira Ferguson, *First Feminists: British Women Writers 1578-1799* (Bloomington, Ind., & Old Westbury, N.Y.: Indiana University Press & Feminist Press, 1985), pp. 257-265;

Ferguson, Introduction to *The Thresher's Labour (Stephen Duck) and The Woman's Labour (Mary Collier)* (Los Angeles: Clark Memorial Library, 1985);

Bridget Hill, *Women, Work, and Sexual Politics in Eighteenth-Century England* (Oxford: Blackwell, 1989), pp. 34-35, 157-161, 236-237;

Donna Landry, *The Muses of Resistance: Laboring-Class Women's Poetry in Britain, 1739-1796* (Cambridge: Cambridge University Press, 1990), pp. 38-40, 56-77;

Landry, "The Resignation of Mary Collier: Some Problems in Feminist Literary History," in *The New Eighteenth Century: Theory, Politics, English Literature*, edited by Laura Brown and Felicity Nussbaum (New York & London: 1987), pp. 99-120;

Roger Lonsdale, *Eighteenth Century Women Poets: An Oxford Anthology* (Oxford & New York: Oxford University Press, 1989), pp. 171-173;

Lonsdale, *The New Oxford Book of Eighteenth Century Verse* (Oxford & New York: Oxford University Press, 1984), pp. 325-326;

Sheila Rowbotham, *Hidden from History: Rediscovering Women in History from the 17th Century to the Present* (New York: Pantheon, 1974), pp. 24-26;

Morag Shiach, *Discourse on Popular Culture: Class, Gender and History in the Analysis of Popular Culture* (Oxford: Polity Press, 1989), pp. 51-53.

Daniel Defoe
(1660 - 24 April 1731)

Spiro Peterson
Miami University

See also the Defoe entry in *DLB 39: British Novelists, 1660-1800.*

SELECTED BOOKS: *A Letter to a Dissenter from His Friend at the Hague, Concerning the Papal Laws and the Test; shewing that the Popular Plea for Liberty of Conscience is not concerned in that Question* (The Hague [i.e., London]: Hans Verdraeght, 1688);

A New Discovery of an Old Intreague: A Satyr Level'd At Treachery and Ambition: Calculated To the Nativity of the Rapparee Plott, and the Modesty of the Jacobite Clergy (London, 1691);

The Character of the Late Dr. Samuel Annesley, By way of Elegy: With a Preface (London: Printed for E. Whitlock, 1697);

An Essay upon Projects (London: Printed by R. R. for Tho. Cockerill, 1697);

The Poor Man's Plea (London, 1698);

The Pacificator. A Poem (London: Printed & sold by J. Nutt, 1700);

The True-Born Englishman. A Satyr (London, 1700 [i.e., 1701]; Philadelphia, 1811);

A New Satyr on the Parliament (London, 1701);

The History of the Kentish Petition (London, 1701);

England's Late Jury: A Satyr, doubtfully attributed to Defoe (London, 1701);

The Mock-Mourners. A Satyr, By way of Elegy on King William (London, 1702);

Reformation of Manners, A Satyr (London, 1702);

Good Advice to the Ladies: Shewing, That as the World goes, and is like to go, the best way for them is to keep Unmarried, doubtfully attributed to Defoe (London, 1702);

The Spanish Descent. A Poem (London, 1702);

The Shortest-Way with the Dissenters; Or Proposals For The Establishment Of The Church (London, 1702);

An Encomium upon a Parliament (London, 1703);

A Collection of the Writings of the Author of The True-Born English-Man (London, 1703);

More Reformation. A Satyr Upon Himself (London, 1703);

Daniel Defoe in 1706 (portrait by Jeremiah Taverner, engraved by Michael Vandergucht). This engraving served as the frontispiece for Jure Divino, *published the same year.*

A True Collection of the Writings Of The Author of The True Born English-man. Corrected by Himself (London, 1703);

A Hymn to the Pillory (London, 1703);

A Hymn to the Funeral Sermon, doubtfully attributed to Defoe (London, 1703);

Review (London, 19 February 1704-11 June 1713); facsimile published as *Defoe's Review,* edited by Arthur Wellesley Secord, 22 volumes (New York: Facsimile Text Society, 1938);

The Address (London, 1704);

The Storm: Or, A Collection Of the most Remarkable Casualties And Disasters Which happen'd in the Late Dreadful Tempest, Both by Sea and Land (London: Printed for G. Sawbridge & sold by J. Nutt, 1704);

An Elegy on the Author of the True-Born-Englishman. With An Essay on the late Storm (London, 1704);

A Hymn to Victory (London: Printed for J. Nutt, 1704);

The Double Welcome. A Poem to the Duke of Marlbro (London: Printed & sold by B. Bragg, 1705);

A Second Volume of the Writings Of the Author Of The True-Born Englishman. Some whereof never before printed. Corrected and Enlarged by the Author (London: Printed & sold by the Booksellers, 1705);

The Consolidator: Or, Memoirs Of Sundry Transactions From the World in the Moon. Translated from the Lunar Language, By the Author of The True-born English Man (London: Printed & sold by Benj. Bragg, 1705);

The Dyet of Poland, A Satyr (Dantzick [i.e., London], 1705);

A True Relation of the Apparition of one Mrs. Veal (London, 1705);

A Declaration without Doors [broadside] (London, 1705);

A Hymn to Peace. Occasion'd, by the Two Houses Joining in One Address to the Queen (London: Printed for John Nutt, 1706);

Defoe's Answer to the Quaker's Catechism, doubtfully attributed to Defoe (London, 1706);

Daniel Defoe's Hymn for the Thanksgiving (London: Printed for the author, 1706);

Jure Divino. A Satyr. In Twelve Books (London, 1706);

The Vision, A Poem (Edinburgh, 1706);

A Reply to the Scots Answer, to the British Vision (Edinburgh, 1706);

Caledonia, &c. A Poem In Honour of Scotland, and the Scots Nation. In Three Parts (Edinburgh: Printed by the Heirs & Successors of Andrew Anderson, 1706);

A Scots Poem: Or A New-years Gift, From a Native of The Universe, To His Fellow-Animals in Albania (Edinburgh, 1707);

The Fifteen Comforts of a Scotch-Man Written by Daniel D'Foe in Scotland, doubtfully attributed to Defoe (London, 1707);

The True-Born Britain, doubtfully attributed to Defoe (London, 1707);

The History of the Union Of Great Britain (Edinburgh: Printed by the Heirs & Successors of Andrew Anderson, 1709);

Resignacón (N.P., 1710; revised, 1712): republished in "Defoe's 'Resignacion' and the Limitations of 'Mathematical Plainness,'" by Frank H. Ellis, *Review of English Studies*, new series, 36 (August 1985): 338-354;

High Church Miracles, or, Modern Inconsistencies [broadside], doubtfully attributed to Defoe (London: Printed & sold by A. Baldwin, 1710);

The Age of Wonders: To the Tune of Chivy Chase [broadside], doubtfully attributed to Defoe (London, 1710);

A Welcome to the Medal; Or, An Excellent New Song, Call'd the Constitution Restor'd in 1711, to the Tune of Mortimer's-Hole (Oxford, 1711);

The Candidate: Being a Detection of Bribery and Corruption as it is just now in Practice all over Great Britain (London: Printed for S. Keimer, 1715);

An Appeal to Honour and Justice, Tho' it be of His Worst Enemies. By Daniel De Foe. Being A True Account of his Conduct in Publick Affairs (London: Printed for J. Baker, 1715);

The Family Instructor, volume 1 (London: Sold by Eman. Matthews & Jo. Button, 1715; Philadelphia: Stewart & Cochran, 1792); volume 2 (London: Printed for Emman. Matthews, 1718);

A Hymn to the Mob (London: Printed & sold by S. Popping, J. Fox, S. Boulter, A. Boulter & J. Harrison, 1715);

Memoirs of the Church of Scotland, In Four Periods (London: Printed for Eman. Matthews & T. Warner, 1717);

Minutes of the Negotiations of Monsr. Mesnager At the Court of England, Towards the close of the last Reign (London: Printed for S. Baker, 1717);

A Vindication of the Press: Or, An Essay on the Usefulness of Writing, on Criticism, and the Qualifications of Authors, doubtfully attributed to Defoe (London: Printed for T. Warner, 1718);

Memoirs of Publick Transactions in the Life and Ministry of his Grace the D. of Shrewsbury (London: Printed for Tho. Warner, 1718);

A History of the Last Session of the Present Parliament (London: Printed & sold by W. Boreham, 1718);

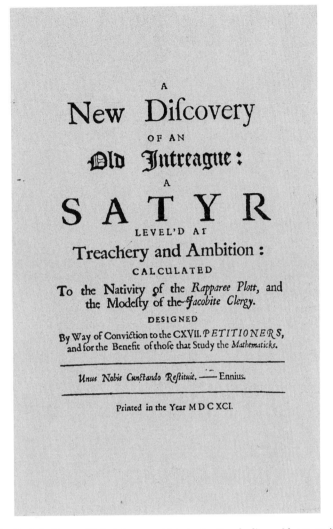

A
New Difcovery
OF AN
Old Intreague:
A
SATYR
LEVEL'D AT
Treachery and Ambition:
CALCULATED
To the Nativity of the *Rapparee Plott*, and
the Modefty of the *Jacobite Clergy*.
DESIGNED
By Way of Conviction to the CXVII. *PETITIONERS*,
and for the Benefit of thofe that Study the *Mathematicks*.

Unus Nobis Cunctando Reftituit. ——— Ennius.

Printed in the Year M D C XCI.

Title page for Defoe's first published poem, a historical satire dealing with events in the 1680s

A Continuation of Letters Written by a Turkish Spy At Paris (London: Printed for W. Taylor, 1718);

The Memoirs of Majr. Alexander Ramkins, A Highland-Officer, Now in Prison at Avignon. Being An Account of several remarkable Adventures during about Twenty Eight Years Service in Scotland, Germany, Italy, Flanders and Ireland (London: Printed for R. King & W. Boreham, 1719 [i.e., 1718]);

The Life and Strange Surprizing Adventures of Robinson Crusoe, Of York, Mariner (London: Printed for W. Taylor, 1719); republished as *The Wonderful Life and Surprizing Adventures of the Renowned Hero Robinson Crusoe* (New York: Printed by H. Gaine, 1775);

The Farther Adventures of Robinson Crusoe; Being the Second and Last Part Of His Life (London: Printed for W. Taylor, 1719);

Memoirs of a Cavalier: Or A Military Journal Of The Wars in Germany, And the Wars in England; From the Year 1632, to the Year 1648 (London: Printed for A. Bell, J. Osborn, W. Taylor, & T. Warner, 1720);

The Life, Adventures, and Pyracies, of the Famous Captain Singleton (London: Printed for J. Brotherton, J. Graves, A. Dodd & T. Warner, 1720);

Serious Reflections During The Life And Surprising Adventures of Robinson Crusoe, With His Vision Of The Angelick World (London: Printed for W. Taylor, 1720);

The Genuine Works of Mr. Daniel D'Foe, 2 volumes (London: Sold by T. Warner, 1721);

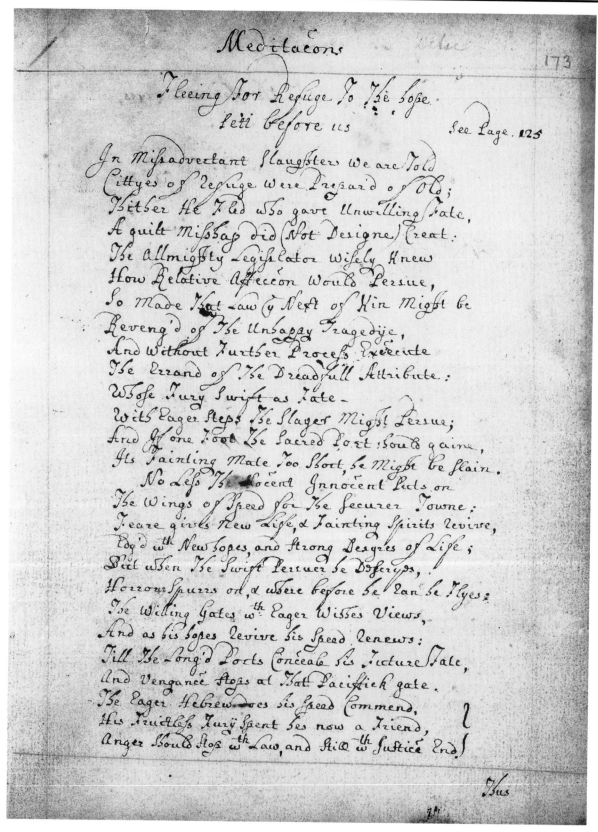

First page of a group of poems written in one of Defoe's notebooks in 1681 and first published in 1946 as The Meditations of Daniel Defoe *(HM 26613; by permission of the Henry E. Huntington Library and Art Gallery)*

The Fortunes and Misfortunes of the Famous Moll Flanders (London: Printed for & sold by W. Chetwood & T. Edling, 1721 [i.e, 1722]);

Due Preparations for the Plague As Well for Soul as Body (London: Printed for E. Matthews & J. Battey, 1722);

Religious Courtship: Being Historical Discourses, On The Necessity of Marrying Religious Husbands and Wives only (London: Printed for E. Matthews, A. Bettesworth, J. Brotherton & W. Meadows, 1722; New York: W. Durrell, 1793);

A Journal of the Plague Year: Being Observations or Memorials, Of the most Remarkable Occurrences, As well Publick as Private, Which happened in London During the last Great Visitation in 1665. Written by a Citizen who continued all the while in London (London: Printed for E. Nutt, J. Roberts, A. Dodd & J. Graves, 1722);

The History and Remarkable Life of the truly Honourable Col. Jacque, Commonly Call'd Col. Jack (London: Printed & sold by J. Brotherton, T. Payne, W. Mears, A. Dodd, W. Chetwood, J. Graves, S. Chapman & J. Stagg, 1723 [i.e., 1722]);

The Fortunate Mistress: Or, A History Of The Life And Vast Variety of Fortunes Of Mademoiselle de Beleau, Afterwards Call'd The Countess de Wintselsheim, in Germany. Being the Person known by the Name of the Lady Roxana, in the Time of King Charles II (London: Printed for T. Warner, W. Meadows, W. Pepper, S. Harding & T. Edlin, 1724);

The Great Law of Subordination Consider'd; Or, The Insolence and Unsufferable Behaviour of Servants in England duly enquir'd into (London: Sold by S. Harding, W. Lewis, T. Worrall, A. Bettesworth, W. Meadows & T. Edlin, 1724);

A General History Of The Robberies and Murders Of the most notorious Pyrates, And also Their Policies, Discipline and Government, From their first Rise and Settlement in the Island of Providence, in 1717, to the present Year 1724, volume 1 (London: Printed for Ch. Rivington, J. Lacy & J. Stone, 1724); volume 2 published as *The History of the Pyrates* (London: Printed for & sold by T. Woodward, 1728);

A Tour Thro' the Whole Island of Great Britain, Divided into Circuits or Journies. Giving A Particular and Diverting Account of Whatever is Curious and worth Observation, 3 volumes (London: Printed & sold by G. Strahan, W. Mears, R. Francklin, S. Chapman, R. Stagg & J. Graves, 1724-1727);

A New Voyage Round the World, By A Course never sailed before (London: Printed for A. Bettesworth & W. Mears, 1724);

The Complete English Tradesman, 2 volumes (London: Printed for Charles Rivington, 1726 [i.e., 1725], 1727);

The Political History of the Devil, As Well Ancient as Modern: In Two Parts (London: Printed for T. Warner, 1726);

The Four Years Voyages of Capt. George Roberts (London: Printed for A. Bettesworth & J. Osborn, 1726);

Mere Nature Delineated: Or, A Body without a Soul: Being Observations Upon The Young Forester Lately brought to Town from Germany. With Suitable Applications. Also, A Brief Dissertation upon the Usefulness and Necessity of Fools, whether Political or Natural (London: Printed for T. Warner, 1726);

Conjugal Lewdness: Or, Matrimonial Whoredom (London: Printed for T. Warner, 1727); republished as *A Treatise Concerning The Use and Abuse Of The Marriage Bed* (London: Printed for T. Warner, 1727);

An Essay on the History and Reality of Apparitions (London: Printed & sold by J. Roberts, 1727);

A New Family Instructor: In Familiar Discourses Between A Father and his Children, On the most Essential Points of the Christian Religion. In Two Parts (London: Printed for T. Warner, 1727);

A Plan of the English Commerce. Being a Compleat Prospect Of the Trade of this Nation, as well the Home Trade as the Foreign. In Three Parts (London: Printed for Charles Rivington, 1728);

The Memoirs of an English Officer, Who serv'd in the Dutch War in 1672. to the Peace of Utrecht, in 1713 (London: Printed for E. Symon, 1728);

Atlas Maritimus and Commercialis; or, A General View of the World, so Far as It Relates to Trade and Navigation; Describing All the Coasts, Ports, Harbours and Noted Rivers, According to the Latest Discoveries and Most Exact Observations (London: Printed for James & John Knapton, William & John Innys, John Darby, Arthur Bettesworth, John Osborn, Thomas Longman, John Senex, Edward Symon, Andrew Johnston & the executors of William Taylor, 1728);

Madagascar: or, Robert Drury's Journal, During Fifteen Years Captivity on that Island (London: Printed & sold by W. Meadows, J. Marshall, W. Worrall, & the author, 1729);

The Compleat English Gentleman, edited by Karl D. Bülbring (London: David Nutt, 1890);

The Meditations Of Daniel Defoe Now First Published, edited by George Harris Healey (Cummington, Mass.: Cummington Press, 1946).

Editions and Collections: *The Novels and Miscellaneous Works of Daniel De Foe*, with prefaces attributed to Sir Walter Scott, 20 volumes (Oxford: Printed by D. A. Talboys for T. Tegg, 1840-1841);

The Works of Daniel De Foe, edited by William W. Hazlitt [the younger], 3 volumes (London: Clements, 1840-1843);

The Novels and Miscellaneous Works of Daniel De Foe, 7 volumes (London: Bell, 1856-1884);

The Earlier Life and Chief Earlier Works of Daniel Defoe, edited by Henry Morley (London & New York: Routledge, 1889);

Romances and Narratives, edited by George A. Aitken, 16 volumes (London: Dent, 1895);

The Works of Daniel Defoe, edited by G. H. Maynadier, 16 volumes (New York: Sproul, 1903-1904);

The Shakespeare Head Edition of the Novels and Selected Writings of Daniel Defoe, 14 volumes (Oxford: Blackwell, 1927-1928);

Daniel Defoe: Selections from His Writings, edited by James T. Boulton (New York: Schocken, 1965);

The Versatile Defoe: An Anthology of Uncollected Writings by Daniel Defoe, edited by Laura A. Curtis (London: Prior, 1979; Totowa, N.J.: Rowman & Littlefield, 1979).

OTHER: "To the *Athenian* Society," preface to *The History of the Athenian Society*, by Charles Gildon (London: Printed for James Dowley, 1692);

Poems on Affairs of State; From the reign of James the First to this Present Year 1703, includes poems by Defoe (London, 1703);

"Parson Plaxton of Barwick in ye County of York turnd inside out," in "Defoe's Yorkshire Quarrel," by Spiro Peterson, *Huntington Library Quarterly*, 19 (November 1955): 71-73;

Frank H. Ellis, ed., *Poems on Affairs of State: Augustan Satirical Verse, 1660-1714*, volumes 6 and 7, includes poems by Defoe (New Haven & London: Yale University Press, 1970, 1975).

How does a poet turn into a novelist, what are the skills or talents that he takes from one art to the other, and what are the preoccupations, themes, or subjects in the poems themselves? These are some of the questions that one raises about Daniel Defoe, who is far better known as a novelist than as a poet. In the not-too-distant past it was more customary to refer to his "verses" than to his poems—and to add such qualifiers as "execrable." In recent years, however, a few critics have begun to pay serious attention to the poems and to discover artistry in them and a reflection of his quick and subtle mind. Defoe is an author still being assessed critically. No complete edition of all of his writings exists. It is not certain that he wrote the 566 works assigned to him by John Robert Moore in the 1971 edition of his *Checklist of the Writings of Daniel Defoe*. Critics are even in the precarious position of not knowing if Defoe is merely a creature we have put together in our heads from works that may or may not be by him. However, the poems discussed here are, for the most part, well established in the canon. They display a sharp mind that is always preoccupied with the social, religious, and political issues of the day.

Defoe wrote some form of poetry all his life, but his great period of poetic composition was from 1699 to 1707. Here and there, especially in the *Review* (the periodical that he wrote singlehandedly from February 1704 to June 1713), he left distichs, lampoons, pasquinades, fragments of songs, and ballads; he also included verses in his novels. One can track the development of his thought in the poems, his attachment to certain ideas, such as reform or morality, his theoretical interests in the language and style of poetry, his habit of casting poems into irony, and his skill in creating large poetic "fictions" that permit him to draw together numerous "characters" in recognizable patterns. Within his lifetime a few poems had considerable popularity, in, for example, the 1703 *Poems on Affairs of State*. "The Author of the *True-Born Englishman*" became a common nom de plume on title pages, both for poems by Defoe and some poems not by him. He was a favorite of the literary pirates; for example, Henry Hill's pieces (including Defoe's) appeared in 1717 as *A Collection of the Best English Poetry*. Giles Jacob, in *The Poetical Register* (1723), observed that two pieces were "very much admir'd by some Persons": *The True-Born Englishman* (1700) and *Jure Divino* (1706). Robert Shiels in Theophilus Cibber's *Lives of the Poets of Great*

King William III and Queen Mary. Defoe praised the king in his first published poem, A New Discovery of an Old Intreague *(1691), and in later works.*

Britain and Ireland (1753) found that "poetry was far from being the talent of De Foe" and yet discussed four verse satires and listed *Caledonia* (1706) and *Jure Divino* in the bibliography. George Chalmers (1785) and the later biographers and critics treat the poems with widely different emphases but generally with scorn or neglect. In the discussion that follows, certain prose works, such as *A Vindication of the Press* (1718), are now controversial as the work of Defoe and are omitted from consideration. The poems are taken up chronologically, with a few exceptions; and some efforts are made to create larger groupings of the poems, such as parliament poems, moral satires, and Scottish poems. The best texts of the poems, with annotations and headnotes, are to be found in *Poems on Affairs of State: Augustan Satirical Verse, 1660-1714*, volumes 6 and 7 (1970, 1975).

Defoe was born in London in the fall of 1660 (as near as can be determined) to James Foe, a tallow chandler, and his wife, Alice. The poems from *The Meditations* (written in 1681; first published in 1946) to *The Character of the Late Dr. Samuel Annesley* (1697) are the products of young Daniel Foe (he began to use "Defoe" more frequently beginning in 1696), ambitious and energetic, turning first from the ministry to the mer-

chant's life, restlessly seeking a place in city politics, and trying out his voice on national issues. The poems in *The Meditations* were written in Defoe's neat hand on twenty-three pages of manuscript (originally titled "Meditacons") and consist of seven highly personal, contemplative pieces on themes of unworthiness, conscience, and guilt-ridden flight. All except one are signed D. F. There is some question as to whether the contents are biblical exegeses or personal experiences, and whether they are in any way related to similar incidents in *Memoirs of a Cavalier* (1720) and *Col. Jack* (1722).

The religion of *The Meditations* is strikingly different from that in any other poem; it has a close affinity to that of the metaphysical poets. Defoe's model here seems to be George Herbert ("The Quip," in *The Temple*, 1633). Like a metaphysical poet, Defoe uses military images, as in "The Seige Raised" (part 7 of *The Meditations*). Most impressive in the light of relationships Defoe will find in future poems between the poet and other artists is "Shall The Clay Say Unto The Potter? &ca" (part 4), wherein "a Rustic Artist" complains that he is "A Drudge" and the pile of clay is "a Dish of qualitye," but the poet is now calmed in his complaint by these observations. Never again in his poetic career would Defoe handle religion with such dramatic immediacy. *The Meditations* reflects the strong puritan education Defoe had received at James Fisher's boarding school at Dorking in Surrey (1672-1676) and the more humanistic learning at Charles Morton's Academy at Newington Green (1676-1679). The poems mirror also the resolution of the conflict in favor of the secular life.

Defoe married Mary Tuffley in 1684, participated in Monmouth's Rebellion, and apparently fought at Sedgemoor in 1685; he was pardoned in 1687. As a hosier in Freeman's Yard, Cornhill, he disliked the excesses of James II and sided with the new rulers, William and Mary. On 29 October 1689 he is described by John Oldmixon, in *The History of England* (1735), as participating fully in a royal regiment of horse made up of "the chief Citizens" who were for the most part Dissenters. *A New Discovery of an Old Intreague* was Defoe's first published poem, appearing sometime before 17 January 1691. The poem is a long satire (666 lines) taking the form of a history of fairly unimportant events in London politics from 1682 to 1691. However, as a satire, it conveys feelings better than facts. *A New Discovery* deals with the theme of the city's freedom gradu-

Stained-glass window honoring Defoe in Butchers' Hall, London. The poet was once a member of the Corporation of Butchers. The window was destroyed during World War II.

William Russell and Henry Cornish. The narrative first takes the events up to the petition by the 117 members of Common Council to parliament. The petition was rejected, but on the return of King William from Ireland the rights were restored to the city. Evidence exists in the poem that, secondly, there was the capture on 31 December 1690 of the Jacobites Lord Preston (Richard Grahame) and John Ashton; they were brought to trial and convicted (17-19 January 1691). The news of this Jacobite threat was a last-minute insertion into the poem.

A New Discovery could have been a major poem eloquently espousing freedom as its larger "fiction" and using its numerous "characters" to reinforce the theme and give it substance. As it is, the poem gropes confusedly for the theme but never grasps the universality requisite in a great satire. For its structure the poet refuses to take "parallels from *Hebrew* times," and will leave "the Jingling Simily to speak" (92-93; hereafter references to lines of the text are given within parentheses). Now and then Defoe hints at the larger structure of the Lord Mayor's pageant–the colorful procession of mayor, sheriffs, and livery companies–but never reaches the brilliant symbolism of Alexander Pope's *Dunciad* (1728). Some of the characters are drawn with realistic details that point to identification of the person: for instance, the fifth Golden Candlestick, in real life Henry Compton, Bishop of London (250-265); Ralph Box (524-533); and Drugestus (534-538), with whom Defoe's focus is on the face and the details drawn from Tom D'Urfey's *The Triennial Mayor* (1691). His techniques for developing characters here will appear again in later poems.

Defoe would complain later in life, as he did in *The Complete English Tradesman* (1725-1727), that it is most difficult to be both a wit and a tradesman. By 1692, as he moved toward his first bankruptcy, he found himself in the company of Peter Anthony Motteux, Nahum Tate, Charles Richardson, and other wits providing prefatory poems to Charles Gildon's *The History of the Athenian Society* (1692). "To the *Athenian* Society," signed D. F., is written in a mode popularized by Abraham Cowley, which would soon become one of Defoe's favorites, the panegyric. With some suggestion of strophe and antistrophe, the poem celebrates the emergence of new knowledge and enlightenment.

A more important early poem is *The Character of the Late Dr. Samuel Annesley*. Annesley had been a well-educated and well-descended minis-

ally being given back by William III. The poem is concerned with events of the 1680s in which tyrants Charles II and James II deprived the city of its charter and silenced leaders such as Lord

Frontispiece for A True Collection of the Writings of The True Born English-man *(1703)*

plicit, the identification of style and action: "*For Honesty and Honour are the same*" (110)–a line his character Roxana was to repeat in a similar context more than a quarter of a century later (in *The Fortunate Mistress*, 1724). He praises Annesley for a sincerity "which made his Actions and his Words agree" (104). The speaker, in the fourth and final section of the poem, finds consolation in the significance of Annesley's death, divine love, again expressed in a Herbert-like relationship to style: "Twou'd be concisely thus, All Heaven is Love" (233).

In *The Pacificator*, published on 15 February 1700, Defoe came closest to imagining the life and mind of a wit and litterateur. Nowhere else in his poetry does he have such a concentrated focus on literature and criticism or include so many names of poets, dramatists, and critics. In some ways it reminds one of greater criticism in verse that lay ahead–Pope's *Essay on Criticism* (1711) or *The Dunciad*. As mock-heroic satire, *The Pacificator* takes the art of innuendo deeply into style, as it imposes one layer of literary reference upon another–for instance, when we are told that John Dryden had some sense until he began to dote and "lately *Deviate into Wit*" (248), neatly echoing "MacFlecknoe," Dryden's poem of 1682.

The structure of the poem causes problems, though, and imposes obstacles to any easy understanding. It is not surprising, therefore, that the poem fell stillborn: not a single contemporary reference or allusion to it has been found. Again, Defoe had avoided the indirection of allegory or biblical parallel. Instead, like Jonathan Swift in *The Battle of the Books* (1704), he creates in *The Pacificator* a "war" between the forces of sense and those of wit. Appropriately, in the period of peace right after the Treaty of Ryswick (signed in February 1697), he describes the "Civil Feuds, and Private Discontent" that broke out. He wants to direct attention to certain recent domestic phenomena that are literary. In the introduction he makes clear his mock-heroic intention. He focuses the theme of sense versus wit on his principal character Nokor, whom he identified as Sir Richard Blackmore in the single marginal note added to the text of *The Pacificator* in his collected works. In the rest of the poem he weaves together two main strands in the personality of Nokor/Blackmore, conspicuously outspoken defender of morality or sense in his epics *Prince Arthur* (1695) and *King Arthur* (1697), as well as in their abrasive prefaces–and just "now," as the poet declares, Nokor/Blackmore has rallied his

ter of St. Helen's Place in St. Giles, Cripplegate, one of the "ejected" (clergy evicted by the Act of Uniformity, 1662, or by the Test Act, 1673). If anyone had been the model of a minister for the young Defoe, it was undoubtedly Dr. Annesley. Among the many funeral sermons and other tributes was Defoe's elegy, filled with echoes of John Milton's *Lycidas* (1638). Compared with the earlier poems *The Character* is unusual in its depth of feeling and strong sense of structure. In particular the emotion over the death of Annesley, a close friend of the Foe family, was centered in character and its relationship to actions. This theme, the identity of the Christian and the gentleman, is woven throughout the poem and gives it an artistic unity not always evident in the early poems. At the high point the speaker (Defoe himself) makes explicit what had thus far been im-

troops in his *Satyr against Wit*, published on 23 November 1699. Defoe seems to have some hint of an "impending stroke," which may be the *Commendatory Verses* (1700), epigrams by Tom Brown and other wits attacking Blackmore. It is at this time of the mock-heroic action that *The Pacificator* appears, with Defoe envisioning himself as a latter-day Lord Rochester or even a successor to the doting Dryden–a litterateur wittily cognizant of the cultural scene. Throughout the entire account of what we now call the Jeremy Collier controversy, Defoe aligns the wit dramatists (Dryden, William Congreve, and John Hughes) and their defenders against the attackers of the stage, principally Collier.

For Defoe's second strand, a subsidiary theme arising from the career of Blackmore as prominent physician, he briefly introduces the somewhat distantly related controversy of the doctors versus the apothecaries, in which Blackmore was mainly opposed to Samuel Garth in a quarrel over the feeding of the poor. Whatever Defoe's posture and pretensions are in *The Pacificator*, he clearly demonstrates that at this stage of his career his ambition is to be a poet and wit, and the resolution he advances in this civil "war" is a truce, a pacification through the combination of qualities from both sense and wit.

In the third and final part Defoe turns from civil war to peace and makes suggestions for repairing Britain's losses. He seeks a compromise between the opposing factions but first defines wit and sense in a brilliant passage of antitheses (355-396). Wit, he declares, is "like a hasty Flood." It is "a Flux, a Looseness of the Brain." "*Sense-abstract*" has too much pride, while "*Wit-unconcoct* is the Extreme of Sloth." Sense like water is "*but Wit condense*"; and wit like air is "*rarify'd from Sense*." Then, wittily, he joins together something literary and something political: "*Wit* is a King without a Parliament, / And *Sense* a Democratick Government." The view of not just wit but of poetry expressed here seems to be the true Defoe. He would say it again, much more forcefully, in *Caledonia*; and it seems to be a deeply held belief. In addition, when he later assigns each kind of writing to a single expert person (419-424), he reserves lampoon for himself, "*F[oe]*." Aside from William Wycherley being assigned to lyric, the pairings are accurate, that is, substantiated by literary history as we now know it. Why Defoe assigned lampoon to himself is not quite clear, except that he did frequently resort to personal satire, and he did see his talent in such writing. Here he shows a keen sense of genres and an understanding of poetic kinds that fall short of poetic theory only because they are somewhat fragmentary.

In the 1690s trade as a means of livelihood was becoming less attractive to Defoe, and politics through pamphlet-writing consumed most of his time and energy. His diversity of interest–social, political, and economic–may be seen best in his prose *Essay upon Projects* (1697). His brick and tile factory at West Tilbury, Essex (Defoe had won government contracts in 1695 and 1696), no longer held his full attention. Minor government posts were temporary and unfulfilling. According to Frank Bastian (*Defoe's Early Life*, 1981), in the winter of 1696-1697 he first showed a keen interest in parliamentary affairs. Defoe found there the themes of the ballads *An Encomium upon a Parliament* (1703), circulating as a manuscript in early May 1699; *A New Satyr on the Parliament*, probably published in June 1701; *England's Late Jury*, published on 4 November 1701; and *The Address*, most likely published in April 1704. All four poems have a similar stanzaic form with radical or "mutinous" overtones, and all four deal with parliamentary issues, at times with an insider's knowledge. The speaker is Legion or "our Legionite," and he is definitely threatening. William III is generally kept from blame but unexpectedly attacked in *A New Satyr* (216-220). None of the ballads is in Defoe's collected works. All four are reprinted as Defoe's in volume 6 of *Poems on Affairs of State* (1970) but with questions on the authorship of *England's Late Jury* and *The Address*.

The True-Born Englishman, published on or about 2 December 1700, shows advances in poetic technique and breadth of subject over anything Defoe had previously attempted. As the xenophobia increased during the second session of the fourth parliament and during the months after John Tutchin's venomous *Foreigners* appeared (published anonymously in 1700), Defoe would rise out of relative obscurity and assume the role of "the unofficial poet laureate" in his staunch defense of William III. Defoe himself said that because of his *True-Born Englishman* King William sought to be acquainted with the author. Defoe's audience in the poem is now the entire nation and even Europe. For with the instinct of the popular artist, he tried to delineate the national character of the English people, the species itself, and to illustrate it with individual characters who anticipate, to an extent, the men and

Queen Anne, during whose reign Defoe was both pilloried and imprisoned for criticizing the government. Nonetheless, he voiced his loyalty to her in several poems, including Jure Divino *(1706).*

women of the novels he would write years later.

How great the poem's popularity was can only be guessed. In the preface to *A Second Volume of the Writings Of the Author Of The True-Born Englishman* (1705), Defoe claimed he had himself seen nine editions through the press, there were twelve editions "by other Hands," and eighty thousand pirated copies had been sold on the streets. The poem was included in *Poems on Affairs of State* (1703), along with *Reformation of Manners* (1702) and *A Hymn to the Pillory* (1703). William Pittis, in *The True-Born-Hugonot* (1703), ridicules the large number of editions (ten) of *The True-Born Englishman*.

The poem, it seems, was being read by almost everyone. Completely unlike the pose of a wit in *The Pacificator*, the speaker of *The True-Born Englishman* takes on a voice very close to the people or folk, again called "Legion." Most of the poem consists of Satyr's response to the speaker, and Satyr frequently makes use of proverb-like language. Most important in the poem's ability to reach the people is its style of rough satire–the poetic theory of which Defoe

clearly understood, and now and then articulated in prefaces or the *Review*–and he looked back to models such as Andrew Marvell, John Cleveland, John Oldham, and John Wilmot, Lord Rochester, as opposed to the style of "fine raillery" of Dryden.

Defoe's motives in writing *The True-Born Englishman* were primarily propagandistic. He was probably both sincere and honest in his autobiographical *Appeal to Honour and Justice* (1715) when he included in the origins of *The True-Born Englishman* "a kind of Rage" at the *Foreigners*. Making use of biblical allegory, this "vile abhor'd Pamphlet" scurrilously attacked the Dutch, and lampooned the King's Dutch favorites, viciously attacked William III, and urged his dethronement (as the anonymous author of the pamphlet *The Examination, Tryall, and Condemnation of Rebellion O[bservato]r* would say in 1703). When *The True-Born Englishman* first came out the evidence of its origin was clearly there, mainly in the satiric character Shamwhig (624-649), obviously John Tutchin. In the following January (1701) Defoe drastically revised the poem, omitting the Shamwhig character and universalizing the satire of Sir Charles Duncombe by eliminating any identification by name. Aware of the relationship between characters that are individual and characters that are general, he clearly moved in the direction of the latter. His interests in character are deep and integral to his artistic purpose.

The main thrust of Defoe's propaganda is not merely to oppose the king's enemies who hated foreigners but to devastate them in such a way that his readers would become advocates of the king. His techniques at times are extremely subtle. The Latin quotation on the title page, "Charta Regis Willielmi Conquisitoris de Pacis Publica . . . (The Charter of King William the Conqueror for the Public Peace . . .), starts the parallel between William the Conqueror and William III, which becomes clearer as Satyr develops the distinction between a de facto and a de jure basis for kingship. Defoe makes the strongest case possible for William's claim to the throne by opposing the de facto argument that would make him a usurper and insists upon William's right to the throne out of the English people's gratitude for a king who saved them from tyranny. The idea of gratitude/ingratitude is central to the poem and becomes its theme. The propaganda here is at times radical, as Pittis pointed out in *The True-Born Englishman: A Satyr, Answer'd, Paragraph by*

Defoe in the pillory on 29 July 1703 (engraving based on a painting by Eyre Crowe); Defoe's Hymn to the Pillory *was published the same day.*

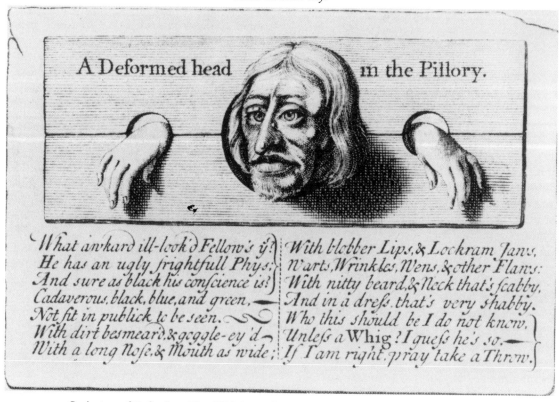

Caricature of Defoe from The Whig's Medley, *1711, an engraving by George Bickham*

Paragraph (1701) when he called Defoe "a Leveller." The poem's speaker identifies himself with Legion and gives the poem a sharp edge (771-778). But beyond propaganda, the poem generates a grand conception that is Gilbert-and-Sullivan comedy in its vast exaggeration, namely, that all Englishmen who are so proud of title, family, ancestry, and wealth are themselves *"Europe's Sink, the Jakes,"* bastards, and so forth (249-250).

As an artistic entity, *The True-Born Englishman* has a structure that reinforces the propaganda. In part 1 Satyr gives a long cosmography of countries and their dominant vices (pride, lust, drunkenness . . .) culminating with England and its own "Devil": Ingratitude. At this point emerges the grand conception mentioned above. Next, in part 2, Defoe turns from the true-born Englishman as a species to individuals–characters, including Shamwhig, who (in spite of preachy writings) betray their benefactors. In stark contrast to the loyal Portland and Schonberg, the speaker introduces "a Modern Magistrate of Famous Note," the longest and best developed character, Sir Charles Duncombe (1045-1063), giving "his own History by Rote and his fine speech" (1064-1190). Defoe's decision in a later edition to depersonalize the fine speech was probably an artistic mistake. The character sketch had been circulating in manuscript in 1699 and was the genesis of the entire poem. Duncombe, in his fine speech, moralizes on ingratitude as the unpardonable sin and rehearses the betrayal of his master Edward Backwell, Charles II, James II, and William III–with the straight face of self-praise. He acknowledges that he surpasses Judas and proudly mentions his old friend the Devil. At the height of revealing his moral misconduct Duncombe bursts out with the question *"A'n't I a Magistrate for Reformation?"* (1182). All the actions Duncombe mentions have real-life counterparts, and they all demonstrate the dominant English vice of ingratitude.

The true-born Englishmen become "the mock mourners" in the poem bearing that title, published on 12 May 1702. King William died on 8 March, and the poems that shortly appeared mourned for the king sincerely, or they turned mourning into severe satire. Defoe's *Mock-Mourners* is a deliberate mixture of genre, presenting both elegy and satire. Defoe says repeatedly in the poem that all praise of William becomes a devastating satire of the praisers because their actions and values were the opposite of his. Still another explanation may be given in that the mixing of genres reflects a highly idiosyncratic way of thinking that we associate with Defoe. The poem, in short, is much more than history.

Defoe says in *The Mock-Mourners*: "So Mad-Men sing in Nakedness and Chains, / For when the Sense is gone, the Song remains" (272-273). If one thinks of the "song" as the poem itself, the lines bear directly on the relationship of panegyric to satire, on Defoe's conception of a difficult time for himself, and on his own role for that occasion. More important, as the poem states explicitly, Defoe's purpose is to "read" the "Modern Character" of King William (346). He asks how "future Ages [will] read his Character?" Again he addresses Satyr and asks that he "Embalm [the King's] Name with Characters of Praise" (520-522). In the future anyone who would be great simply imitates the king. He is the "Example," and youth need only attend to his history. Not until the conclusion of *The Mock-Mourners* does the new reading of King William's character come into focus. The poet responds to the question that Posterity will ask, *What Giant's that?* by turning to "romance" and "legend" (488-519). So important is this passage that Defoe repeated it in the *Review* for 27 March 1707. The poet, at the very end, urges that a substitute be found for Queen Anne among her nobles to provide the military prowess of William III in order to complete the transition of power.

The Mock-Mourners was both the last of the King William poems and the first of the Queen Anne poems. Boldly, as in *The True-Born Englishman*, Defoe marked out his own role of poetic spokesman for the regime. He would continue to write celebratory poems in the general class of occasional poems–public statements, generally in iambic pentameter, of what he would like to be official positions on events. *The Spanish Descent*, probably published in December 1702, is a good early example of such poems. It celebrates the military victory regarded at the time as the most momentous in over a hundred years: Sir George Rooke's capture of the entire Spanish fleet at Vigo. The providential success at Vigo is in sharp contrast to the English failure at Cadiz during the earlier war, 1689-1697. Thus *The Spanish Descent* is history, a poem on state affairs, but because of the ambiguities and ironies inherent in any major historical event and the figurative language of the poem, *The Spanish Descent* is also more than history.

Four poems–*Reformation of Manners, More Reformation* (1703), *A Hymn to the Pillory* and *An*

Justice Hall, London, as it looked when Defoe stood trial there

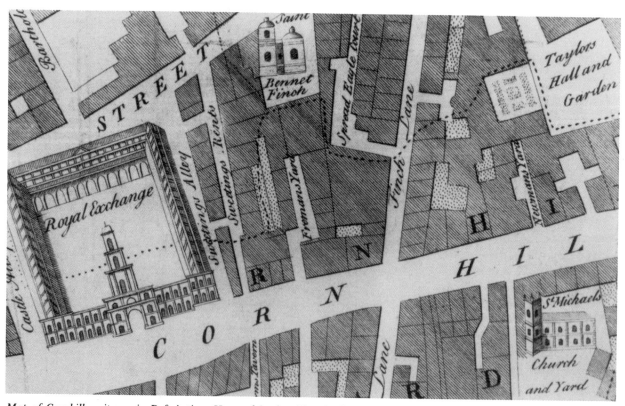

Map of Cornhill as it was in Defoe's time. He stood in the pillory in front of the Royal Exchange, and years later his daughter Mary was buried in St. Michael's churchyard.

Newgate Prison at the time Defoe was incarcerated there as a political prisoner in 1703

Elegy on the Author of the True-Born-English-Man (1704)–are moral satires leading up to and centered on Defoe's imprisonment in Newgate and his standing in the pillory on three successive days, 29-31 July 1703, at the Royal Exchange in Cornhill, Cheapside, and Temple Bar, all places where he was well known. The High Church and Tory prosecutors had expected the pillorying to be harmful to him and perhaps even fatal; it turned out to be triumphant. (In Stefan Heym's fictionalization of the incident–in *The Queen Against Defoe and Other Stories*, 1974–a young man perched high upon a lantern post recites *A Hymn to the Pillory* while a modern-day Defoe stands triumphant, the writer against the East German Commissars.) From Defoe's writings it is known that *A Hymn to the Pillory* was published on 29 July 1703, and the experience of the pillory–including his pursuit, the harassment of his family, his feelings of guilt and isolation, imprisonment, and trial–was central to his own personal and professional development as a writer.

Reformation of Manners, probably published in August 1702, arose out of a powerful emotion, a Juvenalian indignation directed at the hypo-

crites of his time, an upper-class group made up of magistrates, statesmen, clergy, and military leaders–persons who cannot reform the lower classes because they commit the very crimes they rail at. As in his earlier poems Defoe creates a large conception, this two-tiered society, and develops a kind of social symbolism that will recur in his novels. To a certain extent it is this theme of *Reformation of Manners*, with its vast gallery of some thirty-nine characters, that got him into trouble and led to the writing of *More Reformation*– even while he was being pursued by the authorities–and its publication on 16 July 1703. The emotion of this latter poem is much more autobiographical, including more self-discovery, which continues even more powerfully in *A Hymn to the Pillory* and in *An Elegy on the Author of the True-Born-English-Man*, published sometime before 25 July 1704.

Reformation of Manners, containing 1280 lines, is a unique literary phenomenon of its time. The closest counterpart of its rough iambic pentameter may be found in the popular *Poems on Affairs of State* volumes (1703), where it was also included. Defoe's lambasting of highly placed persons is unrelenting and at times vicious. In a long commentary (1120-1181) he interrupts the flow of his narrative to discuss poetry and the role of the poet in a time of reformation; he has clearly gone far beyond the wit / sense debate of *The Pacificator*. Now, says Defoe, if you write for bread, you must please, and so wit, which is often lewd, bawdy, or blasphemous, will prevail over sense. For such are the realities of the marketplace. In vain does one write "Hymns and Histories from sacred Writ." Then follow the well-known lines: "Let this describe the Nation's Character, / One Man reads *Milton*, forty *Rochester*." The preference is for the lewd and not the sublime. The passage is most significant also for its pointed references to "the *Love and Honour*" theme, "the Drunken Stile," and quoted remarks of the bookseller.

With its huge outcroppings of scandalous chronicles, *Reformation of Manners* moves along sluggishly. The structure, however, is simple: the introduction compares the city of London with ancient capitals and outlines the chances now for any honest reformation; part 1 introduces characters of the city; part 2 focuses on characters of the country and the court; and in the conclusion Defoe reiterates his theme of a true reformation. In part 1 the characterizations take the form of nasty lampoons, especially when they arise from Defoe's personal life. No detail of private history, no matter how bizarre or perverted, is exempt from the satirist's scrutiny and exposure. Unremitting is the presentation of high-class rogues of the city: Jeffreys, Lovell, Furnese, Sweetapple and Cole, Clayton, Duncombe, Wills, and Blackbourne. So private are certain references that they are now completely lost to the general reader, and here the artistry suffers. In the midst of this succession of portraits of vile citizens, among the "Tricks and Cheats of Trade," appears suddenly the passage in which Defoe attacks slavery, the bartering of baubles for the souls of men (323-332). The characters of part 2 commit national crimes and so are of a much more serious order: they include Clito or Milo who cannot now be identified, and many others, such as Casco, who can be identified, shockingly, with one of the first families of Hertfordshire. The characters fall into groupings: Tories or High Churchmen, the military, the clergy, the ladies, and finally the "Beau's at *Will's*." In this last group is the couple, dull Flettumasy and Diadora (1082-1119). They seem to be important, for they reappear in *More Reformation* and *A Hymn to*

the Pillory–and as the Fool Husband and Roxana in Defoe's novel *The Fortunate Mistress*.

The main character scrutinized in *More Reformation* is Defoe himself. While some fourteen other characters are drawn, they serve primarily to illustrate a theory that full names are not needed: the character speaks for itself. The response to *Reformation of Manners*, because of the characters, was ferocious; and in *More Reformation*, both in the preface and the poem, Defoe sets out to defend himself and his ideas of satire. The theory he most favors is that the poet's intention should be clear. If the name is necessary, then there is "a Deficiency of Art." In the preface and again in the poem (648-661) he tells of a Dutch painter who was not understood because he did not identify the man and the bear in his painting. The picture, Defoe claims, should be adequate in itself, just as he was obviously the Booby in *Reformation of Manners* without the need of any "*Gazet Marks*." As part of the theory he also counsels against "*Ironies*" (690). In spite of these comments, the method of character-drawing does not seem very different from what it had been in earlier poems, even in those seven characters designed to illustrate the theory. As he describes the motives for writing satire, he gives the character G-----, who from selected details as well as from the "Key" to *The Genuine Works of Mr. Daniel D'Foe* (1721) is known to be Charles Gildon. Such a method of presenting a picture he uses with most of the characters. However, the method does not work effectively for characters who are total unknowns and at the same time uninteresting in their traits. Mainly because of the theory, the characters in *More Reformation* are not as fascinating as earlier ones, except for Flettumasy and Diadora (755-768), who continue as unknowns in real life and yet invite attention.

More Reformation is mainly autobiographical: Defoe intersperses discoveries about himself as a poet. He will not, like Marvell, criticize the king (538-539). He describes how his "*Luxuriant Fancy* soar'd too high, / And scorch'd its Wings," and, like Icarus, fell back into the night (574-577). Somewhat later he calls himself a fool, and (for the second time) claims that he put his own eyes out to open the public's (833). He cites "*Rauleigh's* Cautious Rule" about the true reprover's being hated. The poem closes with tightly controlled emotion as the poet expresses his feelings of betrayal by the Dissenters, his bitterness over a Dissenting minister's praying for a highwayman and not for the poet, and the poet's rejection by "three Petition'd Priests"–in short, his complete abandonment in Newgate.

A Hymn to the Pillory represents the final "stage" of Defoe's tragedy in 1703. Its form is the hymn in highly irregular Pindarics, used both for praise or blame, panegyric or satire. The freedom this form elicited was necessary for the defiant tone that persists throughout the poem. The hymn is an oration addressed to the pillory that modulates from triumph to despair and then to realistic acceptance of the situation. The speaker starts by addressing the pillory, "Hail! *Hi'-roglyphick* State *Machin*"; he continues through a long succession of varied metaphorical references to the pillory: human (brows, face), stage ("modern Scenes," theater), mountain (pinnacles, ridge), military (turrets, counterscarp), scaffold ("Great *Monster of the Law*"), and numerous others. "Stage" seems to be dominant. Rhetorically he inquires after the secret of emblematic ("hieroglyphic") meaning of the pillory. Because of the self-discoveries represented by these references the speaker works his way through different interpretations of the pillory experience and reaches the startling conclusion that the pillory is an absolute subversion of justice, as is the state.

In a sense, then, the pillory is itself a major character; its features dominate the poem and fall into the patterns described. The inquiry and background are given in an introduction, and there follow sections on "criminals" of the past (the most "favorable" being John Selden), inept statesmen, "modern Scenes of Fame" (Vigo, for example), "the Men of Great Employ," judges and magistrates, clergy, lawyers, "heroes," those refusing to take oaths, and high-ranking culprits robbing the state. Up to this point people are fully named when they are out of the past and presented as illustrations (Bastwick and Prynne, for example); and they are designated by initials and blanks when they are contemporaries or recently alive. Altogether eight persons are named, and eight are not.

The poem reaches a climax as the speaker visualizes the great pageant changing its "Dirty Scene" with ladies appearing on the pillory "steps." Sappho is there, and so are "Gay URANIA" (353-360) and the witty French harlot "DIADORA" along with her brainless Flettumasy (361-374). The lines on Flettumasy, it should be noted, were added to the "second edition corrected" (1703) as Defoe was quite aware of the large design of his poem. He has gone from char-

acters inextricably linked to persons in real life, such as Duncombe's mistress in *The True-Born Englishman*, or Diadora in *Reformation of Manners* and *More Reformation*, to the emblematic characters Urania and Diadora in *A Hymn to the Pillory*.

The next poem, still showing the effects of the pillory, but now entirely concerned with himself as a theme, is *An Elegy on the Author of the True-Born-English-Man. With An Essay on the late Storm*. Defoe had been released from Newgate early in November 1703, and he had agreed to certain severe restrictions. He had begun writing and editing the *Review* on 19 February 1704 and would continue this phenomenal task into 1713. Among the penalties he accepted in 1703, the requirement that he give sureties for good behavior during the next seven years particularly aggravated him. In short, he might be charged for any indiscretion he put into print. In *Jure Divino* he saw the penalty as tantamount to silence, a "fancy'd Grave," and explained at the start: "This alludes to the particular Circumstances of the Poet, who having been bound not to Write for Seven Years, had made his own Elegy and suppos'd his Satyr to be Dead." This larger fiction of himself "metaphorically dead" unfolds with all sorts of dramatic flourishes in *An Elegy*. In the preface he describes himself as "a poor abdicated Author," his words appearing everywhere in the "scurrilous Street Ribaldry, and Bear-Garden usage," in both prose and verse. So full of anger is he now, he must retaliate in the "allegory" of the poem. In *An Elegy* Defoe's defense of himself is most prominent, particularly when he poses as an exacerbated writer, now dead and in his grave, rising to strike back at writers who have insulted his muse, "the Whore of Poetry" (107): "*Oppression makes a Poet*; Spleen Endicts" (153). But it is a somewhat chastened muse who introduces characters in the middle section of the poem. Aside from the "great *M[ontagu]*" (Earl of Halifax), the fourteen or so characters are inconsequential, examples of high-class people who commit unnatural crimes or indulge in drunkenness or corrupt the army and navy. There is a possible attack on "young S----," who may be Jonathan Swift, for debauching the House of God (376-381). Most important in the poem is the long section of the poet's self-defense (530-596), wherein he sees himself as comparable to Lord Rochester's "Virtuous Miss" who died with the scandal, but none of the joy, of being a whore (in "Song. Phyllis, be gentler, I advise"). While the specific targets are the same as in other satires, they are given a renewed vitality

*Robert Harley, Earl of Oxford, who rescued Defoe from Newgate Prison and for whom Defoe campaigned and spied
(painting by Godfrey Kneller; by permission of the National Portrait Gallery, London)*

by being made part of a new large fiction. The theme of self builds up to a strong conclusion in which Defoe depicts the allegorical self as a fool.

Curiously joined with *An Elegy* is his *Essay on the Late Storm*, which is actually a poem. Why Defoe calls it an essay is not clear. He does attempt to draw emblematic meanings out of the natural phenomenon of the storm, which occurred from 24 November through 1 December 1703. He visualizes the storm as a providential warning against crimes spread over the "guilty Land." In the extended passage on William III he gives the impression of having known the king personally. He lashes out against cowards in the navy and excoriates the natives' plundering the ship *Goodwin* at Deal. It is also a "High-Church Storm," blow-

ing the steeple down upon the church: "th' Emblem left the Moral in the Lurch" (295-298).

John Dunton wrote about his friend Defoe in 1706 that "by his printing a Poem every day, one would think [he] rhimed in his sleep." Defoe's output of poetry from 1704 to 1706 was unbelievably large. All the poems, still mixing panegyric and satire, were "occasional," each celebrating a public event and surrounding it with considerable history. Now the poet, rescued from Newgate by Robert Harley and feeling an immense gratitude toward him and Queen Anne, brought strong support to the ministry in pamphlets and the *Review*. His strategy for the way he uses poems on his travel missions for Harley can be traced in his letters. Important persons

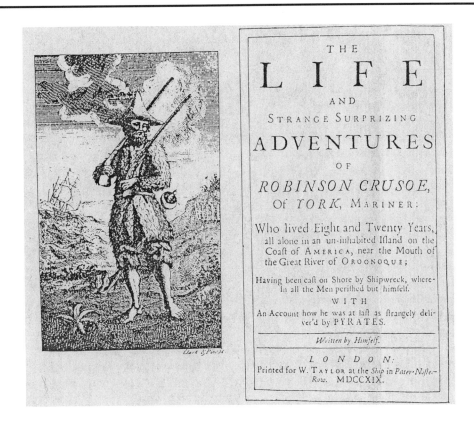

Frontispiece and title page for the first edition of Defoe's most popular work; and Robinson Crusoe and the Footprint, an engraving by Thomas Stothard for a 1790 edition of the novel

like Charles Montagu appreciated the "pretty" turns of phrase in *A Hymn to Victory*, published on 29 August 1704, and *The Double Welcome*, published on 9 January 1705; and he transmitted to Defoe a gift of money from Sarah Churchill, Duchess of Marlborough. In *A Hymn to Victory* Defoe was close to what George Macauley Trevelyan calls the "national mood." Marlborough's victory at Blenheim had shaken all Europe on 10 August 1704: the news had reached England on 18 August. "*Ye Heav'ns!*" says Defoe in his poem, "*What's God a-doing in the World!*" (645). The dedication to the Queen and the conclusion, addressed to the Duke of Marlborough, are signed conspicuously with Defoe's name. In the poem itself, as he addresses Victory, Defoe finds parallel triumphs "at *Cressy, Agin-Court,* and at *Poictiers*" (82); in the battles of William III; and in the military successes of Gustavus Adolphus. The satire is still there, especially directed toward Laurence Hyde, Earl of Rochester, Edward Seymour, and Daniel Finch, second Earl of Nottingham. Characters represent the defeated leader Camille d'Hostun, later Duc de Tallard, as well as the victors, Marlborough and Prince Eugene.

Just over four months later Defoe published *The Double Welcome* honoring the Duke of Marlborough, who while he was not precisely a Whig was a hero of the Whigs and whose land victories seemed to offset the sea victories of Sir George Rooke. In this poem Defoe introduces a new role for the Duke: "*Councils* at Home and *Conquest* from Abroad." As the poet's main thrust, and as he would do also in the prose work *The Consolidator* (1705), he pushed his idea of the consolidator. He pleaded with the Duke "to calm our wild Debates" and balance parties—in short "to *Consolidate*" (309-316). Near the beginning of the poem he argues that it is difficult to differentiate villains from heroes, and then makes another one of his illuminating comments on a sister art: "The Painters thus by Contraries present / The allegorick *Devil* like the *Saint*, / But by some faint Reflection show their Care / *The Cloven Meaning* should not fail t'appear" (50-53). It is not clear how these lines apply to the poem. He urges the use of a plain style as the poet writes about truth, "*'Tis Subject makes a Poet*" (62). He sees himself as entirely abject, "the meanest Poet of the Train" (165). Joseph Addison, in his poem *The Campaign* (published three weeks earlier) represented everything that Defoe despised in poetry. In presenting the "character" of Addison (179-198) Defoe is torn apart by envy over a young poet who

never suffered gaols or "Party-Spleen" and by an artistic sense that in a military poem Addison never described the "how" of battles. Defoe's poem is full of statistics and specific places as he narrates Marlborough's victory at Blenheim, as if he wishes to demonstrate that difficult, exotic names can be turned into poetry in a way that "soft *Boileau*" could not do (209). In particular, Defoe is incensed at Addison, "our Modern *Virgil* " who will not write his poem until he has his pension.

In a later important part of the poem, Defoe describes the "Pulpit War" at home that Marlborough is called upon to settle. Another bill to prevent occasional conformity has been rejected by the House of Lords, and "the strong *Bandity of the Gown*" (that is, Church of England ministers) are up in arms against the Lords (372-379). The occasion gives Defoe the opportunity to draw the not-unfamiliar characters Henry Sacheverell, Charles Leslie, Luke Milbourne, and William Bromley.

The Dyet of Poland, published in July 1705, differs remarkably from occasional poems like *The Double Welcome*. In many respects, it is closer to his earlier ballad-like poems on current parliamentary issues. Unlike them, *The Dyet of Poland* is certainly by Defoe. Like them, it shows him in the role of a keen observer in the House of Commons: he signs himself an "Unconcerned Humble Servant, *Anglipoloski*, of Lithuania." His observations are, first, of men and personalities—of characters, numerous and well developed, altogether about five favorably regarded persons mainly in part 1, and twenty-two satirical ones in both parts. Here he has taken the art of the character farthest along the trajectory that leads to characters in the novels. He presents the character in a short compass, taking full advantage of the virtuosity of language, different styles, contradictions of personality, and above all artistic unities in the relations of characters to one another. The English observer of Polish affairs, the mask or persona, cannot be said to be "unconcerned." His second group of observations concerns his opposition to three bills to prevent occasional conformity that were passed in the House of Commons and rejected in the House of Lords from November 1702 to November 1704. As a part of Anglipoloski's fictional world the three bills are collapsed into a single bill. Defoe's focus as a caustic and at times cynical observer is on the use of such devices as "the Tack" to attach the bill to the Land Tax Bill as was done unsuccessfully in

*Defoe late in life (engraving by
Robert Graves)*

ecution arising from his vitriolic attacks on high-class Tories in *The Dyet of Poland*. The metaphors or allegories are quite transparent. He makes use of current Polish politics, and the "translations" are easily made by the reader: Poland (England), Sweden (France), Cossacks (Dissenters), Sobieski (William III), Augustus (Queen Anne), and so on. He uses "hard Polish Names" that are immediately recognizable for their English counterparts. The characters are wide ranging as if the poet were presenting lives in miniature, not targeted on single quirks of personality but on personality failures over a long period of time. Defoe has in mind the model of Milton's *Paradise Lost*–the large artistic fiction of parliamentary members as orators or speakers in a grand debate. His fallen angels are Tackers, Tookites, or Sneakers, and the debate at his Pandemonium is over the prevention of occasional conformity. The emphasis in presenting a character is on the oratory, rhetoric, or style of a Polander. The alignments are balanced in part 1 with favorable, almost panegyric, treatments for Taguski (Charles Montagu), Ruski (Edward Russell), Rigatski (John Somers), and Cujavia (Thomas Tenison); and satirical treatments for Finski (Daniel Finch, Earl of Nottingham), Lawrensky (Laurence Hyde), old Seymsky (Sir Edward Seymour), and Rokosky (Sir George Rooke). The oratorical skill or lack of it in Finski (295-357) and Seymsky (395-492) catches the attention of Anglipoloski. Defoe's venom in the section on Finski is both personal and political, for it was Finch and John Sheffield, Duke of Buckingham and Normanby (called Bucksky in the poem) who harassed Defoe when he was in Newgate prison awaiting trial and punishment.

Part 2 has a massive display of characters all treated satirically except for Cavensky (William Cavendish), who sided with the Cossacks (Dissenters), opposed the "hasty Priest" (Sacheverell), and brought about the defeat of the bill to prevent occasional conformity. Most of the characters here are presented satirically, that is unfavorably; most are presented as orators; and most are informed with a personal venom, as in the case of Tocoski (John Toke). Part 2 also deals primarily with the Tory Polanders' machinations to pass a bill to prevent occasional conformity. Certain characters appear at greater length, the satire vicious, the banter brilliant, and the innuendo teasingly provocative. Mackreski (Sir Humphrey Mackworth), for instance, becomes the type of the totally ineffectual orator (570-612): "all *Poland* waited on his Chair." In real life Defoe in-

the House of Commons in November 1704. For Defoe to attack certain selected members of the 134 who voted in favor of the tack was clearly dangerous in view of his pillorying in 1703. The broad political parallel between England and Poland is described by Defoe in the preface as being expressed in metaphors and allegories, and he associates the technique with a similar one he had used in *The Consolidator*.

He worked hard at perfecting *The Dyet of Poland*, as he explained to Harley in his letter circa June 1704, in order to bring copies with him on a junket for Harley into "the Country." The poem was thus in gestation for some eleven months. We know about the methods of clandestine distribution of such poems from Pittis's *Whipping Post* (10 July 1705) and *Case of the Church of England's Memorial Fairly Stated* (1705). It is clear also that Defoe was protected by Harley from pros-

tensely disliked Mackworth for his opposing views on occasional conformity and on the poor. Sacharesky (Sacheverell), belonging to a group "that always dealt in *Tropes* and *Similies* absurd" (669), makes use of provocative language (as he did in his sermon *Political Union*, 1702, that at least in part provoked Defoe's *The Shortest-Way with the Dissenters*, 1702). While the character Bromsky (William Bromley) is shown by Defoe as having been full of playful banter and nonsensical statements in Bromley's book *Remarks in the Grande Tour of France and Italy* (1692), the satire has a serious side in that Harley's second edition of the *Remarks* (1705) highlighted Bromley's leanings toward Jacobitism and Catholicism, and thus helped bring about Bromley's defeat for the position of speaker in the House of Commons. Defoe would dredge up the *Remarks* again in the broadside *A Declaration without Doors* (1705). The Bromsky character is severely satirical since this was the man who proclaimed himself the "*Father of the Bill*" (837). For Meersky (Sir Thomas Meres), a Sneaker yet anti-Dissenter, Defoe uses Lord Rochester's comparison of him to "*Jouler the Hound*, a Wiser Beast than he" (898), taken from *A Satyr Against Reason and Mankind* (1679).

In *The Dyet of Poland* Defoe seems to have recognized, as he did also in *The Consolidator*, the emblematic function of character; it is this recognition that advances him closer to the novel as a distinct form of literary discourse. Referring to Tackers and Tookites as being the same, Defoe says in *The Dyet*: "The Emblematick Title's eas'ly known, / Their *Coat of Arms* stands up in *Warsaw* Town" (814-815). Elsewhere in the poem he uses heraldry or a coat of arms to sum up the essence of a character. Bucksky is one of the most brilliantly realized characters (1023-1049) this side of Pope's *Dunciad* partly because it utilizes this emblematic function. About Bucksky's home, the poet says, "the Emblematic sides Describe *his Grace*, / This *Double Front*, and that *a Double Face*." Bucksky is not only like Buckingham House (built in 1703), he is the house. The larger scope of the characterization gets at Bucksky's impotence, which will not allow him to give his mistress what she most desires; it gets at his greed and corruptibility; and the Latin mottoes on his conspicuously lavish house, such as "*Laetentur Lares*" (the household gods delight in such a situation) insinuate that he is also irreligious. This is the man who, with Lord Nottingham, visited Defoe in Newgate and thus earned the wittily expressed hatred here. The character Bucksky

shows Defoe's balance of personal venom and genuine artistry.

In spite of the considerable negativism of *The Dyet of Poland*, the poem strikes more positive notes as it draws to a conclusion. Not only does the poem dramatize in Miltonic terms the defeat of the bill to prevent occasional conformity, it celebrates the purging by Augustus (Queen Anne) of his house, meaning the removal from office of the Tory Lord Nottingham and others. More important, the poem looks forward with considerable affirmation to the joint leadership of Casimir (Sidney Godolphin) as lord treasurer and the Dyet's Marshal (Harley) as secretary of state. Henceforth, these two leaders would bring peace to the land and contentment to the people, including the Cossacks. However, the poem does not end with unmitigated affirmation. The conclusion, as generally happens with Defoe, has more to say about Poland's being saved from knaves who are also fools.

During Defoe's second tour for Harley to bolster his candidates for the general election to parliament, the anonymous poem *A Declaration without Doors* was published on 25 October 1705. It was timed to appear exactly on the opening day of the new parliament and was concerned entirely with the candidacy of the high-flying William Bromley for the position of speaker in the House of Commons. The ballad-like poem is probably but not certainly the work of Defoe on the basis of internal evidence (see volume 7 of *Poems on Affairs of State*, 1975). *A Declaration*, like *The Shortest-Way with the Dissenters*, is all irony. Bromley comes forward and delivers twenty stanzas of his "declaration" for the position of speaker. He brags of all the things he will do for High Church if he is elected to the position. Parts of the poem are richly humorous and deserve an appreciative reading.

A Hymn to Peace, published on 8 January 1706, however is quite different. For the most part it is made up of the near-fatal philosophizing that one finds in *Jure Divino*, on the theme of "Peace and Union" arising from the joint address of the two houses of parliament to Queen Anne shortly before 6 December 1705. Peace, in the poem, is the inner contentment of the poet in this time of political harmony as the treasurer Godolphin puts together a Whig alliance. Rarely does *A Hymn to Peace* come alive, except perhaps in the long account of "sleepy *Momus*" (520-630), who appoints only scandalous justices of the peace all over England.

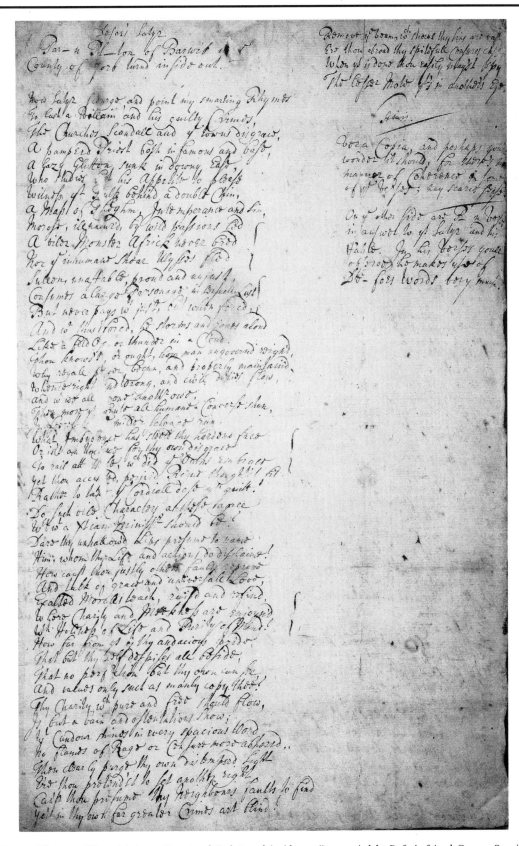

Defoe's "Parson Plaxton of Barwick in ye County of York turnd inside out," as copied by Defoe's friend George Staniland in an 11 May 1709 letter (HM 20340; by permission of the Henry E. Huntington Library and Art Gallery)

More than any other poem *Jure Divino: A Satyr. In Twelve Books* reveals and reflects the mind of Defoe. Published on 18 July 1706, the satire made its appearance ostentatiously, in the full pride of authorship, with an elegant portrait engraved by Michael Van der Gucht as a frontispiece, with the poet's motto "Laudatur et Alget" (honesty is praised, yet starves) with a dedication to Lady Reason, and with verses "To the Author" by A. O. The title page announced the work to be by "The Author of *The True-Born-Englishman.*" *Jure Divino* has been described variously by critics or it has been neglected. Only recently is *Jure Divino* coming into its own as representing the ideological center of Defoe's thought, the breadth of his reading, and the complexity of his mind. It is especially impressive for its political theory.

In the preface Defoe tells of writing the poem "under the heaviest Weight of intolerable Pressures," mostly while he was in prison. He delayed the publication while parliament was in session for a year. He relied upon agents and booksellers in cities like Shrewsbury and Norwich for subscriptions to the book, and he found that the delay caused subscriptions to slump. In letters to friends he constantly pushed subscriptions and in the *Review* announced publication dates and postponements. A piracy of the poem may have appeared even before its official publication. Years later Charles Gildon, in *The Life and Strange Surprizing Adventures of Mr. D-- De F--* (1719), jokingly made Robinson Crusoe boast that Defoe earned five hundred pounds by writing *Jure Divino* in about three weeks "out of this Prolifick Head." Nevertheless, at this time, Defoe was pulling himself out of the bankruptcy and debt the pillory had brought upon him; he was now doing "intelligence" work for Harley; and he seemed to find more time for reading and writing in the frantic pace of his life.

His aim in *Jure Divino* was to write in defense of "the common Right." He starts the preface by saying that he published this work as "the World seem'd to be going mad a second Time with the Error of *Passive Obedience* and *Non-Resistance.*" In the growth of Jacobitism and in a strengthened High Church Tory party Defoe sensed a crisis. The threat was against his own strong belief in monarchy without any divine right and only with the consent of the people as expressed through parliament. Tyrants would therefore be the exact opposites of the limited monarch he had in mind. His larger fiction in *Jure Divino* is to challenge Satyr to trace the history of tyrants right up to the present, to see tyranny as "*the Tincture*" in the blood as created in man by the devil, as he says in the introduction, and to demonstrate that tyranny is inextricably joined with crime and vice. It is quite a dramatic fiction Defoe announces here and then uses to organize the twelve books of his epic. *Jure Divino* has thus the definite structure and unity of the epic. For it does hold the reader through its grand sweep chronologically of vicious tyrants and violent images of lust, murder, and rape, as for instance in the case of the character Sardanapalus (book 8). Defoe has a strong political point about freedom— he even sings a hymn to Liberty in book 5. He views Liberty or emergent Reason as marking the end of tyranny's progress or at least an interruption. He concludes the epic, which is dedicated to Reason (who therefore may be seen as the epic's hero), on a note of vigorous optimism as both William III and Queen Anne represent forces that doom tyranny.

Jure Divino stands out also for its large amount of critical theory about his poetry and art in general. Defoe is especially self-conscious about how poetry is written and observes, for instance (in the preface), that when the poetry is overburdened with argument, he "sacrific'd the Poet to the Reasoning Stile" and used historical notes where the poetry was not "explicit" enough, as Abraham Cowley had done in *Davideis* (1668). By "Reasoning Stile" Defoe has in mind "the legislative style" Dryden defined in the preface to *Religio Laici* (1682) as being apt for instruction. But Defoe also has in mind Milton's *Paradise Lost*, which he mentions frequently and admiringly as it were his model for argumentative verse and "the best Ideas of the Matter of Original Crime, of any Thing put into Words in our Language" (book 7). He continues the exploration of poetry in comparison to painting or the limner's art, stressing the idea that the graphic artist may do the face, but Satyr does the "character" (books 2 and 12). Not infrequently in *Jure Divino*, Defoe will introduce an extended story or character through what he calls a "digression," and at the same time he continues the progress of his narrative as he would do in *A Journal of the Plague Year* (1722) and other books. In *Jure Divino* he also develops the art of integrating adventure and ideology. No better example may be found than the pattern of thought that brings together his ideas of "property," patriarchal theory, consent of the governed, and sovereignty. With the digression on man's compulsion to go to war and with the story of the three men left upon the island of Burmudas—"but these Three Kings fell out about Property" (book 7)—Defoe already has a glimpse in 1706 of Crusoe's island in the distance.

Defoe totally immersed himself in his next mission for Harley. On 13 September 1706 Defoe took horse to Edinburgh, arrived in October, and returned to England on 31 December 1707. He was under Harley's instructions (these seemed always to be arriving late or not at all). It was a lonely, difficult, and dangerous time for Defoe. His assignment was to enter in among the Scots, participate at all levels of society, and report back to Harley on the attitudes of the Scots toward the proposed union between the two countries. Defoe enjoyed playing different roles, assuming half-true disguises, and endlessly improvising.

His job was also to influence and change public opinions about the union. He did this through numerous prose pamphlets and broadsides, the Edinburgh edition of the *Review*, and a few remarkably varied poems. The first of these, *The Vision* (1706), survives in a holograph manuscript that tells us a great deal about Defoe's method of composing, the relationship of one of his manuscripts to the printed texts, and the swift communication between Edinburgh and London in these hectic days of negotiation. John Hamilton, Lord Belhaven, was the principal actor in the verbal altercation that took place on 2 November 1706, when the Scots parliament was debating the article of incorporating union. He delivered a lengthy harangue against the union that was filled with historical parallels and classical allusions. The Jacobite George Lockhart, in his *Memoirs* (1714), suggests that Belhaven "acted a double part." So effective was Belhaven's speech, the vote on the article was delayed over the weekend, and early in the following week Defoe's "Vision" was circulating in manuscript and had a devastating effect on Lord Belhaven's argument. In *The History of the Union* (1709) Defoe reported the entire incident including the Earl of Marchmont's reply to Belhaven: "*Behold he dream'd, but, lo! when he awoke, he found it was a Dream.*" In *The Vision* Defoe brings the art of lampoon to perfection. The entire poem, like *A Declaration without Doors*, is irony, without any revealing of the poet's real attitude toward the union. All the histrionics of Belhaven's original speech are there: "But [he] Let Drop a Few Hypocriticall Teares / So The Crocodile weeps on The Carcass he

Tares" (107-108). And the poem ends with a reminder by the Lord in the North that the betrayal going on in parliament is not very different from Brutus's of Caesar. Almost immediately after the printed version of *The Vision* appeared, Lord Belhaven followed with *A Scots Answer*, and Defoe retaliated with the broadside *A Reply to the Scots Answer, to the British Vision*—entirely focused on Belhaven's language and style in a manner reminiscent of Dryden's "MacFlecknoe."

The poems that followed are at the heart of Defoe's participation in the act of union approved on 1 May 1707. Of the two major poems, *Caledonia, A Poem In Honour of Scotland, and the Scots Nation* had certain embellishments in the Edinburgh edition published in early December 1706: a license from the duke of Queensberry (printed on the verso of the title page) prohibiting any piracy of the poem and a dedication to the duke himself. Publication, as with *Jure Divino*, was by subscription. A few weeks later the poem was issued in London. In contrast to *A Scots Poem: Or A New-years Gift, From a Native Of The Universe, To His Fellow-Animals in Albania* (1707), the earlier poem deliberately avoids any direct advocacy of the union and deals with the theme of "improvements" for Scotland by a recommitment of national energies. *Caledonia* is a panegyric of a nation. Character, says Defoe in the preface, is not the aim of his book, but "a Circumstance like the finishing Strokes of a Fine Picture added to grace the Work: The principal Design was the Climate, Nation, Seas, Trade, Lands, Improvements and Temper of *Scotland* and its People." A stranger to Scotland, he boldly calls upon parliament, upon the owners of the land, of the "property," to bring about the changes.

He carries out the design of the poem in three parts and an epilogue: part 1 focuses on Scotland's geography, climate, soil ("Beauty's best describ'd by Usefulness"), and on the country's wealth in fishery but also on its pervasive poverty; part 2 on "the lab'ring Poor dejected and supprest," on the industry of the people, and most important on the military achievements of Scots abroad who taught warfare to the Swedes, Muscovites, and Poles, and who fought under Gustavus Adolphus in the great battles of 1632 and 1633; and part 3 on Scotland's fame at home, where he introduces the important names, for the most part quick listings, except for the family of Stuart. In part 2 we have a curious foreshadowing of *Memoirs of a Cavalier* in the military exploits of the Scots (567-780). It is in part 3 that

Conjugal Lewdnefs:

O R,

MATRIMONIAL

WHOREDOM.

Loofe Thoughts, at firft, like fubterranean Fires,
Burn inward, fmothering, with unchaft Defires;
But getting Vent, to Rage and Fury turn,
Burft in Volcano's, and like Ætna burn;
The Heat increafes as the Flames afpire,
And turns the folid Hills to liquid Fire.
So fenfual Flames, when raging in the Soul,
Firft vitiate all the Parts, then fire the Whole;
Burn up the Bright, the Beauteous, the Sublime,
And turn our lawful Pleafures into Crime.

LONDON

Printed for T. WARNER, at the *Black Boy* in
Pater-Nofter-Row. M DCC XXVII.

Title page for Defoe's work on some of the pitfalls of marriage, later retitled A Treatise Concerning The Use and Abuse of The Marriage Bed *in 1727 because the original title proved offensive*

Defoe presents a new conception of poetry at some length. As part of Scotland's fame at home, he describes the garden of learning, its epics, strong heroics, lyrics and pastorals, and "Panygericks circled round with Bays" (1096-1101). Knowledge is in the same garden, but wit is constantly "*weeded* of Conceit" (1107). Usefulness is not only a part of the poem's design, it also shares in the practical emphasis that Defoe places on poetry: here the Muses "Wed the Sciences for Wives, / And beat *like Hemp* at *Bridewell* for their Lives" (1145-1148).

A Scots Poem, published in early January 1707, fits exactly the conception of poetry described in *Caledonia*: "No loytring Sing-song Muses trifle here." This long poem, extending to 1125 lines, is cast in the form of a "debate" in which a Scot narrator deliberately confines himself to the present, with only a glance back to "*Eighty Nine,* / When *Scots* did for their *Libertys* appear" (92-93). In the manner of a "miscellany," as Defoe described the poem, he surveys and answers the different factions opposing the union. The issues are specific, mundane, and effectively argued. Just before he takes up the practical issues of the union, the Scot narrator suddenly bursts out in expansive admiration of far-off places (140-196). He has the wanderlust of Robinson Crusoe or Captain Singleton. In the second part of *A Scots Poem*, a favorite character of Defoe's, Britannia, appears and answers the familiar objections to the union raised by "a *Mob* of *Cavillers*" (763-1105).

No other major poem on the union can be identified as the work of Defoe. Practical, but very low in quality, is *The Fifteen Comforts of a Scotch-Man*, published in February 1707, which has the appropriate union-centered content but none of Defoe's style or language. In the *Review* for 11 February 1707, he advanced the cause of the union with what seems to be his own poetical fragment. Another poem, *The True-Born Britain* (1707), was apparently published after the union gained approval. It announces on the title page that it is "*written by the Author of the True-Born Englishman,*" but as in other cases where such a claim is made, the poem remains doubtful as the work of Defoe. One other recently found holograph, "Resignacon," dated July 1708 (published in revised versions in 1710 and 1712), has led its discoverer, Frank H. Ellis, to the conclusion that the poem expresses Defoe's valedictory to an elaborate or figurative style in favor of "mathematical plainness." That he had not abandoned the writing of poems is clear from "Parson Plaxton of Barwick in ye County of York turnd inside out," which survives in a manuscript letter dated 11 May 1709, from a certain George Staniland, written on local Whig politics. (The poem was published in *The Huntington Library Quarterly* in November 1955). *High Church Miracles* and *The Age of Wonders*, both published in 1710, were poems set to music; they were probably written by Defoe, as was *A Welcome to the Medal*, published in September 1711 and added to Defoe's works in volume 7 of *Poems on Affairs of State* (1975). In his last major poem, *A Hymn to the Mob*, published on 14 July 1715, Defoe still uses a large fiction, here a taxonomy of mobs, but without any of the tension or piquancy provided by characters. The content is more relevant to 1710 than to 1715. *A Hymn to the Mob* has all the earmarks of Defoe, the favorite expressions and the illuminating definitions, but most of the poetic fire has gone out.

Defoe's development as a poet was minimal. In the years 1705 and 1706 he poured out the

Defoe's tomb in Bunhill Fields

against the British oppressors. In his own day the author of *The True-Born Englishman* and *A Hymn to the Pillory* was a force to be reckoned with. Between the death of Dryden and the arrival of the young Pope, the ablest satirist was Daniel Defoe the poet.

rhymes, but whether he called the poems hymns or elegies, they came out "rough satires." He admired the Restoration poets rather than the Augustan. In the years of crisis for him (1714-1715), when Robert Harley left the political scene, he turned to the subversive journalism that brought him infamy after his death. His influence as a poet has been slight. After Defoe's death in 1731 there were about a dozen reprints or selections of *The True-Born Englishman*, about five of *A Hymn to the Pillory*, and little more. No praise of Defoe as a poet came from Swift, Pope, Johnson, or Coleridge. William Hone, in *The Right Divine of Kings to Govern Wrong!* (1821), asserted that *Jure Divino* was still apropos and that Defoe was "the ablest politician of his day," but that he was not much of a poet, and Hone set about rewriting the poem. Charles Lamb had only admiration for *A Hymn to the Pillory*. In the early twentieth century, selections of *The True-Born Englishman* were incorporated into *John Bull's Failings* (1904) as Hindu propaganda

Letters:
The Letters of Daniel Defoe, edited by George Harris Healey (Oxford: Clarendon Press, 1955);
Paula R. Backscheider, "John Russell to Daniel Defoe: Fifteen Unpublished Letters from Scotland," *Philological Quarterly*, 61 (Spring 1982): 161-177.

Bibliographies:
Henry C. Hutchins, "Daniel Defoe (1660-1731)," in *The Cambridge Bibliography of English Literature*, edited by F. W. Bateson, 4 volumes (New York: Macmillan / Cambridge: Cambridge University Press, 1941), II: 495-514;
D. F. Foxon, "Defoe: A Specimen of a Catalogue of English Verse 1701-1730," *Library*, 20 (December 1965): 277-297;
John Robert Moore, *A Checklist of the Writings of Daniel Defoe*, second edition, revised (Hamden, Conn.: Archon, 1971);
Maximillian E. Novak, "Daniel Defoe," in *The New Cambridge Bibliography of English Literature*, edited by George Watson, 5 volumes (Cambridge: Cambridge University Press, 1971), II: cols. 880-917;
Foxon, *English Verse 1701-1750: A Catalogue of Separately Printed Poems with Notes on Contemporary Collected Editions*, 2 volumes (Cambridge: Cambridge University Press, 1975).

Biographies:
Theophilus Cibber and Robert Shiels, "Daniel De Foe," in *The Lives of the Poets of Great Britain and Ireland*, 4 volumes (London: R. Griffiths, 1753), IV: 313-325;
George Chalmers, *The Life of Daniel De Foe* (London: John Stockdale, 1785; revised and enlarged edition, 1790);
James Sutherland, *Defoe*, second edition, revised, (London: Methuen, 1950);
John Robert Moore, *Daniel Defoe: Citizen of the Modern World* (Chicago: University of Chicago Press, 1958);
Frank Bastian, *Defoe's Early Life* (Totowa, N.J.: Barnes & Noble, 1981);

Paula R. Backscheider, *Daniel Defoe: His Life* (Baltimore & London: Johns Hopkins University Press, 1989).

References:

Paula R. Backscheider, *Daniel Defoe: Ambition & Innovation* (Lexington: University Press of Kentucky, 1986);

Backscheider, "The Verse Essay, John Locke, and Defoe's *Jure Divino*," *ELH: English Literary History*, 55 (Spring 1988): 99-124;

Harold Bloom, editor, *Daniel Defoe*, Modern Critical Views (New York, New Haven & Philadelphia: Chelsea House, 1987);

Richard C. Boys, *Sir Richard Blackmore and the Wits: A Study of "Commendatory Verses on the Author of the Two Arthurs and the Satyr against Wit" (1700)* (Ann Arbor: University of Michigan Press, 1949);

Charles Eaton Burch, "The Authorship of *A Scots Poem* (1707)," *Philological Quarterly*, 22 (January 1943): 51-57;

Mary Elizabeth Campbell, *Defoe's First Poem* (Bloomington, Ind.: Principia, 1938);

A Catalog of the Defoe Collection in the Boston Public Library (Boston: G. K. Hall, 1966);

Nasarvanji Manecji Cooper, ed., *John Bull's Failings: Being Selections from Daniel Defoe's "The True-born Englishman"* (London: Simpkin, Marshall / Bombay: Cooper, 1904);

Frank H. Ellis, "Defoe's 'Resignačon' and the Limitations of 'Mathematical Plainness,'" *Review of English Studies*, new series, 36 (August 1985): 338-354;

Ellis, "Notes for an Edition of Defoe's Verse," *Review of English Studies*, new series, 32 (November 1981): 398-407;

Ellis, ed., *Poems on Affairs of State: Augustan Satirical Verse, 1660-1714*, volumes 6 and 7 (New Haven & London: Yale University Press, 1970, 1975);

P. N. Furbank and W. R. Owens, "Defoe as Poet," in their *The Canonization of Daniel Defoe* (New Haven & London: Yale University Press, 1988), pp. 134-140;

Charles Gildon, *The Life and Strange Surprizing Adventures of Mr. D-- De F--* (London: J. Roberts, 1719);

Helmut Heidenreich, ed., *The Libraries of Daniel Defoe and Phillips Farewell* (Berlin: Freie Universität Berlin, 1970);

Stefan Heym, *The Queen Against Defoe and Other Stories* (Westport, N.Y.: Hill, 1974);

William Hone, *The Right Divine of Kings to Govern Wrong!*, third edition (London: William Hone, 1821);

Giles Jacob, "Mr. Daniel De Foe," in *The Poetical Register: or, the Lives and Characters of all the English Poets*, revised edition (London, 1723);

John McVeagh, "Rochester and Defoe: A Study in Influence," *Studies in English Literature*, 14 (Summer 1974): 327-341;

John Robert Moore, *Defoe and the Pillory and Other Studies* (Bloomington: Indiana University Press, 1939);

John Bowyer Nichols, ed., *The Life and Errors of John Dunton, Citizen of London*, 2 volumes (London: J. Nichols, Son & Bentley, 1818);

Maximillian E. Novak, *Defoe and the Nature of Man* (London: Oxford University Press, 1963);

Novak, *Realism, Myth, and History in Defoe's Fiction* (Lincoln & London: University of Nebraska Press, 1983);

John Oldmixon, *The History of England* (London: Thomas Cox, Richard Ford & Richard Hett, 1735);

Spiro Peterson, *Daniel Defoe: A Reference Guide 1731-1924* (Boston: Hall, 1987);

Peterson, "Defoe's Yorkshire Quarrel," *Huntington Library Quarterly*, 19 (November 1955): 57-79;

John J. Richetti, *Daniel Defoe* (Boston: Twayne, 1987);

Richetti, *Defoe's Narratives: Situations and Structures* (Oxford: Clarendon Press, 1975);

Pat Rogers, ed., *Defoe: The Critical Heritage* (London & Boston: Routledge & Kegan Paul, 1972);

Rogers, *Robinson Crusoe* (London: Allen & Unwin, 1979);

Albert Rosenberg, "Defoe's *Pacificator* Reconsidered," *Philological Quarterly*, 37 (October 1958): 433-439;

Michael Shinagel, *Daniel Defoe and Middle-Class Gentility* (Cambridge, Mass.: Harvard University Press, 1968);

Henry L. Snyder, "Daniel Defoe, the Duchess of Marlborough, and the *Advice to the Electors of Great Britain*," *Huntington Library Quarterly*, 29 (November 1965): 53-62;

John A. Stoler, *Daniel Defoe: An Annotated Bibliography of Modern Criticism, 1900-1980* (New York & London: Garland, 1984);

James Sutherland, "The Poet," in *Daniel Defoe: A Critical Study* (Cambridge, Mass.: Harvard University Press, 1971), pp. 91-116;

Ian Watt, *The Rise of the Novel: Studies in Defoe, Richardson and Fielding* (London: Chatto & Windus, 1957).

Papers:

Only a few manuscripts of the poems have survived. The holograph of "Meditacons" is at the Henry E. Huntington Library, Los Angeles, and that of *The Vision* is at the University of Notting-

ham Library. "Parson Plaxton of Barwick" is in a manuscript letter not in Defoe's hand at the Huntington Library. A few other manuscripts of poems or parts of poems are at the British Library and the Bodleian Library. *Resignaćon*, in holograph manuscript, remains in private hands. Correspondence between Defoe and Harley is in the Portland Papers, British Library, and correspondence between Defoe and John Russell is in the National Library of Scotland, Edinburgh. Other papers are in the William Andrews Clark Memorial Library, Los Angeles.

Robert Dodsley

(13 February 1703 - 23 September 1764)

Harry M. Solomon
Auburn University

BOOKS: *Servitude* (London: Printed for T. Worrall, 1729); republished as *The Footman's Friendly Advice to his Brethren of the Livery* (London: Printed for T. Worrall, 1731);

An Epistle from a Footman in London to the Celebrated Stephen Duck (London: Printed for J. Brindley, 1731);

A Muse in Livery: or the Footman's Miscellany (London: Printed for J. Nourse, 1732);

The Modern Reasoners (London: Printed for L. Gilliver, 1734);

An Epistle to Mr Pope, Occasion'd by his Essay on Man (London: Printed for L. Gilliver, 1734);

Beauty, or the Art of Charming (London: Printed for L. Gilliver, 1735);

The Toy-Shop (London: Printed for L. Gilliver, 1735; Providence, R.I.: Printed by Carter & Wilkinson, 1794);

The King and the Miller of Mansfield (London: Printed for the Author, 1737; Boston: Printed by Belknap & Hall, 17-?);

The Art of Preaching (London: Printed for R. Dodsley, 1738);

Sir John Cockle at Court (London: Printed for R. Dodsley, 1738);

The Chronicle of the Kings of England, as Nathan Ben Saddi (London: Printed for T. Cooper, 1740; Newport, R.I.: Printed by the Widow Franklin, 1744);

The Blind Beggar of Bethnal Green (London: Printed for R. Dodsley, 1741; Philadelphia: Printed & sold by Robert Bell, 1777);

Colin's Kisses (London: Printed for R. Dodsley, 1742);

Pain and Patience (London: Printed for R. Dodsley, 1742 [i.e., 1743]);

Rex Et Pontifex (London: Printed for M. Cooper, 1745);

Trifles (London: Printed for R. Dodsley, 1745); second edition, enlarged, 2 volumes (London: Printed for J. Dodsley, 1777);

The Museum (London, 29 March 1746-12 September 1747);

Robert Dodsley, circa 1760 (painting by Joshua Reynolds; by permission of the Dulwich Gallery)

The Preceptor, 2 volumes (London: Printed for R. Dodsley, 1748);

The Triumph of Peace (London: Printed for R. Dodsley, 1749);

The Oeconomy of Human Life (London: M. Cooper, 1751 [i.e., 1750]; Boston: Printed & sold by D. Fowle, 1752);

The World (London, 4 January 1753-30 December 1756);

Public Virtue (London: Printed for R. & J. Dodsley, 1753);

Melpomene, or The Regions of Terror and Pity (London, 1757);

Cleone (London: Printed for R. & J. Dodsley, 1758).

PLAY PRODUCTIONS: *The Toy-Shop*, London, Theatre Royal in Covent Garden, 3 February 1735;

The King and the Miller of Mansfield, London, Theatre Royal in Drury Lane, 29 January 1737;

Sir John Cockle at Court, London, Theatre Royal in Drury Lane, 23 February 1738;

The Blind Beggar of Bethnal Green, London, Theatre Royal in Drury Lane, 3 April 1741;

The Triumph of Peace, London, Theatre Royal in Drury Lane, February 1749;

Cleone, London, Theatre Royal in Covent Garden, 2 December 1758.

OTHER: *A Select Collection of Old Plays*, 12 volumes, edited, with a history of drama, by Dodsley (London: Printed for R. Dodsley, 1744-1745);

A Collection of Poems. By Several Hands, 6 volumes, edited, with an introduction, by Dodsley (London: Printed for R. Dodsley, 1748-1758);

Select Fables of Esop and other Fabulists, edited, with
a preface, by Dodsley (Birmingham: Printed
by John Baskerville for R. & J. Dodsley,
1761; Philadelphia: Printed & sold by Joseph Crukshank, 1786); preface published
separately as *Essay on Fable* (Los Angeles:
Clark Memorial Library, 1965);
*The Works in Verse and Prose of William Shenstone,
Esq.*, 2 volumes, edited, with an introduction, by Dodsley (London: Printed for R. &
J. Dodsley, 1764).

When on a tour of Oxford in 1776 Samuel
Johnson was discussing biography with Thomas
Warton, his companion James Boswell suggested
that "Robert Dodsley's life should be written, as
he has been so much connected with the wits of
his time, and by his literary merit had raised himself from the station of a footman" (*Life of Samuel
Johnson*, 1791). As Boswell suggests, Dodsley remains a fascinating figure both because of his
rise from servitude to literary success and because of his significant connections as the most important English publisher of the century, working with Johnson, Daniel Defoe, Alexander Pope,
Edward Young, Mark Akenside, William Shenstone, Samuel Richardson, David Garrick, Joseph
and Thomas Warton, William Collins, Thomas
Gray, Thomas Percy, Horace Walpole, Oliver
Goldsmith, Edmund Burke, Laurence Sterne,
and the Earl of Chesterfield, among many others. Thus, if the concept of literary influence is extended to include not only the influence of
Dodsley's own works but the works of others that
he either initiated or published, a convincing case
can be made that Robert Dodsley was the most influential English man of letters during his lifetime.

Dodsley was born in Mansfield on 13 February 1703 to an ill-paid schoolmaster, also named
Robert, and his wife, whose name is unknown.
As the eldest son, young Robert was apprenticed
to a local stocking weaver. Miserable, he deserted
his indenture and fled from the forests of Sherwood to seek his fortune in London. In the great
city he began at the bottom, entering service as a
footman. Luckily he was hired by the reputed bastard son of Charles II, Charles Dartineuf, an epi-
cure, member of the Kitcat Club, and dinner companion of Pope, Joseph Addison, and Jonathan
Swift. Although an early essay on the "Miseries
of Poverty" (in *A Muse in Livery*, 1732) shows the
demeaning hardships of his first years in town,
an early verse epistle in the same volume ("The

Frontispiece for A Muse in Livery *(1732), Dodsley's first
major publication, a collection of imitative poems that became
very popular with his contemporaries*

Footman") describing his daily duties suggests
that his service was also his polite education. The
only pleasant hour is spent serving at table:

> For whilst I unregarded stand,
> With ready salver in my hand,
> And seem to understand no more
> Than just what's call'd for, out to pour;
> I hear, and mark the courtly phrases,
> And all the elegance that passes;
> Disputes maintain'd without digression,
> With ready wit, and fine expression. . . .

While satire of the period is full of fulmina-
tions against servants who ape their master's mannerisms, Dodsley so successfully appropriated the
norms of high culture that in September 1729 he
published *Servitude*, a short sixpenny pamphlet of
rhyming advice to "excite *Bad* Servants to their
Duty." Although announced as "Written by a Footman," in stressing the need for "Carefulness"
and "Obedience," *Servitude* was calculated more

"Tully's Head," Dodsley's device, which appeared in his books and on the sign for his bookshop in Pall Mall, which he opened in 1735

to distinguish Dodsley from his companions in the pantry than to show solidarity with them. Defoe, that aging chronicler of the proletariat, was persuaded to write a preface, which, added to the novelty of Dodsley's authorship, made the pamphlet popular enough to justify a retitled second edition: *The Footman's Friendly Advice to his Brethren of the Livery* (1731).

Almost simultaneous with the publication of Joseph Spence's *Full and Authentic Account of Stephen Duck* in early 1731, Dodsley published another sixpenny pamphlet, *An Epistle from a Footman in London to the Celebrated Stephen Duck*, drawing an analogy between the rhyming footman and the thresher poet. Although "unlearn'd," they have both tasted the Pierian spring, and Dodsley does not doubt "but that in Time / Our tender Muses, learning now to climb, / May reach Perfection's Top, and grow sublime. / The *Iliad* scarce was *Homer's* first Essay; / *Virgil* wrote not his *Aeneid* in a Day; / Nor is't impossible a Time might be, / When *Pope* and *Prior* wrote like You and Me." In his century's search for "mute inglorious Miltons" of untutored genius, Dodsley became his own publicist. His success may be judged from the five pages of subscribers listed in his first major publication, *A Muse in Livery; or the Footman's Miscellany* (1732). Robert Walpole took four copies, and the impressive list of peers and notable commoners pledged to Dodsley's project suggests the extent of his notoriety; a second edition soon followed. In a self-deprecatory preface, Dodsley begs pardon for his "uncultivated mind," pleading a footman's lack of "a liberal education, or a polite converse," necessities "to shew even the best natural genius in a toler-

able light." The poems themselves are talented imitations of the fashionable miscellaneous verse of Abraham Cowley, John Gay, and Matthew Prior. The tone varies from the elegiac quatrains offered the aging Lady Howe over her husband's death ("But let this thought alleviate / The sorrows of your mind: / He's gone–but he is gone so late / You can't be long behind") to the bawdy conversational couplets of an epistle to a fellow servant ("WHY, *Jack*, how now? I hear strange stories / How *Molly* what-d'ye-call't your whore is / Hold,–blot that word;–rhyme forc'd it in, / Your dear kind mistress, Sir, I mean: / And people say, but whisper that, / That she, poor soul! is big with brat").

On 14 February 1732 Dodsley celebrated the popularity of *A Muse in Livery* by marrying the "Kitty" of his love verses, Catherine Iserloo. He was also emboldened to petition Pope with the manuscript of a short play. On 5 February 1733 Pope wrote that he liked the "morality and satire" of *The Toy-Shop* (eventually published in 1735) and would recommend it to John Rich, manager of Covent Garden. Moreover, Pope undoubtedly encouraged his publisher Lawton Gilliver to issue three of Dodsley's new poems in separate slim folio editions. The most interesting of the three is an *Epistle to Mr Pope, Occasion'd by his Essay on Man*, published in October 1734 shortly after Pope acknowledged authorship of his 1733 work and those poetasters he had attacked in *The Dunciad* (1728) shifted from adulation of the *Essay on Man* to execration. Denouncing "the dunces," Dodsley praises Pope as the "GREAT bard! in whom united we admire, / The sage's wisdom, and the poet's fire."

Rich produced *The Toy-Shop* on 3 February 1735. The one-act afterpiece adapts Thomas Randolph's *Conceited Pedlar* (1650) to Pope's metaphor of "the moving Toyshop" of the heart. The shop owner is, as one character says, "a new Kind of a Satirical Parson, your Shop is your Scripture, and every piece of Goods a different Text, from which you expose the Vices and Follies of Mankind in a very fine Allegorical Sermon." Although the play is less a drama than a series of clever analogies, it was an instant and enormous success. The reviewer for the *Prompter* wrote that it "received the loudest Applauses . . . heard this long while," and it was performed thirty-four times during 1735 alone. Three days after its opening Gilliver published *The Toy-Shop*. A second edition was necessary two weeks later, and four more editions appeared before the end of the

Joseph Spence, Oxford professor of poetry and lifelong friend of Dodsley (mezzotint after a painting by I. Wood)

year. By 1758 the little piece was in its sixteenth legitimate edition and was pirated, translated, and anthologized in almost every eighteenth-century collection of English farces.

Pope's patronage of Dodsley was just beginning. Shortly after the stage success, the *Daily Courant* advertised that volume two of Pope's *Works* was for sale at Gilliver's shop, Homer's Head, and at Tully's Head, the newly opened Pall Mall bookshop of "R. Dodsley, Author of the *Toy-Shop*." Dodsley shared the Ciceronian scepticism in Pope's *Essay on Man*, and Pope may have suggested the name of the shop. Probably Pope had Gilliver teach Dodsley the publishing business, and he certainly gave him a hundred pounds to get started. More importantly, during Dodsley's first years Pope made him joint or sole publisher of various of his works, including his *Letters* (1737).

Dodsley opened the bookshop, which was destined to become London's primary literary meeting place, at an opportune time, as four of the most prestigious publishers, including Jacob

Tonson and Bernard Lintot, died within the year. Uniting a flair for publicity with a genius at identifying and encouraging talented authors, Dodsley became the dominant publisher of the age. In the thirty years between the opening of Tully's Head and his death, Dodsley's name appears on over eleven hundred title pages. Additionally, Dodsley not only selected or commissioned the works he published but, as contemporary correspondence shows, frequently acted as constructive critic and editor.

In 1736, again at Pope's instigation, Dodsley published an edition of Thomas Norton and Thomas Sackville's 1561 play *Gorboduc* with a preface by Joseph Spence, the Oxford professor of poetry who became Dodsley's unlikely lifelong friend. Fascinated by untutored genius, the learned professor united with the former footman to publicize a series of unlettered prodigies. Together with Spence, Dodsley helped create the cult of natural genius. In 1754, when David Hume wished to aid the blind poet Thomas Blacklock, he wrote to Dodsley, who responded by publishing *An Account of . . . Blacklock* written by Spence (1754) and two editions of Blacklock's *Poems* (both in 1756). A footnote to Spence's book lauds Duck, Richardson, and Dodsley as three of his "most intimate Friends, who have been raised purely by their literary Merit and good Characters."

On 29 January 1737 at Drury Lane Dodsley gave the cult of natural genius a moral turn by contrasting artful courtiers to uncorrupted rural peasants in *The King and the Miller of Mansfield*. Lost in Sherwood Forest, the king realizes that his aristocratic trappings are "false Attributes" that must be discarded before the monarch can become a man. The play was so successful that despite its sentimental opposition to aristocratic prerogative and its explicit association of virtue with the laboring classes, the author's third night was staged "by Command of their Royal Highness the Prince and Princess of Wales," both of whom attended the packed theater. The following season Dodsley brought the popular Miller to London in a disappointing sequel, *Sir John Cockle at Court* (23 February 1738). In various guises, a democratic ethos pervades many of the works issued by Tully's Head, including Dodsley's own "Kings of Europe":

Why pray, of late, do Europe's kings
No jester in their courts admit?

They've grown such stately solemn things.
To bear a joke they think not fit.

But tho' each court a jester lacks,
To laugh at monarchs to their face;
All mankind behind their backs
Supply the honest jester's place.

Dodsley's dominance in the publishing of poetry began in April 1737 with his issue of Richard Glover's overvalued epic *Leonidas*. His network expanded with the addition of influential patrons, including Lords Lyttelton and Chesterfield, until his publication list read like a poetic history of the period. For example, in 1738, in addition to separate issues of Pope's "Universal Prayer" and the second dialogue of *One Thousand Seven Hundred and Thirty Eight*, he published three volumes of Henry Brooke's translation of *Tasso's Jerusalem*, three editions of John Dalton's adaptation of Milton's *Comus*, the second and third editions of *Leonidas*, Henry Pemberton's *Observations on Poetry* (which puffed Glover's *Leonidas* as the equal of Homer and Milton), Richard Savage's *Volunteer Laureat*, and the first poem by a bookseller's son from the provinces, *London* by Samuel Johnson.

In the years to follow, Dodsley published most of the poetry of his contemporaries that is still read today, including Young's *Night Thoughts* (1742), Shenstone's *Schoolmistress* (1742), Joseph Warton's *Enthusiast* (1744) and his *Odes* (1746), Thomas Warton's *Pleasures of Melancholy* (1747), various works by Collins, most of Gray, including *Elegy Written in a Country Churchyard* (1751), and Johnson's *Vanity of Human Wishes* (1749). Simultaneously, he published a series of periodicals that printed and reviewed poetry. Moreover, Dodsley also published much of the literary theory and criticism of the period, including Akenside's *Pleasures of the Imagination* (1744), Joseph Warton's *Essay on the Genius and Writings of Mr Pope* (1756), Thomas Warton's *Observations on the Fairie Queene of Spenser* (1754), and Burke's *Philosophical Enquiry into the Origin of our Ideas of the Sublime and Beautiful* (1757). When to this partial list are added such works of fiction as Johnson's *Rasselas* (1759) and Sterne's *Tristram Shandy* (1760), it becomes clear how Johnson could say that it was around Dodsley's dinner table that "the true Noctes Atticae are revived."

During the "Athenian Nights" at Tully's Head, Dodsley not only encouraged individual authors but also initiated a series of larger literary projects that were immensely influential. In

Engraving from a portrait of Dodsley by William Alcock

1743, noting that most pre-Restoration plays had "become exceedingly scarce and extravagantly dear," he solicited subscriptions for *A Select Collection of Old Plays* (1744-1745), which he edited in twelve volumes with his own scholarly "Rise and Fall of the English Stage" as preface. Another of his projects was the best literary magazine of the age. Edited by Akenside, Dodsley's *Museum, or Literary and Historical Register*, in assembling works by the best living authors, both focused and influenced contemporary taste.

Before Dodsley had sufficient issues of the *Museum* to print as collected volumes and, thus, before his competitor Edward Cave of the more humble *Gentleman's Magazine* could breathe easy at the demise of Dodsley's "super-excellent Magazine," Dodsley had already used the *Museum* to preview the two greatest projects of his career: *A Collection of Poems. By Several Hands* and Johnson's *Dictionary*. In January 1748, barely four months after he ceased publication of the *Museum*, Dodsley issued the first three of the six volumes of the collection, an anthology destined to stock the shelves of every poet for the next hundred years. John Butt suggests that study of Dodsley's collection is the most convenient way to ascertain "the state of English poetry at the death of Pope." Unlike the miscellany initiated by John Dryden, which Tonson had reissued as a six-volume collection (in 1716 and 1727), Dodsley's collection contains only contemporary poetry. Thus far Butt is correct; however, his static metaphor fails to emphasize that by excluding earlier poems Dodsley's work allowed his contemporaries a new beginning out from under the massive shadows of Dryden and Pope.

Of course, in addition to creating room for contemporary experimentation, Dodsley's collection bequeathed a canon to subsequent poets. Twenty-eight of the poems had originally appeared in the *Museum* and many in pamphlet publications from Tully's Head that were easily lost and forgotten. Thus, one motive for his anthology is "to preserve to the public those poetical performances, which seemed to merit a longer remembrance than what would probably be secured to them by the MANNER wherein they were originally published." The result is that Dodsley created the canon for all subsequent study of the poetry of his period. With the exception of Young, whose *Night Thoughts* he was publishing simultaneously as separate volumes, Dodsley included, as Raymond Havens notes, "every important poet of the time as well as nearly all the minor figures that are worth while."

In *A Collection* are poems such as Mary Wortley Montagu's "Town Eclogues" and Johnson's august couplet imitations of Juvenal that acknowledge and extend the intimidating influence of Pope; but these jostle with the varied imitations of Pindar, Spenser, and Milton that hindsight would designate as "preromantic." For example, the villain of Gilbert West's "Education" is Custom who trains youth "to wear and hug his chain." Familiarly titled odes abound: "Ode to Fancy," "Ode to an Aeolus's Harp," "Ode. On Melancholy"; and when one reads "A Vernal Ode" and "An Autumnal Ode" remembering Keats's "Ode to May" and "To Autumn," it is difficult not to believe that Dodsley is creating English Romanticism, the more so when we remember that another of Dodsley's projects was Thomas Percy's *Reliques of Ancient English Poetry* (1765), volumes of which William Wordsworth opined that there was not "an able writer in verse of the present day who would not be proud to acknowledge his obligations" (in his introduction to *Lyrical Ballads*, second edition, 1815).

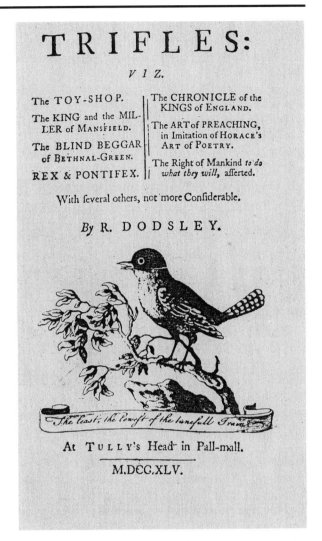

Title page for the first collection of Dodsley's works, its title an example of Dodsley's self-deprecating humor

In contrast to the many fulsome panegyrics to aristocrats in Dryden's *Miscellany*, a democratic spirit pervades Dodsley's volumes; and the town and court focus of the earlier collection changes to a deistic adoration of nature as the locus of virtue, health, and beauty. Volume five opens with Shenstone's image of the "lone *hermit* on the mountain brow . . . his breast to admiration prone," while volume six closes with Gray's "Bard," celebrating from a mountain vantage point both poetic vision and political resistance.

The first notice of Johnson's plan to undertake a dictionary also appeared in Dodsley's *Museum*. As Boswell tells it, Johnson was sitting in Tully's Head when Dodsley suggested "that a Dictionary of the English Language would . . . be well received by the public." After some thought Johnson responded abruptly that he would "not undertake it." Dodsley, however, had been given some suggestions toward a dictionary by Pope; and, doubtless, he used these as an incentive to Johnson to undertake the project. Dodsley suggested to his friend that he dedicate *The Plan of a Dictionary of the English Language* (1747) to Chesterfield, but it is easy to see why Johnson later regarded "Doddy" as his "patron." Dodsley published the plan; praised it in the *Museum*; organized a consortium of publishers to finance the project; and, when the *Dictionary* was ready for release, got Chesterfield to praise it in two essays in the *World*, another of Dodsley's periodicals.

In April 1748 yet another ambitious Dodsley project came to fruition: *The Preceptor*. This two-volume "General Course of Education" provided a liberal education from mathematics to "Human Life and Manners." Remembered now principally for its preface by Johnson and inclusion of what he considered the best thing he ever wrote, "The Vision of Theodore," *The Preceptor* was enormously popular, and forty years later Boswell could still characterize it as "one of the most valuable books for the improvement of young minds that has appeared in any language."

In addition to editing and publishing, Dodsley was actively writing. The deistic *Art of Preaching* (1738) shows his mastery of the Popeian couplet, while, to the pious horror of Dodsley's early editor and biographer Alexander Chalmers, it teaches the "despicable . . . art of casting unmerited obloquy on the clergy." Two years later he published the first of many editions of his pseudobiblical *Chronicle of the Kings of England* (1740), written "in the manner of the Jewish Historians" under the pseudonym Nathan Ben Saddi. The next year an unsuccessful fourth play, *The Blind Beggar of Bethnal Green*, added another proletarian character to Dodsley's group of footman, toy-shop merchant, and honest Mansfield miller. As his plays prove, Dodsley was always a talented songwriter; and in 1742 he published a sixpenny pamphlet of thirteen songs entitled *Colin's Kisses*, the sixth of which—"One kind kiss before we part"—has been frequently praised. During the last twenty years of his life Dodsley suffered debilitating attacks of gout; and in 1743 he published an ode moralizing on *Pain and Patience*.

Early in his London residence he had published several masquelike "Entertainments." However, not until peace was proclaimed with France in February 1749, occasioning the Drury Lane production of his *Triumph of Peace*, was a masque of

his produced. Dodsley had published a more interesting and inflammatory "new species of pantomime" four years earlier. In *Rex Et Pontifex* (1745), a chorus of "pagan, Jewish, Roman, and Mahometan Priests" supports the rule of the allegorical character Tyranny:

Kings the rights of priests defending,
More securely hold their own;
Priests to kings assistance lending,
Merit succour from the throne:
Then give us supreme dominion
Over conscience and the soul!
You shall rule (by our opinion)
Lives and goods without control.

Commanded to worship Imposture, the Muses and the liberal Arts refuse and are rescued by Truth and her entourage of philosophers. Thirteen years later Dodsley published David Hume's *Remarks upon the Natural History of Religion* (1758), and it is not surprising that Voltaire figures prominently among the translations from Tully's Head nor that in 1762 Dodsley published Jean-Jacques Rousseau's *Discourses upon the Origin and Foundations of the Inequality among Mankind*.

Dodsley was consistently described as modest, and many of the poems he had written since *A Muse in Livery* were published with his plays in a 1745 volume self-deprecatingly called *Trifles* (enlarged by his brother to two volumes in 1777). Preceded by *A Select Collection of Old Plays* and followed by his *Collection of Poems. By Several Hands*, his own collected compositions may well have seemed trifling to him. Moreover, he had recently attended Pope on his deathbed and was daily editing the best poetry of Young, Akenside, Collins, Gray, the Wartons, and Johnson. A certain diminished sense of self was perhaps inevitable. In any case, he excluded all but one of his compositions—a short tribute to Pope—from the *Collection of Poems* that was intended to rescue his contemporaries from obscurity.

On 15 November 1750 Dodsley had a literary success that was probably unsurpassed for the rest of the century. Initially attributed to Chesterfield, *The Oeconomy of Human Life* is seventy pages of moral maxims prefaced by an elaborate explanation of the genesis and translation of what purports to be an ancient Hindu manuscript. Influenced by Pope's *Essay on Man*, Dodsley's oriental vade mecum appropriates the biblical language of Proverbs to present deistic ethics. His emphasis on reason, "the bounds of probability," and "the balance of moderation" supports

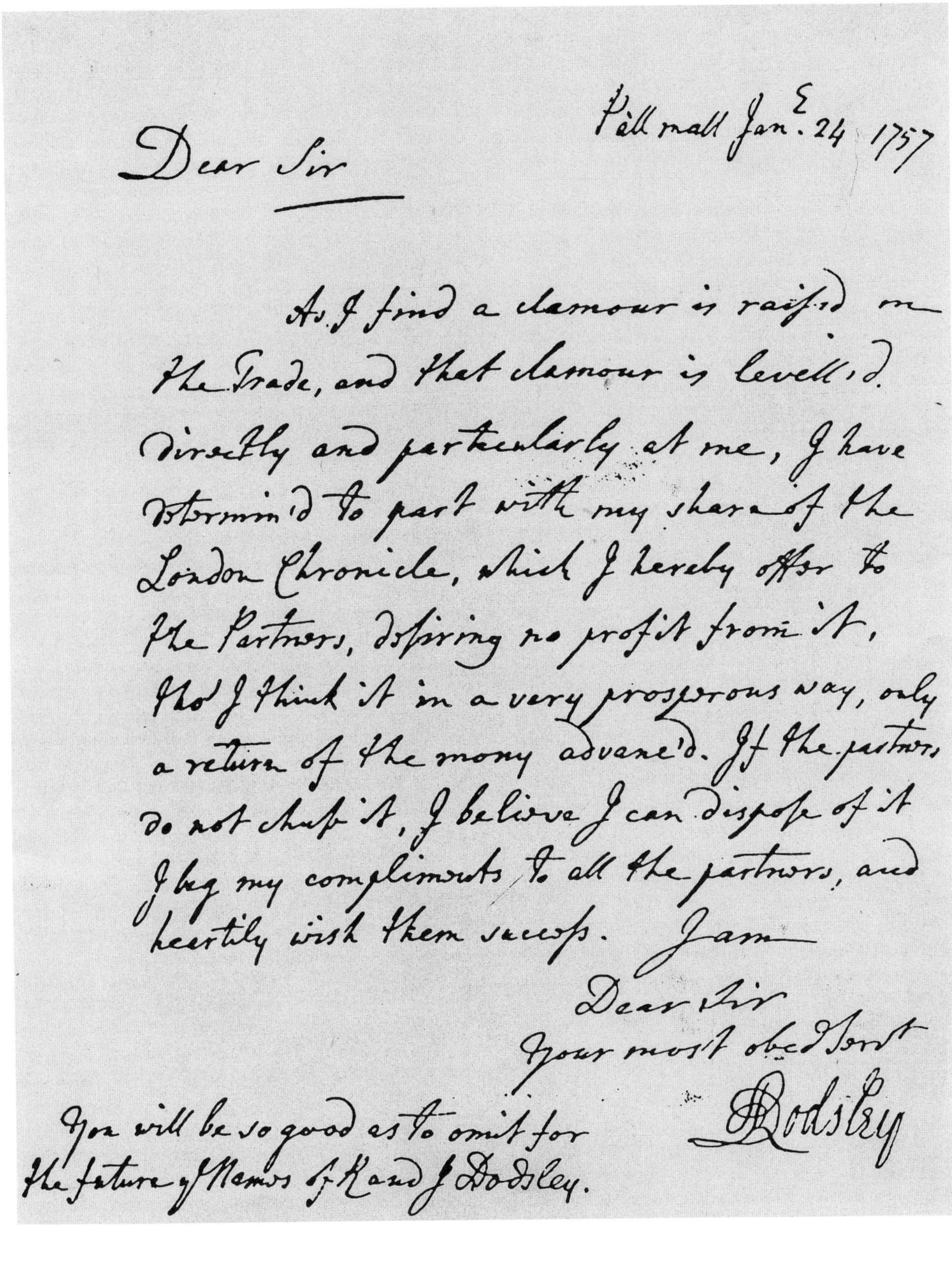

Dear Sir

Pell mall Jan.ᴱ 24 1757

As I find a clamour is rais'd on
the Trade, and that clamour is levell'd
directly and particularly at me, I have
determin'd to part with my share of the
London Chronicle, which I hereby offer to
the Partners, desiring no profit from it,
tho' I think it in a very prosperous way, only
a return of the mony advanc'd. If the partners
do not chuse it, I believe I can dispose of it.
I beg my compliments to all the partners, and
heartily wish them success. I am

Dear Sir
Your most obed.t serv.t
Dodsley

You will be so good as to omit for
the future of Names of R and J Dodsley.

Letter from Dodsley to the printer William Strahan in which he seeks to avoid involvement in the controversies surrounding the Lon-
don Chronicle by giving up his company's share in the paper (from Ralph Straus, Robert Dodsley, *1910)*

43

the traditional moral dichotomies that Blake later reacted against. Within a year seven editions were issued from Tully's Head; and a recent checklist records 142 editions of *The Oeconomy of Human Life* printed from 1750 to 1800 alone. It was quickly translated into Latin, French, German, Italian, Dutch, Spanish, Portuguese, and Hebrew; and it was still so popular in 1810 that Chalmers, in writing a brief biography of Dodsley, thought it "unnecessary to say much on the merit of a piece which is so well known."

In 1753 the indefatigable Dodsley enjoyed another great success and suffered his greatest disappointment. In January, with dramatist Edward Moore as editor and with friends Chesterfield, Horace Walpole, and Richard Owen Cambridge as regular contributors, he initiated the *World*, a periodical more successful than any since the *Spectator*. Collected into volumes, the fashionable journal was reprinted sixteen times before the end of the century. In one issue, with Dodsley in mind, Moore accurately noted that booksellers had superceded the aristocracy as the real patrons of literature. Ironically, it was in the middle of the run of the *World* that Chesterfield wrote the praise of Johnson's *Dictionary* that elicited the scathing letter from Johnson that literary history hears as the death knell of aristocratic patronage. In fact, even social superiors like the Earl of Chesterfield were writing in Dodsley's periodical at Dodsley's suggestion to praise projects initiated and financed by Dodsley, and it was to Dodsley that Chesterfield attempted to justify his conduct when Johnson wrote his caustic rebuff.

In 1753 Dodsley also published *Agriculture*, the first georgic installment of a more massive didactic poem, *Public Virtue*. Although he apologizes for undertaking such an ambitious poem "without the assistance of learning," *Agriculture* is painfully overlearned: the philosophical phraseology of Sir Richard Blackmore's *Creation* (1712) alternates with the scientific periphrasis of James Thomson's *Seasons* (1730). However, Dodsley's imitation of Thomson's Miltonic energy turns turgid, and Dodsley is best when he emulates the aphorisms of Young, as in "The gracious nothing of a great man's nod." Writing hymns to manure and turning Stephen Hales's *Vegetable Staticks* (1727) into immortal blank verse seem doomed enterprises, but *Agriculture* allows Dodsley to say everything about the abuse of the rural poor that Goldsmith wrote later in *The Deserted Village* (1770). Nonetheless, "the miserable poem did not sell," Johnson told Boswell, "and my poor friend

Doddy said, Public Virtue was not a subject to interest the age."

Dodsley's disappointment was more than compensated for five years later when his tragedy *Cleone* gave new splendor to Rich's unfashionable Covent Garden theater. Working to achieve a less grandiloquent and stilted style than was usual at Garrick's Drury Lane, Dodsley had labored long on *Cleone*. In November 1757, while he was rewriting the story of his heroine's traducement and death, attempting to satisfy Garrick's criticisms, Dodsley published *Melpomene, or The Regions of Terror and Pity*, an elaborate ode structured as a series of tragic tableaux, which was instantly the talk of London. Despite Dodsley's celebrity in the tragic mode, Garrick refused the revised *Cleone*, stimulating hostile commentary that Garrick was too proud to stage a tragedy written by a former footman.

Whatever the truth concerning Garrick's refusal, Dodsley's triumph on 2 December 1758 was absolute. Not only was literary London from Chesterfield to Johnson there in support, but the disinterested in the audience hailed a new tragic genius. The Jacobean darkness and violence of Cleone's unmerited abuse and death were decorously chastised by Garrick as cruel, bloody, and unnatural; but Johnson, representatively, argued that had Thomas Otway written *Cleone* none of his other plays would have been remembered. Dodsley denied any comparison to the great dramatist, but, Johnson tells us, Dodsley "went every night to the stage-side and cried at the distress of poor Cleone." Later critics shared Dodsley's compassion. Austin Dobson called *Cleone* "a skilful but a very tragic tragedy"; and Allardyce Nicoll believed it was the only mid-century play that caught the "true tragic note," finding in Cleone's character "something of genuine beauty."

After *Cleone* Dodsley, now rich and renowned, turned over the daily operation of Tully's Head to his brother James. He remained active, contracting Burke to edit the very successful *Annual Register*, publishing Sterne's *Tristram Shandy* and *Sermons of Mr Yorick*, and purchasing the rights to Percy's "old ballads." But his wife's death in 1754 left him free to visit his friends outside London, especially Shenstone and Spence, both of whom helped him compile the *Select Fables of Esop and other Fabulists* that he published in 1761. He prefaced the three-part collection of ancient, modern, and original tales with his own "Essay on Fable," the first full study in English of a very popular genre.

In 1762, ever short of money to maintain his beloved gardens, Shenstone secured Dodsley's aid in publishing a volume of his poems by subscription. Dodsley went to work at once; and when Shenstone suddenly died the following February Dodsley expanded the project to produce a two-volume tribute to his late friend (1764). Despite therapeutic trips with Spence, once to visit the blind Blacklock in Scotland, Dodsley's own health declined. He spent his last days with Spence in Durham. Dodsley was buried outside Durham Cathedral beneath an inscription written by his friend and fellow encourager of natural genius:

> If you have any respect
> for uncommon industry and merit,
> Regard this Place
> in which are interred the Remains
> of
> Mr. Robert Dodsley;
> who, as an Author, raised himself
> much above what cou'd have been expected
> from one in his rank of life
> and without learned Education.
> And who, as a Man, was scarce
> exceeded by any in Integrity of Heart
> & Purity of Manners & Conversation.
> He left this life for a better
> Sept 23d 1764 in the 61 year of his Age.

In the terms of the two weaver's apprentices in William Hogarth's *Idleness and Industry* series, Robert Dodsley is the Francis Goodchild and Stephen Duck the Tom Idle of eighteenth-century untutored genius. Although pensioned by Queen Caroline, Duck, the thresher poet, ended his life in suicide while the stocking weaver's apprentice and footman died immensely successful and universally esteemed. In London he progressed from serving at table to hosting at his own table the "Athenian Nights" celebrated by Johnson and attended by the most distinguished literary and intellectual Londoners of the age.

Dodsley's literary importance may be calculated either narrowly or broadly. Narrowly, his original literary works figured importantly in his own time. His early afterpieces made him, Nicoll contends, the most important sentimental dramatist of the 1730s; and his best play, *Cleone*, may still reasonably be defended as the finest English tragedy of its period. Despite the impetus given to proletarian poetry by the popularity of *A Muse in Livery* and despite the vogue of the melodramatic *Melpomene*, Dodsley's poetry achieved only the modest success accorded good imitation and deserves no more. In contrast, the astonishing popularity of *The Oeconomy of Human Life* warrants fuller study.

If influence be interpreted broadly, on the other hand, it is not absurd to contend that Robert Dodsley is the most influential literary figure of mid century. Indisputably he was the most important publisher; and, patronized by Pope, Dodsley became the patron-publisher of almost every poet of his time still read today. Moreover, when the influence of his six-volume *Collection of Poems*; his varied collaborations with Spence to publicize "natural genius"; and his purchase of Percy's *Reliques* is added to his publication of individual poets, a strong case can be made that Dodsley is the architect of a shift in poetic sensibility from his own couplet allegiance to Pope in *A Muse in Livery* to the grand romantic gestures of his ode *Melpomene*. At the least, if it be argued that Dodsley changed only as the age changed, Tully's Head was nonetheless the focus of the shift.

To this argument on influence must be added his successful periodicals—the *Museum*, the *World*, and the *Annual Register*—as well as the twelve volumes of *A Select Collection of Old Plays*. Moreover, although the influence of his *Preceptor* has been little studied, one scholar contends that it provided the model for the curriculum of the University of Pennsylvania and thereby became a powerful force in American education. The influence of the more than two hundred editions of Dodsley's *Oeconomy* has never been studied.

The cumulative influence of the grammars and dictionaries vended under Dodsley's direction was certainly powerful. Edmund Waller, like Pope later, had lamented that English poets wrote in a "daily-changing Tongue" ("Of English Verse," 1686). As Johnson's preface to the *Dictionary* shows, he shared this anxiety. It is too much to say that Dodsley created "Dictionary Johnson," but it is certain that he was the initiator, publicist, financial coordinator, and publisher of the *Dictionary*; and Johnson always referred to him as his patron and friend. In addition to the *Dictionary*, Dodsley was also the publisher of Robert Lowth's widely influential *Short Introduction to English Grammar* (1762). Together these two publications perhaps did more than any others to slow the rapid changes in English syntax and diction that threatened to make the language of Dryden as obscure as that of Geoffrey Chaucer.

Dodsley's own age regarded him as a genius at judging poetry, and as publisher he was often a kind of coauthor. As Gray wrote to Walpole following the first publication of his *Elegy Written in a Country Churchyard* (1751): "Nurse Dodsley has given it a pinch or two in the cradle, that . . . it will bear the marks of as long as it lives. But no matter: we have suffered under his hands before now." Today, Dodsley is forgotten, and, in a sense, he effaced himself from literary history. Although he included even Duck in his great *Collection of Poems*, the modest Dodsley all but excluded himself. Thus, ironically, he survives today only as a footnote in the biographies of those who eagerly sought the ex-footman's aid and gladly gathered for his Athenian Nights at Tully's Head.

Letters:

The Correspondence of Robert Dodsley, 1733-1764, edited by James E. Tierney (Cambridge: Cambridge University Press, 1989).

Biography:

Alexander Chalmers, "Life of Dodsley," in *The Works of the English Poets, From Chaucer to Cowper* (London: Whittingham, 1810), XXV: 313-323;

Ralph Straus, *Robert Dodsley: Poet, Publisher and Playwright* (London: Lane, 1910).

References:

John Butt, *The Mid-Eighteenth Century*, edited and completed by Geoffrey Carnall (Oxford: Clarendon Press, 1979);

Austin Dobson, "At Tully's Head," in his *Eighteenth Century Vignettes* (London: Chatto & Windus, 1907);

Donald D. Eddy, "Dodsley's *Collection of Poems by Several Hands* (Six Volumes), 1758: Index of Authors," *Publications of the Bibliographical Society of America*, 60 (1966): 9-30;

Eddy, "Dodsley's *Economy of Human Life*, 1750-1751," *Modern Philology*, 85 (May 1988): 460-479;

Eddy, "Dodsley's *Oeconomy of Human Life:* A Partial Checklist, 1750-1800," *Cornell Library Journal*, 7 (Winter 1969); 48-88;

James Gray, " 'More Blood than Brains': Robert Dodsley and the *Cleone* Affair," *Dalhousie Review*, 54 (Summer 1974): 207-227;

Raymond D. Havens, "Changing Taste in the Eighteenth Century: A Study of Dryden's and Dodsley's Miscellanies," *Publications of the Modern Language Association*, 44 (1929): 501-536;

Allardyce Nicoll, *A History of English Drama 1600-1900*, volumes 2 and 3, third edition (Cambridge: Cambridge University Press, 1969);

Lois M. G. Spencer, "Robert Dodsley and the Johnsonian Connection," *New Rambler*, 18 (1977): 1-18;

James E. Tierney, "*The Museum*, the 'Super-Excellent Magazine,' " *Studies in English Literature*, 13 (Summer 1973): 503-515;

Richard Wendorf, "Robert Dodsley as Editor," *Studies in Bibliography*, 31 (1978): 235-248.

Stephen Duck

(1705? - 1756)

Paul Jacob
University of Western Ontario

BOOKS: *Poems on Several Subjects: Written by Stephen Duck, Lately a poor Thresher in a Barn in the County of Wilts, at the Wages of Four Shillings and Six Pence per Week: Which were publickly read by The Right Honourable the Earl of Macclesfield, in the Drawing-Room at Windsor Castle, on Friday the 11th of September, 1730, to Her Majesty. Who was thereupon most graciously pleased to take the Author into her Royal Protection, by allowing him a Salary of Thirty Pounds per Annum, and a small House at Richmond in Surrey, to live in, for the better Support of Himself and Family* (London: Printed for J. Roberts, 1730; Boston: Printed for Richard Fry, 1732; seventh edition, revised and enlarged, London: Printed for J. Roberts, 1730; ninth edition, enlarged, London: Printed for J. Roberts & sold by T. Astley, 1733);

Poems on Several Occasions. By Stephen Duck, Thresher (Dublin: Printed by S. Powell for George Ewing, 1730);

Curious Poems on Several Occasions. Viz. I. On Poverty. II. The Thresher's Labour. III. The Shunamite. All newly corrected, and much amended, by the author Stephen Duck (London: Printed & sold by John Lewis, n.d. [i.e., 1730]);

Royal Benevolence. A Poem. Most humbly address'd to her Majesty Queen Caroline. As it was Presented to the said Queen's Majesty, by the Author, on Friday, the 2nd of October, 1730, at Windsor-Castle. To which is annexed, a Poem on Providence, doubtfully attributed to Duck (London: Printed & sold by W. Harris, 1730);

To His Royal Highness the Duke of Cumberland, on his Birth-day. April the 15th, 1732 (London: Printed for J. Jackson, 1732);

A Poem on the Marriage of His Serene Highness the Prince of Orange, with Ann Princess-Royal of Great Britain. By Stephen Duck. To which are added, Verses to the Author, by a Divine. With the Author's Answer (London: Printed for Weaver Bickerton, 1733-1734);

Truth and Falsehood. A Fable (London: Printed for J. Watts, 1734);

A Poem on Her Majesty's Birth-day (London: Printed for J. Jackson & T. Cooper, 1735);

Poems on Several Occasions (London: Printed for the author, 1736); enlarged as *The Beautiful Works of the Reverend Mr. Stephen Duck, (the Wiltshire Bard)* (London: Printed for the author, 1753);

The Vision. A Poem on the Death of her most Gracious Majesty Queen Caroline (London: Printed for J. Roberts & J. Jackson, 1737);

Alrick and Isabel: or, The Unhappy Marriage. A Poem (London: Printed for J. Roberts, 1740);

Every Man in his Own Way. An Epistle to a Friend (London: Printed for J. Roberts & R. Dodsley, 1741);

Hints to a Schoolmaster. Address'd to the Revd. Dr. Turnbull (London: Printed for J. Roberts & R. Dodsley, 1741);

An Ode on the Battle of Dettingen. Humbly inscrib'd to the King (London: Printed for R. Dodsley & sold by M. Cooper, 1743);

Caesar's Camp; or, St. George's Hill (London: Printed for R. & J. Dodsley & sold by M. Cooper, 1755).

Editions and Collections: *The Shunamite: A Poem from the Fourth Chapter of the Second Book of Kings. Published in 1730–republished in 1830* (Canterbury: Cowan & Brown, 1830);

The Thresher's Labour (London: Swan Press, 1930);

The Thresher's Labour (1736) and The Woman's Labour by Mary Collier (1739) (Los Angeles: Augustan Reprint Society, 1985).

OTHER: "The Two Beavers. A Fable" and "Contentment," in *A Collection of Poems in Six Volumes by Several Hands*, edited by Robert Dodsley (London: Printed by J. Hughs for R. & J. Dodsley, 1755), III: 114-119.

SELECTED PERIODICAL PUBLICATION
UNCOLLECTED: "To Mr. Winter, Agent to General Herbert's Regiment of Dragoon

Stephen Duck, circa 1736 (engraving by G. Bickham, Jr., after a portrait by J. Thornhill; by permission of the National Portrait Gallery, London)

Guards," *Gentleman's Magazine*, 28 (June 1758): 280.

Stephen Duck was a Wiltshire farmhand whose improbable talent for writing verses fascinated a public that fed regularly on wonders. His freakish literary bent caught the interest of powerful patrons and made him a royal favorite, a popular marvel, and finally a dignified clergyman before his puzzling suicide at the height of his career. This fairy-tale transformation started a trend in patronage by encouraging an assortment of other working-class poets and at the same time excited the scorn of the age's most mordant satirists. With few exceptions the appeal of

Duck's poetry is less compelling than the paradoxes of his life. By placing him under an impossible obligation, his good fortune probably scotched the modest ability it should have nurtured. As his public image became a totem of natural virtue available to both friends and detractors for extraliterary purposes, the prodigy was effectively shunted to the margin of his own story, a slave to his celebrity. For the poetical thresher, as for Samuel Richardson's Clarissa and Samuel Johnson's Rasselas, shifting places meant trading one trap for another.

Duck was born, probably in 1705, in Charlton St. Peter, Wiltshire, and received his early education at a local charity school. From the time he left his studies at the age of fourteen, except for a few years when his family held their own small farm, he worked as an itinerant day laborer at the lower end of the scale, mostly as a thresher. Around the time he married his wife, Ann, at the age of nineteen, he felt compelled to recover and improve upon his little formal learning, which was gradually slipping away from him. By working harder than usual he was able to buy arithmetic texts, which he studied at night, and soon felt the satisfaction of surpassing his former knowledge.

The myth of the thresher poet begins with two accounts that offer more and less dependable versions of the phenomenon according to their authors' contrasting interests. Duck was formally introduced to the public in a brief, anonymous preface to the last of seven unauthorized editions of his first book, which appeared in the final quarter of 1730, the year of his first fame. This sketch–probably the work of hack writer and publishing privateer Erasmus Jones–presents a garishly colorful folk hero, pulled out of school by parents who feared that his monstrous appetite for study would spoil him for hard labor, and chastised for favoring the muse at his family's expense by his wife's public complaints of being tied to a madman who mumbled to himself and counted on his fingers for no apparent cause–sure signs of conversation with the devil. However slightly indebted to fact, this caricature, condemned as spurious by the poet, touches the dilemma of a creature at odds with his environment.

A corrective to this travesty appeared in Joseph Spence's *Full and Authentick Account of Stephen Duck, the Wiltshire Poet*, first published as a pamphlet in March 1731 and revised as an introduction to Duck's *Poems on Several Occasions* (1736). Conceived as an empirical case study in the natural history of untutored genius, Spence's biography was based on firsthand observation and whatever facts could be learned directly from the poet during a week of interviews in September 1730. As a friend of Alexander Pope and professor of poetry at Oxford, Spence took an active professional and personal interest in this domestic branch of literary primitivism by befriending several representative writers. Spence explicitly rejects the romance of miraculous inspiration by cataloging specific influences on the poet and by stressing the sequence of early compositions to demonstrate his progress step-by-step.

Frontispiece for the 1733 enlarged edition of Duck's first book, Poems on Several Subjects

Although Duck spent many hours in solitary reading and reflection, the most important factor in his intellectual development, according to Spence, was the mental exercise he enjoyed with a friend, John [?] Lavington, who had a small library that the pair built up to a collection of several dozen volumes. Along with Duck's Bible and math texts their hoard included John Milton's *Paradise Lost*, which was read and reread with dictionary and grammar in hand "as others study the classics"; a complete *Spectator*; Roger L'Estrange's translation of Seneca; François Fénelon's *Telemaque* in English; Joseph Addison's *Defence of Christianity*; Edward Bysshe's *Art of Poetry*; William Whiston's *Josephus*; a volume of seven plays by Shakespeare; works by Ovid, Epictetus, and Edmund Waller; John Dryden's *Virgil*; Matthew Prior's writings; Samuel Butler's

Hudibras; Tom Brown's *Letters from the Dead*; and Ned Ward's *The London Spy*. Spence's re-creation presents Duck as a repository of natural sense, innate taste, and quick feeling, with a modest, strongly moral sensibility that suffers no illusions about the merit of his art. His open, engaging character is reflected in Spence's enthusiastic references to "my friend Stephen," and Spence remained a friend throughout Duck's life.

The Spectator proved the autodidact's most useful tool, both as an introduction to the world of polite culture and as an incitement to emulate the verses scattered throughout its pages. Duck burned his earliest attempts as he wrote them, but when word of the verse-making thresher reached the local clergy and gentry, their encouragement with gifts of money and commissions for works on specific themes led to the more finished products on which his reputation was built. At the time of Spence's interviews these works numbered four: verses "On Poverty"; an epistle written at the request of "a young gentleman of Oxford," Thomas Giffard, who found it unusually well done; an autobiographical poem describing a thresher's annual work, requested by the wife of the most important of Duck's early patrons, Rev. Stanley, recorder of Pewsey; and his most ambitious piece, written for Mrs. Stanley, "The Shunamite," a paraphrase of the fourth chapter of the second book of Kings as a dramatic monologue. These works were collected in 1730 in Duck's first book.

Other of Duck's patrons at this point included Lord Bathurst, Lord Tankerville, Lady Hertford, and the initially skeptical Lord Macclesfield, who, assisted by the dean of Peterborough, subjected the poet to a strict examination and was completely won over. On 11 September 1730 Lord Macclesfield read Duck's poems to the queen, who summoned the author to Windsor; he met his great protectress in Richmond Gardens on 2 October. Caroline's chief agents in bringing the thresher to court were Charlotte Clayton, Lady Sundon, lady of the queen's bedchamber, and Dr. Alured Clarke, prebendary of Westminster and later dean of Exeter. They took kindly pains to ensure the poet's welfare and to help cushion the shock of transition.

Although Spence singled out "The Shunamite" for close critical attention, preferring its evident craft and high seriousness, Duck's signature piece, *The Thresher's Labour*, is also his masterpiece. From its first appearance the poem's vivid rendering of farm life has engaged and amused its audiences. James Thomson's friends at court were apparently put out by readers who, having recently favored the elegant descriptions of nature in *The Seasons* (1730), were momentarily more excited by the novel concreteness and particularity of Duck's poem. Fifty-three years later George Crabbe, launching *The Village* (1783), paid tribute to "honest Duck" as a unique forefather of Crabbe's frankly antipastoral mode. But the realism of *The Thresher's Labour* involves, more than the artless reportage held to be its characteristic strength, an intuitive grasp of the patterns of experience that shape external nature.

Rev. Stanley's suggestion that the fledgling author write about his own life resulted in the invention of a new subgenre. This peasant georgic would become a natural first resort for many of the worker poets who appeared after Duck and was later adapted by Robert Bloomfield, John Clare, Robert Burns, and others; some wrote better poems, but none matched the crude yet forceful economy of Duck's prototype. The humble gratitude of Duck's dedication to his patron, although unquestionably sincere, clashes with the sharp complaint that emerges from the poem as a whole. Yet other inconsistencies often work in his favor. While he wrote as best he could, in keeping with georgic decorum, the verse came out in blunt, sometimes awkward couplets and in a composite of polite and prosy language that, if it struck some readers as ludicrous, served his subject better than more polished diction could. A similarly apt mixture of brief and extended similes is drawn partly from domestic rural life and partly from classical lore, although Duck is careful to restrict mythical allusions to working-class figures: Hercules, Vulcan, Cyclops, and Sisyphus.

The didactic part of georgic verse ordinarily requires a comprehensive prospect in order to describe the time and manner of performing the variety of tasks that make up a total process of production; at some point this view opens out into a patriotic vision of perennial national progress. *The Thresher's Labour* describes the working year in visual, aural, and kinesthetic detail within the strict confines of a purview that is implicitly contrasted with the impatient attitude of the hard-driving master. Duck's foreshortened year measures the seasons disproportionally, as they appear to the thresher who does what he is told when he is told to. Spring and winter are barely mentioned; his main jobs are related in a sequence that suggests the endlessness of work: autumn threshing, summer haymaking, and autumn reaping. The description of each is deliberately paced to render it–both as a discrete operation and as part of a broader annual cadence–according to the worker's distinctive experience of time, which more often than not is painfully monotonous:

> Now in the Air our knotty Weapons fly,
> And now with equal Force descend from high;
> Down one, one up, so well they keep the Time,
> The Cyclops' Hammers could not truer chime;
> Nor with more heavy Strokes could *Aetna* groan,
> When Vulcan forg'd the arms for Thetis' Son.
> In briny Streams our Sweat descends apace,
> Drops from our Locks, or trickles down our Face.
> No Intermission in our Work we know;
> The noisy Threshal must for ever go.
> Their Master absent, others safely play;
> The sleeping Threshal does itself betray.
> Nor yet, the tedious Labour to beguile,
> And make the passing Minutes sweetly smile,
> Can we, like Shepherds, tell a merry Tale;
> The Voice is lost, drown'd by the louder Flail.
> But we may think–Alas! what pleasing thing,
> Here, to the Mind, can the dull Fancy bring?
> Our Eye beholds no pleasing Object here,
> No chearful Sound diverts our list'ning Ear.
> The Shepherd well may tune his Voice to sing,
> Inspir'd with all the Beauties of the Spring.
> No Fountains murmur here, no Lambkins play,
> No Linnets warble, and no Fields look gay;
> 'Tis all a gloomy, Melancholy Scene,
> Fit only to provoke the Muse's Spleen.

The poem's larger and smaller rhythms, combined with a few bald complaints, establish the ironic structural and thematic principle of contrast without real difference. The regular variety that in the master's view ensures prosperity and provides aesthetic refreshment–difference among seasons, places, and tasks–becomes completely illusory from the worker's perspective. The thresher suffers all apparent change as a shabby cheat that cannot mask the dehumanizing sameness of his existence. The poem's exuberant sensory detail is gradually drained of joy as the wheel of time, which turns pleasure and profit for those who control it, grinds into dull resignation the best energies of those who are bound upon it. What little rest is allowed–less and less as the tempo increases during harvest season until work invades the thresher's dreams–is only enough to sharpen the edge of exhaustion; the overgenerous harvest-home supper that concludes the poem merely tricks the workers into momentarily thinking that their yearly labor has an end. Begin-

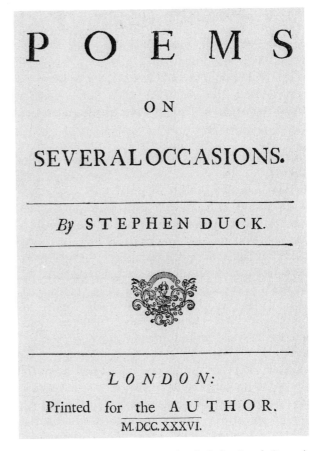

Title page for Duck's collection that includes Joseph Spence's brief biography as an introduction

nings, endings, and finished products are facts of life for masters and poets, oppressive fictions for workers:

> Thus, as the Year's revolving Course goes round,
> No Respite from our Labour can be found:
> Like Sisyphus, our work is never done;
> Continually rolls back the restless Stone.
> New-growing Labours still succeed the past;
> And growing always new, must always last.

The Thresher's Labour was the early high point of Duck's art. "On Poverty," composed just before it, and "The Shunamite," just after, both deal with related topics in the docile, conventional manner typical of the mature poet. The leisure and security that allowed Duck to improve his craft necessarily ended the life-style that had made his writing noteworthy and inspired the best of it. But no one could have wished otherwise; although his early patrons, especially Spence and Clarke, were aware that preferment might prove as dangerous to Duck's welfare as neglect, they saw no real alternative to it. Submissiveness and lack of personal ambition were seemly traits in a royal dependent but precluded the authority that underwrites a distinctive poetic voice. In his new condition Duck needed a Burnsian sense of his dignity and worth if he were to assert himself enough to earn his fame. Lacking those resources, he had little to express except deference, thanks, and praise for his patrons.

The death of Duck's wife, Ann, mother of their three children, while he was en route to Windsor in October 1730 broke his strongest tie to his former self. Installed by the queen in a small house in Richmond with an annual allowance of thirty pounds, he gave himself over to the chore of mastering social and literary protocol. While conceding that his distaste for recent poetry disqualified him for the task, Clarke, assisted by Spence, undertook to guide the poet's education. As Katherine Byerley Thomson reports in her *Memoirs of the Court and Times* (1850), the reading list Clarke devised for the purpose was selected to reinforce Duck's aversion to "drollery, ridicule or jingle" by keeping the finest satire of the day out of his hands. A diet of decent poetry, philosophy, and physico-theology, it was hoped, would encourage Duck's inclination toward the role of a serious, respectful citizen. Unassumingly good-natured and eager to please, Clarke's scholar became a symbol of royal power and a butt of attacks from the unofficial opposition. Reborn into a paper world of partisan turmoil just as the laureateship was about to become a bone of contention after the death of Laurence Eusden, he found that mere innocence was no guarantee of maintaining neutrality.

Alexander Pope, Jonathan Swift, John Gay, and Harry Fielding among anonymous others took notice of Duck soon after his presentation to the queen, and their interest sharpened in November 1730 when, along with Lewis Theobald and Colley Cibber, he was rumored to be a candidate for the post of poet laureate. A barrage of ironic eulogies, exasperated squibs, and witty remarks on the subject peppered the season's poems, plays, journals, and letters. Jonathan Swift's "quibbling epigram" "On Stephen Duck, the Thresher, and favourite Poet" (1730) was the most brilliantly bitter of the lot. Mock essays appeared in the *Grub St. Journal* ironically parsing the "beauties" of Duck's verse, ridiculing the democratization of literature, and offering a caustic learned gloss by Pope on the office of the laureate (reprinted as an appendix to the variorum *Dunciad*, 1729). Pirated editions of Duck's poems

had begun to capitalize on his celebrity before he left Wiltshire, and parodies appeared shortly after, the most ambitious being *The Thresher's Miscellany: or, Poems on Several Subjects, Written by Arthur Duck. Now a poor Thresher . . . though formerly an Eaton-Scholar* (anonymous, 1731).

Although they must have grazed their subject at least, most of these barbs were moderately blunt by contemporary standards. Pope and his friends showed considerable restraint in exploiting so slightly this unhoped-for gift to their "Dunce-ology." In Scriblerian terms Duck represented all the major symptoms of current cultural decline: the spreading plague of scribbler's itch, the pernicious folly of indiscriminate patronage, and the reduction of poetry to flattery or mere amusement. More specifically the thresher-poet provided an unexpected punch line to the rustic dialect mock-pastoral jokes with which Pope and Gay had lampooned Ambrose Philips's experiments in domestic pastoral some years previously. Worse than all these offenses, some overenthusiastic literati at court had hailed the queen's discovery as a greater genius than Pope. Despite these provocations, though he commented satirically on the thresher with amused tolerance in both verse and prose, Pope never attacked Duck publicly by his own name or with personal malice. In her first excitement Caroline had sent Duck's manuscript to the arch-satirist with a cover sewn over the author's name, requesting an impartial opinion. According to William Warburton, Pope, having been informed about the Wiltshire marvel in a letter from Spence written during the course of his first interviews with Duck at Wilton, correctly "guessed" the poet's condition and dismissed his work with the verdict that "most villages could supply verses of the same force." Yet he subscribed to the 1736 volume of Duck's *Poems on Several Occasions* (as did Swift) and behaved with generous cordiality toward the inoffensive newcomer, visiting him regularly at Richmond and helping to establish him at court.

In answering the queen's summons, Duck became a participant in the elaborate public ritual of court life. He was brought to Richmond with the idea that he would work as a gardener, a more theatrical, domestic version of his former occupation. His role became more emblematic with each advancement. In April 1733 (the year the poet married Sarah Big, the queen's housekeeper at Kew) he was made a yeoman of the Guard. In 1735 he was appointed keeper of the queen's li-

TO THE

QUEEN.

M A D A M,

HE great Honour Your Majesty has done me, in giving me leave to prefix Your Royal Name to the following Poems, does not encourage me to presume they are worthy to be laid at Your Feet on any other account, but only as they are an humble

A 2   ble

iv   *D E D I C A T I O N.*

ble Tribute of Duty, offer'd from a thankful Heart to a gracious Benefactress. Your Majesty has indeed the same Right to them, as You have to the Fruits of a Tree, which You have transplanted out of a barren Soil into a fertile and beautiful Garden. It was Your Generosity which brought me out of Obscurity, and still condescends to protect me; like the Supreme Being, who continually supports the meanest Creature, which his Goodness has produc'd.

I have Room here to expatiate upon a very inviting Subject; but Your Majesty has nobly prevented all Panegyric, even from the best Pens, by building Your *Fame* on a much more lasting Basis, than that of *Praise* in *Dedications*. Your Encouragements of *Arts* and *Sciences*, Your Esteem and Friendship for all Defenders of Truth, while they are living,

the

D E D I C A T I O N.   v

the Regard You pay to their Memories when dead, and Your generous Care of their Widows and Orphans, record Your Virtues in such Characters as will ever be legible. Your Christian Love to Mankind, Your zealous Endeavours to promote *Religion*, a Soul made tender to feel our Misfortunes, and a Will inclin'd to redress them, are such amiable and heavenly Qualities, as shine best by their own Light, and can receive no new Lustre from the finest Description.

MAY Heaven long preserve Your Majesty to practise all these Virtues, to be a perpetual Source of Comfort and Joy to our glorious Monarch, a Blessing to the Nation, and a noble Pattern of Beneficence and Generosity to future Queens. Your Majesty's great Goodness to myself draws this Prayer from a Heart fill'd with Gratitude. As there is so

little

vi   *D E D I C A T I O N.*

little Merit in what You now honour with Your Royal Protection, I shall endeavour to supply the Defects, the only way that is in my Power, by my Thanks, and Prayers for Your Majesty: *These* I will ever continue, and always make it my greatest Ambition to shew with what profound Respect I am,

M A D A M,

Your MAJESTY's

Most Grateful,

Most Devoted, and

Most Dutiful Servant,

Stephen Duck.

Duck's dedication to Queen Caroline in his 1736 Poems on Several Occasions

brary at Merlin's Cave, one of Caroline's improvements at Richmond Gardens. Designed by William Kent, this hybrid Palladian cottage contained a small collection of books and half-a-dozen wax figures. As its genius loci Duck became, literally, a living monument to the queen's bounty–intellectual husbandman and tour guide, representing progress as a raw natural resource raised to the level of its natural merit. The spirit of such latter-day pageantry appears as well in the appointment of the poet as master of Duck Island in St. James's Park. At the same time, setting Duck up as a glorified garden ornament was a pragmatic solution to the problem of how to provide the royal protégé some employment that would leave him enough leisure to study and write.

While Merlin's Cave was being built in the summer of 1735 Duck traveled in the counties west and south of the capital and recorded the adventure in "A Description of a Journey to Marlborough, Bath, Portsmouth, etc." (*Poems on Several Occasions*, 1736). He called on earlier patrons, made new friends, toured local landmarks, visited Spithead with the Stanleys, and ended his trip with a reverential stop at Oxford. Duck's return to Great Charlton was a high point of both the journey and the poem. The previous year Lord Viscount Palmerston (to whom "A Description" is dedicated) had bought a plot of land, the annual profits of which were directed to fund a dinner at the local inn each June for the threshers of the parish to honor their famous former colleague–a custom that is still observed at the Charlton Cat. The poet presided at the first of these feasts and described the lively proceedings with a mock-heroic gusto that rarely graces the works he wrote at court: "Abash'd the conscious Heroes stood, / Shook Hands, and thirsted more for *Beer*–than *Blood* . . ." (*Poems*, 1736).

The first authorized collected edition of Duck's poetry was published by subscription in May 1736. *Poems on Several Occasions* implicitly explains as well as demonstrates its author's failure to confirm his early signs of genius. An extravagantly humble dedication to the queen likens the poet to a transplanted tree on a par with God's meanest creature; the preface that follows insistently abjures any claim to merit, a disavowal repeated at secondhand in Spence's revised biographical introduction. These cringing preliminaries make a proper curtsey before a dazzling list of some six hundred subscribers including members of the royal family, the archbishops

of Canterbury and York, and most of the country's nobility and gentry. Most of the works written under the queen's protection read like parodies of the public image that Duck had so thoroughly adopted, as its main components, primitive virtue and pastoral innocence, are paraded in poem after poem. The volume shows competence in a variety of meters and genres: occasional ode, pastoral dialogue, elegy, epigram, dramatic monologue, local description, didactic fable, romantic narrative, imitations of Horace and Claudian, and a paraphrase of Ovid. Yet, except for *The Thresher's Labour* and a few other fresh strokes that recall its vigor–"On Mites," an arch epigram or two, and parts of "Description of a Journey"–the same self-effacing tone and small repertory of obsessions with the evil of avarice and ambition, and the valor of modesty, contentment, and gratitude, recur with a predictability that nullifies the variety of form. Nevertheless, even after the nine pirated editions of *Poems on Several Subjects* published between 1730 and 1733, the new official collected edition saw four printings within two years; a new edition appeared in 1753 and another in 1764, eight years after the poet's death.

With the death of Queen Caroline in 1737 Duck lost his most powerful friend and emotional mainstay. Although he continued to compose and publish sporadically until the end of his life, he seemed to sense that the best of his writing was behind him–an intuition less evident in his elaborate elegy for the queen, *The Vision* (1737), than in a verse epistle written several years later to answer a friend's suggestion that he give up the quill for good. *Every Man in his Own Way* (1741) offers a bolder variant of Duck's standard apology, insisting that, although his verse may be worthless to everyone else, it is the product of an irresistible itch no more harmful to society than certain generally sanctioned foibles. This self-caricature in a sense both affirms and defies contemporary attacks on promiscuous poetasting by comically redefining genius as a natural urge independent of value. Whether or not this defense is prompted by an ongoing need to pay the poet's debt to society, the clarity and good humor with which he faces the issue suggests, perhaps misleadingly, a new degree of personal confidence.

Several paraphrases from Latin in *Poems on Several Occasions* show evidence of the author's progress in classical studies, a course that would eventually qualify him to secure his independence even if his muse should fail. With Spence's encouragement Duck was admitted to Holy Orders in 1746. Having bought his first chaplaincy, he was awarded a chaplain's commission in Ligonier's Dragoons in 1750, and in August of the following year he was promoted to the desirable post of preacher at Kew Chapel, where he drew large crowds of curious worshippers. In January 1752 Duck reached the limit of his clerical career with his appointment as rector of Byfleet in Surrey, Spence's home parish. Although he owed this comfortable living to Spence's influence with the duke of Dorset, the rector performed his offices creditably and won the respect of his parishioners.

The last poem Duck published, a year before his death, is the best known of his later works, having been cited as a likely source for Thomas Gray's *Bard* (1757). *Caesar's Camp; or, St. George's Hill* (1755) gives an ironic symmetry to Duck's oeuvre, obliquely summing up the poet's life as though implicitly in dialogue with *The Thresher's Labour*. It recombines typical themes and motifs both to mark the immeasurable distance between the thresher's lowly viewpoint and the bard's hilltop vista, and to show the identity underlying those complementary personifications of genius. A prospect poem in the mold of John Denham's *Cooper's Hill* (1655) and Pope's *Windsor-Forest* (1713), Duck's patriotic masterpiece blends Pindaric enthusiasm, local description, panegyric, and georgic prophecy in a way that redefines the poet as both medium and messenger of national spirit.

Caesar's Camp surveys the estates surrounding its namesake vantage point, making history and myth extol the heroic stewardship of present masters. Duck's celebration of national prosperity initially culminates in a tribute to the duke of Cumberland as a perfect balance between black warrior (known in some circles as "the Butcher" of Culloden) and green gardener, defender and improver of the land. The poem's double title is thematically justified in a pivotal contrast between the duke's complex creative energy–an extension of St. George's dragon slaying–and the destructive abuse of power during the area's ancient occupation under Caesar. In a dream vision the poet imagines himself bard of the first century B.C., cursing the Roman depredation and prophesying his country's redemption through the husbandry of future generations. This vision of paradise regained becomes so specific in citing names and places as to become indistinguishable from the

Duck, circa 1740 (miniature attributed to Christian Richter; by permission of the National Portrait Gallery, London)

poem's previsionary eulogies. Lincoln (Henry Clinton, Earl of Lincoln), Duck's latest patron, wakes him from his revery and offers thanks for being included in the ongoing project of national restoration. But whereas Pope and Gray subordinate their visions of material progress to the spiritual primacy of poetry that revives Eden in song, Duck literalizes his vision so that art remains a weak reflection of his patrons' power and glory. For all its prophetic paraphernalia, *Caesar's Camp* becomes a parodic antitype of *The Bard* through its unintended caricature of servile genius.

In its portrait of the bard as panegyrist *Caesar's Camp* contains Duck's last attempt to reconcile the level tenor of his art with the steepness of his social ascent. He had been vocally uneasy about that gap since the first stages of his preferment. His repeated professions of contentment were evidently as sincere as his cheerful humility and well-exercised gratitude. Duck stubbornly refused to be silenced, either by a lively sense of his artistic shortcomings or by the lampoons that greeted his debut and persisted well beyond it. By 1755 those jokes had subsided and the quondam thresher was accepted on his own modest strengths both as a priest and as a poet. The *Monthly Review* noticed *Caesar's Camp* graciously if without enthusiasm. Although they supply ample fuel for speculation, Duck's surviving writings offer no evidence of a despair that might have led him to drown himself, as he apparently did at Reading in the spring of 1756.

The idea of the thresher poet proved so much more powerful than his verse that he was hard-pressed to sustain his role as a phenomenon once the novelty of his origins wore off. He wrote one remarkable poem that continued to win him new readers throughout his career and remains readable both as a unique social document and as a rough but rigorous poem of experience. If his other work is, on the whole, undistinguished, it shows a uniformly diligent application to his craft, which was not inferior to that of some of Johnson's or Alexander Chalmers's "standard" poets. But its main interest is as a record of the ways in which the myth of uneducated genius was enlisted to serve nonartistic ends. Throughout the century the example of Duck's success continued to act as a beacon to the would-be worker-bards whose aspirations had been anticipated in the parodies and satirical essays that mocked Caroline's poetical pet. Their numbers included Mary Collier–a washerwoman whose *Woman's Labour* (1739) took issue with the thresher's slighting portrayal of that commodity–as well as a bricklayer, a weaver, a miller, a cobbler, a milkmaid, and a footman. Only the last, Robert Dodsley, prospered independently as a popular poet and influential publisher and bookseller, who published several of Duck's later works. Burns, Bloomfield, and Clare were late heirs of a well-established literary type.

Biographies:

Joseph Spence, *A Full and Authentick Account of Stephen Duck, the Wiltshire Poet* (London: Printed for J. Roberts, 1731); revised as "An Account of the Author," in *Poems on Several Occasions. By Stephen Duck* (London: Printed for the author, 1736), pp. xi-xx;

Rose Mary Davis, *Stephen Duck, the Thresher-Poet*, University of Maine Studies, second series, no. 8 (Orono, Maine: University of Maine Press, 1926).

References:

Edmund Blunden, "The Farmer's Boy," in his *Nature in English Literature* (London: Hogarth, 1929), pp. 106-117;

John Lucas, Introduction to Duck's *Poems on Several Occasions, 1736* (Menston, U.K.: Scolar, 1973);

James M. Osborn, "Spence, Natural Genius and Pope," *Philological Quarterly*, 45 (January 1966): 123-144;

Robert Southey, "Stephen Duck," in his *The Lives and Works of the Uneducated Poets*, edited by J. S. Childers (London: Milford, 1925), pp. 88-113, 182-191;

Katherine Byerley Thomson, *Memoirs of the Court and Times of King George the Second, and His Consort Queen Caroline*, 2 volumes (London: Colburn, 1850), I: 179-206;

Rayner Unwin, "Stephen Duck," in his *The Rural Muse: Studies in the Peasant Poetry of England* (London: Allen & Unwin, 1954);

William Warburton, Introduction and notes to *The Works of Alexander Pope*, 9 volumes, edited by Warburton (London: J. & P. Knapton, 1751);

Raymond Williams, *The Country and the City* (New York: Oxford University Press, 1973), pp. 87-90.

John Dyer

(? August 1699 - December 1757)

David R. Anderson
Texas A&M University

BOOKS: *The Ruins of Rome,* anonymous (London: Printed for Lawton Gilliver, 1740);

The Fleece (London: Printed for R. & J. Dodsley, 1757);

Poems (London: Printed by John Hughs for R. & J. Dodsley, 1761).

Editions and Collections: *The Poetical Works of John Dyer, L.L.B. Carefully Corrected* (London, 1765);

The Poetical Works of John Dyer. With the Life of the Author (Edinburgh: Printed at the Apollo Press by the Martins, 1779);

The Poetical Works of Mark Akenside and John Dyer, edited by Robert Aris Willmott (London: G. Routledge, 1855);

Grongar Hill, edited by R. C. Boys (Baltimore: Johns Hopkins Press, 1941).

OTHER: "The Enquiry," "The Country Walk," "Grongar Hill" (Pindaric version), "An Epistle to A Famous Painter," "To Aaron Hill, Esq.; on a Poem called *Gideon,*" and "To Mr. Savage" in *Miscellaneous Poems and Translations By Several Hands,* edited by Richard Savage (London: Printed for Samuel Chapman, 1726);

"Grongar Hill" (first octosyllabic version) in *A New Miscellany: Being a Collection of Pieces of Poetry, from Bath, Tunbridge, Oxford, Epsom, and other places,* edited by T. Warner (London: Printed for T. Warner, 1726);

"Grongar Hill" (completed octosyllabic version) and "To Aurelia" in *Miscellaneous Poems By Several Hands,* edited by D. Lewis (London: Published by D. Lewis, printed by J. Watts, 1726);

"Wrote at Ocriculum in Italy, 1725" in *A Collection of Moral and Sacred Poems From the Most Celebrated English Authors,* edited by John Wesley, 3 volumes (Bristol: Printed and sold by Felix Farley, 1744).

John Dyer, poet, painter, clergyman, and farmer, wrote one of the best topographical

John Dyer

poems in eighteenth-century literature, "Grongar Hill" (1726). He also wrote the best formal georgic of the period, *The Fleece* (1757). His poetic output was relatively small, and only "Grongar Hill" survives on its artistic merit alone, though *The Fleece* also continues to receive occasional attention. Dyer's work, however, continues to interest critics on other than purely aesthetic grounds, particularly as it reflects his training in painting and his attitudes towards mercantilism and industrialization.

Dyer was born in Aberglasney, Wales, probably in late July or early August 1699, the second son of Robert and Catherine Cocks Dyer, and baptized on 13 August 1699 in the parish of

POEMS.

BY

JOHN DYER, L.L.B.

VIZ.

I. GRONGAR HILL.

II. The Ruins of ROME.

III. The FLEECE, in Four Books.

London: Printed by John Hughs,
For Meſſrs. R. and J. Dodsley, in Pallmall.
MDCCLXI.

*Title page for the first collection of Dyer's poetry, published
almost four years after his death*

Llanfynnydd, Carmarthenshire. He spent his boyhood there and in Aberglasney in the nearby parish of Llangathen. Robert Dyer was a successful attorney who obviously wished to do well by his children, for in about 1713 John was sent to London to be educated at Westminster School. He was apparently not happy there, for, in "Notes Respecting the Life and Family of John Dyer, the Poet," he reports that in 1714 he "Ran from school and my father, on a box of the ear being given me. Strolled for three or four days—found at Windsor." Dyer apparently left Westminster School without finishing his studies, returning to Wales to train for the law in his father's office in Aberglasney. Tradition holds that Dyer's father had little use for poetry or painting, his son's chief interests, and discouraged his endeavors in both.

However, Robert Dyer died on 8 July 1720, leaving John a legacy of six hundred pounds to be paid on his twenty-fourth birthday. Released from his obligation to the law, Dyer went to London in 1720 or 1721 to study painting with Jonathan Richardson, the noted painter and theorist. He also pursued an informal literary education, frequenting Serle's Coffeehouse and joining the circle surrounding Aaron Hill, which included the poets David Mallet and Richard Savage and the artists and collectors Arthur Pond and George Knapton. Dyer participated in the exchange of verses typical of literary coteries, writing complimentary poems to Hill and Savage and amatory verse to "Clio," Mrs. Martha Fowke Sansom.

In the spring of 1724 Dyer journeyed to Italy to continue his study of art, landing at Leghorn and traveling down to Rome and possibly Florence. In Italy he studied the antiquities, the works of the masters, and the countryside. His early biographers report that his health was irreparably injured by the air of the Campagna. Dyer returned to England in late summer or autumn 1725, and after a journey home to Wales settled in London to make his way as a poet and painter.

The year 1726 saw Dyer's first important publications. Six of his poems appeared in Savage's *Miscellaneous Poems and Translations by Several Hands*, among them the Pindaric version of "Grongar Hill." In the same year Dyer published another version of "Grongar Hill"—this one in octosyllabic couplets—in *A New Miscellany*, and a completed octosyllabic version in *Miscellaneous Poems By Several Hands*, edited by his friend David Lewis.

"Grongar Hill," in its final octosyllabic version, is Dyer's best and best-known poems. It belongs to the genre that Samuel Johnson, in the life of John Denham, in volume 1 of his *Lives of the Poets* (1779-1781), called "*local poetry*, of which the fundamental subject is some particular landscape to be poetically described, with the addition of such embellishments as may be supplied by historical retrospection or incidental meditation." Since Dyer grew up at the foot of Grongar Hill, this is a "local" poem in the deepest sense, for it treats a landscape that is not only picturesque but also resonant with personal meaning for the poet.

The poem begins with an address to Fancy, "Silent Nymph, with curious eye!," whom the speaker invites, along with her "sister Muse" to "Draw the landskip bright and strong." In the best poems of this kind, vision and contemplation merge to become a unified form of apprehension. The two are linked early in Dyer's poem as the speaker remembers how often he has sat on

Illustration for "Grongar Hill" in Dyer's Poems *(1761)*

the hill and gazed at the Towy river and the houses below, " 'Till Contemplation had her fill." The speaker then begins to climb Grongar Hill, and the prospect, and the poem's thematic concerns, widen as he ascends. From the top of the hill, for example, the speaker sees the ruins of old castles on the surrounding cliffs, a sight which prompts the famous lines, "A little rule, a little sway, / A sun beam in a winter's day, / Is all the proud and mighty have, / Between the cradle and the grave." The entire scene becomes charged with meaning for the speaker: not only the artifacts but also the structure of the landscape itself hold significance. Gazing down at the river below, the speaker reflects, "Thus is nature's vesture wrought, / To instruct our wand'-ring thought."

The instruction supplied by nature as seen from atop Grongar Hill is clarified in the last four stanzas. The speaker, reflecting that distance distorts the landscape, making far-off

streams seem narrow and meadows tiny, observes that the same distortion occurs when humans gaze into the future "thro' hope's deluding glass." To avoid the unhappiness of those who ignore present reality in favor of the delusive future, the speaker prays, "may I with myself agree, / And never covet what I see: / Content me with an humble shade, / My passions tam'd, my wishes laid; / For while our wishes wildly roll, / We banish quiet from the soul."

Criticism of "Grongar Hill" has focused chiefly on two issues: how well Dyer succeeds at integrating description and commentary and the degree to which he treats landscape in a painterly way. Opinion divides somewhat on both issues. Contemporary and modern readers have mostly found Dyer's integration of thematic material into natural description deft and graceful—perhaps excessively so, however, for the poem has not often been thought profound. As to the second matter, William Gilpin's *Observations On the River Wye* (1782) criticizes Dyer's handling of distances in "Grongar Hill" as unpainterly, but more recently the poet's ability to translate painterly vision into words has been regarded as exemplary.

In July 1729, in his thirtieth year, a crucial change occurred in Dyer's life when he left the literary life of London for rural Herefordshire, where he lived for the next six years. His first years there were spent traveling around the countryside, painting various subjects. However, in April 1734 Dyer took up residence at Mapleton, a farm he stood to inherit. When Dyer arrived Mapleton was in financial difficulty, and he took over supervising not only the farm's finances but also its day-to-day operations. He was apparently successful at restoring it to profitability, in the process becoming one of the few high-culture English poets of rural life ever to concern himself on a daily basis with such issues as the price of hops. Dyer's firsthand knowledge of farming gained at Mapleton and other farms he operated helped inspire *The Fleece*, his georgic poem on sheep farming, which was not published for another twenty-three years.

In 1736 Dyer moved to Worcester, where in addition to his continued supervision of Mapleton he completed a first draft of *The Ruins of Rome* (1740), a poem that had been gestating since his journey to Italy in 1724. He began work in 1737 on "The Commercial Map of England," a work in which he planned to indicate by symbols on a map the location of natural resources

Illustration for The Ruins of Rome *in Dyer's* Poems

and industries in England. This work was never published. Also in 1737 Dyer sold Mapleton and bought two farms in Leicestershire, where he moved in 1738. At some time during this period he married a twenty-six-year-old widow, Sarah Ensor Hawkins, who claimed to be a descendent of William Shakespeare. Their son, John, was baptized on 26 July 1739.

The Ruins of Rome was finally published (anonymously) in February or March 1740. It connects with "Grongar Hill" because of its focus on memorials of the passage of time. In the earlier poem the sight of ruined medieval castles had prompted the speaker to meditations on the transience of power; in *The Ruins of Rome,* the ruins of the ancient city prompt meditations on that theme as well as on the speaker's personal vocation and on various patriotic themes. *The Ruins of Rome,* however, belongs to a very different mode than "Grongar Hill," as the opening lines indicate: "Enough of Grongar, and the shady dales / Of winding Towy, Merlin's fabled haunt / I sung

inglorious." Situated somewhere between the "progress" poem and a meditation among the tombs, it casts an elegiac eye backward, seeking guidance for the present among the ruins of the past.

Like "Grongar Hill" the poem is structured chiefly around a walk up a hill–the Palatine– and the prospect and resultant meditations are achieved from there. No longer the solitary country walker, however, the speaker shares his quest with "the delicate of mind, / Curious and modest, from all climes . . . / Grateful society!" Throughout the poem he is torn between awe at the profound majesty of the ruins and a sense of the urgency of the lessons they teach. In the poem's best moments these two responses combine, as when the ruined statues of great Romans prompt the speaker to resolve to serve his country: "Me now, of these / Deep-musing, high ambitious thoughts inflame / Greatly to serve my country, distant land, / And build me virtuous fame."

The chief subject of *The Ruins of Rome* is liberty: how Rome gained and lost it, how Britain has gained it, how valuable liberty is, and what must be done to prevent its loss in the speaker's native land. Liberty (personified) is valuable in part because his "hand benign / Teaches unwearied toil to cloth the fields, / And on his various fruits inscribes the name / Of Property." This mercantile patriotism reflects Dyer's interest in the "Commercial Map of Britain" at this time and looks forward to a central concern of *The Fleece. The Ruins of Rome* concludes with an exhortation to Britons to heed the example of the Romans and not to permit either tyranny or luxury to threaten their own liberty.

Dyer's second child, Elizabeth, was baptized on 7 August 1741, and the following month, on 20 September 1741, he was ordained as a deacon. He was then ordained a priest on 18 October 1741, and in 1742 Dyer moved with his family to the village of Catthorpe in Leicestershire to begin his duties as a country parson. Here he also began work on the poem by which he wished to be remembered, *The Fleece.* Little remains in Dyer's records to explain his turn to a religious vocation in his early forties. His biographers have noted his latent seriousness of mind, deepened by his own experience of poor health, and his enjoyment of a retired life as contributing to his turn to the church. The size of Dyer's family increased rapidly at Catthorpe: a second daughter, Sarah, was baptized on 12 August 1744; a third daughter, Catherine, was baptized on 11 August 1745; and a second son, also named John, was baptized on 30 January 1750.

Later in 1750 Dyer traveled to London with the manuscript of book 1 of *The Fleece*. There he was introduced to Philip Yorke, son of the earl of Hardwicke, and his wife, who became Dyer's patrons, arranging for him to receive in 1751 the livings of Belchford and Coningsby in Lincolnshire. Dyer resigned his living at Catthorpe in favor of the ones in Lincolnshire, which significantly increased his income. Yorke's father was high steward of Cambridge, and Yorke also began proceedings to secure for Dyer a degree from that university, which he received in August 1751. In 1755 Dyer received from his patrons the living of Kirkby on Bain with Tumby in exchange for Belchford. His new parish adjoined Coningsby and paid a higher salary.

The Fleece was finally published on 15 March 1757, after extensive revision and consultation with a "board of critics," including Mark Akenside, author of *The Pleasures of Imagination* (1744). Dyer's most ambitious work, written in four books of blank verse and closely modeled on Virgil's *Georgics*, it did not find favor with the reading public, and it is little read today except by specialists, though detailed readings of the poem continue to appear periodically. *The Fleece* combines some practical instruction on raising sheep (book 1) with praise of trade and manufacture generally and of the British woolen industry in particular. It is informed, exuberant, and patriotic, but–some would say–complacent.

Book 1 announces its subject unequivocally– "The care of Sheep, the labours of the Loom, / And arts of Trade, I sing"–and specifies its audience and theme: "ye good, of all / Degrees, all sects, be present to my song. / So may distress, and wretchedness, and want, / The wide felicities of labour learn." The poem begins on a practical note as the speaker discusses the different kinds of pastures fit for sheep and suggests ways to remedy the faults of each. This faith in the power of human ingenuity to "improve" both upon nature (by improving the soil) and upon art (by labor-saving inventions for processing wool) typifies the optimism, or naiveté, with which Dyer approaches his topic. Such an attitude appears again in book 2 in the famous lines, " 'Tis art and toil / Gives nature value, multiplies her stores, / Varies, improves, creates. . . ." Book 1 continues with praise of Britain's climate ("Rich queen of mists and vapours!"), which introduces early on another of the poet's chief concerns, a pa-

Portrait of the Dyers' second daughter, Sarah, painted by her father, circa 1752-1753 (private collection; from Ralph Williams, Poet, Painter, and Parson: The Life of John Dyer, *1956)*

triotic belief in the inherent superiority of British production and commerce. The poet discusses different breeds of sheep in Britain and elsewhere, what to feed sheep, how to treat their diseases, what shepherds should have on hand, and how to deal with the breeding season, the castration of lambs, and similar matters. Book 1 concludes with a passage upon which modern commentators have focused: a description of a shearing festival, featuring a pastoral eclogue between the characters Damon and Colin that celebrates the virtues of country life in contrast to the physical and moral dangers of city life. This passage seems to contradict the poem's later praise of northern industrial towns and industrialization in general, but the speaker makes it plain that the eclogue, though pleasing, belongs to a former time: "Could I recall those notes, which once the muse / Heard at a shearing, near the woody sides / Of blue-topp'd Wreakin! Yet the carols sweet, / Through the deep maze of the memorial cell, / Faintly remurmur." Moreover, as the poet steps back from the pastoral scene for a broader prospect, his sweep of vision takes in not only happy swains but also a merchant ship anchored in the distance, its sails furled, peacefully a part of the country scene.

In the three remaining books the poet's attention turns sharply from the practical and pastoral to the celebratory as Dyer takes up the subject of the benefits of labor, the virtues of trade, and the glories of the woolen industry. Book 2, for example, begins with a pastoral vision of the communion between the human and natural worlds typified by the willingness of sheep to sacrifice their fleece each year. However, the poem quickly turns to the subject of what happens to the fleece, after it has been bought from the farmer, as it is transported to town, processed, and sold around the world. These latter parts of the poem raise the question of the adequacy and humanity of Dyer's vision. He praises Belgian industry, for example, where "the tender eye / May view the maim'd, the blind, the lame, employ'd, / And unrejected age; ev'n childhood there / Its little fingers turning to the toil / Delighted." In another passage in book 2 he praises the practice of enclosing common fields and later implies that trade is a manifestation of divine providence. Book 3 argues that laborers should not fear the advent of machines that do their work, since "Yours, with the public good, shall ever rise," and calls for workhouses throughout England where "children of affliction" will be "compell'd / To happiness."

In one key respect the poem is not as relentlessly optimistic as it might appear, especially to readers who recall the gravity of *The Ruins of Rome*. Dyer does not allow the reader to forget the fate of the seemingly invincible Roman empire celebrated in Virgil's *Georgics*. In Dyer's reading of history, loss of political independence and a decadent taste for luxury brought down Rome, and the possibility always remains that the same could happen to England, despite its current glory. This moral is the focus of Dyer's recounting of the story of Jason and the Argonauts, who found that the possessors of the Golden Fleece " 'gan to slight / The shepherd's trade, and turn to song and dance: / Ev'n Hydrus ceas'd to watch. . . ." The results were the theft of the fleece, loss of trade, and poverty and servitude. The frequent calls to labor and the praise of industry in the poem spring in part from Dyer's faith in the mercantile economy but also from a dark awareness of history and of the sober parallels between Augustan Rome and Augustan England.

In terms of form, *The Fleece* is more focused than other long eighteenth-century poems with

Illustration for The Fleece, *Dyer's formal georgic, in* Poems

georgic elements, such as James Thomson's *The Seasons* (1730). Digressions, like Dyer's retelling of the story of Jason and the Golden Fleece in book 2, sanctioned by the Virgilian model, never obscure the overall design of the poem, as they threaten to do in Thomson's work. At the same time, especially in book 4, which concentrates on exports, *The Fleece* exhibits a global vision as the speaker's muse carries him to Russia, China, America, and beyond, waxing sublime in pursuit of the full story of fleece. Dyer is patriotic but not xenophobic: his poem also welcomes to Britain exiles who come to contribute to its mercantile system.

Finally, however, the central question regarding *The Fleece* remains that of the quality of its vision. Contemporary readers did not warm to its theme, and subsequent readers have paid it less attention than a poem like *The Seasons*. Dyer's conception of a world where "man, / With man united, is a nation strong; / Builds tow'ry cities, satiates ev'ry want, / And makes the seas profound, and forests wild, / The gardens of his joys. Man, each man's born / For the high business of the public good," while aesthetically complete in the poem, does not seem to accord with the social realities of his day or of modern times. Dyer succeeds poetically in uniting the pastoral and mercantile with the georgic vision of life, but that union seems strained and incomplete in reality.

The story of Dyer's life after the publication of *The Fleece* is chiefly one of rapidly worsening disease. He died in December 1757 and was buried on the fifteenth in his church at Coningsby. He remains a significant, though a minor, voice in eighteenth-century poetry. As the author of one of the finest "local poems" and the most ambitious formal georgic of the period, he continues to repay study by social historians, historians of pictorialism, and students of poetry generally.

Letters:

Letters, By Several Eminent Persons Deceased. Including the Correspondence of John Hughes, Esq. (Author of the Siege of Damascus) And Several Of His Friends, Published From The Originals: With Notes Explanatory and Historical, edited by John Duncombe, 3 volumes, second edition, enlarged (London: Printed for J. Johnson, 1773), pp. 56-75.

Biographies:

Samuel Johnson, "Dyer" in *Lives of the English Poets* (1779-1781), edited by George Birkbeck Hill (Oxford: Clarendon Press, 1905), III: 343-347;

William Hylton Dyer Longstaffe, "Notes Respecting the Life and Family of John Dyer, the Poet," in *The Patrician*, edited by J. B. Burke, 6 volumes (London: 1846-1848), IV: 7-12, 264-268, 420-426; V: 75-81, 218-235;

Ralph M. Williams, *Poet, Painter, and Parson: The Life of John Dyer* (New York: Bookman Associates, 1956).

References:

John Barrell, *English Literature in History: An Equal, Wide Survey* (New York: St. Martin's, 1983), pp. 51-109;

John Chalker, *The English Georgic: A Study in the Development of a Form* (Baltimore: Johns Hopkins Press, 1969), pp. 34-65;

Richard Feingold, *Nature and Society: Later Eighteenth-Century Uses of the Pastoral and Georgic* (New Brunswick, N.J.: Rutgers University Press, 1978), pp. 83-119;

William Gilpin, *Observations on the River Wye* (London: R. Blamire, 1782), pp. 57-65;

Mary Theresa Griffin, "Dyer's Grongar Poems and 'Picturesque' Sensibility," *Studies in English Literature, 1500-1900,* 21 (Summer 1981): 457-469;

John F. Reichert, " 'Grongar Hill': Its Origins and Development," *Papers on Language and Literature,* 2 (Spring 1969): 123-129;

John Scott, *Critical Essays on Some of the Poems of Several English Poets* (London: James Phillips, 1785), pp. 97-152;

O. H. K. Spate, "The Muse of Mercantilism: Jago, Grainger, and Dyer," in *Studies in the Eighteenth Century I: Papers Presented at the David Nichol Smith Memorial Seminar, Canberra, 1966,* edited by R. F. Brissenden (Toronto: University of Toronto Press, 1968), pp. 119-131.

Papers:

Dyer's papers and manuscripts have been dispersed and lost, and there is no significant repository of them. Further details about the history of Dyer's papers may be found in the *Index of English Literary Manuscripts,* volume 3, part 1, compiled by Margaret M. Smith and Penny Boumella (London: Mansell, 1986), pp. 341-353.

Anne Finch, Countess of Winchilsea
(April 1661 - 5 August 1720)

Jamie Stanesa
Emory University

BOOKS: *Upon the Death of King James the Second,*
anonymous (London, 1701);

The Tunbridge Prodigy (London: Printed & sold by
John Morphew, 1706);

The Spleen, A Pindarique Ode. By a Lady (London:
Printed & sold by H. Hills, 1709);

Free-thinkers: A Poem in Dialogue (London, 1711);

*Miscellany Poems, on Several Occasions. Written by a
Lady* (London: Printed for John Barber &
sold by Benj. Tooke, William Taylor &
James Round, 1713).

Editions & Collections: *The Poems of Anne Countess of Winchilsea,* edited by Myra Reynolds
(Chicago: University of Chicago Press,
1903);

Selected Poems of Anne Finch, Countess of Winchilsea
(Hull, Que.: Orinda, 1906);

Poems, by Anne, Countess of Winchilsea, compiled by
John Middleton Murray (London: Cape,
1928);

Selected Poems, edited by Katharine M. Rogers
(New York: Ungar, 1979);

Selected Poems, edited by Denys Thompson (Manchester: Carcanet Press, 1987; New York:
Fyfield, 1987);

*The Wellesley Manuscript Poems of Anne Countess of
Winchilsea,* edited by Jean M. Ellis D'Alessandro (Florence: Universita degli Studi di Fi-
renze, 1988).

OTHER: *Poems and Extracts chosen by William Words-
worth for an album presented to Lady Mary
Lowther,* includes poems by Finch (London:
Henry Frowde, 1905);

Minor Poets of the Eighteenth Century, edited by
H. I'A. Fausset, includes poems by Finch
(N.p.: Everyman's Library, 1930).

Although she enjoyed some fame during
the eighteenth and nineteenth centuries, Anne
Finch, Countess of Winchilsea, has only recently
received greater praise and renewed attention as
a poet. Her diverse and considerable body of
poems record her private thoughts and personal
struggles but illustrate as well her awareness of
the social and political climate of her age. Not
only do Finch's poems reveal a sensitive mind
and a religious soul, but the body of her work exhibits great generic range and demonstrates her
fluent use of Augustan diction and forms.

Descended from an ancient Hampshire family, Finch was born in April 1661, the third and
youngest child of Anne Haselwood and Sir William Kingsmill. Her father died when she was
five months old. Her mother soon remarried and
bore another daughter, Dorothy, to whom Finch
remained close throughout her life. When Anne
Haselwood died, her second husband, Sir
Thomas Ogle, was left alone to raise four children under the age of seven. Little else is known
of Finch's early life until, at the age of twenty-
one, she was appointed one of six maids of
honor to Mary of Modena, wife of the duke of
York, in the court of Charles II. Her interest in
verse writing began during this period and was
probably encouraged by her friendships with
Sarah Churchill and Anne Killigrew, also maids
of honor and women of literary interests. They
read romances aloud to one another, acted in
masques, and enjoyed regular musical performances at court. Later in her life Finch fondly recalled those days "when trifles pleas'd & every
pleasure charm'd" in her 1718 poem "On the
Death of the Queen."

During her residence in the court of
Charles II she met Col. Heneage Finch, uncle of
the fifth earl of Winchilsea and gentleman to the
duke of York, who fell in love with her and
courted her persistently until they married. She resigned her post, although Heneage Finch continued to serve in various government positions.
Their marriage was a happy one, as attested by
his letters and several of her early poems. They
led a quiet life, residing first in Westminster and
then in London, as Heneage Finch became more
involved in public affairs with the accession of
James II in 1685. The couple wholly supported
James throughout his brief and difficult reign

Anne Finch, Countess of Winchilsea (miniature by Lawrence Crosse; by permission of the National Portrait Gallery, London)

and remained forever sympathetic to the interests of the Stuart court.

Following the revolution and deposition of James in 1689, Finch lost his government position and permanently severed himself from public life by refusing allegiance to the incoming monarchs, William and Mary. The subsequent loss of income forced the Finches to take temporary refuge with various friends in London until Heneage's nephew Charles invited them to settle permanently on the family's estate in Eastwell in 1689 or 1690, where they resided for more than twenty-five years.

It was during the happy yet trying years of her early married life that Anne Finch began to pursue more seriously her interest in writing poetry. She adopted the pseudonym Ardelia, and not surprisingly, many of her earliest poems are dedicated to her "much lov'd husband," who appears as "Dafnis" in her work. In a "Letter to Dafnis" written in 1685, Finch expresses her love to Heneage during his absence from court, describ-

ing the details of her husband's persistent quest to "win a stubborn, and ungrateful heart." In "A Letter to the Same Person," she draws a connection between the passions of love and of poetry, indicating that neither is as fine without the other:

> Love without Poetry's refining Aid
> Is a dull Bargain, and but coarsely made;
> Nor e'er cou'd Poetry successful prove,
> Or touch the Soul, but when the Sense was Love.
>   Oh! cou'd they both in Absence now impart
> Skill to my Hand, but to describe my Heart; . . . .

This connection between her love for Heneage and her expression of that love through poetry appears repeatedly in Finch's work, intimating more generally that her verse is the vehicle through which she could express her deepest, most heartfelt passions.

Finch's early poems to her husband demonstrate her awareness of seventeenth-century poetic conventions yet point as well to the problems those conventions pose to the expression of such intimate thoughts. In "To Mr. F. Now Earl of Winchilsea," for example, she appropriately invokes the Muses for inspiration, but finally only Urania, the Muse of heavenly love, tells the poet that true love can be expressed without such inspiration:

> She whisp'ring did impart:
> They need no Foreign Aid invoke,
>   No help to draw a moving Stroke,
> Who dictate from the Heart.
>
> Enough! the pleas'd ARDELIA cry'd;
> And slighting ev'ry Muse beside,
>   Consulting now her Breast,
> Perceiv'd that ev'ry tender Thought,
> Which from abroad she'd vainly sought,
>   Did there in Silence rest. . . .

She demonstrates her awareness of conventional invocation, yet alters it, rejecting ultimately the Muse in favor of her own emotion.

Finch's earliest verse records her own frustration and sense of loss following her departure from court in 1689. She and her husband remained loyal to the Catholic Stuarts, a tenuous stance to assume given the popularity of the Protestant William and Mary in Britain in the 1690s. In "Fragment" Finch recalls that her "early Time" in court, "with all its glorious Show / Was sure above the rest, and Paradise below." Too soon, however, the "wheels inevitable Round" removed James from power, dashing her own aspirations. Like James, she too was exiled, forced to "Abandon the Pleasures of the court in Monastick Walls" and to accept her retirement, "which the World *Moroseness* calls." Ardelia turns finally toward God, recognizing that since her aspirations for heaven on earth were destroyed, she must "wait with chearful hope, till Heaven be known in Heaven."

Her most explicit recognition of the problem of succession and of the difficulty of her relationship to the Stuarts appears in Finch's first published poem, an elegy for James II anonymously published in 1701. In *Upon the Death of King James the Second* the speaker begins by imagining the kind of "weeping Elegies" and "melancholy Dirges" poets would have sung to James's "acknowledg'd worth" had he left the throne because of death rather than by ejection. She laments that the "noblest Subjects for the Pen are lost" and thus writes the elegy herself, since "abler Writers" refuse to honor the unpopular James. The speaker calls to those loyal to James

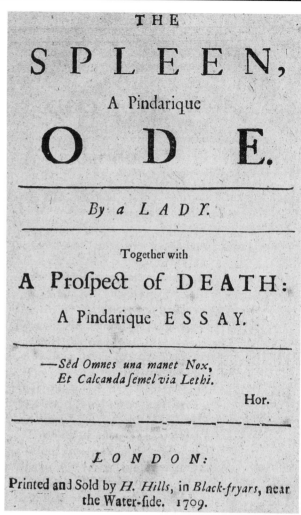

Title page for Finch's well-received description in verse of maladies associated with the spleen, including melancholia (RB 226671; by permission of the Henry E. Huntington Library and Art Gallery)

to "let your Tears a heavier Tribute pay." She acknowledges the problem of succession, since James was robbed of the throne by his daughter and her foreign husband, although it was James's "right by birth." The speaker then focuses on Mary of Modena's grief since, as Carol Barash suggests, all Mary can share now with her husband is death: his body lies "unmolested" in the grave, finally beyond the threat of political opposition. The poem ends with an appeal to Britain's "Maternal Bosome"–an attack on William and possibly on the currently reigning queen as well–to honor "Rightful Kings" and "All who shall intend thy Good." Curiously, the speaker retreats in the final lines:

> May all who Shield Thee [Britain] due Applauses
>   have

Whilst for myself like solitary men
Devoted only to the Pen
I but a safe Retreat amidst thee Crave
Below th' ambitious World and just above my
    Grave.

Finch's benign acceptance of her safe retreat may well reflect the comfort of retirement in Eastwell. Yet the reversal of her initially bitter attitude is ironic, attesting to the poem's politically unpopular and even dangerous attitude and to her own inability to speak very openly of her loyalty to the Stuart court.

Although her sense of loss seemed to dissipate after the turn of the century as she became more comfortable with her husband's family in Eastwell, Finch never forgot those happy days at court nor the devastation she felt after 1689. She acknowledges her precarious position in a letter to Arabella Marow in 1716. Apologizing for tardiness in answering her friend's note, Finch remarks that she was "still detain'd by reflecting on the great cautiousness with which we must write to our friends under the present posture of affairs & I was very unwilling when addressing my self to you to be under that necessity of being dull which that great reserve imposes." Even as late as 1717, in "A Supplication for the joys of Heaven," Finch refers to her deep sense of loss and subsequent bitterness following the revolution, turning once again to God and Heaven for comfort:

With the Heroick Spirits of the brave
Who durst be true then threatn'd with the Grave
And when from evil in triumphant sway
Who e'er departed made himself a prey
To sanguine perils to penurious care. . . .
Unsuccour'd losses and imputed faults
With these let me be join'd when Heaven reveals
The judgement which admits of no appeals
And having heard from the deciding throne
Well have ye suffer'd wisely have ye done
Henceforth the Kingdom of the blest is yours. . . .

As her work developed more fully during her retirement at Eastwell, Finch demonstrated an increasing awareness of poetic traditions of her own period as well as those governing much seventeenth-century verse. Her work's affinity with the metaphysical tradition is evident in poems such as "The Petition for an Absolute Retreat," which represents the distanced perspective of the speaker through the image of the telescope, an emblem common to much religious poet-

ry of the seventeenth century. The images of foundation and construction in "On Affliction" are reminiscent of George Herbert's architectural imagery in *The Temple* (1633), as is the speaker's personal allegory depicted through biblical allusions. The speaker thinks forward to the time when she will accomplish "Babel's aim" and reach "th' Almighty's hill" where heaven is revealed in glorious light. The third stanza of the poem is also metaphysical in the geometrical "line" figure:

Affliction is the line, which every Saint
    Is measur'd by, his stature taken right;
So much it shrinks, as they repine or faint,
    But if their faith and Courage stand upright,
    By that is made the Crown, and the full robe of
        light.

The logic of the shrinking measure seems paradoxical, as does the shift from the image of the "line" to the encircling "Crown, and full robe of light." The lines initially suggest that affliction increases when Christians "repine and faint," and decreases when they are courageous. But as with John Donne's poetry, the striking inversion at the end of the poem is more than a mere paradox. As Reuben Brower suggests, the image corresponds as well to the realities of experience, the attainment of Christian salvation through faith and endurance.

Finch first followed the stylistic standards set forth by John Dryden at the end of the seventeenth century in her preference for heroic couplets and in her often excessive elision. Her later work is more typically Augustan in both form and content. Finch experimented with rhyme and meter and imitated several popular genres, including occasional poems, fables, satirical verse, and religious meditations.

Fables comprise the largest portion of her oeuvre, about one-third of her poetic output. Most likely inspired by the popularity of the genre at the turn of the century, Finch wrote dozens of these often satiric vignettes between 1700 and 1713. Most of them were modeled after the short tales of Jean La Fontaine, a French fable writer whose work Charles II introduced at court in 1660 following his exile in France. Finch mocked these playful trifles; her fables offer interesting bits of social criticism and thus blend with the satiric spirit of her age.

However, Finch's more serious poems have received greater critical attention than her fables during and since her own time. "A Nocturnal Reverie," for instance, is clearly Augustan in its perspective and technique, although many admirers have tended to praise the poem as a pre-Romantic work since William Wordsworth mentioned its "new images of external nature" in his "Essay, Supplementary to the Preface" in the second edition of his *Lyrical Ballads* in 1815. Finch's poem opens with classical references and proceeds through characteristically Augustan descriptions of the foxglove, the cowslip, the glowworm, and the moon. Finch imitates Augustan preferences for decorum and balance in her use of heroic couplets and the medial caesura in setting the peaceful, nocturnal atmosphere of the poem:

> Or from some Tree, fam'd for the *Owl's* delight,
> She, hollowing clear, directs the Wand'rer right:
> In such a *Night*, when passing Clouds give place,
> Or thinly vail the Heav'ns mysterious Face; . . .
> When Odours, which declin'd repelling Day,
> Thro' temp'rate Air uninterrupted stray; . . . .

The tone is sedate and peaceful; animals graze in twilight, and the spirit is content, undisturbed by "fierce Light." This peace, however, like the night, is short-lived; the "solumn Quiet" of evening is interrupted again by morning, where "All's confused again; / Our Cares, our Toils, our Clamours are renew'd, / Our Pleasures, seldom reach'd, again pursu'd."

While Finch's verse occasionally displays slight antitheses of idea and some structural balances of line and phrase, she never attains the epigrammatic couplet form that Alexander Pope perfected in the early eighteenth century. Her admission in "A Nocturnal Reverie" that her verse attempts "Something, too high for Syllables to speak" might be linked to the Romantic recognition of the discrepancy between human aspiration and achievement. But ultimately she retreats to God and solitude and displays a more properly Augustan attitude in the acceptance of her human limitations. At times her descriptions of natural detail bear some likeness to mid-eighteenth-century poets such as James Thomson. But Finch's expression is more immediate and simple, and her versification ultimately exhibits an Augustan rather than a pre-Romantic sensibility.

Another form Finch appropriates is the Pindaric ode. Between 1694 and 1703 she wrote three such odes in the form introduced in England by Abraham Cowley in the 1650s, following his preference for complex and irregular stanzaic structures and rhyme schemes. These poems—"All is Vanity," *The Spleen* (1709), and

"On the Hurricane"—all depict metaphysical entities working against humanity to test its strength and faith in God. Vanity is destructive to humanity, the spleen (melancholy) is destructive to a person's mind and soul, and the hurricane is destructive of earth, humanity, and human works. As Jean M. Ellis D'Alessandro suggests, Finch moves from vanity, an abstract personification of evil, to melancholy, a physically and mentally overpowering ailment, and finally to the hurricane, an adversary to the whole of creation.

The Spleen is possibly Finch's most well-known poem, rivaled only by "A Nocturnal Reverie." First published anonymously in 1709, the ode was immediately popular and received much attention for its accurate description of the symptoms of the disease. Throughout her life Finch suffered from melancholia, a condition often synonymous with the spleen, which probably prompted her poetic presentation of the ailment. The speaker begins by acknowledging the hypochondria often associated with the spleen, the "pretended Fits," the "sullen *Husband's* feign'd Excuse," and the coquette's melancholy pose, "careless Posture, and the Head reclin'd." She then proceeds to undermine these portraits of feigned illness, treating the disease as a real and terrifying affliction:

> From Speech restrain'd, by thy Deceits abus'd,
> To Deserts banish'd or in Cells reclus'd,
> Mistaken Vot'ries to the Pow'rs Divine,
> Wilst they a purer Sacrifice design,
> Do but the *Spleen* obey, and worship at thy Shrine.

In "Ardelia to Melancholy" Finch similarly presents a struggle against melancholy and depression. In the first stanza Ardelia describes melancholy as her "inveterate foe," which she cannot overcome by any means. Ardelia then seeks the "sov'rain aid" of friendship to "conquer" melancholy by "united charge." But her resolve is not strong enough. Ardelia invokes a Muse, hoping to use "troops of fancies" to "guard" her from the "Tyrant pow'r" that threatens to banish her rest. Her conquest fails, however, as even poetry writing yields her "captive" to melancholy. Once again Ardelia turns to God for relief, as "heav'n, alone" can set her "free." The poem shifts from the first to the third person in the last four lines, thus generalizing Ardelia's particular experience to encompass all those who suffer from melancholia: "All, that cou'd ere thy ill got rule, invade, / Their uselesse arms, before thy feet have laid; / The Fort is thine, now ruin'd, all within, / Whilst

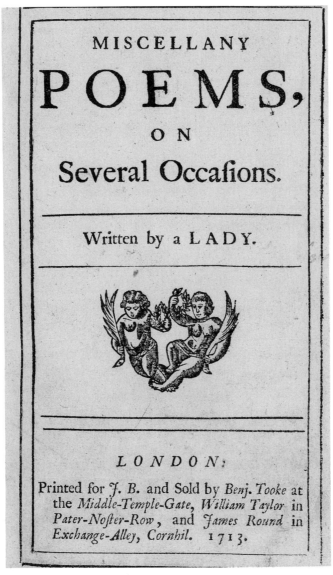

MISCELLANY

POEMS,

ON

Several Occasions.

Written by a LADY.

LONDON;

Printed for J. B. and Sold by Benj. Tooke at
the Middle-Temple-Gate, William Taylor in
Pater-Noster-Row, and James Round in
Exchange-Alley, Cornhil. 1713.

*Title page for the only collection of Finch's poetry published in her lifetime; also published with another title page, dated 1714,
which bears her name (RB 83550; by permission of the Henry E. Huntington Library and Art Gallery)*

by decays without, thy Conquest too, is seen."
The generalized ending portrays all those people
unfairly invaded by melancholy's conquest; the victims' "arms" are useless except to obey, to bow
down to the powers of melancholy. Thus, with
an effort toward accuracy, Finch represents the
spleen as a tyrant that banishes its victims to de-
serts or holds them captive. The imperial language of the poem might also suggest a more abstract relation between her submission to the
spleen and her necessary retirement as a political
exile.

Finch wrote two plays and attempted some
satire and verse criticism, though hers differed
markedly from the caustic variety most popular

during the Restoration and early eighteenth century. Sensitive to the ridicule faced by James's entourage following the revolution, she expressed
her distaste for such lampoons in the preface to
her *Miscellany Poems* (1713) and then later in "On
my being charged with writing a lampoon at Tunbridge." Finch defends herself, insisting throughout that she "scorns lampoon" and whoever accuses her of satire "Knows not the style of [her]
well-temper'd muse."

The Christian consolation suggested at the
end of many of Finch's early poems foreshadows
the more solemn religious writing of her later
life, illustrated in the final lines of one of her last
poems, written in 1715 after a fit of illness:

For Providence my ample field
My food my raiment and my shield
   Thro' life my trust
   Rejoice I must
And Allelujahs yield. . . .

In Allelujahs who'l proceed
Shall find all objects praises breed
   Nor fear the spleen
   Shou'd come between
By Allelujahs freed.

Many of Finch's later poems once again demonstrate her turn from friendship and poetry toward God, as in "A Act of Contrition" [*sic*]:

O place of the Sufferings of thy Son between
Through him regard O Lord my trembling Soul
And speak the Word that makes thy Creature
   whole
Then for the time which I have yet to see
Be Thou my God thy Servant I will be.

And, in the final poem in her notebook, "A Contemplation," written sometime in 1716 or 1717, she writes:

From Gratitude what Graces flow
   What endlesse spring
From Prayers whilst we remain below
   Above whilst Praises we sing . . .

Whilst to this Heav'n my Soul Aspires
   All Suff'rings here are light
He travells pleas'd who but desires
   A Sweet Repose at Night.

Finch circulated two manuscripts of her work before she published *Miscellany Poems*, and several of her poems were published individually in broadsheets and smaller collections. The 1713 volume includes a play and eighty-one poems, forty-five of which had not appeared before. Two title pages were used. The first, dated 1713, has a woodcut of two winged cherubs bearing laurel wreaths and palm branches. The second, dated 1714, omitted the cherubs and identified the lady poet as the "Right Hon'ble Anne, Countess of Winchilsea," denoting perhaps her growing sense of confidence in her own poetic abilities.

After the publication of her *Miscellany Poems*, Finch experienced some additional, though limited, recognition. Richard Steele, for instance, published several of her poems in his *Miscellanies* of 1714. She was personally acquainted with both Swift and Pope, though the full extent of her relationships with them is unknown. Pope initially seemed supportive of her work, printing one of her poems in the quarto edition of his *Works* in 1717. He is thought to have sneered at her elsewhere, however, as he did at "female wits" in general in his later work. Finch is mentioned as well in several compilations, memoirs, and literary dictionaries during the eighteenth century, and to a lesser extent, in the nineteenth century. Only recently has Finch received sustained attention. The first modern edition of her work, though incomplete, appeared in 1903. Since then, other shorter collections of her poems and an edition of her later notebook have been published, and selections of her work currently appear in major literary anthologies.

Much of the recent interest in Finch arises from current academic efforts to recover the work of previously neglected women writers, exploring how those writers depict themselves as poetic subjects and examining the ways in which they adopt and alter the poetic standards of a particular period. In addition to her depictions of the spleen–an affliction common to women throughout the eighteenth century–Finch also called attention to the need for the education of women and recorded the isolation and solitude that marked women's lives. In "The Bird and the Arras," for instance, a female bird enclosed in a room mistakes the arras for a real scene and flies happily into it. But she is soon trapped, "Flutt'ring in endless circles of dismay" until she finally escapes to "ample space," the "only Heav'n of Birds." Such images of entrapment and frustration are echoed in Finch's description of the limitations of women's social roles in England at the turn of the eighteenth century. In "The Unequal Fetters," the speaker notes her fear of fading youth, but later refuses to be a "pris'ner" in marriage: "Free as Nature's first intention / Was to make us, I'll be found / Nor by subtle Man's invention / Yield to be in Fetters bound / By one that walks in freer round." Finch admits that marriage does "slightly tye Men," yet insists that women remain "close Pris'ners" in the union, while men can continue to function "At the full length of all their chain." For the most part, however, Finch's message is subtle in its persistent decorum and final resignation and consolation in God. Although she was certainly aware of the problems many of her countrywomen faced, and particularly of the difficulties confronting women writers, Finch offers a playful yet firm protest rather than an outspoken condemnation of the social position of women in eighteenth-century England. And although she endured a loss of affluence with James's deposition, there is little evidence that she abhorred her twenty-five-year retirement in Eastwell, which afforded her the leisure hours in which to pursue her creative interests.

Finch died quietly on 5 August 1720 after several years of increasingly ill health. Following her funeral, Heneage Finch, as quoted by Myra Reynolds, praised her Christian virtues and persistent loyalty to her friends and family, noting as well her talents as a writer: "To draw her . . . just character requires a masterly pen like her own. We shall only presume to say she was the most faithfull servant to her Royall Mistresse, the best wife to her noble Lord, and in every other relation public and private so illustrious an example of all moral and divine virtues: in one word a Person of such extraordinary endowments both of Body and Mind that the Court of England never bred a more accomplished Lady nor the Church of England a better Christian." Much of the immediate appeal of Finch's verse to a post-Romantic modern audience lies in the sincerity with which she expressed the Christian values her husband recalls in his eulogy. But clearly Anne Finch belongs to her age and merits greater appreciation for her poetic experimentation and her fluent use of Augustan diction and forms. Her voice is clear and self-assured, evidence of the controlled and confident poise of an aristocratic poet.

References:
Carol Barash, "Augustan Women's Mythmaking: English Women Writers and the Body of the Monarchy, 1660-1720," Ph.D. dissertation, Princeton University, 1989;

Reuben A. Brower, "Lady Winchilsea and the Poetic Tradition of the Seventeenth Century," *Studies in Philology*, 42, no. 1 (1945): 61-80;

Jean M. Ellis D'Alessandro, "Anne Countess of Winchilsea and the Whole Duty of Women: Socio-Cultural Inference in the Reading of 'The Introduction,' " *Le Lingue del Mondo*, 52, nos. 5-6 (1988): 9-15;

D'Alessandro, "Lady Anne Winchilsea's 'Preface' and the Rules of Poetry," *Filologia Moderna* (1988);

Elizabeth Hampsten, "Petticoat Authors: 1660-1720," *Women's Studies*, 5, nos. 1-2 (1980): 21-38;

Ann Messenger, "Publishing Without Perishing: Lady Winchilsea's *Miscellany Poems* of 1713," *Restoration*, 5, no. 1 (1981): 27-37;

Messenger, "Selected Nightingales: Anne Finch, Countess of Winchilsea, et al.," in her *His and Hers: Essays in Restoration and Eighteenth-Century Literature* (Lexington, Ky.: University Press of Kentucky, 1986), pp. 71-83;

Katharine Rogers, "Anne Finch, Countess of Winchilsea: An Augustan Woman Poet," in *Shakespeare's Sisters: Feminist Essays on Women Poets*, edited by Sandra M. Gilbert and Susan Gubar (Bloomington: Indiana University Press, 1979), pp. 37-46.

Papers:
A manuscript collection containing Finch's poems written after 1713 and some letters is at Wellesley College, Wellesley, Massachusetts.

Samuel Garth
(1661 - 18 January 1719)

Richard I. Cook
Kent State University

BOOKS: *Oratio Laudatoria: In Aedibus Collegii Regalis Med. Lond.* (London: Printed for Abel Roper, 1697);

The Dispensary: A Poem in Six Cantos (London: Printed for John Nutt, 1699; revised and enlarged, 1700; sixth edition, revised and enlarged again, 1706; seventh edition, enlarged again, London: Printed for Jacob Tonson, 1714; eighth edition, enlarged again, 1718; ninth edition, enlarged again, Dublin: Printed by Pressick Rider & Thomas Harbin, for Pat. Dugan, 1725; London: Printed for J. T. & sold by Tho. Astley, 1726);

Claremont: Address'd to the Right Honourable the Earl of Clare, anonymous (London: Printed for J. Tonson, 1715).

Collection: *The Poetical Works of Sir Samuel Garth. With the Life of the Author* (London: Printed for John Bell, 1791).

OTHER: "The First Philippick," translated by Garth, in *Several Orations of Demosthenes* (London: Printed for Jacob Tonson, 1702);

Dedication for *The Latin Edition of Lucretius,* translated and edited by John Oldmixon (London: Printed for John Roberts, 1714);

Ovid's Metamorphoses: Translated into English Verse, edited, with an introduction, by Garth (London: Printed for Jacob Tonson, 1717);

"Garth's Poems," in *The Works of Celebrated Authors,* volume 1 (London: Printed for Jacob Tonson & John Draper, 1750);

"Garth's Poems," in *The Works of the English Poets,* volume 20, edited by Samuel Johnson (London: Printed for J. Buckland, 1790);

"Life of Otho," translated by Garth, in *Plutarch's Lives,* edited by A. H. Clough (New York: Bigelow, Brown, 1911).

Upon the publication of his mock-epic poem, *The Dispensary,* in 1699, Samuel Garth achieved an overnight fame that led many to hail him as the logical heir to John Dryden as

Samuel Garth (painting by Godfrey Kneller; by permission of the National Portrait Gallery, London)

England's reigning poet. In the early years of the eighteenth century Garth's wit, the facility of his verse, and the importance of his work in refining and demonstrating the possibilities of the heroic couplet as a satiric vehicle all recommended him to his contemporaries. With the later emergence of more polished and prolific practitioners in the same mode (most notably Alexander Pope, who greatly admired Garth and generously acknowledged his influence and example) Garth's reputation diminished significantly, though his works continued to be read, praised, and emulated throughout the century. After having been largely forgotten during the nineteenth century, Garth has more recently come to be recognized as one of the more talented and interesting poets of his age.

Garth was born in 1661 in Bolam, Durham, where his father, William, was a landed proprietor of sufficient wealth to underwrite his son's expensive and protracted education. After attending school at Ingleton, Garth entered Cambridge (Peterhouse College) in 1676, taking his B.A. in 1679, his M.A. in 1684, and eventually his M.D. in 1691. The exceptional duration of Garth's medical training is accounted for by two lengthy trips in the late 1680s to the Continent, where he pursued his studies in hospitals, the University of Leyden, and possibly in military campaigns. With his medical degree finally in hand, Garth married Martha Beaufoy, daughter of Sir Henry Beaufoy, and moved to London, where in 1693 he was elected as a fellow of the Royal College of Physicians, in which organization he was to remain prominent for the rest of his career. His early reputation with the college seems to have derived as much from his talents as a Latin orator as from his medical skills. In 1694 he was appointed Gulstonian Lecturer (his topic being "De Respiratione"), and in 1697 he was assigned the signal honor of delivering the annual Latin Harveian Oration, printed later that year as Garth's first known publication. In that speech Garth addresses himself, among other things, to the division in the college ranks over a proposed charity clinic for the poor—a subject which two years later, with the publication of his comic epic *The Dispensary*, was to bring him fame.

The controversy in which Garth's literary contribution was to figure so prominently had been brewing for a generation or more. By royal charter dating back to Henry VIII the members of the College of Physicians enjoyed sole rights to the practice of medicine within London and its environs—just as the London Apothecaries Society had been granted by its charter of 1617 an exclusive franchise on the preparation and sale of drugs. In practice neither monopoly proved enforceable, and recriminations in the form of accusatory pamphlets had been common between the two groups since the Restoration. To the physicians, the apothecaries, with their inferior educations and generally humble social origins, appeared mere greedy tradesmen quick to exploit the credulity of the ignorant; while to the apothecaries, the physicians seemed arrogantly deter-

Garth, circa 1705-1710 (painting by an unknown artist; by permission of the National Portrait Gallery, London)

mined to bar all claimants to medical knowledge other than themselves. When the physicians complained about apothecaries practicing medicine, the latter maintained that their patients were mostly among the poor, who could not afford a doctor's fee in any case.

It was in response to this telling argument that the author (identified only as "Dr. T. C.") of *Some Papers Writ . . . Concerning the Practice of Physick in England* (1670) urged his fellow doctors to establish a dispensary in which free treatment and drugs would be given to the poor. Not only did the apothecaries (who feared for their livelihood) oppose this plan, but a significant minority in the college itself—the so-called "Apothecaries's Physicians"—objected, thereby incurring the special wrath of the dispensarian faction and their spokesman Garth, who in his Harveian Oration ascribes such opposition to pure avarice. After complex debate, delaying tactics, and pamphlet warfare, the "Repositorie well furnished with Druggs for the help of the poor" called for by Garth finally opened its doors in 1698, though the occasion was somewhat marred by, as Garth describes it in *The Dispensary,* "a Feud that hapned in the *Dispensary,* betwixt a Member of the College with his Retinue, and some of the Servants that attended there, to dispence the Medicines." This unseemly scuffle, evidently involving an irate Apothecaries' Physician, became the inspiration for Garth's six-canto poem, a more fully conceived mock-epic than had hitherto appeared in the English language.

Garth's sudden emergence as a poet is all the more surprising since it was quite unheralded. The technical facility of *The Dispensary* suggests considerable practice, but prior to this, his masterpiece, Garth had published no verse, nor have any apprentice works by him survived. Yet so well received was *The Dispensary* (within a month of its issuance two further editions were called for) that when Dryden died a year later, the anonymous author of an *Epistle to Sr. Richard Blackmore* (1700) was merely endorsing a widespread opinion when he hailed Garth as Dryden's natural heir: "Tho *Con*[greve] may in time, when he has merit, / The Prophet's [Dryden's] Throne in peaceful sway inherit, / The Poets all with one consent agree / His mantle falls to G[arth] by Destiny." The poetical ancestry here suggested seems appropriate, since Garth was a friend of Dryden's in that poet's later years and helped to organize the elder poet's funeral, at which he delivered a Latin eulogy. Likewise Dryden's example and influence are everywhere apparent in *The Dispensary.*

Both from Dryden's work (*Absalom and Achitophel,* 1681, and *MacFlecknoe,* 1682) and from his critical precepts (*The Original and Progress of Satire,* 1693), Garth learned important lessons concerning comic tone, authorial stance, and the effective use of the heroic style in satire. More particularly Garth elaborated so well upon Dryden's employment of the closed iambic pentameter couplet as a vehicle for epigram, antithesis, and symmetry that, in the words of George Saintsbury in *The Cambridge History of English Literature* (volume 9, 1933), *The Dispensary* "represents, as a sort of practical *Ars Poetica* . . . , the stage between Dryden and Pope, and, without exaggeration, may be said to be the first draft—and not a very rough first draft—of the couplet versification and the poetic diction which were to dominate the whole eighteenth century."

Another major influence on *The Dispensary* was Nicolas Boileau-Despréaux's *Le Lutrin* (1683), a mock-epic about bickering clerics in the church of Sainte Chapelle. The superficial resemblances between the two works were so close that many of Garth's contemporaries (especially those among the antidispensarians) criticized the English work as little better than an imitation of the French poem. In response Garth both acknowledged his debt to Boileau and sought to minimize it by claiming he had followed *Le Lutrin* only in three or four images. A more detached judgment suggests that, although Garth did derive much of his general scheme, some of his personified abstractions, and a few of his descriptive passages from Boileau, Garth's use of sustained heroic diction, elaborate structure, and a variety of adaptations of epic conventions make his work by far a more carefully rendered mock-epic than its predecessor.

In the course of the two decades between its initial publication and his death, Garth revised *The Dispensary* extensively, seldom deleting, but adding further detail, illustration, and analogy until the 1,418 lines of the first edition had grown to the 1,848 of the eight, the last edition published in Garth's lifetime. In its completed form *The Dispensary,* after a formal invocation and proposition, opens with a brief history of the College of Physicians and its lofty purpose, which has lately been rendered so ineffectual by factionalism that Sloth has taken up residence in the college headquarters. His slumbers are disturbed by the sounds of the new charity dispensary being constructed. After a speech of complaint, Sloth sends his servant to rouse Envy, who from her baleful grotto assumes the form of Colon, an apothecary, and goes to warn Horoscope, another apothecary, of this threat to their income. Overwhelmed by the shock, Horoscope is revived only when his assistant applies the vapors from a urinal. After a sleepless night, Horoscope assembles the apothecaries for a strategy session, meanwhile building an altar to Disease, to whom he prays for aid in the coming struggle. At the assembly (in canto 3) several apothecaries give heroic orations, variously advocating conciliation, a fight to death, and a policy of quiet subversion. The proceedings end inconclusively and in confusion when a supply of fulminate of gold stored in the basement explodes.

As canto 4 begins we meet the Apothecaries' Physicians, who have assembled to subvert the college's plans from the inside. Whereas Horoscope's prayers to Disease have gone unanswered, the goddess appears at once when invoked by the disaffected physicians, and, after promising her help, she raises a whirlwind that transports Horo-

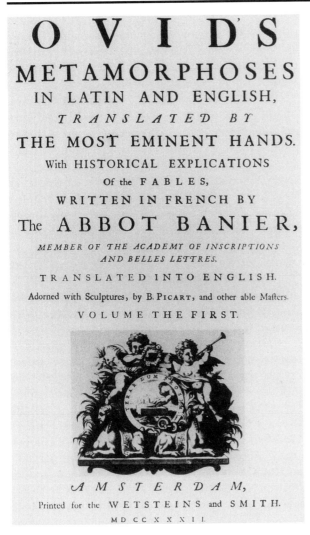

O VID'S
METAMORPHOSES
IN LATIN AND ENGLISH,
TRANSLATED BY
THE MOST EMINENT HANDS.
With HISTORICAL EXPLICATIONS
Of the F A B L E S,
WRITTEN IN FRENCH BY
The A B B O T B A N I E R,
*MEMBER OF THE ACADEMY OF INSCRIPTIONS
AND BELLES LETTRES.*
TRANSLATED INTO ENGLISH.
Adorned with Sculptures, by B. PICART, and other able Masters.
VOLUME THE FIRST.

A M S T E R D A M,
Printed for the WETSTEINS and SMITH.
MDCCXXXII.

*Title page for volume 1 of the Dutch edition of Ovid's major
work as translated by Garth and others*

scope (with much descriptive detail) to the Fortunate Islands. There he consults Fortuna, who cryptically prophesies success and failure for both sides in the coming conflict. Back at the college headquarters, the Apothecaries' Physicians—inspired by an eloquent call to arms from the goddess Discord and joined by a motley army of apothecaries and other submedical pretenders—prepare to launch their attack. The dispensarians, however, are warned by Fame, and the two sides soon join in a furious confrontation in which the weapons are syringes, gally-pots, bedpans, and other sickroom paraphernalia. At the height of the conflict, the goddess Health appears, stops the fighting, and takes Celsus, one of the leaders of the dispensarian doctors, to the Elysian Fields to ask the ghost of William Harvey how the issue should be settled. Much of the final section of

the poem is taken up with close description of this trip, and the poem ends with Harvey's ghost advising the combatants to place their trust in Atticus (Lord Somers, head of the Royal Society and then lord chancellor), who will restore the healing arts to their former dignity.

The work is sustained throughout by an elevation of diction and reference that neatly exploits the essence of the mock-heroic—namely the comic discrepancy that results when a prosaic, trivial, or sordid topic is dealt with in lofty terms. The contrast between Garth's meanly bickering disputants and the epic heroes whose world is evoked by his language and allusion is underlined by parodic versions of such standard epic devices as the catalogue of warriors, the extended simile, the visit to the underworld, the machinery of participating gods and goddesses, and others. Even the frequent scatological humor is made all the more pointed by the straight-faced solemnity with which Garth delivers it.

The reductive nature of the mock-heroic mode tends to make all participants in the action it describes seem at least partly ridiculous, but Garth, as an avowed partisan in the dispute he is satirizing, does not pretend to an above-the-battle impartiality. Although he issues little direct praise of the dispensarian forces and even occasionally mocks (albeit gently) their professional pomposity, the antidispensarians are unrelievedly ignoble, their overriding motive being an insatiable avarice so ingrained as to eclipse all claims of charity or public good. Such rapacity in the lowly apothecaries (where he no doubt thought it only to be expected) Garth treats with amused scorn; the same sort of greed, as displayed among the disloyal physicians (who presumably should have known better) he views as a professional betrayal, and accordingly it is toward them that he directs his sharpest and most personal attacks.

Almost as prominent a feature of *The Dispensary* as its satiric energy are the numerous straightforward descriptive passages, philosophical reflections, and moral sententiae which Garth included in an evident attempt to enhance the work's dignity. Such material, which alleviates the otherwise predominantly unedifying atmosphere engendered by the principals and their actions, especially commended the poem to Garth's contemporaries, for whom the intricacies of medical politics were of minimal interest. The success of *The Dispensary* was by no means limited to readers who could identify the thinly disguised main characters or savor the more particularized allusions; to the general reader (as the anonymous author of a letter to *Mist's Weekly Journal* put it in 1728), "the admired and elegant reflections which are the Beauties of Garth" were as important as his comic verve.

The fame of *The Dispensary* and the wit and urbanity which contributed so largely to that fame won for Garth an entrée into some of the most eminent social and literary circles of the day. Thus, through his friend and subsequent publisher, Jacob Tonson, Garth became a member of the famous literary-political Kit-Kat Club, where he was the social intimate of such powerful figures as the Lords Dorset, Essex, Somerset, Sunderland, Somers, Marlborough, and Newcastle, as well as such distinguished literary men as Joseph Addison, Richard Steele, William Congreve, John Vanbrugh, and Matthew Prior. Garth also became the friend of other important authors, such as Lady Mary Wortley Montagu, Jonathan Swift (though political differences led to later alienation), and the young Alexander Pope, who throughout his life spoke of Garth as an especially valued poetic mentor as well as friend. Along with Garth's literary and social success, his medical career advanced in the opening years of the eighteenth century. In 1702 he was elected to the important post of censor within the College of Physicians, and in 1706 he became a fellow of the Royal Society, with whose secretary and later president, Sir Hans Sloane, he was professionally close. Concomitantly his medical practice grew. Appropriately enough for the author of a work advocating a charity clinic, Garth devoted a considerable portion of his time to serving the poor, but he likewise had notable persons as patients, including many of his famous literary and political friends and even King George I, by whom he was appointed royal physician-in-ordinary in 1715.

For all the lavish praise *The Dispensary* elicited and all the extraliterary success it helped him achieve, Garth showed no signs of seriously aspiring to wear the poetic crown so many urged upon him. In his remaining career, his concerns as a doctor and his involvement in Whig politics took precedence over authorship. Yet these three areas of his life were inextricably intertwined, and Garth, though never a prolific writer, continued to produce a steady stream of occasional pieces, light verse, topical commentary, and literary translations. Of Garth's lighter verse, usually elicited by some social event or circumstance (first collected in *The Works of Celebrated Authors*,

1750), typical examples are "To the Merry Poetaster" (1700), a gibe at his medical and literary rival, Sir Richard Blackmore; "Verses Written for the Toasting-Glasses of the Kit-Kat Club in the Year 1703"; "To the Lady Louisa Lenos"; and "To the Earl of Burlington." Garth wrote several poems as theatrical prologues or epilogues, most notably "Prologue to [Nicholas Rowe's] *Tamerlane*" (1701), "Prologue to *Squire Trelooby*" (a 1704 adaptation by John Vanbrugh, William Congreve, and William Walsh of Molière's *Monsieur de Pourceagnac*), "Prologue Spoken at the Opening of the Queen's Theatre in the Haymarket" (1705), and "Epilogue to [Joseph Addison's] *Cato*" (1713). Garth also produced poetical commentary on political events, such as his verses "On the King of Spain" (1706), "To the Earl of Godolphin" (1710), "On Her Majesty's Statue in St. Paul's Church-Yard" (1715), and "On the New Conspiracy, 1716."

Aside from *The Dispensary* Garth's most substantial poem is *Claremont* (1715), a "place" poem in the tradition of John Denham's *Cooper's Hill* (1642) and Alexander Pope's *Windsor-Forest* (1713). *Claremont* celebrates the building of the country house of that name by Thomas Pelham-Hobbes (earl of Clare and duke of Newcastle), a young nobleman who was Garth's friend, patient, and sometime patron. After the customary introduction in praise of Pelham-Hobbes's ancestry, learning, and generosity, Garth devotes the bulk of the 329-line poem to a fanciful "explanation" of how the villa was named, describing how in ancient times its hillside setting was the scene of an Ovidian drama of thwarted love between the nymph, Echo, and "the fair Montano, of the sylvan race." Subsequently, Garth explains, the hill became a holy place to the Druids, and in time became known as Claremont, "the celebrated hill" (from the Latin *clarus*, meaning, among other things, "famous" or "noteworthy"). The poem ends with a Druid high priest offering a prophecy for the period up to the time of George I, during whose benign reign the earl of Clare will one day build his house on this hallowed ground. *Claremont* is a graceful and polished performance in the stylized manner of its genre, and in its day it was, among Garth's poems, second only to *The Dispensary* in popularity.

Along with his works in English, Garth was noted for some Latin compositions and for his renditions into English of both Latin and Greek originals. His first publication, *Oratio Laudatoria* (1697), was, of course, in Latin. In 1700 Garth

P. OVIDII NASONIS
METAMORPHOSEON
LIBER QUARTUS DECIMUS.
F A B. I.   *Scylla changed into a Monster.*

THE ARGUMENT.

Circe grows enamoured of Glaucus, who complains to her of Scylla's Indifferency. She endeavours to make him leave his ungrateful Mistress for her; but without Success. In Revenge she poisons the Fountains where that Nymph used to bathe, and communicates to her a hideous Form; which is so insupportable to her, that she throws herself into the Sea, and is transformed into a Rock.

First page of Garth's translation of Metamorphoses, *book 14, from the 1732 Dutch edition*

translated the "Life of Otho" from the Greek (included in *Plutarch's Lives*, 1911), and in 1702 he translated the "First Philippick" for a volume of *Several Orations of Demosthenes*. His most important excursion into classical translation, however, came in 1717 with the appearance of a new rendition into English of Ovid's *Metamorphoses*, for which Garth not only served as general editor but translated a substantial 902 lines (book 14 and a portion of 15). Undertaken at the behest of its eventual publisher, Tonson, this translation (with a critical introduction by Garth) was to become, in the considered opinion of Douglas Bush, in *Mythology and the Romantic Tradition* (1937), "the chief Augustan version of the *Metamorphoses*" and in the opinion of F. Seymour Smith, in *The Classics in Translation* (1930), "the best of the eighteenth century translations ...

[with] parts which have yet to be excelled."

Throughout his adult life Garth's politics were strongly Whiggish. Though he never held or, as far as is known, sought political office, his surviving correspondence indicates that in his travels at home and abroad he sometimes served the Duke of Newcastle and others as a collector of political intelligence and as a courier of sensitive messages, especially to the duke and duchess of Marlborough, with whom he was close. It was because of such service, along with his staunch Hanoverian sympathies (there is a lavish eulogy of George I in *Claremont*), that in 1715 Garth received the first knighthood conferred by that monarch and was further appointed as one of the royal physicians and as physician-general to the army. Toward the end of his life Garth twice visited the Continent (1715-1716 and 1718), and on both occasions he served as an unofficial emissary to the deposed Tory minister Henry St. John, Viscount Bolingbroke, who, after the Whig ascendancy in 1714, had fled to France, but who, it was thought, might be receptive to Whig proselytizers. It was in furtherance of so politically valuable a conversion that Garth, an old friend of Bolingbroke's, was twice sent to sound him out, though nothing came of either effort.

On his 1718 trip Garth had planned to visit Italy, but ill health forced him to return to London after a stay in France. The illness, the exact nature of which is unknown, proved fatal on 18 January 1719. Garth had bequeathed his entire modest estate to his daughter Martha, the sole issue of his marriage to Martha Beaufoy (who had died in 1717). Garth's behavior and state of mind during his final weeks soon became the subject of various rumors and anecdotes in which he was described as having been wittily dismissive of Christianity and the idea of an afterlife. In contrast to such stories, his friend Pope (who once characterized Garth in a letter as "a good Christian without knowing himself to be so") is cited by Joseph Spence, in *Observations, Anecdotes, and Characters of Books and Men* (1820), as claiming that Garth had embraced Roman Catholicism on his deathbed. Whatever the actual nature of his religious beliefs or lack thereof, almost all who knew him united in praising the amiability of his character and especially his generosity—as evidenced both by his advocacy of institutional philanthropy in *The Dispensary* and by personal charities which, in the opinion of one newspaper obituarist (anonymous, *Weekly Packet*, 17-24 January 1719), accounted for the smallness of his estate. That such praise sprang from something more than the customary funeral pieties is suggested by the fact that of Garth's surviving thirty-one letters no fewer than twelve are concerned with conferring aid or soliciting it on behalf of some needy third party.

Aside from his considerable literary talents, Garth's enormous contemporary reputation doubtless owed something to both the popularity of the dispensarian cause and to the paucity of formidable poetic rivals in the years between the death of Dryden and the rise of Pope. It is not surprising, therefore, to find that as the century progressed Garth's standing as a poet was realistically adjusted downward, although his works continued to be read and frequently anthologized. While there were those (such as Horace Walpole) who continued to rank Garth highly, as

well as others (such as Charles Churchill) who disparaged his work, the majority by the latter part of the eighteenth century seemed to recognize *The Dispensary* as a minor classic and its author as deserving of a place somewhere on the lesser slopes of Parnassus. In the nineteenth century, however, given the general disfavor into which Augustan verse fell, Garth's reputation declined precipitously, with his masterwork most often dismissed as having more historic than literary appeal. In our own century Garth has largely recovered from his near eclipse and is once more coming to be acknowledged as a poet whose accomplishments place him well forward in the secondary rank of eighteenth-century verse satirists.

Letters:
"The Letters of Samuel Garth," edited by John F. Sena, *Bulletin of the New York Public Library,* 78 (Autumn 1974): 69-94.

Biographies:
Robert Shiells, *The Lives of the Poets of Great Britain and Ireland* (London: Robert Griffiths, 1753), IV: 266-271;

Samuel Johnson, *Lives of the English Poets* (London: J. Buckland, 1790), XX: 60-63;

Harvey Cushing, "Dr. Garth: The Kit-Kat Poet," *Bulletin of the Johns Hopkins Hospital,* 17 (January 1906): 1-17;

William H. Cornog, "Sir Samuel Garth, a Court Physician of the 18th Century," *Isis,* 29 (July 1938): 29-42;

Daniel McCue, "Samuel Garth, Physician and Man of Letters," *Bulletin of the New York Academy of Medicine,* 53 (March 1976): 368-402.

References:
C. C. Booth, "Samuel Garth, The Dispensary Poet," *Notes and Records of the Royal Society,* 40 (1986): 125-145;

Benjamin Boyce, "*The Dispensary,* Sir Richard Blackmore, and the Captain of the Wits," *Review of English Studies,* 14 (October 1938): 453-458;

Richard I. Cook, "Garth's *Dispensary* and Pope's *Rape of the Lock,*" *C.L.A. Journal,* 6 (December 1962): 107-116;

Cook, *Sir Samuel Garth* (Boston: Twayne, 1980);

Frank H. Ellis, "The Background of the London Dispensary," *Journal of the History of Medicine,* 20 (Fall 1965): 197-212;

Ellis, "Garth's Harveian Oration," *Journal of the History of Medicine,* 18 (Spring 1963): 8-19;

D. W. Hopkins, "Dryden's Cave of Sleep and Garth's *Dispensary*," *Notes and Queries*, 23 (May-June 1976): 243-245;

Philip E. Roberts, "The Background and Purpose of Garth's *Dispensary* (1699)," *Journal of the Royal College of Physicians of London*, 2 (Summer 1968): 154-160;

Pat Rogers, "The Publishing History of Garth's *Dispensary:* Some 'Lost' and Pirated Editions," *Transactions of the Cambridge Bibliographical Society*, 5 (1971): 161-177;

Albert Rosenberg, "The Last Days of Sir Samuel Garth: A Footnote to a Pope Letter," *Notes and Queries*, 204 (July-August 1959): 272-274;

Rosenberg, "The London Dispensary for the Sick-Poor," *Journal of the History of Medicine*, 14 (Spring 1959): 41-56;

Rosenberg, "The Sarah Stout Murder Case: An Early Example of the Doctor as an Expert Witness," *Journal of the History of Medicine*, 12 (Fall 1957): 41-56;

Theodor Schenk, *Sir Samuel Garth und Seine Stellung zum Komischen Epos* (Heidelberg: Carl Winter's Universitätsbuchhandlung, 1900);

Duane B. Schneider, "Dr. Garth and Shakespeare: A Borrowing," *English Language Notes*, 1 (March 1964): 200-202;

John F. Sena, *The Best-Natured Man: Sir Samuel Garth, Physician and Poet* (New York: A.M.S. Press, 1986);

Sena, "Samuel Garth's *The Dispensary*," *Texas Studies in Literature and Language*, 15 (Winter 1974): 639-648;

Joseph Spence, *Observations, Anecdotes, and Characters of Books and Men*, edited by Edmund Malone (London: John Murray, 1820); modern edition, edited by James Osborn (Oxford: Clarendon Press, 1966), I: 208-209.

John Gay

(30 June 1685 - 4 December 1732)

Anne McWhir
University of Calgary

See also the Gay entry in *DLB 84: Restoration and Eighteenth-Century Dramatists.*

BOOKS: *Wine, A Poem,* anonymous (London: Printed for William Keble, 1708);

The Present State of Wit, in a Letter to a Friend in the Country, anonymous (London, 1711);

An Argument Proving from History, Reason, and Scripture, that the present Mohocks and Hawkubites are the Gog and Magog mention'd in the Revelations [broadside] (London: Printed for Bernard Lintott, 1712);

The Mohocks: A Tragi-Comical Farce. As it was Acted near the Watch-house in Covent Garden. By Her Majesty's Servants (London: Printed for Bernard Lintott, 1712);

Rural Sports. A Poem. Inscribed to Mr. Pope (London: Printed for Jacob Tonson, 1713; revised, 1713);

The Wife of Bath. A Comedy. As it is Acted at the Theatre-Royal in Drury-Lane, By Her Majesty's Servants (London: Printed for Bernard Lintott, 1713); revised as *The Wife of Bath. A Comedy. As it is Acted at the Theatre-Royal in Lincoln's Inn Fields* (London: Printed for Bernard Lintott, 1730);

The Fan. A Poem. In Three Books (London: Printed for Jacob Tonson, 1714 [i.e., 1713]);

The Shepherd's Week: In Six Pastorals (London: Printed & sold by Ferd. Burleigh, 1714);

A Letter to a Lady. Occasion'd by the Arrival of Her Royal Highness, the Princess of Wales (London: Printed for Bernard Lintott, 1714);

The What D'Ye Call It: A Tragi-Comi-Pastoral Farce (London: Printed for Bernard Lintott, 1715);

Trivia: or, The Art of Walking the Streets of London (London: Printed for Bernard Lintott, 1716);

Three Hours after Marriage. A Comedy, As it is Acted at the Theatre-Royal (London: Printed for Bernard Lintott, 1717);

Daphnis and Chloe [broadside] (London, 1720);

Two Epistles; One, to the Right Honourable Richard Earl of Burlington; The Other, to a Lady (London: Printed for Bernard Lintot, [1720]);

Poems on Several Occasions (London: Printed for Jacob Tonson & Bernard Lintot, 1720)– includes *Dione. A Pastoral Tragedy;*

A Panegyrical Epistle to Mr. Thomas Snow (London: Printed for Bernard Lintot, 1721);

An Epistle to her Grace Henrietta, Dutchess of Marlborough (London: Printed for Jacob Tonson, 1722);

The Captives. A Tragedy. As it is acted at the Theatre-Royal in Drury-Lane, By His Majesty's Servants (London: Printed for Jacob Tonson, 1724);

The Poor Shepherd [broadside] (London, 1724?);

To a Lady on her Passion for Old China (London: Printed for J. Tonson, 1725);

Fables (London: Printed for Jacob Tonson & John Watts, 1727; Philadelphia: Printed for Mathew Carey, 1794);

The Beggar's Opera. As it is Acted at the Theatre-Royal in Lincoln's-Inn-Fields (London: Printed for John Watts, 1728; Boston: Wells & Lilly, 1822; facsimile, Larchmont, N.Y.: Argonaut, 1961); enlarged as *The Beggar's Opera. The Second Edition: To which is Added The Overture in Score; And the Musick prefix'd to each Song* (London: Printed for John Watts, 1728);

Polly: An Opera. Being the Second Part of The Beggar's Opera (London: Printed [by William Bowyer] for the author, 1729);

Acis and Galatea: An English Pastoral Opera. In Three Acts. As it is Perform'd at the New Theatre in the Hay-Market. Set to Musick by Mr. Handel (London: Printed for John Watts, 1732);

Achilles. An Opera. As it is Perform'd at the Theatre-Royal in Covent-Garden (London: Printed for John Watts, 1733);

Fables. By the late Mr. Gay. Volume the Second (London: Printed for J. & P. Knapton & T. Cox, 1738);

The Distress'd Wife. A Comedy (London: Printed for Thomas Astley, 1743);

John Gay

The Rehearsal at Goatham (London: Printed for Thomas Astley & sold by R. Baldwin, 1754).

Editions and Collections: *Plays written by Mr. John Gay . . . To which is added, An Account of the Life and Writings of the Author* (London: Printed for J. & R. Tonson, 1760);

The Works of Mr. John Gay, 4 volumes (London: Printed for J. Bell, 1772);

The Poetical Works of John Gay. Including his Fables (Edinburgh: Printed for John Bell at the Apollo Press by Jno [*sic*] Martins, 1777);

The Poetical, Dramatic, and Miscellaneous Works of John Gay . . . To which is prefixed, Dr. Johnson's Biographical and Critical Preface, 6 volumes (London: Printed for Edward Jeffery, 1795);

Fables by Mr. John Gay, edited by Austin Dobson (London: Kegan Paul, Trench, 1884);

The Poetical Works of John Gay: including Polly, The Beggar's Opera, and selections from the other dramatic work, edited by G. C. Faber (Oxford: Oxford University Press, 1926);

John Gay: Poetry and Prose, edited by Vinton A. Dearing and Charles E. Beckwith, 2 volumes (Oxford: Oxford University Press, 1974);

John Gay: Dramatic Works, edited by John Fuller, 2 volumes (Oxford: Clarendon Press, 1983).

PLAY PRODUCTIONS: *The Wife of Bath*, London, Theatre Royal in Drury Lane, 12 May 1713; revised version, London, Theatre Royal, Lincoln's Inn Fields, 19 January 1730;

The What D'Ye Call It, London, Theatre Royal in Drury Lane, 23 February 1715;

THE

MOHOCKS.

A

Tragi-Comical Farce.

As it was Acted near the

Watch-houfe in *Covent-Garden.*

BY

Her MAJESTY's Servants.

*Quo, quo, fcelefti, ruitis? aut cur dexteris
Aptantur enfes conditi?* Hor.

LONDON:

Printed for *Bernard Lintott,* at the *Crofs-Keys* between the two *Temple-Gates,* in *Fleet-ftreet.* 1712.

Title page for Gay's first play. Based on stories about London street gangs called the Mohocks, the work was never staged.

Three Hours after Marriage, London, Theatre Royal in Drury Lane, 16 January 1717;

Acis and Galatea, libretto by Gay and music by G. F. Handel, Canons, Middlesex, private performance, circa 1718; London, Theatre Royal, Lincoln's Inn Fields, 26 March 1731; London, New Theatre in the Hay-Market, 17 May 1732;

The Captives, London, Theatre Royal in Drury Lane, 15 January 1724;

The Beggar's Opera, London, Lincoln's Inn Fields, 29 January 1728;

Achilles, London, Theatre Royal in Covent Garden, 10 February 1733;

The Distress'd Wife, London, Theatre Royal in Covent Garden, 5 May 1734;

Polly, London, Haymarket Theatre, 19 June 1777.

OTHER: "To the Learned Ingenious Author," in *Licentia Poetica Discuss'd,* by William Coward (London: Printed for W. Carter, 1709);

"The Story of Arachne" and "On a Miscellany of Poems," in *Miscellaneous Poems and Translations* (London: Printed for Bernard Lintot, 1712);

Untitled essay, *Guardian,* no. 149, 1 September 1713;

"Panthea," "Araminta," "A Thought on *Eternity,*" and "A Contemplation on *Night,*" in *Poetical Miscellanies,* edited by Richard Steele (London: Printed for Jacob Tonson, 1714 [i.e., 1713]);

"The Toilette," in *Court Poems,* edited by Edmund Curll (London: Printed for J. Roberts, 1706 [i.e., 1716]);

"Ovid's Metamorphoses, Book IX," in *Ovid's Metamorphoses in Fifteen Books. Translated by the most Eminent Hands,* edited by Samuel Garth (London: Printed for Jacob Tonson, 1717);

"An Answer to the Sompner's Prologue," in *Poems on Several Occasions,* edited by Alexander Pope (London: Printed for B. Lintot, 1717);

"Newgate's Garland," in *Harlequin Sheppard,* by John Thurmond (London: Printed for J. Roberts, 1724);

"The Coquet Mother and the Coquet Daughter," in *Poetical Miscellanies,* edited by Richard Steele (London: Printed for J. Tonson, 1727);

"Ballad," "A Ballad on Quadrille," "A New Song of New Similies," and "Ay and No," in *Miscellanies,* edited by Pope and Jonathan Swift (London: Printed for Benjamin Motte, 1727 [i.e., 1728]);

"A True and Faithful Narrative," in *Miscellanies,* edited by Pope and Swift (London: Printed for B. Motte & L. Gilliver, 1732);

"To the most Honourable the Earl of Oxford" and "A Pox of all Senders" [Scriblerus Club invitation], in Jonathan Swift, *The Letters of Jonathan Swift,* edited by John Hawkesworth, 3 volumes (London: Printed for T. Davies, 1766);

"The Story of Cephisa," "A Ballad. On Ale," "An Elegiac Epistle to a Friend," and "The Man-Mountain's Answer," in *Miscellaneous Works* (London: Printed for J. Bell, 1773);

"Mr. Pope's Welcome from Greece" [1720] and "A Motto for the Opera of Mutius Scaevola" [1721], in *Additions to the Works of Alexander Pope,* edited by William Cooke [?] or George

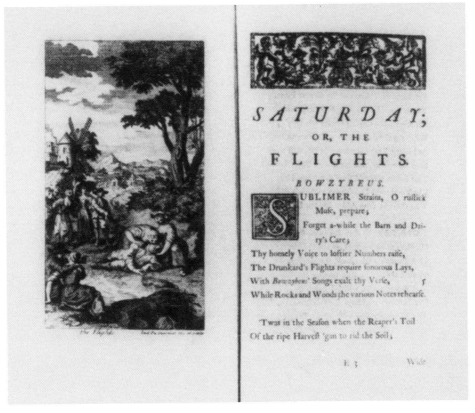

Illustration and opening page for the last poem in Gay's Shepherd's Week *(1714), modeled on* The Shepheardes Calendar *by Spenser*

Steevens [?] (London: Printed for H. Baldwin, 1776);

"Verses in a Letter to Mrs. Howard" [9 August 1729], in *Letters to and from Henrietta, Countess of Suffolk*, edited by John Wilson Croker (London: J. Murray, 1824), I: 354-359;

"My Lord, forsake your Politick Utopians" [Scriblerus Club invitation], in *The Poems of Jonathan Swift*, edited by Harold Williams (Oxford: Clarendon, 1937), I: 187-188;

"Verses in a letter to Thomas Parnell" [1714], in "Some Unpublished Letters of Pope and Gay; and Some Manuscript Sources of Goldsmith's Life of Thomas Parnell," by C. J. Rawson, *Review of English Studies*, new series, 10 (1959): 376.

SELECTED PERIODICAL PUBLICATIONS–UNCOLLECTED: "The Quidnuncki's," *Weekly Journal or Saturday's Post*, 14 March 1724;

"Molly Mogg," *Mist's Weekly Journal*, 27 August 1726.

Even if John Gay had never written his best-known poems and plays–*The Shepherd's Week* (1714), *Trivia* (1716), *Fables* (1727), and *The Beggar's Opera* (1728)–we would know him through his friends, some of the wittiest and most influential writers, poets, courtiers, and politicians of early-eighteenth-century England. While he had friends in high places, however, Gay's familiarity with the life of the streets, the calculated ambiguity of his poetry, and his lack of success at court make him a congenial figure for the common reader. But John Gay has usually been denigrated, not respected, for his comparative powerlessness. According to Samuel Johnson, for example, in his *Lives of the Poets* (volume 2, 1779) Gay's friends "regarded him as a play-fellow rather than a partner, and treated him with more fondness than respect." Recently scholars and critics have challenged such a judgment, recognizing that Gay happened to excel at lyric poetry at a time when epic and satire were most prestigious, and valuing his generic inventiveness. But the habit of ascribing his work to others goes back to Gay's own time and is especially hard to combat be-

Henrietta Howard, Gay's close friend and the mistress of the Prince of Wales

selves than for their political allegiance. In an early pamphlet he claims that he "never cared one Farthing either for *Whig* or *Tory*"; and while this may have damaged his hopes of preferment, it also allowed him to choose his friends freely and to look at the world and at human behavior with, for the most part, clear vision. In spite of Gay's obvious hopes of a lucrative court appointment, he wrote to Swift in 1726, "I still despise Court Perferments [*sic*] so that I lose no time upon attendance on great men, and still can find amusement enough without Quadrille, which is here [at Whitehall] the Universal Employment of Life." Despite years of bad health, Gay kept himself and his friends amused, and his best poems and plays show that he still has the power to amuse modern readers. But the amusement is not shallow. Gay may have been "inoffensive" to his friends, one of whom (probably Pope) described him as such in Gay's obituary in the *Universal Spectator*, 9 December 1732, but as a satirist he was not without the power to instruct and sometimes offend. It would be hard to read his poetry without remembering that Pope's epitaph for him in Westminster Abbey assigns to Gay "virtuous rage" as well as childlike simplicity.

Born in Barnstaple, Devon, on 30 June 1685, Gay was the youngest of four surviving children and was baptized at Barnstaple Old Church on 16 September. Barnstaple was an important port, and Gay's family included tradesmen, clergymen, and soldiers. His early life suggests that Gay was well prepared to write about people from different occupational groups and social classes, for his own experience was remarkably broad. After the death of his parents, William and Katherine Hanmer Gay, when he was ten, Gay continued to live in Barnstaple with his uncle Thomas Gay. He was educated at the local grammar school, where Robert Luck encouraged the boys to translate from the classics into English verse and to perform plays. Later, addressing Gay's patron the duke of Queensbury, Luck would make the exaggerated claim that it was he who "taught ... *Gay* to sing" (*Miscellany of New Poems*, 1736). At Barnstaple, Gay's schoolfellows included William Fortescue, the "sincere, experienc'd friend" in Gay's *Trivia*, an acquaintance of Gay and Pope who became Master of the Rolls and member of the Privy Council, and Aaron Hill who, like Gay himself, later collaborated with George Frideric Handel. Possessing neither land nor sufficient wealth for the life of an independent gentleman, Gay went into trade, like

cause some of his works were, in fact, collaborative. Hearing Pope read part of a transcription of one of Gay's plays, according to Joseph Spence, Colley Cibber, "upon seeing a knife with the name of J. Gay upon it, . . . said: 'What, does Mr. Pope make knives too?'" It is worth demonstrating that Gay could use his own verbal knife effectively. But if Gay is interesting and amusing on his own, he is all the more so for readers who know the work of some of his friends and contemporaries and who are alert to intertextual relationships as well as to personal ones.

Gay had a gift for friendship. In "A Farewell to London" (1715) Pope describes him as "lov[ing] all Mankind, but flatter[ing] none." Gay was fat: Spence quotes a letter in which William Congreve remarks to Pope, "As the French philosopher used to prove his existence by *cogito ergo sum*, the greatest proof of Gay's existence is *edi ergo est*" (the gist of this imprecise Latin being "he eats, therefore he is"). Gay was so careless with money, says Spence, that "latterly the Duke of Queensbury [i.e., Queensberry] took his money into his keeping, and let him have only what was necessary out of it." But Gay was also affectionate, charming, observant, witty, sincere to a fault, and more interested in people for them-some of his relatives before him. He was apprenticed to a silk mercer in London about 1702 but gained release from his articles by the summer of 1706, possibly because of bad health. Returning home to Barnstaple, he lived for a short time with his mother's brother, John Hanmer, a dissenting minister.

After Hanmer's death the following year Gay went back to London and worked as secretary to his school friend Hill, who had sufficient money and influence to support various literary projects. For the first time Gay became part of the London literary scene, meeting a growing circle of friends and visiting Will's and Button's coffeehouses, where the wits congregated. His first poem, *Wine*, a blank-verse Miltonic burlesque with appropriately drunken shifts of tone, was published anonymously in folio in May 1708. It is not a subtle poem, and Gay chose not to include it in his 1720 collection *Poems on Several Occasions*. But it is high-spirited and amusing, foreshadowing some of his later poetry in its alternating ridicule and praise. Toasts to the queen and her ministers come near the end of a poem in which the poet has also celebrated the "matchless worth" of wine and which ends with the departure of the speaker's company—oddly dignified, though "of Cares and Coin bereft"—into the early-morning London streets.

On 3 May 1711, by which time Hill's question-and-answer periodical the *British Apollo* had been eclipsed by Richard Steele's *Tatler*, Gay published a threepenny pamphlet, *The Present State of Wit, in a Letter to a Friend in the Country*. This pamphlet gave an account of contemporary periodical literature, including the *Examiner*, the *Spectator*, and the *Tatler*, while disclaiming party allegiance. Jonathan Swift, by now a Tory, mentions this pamphlet in the *Journal to Stella* (1711) asserting, on the basis of Gay's praise of Joseph Addison and Steele, that the anonymous author is a Whig.

In response to gangs of town rakes, some called the Mohocks, who were terrorizing people in the London streets, on 18 March 1712 Gay published a penny broadside, *An Argument Proving from History, Reason, and Scripture, that the present Mohocks and Hawkubites are the Gog and Magog mention'd in the Revelations*. Gay's tragicomical farce, *The Mohocks*, was published by Bernard Lintot in April 1712 after an unsuccessful attempt to have it produced. The ironic dedication of *The Mohocks* to the critic John Dennis, who in

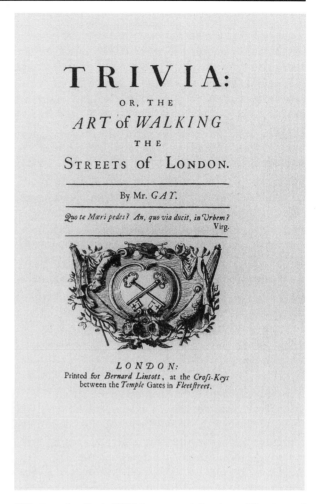

Title page for Gay's 1716 poem, an elaborate walking tour of the city, graphically describing its danger as well as its beauty

1711 had attacked Pope's *Essay on Criticism*, was probably intended to avenge and flatter Pope.

Gay and Pope had met in the late spring of 1711; they became lifelong friends. In October 1711 Gay submitted to Pope a translation from Ovid, "The Story of Arachne," for publication in a miscellany. Gay followed its acceptance by submitting through his friend Henry Cromwell— "honest, hatless *Cromwell*, with red breeches" as Gay later described him in "Mr. Pope's Welcome from Greece" (1720)—a poem called "On a Miscellany," which included praise of Pope, editor of the volume for the publisher Lintot: "His various Numbers charm our ravish'd Ears, / His steady Judgment far out-shoots his Years, / And early in the Youth the God appears." Pope published Gay's translation and poem (and the two-canto version of his own *The Rape of the Lock*) in Lintot's *Miscellaneous Poems and Translations* of May 1712.

In December 1712 Gay was appointed domestic steward and secretary to the duchess of Monmouth, widow of the duke executed in 1685–the Absalom of Dryden's *Absalom and Achitophel*. In January 1713, Gay published *Rural Sports*, "Inscrib'd to Mr. *POPE*." Gay's claim in the first edition that he "in Attendance wasted Years in vain" refers to his efforts to promote himself at court and to recommend himself to wealthy patrons. Later in his life, in spite of his many friends, he was sometimes a little bitter at his failure at court. But at this early stage of his career the hint of complaint is probably inappropriate; perhaps because of his new place in the duchess of Monmouth's household, Gay removed the reference to his struggle for patronage when he prepared a second edition of *Rural Sports* later in 1713. When Gay revised *Rural Sports* yet again for inclusion in his 1720 collection, he called it a georgic, suggesting a significant connection between this poem about country sports and Virgil's *Georgics*, with its account (in four books) of tillage, the cultivation of vines and fruit trees, animal breeding, and beekeeping.

Rural Sports begins as a poem of pastoral retreat, following the course of a spring day from "morning lark" through the "sultry hours" of midday to the ploughman "trudging homeward." Observing the labors of the English swain in an English landscape, the poet superimposes a literary landscape and the "labours of *Italian* swains," conflating the English countryside with classical pastoral and georgic literature, and combining mythological gods and goddesses with an Addisonian "survey" of "the works of providence." The course of the sun across the sky and the cycle of the seasons find their parallel in "circling pleasures": fishing, hunting, and, at the end of the second canto, the innocent love associated with a sentimental pastoral ideal. Sometimes, as in its conclusion, the poem is merely conventional but at its best it is meticulously observed, spreading out panoramic landscapes on the one hand and, on the other, focusing on such details as how fishermen should make flies. Gay, former silk mercer's apprentice, would-be courtier, and reader of Pope's *Rape of the Lock*, finds the betrayal and deceit of the drawing room even in the trout stream:

> Silks of all colours must their aid impart,
> And ev'ry fur promote the fisher's art.
> So the gay lady, with expensive care,
> Borrows the pride of land, of sea, and air;

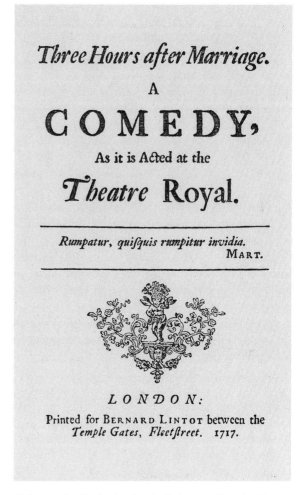

Title page for Gay's play that includes some lines by Alexander Pope and John Arbuthnot. The work caused bad publicity when it was labeled "pornographic" by critics and audiences alike.

> Furs, pearls, and plumes, the glittering thing
> 　displays,
> Dazles our eyes, and easie hearts betrays.

The effect of the poem is often heightened by the literary context it evokes. For example, giving advice to the fisherman, Gay gives us the predator's point of view–"Let not thy wary step advance too near, / While all thy hope hangs on a single hair"–in language that recalls the point of view of the victim in *The Rape of the Lock*: "Fair Tresses Man's Imperial Race insnare, / And Beauty draws us with a single Hair." We have here an intertextual connection that blurs the boundaries between texts, forming part of the pleasure of reading the works of Gay and his friends. Gay's shifting point of view, however, leads to the disturbing knowledge that his speaker, like his fisherman, can be both predator

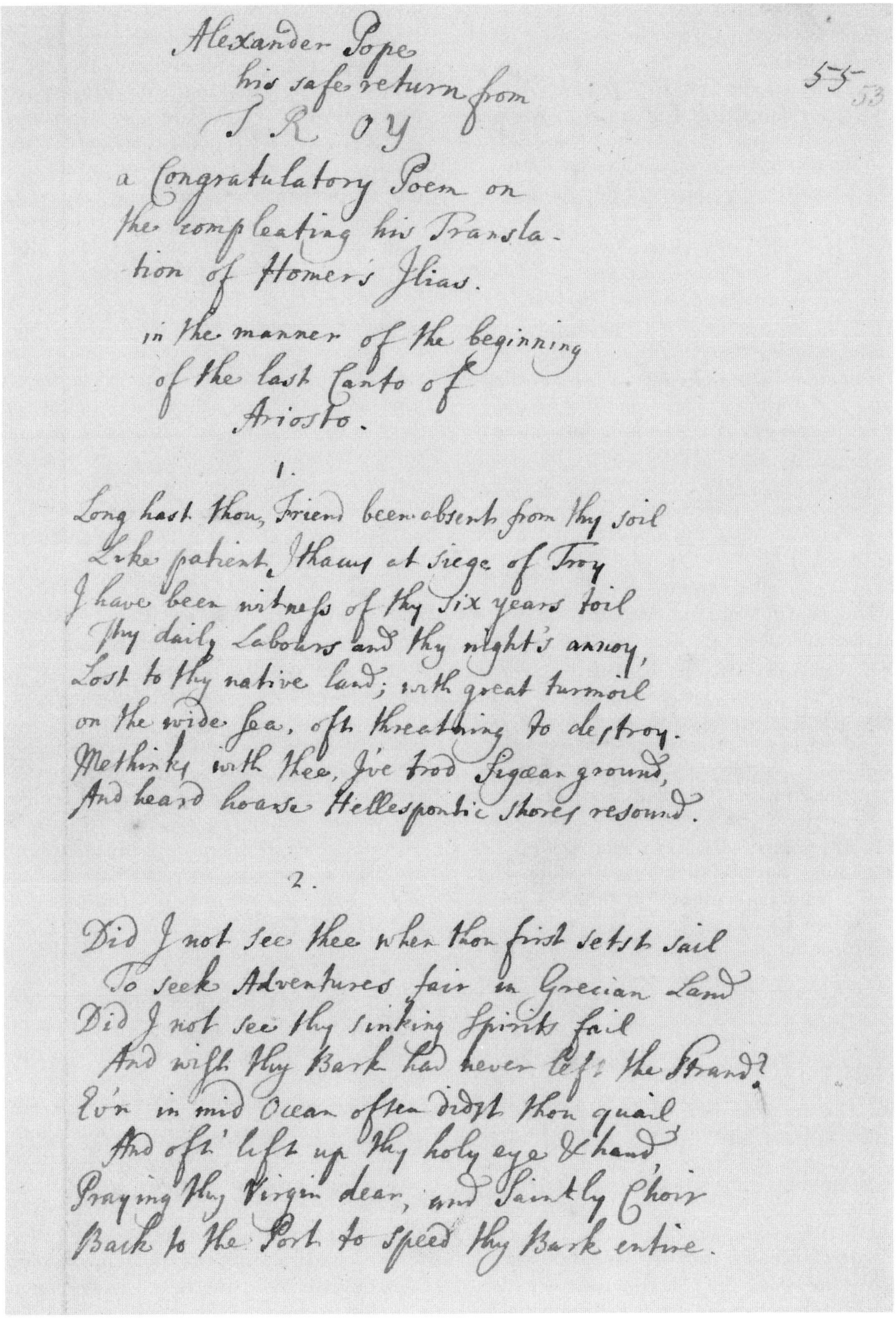

Alexander Pope
his safe return from
T R O Y
a Congratulatory Poem on
the compleating his Translation of Homer's Ilias.

in the manner of the beginning
of the last Canto of
Ariosto.

1.

Long hast thou, Friend been absent from thy soil
Like patient Ithacus at Siege of Troy
I have been witness of thy Six years toil
Thy daily Labours and thy night's annoy,
Lost to thy native land; with great turmoil
on the wide Sea, oft threatning to destroy.
Methinks with thee, I've trod Sigaean ground,
And heard hoarse Hellespontic shores resound.

2.

Did I not see thee when thou first setst sail
To seek Adventures fair in Grecian Land
Did I not see thy sinking Spirits fail
And wish thy Bark had never left the Strand?
Ev'n in mid Ocean often didst thou quail
And oft' lift up thy holy eye & hand,
Praying thy Virgin dear, and Saintly Choir
Back to the Port to speed thy Bark entire.

Page from Gay's 1715 manuscript for "Mr. Pope's Welcome from Greece," published in 1720 in Poems on Several Occasions
(by permission of the British Library)

and prey. In some of his later poetry Gay used this ambivalence more deliberately.

Gay's comedy *The Wife of Bath* was performed at Drury Lane in May 1713, immediately after the great success of Addison's *Cato*. It was not a success, but one of its songs, "There was a Swain full fair," became popular in an arrangement by John Barrett, whose "Ianthe the lovely" is used in *The Beggar's Opera*. Several of the lyrics and ballads from Gay's plays were successful, even if the plays themselves were less so: " 'Twas when the Seas were roaring," from *The What D'Ye Call It* (1715), with music traditionally attributed to Handel, was another that made its way into the miscellanies. Later in his career Gay's successful lyrics for music included *Daphnis and Chloe*, which first appeared as a broadside in 1720 and was included in his collected poems the same year, and *The Poor Shepherd*, written about 1724. *The Beggar's Opera* ensured Gay's lasting reputation as a writer of words for songs.

In the fall of 1713 Gay contributed to the *Guardian* (1 September) an essay mockingly applying the language of literary criticism to the description of fashionable dress; here Gay's years as a silk mercer's apprentice merge with his knowledge of classical genres. On 8 December 1713 he published *The Fan* (dated 1714 on its title page), a poem similarly concerned with "Th' inconstant Equipage of Female Dress," though far less detailed in descriptions of clothing than *Trivia* would be a few years later. *The Fan* was influenced by Pope, especially by *The Rape of the Lock*, and Pope may have helped with revisions. But *The Fan* depends structurally on rather a slight idea: Strephon appeals to Venus to help him win Corinna's love by showing him "some bright Toy" that will please her; Venus goes to the forge where the trinkets of love and vanity are made; Diana, Momus, and Minerva each have a turn to describe the scenes that should be painted on the newly invented fan; finally, in the 1713 version, Corinna snatches the fan from Strephon and turns away from him to flirt with a new, foppish lover. (When Gay revised *The Fan* for inclusion in his 1720 collection, he changed the ending so that Corinna was moved to love Strephon by his gift and by the scenes painted on it.)

The Fan suffers by the inevitable comparison with *The Rape of the Lock*: it is slow, sometimes dull, excessively reliant on predictable machinery and rather static mythological set pieces. The modern reader may agree with Samuel Johnson's remark in *Lives of the Poets* (volume 2): "The atten-

tion naturally retires from a new tale of Venus, Diana, and Minerva." Moreover, in spite of a conventional epic opening and a council in heaven in Book II, *The Fan* is not really effective as mock-epic. The action takes place only within the Ovidian scenes, and the framing story is narrowly, prettily pastoral. Rather as *Wine* offers seriously exalted moments in a mock-epic, so *The Fan* has sections that contrast with its structure and dominant tone. A contrast between Gay and Pope makes this point clearer.

When Pope alludes in *The Rape of the Lock* to Dido's hair (clipped by Iris so that Dido can die at last), he does so subtly and delicately, so that the reader who wants to catch the allusion can smile once again at Belinda's grief by contrasting it with Dido's tragedy. But when Gay tells the story of Dido in *The Fan*, he does so for the story's own sake, letting his speaker, Diana, draw a moral that may be conventional, even ironic in its inevitability, but which hardly undercuts the pathos of Dido's story: "View this, ye Maids, and then each Swain Believe, / They're *Trojans* all, and vow but to Deceive." Gay's tone tends to shift, allowing for directly serious passages within a mock-epic context. In his early poems Gay's inconsistency of tone and his clashing voices seem to weaken the coherence of poems. But Gay does begin to show how laughter is not incompatible with seriousness, how one can laugh at Corinna's frivolity without losing sight of Dido's tragedy. In the revised ending of *The Fan* Corinna, having learned Minerva's lesson of faithful love, chooses Strephon's merit and constancy over Leander's more superficial charms. But the conversion of such a flirt as Corinna seems whimsical, a mere flirtation with commitment. The pastoral flippancy of the first ending, where she turns away from the gift giver to flirt with the fop, is equally appropriate to the mixture of pleasure and wisdom, innocence and smiling cynicism that is at the heart of the poem.

Four of Gay's poems appeared in Steele's *Poetical Miscellanies* at the end of December 1713: "Panthea," a pastoral love elegy indebted to Theocritus and Virgil; "Araminta," the first English "town-eclogue," in which Virgil's Eclogue VIII is adapted to the circumstances of the fashionable urban world; and "A Thought on *Eternity*" and "A Contemplation on *Night*," two religious poems. But by this time Gay was at work on *The Shepherd's Week*, his first major success, published on 15 April 1714. Historically, it forms part of the controversy about pastoral poetry in which Pope was engaged in the *Guardian* the previous year, for it makes the native rustic pastoral practiced by Ambrose Philips and mocked by Pope in the *Guardian* deliberately absurd through complex allusion and exaggeration. But the interest of the poem goes well beyond that.

Gay's prose Proeme and verse Prologue are deliberately reminiscent of E. K.'s preliminary dedication and argument in Edmund Spenser's *Shepheardes Calender*, the model for native, rather than classical, pastoral; Gay's Proeme, Prologue, and footnotes are parodic in the sense that the Apology and Epistle Dedicatory to Swift's *A Tale of a Tub*, or the notes to Pope's *Dunciad*, are parodic. Gay manages simultaneously to mock learning (by the pedantic, pompous tone of his Proeme, where Theocritus is quoted in Greek, but native "uncouth Pastoral Terms" must be glossed) and to show off the extent of his learning with the intention of mocking Philips. But if the Gay of the Proeme is pedantic, the Gay of the Prologue is a bumbling shepherd poet from a literary never-land, dazzled by real court ladies and content to rush his work into print at the command of Henry St. John, Viscount Bolingbroke (a dominant figure in the Tory party under Queen Anne). Court and country, real world and literary fantasy come together, as the poet—or his naive persona—addresses the great man: "Lo here, thou hast mine Eclogues fair, / But let not these detain thine Ear. / Let not Affairs of States and Kings / Wait, while our *Bowzybeus* sings." "Bowzybeus" is one of the more original of Gay's pastoral names (analogous to Alphesiboeus and Meliboeus in Virgil); others are Blouzelinda and Buxoma. Most of his other names are either Spenser's or Philips's—or some variation, names intended to suggest, and laugh at, a native pastoral tradition. Similarly the structure of Gay's poem—six eclogues, one for each day of the week except Sunday—is modeled on the structure of *The Shepheardes Calender*.

"*Monday*; or, The Squabble" is a singing contest between Lobbin Clout and Cuddy. The structure of the poem is classical, the *carmen amoeboeum* or alternate song of Theocritus and Virgil, practiced by Philips in his sixth pastoral. Philips places the contest in an English landscape and refers to a native context: Eliza, Albion (England), Sidney, and Merlin. Gay takes the naturalization of classical pastoral several steps further, telling of country lore ("pricking Corns foretold the gath'ring Rain") and, through footnotes, the meanings of unfamiliar words. The effect is both

eccentrically learned and disingenuous. For example, the poet's insistence that he does not use "queint" in an obscene sense directs the reader to an otherwise obscure context for the word in Chaucer's "Miller's Tale." Thus the reader becomes a coconspirator in a literary game, finding allusions to Theocritus, Virgil, Chaucer, Spenser, Philips, Thomas D'Urfey, and others throughout the poem.

"*Tuesday*; or, The Ditty" is the character Marian's love lament for Colin Clout. Here Gay manages to convey pathos without sacrificing parody. The substitution of rural superstitions and humble toil for more idealized pastoral themes may make the reader smile, but Marian's love for her staring oaf is nevertheless convincing. In "*Wednesday*; or, The Dumps" Sparabella (like the character in Damon's part of Virgil's Eclogue VIII) laments the loss of a lover—in this case, Bumkinet. Sparabella's version of a pastoral cliché, the description of a world of antipastoral disorder, is characteristic of Gay's control of tone in *The Shepherd's Week*. The passage is conventional, but vividly imagined and just exaggerated enough to point up the possibilities for absurdity in familiar conventions:

> Sooner shall Cats disport in Waters clear,
> And speckled Mackrels graze the Meadows fair,
> Sooner shall scriech Owls bask in Sunny Day,
> And the slow Ass on Trees, like Squirrels, play,
> Sooner shall Snails on insect Pinions rove,
> Than I forget my Shepherd's wonted Love!

"*Thursday*; or, The Spell" is Hobnelia's account of how she drew Lubberkin home from the town with her magic, in the manner of the second part of Virgil's Eclogue VIII. Here Gay returns to the opposition of country and town that is so important in the Proeme and Prologue. The town appears throughout *The Shepherd's Week* as the sophisticated literary context of these poems about country people and country pursuits. Out of a series of tensions—town or court and country, sophistication and naiveté, laughter and tears, skepticism and superstition—emerges the truth of what Gay claims in his Proeme: the language of his shepherds is "such as is neither spoken by the country Maiden nor the courtly Dame.... It having too much of the Country to be fit for the Court; too much of the Court to be fit for the Country, too much of the Language of old Times to be fit for the Present, too much of the Present to have been fit for the Old, and too much of both to be fit for any time to come."

Portrait of Gay by Godfrey Kneller (by permission of the National Portrait Gallery, London)

Thus through carefully contrived contradictions Gay undercuts the language of his own poem. Not only is it neither a court poem nor a true pastoral, it has its own language, subversive of both, and its own perspective, familiar with the conventions of both worlds, and therefore invites the reader to laugh at *and* to praise both.

Not surprisingly, *"Friday"* is subtitled "The Dirge": after so many laments for lost lovers the reader may expect a pastoral elegy. Blouzelinda dies, and the shepherds grieve until Susan comes along to console them with "Ale and Kisses." *"Saturday*; or, The Flights" ends the week with the wonderful drunken song of Bowzybeus, Gay's Silenus, who sings of nature lore, of "Fairs and Shows," and of folktales, ballads, and religious enthusiasm, until he falls asleep as the sun sets and the poem comes to an end.

Some years later, in a letter to Gay (8 January 1723), Swift suggested that the Prologue to *The Shepherd's Week*, addressed to Bolingbroke, may have damaged Gay's prospects of preferment at court after the accession of George I; for by 1714 Gay was firmly associated through Pope with Swift, Thomas Parnell, and Dr. John Arbuth-

not, physician to Queen Anne, all of whom were Tories. Under the patronage of Robert Harley, earl of Oxford and lord treasurer, they formed the Scriblerus Club, with the object of ridiculing, according to Spence, "all the false tastes in learning, under the character of a man of capacity enough that had dipped into every art and science, but injudiciously in each." The relation of the Scriblerus Club to such a literary parody as *The Shepherd's Week* is suggested by an invitation by Gay to a meeting of the club, in which the Prologue to Bolingbroke is turned upside down: "Leave Courts, and hye to simple Swains, / Who feed *no* Flock upon *no* Plains." Harley came from a real court to play the serious game of the Scriblerians. The other five members must have expected great things from his membership, not knowing that he, along with his colleague and rival Bolingbroke, would be impeached the following year by the Commons for high treason.

Without strong political allegiance of his own, Gay was affected by the political currents of his day. Shortly after the publication of *The Shepherd's Week* he left the household of the duchess of Monmouth to take up the position of secretary

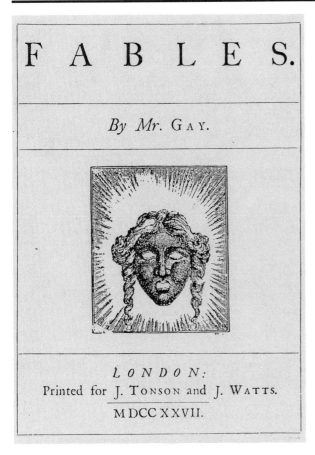

Title page for Gay's collection of fifty poems that present moral lessons in the tradition of Aesop

to Lord Clarendon's Tory embassy to the court of Hanover. Briefly, disregarding politics, Gay had hopes of success at court: Princess Caroline of Anspach (soon to be princess of Wales) requested copies of *The Fan* and *The Shepherd's Week.* But after Queen Anne's death on 1 August 1714, Lord Clarendon was recalled to England. Because some of them had Jacobite sympathies, the Tories were generally discredited. Arbuthnot lost his royal appointment and failed to obtain the legacy promised by Queen Anne; Swift and Parnell returned to Ireland: the heyday of Martinus Scriblerus was over, though many years later, in his *Works in Prose* (1741), Pope published *The Memoirs of Martinus Scriblerus,* including "Memoirs of P. P. Clerk of this Parish" on which he and Gay had collaborated. Some of the best work of Pope and Swift is related in spirit to the Scriblerian project: *The Dunciad, A Tale of a Tub,* and *Gulliver's Travels.* The letter from Gulliver's cousin, "Richard Sympson," offering Gulliver's memoirs to the publisher in 1726, appears to be in Gay's handwriting.

Gay's attempt to find court patronage lasted throughout the reign of George I. His *Letter to a Lady* (1714) refers to this predicament: "Places, I found, were daily giv'n away, / And yet no friendly Gazette mention'd *Gay.*" In this poem Gay indirectly appeals to Princess Caroline. But while many of Gay's friends and acquaintances did well under the new regime, Gay himself, in spite of his popularity and his connection with Princess Caroline and the court, failed to find a place during the reign of George I. Gay's modern biographer, William Henry Irving, speculates that Addison, whose *Cato* was one of the plays ridiculed in Gay's "tragi-comi-pastoral farce" *The What D'Ye Call It* (produced and published in February 1715), may have had something to do with Gay's failure; this possibility is supported by the story in Spence's *Anecdotes* that Addison confessed to Gay on his deathbed that he had "injured him greatly." Most modern scholars agree that Pope had a hand in *The What D'Ye Call It,* but disagree about the extent of collaboration. One sometimes suspects that Pope's generous insistence that Gay be given chief credit for collaborative works may have been, at least partly, an attempt to distance himself from notoriety.

In spite of Gay's failure to find a place at court, he found patrons, at this time notably Lord Burlington, and friends—including Henrietta Howard, who became the mistress of Princess Caroline's husband, the Prince of Wales. The Scriblerians offered Gay help and support, some of it more loyal than useful, such as Pope's notorious attack on the bookseller Edmund Curll. On 26 March 1716, without authorization, Curll published Gay's "The Toilette," a town eclogue about an aging beauty, in *Court Poems.* This volume also contained poems by Lady Mary Wortley Montagu, notably "The Drawing Room," attacking certain distinguished ladies, including Princess Caroline. Readers were encouraged by Curll's advertisement to attribute authorship of the scurrilous poems to Gay or Pope, as well as to Lady Mary. Not only angered on his own and Lady Mary's account, but also remembering Gay's hopes for preferment at court, Pope took revenge on Curll by giving him an emetic and recording the effects in a pamphlet: *A Full and True Account of a Horrid and Barbarous Revenge by Poison On the Body of Mr. Edmund Curll, Bookseller* (1716).

In January 1716 Gay had published *Trivia: or, The Art of Walking the Streets of London,* a poem that may owe something to Swift's "Morning" and

Pages from the score for The Beggar's Opera, *with an illustration depicting Polly Peachum*

Act 3, scene 2 of The Beggar's Opera *(1728), Gay's most popular work, as painted by William Hogarth (by permission of the National Gallery of Art, Washington, D.C.; Paul Mellon Collection)*

"A Description of a City Shower." But in its complex play with the conventions of pastoral, georgic, and epic, in its wit, and in the vividness of its descriptions of contemporary London, the poem is far more than merely derivative. The first copies seem to have been popular, Pope suggesting that Gay might make £150 from it.

Trivia is a georgic in the sense that it is a poem about how to do something; as such, its classical model is Virgil's *Georgics*. But the poem's epigraph and the quotation in the advertisement are from the *Eclogues*, for *Trivia* is also an urban pastoral, the town poet's answer to the country poet of *The Shepherd's Week*. This poet of urban pastoral and urban georgic aspires to epic flight, burning "with Thirst of Fame" and setting out, with an ironic lack of self-interest, to bring profit to his country. If *The Shepherd's Week* brings the country to the town (as Gay the countryman goes to court to see Arbuthnot in its Prologue), *Trivia* brings the unfamiliar town to naive readers who know nothing about urban survival. At the same time, Gay characteristically blurs the distinction between town and country, presenting the city as a place of swains as well as fops, and telling mock-rural folktales about such humble subjects as the invention of pattens (forerunners of modern overshoes).

Trivia has been read as a tourist guide in verse, but it is also a highly sophisticated and literary poem. Trivia, the inspiring goddess whom the poet invokes, corresponds to Diana, the three-formed goddess of classical mythology, associated with the crossroads, where three roads come together. She is therefore evoked by the figure of the blind Oedipus groping his way through the streets of Thebes in Book III, having killed his father at a place where three roads meet; but she may also recall the "mighty contests [rising] from trivial things" in *The Rape of the Lock*. Rather than laughing at trivialities by describing them in epic language as Pope does, Gay shows that high seriousness is not something altogether distinct from the familiar and commonplace. Rather than using the language of mock epic to show how inappropriate some subjects are for epic treatment, Gay blurs generic distinctions in order to suggest that trivial things can be centrally important and that prestige alone is not a sufficient indicator of virtue or enduring value. While Pope's mock epic tends through deliberate confusion to reassert hierarchy, both social and generic, Gay's tends to assault it by placing characters from different conventional categories on the same level. The comic

mythological figures of *Trivia*–such as Doll the apple seller in Book II, whose fate resembles that of Orpheus; such as the pickpockets, bullies, and whores of the London streets–all have moral and imaginative power and are no less important, no less central to the poem, than heroic mythological figures or the ladies and gentlemen of contemporary London.

This poem about walking begins, practically enough, with a discussion of shoes, coats, and canes. *The Shepherd's Week* introduces the urban reader to country lore; *Trivia* turns the urban walker's experience into similar lore, applying the manner of georgic to an urban context. The poet warns the reader, "when too short the modish Shoes are worn, / You'll judge the Seasons by your shooting Corn," and describes "sure Prognosticks," everything from fires burning more brightly to ladies appearing in more colorful dresses, by which the urban dweller can foretell the weather. By Book II such lore is taken for granted, treated briefly and dismissively and glossed in the margin as "Precepts vulgarly known." Book I warns against urban superstitions (rather as *The Shepherd's Week* makes one laugh at rural ones). The reader is given a vivid description of a foolish walker caught in the rain, "spatter'd" with mud (an indirect comment on a foppishly dressed man earlier, who has his cloak "be-spatter'd o'er with Lace"). After a description of women's umbrellas and pattens, Book I ends with a digressive episode: Vulcan falls in love with a village maiden called Patty and invents pattens for her, rather as Cupid invented the fan for Corinna in *The Fan*.

In Book II Gay considers the dangers of walking London's streets: the dirt, the bullies, and the possibility of getting lost in the labyrinthine streets and alleys. The "spatt'ring" mud and dirt of Book I are everywhere in Book II, drying on the calves of unwary walkers and–in another mythological episode–on the face of a "mortal Scavenger" beloved by Cloacina, goddess of the sewers. Their son, abandoned at birth, is first a beggar; then, like an epic hero blessed by a divine mother, he receives from Cloacina the implements of a more exalted destiny, that of a bootblack.

But after pausing for the Cloacina episode, the poet moves on, past a culprit in the stocks, past horses and wagons clashing in narrow streets, past the stink of Fleet ditch, to Pall Mall. Bombarded by sight and sound and smell, by cruelty and uncertainty, he retreats to an alley; but

even there lechery, extravagance, "Jealousies and Cares" are unavoidable, even by one who knows the town as well as he. A country visitor (Gay calls him a "Clown," recalling the speaker's role in the Proeme to *The Shepherd's Week*) would be susceptible to further dangers: charlatans, more mud, and the sight of self-styled wits "discharg[ing] their Tea" in public. Book III will warn against even more serious dangers.

In Book II, after some vivid descriptions of the frozen Thames in winter, Gay provides an explicit counterpart to the shepherd's week, describing a week in the life of the city, based on what is for sale in the shops and stalls. Similarly, he describes the characteristic cries of the year's cycle, ending the year with Christmas and the charity of the walker, who cannot remove himself from human suffering. Walking along the Strand with William Fortescue (the friend with whom Gay had visited Exeter in the summer of 1715), the poet moves into a more social world. He admires the houses of the great, ending Book II with a description of the opportunities and abundance of the city: meat, cheese, fruit, and stalls of second-

hand books and clothes. But the walker who is offered all this will not escape knowledge of suffering. Such knowledge, and the understanding of charity that should flow from it, allow the poet to make moral judgments, ending the book with an overtly satiric, even Juvenalian passage:

> See, yon' bright Chariot on its Braces swing,
> With *Flanders* Mares, and on an arched Spring,
> That Wretch, to gain an Equipage and Place,
> Betray'd his Sister to a lewd Embrace.
> ....
> Here the brib'd Lawyer, sunk in Velvet, sleeps;
> The starving Orphan, as he passes, weeps;
> ....
> That other, with a clustring Train behind,
> Owes his new Honours to a sordid Mind.
> This next in Court Fidelity excells,
> The Publick rifles, and his Country sells.

The generic blurring of pastoral, georgic, and epic here includes satire as well. The poem challenges traditional generic distinctions, for the poet is at once pastoral singer, upstart epic poet, moral prophet, and self-proclaimed lover of trivia. There is no need to reconcile these roles, for absolute consistency would be a suspect stance in Gay's world of confusion and diversity. But the reader is left with the difficulty of determining the tone of particular passages in context.

Book II ends with the positive and the negative sides of the wealth and power–the houses of the great and the decadence of ostentatious hypocrites. Book III turns to the teeming life of the streets at night. Gay describes a traffic jam as if it were a scene of epic warfare, moving from one scene of congestion to another as pickpockets move slyly through a crowd while ballad singers distract people's attention. The emphasis throughout Book III is on vigilance: the dangers are great, but the circumspect walker can evade them. Besides, the law is on his side, for in spite of its dangers London is "Happy *Augusta*! Law-defended Town!" The reader is warned against quarreling and is reminded of Oedipus, who met his father unknowingly at a place "Where three Roads join'd": "Hence wert thou [Oedipus] doom'd in endless Night to stray / Through *Theban* Streets, and cheerless groap thy Way." The night of Oedipus's blindness makes the danger of a London night all the more oppressive. The Cretan labyrinth, unwound with Ariadne's help, is evoked in Book II in order to warn the reader against another, more sinister "female Guide." In Book III she appears again, haunting "*Drury*'s mazy Courts" to lure strangers and visiting country swains to their destruction. Prostitution is one of Gay's symbols of moral evil, for, like the hypocrisy of the elevated rich at the end of Book II, it uses disguise and trickery in order to ensnare and entrap, revealing the predator at the heart of the labyrinthine city.

Through the image of the labyrinth, London becomes the universal city; through the final image of fire, this universality becomes archetypal, conflating images of the burning city of Troy, Nero's Rome, and Naples destroyed by a volcanic eruption. The language and imagery are apocalyptic. Gay achieves for a moment the high seriousness of epic before finally reverting to a parody of the last lines of *The Rape of the Lock*: "High-rais'd on *Fleetstreet* Posts, consign'd to Fame, / This Work shall shine, and Walkers bless my Name."

But "mock-epic" is an inadequate term to describe the effect of *Trivia* as a whole. The poem *is* epic, although it is also parodic, finally mocking itself; the reader must manage to read without insisting that it be either one thing or another, for it defines itself, holding itself up at once to fame and to ridicule. *Trivia* is to be read seriously as Gay's celebration of his law-defended city; the reader also recognizes the presence of suffering, danger, and lawlessness. Occasionally disparaging his own claims to be taken seriously, Gay presents a world where order emerges only out of confusion and cannot be taken for granted, but where the poet can construct a seriously good-humored model of human order.

In Book II Gay mentions the earl of Burlington, whose "fair Palace" (Burlington House, Piccadilly) is an image of such ideal order: "Beauty within, without Proportion reigns. / Beneath his [Burlington's] Eye declining Art revives, / The Wall with animated Picture lives." In the summer of 1716, some months after the publication of *Trivia*, Burlington sent Gay on a visit to Devonshire, where Gay had been with Fortescue the previous year. Gay responded with an account of his journey in "An Epistle to the Earl of Burlington," published with another letter in 1720 as *Two Epistles*, after having first circulated in manuscript. Here Gay, a fat bard on horseback, goes on a Chaucerian pilgrimage to his "native Land," eating, drinking, flirting, and looking back to town with a gently satiric eye.

In the advertisement to *Trivia* Gay referred to critics who denied him the authorship of his own works. The play *Three Hours after Marriage*, a collaboration of Pope, Gay, and Arbuthnot, was first performed at Drury Lane on 16 January 1717 and published later the same month. Gay signed the advertisement, admitting "the Assistance [he had] receiv'd in this Piece from two of [his] Friends," but in this case authorship brought only bad publicity, as people rushed to identify the originals of the characters in the play and to label it pornographic. In the midst of the uproar following the play's production, Gay wrote to Pope in high spirits: "I will (if any Shame there be) take it all to myself, as indeed I ought, the Motion being first mine, and never heartily approv'd of by you." The same year, Gay contributed a translation of Book IX of the *Metamorphoses* to Samuel Garth's version of Ovid, published in July 1717. "An Answer to the Sompner's Prologue," an attempt to imitate Chaucer's style and language (and the scatological humor of Chaucer's *fabliaux*), was included in a miscellany edited by Pope, *Poems on Several Occasions* (1717).

In the summer of 1717 Gay accompanied William Pulteney, later earl of Bath, to France, where he wrote "To My Ingenious and Worthy Friend W[illiam] L[owndes] Esq.," an ironically commendatory poem addressed to the author of a land-tax bill. This poem was published in the "Miscellanies" section of Gay's *Poems on Several Occasions*. The 1717 expedition to France was later (probably in 1719) commemorated in Epistle III, "To the Right Honourable William Pulteney Esq.," also published in the 1720 collection. Here Gay describes French fops who are more foolish than anyone in *Trivia* and women even more vain, frivolous, and promiscuous than they are in London. Explicitly France is to England as city is to country; a Frenchman tells the poet: "*now you've* Paris *seen, you'll frankly own* / *Your boasted* London *seems a country town.*" But the poet prefers England, defending in himself the very xenophobia he condemns in the French by insisting that he would love his country less were it not for her spirit of liberty. The poem depends on stereotypes distasteful to most modern readers, but it is saved by some wonderful passages, such as this evidence of spontaneous stolen love: "*Chelsea's* meads o'erhear perfidious vows, / And the prest grass defrauds the grazing cows." Gay is characteristically witty and ambivalent in his description of an England where perfidy and fraud take on a quality of pastoral innocence. In France, predictably, love is a more heated and dangerous affair, as it once was in England in the days of Charles

PREFACE.

AFTER Mr. Rich and I were agreed upon terms and conditions for bringing this Piece on the stage, and that every thing was ready for a Rehearsal; The Lord Chamberlain sent an order from the country to prohibit Mr. Rich to suffer any Play to be rehears'd upon his stage till it had been first of all supervis'd by his Grace. As soon as Mr. Rich came from his Grace's secretary (who had sent for him to receive the before-mentioned order) he came to my lodgings and acquainted me with the orders he had received.

Upon the Lord Chamberlain's coming to town, I was confined by sickness, but in four or five days I went abroad on purpose to wait upon his Grace with a faithful and genuine copy of this Piece, excepting the errata of the transcriber.

It was transcribed in great haste by Mr. Stede the Prompter of the Play-house, that it might be ready against his Grace's return from the country: As my illness at that time would not allow me to read it over, I since find in it many small faults, and here and there a line or two omitted. But left it should be said I had made any one alteration from the copy I deliver'd to the Lord Chamberlain: I have caused every error in the said copy to be printed (litteral faults excepted) and have taken notice of every omission. I have also pointed out every amendment I have made upon the revisal of my own copy for the Press, that the reader may at one view see what alterations and amendments have been made.

A   E R-

PREFACE.

ERRORS as they stood in the copy delivered to the Lord Chamberlain (occasion'd by the haste of the transcriber) corrected in this edition; by which will appear the most minute difference between that and my own copy.

P for page. l for line. sc. for scene. what was added mark'd thus *. What was left out, thus †.

The names of all the tunes †. The scenes not divided and number'd. The marginal directions for the Actors were often omitted.

EMENDATIONS of my own copy on revising it for the Press.

* Is the mark for any thing added.
† The mark for what is left out.
‡ The mark of what stood in the original Copy.

Excepting these errors and emendations, this Edition is a true and faithful Copy as I my-self in my own hand writing delivered it to Mr. Rich, and afterwards to the Lord Chamberlain, for the truth of which I appeal to his Grace.

PREFACE.   iii

As I have heard several suggestions and false insinuations concerning the copy: I take this occasion in the most solemn manner to affirm, that the very copy I delivered to Mr. Rich was written in my own hand from the Bath from my own first foul blotted papers; from this, that for the Playhouse was transcribed, from whence the above-mention'd Mr. Stede copied that which I delivered to the Lord Chamberlain, and excepting my own foul blotted papers; I do protest I knew of no other copy whatsoever, than those I have mention'd.

The Copy I gave into the hands of Mr. Rich had been seen before by several Persons of the greatest distinction and veracity, who will be ready to do me the honour and justice to attest it; so that not only by them, but by Mr. Rich and Mr. Stede, I can (against all insinuation or positive affirmation) prove in the most clear and undeniable manner, if occasion required, what I have here upon my own honour and credit asserted. The Introduction indeed was not shown to the Lord Chamberlain, which, as I had not then quite settled, was never transcribed in the Playhouse copy.

'Twas on Saturday morning December 7th, 1728. that I waited upon the Lord Chamberlain; I desir'd to have the honour of reading the Opera to his Grace, but he order'd me to leave it with him, which I did upon expectation of having it return'd on the Monday following, but I had it not 'till Thursday December 12, when I receiv'd it from his Grace with this answer; that it was not allow'd to be acted, but commanded to be suppress't. This was told me in general without any reasons assign'd, or any charge against me of my having given any particular offence.

Since this prohibition I have been told that I am accused, in general terms, of having written many disaffected libels and seditious pamphlets. As it hath ever been my utmost ambition (if that word may be us'd upon this occasion) to lead a quiet and inoffensive life, I thought my innocence in this particular would never have requir'd a justification; and as this kind of writing is, what I have ever detested and never practic'd, I am persuaded so groundless a calumny can never be believ'd but by those who do not know me. But when general aspersions of this sort have been cast upon me, I think my-self call'd upon to declare my principles; and I do with the strictest truth affirm, that I am as loyal a subject and as firmly attach'd to the present happy establishment as any of those who have the greatest places or pensions. I have been inform'd too, that in the following Play, I have been charg'd with writing immoralities; that

A 2   it

PREFACE.   iv

it is fill'd with slander and calumny against particular great persons, and that Majesty it-self is endeavour'd to be brought into ridicule and contempt.

As I knew that every one of these charges was in every point absolutely false and without the least grounds, at first I was not at all affected by them; but when I found they were still insisted upon, and that particular passages which were not in the Play were quoted and propagated to support what had been suggested, I could no longer bear to lye under these false accusations; so by printing it, I have submitted and given up all present views of profit which might accrue from the stage, which undoubtedly will be some satisfaction to the worthy gentlemen who have treated me with so much candour and humanity, and represented me in such favourable colours.

But as I am conscious to my-self that my only intention was to lash in general the reigning and fashionable vices, and to recommend and set virtue in as amiable a light as I could; to justify and vindicate my own character, I thought my-self obliged to print the Opera without delay in the manner I have done.

As the Play was principally design'd for representation, I hope when it is read it will be considered in that light: And when all that hath been said against it shall appear to be intirely misunderstood or misrepresented; if, some time hence, it should be permitted to appear on the stage, I think it necessary to acquaint the publick, that as far as a contract of this kind can be binding; I am engag'd to Mr. Rich to have it represented upon his Theatre.

March 25. 1729.

ERRATA.

Air 5. l. 15. read Neighbours.   Air 9. l. 1. r. all my senses.

INTRO-

Gay's preface to Polly (1729), a sequel to The Beggar's Opera that was prohibited from performance in 1728 by the Lord Chamberlain and not staged until 1777

II, before "the rural taste [was] lost," as Gay remarks, returning with more irony than ever to the blurring and reversal of town and country, decadence and simplicity.

Gay spent the summer of 1718 at Stanton Harcourt in Oxfordshire, where Pope was working on his translation of Homer. Here two lovers, John Hewet and Sarah Drew, were struck by lightning while at work in the fields, and Gay told the story in a letter to Fortescue; Pope and Gay wrote a collaborative epitaph (one of three–Pope also contributed a more conventionally pious one, Lady Mary Wortley Montagu, a two-line irreverent epigram). The events of the winter of 1718 are obscure. Gay was probably at work on the libretto to *Acis and Galatea*, which, with music by Handel, was performed privately at Canons (the palace of Handel's patron the duke of Chandos) in 1718.

After spending the summer of 1719 alone in Belgium and France, Gay returned to London in November in need of money. For some unknown reason his pastoral tragedy *Dione* (published in his collection later that year), which was to have been produced in February 1720, was never performed. But *Daphnis and Chloe* was published as a broadside in January 1720. Then, on 20 May, the same month that the last volumes of Pope's *Odyssey* appeared, Tonson and Lintot jointly published *Poems on Several Occasions* in two quarto volumes (together in one book), with a frontispiece by William Kent.

The first volume consists wholly of reprinted poems, with some considerable revisions: *Rural Sports, The Fan, The Shepherd's Week, Trivia*, and *The What D'Ye Call It*. The second volume consists mostly of previously unpublished work, including epistles ("To . . . William Pulteney" and "To the Right Honourable Paul Methuen"), tales (including "The Mad-dog"), eclogues (including a parody of Virgil's Eclogue IV, "The Birth of the Squire"), miscellanies (including "W[illiam] L[owndes]" and "Sweet William's Farewell to Black-Ey'd Susan"), and *Dione*. The impressive list of subscribers included the names of many famous and powerful people: Lords Burlington, Chandos, Bathurst, and Warwick, Robert Walpole, and the duke and duchess of Queensberry, to list only a few. Subscriptions earned Gay a thousand pounds, which he invested in the South Sea Company. He was encouraged to make this investment by a gift of stock from the secretary of state, James Craggs the younger, described by Gay (in "Mr. Pope's Welcome from Greece") as

"Bold, gen'rous *Craggs* whose heart was ne'er disguis'd."

The market crashed in August 1720, and Gay lost most if not all his investment. He spent the spring of 1721 at Chiswick with Lord Burlington, visiting such other friends as the Pulteneys. Then in August 1721, suffering from intestinal trouble (perhaps exacerbated by financial stress and by the death of his friend Lord Warwick), Gay went to Bath, where he returned for a somewhat livelier holiday the following summer. Scholars disagree about the extent and the effects of Gay's financial loss, but clearly he himself worried about his rather precarious dependence, writing such panegyrics as *An Epistle to her Grace Henrietta, Dutchess of Marlborough* (1722) in an effort to win favor. "I lodge at present in Burlington house," he wrote to Swift on 22 December 1722, "and have received many Civilitys from many great men but very few real benefits. They wonder at each other for not providing for me, and I wonder at 'em all." Walpole's rise to power may have encouraged Gay's hopes of preferment, though Walpole was not particularly fond of poets or intellectuals, nor of Tories like Swift, Bolingbroke, or Pulteney and their friends. Swift claimed in the *Intelligencer* that Walpole suspected Gay of writing a lampoon against him. For whatever reason Gay was forced to settle for less than he had hoped for: in 1723, perhaps through the influence of Pulteney or Burlington, he was appointed a lottery commissioner, drawing a salary of £150 a year until 1731, and the earl of Lincoln found apartments for him at Whitehall.

However, Gay was depressed. He trusted such friends as Henrietta Howard, later the countess of Suffolk, to speak on his behalf at court, but her power was limited. Princess Caroline, not Mrs. Howard, guided the prince, who became king in 1727; and Caroline was influenced by Walpole. Gay's letters of these years show him dashing back to London from various visits in the hope of some appointment or other, only to be repeatedly disappointed. In 1724 his tragedy *The Captives* was acted at Drury Lane, after a special reading for Princess Caroline, to whom the printed version is dedicated. But however friendly the princess may have been, she offered no concrete help. Although *The Captives* did well, bringing Gay more than one thousand pounds, his search for patronage continued. In October 1725 he wrote to Brigadier James Dormer that he was working on "a Book of Fables, which I hope to have leave to inscribe to Prince William," the duke of Cumberland, Princess Caroline's third son.

The first volume of *Fables* was published in 1727 with plates designed by Kent, and it was well received. Following the tradition of Aesop, of Chaucer (in "The Nun's Priest's Tale"), and of La Fontaine and L'Estrange, Gay wrote fifty poems drawing moral lessons for human life and usually, though not always, using animal characters. But in Swift's defense of *The Beggar's Opera* (*Intelligencer*, no. 3), he mentions that "even in his Fables . . . for which he was PROMISED a Reward, [Gay] hath been thought somewhat too bold upon *Courtiers*." There is some truth to this accusation. Although Gay claimed to have written them for a five-year-old duke, the fables are not really poems for children. They are satiric pieces in which the role of the satirist, who tells the truth even if he must employ masks and fictions to do so, is implicitly contrasted with the role of the flatterer—the liar who is successful at the courts of princes.

Gay asserts his moral stance in the introduction to *Fables*, in which a swain teaches a philosopher the lessons of nature:

> Pride often guides the author's pen,
> Books as affected are as men,
> But he who studys nature's laws
> From certain truth his maxim draws,
> And those, without our schools, suffice
> To make men moral, good and wise.

But elsewhere, as in Fable XVIII, Gay demonstrates that he has learned the lessons of courts as well; one question raised by *Fables* is whether pride ever guides *this* author's pen. There is some truth to Johnson's dismissive comment (in *Lives of the Poets*, volume 2) on the *Fables*: "from some, by whatever name they may be called, it will be difficult to extract any moral principle." But Johnson expected a consistency of writerly vision that, as we have already seen, Gay refuses to grant his readers. The swain's "certain truths" are elusive; the philosopher's grip on them wavers; and, besides, the poet who refuses to flatter may sell books anyway. The line between the satirist and the flatterer may be less clear than it seems at first, for it partly depends on the reader's response. Once again Gay refuses to draw clear lines: the language of the fabulist, like the language of the clown-courtier in *The Shepherd's Week*, is such a language as no one ever speaks, at least to conduct the business of a court.

The painter of Fable XVIII, who has shown people as they really are, becomes successful after he acquires busts of Venus and Apollo as models. As the painter's reputation soars, the poet asks: "Had he the real likeness shown, / Would any man the picture own? / But when thus happily he wrought, / Each found the likeness in his thought." The fabulist's world, however, is more complex than the painter's: his real likenesses are *also* disguise and pretense, for he attempts to show men and woman as they really are by giving them the appearance and sometimes the qualities of animals. However, even the animal likeness, intended to cut through appearance, can mislead. The lion cub of Fable XIX, who has learned to bray like an ass, is rejected by his own kind as a fool; but the lion of Fable I, accepting flattery, has shown his resemblance to human tyrants. Not every king of the beasts is a good king, and some kings are asses. In the last poem, Fable L, "The Hare and many Friends," Gay presents himself as a victim—"A Hare, who, in a civil way, / Comply'd with ev'ry thing, like *Gay*"—and shows how, rejected by a succession of friends including a "trotting calf" (the young prince?), he confronts the approaching hounds as the volume of fables comes to an end.

Volume 1 of *Fables* is generally good-humored, though it is hard to think of its author as compliant. Gay's sense of himself as a victim was partly borne out by circumstances. When Caroline's husband, the Prince of Wales, became George II in 1727, Gay was finally offered his appointment at court, as gentleman-usher to the two-year-old Princess Louisa. This he turned down in disappointment, writing to Pope in October 1727, "O that I had never known what a Court was! . . . Why did I not take your Advice before my writing Fables for the Duke, not to write them?" The final irony of *Fables*, of course, is that in spite of their satire they were immensely successful. The same is even more true of Gay's next work, *The Beggar's Opera*.

Walpole's biographer, J. H. Plumb, calls the appointment as gentleman-usher "a callous gesture by Walpole that was to call forth in *The Beggar's Opera* a musical satire of wonderful versatility" (*Sir Robert Walpole*, volume 2, 1960). But the first idea for Gay's ballad opera, which was already finished by the end of 1727, may have been Swift's: "I believe," he wrote to Pope on 30 August 1716, "the Pastoral ridicule is not exhausted; and that a porter, foot-man, or chairman's pastoral might do well. Or what think you of a Newgate pastoral among the whores and thieves there?" By 1723 Gay had clearly made the association between low and high life–with Walpole a chief example of the latter–on which *The Beggar's Opera* depends, writing to Mrs. Howard in August: "I cannot indeed wonder that the Talents requisite for a great Statesman are so scarce in the world since so many of those who possess them are every month cut off in the prime of their Age at the Old-Baily." At the same time, the form of the ballad opera allowed Gay to offer a mocking alternative to Italian opera. On 15 February 1728 he wrote to Swift: "I fear I shall have remonstrances drawn up against me by the Royal Academy of Musick" (the body which sponsored Italian opera).

The Beggar's Opera opened on 29 January 1728 at Lincoln's Inn Fields, with Tom Walker as Macheath and Lavinia Fenton as Polly. A note in *The Dunciad* summarizes its success; the play was revived the next season and acted throughout Britain. Pictures of the scene in which Polly and Lucy plead for Macheath were painted by William Hogarth, and William Blake made an engraving based on one of the paintings in 1790, showing among the spectators John Rich (the producer), the duke of Bolton (who eloped with Fenton and later married her), and Gay himself. Whether or not the play made Gay rich (according to the *Craftsman*, 3 February 1728, "the Waggs [said] it has made *Rich* very *Gay* and . . . *Gay* very *Rich*"), it certainly made *Rich* rich–to the extent of four thousand pounds.

Gay completed a sequel, *Polly*, but production of the new play was prohibited by the duke of Grafton, Lord Chamberlain, acting on the king's instructions and probably under Walpole's influence. *Polly* was not performed for the first time until 1777. Opponents of the court became supporters of the sale of *Polly* in book form. The duchess of Marlborough gave a hundred pounds for a single copy, and the duchess of Queensberry was dismissed from court for soliciting subscriptions within the precincts of St. James's. But while the inoffensive Gay stirred up trouble at court and fell into greater disfavor than ever, the publication of *Polly* brought him between eleven hundred and twelve hundred pounds. Ironically the end of his hopes of court patronage was also the end of financial insecurity.

Early in 1728 Gay suffered a serious attack of fever, followed by a relapse after the prohibition of *Polly* on 12 December. Thereafter he probably stayed with the duke and duchess of Queens-

berry for the rest of his life. In 1730 a revised version of *The Wife of Bath* was produced; *Acis and Galatea* was performed in 1731, and its libretto–excerpts of which had been appearing since 1722–was published the following year. Gay's last years were productive and prosperous, his savings exceeding thirty-four hundred pounds. By December 1731 he had begun a second volume of *Fables* (published posthumously in 1738 with a frontispiece illustrating Gay's tomb). He probably also wrote the plays *The Distress'd Wife* and *The Rehearsal at Goatham* during his years with the Queensberrys. By the spring of 1732 he was at work on the opera *Achilles*, produced at Covent Garden in February 1733. Gay did not live to see it. After a trip to London in November 1732 to make arrangements for its production, he contracted a fever and died three days later on December 4 at the age of forty-seven.

On 23 December he was buried in Westminster Abbey, next to Chaucer's tomb. There the duke and duchess of Queensberry erected a monument by John Rysbrack on which appears the epitaph, with its witty and inscrutable "now," that Gay first published in the *Poems* of 1720: "Life is a jest, and all things show it, / I thought so once; but now I know it." To balance this mocking summation is Pope's epitaph, with its famous description of Gay, "In wit, a man; simplicity a child":

> With native humour temp'ring virtuous rage,
> Form'd to delight at once and lash the age:
> Above temptation, in a low estate,
> And uncorrupted, ev'n among the great:
> A safe companion, and an easy friend,
> Unblam'd through life, lamented in thy end. . . .

Whatever one thinks of these lines, which Johnson condemned (in his account of Pope's epitaphs in *Lives of the Poets*, volume 2), there is no doubt that they commemorate in traditional terms Pope's personal friendship for Gay, as they continue: "These are Thy Honours! Not that here thy Bust / Is mix'd with Heroes, or with Kings thy dust; / But that the Worthy and the Good shall say, / Striking their pensive bosoms– *Here* lies Gay."

The traditional view of Gay is of a poet whose personal virtues mitigated against his public success. Because he lacked the savage indignation of Swift or the sustained energy of Pope, he has until quite recently been marginalized, discussed with the kind of patronizing affection traditionally applied to women and children. He has been regarded as the friend of great poets, but hardly as more than a secondary figure, the "play-fellow" whom they treated "with more fondness than respect," to recall Johnson's words. Even his twentieth-century biographer William Henry Irving regards his wit as "superficial," and accepts at face value Gay's own description of himself as compliant. But at a time when the need to distinguish great poets from minor ones is no longer as pressing as it once was, and when readers of eighteenth-century literature are increasingly interested in the complex and changing social patterns that poets help to articulate, John Gay has special interest. His poetry questions what it asserts, existing in a space between assertion of cultural hegemony and skeptical laughter. It tells the truth from behind a whole series of shifting, elusive masks, its point of view typified by Gay's complex, self-conscious epitaph, a couplet once dismissed (by Austin Dobson in the *Dictionary of National Biography*) as merely flippant.

Letters:

The Letters of John Gay, edited by C. F. Burgess (Oxford: Clarendon Press, 1966).

Bibliographies:

G. C. Faber, Bibliography of Gay's works, in *The Poetical Works of John Gay, Including Polly, The Beggar's Opera, and Selections from the other Dramatic Work*, edited by Faber (London: Oxford University Press & Humphrey Milford, 1926);

Julie T. Klein, *Gay: An Annotated Checklist of Criticism* (Troy, N.Y.: Whitston, 1974).

Biographies:

Samuel Johnson, "Gay," in *Lives of the Poets*, volume 2 (London: Printed by J. Nichols for C. Bathurst, 1779);

Lewis Melville [Lewis S. Benjamin], *Life and Letters of John Gay* (London: O'Connor, 1921);

William Henry Irving, *John Gay: Favourite of the Wits* (Durham, N.C.: Duke University Press, 1940).

References:

John M. Aden, "The 1720 Version of *Rural Sports* and the Georgic Tradition," *Modern Language Quarterly*, 20 (1959): 228-232;

Dianne S. Ames, "Gay's *Trivia* and the Art of Allusion," *SP*, 75 (April 1978): 199-222;

Sven M. Armens, *John Gay, Social Critic* (New York: Octagon, 1954);

William D. Ellis, Jr., "Thomas D'Urfey, the Pope-Philips Quarrel and *The Shepherd's Week*," *PMLA*, 74 (1959): 203-212;

J. V. Guerinot and Rodney D. Jilg, *Contexts I: The Beggar's Opera* (Hamden, Conn.: Archon, 1976);

Charles Kerby-Miller, ed., *Memoirs of the Extraordinary Life, Works, and Discoveries of Martinus Scriblerus* (New York: Russell & Russell, 1966);

Maynard Mack, *Alexander Pope: A Life* (New York & London: Norton, 1985; New Haven & London: Yale University Press, 1985);

Anne McWhir, "The Wolf in the Fold: John Gay in *The Shepherd's Week* and *Trivia*," *Studies in English Literature*, 23 (Summer 1983): 413-423;

John Robert Moore, "Gay's Burlesque of Sir Richard Blackmore's Poetry," *Journal of English and Germanic Philology*, 50 (1951): 83-89;

Alexander Pope, *The Correspondence of Alexander Pope*, edited by George Sherburn, 5 volumes (Oxford: Oxford University Press, 1956);

Arthur Sherbo, "Virgil, Dryden, Gay, and Matters Trivial," *PMLA*, 85 (1970): 1063-1071;

Patricia Meyer Spacks, *John Gay* (New York: Twayne, 1965);

Joseph Spence, *Anecdotes, Observations and Characters of Books and Men*, edited by S. W. Singer (Carbondale: Southern Illinois University Press, 1964);

James Sutherland, "John Gay," in *Pope and His Contemporaries: Essays Presented to George Sherburn*, edited by James L. Clifford and Louis A. Landa (Oxford: Clarendon Press, 1949), pp. 201-214;

Hoyt Trowbridge, "Pope, Gay, and *The Shepherd's Week*," *Modern Language Quarterly*, 5 (1944): 79-88.

Papers:

C. F. Burgess, the editor of Gay's letters, acknowledges manuscript sources as follows: the Bodleian Library, the British Museum, the Houghton Library, the Historical Society of Pennsylvania, the Huntington Library, the Pierpont Morgan Library, Trinity College Library (Dublin), and Yale University Library.

Richard Glover

(1712 - 25 November 1785)

Gregory G. Kelley
Emory University

BOOKS: *Leonidas, A Poem* (London: Printed for R. Dodsley, 1737; revised and enlarged edition, 2 volumes, London: Printed for T. Cadell and Richardson & Urquhart, 1770; Baltimore: Neal, Wills & Cole, 1814);

London: Or, The Progress of Commerce, A Poem (London: Printed for T. Cooper, 1739);

Admiral Hosier's Ghost: to the Tune of, Come and Listen to My Ditty [broadside], anonymous (London: Printed for Mr. Webb, 1740);

A Short Account of the Late Application to Parliament Made by the Merchants of London upon the Neglect of their Trade (London: Printed for T. Cooper, 1742);

Boadicia: A Tragedy; As It is Acted at the Theatre-Royal in Drury-Lane (London: Printed for R. & J. Dodsley; & M. Cooper, 1753);

Medea: A Tragedy (London: Printed by H. Woodfall; and sold by J. Morgan, 1761);

The Substance of the Evidence Delivered to a Committee of the Honourable House of Commons by the Merchants and Traders of London, Concerned in the Trade to Germany and Holland, . . . as Summed Up by Mr. Glover. To Which is Annexed, His Speech, Introductory to the Proposals Laid before the Annuitants of Mess. Douglas, Heron and Co. . . . (London: Printed for J. Wilkie, 1774);

The Substance of the Evidence on the Petition Presented by the West-India Planters and Merchants to the Hon. House of Commons, as It Was Introduc'd at the Bar, and Summ'd Up by Mr. Glover on Thursday the 16th of March, 1775 (London: Printed by H. S. Woodfall for T. Cadell & sold by J. Wilkie, 1775; New York: Reprinted by H. Gaine, 1775);

The Athenaid: A Poem, by the Author of Leonidas, edited by Mrs. Halsey, 3 volumes (London: Printed for T. Cadell, 1787);

Jason: A Tragedy in Five Acts (London: Printed for J. Debrett, 1799);

Memoirs of a Celebrated Literary and Political Character, anonymous, edited by R. Duppa (London: Murray, 1813).

Engraving by B. Granger, 1800 (by permission of the National Portrait Gallery, London)

PLAY PRODUCTION: *Boadicia: A Tragedy,* London, Theatre-Royal in Drury Lane, 1 December 1753.

OTHER: "A Poem on Sir Isaac Newton," in *A View of Sir Isaac Newton's Philosophy,* by Henry Pemberton (London: Printed by S. Palmer, 1728).

Although now largely ignored, Richard Glover was in his own time one of England's most famous poets. In addition to his substantial literary reputation, he acquired a formidable body of classical learning, participated in the growing commercial activities of mid-eighteenth-century London, and made himself a man of considerable political influence. When Glover is remembered today, it is chiefly for his blank-verse epic *Leonidas,* a recounting of Greece's defense of Thermopylae during the war with Persia in the fifth century B.C., a poem viewed by his contemporaries as an attack on the ministry of Robert Walpole.

Glover was born in London at St. Martins Lane, Cannon Street, in 1712, the son of Mary and Richard Glover, a merchant engaged in the trade with Hamburg. He was later to follow his father into this profession. His attainments as a scholar are remarkable considering his education, solid enough for a trader but not rigorously classical, at Cheam in Surrey. He must have applied himself well, however, for his knowledge of ancient literature revealed itself early.

In 1728, when Glover was only sixteen, he provided the prefatory poem to a work of scientific popularization entitled *A View of Sir Isaac Newton's Philosophy* by Henry Pemberton, who would remain a lifelong patron. In an introductory note Pemberton asks indulgence for the poet's tender years but insists that the "boldness of the [work's] digressions" would be "best judged by those who are acquainted with Pindar." It does indeed sound a reverberant tone: "Newton demands the muse." The poem belongs to the class of moral and scientific didacticism then being perfected by James Thomson in *The Seasons* (1730), and it successively touches upon Newton's discoveries in cosmology, optics, gravitation, and acoustics. On this last point Glover gets out of his depth. Digressing boldly in comparing Newton's achievement to that of the ancients, the youthful poet allows Orphic and empiricist language to clash dissonantly: "O might'st thou, Orpheus, now again revive, / And Newton should inform thy list'ning ear, / How the soft notes were on the wind conveyed. / He taught the Muse, how sound progressive floats / Upon the waving particles of air." The poem did indicate Glover's great promise, and it is a livelier performance than many of his mature works. In the future Glover's didacticism would be more historical than scientific and his digressions more Homeric than Pindaric.

Glover's financial situation was not always consistent, but the 1730s saw him advancing in the world of commerce. His marriage to Hannah Nunn, on 21 May 1737, was a profitable one. Although it was dissolved in divorce in 1756, a pro-

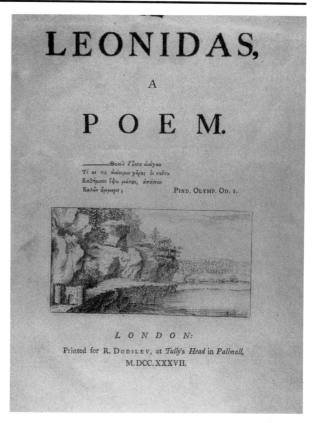

Title page for Glover's best-known poem (Special Collections, Thomas Cooper Library, University of South Carolina)

cess that then required an act of Parliament, the union had been accompanied by a dowry from Miss Nunn of substantial property holdings, which Glover apparently kept. Glover's pecuniary improvement during this period occasioned a rise in his political influence. He was increasingly drawn toward the circle of "patriot poets," including Thomson, David Mallet, and Mark Akenside, who rallied around Lord Lyttleton and Frederick, Prince of Wales. This group, distinguished as much by their opposition to Prime Minister Walpole as by their fondness for blank verse, frequently puffed each other's works in Lyttleton's periodical journal *Common Sense* and excoriated the hacks who propagated Walpole's *Daily Gazetteer.* Meanwhile, Viscount Bolingbroke was making his call for a "Patriot King" to rise up and lead England to glory.

It was in this atmosphere of patriotic opposition that Glover began to write the epic *Leonidas.* Not every member of his clique believed that such a task was within the young merchant's ability; Thomson was reputed to have exclaimed, as reported by Alexander Chalmers, "He write an epic poem! a Londoner, who has never seen a mountain!" Glover did manage to complete the work, however, and in 1737 brought out the earliest version of *Leonidas,* in nine books. It was an immediate success, going through four English and two Irish editions within the first two years of its publication. The sensation the poem caused is reflected in a 31 May 1737 letter from Jonathan Swift in Dublin to Alexander Pope asking, "Pray who is that Mr. Glover, who writ the epic poem called Leonidas, which is reprinted here, and hath great vogue?"

The story tells of Leonidas, king of Sparta, who, in obedience to an oracle, vows to die in hopeless battle along with three hundred citizens in order to prevent the conquest of his homeland by the invading tyrant, Xerxes. In addition, following closely the accounts of the ancient historians, the narration rehearses the campaigns of the Greek commanders Dieneces, Diomedon, and Dithyrambus and the Persian generals Hyperanthes and Teribazus. The priestess Melissa, added in the poet's 1770 revision, hovers over the action like a human embodiment of the "goddess Liberty."

With its first appearance the poem quickly drew the praise of Henry Fielding in the *Champion* and lavish, if not unexpected, encomiums from Lyttleton and from Glover's old friend Pemberton. The members of the anti-Walpole party were quick to seize upon the polemical possibilities of an epic that shrilled, "All is due / To liberty against a tyrant's pride." In his preface to the work Glover himself implied that "such disinterested public service [as Leonidas showed] did once exist," in pointed contrast to that demonstrated by the current ministry. The dedication to Lord Cobham, Lyttleton's uncle, further identified the epic as an opposition tract. *Leonidas* was thus declared to be a call for the people of England, threatened with slavery, to resist the assaults of the modern Xerxes, Walpole. The fallacy of reducing the poem to an attack on the government is obvious, at least today, for it sticks too closely to established historical record to be seen as merely topical political allegory. Styling the epic as a fashionable attack certainly inflated its early readership, but as the controversy into which *Leonidas* had been enlisted went away, so did much of its appeal.

As an epic in blank verse *Leonidas* shows Glover avoiding almost all stylistic affinities with the great seventeenth-century predecessor, John Milton's *Paradise Lost.* In an empiricist era Glover felt it necessary to dispense with the mythological

machinery that previous epic poets, including Milton, had deemed necessary. The era's demand that literature instruct did not require that historical verse read like a chronicle. More damaging is the poet's decision to renounce virtually all metrical variation, as if the heroic poem in blank verse would tolerate no foot except the iambic. The hero's harangue to his generals is typical: "Illustrious warriors hail, / Who thus undaunted signalize your faith, / And gen'rous ardour in the common cause. / But you, whose counsels prop the Grecian state, / O venerable synod, whose decrees / Have call'd us forth, to vanquish, or to die." Even when a touch of variety does enter the poem it is vitiated by the monotonous habit of rigidly mid-stopped lines. These caesurae begin to resemble a tic: "Meantime the shades of night, / Retiring, wake Dieneces. He gives / The word. His pupil seconds. Ev'ry band / Is arm'd. Day opens. Sparta's king appears. / Oïileus greets him."

With these defects invisible to Glover's contemporaries, or at least to his partisans, he quickly built upon the success of *Leonidas* with a different kind of poem, though still firmly oppositional: the ballad *Admiral Hosier's Ghost,* published in 1740. It commemorates the events of 1726 when Vice-Admiral Francis Hosier had commanded a British blockade of the Spaniards at Porto Bello. The deaths of thousands of sailors from fever and Hosier's own subsequent death, supposedly "of a griev'd and broken heart," were attributed by the opposition at that time to the government's restraint of naval activity. The poem begins when the anti-Walpole forces were attempting again to inflame hostilities against Spain. In it, Hosier's ghost returns to Porto Bello to congratulate Admiral Vernon (a member of Glover's opposition party) on his recent success there but adds a warning for his "patriot friends" to "Think on vengeance for my ruin, / And for England sham'd in me."

A fairly blatant piece of propaganda, *Admiral Hosier's Ghost* seemed particularly appropriate during the brouhaha over Jenkins's ear. (In 1731 Jenkins, an English seaman, had traveled around Britain with his severed ear preserved in a bottle, claiming the Spanish had so disfigured him.) According to the custom for broadside poems, Glover published the work anonymously. Ironically it has enjoyed a better fate than *Leonidas,* the poet's great public gesture, surviving in readers' attention longer than any other of Glover's works. It was included in Thomas Percy's *Re-*

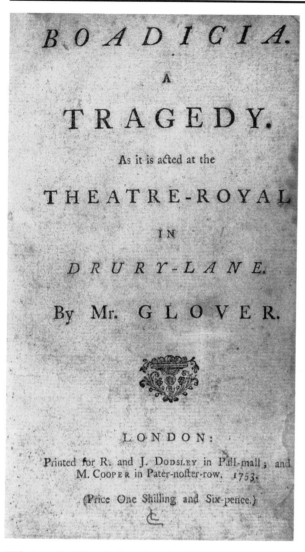

Title page for Glover's first play (Special Collections, Thomas Cooper Library, University of South Carolina)

liques of Ancient English Poetry (1765), a book that inspired another century's poets, and it was considered at least readable into the twentieth century.

Glover continued the political agitations of 1739 in *London: Or, The Progress of Commerce*. This poem rebukes Spain as an "Insatiate race! the shame of polish'd lands! / Disgrace of Europe! for inhuman deeds / And insolence renown'd!" Beyond these assertedly topical references, in *London* Glover proposed to trace England's favored destiny in the allegorical style of the eighteenth century's many so-called progress poems. Commerce is born in ancient days, the product of Neptune's rape of Phoenice (Phoenicia), and after traveling bombastically through all of the lands that have encouraged trade, she (Commerce) settles in England. Like a good opposition propagandist

she warns the citizens there that all should prepare for war who have "vainly deem'd, that wealth / Could purchase lasting safety, and protect / Unwarlike freedom." The poem opens with an uncharacteristically personal note; the speaker asks for fair winds to guide his ships from Germany so that "dispossess'd of care, / And free from every tumult of the mind" he may concentrate on his poetic task. Thus we catch a rare glimpse of the merchant-poet in his labors and anxieties before the vast, abstract form of Commerce dispenses the empire-shaping gifts of numbers, letters, and mechanical invention.

As the Walpole ministry began to fade in 1742 Glover made a speech before Parliament, reprinted several times, to protest the alleged neglect by the government of English commercial interests. Later in that same year Walpole resigned as prime minister, leaving Glover's party in the ascendancy. Glover seems to have derived no direct benefit from the victory, however, and, about that time, he apparently became financially distressed. However, in 1744, when the duchess of Marlborough left five hundred pounds in her will for Glover and Mallet to write a biography of her late husband, Glover, to his credit, refused this act of servility.

Not until 1751 did Glover feel the time right for him actively to broaden his own political ambitions. His calculations proved amiss, however, for he was defeated by Thomas Harrison in the election for the office of chamberlain of London. His speech conceding defeat was a model of magnanimity and stoical acceptance. The misfortunes of that year continued with the death of Frederick, Prince of Wales, a patron who had earlier provided Glover such gifts as an expensively bound set of the classics.

Although Glover was not yet a full-fledged member of the government, he participated extensively in political affairs during the 1740s and 1750s as evidenced by his memoir of the period, *Memoirs of a Celebrated Literary and Political Character* (posthumously published in 1813). This dry and depressing record of alliances and intrigue was probably never intended for publication, and it remained hidden for almost thirty years after its author's death. A revealing digression from the otherwise tedious account reveals Glover's apparently growing pessimism about the state of George II's England. He despairs to describe adequately the nation's "subjects without subordination, laws uninforced, magistrates without authority, fleets and armies without discipline in the

RICHARD GLOVER ESQ.ᴿ

*Engraved by T. Holloway 1786 from an Original
Painted by Mr. Hone 1756.*

Engraving based on a portrait by Nathaniel Hone (by permission of the National Portrait Gallery, London)

midst of an unsuccessful war, . . . the supineness of an effeminate gentry, the corruption of a servile and dependent senate . . . under a doting, mean, spiritless, covetous, prejudiced, undiscerning Prince." Such feelings may have inspired the poet's recourse to tragedy soon after the events described in the *Memoirs*.

In 1753 Glover began his first forays into drama with *Boadicia*, presented at Drury Lane for nine nights in December of that year. In the play ancient England's Celtic inhabitants vie with their Roman conquerors in arms and stoic honor. Boadicia, queen of the Icenians, ferociously leads her tribe to disaster. Her merciless but ineffectual blood lust may reflect a revisionary attitude

in Glover toward the bellicose sentiments of *London* and *Admiral Hosier's Ghost*. The action focuses more closely, however, on the pathetic situation of Dumnorix (originally played by the famous actor David Garrick) and Venusia, king and queen of the Trinobantians, who choose Roman-like suicide over dishonor. The love between the Roman soldier Flaminius and a Trinobantian princess provides a mildly interesting subplot.

His high renown as a poet notwithstanding, Glover knew little of stagecraft. Thomas Davies's biography of Garrick amusingly relates how Glover insisted upon reading his play to the assembled cast despite the fact that "his voice was harsh and his elocution disagreeable." The play reflects a similar insensibility to audience response; John Bell's introduction to an early published edition (1791) granted the tragedy "more poetic than histrionic powers." Glover's *Medea* (1761) shows even less of either. Following Seneca more closely than it does Euripides, it retells the story of the spurned witch who wreaks her vengeance on her lover, the hero Jason. This drama is of a ranting kind that mid-eighteenth-century audiences had justly wearied of. Nevertheless, it was performed for the benefit of Mrs. Mary Ann Yates three times, in 1767, 1768, and 1776. A sequel, *Jason,* was never performed during the author's lifetime, but was published in 1799, fourteen years after his death. It is, if anything, less interesting than its predecessor, since it begins after the action has already been exhausted.

Glover finally succeeded in his political ambitions, being elected to Parliament in 1761 and representing Weymouth until 1768. His only recorded speech, opposing a subsidy to Portugal on 13 May 1762, is undistinguished, but he is said to have played a prominent role in the complicated direction of policy toward India. Of more note were his summations of evidence before the House of Commons in 1774 and 1775, which, like his speech of 1742, sought redress for merchants' grievances. When the summations were published, the West India merchants rewarded Glover with a piece of silver plate worth three hundred pounds. He demonstrated similar commercial good sense in his handling of the affairs of the Scottish bank of Douglas, Heron, and Company, following its failure in 1762.

Glover's last public literary act was his revision of *Leonidas* from nine books to twelve in 1770. It has been conjectured that this poetic return to the Persian war stimulated him to write *The Athenaid,* a sequel, but it is not known when the latter work was in fact begun. Published posthumously (1787) by Glover's daughter, Mrs. Halsey, this epic narrates the events that followed the defense of Thermopylae. *The Athenaid* suffers even more than its predecessor from being versified classical historiography and at thirty books is vastly too long.

Barring a cataclysmic alteration of canons, Richard Glover is not likely to regain the position he once held as one of the major English poets. Yet in his day he was acclaimed (by members of his own party) as second only to Milton and as the equal of Pope. Indeed, he triumphed, it was said, by writing an epic when Pope had only produced translations of epics. He outlived his own popularity; by the time of his death on 25 November 1785 his poems were already headed for oblivion. If only by virtue of its transitoriness, the great vogue for Glover's works should be of interest to historians of taste. He united accomplishments in areas today considered utterly distinct if not mutually exclusive: commerce, politics, and literature. His versatility remains estimable even if the bulk of his poetry does not.

Biographies:

Alexander Chalmers, *The Works of the English Poets from Chaucer to Cowper,* volume 17 (London: Printed for J. Johnson, 1810), pp. 3-12;

J. G. Schaaf, *Richard Glover: Leben und Werke* (Leipzig: Grafe, 1900).

References:

The Correspondence of Jonathan Swift, D.D., volume 6, edited by F. Elrington Ball (London: Bell, 1914);

Thomas Davies, *Memoirs of the Life of Garrick* (London: Printed for T. Davies, 1780), pp. 172-174;

Lewis Namier and John Brooke, *The House of Commons: 1754-1790* (London: History of Parliament Trust, 1964).

Samuel Johnson

(7 September 1709 - 13 December 1784)

Martine Watson Brownley

Emory University

See also the Johnson entry in *DLB 39: British Novelists, 1660-1800.*

SELECTED BOOKS: *London: A Poem in Imitation of the Third Satire of Juvenal,* anonymous (London: Printed for R. Doddesley [*sic*], 1738);

Marmor Norfolciense; or, An Essay on an Ancient Prophetical Inscription, in Monkish Rhyme, Lately Discover'd Near Lynn in Norfolk, as Probus Britannicus (London: Printed for J. Brett, 1739);

A Compleat Vindication of the Licensers of the Stage from the Malicious and Scandalous Aspersions of Mr. Brooke, Author of Gustavus Vasa, with a Proposal for Making the Office of Licenser More Extensive and Effectual, by an Impartial Hand (London: Printed for C. Corbett, 1739);

Proposals for Printing a Medicinal Dictionary (London, 1741);

An Account of the Life of Mr. Richard Savage, Son of the Earl Rivers, anonymous (London: Printed for J. Roberts, 1744);

An Account of the Life of John Philip Barretier, Who Was Master of Five Languages at the Age of Nine Years (London: Printed for J. Roberts, 1744);

Miscellaneous Observations on the Tragedy of Macbeth, with Remarks on Sir T. H.'s Edition of Shakespear; to Which Is Affix'd Proposals for a New Edition of Shakeshear [sic] *with a Specimen* (London: Printed for E. Cave & sold by J. Roberts, 1745);

The Plan of a Dictionary of the English Language, Addressed to the Right Honourable Philip Dormer, Earl of Chesterfield, One of His Majesty's Principal Secretaries of State, anonymous (London: Printed for J. & P. Knapton, T. Longman & T. Shewell, C. Hitch, A. Millar & R. Dodsley, 1747);

Prologue and Epilogue, Spoken at the Opening of the Theatre in Drury-Lane (London: Printed by E. Cave & sold by M. Cooper & R. Dodsley, 1747);

The Vanity of Human Wishes: The Tenth Satire of Juvenal, Imitated by Samuel Johnson (London: Printed for R. Dodsley & sold by M. Cooper, 1749); revised version, in *A Collection of Poems by Several Hands,* volume 4 (London: Printed for R. Dodsley, 1755);

Irene: A Tragedy, as It Is Acted at the Theatre Royal in Drury-Lane (London: Printed for R. Dodsley & sold by M. Cooper, 1749);

A New Prologue Spoken by Mr. Garrick, Thursday, April 5, 1750, at the Representation of Comus, for the Benefit of Mrs. Elizabeth Foster, Milton's Granddaughter, and only Surviving Descendant (London: Printed for J. Payne & J. Bouquet, 1750);

The Rambler, 8 volumes (Edinburgh: Sold by W. Gordon, C. Wright & the other booksellers, 1750-1752; revised edition, 4 volumes, Dublin, 1756; New York: Printed for Samuel Campbell, 1800);

A Dictionary of the English Language, in Which the Words are Deduced from Their Originals, and Illustrated in Their Different Significations by Examples from the Best Writers; to Which are Prefixed a History of the Language and an English Grammar, 2 volumes (London: Printed by W. Strahan for J. & P. Knapton; T. & T. Longman; C. Hitch & L. Hawes; A. Millar; & R. & J. Dodsley, 1755; 4 volumes, Philadelphia: Moses Thomas, 1818);

A Dictionary of the English Language . . . Abstracted from the Folio Edition, 2 volumes (London: Printed for J. Knapton; C. Hitch & L. Hawes; A. Millar; R. & J. Dodsley; M. & T. Longman, 1756; 1 volume, Philadelphia: J. Johnson, 1805);

Proposals for Printing, by Subscription, the Dramatick Works of William Shakespeare, Corrected and Illustrated by Samuel Johnson (London: J. & R. Tonson; J. Knapton; C. Hitch & L. Hawes; & M. & T. Longman, 1756);

The Prince of Abissinia: A Tale, 2 volumes (London: Printed for R. & J. Dodsley & W. Johnston, 1759; revised, London, 1759); repub-

Samuel Johnson (portrait by Joshua Reynolds, circa 1778; by permission of the Tate Gallery)

lished as *The History of Rasselas, Prince of Abissinia: An Asiatic Tale* (Philadelphia: Printed by Robert Bell, 1768); modern edition, edited by Geoffrey Tillotson and Brian Jenkins (London: Oxford University Press, 1971);

The Idler, 2 volumes (London: Printed for J. Newbery, 1761; Philadelphia: Printed by Tesson & Lee for S. F. Bradford & J. Conrad, 1803);

Mr. Johnson's Preface to His Edition of Shakespear's Plays (London: J. & R. Tonson, H. Woodfall, J. Rivington & others, 1765);

The False Alarm (London: Printed for T. Cadell, 1770);

Thoughts on the Late Transactions Respecting Falkland's Islands, anonymous (London: Printed for T. Cadell, 1771);

The Patriot, Addressed to the Electors of Great Britain, anonymous (London: Printed for T. Cadell, 1774);

Taxation No Tyranny: An Answer to the Resolutions and Address of the American Congress, anony-

mous (London: Printed for T. Cadell, 1775);

Political Tracts (London: Printed for W. Strahan & T. Cadell, 1775);

A Journey to the Western Islands of Scotland (London: Printed for W. Strahan & T. Cadell, 1775; Baltimore: P. H. Nicklin / Boston: Farrand, Mallory, 1810);

Prefaces, Biographical and Critical, to the Works of the English Poets, 10 volumes (London: Printed by J. Nichols for C. Bathurst, J. Buckland, W. Strahan & others, 1779-1781); republished as *Lives of the Most Eminent English Poets; with Critical Observations on Their Works*, 2 volumes (Philadelphia: Benjamin Johnson, 1803);

Prayers and Meditations, Composed by Samuel Johnson LL.D., and Published from His Manuscripts, edited by George Strahan (London: Printed for T. Cadell, 1785);

Debates in Parliament by Samuel Johnson LL.D., edited by George Chalmers, 2 volumes (London: Printed for John Stockdale, 1787);

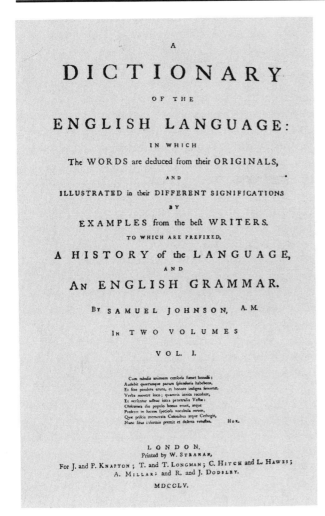 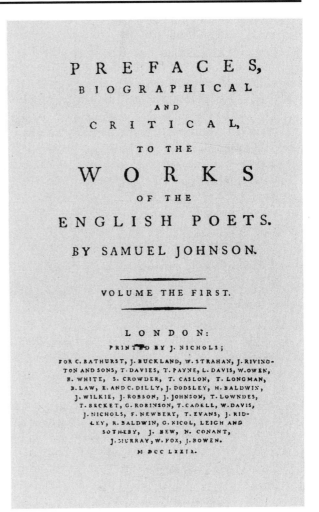

Title pages for Johnson's best-known works

An Account of the Life of Dr Samuel Johnson, from his Birth to his Eleventh Year, Written by Himself, edited by Richard Wright (London: Richard Phillips, 1805).

Editions and Collections: *The Works of Samuel Johnson, LL.D.,* 9 volumes (Oxford: Talboys & Wheeler, 1825);

The Lives of the Poets, edited by G. B. Hill, 3 volumes (Oxford: Clarendon Press, 1905; New York: Octagon Press, 1967);

The Poems of Samuel Johnson, edited by D. Nichol Smith and E. L. McAdam (Oxford: Clarendon Press, 1941; revised, 1962);

The Yale Edition of the Works of Samuel Johnson, 15 volumes, continuing, includes *Poems* (volume 6, 1964), edited by McAdam and George Milne (New Haven: Yale University Press, 1958-);

Samuel Johnson: Selected Poetry and Prose, edited by

Frank Brady and W. K. Wimsatt (Berkeley: University of California Press, 1977);

Samuel Johnson on Literature, edited by Marlies K. Danziger (New York: Ungar, 1979).

PLAY PRODUCTION: *Mahomet and Irene,* London, Theatre Royal in Drury Lane, 6 February 1749.

OTHER: *The Messiah,* translated (into Latin) by Johnson, in *A Miscellany of Poems by Several Hands, Publish'd by J. Husbands* (Oxford: Printed by L. Lichfield, 1731);

A Voyage to Abyssinia, by Father Jerome Lobo, a Portuguese Jesuit. . . . With a Continuation of the History of Abyssinia down to the Beginning of the Eighteenth Century, and Fifteen Dissertations by Mr. Legrand, from the French, translated by

Johnson (London: Printed for A. Bettesworth & C. Hitch, 1735);

Introduction to *The Harleian Miscellany*, edited by W. Oldys, 8 volumes (London, 1744-1746);

The Plays of William Shakespeare, in Eight Volumes, with the Corrections and Illustrations of Various Commentators; to Which Are Added Notes by Sam. Johnson, edited by Johnson, 8 volumes (London: Printed for J. & R. Tonson, C. Corbet, H. Woodfall, J. Rivington, R. Baldwin, L. Hawes, Clark & Collins, W. Johnston, T. Calson, T. Lownds & the executors of B. Dodd, 1765);

Anna Williams, *Miscellanies in Prose and Verse*, includes a preface and poems by Johnson (London, 1766).

Samuel Johnson, the premier English literary figure of the mid and late eighteenth century, was a writer of exceptional range: a poet, a lexicographer, a translator, a journalist and essayist, a travel writer, a biographer, an editor, and a critic. His literary fame has traditionally—and properly—rested more on his prose than on his poetry. As a result, aside from his two verse satires (1738, 1749), which were from the beginning recognized as distinguished achievements, and a few lesser pieces, the rest of his poems have not in general been well known. Yet his biographer James Boswell noted correctly that Johnson's "mind was so full of imagery, that he might have been perpetually a poet." Moreover, Johnson wrote poetry throughout his life, from the time he was a schoolboy until eight days before his death, composing in Latin and Greek as well as English. His works include a verse drama, some longer serious poems, several prologues, many translations, and much light occasional poetry, impromptu compositions or jeux d'esprit. Johnson is a poet of limited range, but within that range he is a poet of substantial talent and ability.

Johnson, the son of Sarah and Michael Johnson, grew up in Lichfield. His father was a provincial bookseller prominent enough to have served as sheriff of the town in 1709, the year of Samuel's birth, but whose circumstances were increasingly straitened as his son grew up. Samuel was a frail baby, plagued by disease. He contracted scrofula (a tubercular infection of the lymph glands) from his wet nurse, which left him almost blind in one eye and nearsighted in the other, deaf in one ear, and scarred on his face and neck from the disease itself and from an operation for it. He also was infected with smallpox.

These early and traumatic illnesses presaged the continuing physical discomfort and ill health that would mark his entire life.

The Johnson household was not a particularly happy one, for financial difficulties only exacerbated his parents' incompatibilities. The serious psychological problems Johnson experienced throughout his life were undoubtedly connected in part with the troubled domestic situation of his childhood. Johnson's major advantage from the beginning was his mind, for the intellectual powers that were to astonish his associates throughout his life appeared early. He excelled at the Lichfield Grammar School, which he attended until he was fifteen.

According to his boyhood friend Edmund Hector, Johnson's first poem, "On a Daffodill, the first Flower the Author had seen that Year," was composed between his fifteenth and sixteenth years (in 1724). Written in heroic quatrains, the poem is largely an accumulation of traditional lyric conventions typical of poets from Robert Herrick to Matthew Prior. At moments, however, its weighted seriousness, and particularly the melancholy sense of process and the moral that ends it, suggests some of the points where the poetic strengths of the mature Johnson would focus. The poem poses no serious challenge to William Wordsworth but is not an entirely inauspicious beginning. Hector later told Boswell that Johnson "never much lik'd" the poem because he did not feel "it was . . . characteristic of the Flower." Significantly, even so young, Johnson recognized the need for the concreteness and specificity that in his later poems would infuse the more abstract intellectual conceptions that dominated his first effort.

Johnson spent the next year at Stourbridge. Initially he made a protracted visit to his older cousin Cornelius Ford, enjoying the company of this genial, witty, and worldly relative and access to a social world significantly wider than life at Lichfield had offered. Later Johnson worked at the Stourbridge Grammar School with the headmaster, John Wentworth. About a dozen of Johnson's poems from this period survive, mainly translations. Most of them were school exercises, such as his translations of Virgil's first and fifth eclogues and the dialogue between Hector and Andromache in the sixth book of the *Iliad*. Johnson later told Boswell that Horace's odes were "the compositions in which he took most delight," and he had already translated the *Integer vitae* ode (I:xxii) before studying with Went-

ANNALS.

I. 1709-10.

SEPT. 7*, 1709, I was born at Lichfield. My mother had a very difficult and dangerous labour, and was assisted by George Hector, a man-midwife of great reputation. I was born almost dead, and could not cry for some time. When he had me in his arms, he said, "Here is a brave boy †."

* 18 of the present stile. *Orig.*
† This was written in January, 1765. *Edit.*

Johnson's birthplace in Lichfield, Staffordshire—his father's bookshop was on the ground floor of the house (watercolor by Clarkson Stanfield, 1835; private collection; from Samuel Johnson 1709-84: A Bicentenary Exhibition, *Arts Council of Great Britain, 1984); and page 1 of* An Account of the Life of Dr Samuel Johnson, from his Birth to his Eleventh Year, Written by Himself, *first published in 1805*

worth. At Stourbridge he translated three other odes (II: ix, xiv, and xx) and two epodes of Horace's (II and XI). All are capable and fairly accurate performances, although the epodes show more energy. The most interesting of his early translations is that of Joseph Addison's Latin poem "The Battle of the Pygmies and the Cranes" (1698), for it anticipates the vigor, the sympathetic involvement and resulting moral poignance, and the ability to revivify known truths that are characteristic of Johnson's greatest poems.

Two more school exercises, "Festina Lente" (Make Haste Slowly) and "Upon the Feast of St. Simon and St. Jude," are original poems. The latter, written in the stanzaic form that Christopher Smart would employ over three decades later in the *Song to David* (1763), is singular among Johnsonian poems for what it terms "extatick fury," and it shows his youthful willingness to experiment with verse forms and varieties of poetic expression. Despite its interest, it is in many ways the

"rude unpolish'd song" that it claims to be, and it suggests that Johnson's decision to confine himself to couplets and quatrains was not unwise. Wentworth's preservation of Johnson's early pieces reflects his high opinion of his pupil's talent and skill, and the early poems show an increasing command of diction and rhythm. W. Jackson Bate has pointed out that although merely school exercises, they are "as good as the verse written by any major poet at the same age."

Johnson returned to Lichfield in the fall of 1726 and spent two more years there, working and also reading in his father's bookshop. Once again he found a mentor, this time Gilbert Walmesley, a scholarly, sophisticated, hospitable lawyer who was registrar of the Ecclesiastical Court at Lichfield. In 1728, when Johnson was nineteen, his parents managed to scrape together enough money to send him to Pembroke College, Oxford. In his first interview he impressed his tutor by quoting Macrobius, and with the wide knowledge he had accumulated over his years of

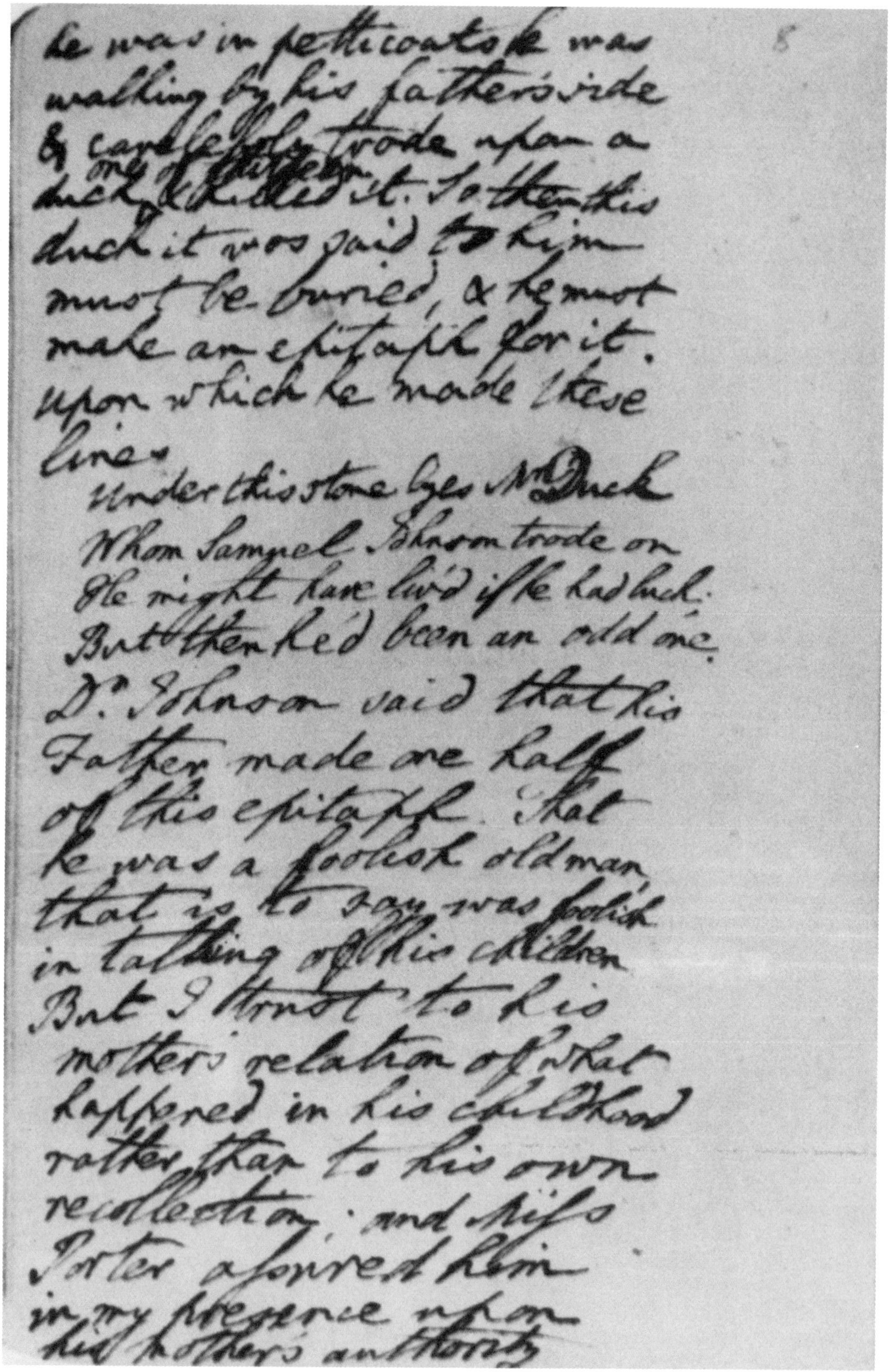

he was in petticoats & he was
walking by his father's side
& carelessly trode upon a
one of the ducks & killed it. So then this
duck it was said to him
must be buried, & he must
make an epitaph for it.
upon which he made these
lines·

> Under this stone lyes Mr Duck
> Whom Samuel Johnson trode on
> He might have liv'd if he had luck.
> But then he'd been an odd one.

Dr Johnson said that his
Father made one half
of this epitaph. That
he was a foolish old man,
that is to say was foolish
in talking of his children
But I trust to his
mothers relation of what
happened in his childhood
rather than to his own
recollection; and Miss
Porter assured him
in my presence upon
his mother's authority

*Page from James Boswell's notebook on which he recorded Lucy Porter's account of what may have been Johnson's first poem,
composed when he was three (Hyde Collection; by permission of the Viscountess Eccles)*

reading, he continued to impress members of the college with his intellectual prowess. Although a desultory and often irresponsible student, he loved college life. His reading of William Law's *A Serious Call to a Devout and Holy Life* (1728) during this period led him to think seriously about religion, and he gradually developed the deep, though troubled, acceptance of the Christian faith and its principles that marked his life.

As a youth in Lichfield, Johnson had first attempted Latin verse in a now-lost poem on the glowworm, but several of his Latin poems composed as college exercises survive. Of these the most important is a translation of Alexander Pope's *Messiah* (1712), made as a 1728 Christmas exercise at the suggestion of his tutor. Working through Isaiah, Virgil, and Pope, Johnson produced his own Latin poem of 119 lines at remarkable speed, writing half of it in an afternoon and completing the rest the next morning. This kind of facility in poetic composition was characteristic of Johnson, whether he was writing original poetry or translating, just as he later wrote prose with incredible speed. He could effectively organize and even edit in his mind; he later explained to Boswell that in composing verses, "I have generally had them in my mind, perhaps fifty at a time, walking up and down in my room; and then I have written them down, and often, from laziness, have written only half lines." The manuscript of *The Vanity of Human Wishes* (1749) reflects this practice, for the first half of many lines is written in different ink than the last half.

The translation of *The Messiah* was received enthusiastically at Pembroke. Although the extant evidence is conflicting, one close friend said that Johnson's father had it printed without his son's knowledge and even dispatched a copy to Pope. Johnson, who had always experienced difficulties in getting along with his father, was furious at the interference, for he had his own plans for having the poem presented properly to the English author. Whatever actually happened in this connection, the translation was Johnson's first published poem, for in 1731 it was included in *A Miscellany of Poems*, edited by John Husbands, a Pembroke tutor. But by the time it appeared, lack of money had forced Johnson to leave Oxford and return once more to Lichfield.

Johnson's early translations and his Latin verse reflect two poetic modes that he would pursue for the rest of his life. Other poems extant from his earlier years show his abilities in the

James Boswell (painting by Joshua Reynolds; National Portrait Gallery, London)

kind of occasional or impromptu verses that appear in large numbers in his later writings. In addition to the more serious and substantial "Ode on Friendship," there are the complimentary verses "To a Young Lady on Her Birthday" and "To Miss Hickman Playing on the Spinet," along with "On a Lady leaving her place of Abode" and "On a Lady's Presenting a Sprig of Myrtle to a Gentleman," the latter composed hastily to help a friend. A Latin quatrain, "To Laura," resulted when a friend proposed a line and challenged Johnson in company to finish it; he complied instantly. Finally, an epilogue written for a play acted by some young women at Lichfield presages his later theatrical pieces, while "The Young Author" prepares for the future treatment of a similar theme in one of his great verse satires. Almost the entire range of Johnson's mature poetic interests is represented in his early pieces.

Barred from returning to Oxford because of his family's increasingly desperate financial situation, Johnson lacked an occupation, had no prospects of one, and faced a bleak future on his return to Lichfield. Worst of all was his psychological state. For him the early years of the 1730s were a period of despair, ultimate breakdown, and only gradual recovery. Indolence had always been a problem for him; indeed, it would plague him throughout his life. But during this period, despite his best efforts to pull himself together and focus his life, he could not break the terrible lassitude afflicting him. Deeply depressed, paralyzed with guilts and fears, he suffered a massive emotional collapse that lasted for about two years and left him unsteady for three more. He later dated his constant health problems from this period, writing in a letter in his early seventies that "My health has been from my twentieth year such as seldom afforded me a single day of ease" (*Letters of Samuel Johnson*, II: 474). In addition, during this time he developed the convulsive gestures, tics, and obsessional mannerisms that contributed to making his demeanor so odd. Johnson was a large, powerful man, but his awkwardness, his scrofula and smallpox scars, and his compulsive mannerisms, combined with his disheveled and slovenly dress, created a grotesque initial impression.

After failing in attempts to secure several positions, Johnson was briefly employed in 1732 as an undermaster at Market Bosworth Grammar School in Leicestershire. He hated the job and particularly the chief trustee who controlled the school, and he quit during the summer. In the autumn he visited his old friend Hector in Birmingham and lived there for over a year, still trying to settle his mind and his life. By 1734 he managed to complete a translation of Father Jeronymo Lobo's account of Abyssinia, Johnson's first published book (1735). He had not forgotten poetry. Returning to Lichfield, he published proposals for a subscription edition of the Latin poems of the fifteenth-century writer Politian, with a history of Latin poetry from the age of Petrarch to Politian. Like most of his endeavors during this bleak period, the project failed.

In July 1735 Johnson married Elizabeth Jervis Porter, whom he referred to as "Tetty," a widow twenty years his senior. To this unusual marriage, which he always described as a love match, she brought a substantial amount of money, and with it Johnson began a small school at Edial. It opened in the fall with only three students, among them David Garrick, who was to become the greatest actor of the century. As the school rapidly declined, Johnson decided to try to earn money—and perhaps to make a name for himself—by writing a blank-verse tragedy, a historical drama in the vein that Addison's *Cato* (1713) had popularized. Usually a rapid writer, this time

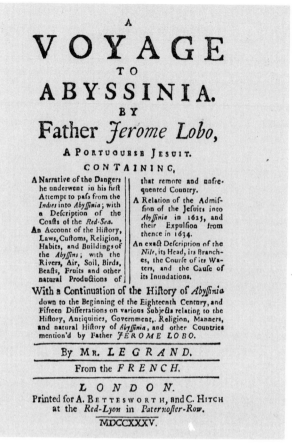

Title page for the anonymous translation that became Johnson's first published book

he was unable to proceed with any celerity on his ill-fated play *Irene* (not published until 1749). He had completed only half of it when the school failed. With Tetty's resources now steadily diminishing, he decided to go to London, where he hoped to find work writing for journals and translating and to complete and sell *Irene*. Tetty stayed behind. On 2 March 1737 Johnson and young Garrick set out for London, sharing a single horse between them. In London and then in Greenwich, Johnson continued to work on *Irene*, but in the summer he returned to Lichfield, and after three months there he finally finished the drama. No evidence exists to indicate that any other work cost Johnson as much effort as *Irene*. The manuscript of his first draft is extant, and it shows his extensive research, his careful organization, and his detailed descriptions of scenes and characters.

Johnson and Tetty moved back to London in October, and Johnson sought unsuccessfully to get *Irene* produced. Meanwhile he began to do some work for Edward Cave on the *Gentleman's Magazine*. In March 1738 his first contribution to it appeared, an elegant and dignified Latin poem, "To Sylvanus Urban" (Cave's editorial pseudonym), which defended Cave against current attacks by rival booksellers. Other poems that year included light complimentary verses to Elizabeth Carter and Lady Firebrace, and Latin and Greek epigrams to Carter, Richard Savage, and Thomas Birch.

As he worked for Cave, Johnson also sought something to write on his own that might sell. A natural choice was the "imitation," a popular contemporary poetic form. Dryden in his *Preface to Ovid's Epistles* (1680) had described the imitation as a kind of translation, "where the translator (if now he has not lost that name) assumes the liberty not only to vary from the words and sense, but to forsake them both as he sees occasion; and taking only some general hints from the original, to run division on the groundwork, as he pleases." Johnson himself would later define it in the *Life of Pope* (volume 7 of *Prefaces, Biographical and Critical*, 1779-1781) as "a kind of middle composition between translation and original design, which pleases when the thoughts are unexpectedly applicable and the parallels lucky." Pope, whose *Imitations of Horace* had been appearing during the 1730s, was the acknowledged master of the mode, which had been developed extensively during the Restoration by such poets as Abraham Cowley, John Wilmot, Earl of Rochester, and John Oldham and had also been employed by Swift. Johnson turned to the Latin poet Juvenal and imitated his *Satura III* on urban life in *London*. Late in March 1738 he sent a copy of the poem to Cave, with a letter in which he claimed to be negotiating for a needy friend who had actually composed the poem. He even offered to alter any parts of it that Cave disliked. Cave printed *London* and arranged for Robert Dodsley, who was well known for his abilities to promote poetry, to publish it. From Dodsley, Johnson received ten guineas for the copyright, because, as he explained to Boswell years later, the minor poet Paul Whitehead had recently gotten ten guineas for one of his pieces, and he would not settle for less than Whitehead had earned. *London* was published on 13 May 1738.

In Juvenal's third satire his friend Umbricius pauses at the archway of the Porta Capena to deliver a diatribe against city life as he leaves Rome forever for deserted Cumae. Johnson's Thales in *London* similarly rails as he waits on the banks of the Thames at Greenwich to depart for Wales. (Much ink has been spilled

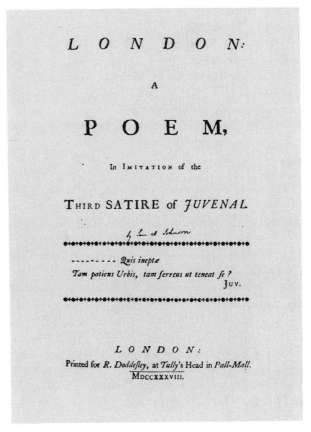

Title page for Johnson's first major published poem, for which bookseller Robert Dodsley paid him ten guineas

over whether or not Thales is modeled on Johnson's friend Savage, but the best evidence suggests that Johnson had not met Savage at the time he wrote the poem.) Following the example of Pope and others, Johnson insisted that the relevant passages from Juvenal's satire be published with his own poem at the bottom of the pages, because he believed that part of any beauty that *London* possessed consisted in adapting Juvenal's sentiments to contemporary topics. Thus Juvenal's work provides a natural point of departure for evaluating Johnson's achievement.

Between an introduction and conclusion, Juvenal's original satire is broken into two major sections. The first focuses primarily on the difficulties faced by an honest man trying to make a living in the city, while the second part considers the innumerable dangers of urban life (falling buildings, fires, crowds, traffic, accidents, and crimes). Johnson in general follows Juvenal's structure, but as he reworks the subject, the sections he retains and those he alters reveal his own particular concerns.

Johnson when he wishes can capture Juvenal's meanings exactly. "SLOW RISES WORTH, BY POVERTY DEPREST" is a classic example, as he powerfully restates Juvenal's "haud facile emergunt quorum virtatibus obstat / Res angusta domi" (it is scarcely easy to rise in the world for those whose straitened domestic circumstances obstruct their abilities). Johnson can also use balance and antithesis in the couplet to juxtapose for satirical effect in a manner reminiscent of Pope; a fawning Frenchman, for example, will "Exalt each Trifle, ev'ry Vice adore, / Your Taste in Snuff, your Judgment in a Whore." But Johnson does not usually concentrate either on details or on close rendition of Juvenal, and because of his different satiric emphases, *London* becomes in important ways his own poem.

First of all Johnson's treatment of country life includes significant additions to Juvenal. Early in *London*, with no Juvenalian basis whatsoever, he adds two lines describing what Thales expects to find in the country: "Some pleasing Bank where verdant Osiers play, / Some peaceful Vale with Nature's Paintings gay." This couplet sets the tone for Johnson's subsequent rural depictions. In *Satura III* Juvenal lauds the country not for its beauty or the ease of life there, but as the only possible alternative to the city. Johnson, however, takes Juvenal's simple descriptions of country life and produces a combination of eighteenth-century garden (with pruned walks, supported flowers, directed rivulets, and twined bowers) and Miltonic Paradise (including nature's music, healthy breezes, security, and morning work and evening strolls). Such idealization of the country is totally incongruous with Johnson's views; he loved the bustling life of London and, like George Crabbe, always emphasized that human unhappiness emanates from the same causes in both the city and the country. His treatment of the country in *London* reflects prevailing poetic convention rather than conviction; his predominantly conventional additions to Juvenal in this area highlight the extent to which *London* is very much the work of a young poet eager to please, who played to contemporary tastes accordingly.

If Johnson's additions to Juvenal in the rural depictions are significant, his omissions in portraying the wretched life of the urban poor are even more telling. "SLOW RISES WORTH," justly the best-known line in the poem, has had impact enough to obscure the fact that Johnson's general treatment of poverty in *London* is cursory, particularly when compared to Juvenal's. He leaves

out fully half of Juvenal's section on the general helplessness of the poor in making a living in the city. In surveying urban vexations, he omits Juvenal's sections on crowds, traffic, accidents, and thefts, leaves out the falling buildings (although collapsing older houses were a frequent hazard in eighteenth-century London), and condenses the fight scene. In the process he loses some of Juvenal's most telling episodes, for urban life is, of course, made intolerable not so much by huge disasters as by incessant small annoyances. The noise, the loss of sleep, and the difficulties in getting from one place to another disappear in Johnson's version because he is not interested in the small personal perils of city life.

No one, however, could accuse Johnson of not caring deeply about the conditions of the urban poor. He told Boswell that the true test of civilization was a decent provision for the poor, and he personally offered such provision to unfortunates whenever he could. Although his passages on the poor in *London* are usually competent and occasionally eloquent, he drastically condensed Juvenal's treatment because he wanted to focus his own poem on political rather than personal conditions.

The accuracy of Boswell's description of *London* as "impregnated with the fire of opposition" is clear from the many political references that Johnson adds to Juvenal. He expands Juvenal's introductory section to include nostalgic references to the political and commercial glories of the Elizabethan age and several times in the poem opposes Spanish power. In elaborating Juvenal's passage on crimes and the jail, he manages to attack Walpole's misuses of special juries and secret-service funds, the House of Commons, and the king himself. Johnson never forgets politics in *London*, even when he is at his most conventional. For example, the lines on the country include references to the seat of a "hireling Senator" and the confections of a "venal Lord."

Johnson's emphasis on politics in *London* was undoubtedly due to factors in the contemporary political scene as well as his personal life at the time. The year 1738 was one of widespread popular unrest, and the nation, already in ferment over the court and Walpole's ministry, was outraged over alleged Spanish oppression of British commerce. In the midst of the uproar Johnson, a newcomer to London, unsure of himself and his ability to achieve success anywhere, associated with various acquaintances who opposed the

Two of Johnson's residences in London: Inner Temple Lane, his home in the early 1860s; and Bolt Court, Fleet Street, where he lived from 1776 until his death

government as he eked out the barest of livings in the great capital. Young and frustrated, he was understandably eager enough to view the current political situation as the direct cause of adverse personal as well as national conditions. During his first few years in the city he produced the most violent political writings of his life. The year after *London*, he published *Marmor Norfolciense* (1739), a feigned prophetical inscription in rhymed Latin verse with a translation and long commentary attacking Walpole. This satire was so virulent that, according to Johnson's early biographer James Harrison, even a government inured to invective issued a warrant for his arrest.

London in many places shows Johnson's technical proficiency in employing the heroic couplet. It is an exuberant poem, full of life and high spirits. *London* does not finally bring out all of Johnson's powers, because the satire is weakened in places by the false stances into which he is forced by convention and political themes. But it is an impressive performance, and certain passages, such as the description of the dangers of friendship with great men, reflect Johnson's full poetic abilities. The final lines of this passage show Johnson rising above the specific poetic situation to present the overview of the moralist. The movement of satire into reflection here, but-

A London Chop House, a 1781 engraving by H. Burnbury. Boswell and Johnson are seated at the table on the right.

tressed by the enlargement and extension of the particular into the general, is characteristic of Johnson at his best. Indeed, these movements from satire to meditation and from the particular to the general combine a decade later with a more mature view, sometimes savage about life itself but always sympathetic to the struggles of suffering individuals, to produce *The Vanity of Human Wishes* (1749), Johnson's second Juvenalian imitation.

Pope's *One Thousand Seven Hundred and Thirty Eight*, another of his Horatian imitations, was published–also by Dodsley–a few days after *London*, and the two poems were favorably compared. Boswell reports that Pope himself responded generously to his putative rival; he asked Jonathan Richardson to try to discover who the new author was, and when told that he was an obscure man named Johnson, Pope commented that he would not be obscure for long. The popular success of the poem seemed to support Pope's prediction. Within a week a second edi-

tion was required, a third came out later that year, and a fourth in the next year. It was reprinted at least twenty-three times in Johnson's lifetime. However, the political topicality and the poetic conventionality that contributed so much to the contemporary success of *London* considerably lessened its later appeal. Its status as a major Johnsonian poem has always been secure and its substantial poetic power recognized. But it has also suffered from inevitable comparisons with *The Vanity of Human Wishes*. Modern readers have uniformly preferred the second poem for its moral elevation, its more condensed expression, and its treatment of more characteristic Johnsonian themes and ideas. Many of these elements are present in *London*, but to a lesser degree.

During this early period in London it was increasingly clear that Johnson's marriage was in trouble. Bruised by this second marriage to which she had brought so much and which had so reduced her circumstances, Tetty was retreating steadily from Johnson and also from life in general. The two gradually began to live apart much of the time, as Tetty steadily deteriorated, ultimately taking refuge in alcohol and opium and in her final years seldom leaving her bed. Johnson did all that he could to support her, writing furiously and stinting himself to provide for his wife. He sometimes walked the streets all night because he lacked money for even the cheapest lodging. For the next fifteen or twenty years he was a journalist and a hack writer of incredible productivity and variety. He became a trusted assistant to Cave on the *Gentleman's Magazine* from 1738 until the mid 1740s, writing many reviews, translations, and articles, including a long series of parliamentary debates from 1741 until 1744. He helped to catalog the massive Harleian Library and worked on the eight volumes of *The Harleian Miscellany* (1744-1746). In addition to a series of short biographies for Cave, he contributed biographical entries to *A Medicinal Dictionary* (1743-1745) by his friend Dr. Robert James, for whom he had composed the *Proposals* for the work (1741). His own *Account of the Life of Mr. Richard Savage*, a short masterpiece of biography, appeared in 1744. In 1745 he published a proposal for a new edition of Shakespeare, composing *Miscellaneous Observations on the Tragedy of Macbeth* to illustrate his critical approach. This project did not materialize, but a greater one did. The next year he signed a contract with a group of publishers to produce an English dictionary, on which he labored for the next seven years in the garret of the house he rented at 17 Gough Square. Even as he worked on it, however, he always continued with many other miscellaneous writing projects.

During these years Johnson wrote substantially more prose than poetry, but he did publish various minor poems in the *Gentleman's Magazine*. An epitaph on the musician Claudy Phillips, composed almost extemporaneously and years later set to music, appeared there in September 1740. He revised several of his early poems (the *Integer Vitae* ode, "The Young Author," the "Ode to Friendship," and "To Laura") and published them in the magazine in July 1743, along with a Latin translation, described as "the casual amusement of half an hour," of Pope's verses on his grotto. When Cave needed a revision of Geoffrey Walmesley's Latin translation of John Byrom's "Colin and Phebe" in February 1745, Johnson and Stephen Barrett alternated distiches, rapidly passing a sheet of paper between them "like a shuttlecock" across the table. In 1747, when the editor of the poetry section of the magazine was

away and the copy available for the May issue was insufficient, Johnson contributed some half-dozen poems. Most were light occasional pieces written years before, including "The Winter's Walk," "An Ode" on the spring, and several complimentary poems to ladies, but a more substantial English poem loosely based on the Latin epigraph of Sir Thomas Hanmer also appeared.

In the same year Johnson also supplied a prologue for the celebration of the reopening of the Drury Lane Theatre under his friend Garrick's management. He had already helped Garrick out by writing a preface for his first play, *Lethe*, for a benefit performance for Henry Gifford in 1740. The *Prologue Spoken at the Opening of the Theatre in Drury-Lane* was a much more considerable piece. Johnson later said that the whole poem was composed before he put a line on paper and that he subsequently changed only one word in it, making that alteration solely because of Garrick's remonstrances. The Drury Lane prologue offers an overview of the history of English drama, tracing it from "immortal" Shakespeare's "pow'rful Strokes" through Ben Jonson's "studious Patience" and "laborious Art" and the "Intrigue" and "Obscenity" of Restoration wits to the playwrights of his own age. After censuring contemporary tragedy and the taste for pantomimes and farces, he speculates pessimistically on the future of the stage, closing by reminding the audience that "The Stage but echoes back the publick Voice" and urging them to "bid the Reign commence / Of rescu'd Nature, and reviving Sense". The prologue is a fine poem that reflects premises Johnson would later employ in his dramatic criticism, particularly in his edition of Shakespeare. When published a few weeks after the opening, it did not bear Johnson's name, and the public was left to assume that Garrick was the author.

In each of the next three decades Johnson wrote one prologue, and they can be considered as a group, despite their chronological dispersion. In 1750 Johnson learned that John Milton's only surviving granddaughter, Elizabeth Foster, was living in poverty, and he convinced Garrick to put on a benefit performance of *Comus* (1637) to aid her. The new prologue Johnson composed lauds "mighty" Milton's achievement and the fame he has garnered, but characteristically Johnson also praises "his Offspring" Mrs. Foster for "the mild Merits of domestic Life" and "humble Virtue's native Charms." Late in 1767 he wrote a prologue that he had promised long before to Oli-

Engravings from Thomas Rowlandson's Picturesque Beauties of Boswell *(1786) depicting Johnson's biographer as "The Journalist" and with Johnson on the High Street in Edinburgh*

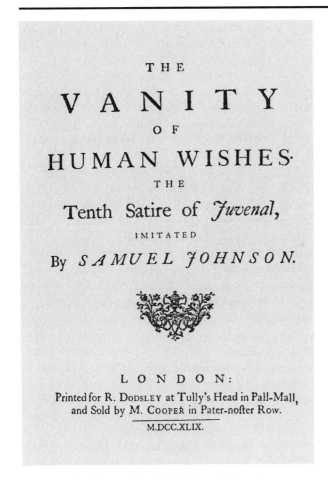

THE

VANITY

OF

HUMAN WISHES·

THE

Tenth Satire of *Juvenal*,

IMITATED

By *SAMUEL JOHNSON.*

LONDON:

Printed for R. DODSLEY at Tully's Head in Pall-Mall,
and Sold by M. COOPER in Pater-noſter Row.

M.DCC.XLIX.

*Title page for the poem in which Johnson follows the structure
of Juvenal's satire but puts more emphasis on spiritual and
psychological concerns*

ver Goldsmith for his comedy, *The Good Natur'd
Man* (1768). With a parliamentary election approaching, Johnson, in a rather gloomy piece
that, unsurprisingly, was not very popular, compared the pressures on the playwright and the politician to please the rabble. Thomas Harris, the
manager of Covent Garden, solicited Johnson's
last prologue in 1777 for a performance of
Hugh Kelly's *A Word to the Wise* (1770) to benefit
the author's widow and children. When first produced in 1770 the play had been disrupted by
Kelly's political enemies, and Johnson's conciliatory and well-received prologue asked the audience to "Let no resentful petulance invade / Th'
oblivious grave's inviolable shade." All Johnson's
prologues resulted from the generosity to friends
and to those in need so characteristic of him
throughout his life. All of them are competent examples of the genre, while the poem for the opening of the Drury Lane Theatre, and to a lesser
extent the prologue for *Comus*, rise to real excellence. The Drury Lane prologue has long re-

mained one of Johnson's best-known poems.

In the fall of 1748 Johnson had returned to
Juvenal, and in *The Vanity of Human Wishes*, an imitation of Juvenal's tenth satire, he wrote his greatest poem. He later said that he wrote the first seventy lines of it in one morning, while visiting
Tetty at Hampstead. Like the Drury Lane prologue, the entire section was composed in his
head before he put a line of it on paper. He also
mentioned to Boswell in another connection that
he wrote a hundred lines of the poem in one
day. A receipt in Johnson's handwriting dated 25
November 1748 assigns the copyright of *The Vanity of Human Wishes* to Robert Dodsley for fifteen
guineas, and it was published on 9 January 1749.
Significantly, it was the first of Johnson's works
in which his name appeared on the title page.

Satura X is Juvenal's greatest satire, and in
The Vanity of Human Wishes Johnson produced a
poem of equal worth. He directly shares some of
Juvenal's concerns, for both use the theme of the
folly of human desires and petitions for wealth,
power, long life, and beauty, and early in each
poem both emphasize the importance of using reason to guide one's choices. As they focus on various wishes, each poet introduces the theme of
the liabilities inherent in the process of desiring.
In both *Satura X* and *The Vanity of Human Wishes*
fulfillment of desire is followed by envy from others and ultimately by personal dissatisfaction with
the gain. Although inherent in Juvenal, this latter theme of the insatiability of the human imagination is emphasized much more in Johnson,
who is concerned with general psychological factors, with the human mind and heart, while Juvenal is more interested in specific events and their
influences on individuals. Johnson amplifies Juvenal's initial four-and-a-half lines to eleven lines,
to present through images of moving and crowding the effect and extent of the emotions produced by the imagination, and he also specifically
names some of these emotions. In considering
each of these desires later in his poem he explores the additional theme of their treachery
and their betrayal of the human being's best interests.

In *The Vanity of Human Wishes* Johnson followed Juvenal's basic structure, as he had in *London*, altering it to emphasize the concerns of his
own poem. Juvenal's *Satura X* has 365 lines; that
Johnson managed to imitate it in only 368 lines
suggests his massive and masterly condensation,
particularly since couplet verse often requires expansion and amplification. Both poems contain

seven sections: an introduction and a conclusion enclose five sections on politics, eloquence or learning, war, long life, and beauty. The relative importance of the topics in each poem is clear from the amount of attention devoted to them by the two poets.

Juvenal throughout *Satura X* emphasizes the physical, the sensuous, and the licentious, while Johnson in *The Vanity of Human Wishes* is most concerned with the spiritual and the psychological. He is not particularly interested in the sins of the flesh. In the section on old age, for example, Juvenal dwells at length on physical decrepitude, while Johnson refers only briefly to such infirmities and presents the avarice of an old man, a vice not mentioned by Juvenal. Significant differences also appear in the passages on beauty in the two poems. Juvenal presents a long section on masculine beauty, centered on graphic details of scandalous individual misconduct, which Johnson omits completely, preferring to focus on more general human problems. On the other hand, in the passages on female pulchritude Juvenal contents himself with brief references to the dangers that beset beautiful women, while Johnson traces the complete moral disintegration of a beautiful young woman by using abstract terms (for example, "The Guardians yield, by Force superior ply'd; / By Int'rest, Prudence; and by Flatt'ry, Pride"). The whole passage exemplifies Johnson's careful development of the theme of the treachery of human desires, which lead people astray while they remain until the end ignorant of their gradual destruction.

Juvenal's orator becomes in *The Vanity of Human Wishes* Johnson's scholar, in part for autobiographical reasons. At some point near the time he left Oxford, Johnson had written a poem entitled "The Young Author," which in revised form he had published in the *Gentleman's Magazine* in 1743. This poem in many ways anticipates the mature treatment of the quest for scholarly renown in *The Vanity of Human Wishes*. Hester Thrale (later Piozzi) wrote that years later, when reading *The Vanity of Human Wishes* to the family and a friend at Streatham, Johnson burst into tears while reading the section on the scholar. Events in his life also dictated one famous emendation in the passage. Johnson had originally listed the problems besetting the scholarly life as "Toil, Envy, Want, the Garret, and the Jail." Boswell indicates that after experiencing difficulties with Lord Chesterfield over his putative patronage of Johnson's *Dictionary*, Johnson in his 1755 revision

of the poem (in Robert Dodsley's *Collection of Poems by Several Hands*, volume 4) changed "the Garret" to "the Patron."

In the last passage of his poem Johnson amplifies Juvenal's succinctly abrupt "nil ergo optabunt homines?" (Is there nothing, therefore, that people should pray for?) to six lines of deeply moving rhetorical questions about human fate. This amplification again shows the plethora of emotions produced by the human imagination, and in addition emphasizes another theme of the poem, the overwhelming human desire to be free from the emotions that simultaneously bind and blind. Juvenal becomes flippant, but Johnson turns fervently serious when each advises turning to prayer. Juvenal's Stoicism and Johnson's Christianity dominate the endings of their respective poems. Both urge leaving individual destiny to heaven, and both assert that higher powers know what is best for human beings. Both poets urge people to pray for endurance, for acceptance of death, and for a healthy mind. (Johnson omits the last half of Juvenal's famous "mens sana in corpore sano" [a sound mind in a sound body], in part because he knew from personal experience that humans can endure despite the most debilitating physical ailments.) But Juvenal's Stoicism prompts him to say that humans themselves can do all that is necessary to have a tranquil life–"monstro quod ipse tibi possis dare" (I am pointing out what you are able to do for yourself)–while Johnson emphasizes the Christian concept of dependence on God: "celestial Wisdom calms the Mind, / And makes the Happiness she does not find." Johnson's closing lines emphasize that the human desire to free the self from the many treacherous emotions generated by the imagination can be fulfilled only by going beyond the self and worldly concerns and by relying on divine omniscience in order to compensate for the limitations in human knowledge that lead to folly.

Thus *The Vanity of Human Wishes* includes biblical as well as classical overtones. As its title suggests, it has close affinities with the Book of Ecclesiastes and shares many of its themes. The insufficiency of earthly goods and values and the concomitant need for religious faith as the only bulwark are traditional arguments in Christian apologetics from Augustine on, including Jeremy Taylor and the Renaissance divines whose works Johnson knew so well, and also William Law, whose *Serious Call to a Devout and Holy Life* so deeply influenced the young Johnson.

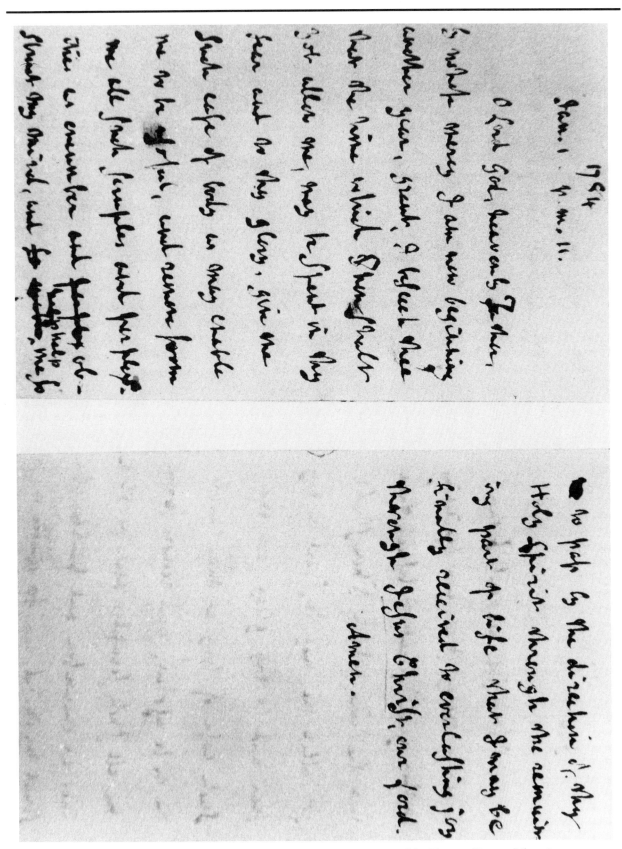

Manuscript for one of Johnson's prayers (MA 206; by permission of the Pierpont Morgan Library)

Juvenal in his poetry assumes a dual persona. On the one hand he writes as a stern moralist castigating wrongdoing, but he also writes as a rhetorician and particularly as a wit, delighting in invective, exaggeration, and filth. Johnson recognized these two sides when he wrote in the *Life of Dryden* (volume 1 of *Prefaces, Biographical and Critical*) that Juvenal was "a mixture of gaiety and stateliness, of pointed sentences [epigrams], and declamatory grandeur." Johnson in his own imitation chose to reproduce mainly Juvenal's "stateliness" and "declamatory grandeur." Johnson's slow and dignified couplets abound in vivid personified abstractions that with characteristic compression render an impression of philosophic generality. *The Vanity of Human Wishes* is marked by a moral elevation and seriousness that *Satura X* does not, on the whole, share. Juvenal delights in the narrowly personal; for example, hilarious conversations following Sejanus's fall vividly depict personal reactions. Johnson, in contrast, uses no dialogue in his poem, for he is concerned with general human feelings on a broader scale. He does, of course, use individual men and women as examples, and his replacement of Juvenal's classical personalities with more contemporary figures (Charles XII for Hannibal, for instance, and Marlborough and Swift for Marius, Pompey, and the Catilinian conspirators) is masterfully done. However, Johnson does not name individuals nearly as often as Juvenal does, and in many sections, such as the early stanzas on wealth, Johnson deals in generalities while Juvenal freely intersperses specific names.

The moral elevation and large vision so characteristic of *The Vanity of Human Wishes* are one reflection of the ways that Johnson moves from *Satura X* as a base to take his own poem beyond satire. Johnson's anger, his aggressiveness, and his capacity for savage and brutal wit made him eminently suited for writing satire, but his satiric urges were indulged more in his conversation than in his writings. Mrs. Thrale wrote that Johnson did not "encourage general satire," and that he had an "aversion" to it—an aversion that accounts in part for his unfairness to Swift in the *Lives of the Poets (Prefaces, Biographical and Critical)*. Johnson's personal struggles to control his aggressive tendencies, to maintain good humor, and to be good-natured made him leery of releasing a satiric urge that might be so strong that it could only be destructive rather than constructive. Moreover, because of his recognition of his own pride, fears, vanity, and anxieties, he felt a sympathy

with others that prevented him from attacking them too harshly. His keen understanding of his own shortcomings led him to the kind of sense of participation that makes strong, vicious satire impossible.

Johnson was finally more comfortable as a moralist than as a satirist. Bate has called Johnson's characteristic procedure in many of his great writings "satire *manqué*," or "satire foiled," a process in which satiric potential dissipates through understanding and compassion. Bate describes it as "a drama of thought and expression always moving from the reductive to explanation and finally to something close to apology." Johnson's tendency to employ satire manqué is shown at some points in *London*, but in that poem his youthful exuberance and self-consciousness, along with the political focus and obeisance to contemporary poetic practices, led him to a greater proportion of actual satire. The fact that *The Vanity of Human Wishes* is much more satire manqué than satire accounts for a great deal of its power.

Juvenal's professed aim in his satires was to shame the men of his time out of the vices they practiced in their private lives, but Johnson's largeness of thought and feeling led him far beyond Juvenal's tactics and topics. In *The Vanity of Human Wishes* Johnson is concerned with a human problem more pervasive, more insidious, and more important than deliberate wrongdoing, for he focuses finally on the errors that people are unwittingly led to commit. Intentional vice chosen for pleasure can be unmercifully castigated, but the ignorance that leads people to pursue unworthy ends and thus lose their potential as human beings cannot be combated effectively by mere invective. To meet the challenge of this ignorance Johnson uses the satirical mode but elevates it above the petty limitations of bitter humor, vile invective, and grim epigram aimed at individuals in order to encompass humanity as a whole with sympathy and a sense of participation so that he can offer his corrective vision. The affinities of the poem with tragedy are in certain ways stronger than its ties to satire.

Bate has also pointed out that *The Vanity of Human Wishes* inaugurates a brilliant decade of moral writing for Johnson and has noted that these writings could be described as "an extended prose application" of the poem. In his periodical essays—in the *Rambler* (1750-1752), the *Adventurer* (1753-1754), and the *Idler* (1758-1760, collected in 1761)—he deals collectively and indi-

The engraving by James Heath, based on a 1756 portrait by Reynolds, that served as the frontispiece for Boswell's biography of Johnson

vidually with the same clutter of human emotions and their treachery that he delineates in the poem. *Rasselas (The Prince of Abissinia*, 1759) also treats similar themes in detail. *The Vanity of Human Wishes* stands on its own as a major poem and can also function as an excellent introduction to these writings. But more than this, in the context of Johnson's work as a whole, this poem, as a condensed presentation of the themes that Johnson explores in all of his writings, is a good introduction to the dominant concepts of Johnson's thought as a moralist and a humanist.

Commenting that *The Vanity of Human Wishes* "has less of common life, but more of a philosophical dignity" than *London*, Boswell noted that more readers would be delighted with the "'pointed spirit'" of the latter than with the "profound reflection" of the former. He exactly reflected the general eighteenth-century reaction to the poem. Johnson's contemporaries admired his second Juvenalian imitation, but their response to it was muted. As Boswell reports, Garrick jokingly remarked that "When Johnson lived much with the Herveys, and saw a good deal of

what was passing in life, he wrote his 'London,' which is lively and easy. When he became more retired, he gave us his 'Vanity of Human Wishes,' which is as hard as Greek. Had he gone on to imitate another satire, it would have been hard as Hebrew." Modern critics who compare the two poems have drawn exactly the opposite conclusion, universally praising *The Vanity of Human Wishes* as Johnson's greatest poem.

As for Garrick's putative third satire that would have been "hard as Hebrew," Johnson never wrote poems of this sort again. Once when Boswell regretted that Johnson had not imitated more of Juvenal's satires, Johnson responded that "he probably should give more, for he had them all in his head." Boswell took the reply to mean that "he had the originals and correspondent allusions floating in his mind, which he could, when he pleased, embody and render permanent without much labour." (Characteristically, Johnson added that some of Juvenal's satires were "too gross for imitation.") In the years to come he continued to write some poetry, and

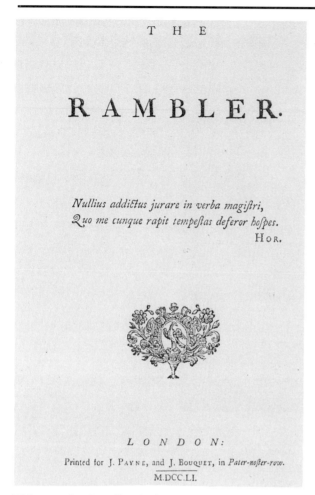

THE

RAMBLER.

Nullius addictus jurare in verba magistri,
Quo me cunque rapit tempestas deferor hospes.
HOR.

LONDON:

Printed for J. PAYNE, and J. BOUQUET, in *Pater-noster-row.*
M.DCC.LI.

*Title page for the collected edition of the periodical Johnson
wrote singlehandedly twice a week from 1750 to 1752*

he composed many jeux d'esprit with friends, but his major works would be in prose.

In 1749 Garrick as manager of the Drury Lane Theatre was able to have Johnson's *Irene* produced at last. He assembled a strong cast, including himself, prepared magnificent scenery and costumes, and fought fiercely with Johnson for alterations to make the play more suitable for actual performance. Though Johnson complained that Garrick "wants me to make Mahomet run mad, that he may have an opportunity of tossing his hands and kicking his heels," he finally relented, also allowing Garrick to retitle it *Mahomet and Irene*. Johnson was in the audience in a scarlet waistcoat with gold lace when the curtains rose on the evening of 6 February 1749.

Johnson based *Irene* on a story in Richard Knolles's *The Generall Historie of the Turkes* (1603), substantially altering Knolles's account to create a drama of temptation that would inculcate moral truths. In Johnson's version, after the fall of Con-

stantinople to the Turks in 1453, the sultan Mahomet falls passionately in love with the beautiful Greek Irene, a Christian captive. He wants her to be his queen but demands that she first renounce her religion for his. Urged to Christian fidelity by the virtuous Aspasia, Irene wavers, while a mutiny is developing among Mahomet's officers and certain Greeks. Irene finally chooses earthly rewards over spiritual ones, but after wavering yet again she is killed when slander leads Mahomet to believe her treacherous.

Though not without suspense and psychological complexity, *Irene* remains static, stiff, and stylized like most of its precursors in the genre. Deliberately indistinct in time and place, its effects are also remote, for Johnson tends to describe emotions rather than to depict them through the characters' actions. But it is above all in the poetry, in particular in its versification, that *Irene* is flawed. Johnson's blank verse functions like unrhymed couplets, and despite its elevated and often eloquent style, the monotonous regularity of its meter detracts from the sense. The results of his efforts with *Irene* undoubtedly contributed to Johnson's later critical view that blank verse was best avoided, except by exceptional talents such as Milton.

Garrick managed nine performances of *Irene*, so that Johnson could three times receive the third-night profits designated for authors. The reception was never enthusiastic, although audience response improved after the first night, when Garrick's unfortunate decision to have Irene strangled onstage created so much uproar that her death subsequently had to be moved offstage, as Johnson had originally intended. Johnson ultimately made almost three hundred pounds from *Irene*, including his profits from the production and publication of the play. No one revived the play during Johnson's lifetime, and it apparently has not been produced since. Years later, according to Boswell, when informed that someone named Pot had called *Irene* "the finest tragedy of modern times," Johnson responded: "If Pot says so, Pot lies." At another time, while the play was being read aloud by friends, he left the room and, when asked why, responded simply: "I thought it had been better." Modern critics and readers have uniformly agreed with his assessments, largely because of the difficulties in the blank verse and problems inherent in the genre. *Irene* remains the least read of Johnson's major works.

A meeting of The Club at Joshua Reynolds's house, showing (left to right) Boswell, Johnson, Reynolds, David Garrick, Edmund Burke, Pasquale Paoli, Charles Burney, Thomas Warton, and Oliver Goldsmith (engraving by William Walker after a painting by James Doyle)

Boswell, Goldsmith, and Johnson at the Mitre Tavern in London (engraving by R. B. Parkes after a painting by Eyre Crowe)

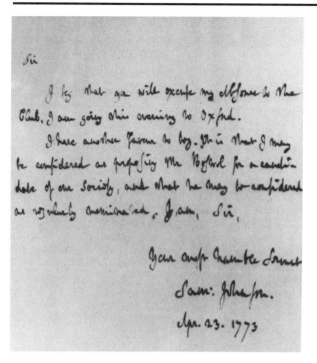

Letter from Johnson to Goldsmith, asking him to accept Boswell as a member of The Club (by permission of the trustees of Dr. Johnson's House, Gough Square)

Many find the essence of Johnson in the series of moral writings he composed during his forties, stretching from *The Vanity of Human Wishes*, through the essays he wrote for three different periodicals, and ending with *Rasselas*. In these works Johnson's own experiences of suffering and endurance, his extensive knowledge of human nature, his psychological acumen, and his abiding honesty and sympathy coalesced to deal with life as it is in order to help his readers through it. A great literary figure, Johnson also was preeminently a moralist. From 1750 to 1752 every Tuesday and Saturday he wrote the *Rambler*, his own periodical series and his favorite of all his works. Originally the mottoes and quotations in each *Rambler* were untranslated, but when an Edinburgh edition appeared with translations, Johnson added them in his revised edition (1756). About 250 of these were in verse, of which Johnson himself produced over sixty, filling in the rest from friends and contemporaries, from Dryden's translations of Virgil and Juvenal, from Philip Francis's versions of Horace, and from other sources. Some of the translations were reprinted in the *Gentleman's Magazine* in October 1752. The selection ended with Johnson's own translations of verses from Boethius and Lucanus, the mottoes before *Rambler*s 7 and 12, and with a wish that Johnson "would oblige the

world with more of his poetical compositions." But he seems to have been writing little poetry at that time, although in April of the same year he had revised his college translation of *The Messiah* before it was published in the *Gentleman's Magazine* with Pope's poem in parallel columns.

A year after completing the *Rambler*, Johnson contributed essays to another periodical, John Hawkesworth's *Adventurer*. He is believed to have been responsible for selecting various mottoes and also for translating them and other quotations as he did in the *Rambler*. The *Idler*, Johnson's final series of essays, was contributed to a weekly newspaper (the *Universal Chronicle*) and was written in an easier style than his earlier pieces, as Johnson tried consciously to replicate the lighter tone of Addison and Steele. Johnson undertook the *Rambler* and his contributions to the *Adventurer* in part to get relief from his drudgery on the dictionary, while the *Idler* provided breaks from his work on Shakespeare. He also wrote the essays to earn money. But in addition, in all three series he was concerned with making a serious moral impact.

The 1750s were years of both triumph and pain for Johnson. In 1752 Tetty died, and Johnson was devastated. For many years at regular intervals he inserted prayers for her in his diaries. In 1755 Oxford awarded him an M.A. to honor him for the *Dictionary of the English Language*. This monumental work appeared later that year, and as its preface emphasizes, the achievement was uniquely Johnson's own: "the English Dictionary was written with little assistance of the learned, and without any patronage of the great; not in the soft obscurities of retirement, or under the shelter of academick bowers, but amidst inconvenience and distraction, in sickness and in sorrow." The dictionary established Johnson's reputation, but he still lacked financial security. In the year after it was published he was arrested for debt, extricating himself with a loan from Samuel Richardson. To earn money he continued to write. For over a year he was involved in editing and writing articles and reviews for a new periodical, the *Literary Magazine*, and he also composed many prefaces and dedications for his friends' works as favors. Like Johnson's hack writing in the 1740s, the quality of these ephemeral writings was unusually high, reflecting an extraordinary range of knowledge.

In 1756, ten years after he had first proposed to edit Shakespeare, he signed a contract with the publisher Jacob Tonson to prepare an

Mrs. Hester Thrale as she looked when Johnson met her in 1765 (painting by Richard Cosway; Hyde Collection; by permission of the Viscountess Eccles)

edition in eighteen months. But the project stretched on, and in 1758 Johnson was once more arrested for debt, saved this time by Tonson. Early the next year he learned that his mother was seriously ill, and to get money to visit her and also to help with her medical bills, he composed *Rasselas* in the evenings of one week. The last of his great moral writings of the 1750s, this generic amalgam of story, novel, and extended essay converts the popular form of the oriental tale into a serious didactic and philosophical vehicle. Johnson's relationship with his mother had always been a troubled one, for he had never gone to see her in the two decades after he left Lichfield. She died before he could leave London.

In 1762 the government awarded Johnson a pension of three hundred pounds a year for his services to literature. The pension freed him from the endless hackwork on which he had been forced to labor for so long, giving him financial security at last. A year later he met Boswell for the first time, and in 1764 Johnson's famous club–known simply as "The Club"–had its initial

meeting. Originally proposed by Joshua Reynolds, The Club ultimately included the most distinguished and talented men of the period, among them Goldsmith, Garrick, Edmund Burke, Richard Brinsley Sheridan, Charles James Fox, Adam Smith, and Edward Gibbon. In 1765 Trinity College, Dublin, awarded Johnson an honorary LL.D.

After decades of hardship, life seemed finally to be offering Johnson stability and even some comfort. But the enormous effort and willpower that he had continuously expended to survive and excel had taken a fierce toll. In the early 1760s the same kind of depression and lassitude that had crippled him after leaving Oxford began to recur with increasing severity, and he found himself less and less capable of functioning. By 1764 he was dangerously near to another breakdown, and he would continue in this fragile state for the next few years. With massive effort he managed in 1765 to complete the edition of Shakespeare for which he had contracted with Tonson in 1756. The eighteen months stipulated in the contract, overly optimistic by any standards, had stretched to nine years. Despite his grim mental state, the superb preface he wrote for the edition was one of his greatest pieces of literary criticism. Moreover, by the time the work appeared in October 1765, he had already met the friends who would eventually enable him once again to pull himself together and continue.

On 9 January 1765 Johnson's friend Arthur Murphy introduced him to Henry and Hester Thrale. Thrale was a well-educated and fashionable man with a fortune from the family brewery; his wife was witty, charming, and intelligent. Johnson got along well with them, and they began to see him regularly. Mrs. Thrale was a woman of wide literary interests, who had been composing poems and translations since she was a young girl. Johnson, who was planning to translate Boethius's *Consolation of Philosophy* (circa A.D. 520), immediately involved her in the project. He assigned her to do an ode for each Thursday, when he and the Thrales met for dinner, and he also did some of the odes himself. Still others they worked on together. They stopped abruptly when Johnson discovered that a poor author was engaged in the same work, for he did not want to diminish the other translator's profits.

In 1766 Johnson asked Mrs. Thrale for verses he could insert to help fill up a volume he was preparing of the poems of Anna Williams. The blind Miss Williams, originally his wife's

Mezzotint of Johnson by James Watson based on a 1769 portrait by Reynolds showing Johnson's characteristic involuntary gesticulations

friend, was among the assorted inmates of Johnson's house, a group of living examples of Johnson's charity to the unfortunate. Since in both quantity and quality Miss Williams's verses were slight, Johnson revised them for publication and added some of his own lighter poems that might seem to be hers to her *Miscellanies*, which appeared on 1 April 1766. He told Boswell that in his revision of one of her poems ("On the Death of Stephen Grey") only two of her original lines remained, and he made substantial changes in others. Among the poems he contributed were his early friendship ode, the epitaphs on Philips and Hanmer, and several of his light complimentary verses to ladies. His poem "The Ant," based on Proverbs 6:6, opens the volume. Previously unpub-

lished, it was probably written soon after he completed his *Rambler* essays; an appendix to Wordsworth's preface to the *Lyrical Ballads* (1802) quotes it rather unfairly to illustrate "extravagant and absurd" features of poetic diction.

During the second year of their friendship with Johnson, the Thrales became increasingly concerned as they saw his condition worsening. When they dropped by to visit him one morning in June 1766 and found him in a terrible state, they promptly moved him to their beautiful country estate at Streatham to take care of him. In these luxurious surroundings Johnson began slowly to mend, and as he did so over this period, he gradually became an integral part of the Thrale household. The Thrales gave him his

Mrs. Thrale with her eldest daughter, Queeney (Hester Maria), whose birthday, falling one day before Johnson's, was celebrated with his at Streatham Park, the Thrales' house in Surrey (by permission of the Beaverbrook Art Gallery)

Engraving of Streatham Park

own rooms both at Streatham and in their city residence in Southwark by the brewery. For the next sixteen years Johnson generally spent more time with them than he did at his own house. Mrs. Thrale later wrote that she "in some measure, with Mr. Thrale's assistance, saved from distress at least, if not from worse, a mind great beyond the comprehension of common mortals." The only aspect that she perhaps overstates is her husband's contribution.

Mrs. Thrale looked after Johnson, keeping him company, listening to his problems, nursing his illnesses, sharing his confidences, and soothing his fears. The sympathy, understanding, and affection she so lavishly extended to him were thoroughly reciprocated. She had led a fairly restricted and isolated life since her marriage, and Johnson expanded the dimensions of her world, encouraging her intellectually and bringing his distinguished friends to Streatham. The two collaborated on everything from chemical experiments to charitable projects. Mrs. Thrale was the most conscientious of mothers, and Johnson became actively involved with the Thrale children, playing with them as well as educating them. The oldest daughter's birthday was the day before Johnson's, and each year the Thrales celebrated both with one big party. Very much a part of the family, he vacationed with the Thrales at Brighton and also traveled with them to Wales (1774) and to France (1775).

The direct result of such an environment was the return of Johnson's stability; important indirect results were various writing projects. Mrs. Thrale wrote that "To the assistance we gave him, the shelter our home afforded to his uneasy fancies, and to the pains we took to soothe or repress them, the world perhaps is indebted for the three political pamphlets, the new edition and correction of his Dictionary, and for the Poets' Lives, which he would scarce have lived, I think, and kept his faculties entire, to have written, had not incessant care been exerted at the time of his first coming to be our constant guest in the country; and several times after that." Henry Thrale was an active member of Parliament, and from the beginning of their friendship Johnson had composed election addresses for him. One of Johnson's political pieces, *The Patriot* (1774), was a short election pamphlet composed for Thrale in a day. In the early 1770s Johnson also wrote three other polemical pamphlets: *The False Alarm* (1770), defending John Wilkes's exclusion by the House of Commons; *Thoughts on*

the Late Transactions Respecting Falkland's Islands (1771), opposing war with Spain over the disputed territory; and *Taxation No Tyranny* (1775), answering resolutions of the American Continental Congress. Joseph (Giuseppe) Baretti, an Italian critic and friend of Johnson, then living in England and acting as tutor for the Thrales's children, later indicated that the Thrales urged Johnson to compose these pieces, and that the last two were written only because Baretti and Mrs. Thrale challenged Johnson by making wagers.

It was the prospect of his trip to Wales with the family that spurred Johnson to write his *Journey to the Western Islands of Scotland* (1775), his account of the rough and exhilarating three-month tour of the region he had taken with Boswell in 1773. Using the letters he had written on the trip to Mrs. Thrale to refresh his memory, he completed the travel book in twenty days in June 1774, although it was not published until the next January. But his most important production was the *Lives of the Poets*, which he began in 1777. When a group of London booksellers had decided to publish an elaborate edition of the works of the English poets since 1660, they asked Johnson to write brief prefatory biographies for each of the poets in the collection. In Johnson's hands this basically commercial project became a landmark in English literary criticism. Some of the pieces were brief, but the lives of the major poets were lengthy and detailed, with a biographical section, a short character sketch of the poet, and a critical evaluation of the works. The *Life of Pope* has always been considered the best, but each one of the prefaces contributes to the cumulative effect of the entire collection, which offers a richness of biographical and critical insight that gives an incomparable overview of Augustan literary culture. There could be no more fitting final achievement for one of the masters of that tradition.

Mrs. Thrale, the central figure in stabilizing Johnson's life during this period, also played a role in the story of his poetry from the time of their joint translations of Boethius. Since she loved poetry and wrote it herself, she was naturally interested in Johnson's. She stimulated his poetic abilities in many different ways. One night he accompanied her to an oratorio at the Covent Garden Theatre. Usually prone to loud talking during performances that in any case he was unable to hear well, to Mrs. Thrale's relief he was uncharacteristically quiet during that evening. She

Johnson at age sixty (etching by Mary Palgrave Turner based on a portrait by Ozias Humphry)

thought Johnson was for once listening to the music, but as soon as they got home he recited "In Theatro," a Latin poem he had composed during the oratorio. He then challenged her to translate it by breakfast the next morning.

His journey to Scotland with Boswell resulted in three other Latin poems: an ode on the Isle of Skye, verses on Inchkenneth, and an ode to Mrs. Thrale. The poem to "Thralia dulcis" (sweet [Mrs.] Thrale) depicts his thinking of her often while he is in a strange and remote land, wondering what she is doing, and hoping that she remembers him. The culminating image emphasizes his admiration of her: "meritoque blandum / Thraliae discant resonare nomen / Littora Sciae" (deservedly let the shores of Skye learn to reecho the charming name of [Mrs.] Thrale). Written on Skye on 6 September 1773, the ode was enclosed in a letter to Henry Thrale mailed from Inveraray on 23 October. Johnson refused to give Boswell a copy of it, but told him

that Mrs. Thrale could give him one if she wished.

With Mrs. Thrale, Johnson always felt free to indulge the playful side of his nature, and she especially brought out the talent that he had shown throughout his life in making impromptu verses. Mrs. Thrale recorded that even Baretti, to whom Johnson had written verses, admitted that Johnson could improvise poetry "as well as any Italian of us all if he pleases," and she agreed that he possessed an "almost Tuscan power of improvisation." On his trip to France with the Thrales he made humorous French distiches on towns they visited. On the morning of Mrs. Thrale's thirty-fifth birthday, she went into his room and complained that no one sent her verses any longer because she was thirty-five, although Swift's Stella had received them until the age of forty-six. On the spot Johnson improvised and recited a poem with "Thirty-five" as the rhyming word in alternate lines, ending with "And those who wisely wish to wive, / Must look at Thrale at Thirtyfive." As Mrs. Thrale was writing the verses down, Johnson commented: "And now . . . you may see what it is to come for poetry to a Dictionary-maker; you may observe that the rhymes run in alphabetical order exactly."

With Johnson and Mrs. Thrale in the same household, poetry became an integral part of everyday life. Streatham rang with constant improvisations; the group played with poetry as only those who deeply care about it can do. When Mrs. Thrale's oldest daughter was trying to decide whether to wear a new hat to dinner at Mrs. Elizabeth Montagu's, Johnson immediately cried, "*do* my darling," and provided a quatrain. He also improvised verses for Fanny Burney, who joined him and Mrs. Thrale in producing alternate lines for an extemporary elegy on "a Woman of the Town." There were also many impromptu translations, reflecting Johnson's linguistic abilities as well as his poetic skills: the opening of the Spanish ballad "Rio Verde," a burlesque of lines by Lope de Vega, Italian verses by Metastasio and Baretti, Du Bellay's Latin epigram on a dog, and French lines by Benserade. Often when Mrs. Thrale mentioned her fondness for certain verses, he would instantly translate them for her. At other times her commendation of a particular translation would lead him to show that he could do it better himself.

Johnson also wrote more serious translations during his years with the Thrales. In 1777 he translated a song from Izaak Walton's

Long-expected one and twenty

Ling'ring year at last is flown,

Pomp and Pleasure, Pride and Plenty

Great Sir John, are all your own.

Loosen'd from the Minor's tether,

Free to mortgage or to sell,

Wild as wind, and light as feather

Bid the slaves of thrift farewell.

Call the Bettys, Kates, and Jennys

Ev'ry name that laughs at care,

Lavish of your Grandsire's guineas,

Show the Spirit of an heir.

Manuscript for Johnson's "Short Song of Congratulation," which he sent to Mrs. Thrale in 1780 after learning that Henry Thrale's extravagant nephew, John Lade, had attained the age of twenty-one and inherited his father's money (HM 2583; by permission of the Henry E. Huntington Library and Art Gallery)

All that prey on vice and folly
Joy to see their quarry fly,
Here the Gamester light and jolly
There the Lender grave and sly.

Wealth, Sir John, was made to wander,
Let it wander as it will;
See the Jockey, see the Pander,
Bid them come, and take their fill.

When the bonny Blade carouses,
Pockets full, and Spirits high,
What are acres? what are houses?
Only dirt, or wet or dry.

If the Guardian or the Mother
Tell the woes of wilful waste,
Scorn their counsel and their pother,
You can hang or drown at last.

Johnson at sixty-four, a 1786 engraving by Thomas Trotter based on a description by Boswell in his Journal of a Tour to the Hebrides

Compleat Angler (1653) into Latin. A year later he announced to Mrs. Thrale that he had translated Anacreon's "Dove" (Ode IX) into English, saying, "if you will get the pen and ink, I will repeat [it] to you . . . directly." Noting that it had been a boyhood favorite of his that had continued to please him, he told her that he had intended to translate it when he was sixteen and had never gotten around to doing so until he was sixty-eight. Ever willing to help his friends, he provided both Latin and English versions of an epilogue for performances of Baretti's musical adaptation of Horace's *Carmen Seculare* (1779). Earlier that year he had translated a favorite passage from Euripides' *Medea* for Dr. Charles Burney's *General History of Music* (1776-1789). He soon after produced a second translation of the same lines burlesquing the turgid and awkward style of Robert Potter, a contemporary translator of Aeschylus. The next morning over breakfast in the Streatham library he and Mrs. Thrale presented the burlesque version as Potter's work to Burney,

who had dropped in to visit. After reading a single stanza Burney, according to a 1 August 1779 letter by his daughter Susan, exclaimed that the verses were "*worse* than Potter," and as Johnson and Mrs. Thrale burst into laughter, Burney commented that the lines beat Potter with his own weapons. At some point Johnson returned to the passage to translate it again seriously, this time into Latin.

Johnson's skill at impromptu poetic caricatures delighted his friends at Streatham and elsewhere, but the objects of it were often not as appreciative. Indeed, Johnson refused to allow Burney to take a copy of the burlesque of Potter because an earlier experience with Bishop Thomas Percy had made him hesitant to allow such verses into circulation. In her diary Mrs. Thrale had copied a parody of Percy's modern ballad, *The Hermit of Warkworth* (1771), that Johnson produced one day at Streatham, and Boswell recorded another on the same subject that was being widely quoted. Percy was for a while angry, although apparently he soon calmed down; yet a third similar parody exists that Johnson improvised in Percy's presence. Johnson had urged Percy to publish the *Reliques of Ancient English Poetry* (1765), his famous collection of ballads, and while on a visit to him in Northamptonshire had written a dedication and also helped with the glossary for it. But when Percy decided to compose an original ballad, and when others began lauding its "simplicity" and treating it as a serious poetic achievement, Johnson teased Percy while ridiculing what he saw as literary affectation. He treated Thomas Warton similarly, although having learned from the experience with Percy, he was more discreet. In 1777 when Warton's poems were first published, Johnson told Mrs. Thrale he had "written Verses to abuse them" and warned her not to mention the parodies: "for I love Thomas look you–tho' I laught at him." Johnson disliked what he considered the unnecessary obscurity and antiquated diction in the poetry of Warton and others like him, and he made fun of this artificiality. Later with Boswell he improvised a second ludicrous parody of Warton that both Boswell and Mrs. Thrale eventually transcribed.

With Mrs. Thrale, Johnson felt free to share any poetic foray he might make. After her irresponsible and hapless nephew John Lade came of age in 1780, Johnson sent her what he described in a covering letter as a "Short Song of Congratulation," a set of rollicking satiric quatrains. The kind of relationship they had is sug-

Johnson and Boswell visiting Flora and Allan Macdonald in Kingsburgh in 1773 (anonymous painting; by permission of the Trustees of Dr. Johnson's House, Gough Square)

gested by his remarks in the letter, in which he cautioned her not to show the verses to anyone, adding that "It is odd that it [the poem] should come into any bodies head." He also comments: "I hope you will read it with candour, it is, I believe, one of the authours first essays in that way of writing, and a beginning is always to be treated with tenderness." Three weeks before he died Johnson repeated the poem "with great spirit" to some friends and noted that he had never given but one copy of it away. The "Short Song" resembles the verse of A. E. Housman's *A Shropshire Lad* (1896), although no specific indebtedness has been established.

Mrs. Thrale carefully preserved "A Short Song of Congratulation," as she did all of Johnson's poems. Even a distich as minor as the Latin motto he composed for the collar of Joseph Banks's well-traveled goat did not escape her vigilance. Sometimes Johnson would dictate his poems to her for her diaries. At other times she would record his impromptu verses from memory, rescuing for posterity the ephemeral jeux d'esprit of Streatham evenings that could so easily have been lost. Though not of surpassing liter-

ary importance, these light verses illumine the playful and frolicsome side of his personality, an element in his character that is revealed in few other places with the same kind of impact. Mrs. Thrale also questioned Johnson about various early works, and her identifications are often the sole authority for some of his minor verses. Because her interest extended to all of his poems, not just the ones composed in the years she knew Johnson, Mrs. Thrale's records are one of the major sources of information about his poetry.

The golden life at Streatham began to fade in 1779, when Henry Thrale suffered a stroke from which he never entirely recovered. Concern for him darkened the two following years until his death in 1781. Although afterward Mrs. Thrale continued to do a great deal for Johnson, he recognized that the conditions of her life had altered in ways that were leading her gradually to withdraw from him. For many reasons Mrs. Thrale was finding their relationship more and more difficult to maintain. In particular, her growing attraction to Gabriel Piozzi, her daughters' music tutor, was encouraging her to see new possibilities for future happiness. Johnson, increas-

Manuscript for a Latin poem Johnson wrote for his friend and physician Dr. Thomas Lawrence (HM 675; by permission of the
Henry E. Huntington Library and Art Gallery)

ingly suffering from ill health, was hurt and bewildered as his ties with Mrs. Thrale loosened.

One minor attraction of the Thrale household for Johnson was undoubtedly that it allowed him to escape from the incessant quarreling of the strange and pathetic assortment of people he supported under his own roof. Among this group who, according to Mrs. Thrale, "shared his Bounty, and increased his Dirt," was Dr. Robert Levet, whom Johnson had known since 1746. An awkward, taciturn man, he had a large medical practice among the poor people widely scattered in the slums across London, serving them devotedly for minimal pay. On 17 January 1782 Levet died suddenly of a heart attack. Johnson told a friend that only the night before he had been thinking that wherever he might move in the future, or however he might live, he would endeavor to keep Levet around him. At some point during the next three months, as he tried to assimilate yet another loss, he composed "On the Death of Dr. Robert Levet." His first and only serious elegy, the poem shows all the techniques characteristic of Johnson's finest verse.

Firmly anchored in the particular, the poem gives an honest depiction of Levet, "Obscurely wise, and coarsely kind," the possessor of "merit unrefin'd." Johnson refuses to exaggerate or overstate. At the same time, the accurate portrayal of a friend is embedded in commentary on more general conditions of human life itself, whether the inevitable limitations of "letter'd arrogance" or the beneficent influence of "The single talent well employ'd." (With his acute awareness of his own powers and abilities and his lifelong feeling that his accomplishments had failed to live up to his potential, Johnson was always haunted by the biblical parable of the talents.) In addition to these characteristic moves between the specific and the general, the poem on Levet shows the powerful imagery ("hope's delusive mine") and the personified abstractions that retain a concrete vividness ("Death" breaking "at once the vital chain") always typical of Johnson's poetry at its best. Finally, "On the Death of Dr. Robert Levet" reflects the precise attention to the meanings of words characteristic not only of Johnson's poetry, but of all his writings. In describing Levet as "Officious," for example, Johnson draws on the original meaning of the word, which is "obliging," "dutiful," or "full of kind offices." Straightforward yet economic, restrained yet full of feeling, this elegy suggests some of the reasons why Johnson reacted so strongly against Milton's *Lycidas* (1638)

John Opie's 1783 portrait of Johnson, painted less than a year before his death (by permission of the National Galleries of Scotland)

and so vehemently criticized its artificiality and lack of sincerity. Widely reprinted after Johnson first composed it, "On the Death of Dr. Robert Levet" has continued to be widely anthologized and has always been one of Johnson's best-known poems.

Later in 1782 Mrs. Thrale, who was planning a trip to Italy without Johnson, rented Streatham for three years. Johnson was desolate at leaving the place for what he suspected would be the last time. Mrs. Thrale retired to Bath to agonize over whether or not to marry Piozzi; much as she had come to love him, she recognized the scandal that a marriage to an Italian Catholic who was unequal to her in financial and social status would create. While she was away, Johnson suffered a stroke in June 1783. Though the two kept in touch over the next year, she informed him only at the last minute (30 June 1784) of her plans to marry Piozzi. An angry exchange of letters dissolved the friendship that had so long sustained him.

In addition to writing his own poems, Johnson was throughout his life generous in helping others with their works. The earliest known sub-

Page from a letter from Johnson to Hester Thrale, written in London on 6 October 1783 (Maggs Bros., catalogue number 527, December 1929)

stantial revision that he did was for Samuel Madden's *Boulter's Monument*, which appeared in 1745. As Boswell reports, Johnson said that he "blotted a great many lines" in it, and although Madden did not acknowledge Johnson's assistance within the volume, he more substantively thanked him with ten guineas. Boswell mentions Johnson's revisions for the poet Mary Masters, and Johnson also gave John Hawkesworth a couplet for his tragedy, *Edgar and Emmeline* (1761). During the process of helping Garrick with an epitaph on William Hogarth that the painter's wife had requested, he produced stanzas of his own superior to Garrick's final version inscribed on the monument. Goldsmith requested Johnson's assistance with the proofs of *The Traveller* (1764), to which Johnson contributed at least nine lines, including four of the five couplets at the end. He also composed the two final couplets of Goldsmith's *Deserted Village* (1770). Early in 1776 Johnson came to tea with Hannah More and that evening made some alterations for her in *Sir Eldred*, her recently published tale, and wrote an additional stanza for it. James Grainger sent him the second canto of *The Sugar Cane* (1764), and Crabbe got Joshua Reynolds to submit the manuscript of *The Village* (1783) to Johnson, which he returned with some suggested alterations. He also read and revised the poems of Reynolds's sister Frances, in particular changing some bad rhymes. Given the number of people anxious for Johnson to read their works and his characteristic generosity, he undoubtedly rendered a good deal of poetic assistance for which no records survive.

In the 1780s the majority of the poems that Johnson himself wrote were in Latin. He had for years instinctively turned to Latin for poems focused on his more personal concerns; it apparently provided a certain formal distance that he needed to feel comfortable in writing on such topics. Two of his best and most revealing Latin poems are occasional meditations. The impressive and poignant "Gnothi Seauton (Post Lexicon Anglicanum Auctem et Emendatum)"–Know Thyself (After the Revision and Correction of the English Dictionary)–was dated 12 December 1772, when he was sixty-three years old. Johnson had worked sporadically for well over a year (summer 1771–October 1772) on revisions for the fourth edition of his *Dictionary*, and he recognized that this edition was probably the last he would prepare. The first half of the poem focuses on Joseph Scaliger, the Renaissance scholar who went on from his Arabic dictionary to

Page from a catalogue for the May 1816 auction of Mrs. Hester Thrale Piozzi's furniture, listing the contents of Johnson's room above the library (by permission of the National Portrait Gallery, London)

greater tasks. A contrasting second part considers Johnson's own situation, his indolence, his melancholy, and his unending search for peace and relief, as he ponders what he should do in the time that remained for him. "In Rivum a Mola Stoana Lichfeldiae diffluentem" (By the River, at Stowe Mill, Lichfield, Where the Streams Converge) was composed on one of his visits there in his later years. Disturbed at finding the spot where he had swum as a boy sadly altered, he reminisces nostalgically about its beauty and his youthful experiences as his father taught him how to swim. Johnson never wrote poems in English reflecting the kind of deep personal feelings that appear in these two poems.

Several Latin poems are connected in various ways with difficulties with his health. While confined with eye trouble in 1773 Johnson addressed a Latin poem in hexameters to Dr. Thomas Laurence, his physician, and he also wrote another brief poem on recovering the use of his eyes. Other Latin verses to Laurence, ranging from a two-line note summoning him to attend a friend, to an ode to him, also survive. When Johnson suffered a paralytic stroke that briefly deprived him of his power of speech during the night of 16 June 1783, he turned immediately to compose a Latin verse prayer to assess any mental damage. As he explained a few days later in a letter to Mrs. Thrale, "The lines were not very good, but I knew them not to be very good: I made them easily, and concluded myself to be unimpaired in my faculties."

At other times Johnson also used Latin verse as a way of testing and controlling his mind. Toward the end of his life he apparently amused himself by translating numbers into Latin hexameters, and he used the numerical computations in Thomas Templeman's *A New Survey of the Globe* (1729) for a fragmentary "Geographica Metrica." Throughout his life Johnson had enjoyed composing and translating Latin epigrams; during his early years in London he had given Latin verse translations of two inscriptions from the *Greek Anthology* (circa A.D. 900) in his "Essay on Epigraphs" for the *Gentleman's Magazine* (1740). In the winter of 1783-1784, to while away the long sleepless nights, he again occupied himself by turning many of the epigrams in the *Anthology* into Latin.

Aside from his early and uncharacteristic "Upon the Feast of St. Simon and St. Jude," Johnson's poems on religious subjects are all in Latin. Acutely aware of the gulf between the demands of the topic and the limits of human comprehension and ability, as a critic, particularly in the *Lives of the Poets*, he was generally negative about religious verse and prospects for success in it. His own devotional poems, marked by earnestness and humility, were composed sporadically throughout his life, but most of them cluster in his later years. Many are occasional, such as those composed on Christmas Day (1779, 1782) and Good Friday (1781) and the short poem on hope written on the Wednesday of Holy Week in 1783. In addition to a version of Psalm 117 and the longer "Christianus Perfectus," there are several meditations and seven Latin prayers, the majority

of them based on the Collects in The Book of Common Prayer. In David Nichol Smith's opinion (in "Samuel Johnson's Poems"), these verses "are preserved for us in sufficient numbers to rank [Johnson] as a religious poet, though a minor one."

Appropriately enough Johnson's last extant poem in English, composed in November 1784, was a translation of a Horatian ode on human mortality. Johnson had traveled a long road since his first schoolboy translations of the poet he loved. Eight days before his death, when on 5 December 1784 he received the sacrament for the last time, he composed his final poem, a loose paraphrase in Latin of the Collect of the Communion Service.

Johnson's contemporaries buried him in the Poet's Corner in Westminster Abbey, near the foot of Shakespeare's monument. Beneath his statue in St. Paul's Cathedral they placed the word "POETA." His poetry was generally disliked and disregarded during the nineteenth century, but in the next century interest in it began to revive, and the reaction became much more positive. Donald Greene and John A. Vance's 1987 *Bibliography of Johnsonian Studies* shows that from 1970 to 1985 the most popular area of study among all the genres in which Johnson wrote was his poetry. Among writers of heroic-couplet verse, Johnson ranks with Goldsmith just below Pope and Dryden as masters of the form. More generally Johnson's overall stature as a poet depends on the amount of emphasis the individual critic places on poetic range and scope and on uniformity of excellence over many works. T. S. Eliot, for example, wrote in "Johnson as Critic and Poet" that the claim of an author to be a major poet "may, of course, be established by *one* long poem, and when that long poem is good enough, when it has within itself the proper unity and variety, we do not need to know, or if we know we do not need to value highly, the poet's other works. I should myself regard Samuel Johnson as a major poet by the single testimony of *The Vanity of Human Wishes*. . . ." But however Johnson is finally ranked, the importance of his poetry both in the context of his own literary output and in the larger context of his age is unquestionable.

Letters:

The Letters of Samuel Johnson, edited by R. W. Chapman, 3 volumes (Oxford: Clarendon Press, 1952);

Portrait of Johnson, circa 1775, by Reynolds (by permission of Courage Limited)

Mary Hyde, " 'Not in Chapman,' " in *Johnson, Boswell and Their Circle: Essays Presented to Lawrence Fitzroy Powell*, edited by Mary M. Lascelles and others (Oxford: Clarendon Press, 1965), pp. 286-319.

Bibliographies:
William P. Courtney and D. Nichol Smith, *A Bibliography of Samuel Johnson* (Oxford: Clarendon Press, 1915);
Robert William Chapman and Allen T. Hazen, "Johnsonian Bibliography: A Supplement to Courtney," in *Proceedings of the Oxford Bibliographical Society*, 5 (1939): 119-166;
James L. Clifford and Donald J. Greene, *Samuel Johnson: A Survey and Bibliography of Critical Studies* (Minneapolis: University of Minnesota Press, 1970);
Donald Greene and John A. Vance, *A Bibliography of Johnsonian Studies, 1970-1985*, ELS Monograph Series, no. 39 (Victoria, B.C.: University of Victoria, 1987).

Biographies:
James Harrison, *Life of Dr. Samuel Johnson* (London, 1786);

Hester Lynch Thrale Piozzi, *Anecdotes of the Late Samuel Johnson, LL.D., During the Last Twenty Years of His Life* (London: Printed for T. Cadell, 1786);
John Hawkins, *The Life of Samuel Johnson, LL.D.* (London: Printed for J. Buckland, 1787); republished as *The Life of Samuel Johnson, LL.D., by Sir John Hawkins, Knt.*, edited and abridged by Bertram H. Davis (New York: Macmillan, 1961);
James Boswell, *The Life of Samuel Johnson, LL.D.* (London: Printed by Henry Baldwin for Charles Dilly, 1791); republished as *Boswell's Life of Johnson*, edited by George Birkbeck Hill, revised and enlarged by Lawrence F. Powell, 6 volumes (Oxford: Clarendon Press, 1934-1950);
James L. Clifford, *Young Sam Johnson* (New York: McGraw-Hill, 1955);
O. M. Brack, Jr., and Robert E. Kelley, *The Early Biographies of Samuel Johnson* (Iowa City: University of Iowa Press, 1974);
W. Jackson Bate, *Samuel Johnson* (New York: Harcourt Brace Jovanovich, 1977);
Clifford, *Dictionary Johnson: Samuel Johnson's Middle Years* (New York: McGraw-Hill, 1979).

References:
W. Jackson Bate, "Johnson and Satire *Manqué*," in *Eighteenth Century Studies Presented in Memory of Donald F. Hyde*, edited by W. H. Bond (New York: Grolier Club, 1970), pp. 145-160;
Edward A. and Lillian D. Bloom, "Johnson's *London* and its Juvenalian Texts," and "Johnson's *London* and the Tools of Scholarship," *Huntington Library Quarterly*, 34 (1970-1971): 1-23, 115-139;
Bertrand H. Bronson, "Johnson's 'Irene,' " in his *Johnson Agonistes and Other Essays* (Berkeley: University of California Press, 1944; Cambridge: Cambridge University Press, 1945), pp. 100-155;
John Butt, "Pope and Johnson in Their Handling of the Imitation," *New Rambler* (June 1959): 3-14; reprinted as "Johnson's Practice in the Poetical Imitation," in *New Light on Dr. Johnson: Essays on the Occasion of His 250th Birthday*, edited by Frederick W. Hilles (New Haven: Yale University Press, 1959), pp. 19-34;
William Edinger, *Samuel Johnson and Poetic Style* (Chicago: University of Chicago Press, 1977);

T. S. Eliot, "Johnson as Critic and Poet," in his *On Poetry and Poets* (New York: Noonday Press, 1961), pp. 184-222;

Eliot, Preface to *London: A Poem and The Vanity of Human Wishes* (London: Etchells & Macdonald, 1930); reprinted in *English Critical Essays: Twentieth Century*, edited by Phyllis M. Jones (London: Oxford University Press, 1933), pp. 301-310; reprinted as "Poetry in the Eighteenth Century," in *The Pelican Guide to English Literature*, 4 (Baltimore: Penguin, 1957), pp. 271-277;

Macdonald Emslie, "Johnson's Satires and 'The Proper Wit of Poetry,' " *Cambridge Journal*, 7 (March 1954): 347-360;

F. W. Hilles, "Johnson's Poetic Fire," in *From Sensibility to Romanticism*, edited by Hilles and Harold Bloom (New York: Oxford University Press, 1965), pp. 67-77;

Ian Jack, " 'Tragical Satire': *The Vanity of Human Wishes*," in his *Augustan Satire* (Oxford: Clarendon Press, 1952), pp. 135-145;

Mary Lascelles, "Johnson and Juvenal," in *New Light on Dr. Johnson: Essays on the Occasion of His 250th Birthday*, pp. 35-55;

F. R. Leavis, "Johnson as Poet," in his *The Common Pursuit* (London: Chatto & Windus, 1952; New York: George W. Stewart, 1952), pp. 116-120;

Helen Harrold Naugle, ed., *A Concordance to the Poems of Samuel Johnson* (Ithaca, N.Y. & London: Cornell University Press, 1973);

John E. Sitter, "To *The Vanity of Human Wishes* through the 1740s," *Studies in Philology*, 74 (October 1977): 445-464;

D. Nichol Smith, "The Heroic Couplet–Johnson," in his *Some Observations on Eighteenth Century Poetry* (Toronto: University of Toronto Press, 1937), pp. 31-55;

Smith, "Samuel Johnson's Poems," *Review of English Studies*, 19 (January 1943): 44-50; reprinted in *New Light on Dr. Johnson: Essays on the Occasion of His 250th Birthday*, pp. 9-17, and in *Samuel Johnson: A Collection of Critical Essays*, edited by Donald J. Greene (Englewood Cliffs, N.J.: Prentice-Hall, 1965), pp. 63-69;

Susie I. Tucker and Henry Gifford, "Johnson's Latin Poetry," *Neophilologus*, 41 (July 1957): 215-221;

Tucker and Gifford, "Johnson's Poetic Imagination," *Review of English Studies*, new series, 8 (August 1957): 241-248;

Marshall Waingrow, "The Mighty Moral of *Irene*," in *From Sensibility to Romanticism*, pp. 79-92;

Howard D. Weinbrot, *The Formal Strain: Studies in Augustan Imitation and Satire* (Chicago: University of Chicago Press, 1969), pp. 165-191, 193-217;

Weinbrot, "Johnson's *London* and Juvenal's Third Satire: The Country as 'Ironic' Norm," *Modern Philology*, 73 (May 1976): S56-S65;

Anne Williams, "Satire into Lyric: *The Vanity of Human Wishes*," in her *The Prophetic Strain: The Greater Lyric in the Eighteenth Century* (Chicago: University of Chicago Press, 1984), pp. 79-82.

Papers:

Over forty holograph manuscripts of Johnson's poems survive, and there are also many contemporary transcripts of his works by others. The Hyde Collection at Somerville, N.J., the largest collection of Johnson's manuscript poetry, includes holographs of *The Vanity of Human Wishes*, sections from *London* and *Irene*, and many of Johnson's other poems. A complete draft of *Irene*, along with a transcript by Bennet Langton, is in the British Museum. Other manuscripts of individual poems are scattered in various locations, including the Bodleian Library and Pembroke College, Oxford, and the Yale University Library. For further information see J. D. Fleeman, *A Preliminary Handlist of Documents & Manuscripts of Samuel Johnson* (Oxford: Oxford Bibliographical Society/Bodleian Library, 1967).

Lady Mary Wortley Montagu
(26 May 1689 - 21 August 1762)

Carol Barash
Rutgers University

BOOKS: *Virtue in Danger: Or Arthur Gray's last Farewell to the World. Written by a Gentleman at St. James's; (Tune, of Chivy Chase)* [broadside], anonymous (London, n.d.);

Court Poems (London: Printed for J. Roberts, 1706 [i.e., 1716]);

The Genuine Copy of a Letter written from Constantinople by An English Lady . . . to a Venetian Nobleman (London: Printed & sold by J. Roberts & A. Dodd, 1719);

VERSES Address'd to the IMITATOR of the FIRST SATIRE of the Second Book of Horace, by Montagu and John, Lord Hervey (London: Printed for A. Dodd, 1733);

An Elegy to a Young Lady, in the manner of Ovid . . . With an answer. By a Lady, author of the Verses to the Imitator of Horace, by Montagu and James Hammond (London: Printed for J. Roberts, 1733);

The Dean's Provocation for Writing the Lady's Dressing-Room (London: Printed for T. Cooper, 1734);

The Nonsense of Common Sense, 9 issues (London, 16 December 1737-14 March 1738); modern edition, edited by Robert Halsband (Evanston, Ill.: Northwestern University Press, 1947);

Six Town Eclogues. With Some Other Poems, edited by Horace Walpole (London: Printed for M. Cooper, 1747);

Letters of the Right Honourable Lady M--y W---y M----e [sic]*: Written during her Travels in Europe, Asia and Africa, to Persons of Distinction, Men of Letters, &c. in different parts of Europe*, 3 volumes (London: Printed for T. Becket & P. A. De Hondt, 1763; New York, 1766); enlarged as *Letters of the Right Honourable Lady M--y W----y M----e* [sic] *. . . A New Edition. To Which Are Now First Added, Poems, by the Same Author*, 2 volumes (London: Printed for T. Cadell, T. Evans, J. Murray & R. Baldwin, 1784).

Editions and Collections: *The Poetical Works of the Right Honourable Lady M-y W-y M-e* [sic], ed-

Lady Mary Wortley Montagu (painting by Jonathan Richardson; by permission of the Harrowby Manuscripts Trust, Sandon Hall, Stafford)

ited by Isaac Reed (London: Printed for J. Williams, 1768; Philadelphia: Printed by Robert Bell, 1769);

The Works of the Right Honourable Lady Mary Wortley Montagu. Including her correspondence, poems and essays, edited by James Dallaway, 5 volumes (London: R. Phillips, 1803);

The Letters and Works of Lady Mary Wortley Montagu, edited by James, Lord Wharncliffe, 2

Page from a 15 August 1712 letter from Lady Mary Pierrepont to her future husband, Edward Wortley Montagu (Wortley MSS i.170; by permission of the Harrowby Manuscripts Trust, Sandon Hall, Stafford)

volumes (London: R. Bentley, 1837); third edition, revised by W. Moy Thomas (London: Bohn, 1861);

"A Critical Edition of the Verse of Lady Mary Wortley Montagu," edited by Isobel Grundy, Ph.D. dissertation, Oxford University, 1970;

Court Eclogs Written in the year, 1716: Alexander Pope's autograph manuscript of poems by Lady Mary Wortley Montagu, edited by Robert Halsband (New York: New York Public Library & Readex, 1977);

Essays and Poems and Simplicity A Comedy, edited by Halsband and Grundy (Oxford: Clarendon Press, 1977).

OTHER: "Constantinople To ----," in *A New Miscellany*, edited by Anthony Hammond (London: Printed for T. Jauncy, 1720);

Robert Dodsley, ed., *A Collection of Poems by Several Hands*, 3 volumes, includes poems by Montagu (London: Printed for R. Dodsley, 1748);

George Colman, ed., *Poems by Eminent Ladies*, 2 volumes, includes poems by Montagu (London: Printed for R. Baldwin, 1755).

Best known as a letter writer, Lady Mary Wortley Montagu wrote verses all her life and frequently referred to herself as a "poet." From the young girl, as she later described herself, "trespassing" in Latin and Greek sources to the old woman haunted "by the Daemon of Poesie" (as quoted by Isobel Grundy in *Essays and Poems*, 1977), Montagu repeatedly turned to the forms of Augustan verse–satires, verse epistles, mock epics, translations, essays, ballads, and songs–to respond to events around her and, indirectly, to give public form to her private feelings.

Montagu was born on 26 May 1689, the first daughter of Evelyn and Mary Pierrepont. Her father became earl of Kingston the year after her birth. Montagu's early influences were the same as those of her male contemporaries: the classics, John Dryden, and French romances. However, denied a classical education because she was a woman, she was educated at home and taught herself Latin in her father's library. Her earliest poetic endeavors were based on Roman sources and carefully transcribed in manuscript volumes, the most complete of which she titled "The Entire Works of Clarinda" (collected by Grundy in her Ph.D. dissertation, 1970). In 1710 she translated the *Enchiridion* of the Greek stoic

Edward Wortley Montagu

philosopher Epictetus from Latin and sent a copy to Bishop Gilbert Burnet with a long letter defending women's right to formal education.

Although Montagu imitated other classical sources, the influence of Ovid is particularly evident in her juvenilia and also in her later poetry. She claimed, according to Joseph Spence, that the pleasures of reading Ovid's *Metamorphoses* originally "set [her] upon the thoughts of stealing the Latin language." She frequently reworked Ovidian sources, particularly the *Heroides*, in poems that probe different aspects of eighteenth-century sexual inequality. She uses the form of the heroic epistle in her "Epistle from Mrs. Y[onge] to Her Husband" (1724; collected in *Essays and Poems*), in which a woman accused of adultery lashes out against her flagrantly adulterous husband, against the patriarchal legal system that allows him to profit economically from their divorce, and against what she sees as women's enslavement in marriage: "Defrauded Servants are from Service free, / A wounded Slave regains his Liberty. / For Wives ill us'd no remedy remains, / To daily Racks condemn'd, and to eternal Chains." Montagu used the *Heroides* to show victims of class difference and sexual exploitation condemning their attackers. As she writes in the "Epistle from Mrs. Y[onge]," "Th' Oppress'd and

Injur'd allways may complain." The "Epistle From Arthur G[ra]y to Mrs. M[urra]y" (1721; in *Six Town Eclogues*, 1747), written in the voice of a working-class man who has been accused of raping his employer's sister, transforms the speaker into a romantic hero denied access to his love because of his class. He describes both himself and the woman he loves as subservient to middle-class men, "Trifflers that make Love a Trade."

As an aristocrat Montagu was in many respects different from other feminist thinkers of her time. In her discussions of the need for women's education, she seems to have desired the privileges granted to men of her class, but was less vigorous in pressing for the education, much less the equality, of women in general. Critics have long called Montagu's poetry, "masculine," an unfortunate epithet that indirectly mocks the most remarkable aspects of her writing: she was capable of extremely stringent satire, and particularly in published attacks on Alexander Pope and Jonathan Swift, she engaged in poetic warfare with the best of her male contemporaries. She was also friends with Mary Astell, whose *Serious Proposal To the Ladies, For the Advancement of their true and greatest Interest* (2 volumes, 1694, 1697) proposed a retreat where unmarried women might educate themselves in religious and intellectual matters while protecting themselves from the economic demands of early marriage; and as a young girl Montagu thought of herself as one who would thrive in such a retreat rather than in the ordinary path of marriage. Although she occasionally satirized women's vanity and the follies resulting from it, Montagu wrote essays and poems describing the benefits of women's education and of more equitable marriage arrangements.

The impetus for Montagu's feminism was at least partly personal experience. After her mother's death in 1693, Montagu was groomed to keep house for her father, then a Whig M.P. As her father's eldest daughter, her roles included presiding over his dinner table and carving up meats for his guests. According to her granddaughter Louisa Stuart, at the age of eight Montagu was made the "toast" of the Whig Kit-Cat Club, after which she "went from the lap of one poet, or patriot, or statesman, to the arms of another, was feasted with sweetmeats, [and] overwhelmed with caresses." She claimed that "the love of admiration, which this scene was calculated to excite . . . could never again be so fully gratified."

Engraving of Montagu, with verses showing her reputation among her contemporaries

Despite her initial resistance to marriage and after prolonged negotiations with her father and her future husband, she eloped with Edward Wortley Montagu, also a Whig M.P., in 1712. A stingy and possessive man, he wished to control Montagu even more than her overbearing father had. Although the marriage quickly proved miserable for both partners, it was through her husband's close friendship with Joseph Addison that Montagu was introduced to other writers of her generation. In 1713 she wrote a critique of Addison's *Cato*; although her remarks were not published in her lifetime, Addison took them to heart, making several of the changes she recommended.

Montagu's first published writing appeared in Addison's *Spectator* in 1714, where she wrote under the pseudonym Lady President. In this period she also became friends with Pope and John Gay, and in 1716 they wrote a group of "court eclogues," poems that describe upper-class rituals such as card playing and that mock immorality in the court of George I. In "Satturday, The Small Pox, Flavia" (1716; in *Six Town Eclogues*) Montagu describes her own experience of smallpox as taking her away from polite society:

> Adieu ye Parks, in some obscure recess,
> Where Gentle streams will weep at my Distress,
> Where no false Friend will in my Greife take part,
> And mourn my Ruin with a Joyfull Heart,
> There let me live, in some deserted Place,
> There hide in shades this lost Inglorious Face.
> Ye Operas, Circles, I no more must view!
> My Toilette, Patches, all the World Adieu!

Three of Montagu's eclogues were published in *Court Poems*, 1716, the first of many poems throughout her life intended only for manuscript circulation among her friends but published quickly and sloppily without her permission—and often, as a result, attributed to other authors.

Later in 1716 Montagu traveled with her husband to Constantinople, where he was to be the English ambassador to Turkey. In Turkey she saw smallpox innoculation performed, and when she returned to England she had her son, Edward, Jr., innoculated. In September 1722 she wrote a biting letter to *The Flying-Post: or, Post-Master* in which she defended the practice and criticized English doctors who failed to perform the procedure correctly. While traveling, Montagu also began writing what became her best-known work, the "Turkish Embassy Letters" (published in 1763 as *Letters of the Right Honourable Lady M--y W---y M----e [sic]*). Some of these letters were written to specific friends, but the majority are aimed at a larger public audience. Montagu had Astell's introduction to the letters bound with her own manuscript, and she seems to have wanted the letters to be published after her death, as they were one year thereafter.

An outspoken woman of strong convictions, Montagu seems to have assumed that her class status justified a certain amount of flamboyant behavior, and allowed her to imitate the freedoms granted to aristocratic men: she was often mocked for refusing to wear wigs, for taking snuff, and for sporting elaborate Turkish dress. Unlike Anne Finch, Countess of Winchilsea, who organized her manuscript poems and reworked many of them for publication in 1713, Monta-

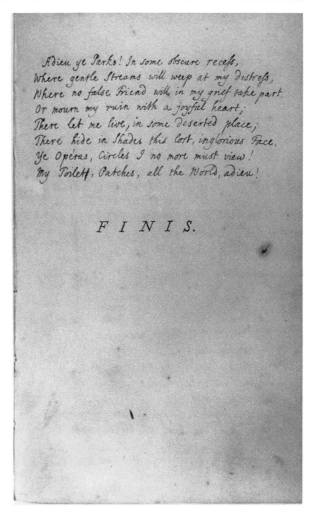

Last stanza of Montagu's "Satturday, The Small Pox, Flavia" (1716), as Alexander Pope transcribed it in a manuscript copy of her court eclogues prepared by Montagu and Pope (by permission of the Arents Tobacco Collection, New York Public Library)

gu, as a female aristocrat, scorned publication through booksellers and circulated her early poems primarily in manuscript. However, she seems indirectly to have allowed some of her later satires into print, and she had a strong sense of possessing the verses she had written. According to Spence, when Pope attempted to edit one of her poems, she told him, "No, Pope, no touching, for then whatever is good for any thing will pass for yours, and the rest for mine." And in her copy of Pope's *Eloisa to Abelard* (1720), she wrote "mine" in the margin beside a couplet she believed he had stolen from her. There were numerous similar episodes in the long and fierce battle between Montagu and Pope.

Written ~~at~~ ~~Constantinople~~

January 1718

in the chiosk at Pera

overlooking Constantinople

Give me Great God (said I) a little Farm

in Summer shady, & in Winter warm

where a cool spring gives birth ~~to~~ a clear brook

by Nature slideing down a mossy Rock

Not artfully in Leaden Pipes convey'd

Or greatly falling in a forc'd Cascade

Pure & unsully'd winding throu' yᵉ Shade.)

All bounteous Heaven has added to my Praier

a softer climate and a purer Air.

Our Frozen Isle now chilling Winter binds

Deform'd by Rains, & rough wᵗʰ blasting Winds

yᵉ wither'd Woods grown white wᵗʰ hoary Frost

by Driving Storms their scatter'd beautys lost

The Trembling birds their leaveless coverts shun

And seek in distant Climes a warmer Sun

The Water Nymphs their silenc'd Urns deplore

Even Thames benumb'd a River now no more

The barren Meadows give no more delight

by glist'ning Snows made painfull to yᵉ Sight

First two pages of Montagu's "Constantinople, To---" from the manuscript copy of her court eclogues prepared by Montagu and Pope (by permission of the Arents Tobacco Collection, New York Public Library)

Here Summer reigns wth one eternal Smile
And double Harvests bless ye happy Soil.
Fair, fertile Fields to w^m Indulgent Heaven
Has every charm of every Season given!
No killing Cold deforms ye Beauteous Year
The springing Flowers no coming Winter fear
But as ye Parent Rose decays & dies
ye Infant Buds wth brighter Colours rise
And with fresh sweets ye Mother-scent supplys
Near y^m the Vi'let glows wth odours blest
And blooms in more than Tyrian Purple drest
The rich Jonquils their golden gleam display
And shine in glorys emulateing Day.
Tßese chearfull Groves their living Leaves retain
The Streams still murmur undefil'd by Rain
And growing Green adorns ye Fruitfull Plain
The warbling Kind uninterupted Sing,
Warm'd wth Enjoyment of perpetual Spring.

    Here from my Window I at once survey
The crouded City, & resounding Sea
In distant Views see Assian Mountains rise
And lose their Snowy Summits in y^e Skies
Above those Mountains high Olympus Tow'rs
The Parliamental Seat of Heavenly Powers.

Montagu in Turkish attire with her son, Edward, Jr., and attendants, circa 1717 (painting by J. B. Vanmour; by permission of the National Portrait Gallery, London)

Early in their relationship Pope was much taken with Montagu's wit and vivacity, as well as her class; he wrote her flirtatious letters and poems and thought of himself almost as her suitor. There are many conflicting versions of their falling-out in 1722, including a story of Montagu laughing openly when Pope finally declared his love to her. Pope subsequently attacked her as the dirty "Sappho" in some of his satiric works, until she was finally enraged by the characterization in his *First Satire of the Second Book of Horace Imitated* (1733). Joining forces with her sometime collaborator, John, Lord Hervey, whose name had also been dragged through the mud by Pope, Montagu helped to produce *VERSES Address'd to the IMITATOR of the FIRST SATIRE of the Second Book of Horace* (1733), which many critics consider the best satire of Pope written at that time. Manuscript evidence suggests that, while Hervey was more involved in the satire's publication, Montagu predominated in the poem's composition.

In the satire she mocks Pope's "obscure" birth and makes his hunchbacked body the symbol of his status as outsider to the human race:

> Thine is just such an Image of [Horace's] Pen,
> As thou thy self art of the Sons of Men:
> Where our own Species in Burlesque we trace,
> A Sign-Post Likeness of the noble Race;
> That is at once Resemblance and Disgrace.

She claims that, like his body, his satire is unsightly, diseased, and out of control:

> *Satire* shou'd, like a polish'd Razor keen,
> Wound with a Touch, that's scarcely felt or seen,
> Thine is an Oyster-Knife, that hacks and hews;
> The Rage, but not the Talent, to Abuse;
> And is in *Hate*, what *Love* is in the Stews.

Whereas Pope's depiction of "Sappho" had been fairly general, many people in addition to Montagu believing themselves the objects of his attack, Montagu's revenge was quite specific, flaunting the class privilege that allowed her to look down on Pope with scorn.

While Montagu's scathing satire against Pope was the result of a complicated friendship turned sour, her "Reasons that Induced Dr. S[wift] to write a Poem call'd the Lady's Dressing Room" (published as *The Dean's Provocation for*

Writing the Lady's Dressing Room, 1734) was born out of lifelong distrust. In Swift's *The Lady's Dressing Room* (1732), the voyeuristic Strephon goes to his mistress's chamber when she is not there, and after looking through piles of filthy laundry and pots of saliva and excrement, he runs from the room in disgust. Montagu's riposte suggests that Swift's own sexual failure is the event that precedes the poem and engenders the author's contempt for the materiality of the female body:

> The Reverend Lover with surprize
> Peeps in her Bubbys, and her Eyes,
> And kisses both, and trys—and trys.
> The Evening in this Hellish Play,
> Beside his Guineas thrown away,
> Provok'd the Priest to that degree
> He swore, the Fault is not me.

She accuses Swift of being both impotent and cheap, threatening to write verses because the prostitute refuses to return his money. The poem's final couplet responds to Swift's line, "Celia, Celia, Celia shits": "She answer'd short, I'm glad you'l write, / You'l furnish paper when I shite." Montagu wrote many of her strongest lines in these satiric poems, which she clearly intended as public attacks and which she allowed to appear in print.

Other aspects of Montagu's sense of herself as public judge and critic are seen in her numerous manuscript poems that address the situations of women in extreme circumstances: horrid marriages, divorces, and attempted rapes. One of her earliest poems (written in 1712 or 1713), "Written ex tempore in Company in a Glass Window the first year I was marry'd" (published as "The Lady's Resolve," *Plain Dealer*, 27 April 1724), anticipates her fascination with women's unhappiness in marriage and their potential adultery: "In part to blame she is, who has been try'd; / Too near he has approach'd, who is deny'd." While this early poem seems to blame women for men's sexual advances, her later work often speaks out against the institution of marriage and comes very close to defending women who, like Montagu herself, find a variety of pleasures with men other than their husbands. Speaking in the voice of a woman who shuns her lover's proposal in "The ANSWER to the foregoing ELEGY" (in *An Elegy to a Young Lady*, 1733), she likens marriage to bondage:

> For would'st thou fix Dishonour on my Name,
> And give me up to Penitence and Shame!

> Or gild my Ruin with the Name of Wife,
> And make me a poor *Virtuous* Wretch for Life?
>   Could'st thou submit to wear the Marriage-
>   Chain,
> (Too sure a Cure for all thy present pain). . . .

> Tho' ev'ry softer Wish were amply crown'd,
> *Love* soon would cease to smile, when *Fortune*
>   frown'd.

She writes of a young woman sexually abused—if not murdered—by her husband in "Written ex tempore on the Death of Mrs. Bowes" (*Weekly Journal or Saturday's-Post*, 26 December 1724), and in her 1731 "Song" she urges a young widow to forget her grief, to find an appealing young lover instead (the poem was collected in *The Works* of 1803).

Many of Montagu's best poems seem to have been written "extempore"; she wrote quickly, without much revision, when events provoked her. She also wrote several more contemplative poems, including "Constantinople, To ---" (in *A New Miscellany*, 1720) and "The 5th Ode of Horace Imitated" (*London Magazine*, September 1750), which concludes with these lines:

> For me, secure I view the raging Main,
> Past are my Dangers, and forgot my Pain,
>   My Votive Tablet in the temple shews
>   The Monument of Folly past,
> I paid the bounteous God my gratefull vows
>   Who snatch'd from Ruin sav'd me at the last.

Indeed, by the end of her life, Montagu had spent considerable time away from her husband and England, estranged from many who had once been close friends. Living almost in genteel poverty, she still entertained those who sought her out in her retreats in France and Italy. After years of her poems being sneaked into print a few at a time, without her knowledge of their publication, she was outraged to discover that they had been sloppily edited and some of them attributed to others when they appeared in Dodsley's *Collection of Poems by Several Hands* in 1748.

Although her daughter, Mary, Lady Bute, destroyed Montagu's diaries, there is still a considerable amount of primary material relating to her career. Montagu remains the one eighteenth-century woman poet of whom there is both a standard edition and a critical biography; she would have been pleased to see other eighteenth-cen-

Page from a letter Montagu wrote to her daughter, Mary, Countess of Bute, on 23 January 1755 (Wortley MSS iii.127; by permission of the Harrowby Manuscripts Trust, Sandon Hall, Stafford)

Lady Mary Wortley Montagu (miniature by C. F. Zincke, 1738; private collection)

tury women poets given such scholarly attention and respect.

Letters:

The Genuine Copy of a Letter written from Constantinople by An English Lady . . . to a Venetian Nobleman (London: Printed & sold by J. Roberts & A. Dodd, 1719);

Letters of the Right Honourable Lady M--y W---y M----e [sic]: Written during her Travels in Europe, Asia and Africa, to Persons of Distinction, Men of Letters, &c., in different parts of Europe, 3 volumes (London: Printed for T. Becket and P. A. De Hondt, 1763);

The Letters and Works of Lady Mary Wortley Montagu, edited by James, Lord Wharncliffe, third edition, revised by W. Moy Thomas (London: Bohn, 1861);

The Complete Letters of Lady Mary Wortley Montagu, edited by Robert Halsband, 3 volumes (Oxford: Clarendon Press, 1965-1967).

Biographies:

Louisa Stuart, "Biographical Anecdotes of Lady Mary Wortley Montagu," in *The Letters and Works of Lady Mary Wortley Montagu*, third edition (London: Bohn, 1861);

George Paston [i.e., Emily Morse Symonds], *Lady Mary Wortley Montagu and Her Times* (London: Methuen, 1907);

Lewis Melville [i.e., Lewis Saul Benjamin], *Lady Mary Wortley Montagu: Her Life and Letters* (London: Hutchinson, 1925);

Iris Barry, *Portrait of Lady Mary Wortley Montagu* (Indianapolis: Bobbs-Merrill, 1928);

Lewis Gibbs [i.e., Joseph Walter Cove], *The Admirable Lady Mary; the Life and Times of Lady Mary Wortley Montagu* (London: Dent, 1949);

Robert Halsband, *The Life of Lady Mary Wortley Montagu* (Oxford: Clarendon Press, 1956).

References:

Anonymous, *Advice to Sappho. Occasioned by her Verses on the Imitator of the first satire of the second book of Horace. By a Gentlewoman* (London: Printed for the author & sold by J. Roberts, 1713);

Robert Bataille, "The Dating of *The Lady's Curiosity* and Lady Mary's 'The Fifth Ode of Horace Imitated,'" *American Notes and Queries*, 18, no. 6 (1980): 87-88;

Miriam Benkovitz, "Some Observations on Women's Concept of Self in the Eighteenth Century," in *Woman in the Eighteenth Century and Other Essays*, edited by Paul Fritz and Richard Morton (Toronto & Sarasota; Hakkert, 1976);

Jeremy Black, "Lady Mary Reports," *Scriblerian*, 17, no. 1 (1984): 82;

Marie-Louise Dufrenoy, "Lady Mary Wortley Montagu et la satire orientale," in *Proceedings of the IVth Congress of the International Comparative Literature Association*, edited by François Jost (The Hague: Mouton, 1966), II: 1332-1343;

Isobel Grundy, " 'The Entire Works of Clarinda': Unpublished Juvenile Verse by Lady Mary Wortley Montagu," *Yearbook of English Studies*, 7 (1977): 91-107;

Grundy, "A Moon of Literature: Verse by Lady Mary Wortley Montagu," *New Rambler*, 112, no. 1 (1972): 6-22;

Grundy, "Ovid and Eighteenth-Century Divorce: An Unpublished Poem by Lady Mary Wortley Montagu," *Review of English Studies*, new series, 23, no. 92 (1972): 417-428;

Wrote in the Year 1755 at Louvere

Wisdom! slow product of experienc'd Years,
The only Fruit that lifes' cold Winter bears!
Thy sacred seeds in vain in Youth we lay
By the Fierce storms of Passion torn away;
Should some remain in a rich Generous soil
They long lie hid, & must be rais'd with Toil;
Faintly they struggle with inclement skies,
No sooner born, than the poor Planter dyes

Song

How happy is the Harden'd Heart
where Interest is the only view
Can sigh and meet, or smile & part
nor pleas'd, nor greiv'd, nor false; nor True.

Yet have they truly peace of mind?
Or do they ever truly know,
The bliss sincerer tempers find
Which Truth & virtue can bestow?

Fair copy of two of Montagu's poems (MS. 256. f. 57; by permission of the Harrowby Manuscripts Trust, Sandon Hall, Stafford)

Page from Montagu's commonplace book for the year 1760 (by permission of the Fisher Library, University of Sydney)

Grundy, "The Politics of Female Authorship," *Book Collector*, 31, no. 1 (1982): 19-37;

Grundy, "Pope, Peterborough, and the Characters of Women," *Review of English Studies*, new series, 20, no. 80 (1969): 461-468;

Grundy, "Verses Address'd to the Imitator of Horace: A Skirmish between Pope and Some Persons of Rank and Fortune," *Studies in Bibliography*, 30 (1977): 96-119;

Robert Halsband, "Algarotti as Apollo: His Influence on Lady Mary Wortley Montagu," in *Friendship's Garland: Essays Presented to Mario Praz on his Seventieth Birthday*, edited by Vittorio Gabrieli (Rome: Storia e Letteratura, 1966), I: 223-241;

Halsband, "Ladies of Letters in the Eighteenth Century," in *The Lady of Letters in the Eighteenth Century; Papers Read at a Clark Library Seminar, January 18, 1969* (Los Angeles: Clark Memorial Library, 1969), pp. 31-51;

Halsband, "Lady Mary Wortley Montagu and Eighteenth-Century Fiction," *Philological Quarterly*, 45, no. 1 (1966): 145-156;

Halsband, "Lady Mary Wortley Montagu as a Friend of Continental Writers," *John Rylands Library Bulletin* (University of Manchester), 39, no. 1 (1956): 57-74;

Halsband, "Lady Mary Wortley Montagu as Letter-Writer," *PMLA*, 80, no. 3 (1965): 155-163;

Halsband, "Lady Mary Wortley Montagu's Answer to Dorset's Ballad," *Huntington Library Quarterly*, 30, no. 4 (1950): 409-413;

Halsband, " 'The Lady's Dressing Room' Explicated by a Contemporary," in *The Augustan Milieu: Essays Presented to Louis A. Landa*, edited by Henry K. Miller, Eric Rothstein, and George S. Rousseau (Oxford: Clarendon Press, 1970), pp. 225-231;

Halsband, *Lord Hervey, Eighteenth-Century Courtier* (Oxford: Clarendon Press, 1973);

Halsband, "Pope, Lady Mary, and the *Court Poems* (1716)," *PMLA*, 68, no. 1 (1953): 237-250;

Alice Hufstader, *Sisters of the Quill* (New York: Dodd, Mead, 1978);

Ruth Perry, *The Celebrated Mary Astell* (Chicago & London: University of Chicago Press, 1986);

Valerie Rumbold, *Women's Place in Pope's World* (Cambridge: Cambridge University Press, 1989);

Arthur Sherbo and Isobel Grundy, "A 'Spurious' Poem by Lady Mary Wortley Montagu?," *Notes and Queries*, new series, 27 (October, 1980): 407-410;

Hilda Smith, *Reason's Disciples; Seventeenth-Century English Feminists* (Urbana, Ill., Chicago & London: University of Illinois Press, 1982);

Warren H. Smith, ed., *Horace Walpole: Writer, Politician, Connoisseur* (New Haven: Yale University Press, 1967), pp. 215-226 and Appendix III: 339;

Joseph Spence, *Anecdotes, Observations, and Characters of Books and Men* (London: J. Murray, 1820).

Papers:

The major manuscripts are those held by Harrowby Manuscripts Trust, Sandon Hall, Stafford, and those held with the Wharncliffe Muniments on deposit in the Sheffield City Library. Other important collections of Montagu's papers and related material are at the Bodleian Library, Oxford; the British Library; Cornell University; the Fisher Library, University of Sydney, Australia; the Henry E. Huntington Library, San Marino, Cal.; the John Rylands Library, University of Manchester; the New York Public Library; the Pierpont Morgan Library, New York; the Pforzheimer Library, New York; the University of Nottingham Manuscript Library; the Firestone Library, Princeton University; and the Beinecke Rare Book Library, Yale University.

Thomas Parnell

(1679 - 24 October 1718)

Thomas M. Woodman
University of Reading

BOOKS: *An Essay on the Different Stiles of Poetry* (London: Printed for Benj. Tooke, 1713);

Homer's Battle of the Frogs and Mice, with the remarks of Zoilus, To which is prefix'd the life of the said Zoilus (London: Printed for Bernard Lintot, 1717);

Poems on Several Occasions, edited by Alexander Pope (London: Printed for B. Lintot, 1722 [i.e., 1721]).

Editions and Collections: *The Works, in Verse and Prose . . . Enlarged with variations and poems, not before publish'd* (Glasgow: Printed & sold by R. & A. Foulis, 1755);

The Posthumous Works . . . Containing poems moral and divine: and on various other subjects (Dublin: Printed for Benjamin Gunne, 1758);

The Poetical Works, edited by George Aitken (London: Bell, 1894);

Collected Poems, edited by C. J. Rawson and F. P. Lock (Newark: University of Delaware Press / London & Toronto: Associated University Presses, 1989).

OTHER: *Poetical miscellanies, consisting of original poems and translations . . . Published by Mr. Steele*, includes poems by Parnell (London: Printed for Jacob Tonson, 1714);

"Essay on the Life, Writings and Learning of Homer," in *The Iliad of Homer Translated by Mr. Pope* (London: Printed by W. Bowyer for Bernard Lintot, 1715);

Works of the English Poets, edited by Alexander Chalmers, volume 9, includes all of Parnell's poems then published (London: Whittingham, 1810).

Thomas Parnell (mezzotint by Thomas Davies, based on a painting by Godfrey Kneller; by permission of the National Portrait Gallery, London)

Thomas Parnell's fame has often seemed to depend more on his important friendships and the considerable influence of a tiny handful of his poems than on his total literary achievement. Recent criticism, however, has established that his work is the epitome of early-eighteenth-century polite poetry, combining polished classicism with Christian sentiment. It is better to envision him as contributing to an expanded sense of the possibilities of poetry in his own period than to imagine him as the herald of something new.

Parnell was born in Dublin in the autumn of 1679. His family had long been settled in Congleton in the county of Cheshire, England, but they had Irish connections; his parents, Thomas and Anna Parnell, decided to move to Ireland just after the Restoration because of their previous support for Oliver Cromwell. They were Anglicans, however, rather than Presbyterians, and Parnell was early destined for a career in the church. He was admitted to Trinity College, Dublin, at the early age of thirteen and received his bachelor's degree in 1697. Three years later he was ordained a deacon by his influential guardian, William King, later archbishop of Dublin. A period of indecision about the priesthood followed, but he was ordained in 1704 and installed the same year as minor canon at St. Patrick's Cathedral, Dublin. In 1706 King was able to help his protégé become archdeacon of Clogher. That same year Parnell married Anne Minchin, to whom he addressed an early version of his song "When thy beauty appears," later collected by Alexander Pope in *Poems on Several Occasions* (1722).

Protestant influences in Parnell's background and the family's church connections are reflected in the piety of his early poems, the lengthy biblical paraphrases that constitute his apprentice work. From a literary point of view these are works of little merit. In heavy heroic couplets the young poet versifies large tracts of the Old Testament and presents himself as the inspired prophetic poet of the "biblical sublime" tradition of Guillaume du Bartas. Only of slightly more interest are the shorter religious lyrics and hymns that seem to express a warm personal devotion but lack artistic control.

The whole essence of Parnell's development as a poet lies in the movement toward polish and wit brought about by his important contacts in the Irish and, later, the London literary world. His friendship with Jonathan Swift was the earliest of these, dating perhaps from the time when both held minor offices in St. Patrick's Cathedral. Parnell's visits to London began before the death of his wife in 1711. It was probably through the influence of Swift that Parnell made contact with the Whig writers Joseph Addison and Richard Steele, from whom Swift was not yet estranged. On 18 August and 4 October 1711 Parnell contributed allegorical papers to the *Spectator* (nos. 460 and 501), the first of his works to appear in print. In 1713, he contributed two untitled essays to the *Guardian* (nos. 56 and 66). His first poems to be published were several lyrics including the "Hymn to Contentment" that appeared in Steele's *Poetical Miscellanies* of 1714.

Through attachment to the interests of the church and through the influence of Swift, Parnell was increasingly drawn to side with the Tories. Swift in fact hoped to obtain a government diplomatic post for his friend, but the plan fell

through. It was at this time that Parnell was completing his verse treatise *An Essay on the Different Stiles of Poetry* (1713), and Swift prevailed upon his friend to turn the conclusion into a compliment to the leading Tory figure, Henry St. John, Viscount Bolingbroke. The poem, in the tradition of Horace's *Ars Poetica* (12-8 B.C.) and Pope's *Essay on Criticism* (1711), is an eloquent statement of neoclassical ideals, describing, as Addison had in the *Spectator*, various regions of false wit before coming to the realm of true poetry.

In the same year that his essay was published Parnell began to meet informally with Pope, Swift, John Gay, and Dr. John Arbuthnot, the nucleus of what was soon to become the Scriblerus Club. Parnell's exact contribution to the club's literary projects cannot now be determined, though it is clear from remarks by the other members that he was valued for his learning and his social gifts. One amusing anecdote from this time (reported by Oliver Goldsmith in his "Life of Parnell," 1770) tells how Parnell memorized an extract from a draft of *The Rape of the Lock* (1714) as Pope read it to them and, turning it later that night into Latin verse, was able the next day to accuse Pope of plagiarism.

Parnell's friendship with Pope blossomed; he stayed with him at Binfield and spent considerable time helping him with the scholarly aspects of translating Homer. Such assistance was crowned by Parnell's "Essay on the Life, Writings and Learning of Homer" that appeared at the front of Pope's *Iliad* in 1715.

With the fall of the Tories in 1714 Parnell returned to Ireland, and he was presented with the vicarage of Finglass there in 1716. Yet he felt, as he wrote in "To Mr. Pope," "Far from the joys that with my soul agree, / From wit, from learning ... from thee." His thoughts were still with the literary controversies of London, and he worked after his return on his translation of a mock-heroic poem attributed to Homer, the *Battle of the Frogs and Mice*, which Parnell published in 1717 together with his prose satire *The remarks of Zoilus, To which is prefix'd the life of the said Zoilus*. This book has the distinction of being the first of the Scriblerus Club products to be published. In its lightness of tone and brilliant use of perspective the translation is one of Parnell's best performances. It has been shown to relate closely to Pope's own translation (1715-1720), exemplifying its principles and at the same time burlesquing it in an affectionate way. The life of Zoilus, the notoriously pettifogging critic of Homer, indi-

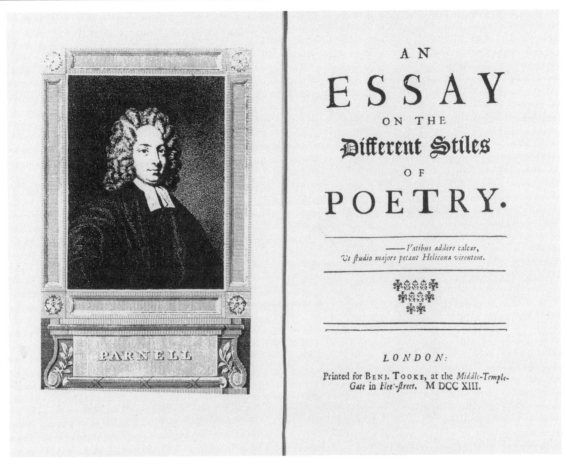

AN
ESSAY
ON THE
Different Stiles
OF
POETRY.

—— *Vatibus addere calcar,*
Ut studio majore petant Helicona virentem.

LONDON:

Printed for BENJ. TOOKE, at the *Middle-Temple-*
Gate in *Fleet-street.* M DCC XIII.

Frontispiece and title page for Parnell's first book, a poem in the tradition of Horace's Ars Poetica, *that delineates Parnell's neoclassical aesthetics*

rectly deals with Pope's detractors. Pope's letters make it clear that he was delighted with the whole work.

Parnell died suddenly at Chester on 24 October 1718, at the age of thirty-nine, on the return journey to Ireland after a summer visit to England. It was believed that his death was hastened by the excessive drinking and melancholy that began after the death of his wife.

The greatest memorial to Parnell's friendship with Pope was the posthumous volume of Parnell's *Poems on Several Occasions* that Pope edited and published at the end of 1721 (with 1722 on the title page). The volume is prefaced by Pope's dedicatory poem to Robert Harley, Lord Oxford, in which Pope praises Parnell as one "with gentlest manners, softest arts adorn'd" and as a poet who is "blest in ev'ry strain." The volume, which consists of poems Parnell had written from just before his first meeting with Pope to a few months before his death, is well arranged to

make the best of Parnell's talents as a poet of classical poise, polished finish, and sweet sentiment. It begins with a striking achievement, "Hesiod; or, The Rise of Woman," a carefully patronizing, archly noncommital satiric account of the gods' creation of women as a punishment for men. The poem deserves more attention than it has received as an analogue to *The Rape of the Lock* and as a good example of the way early-eighteenth-century reverence for "the fair" may be used to mask traditional misogyny.

The main body of the collection establishes Parnell's mastery in a miscellany of lighter verse. The song "When thy beauty appears," for example, is a deservedly popular and graceful love compliment. "A Fairy Tale in the Ancient English Style" is significant as an early response to Addison's well-known *Spectator* essay on "the fairy way of writing" (12 July 1712), though it is important to notice that Parnell's exploration of the poetic charm of the world of fairies is heavily moralized at the conclusion and that Parnell distances

Illustration for "Hesiod; or, The Rise of Woman"; published as the frontispiece for the 1770 edition of Parnell's Poems on Several Occasions

himself by attributing the tale to his childhood nurse.

Parnell's deft classicism is evident not only in the translation of "The Battle of the Frogs and Mice" but also in the elegant version of the "Vigil of Venus." "The Flies: An Eclogue" combines the mock-heroic of the former with the nature poetry of the latter and creates an ironic picture of careless poetic flies in an age dominated by the workmanlike ants. More moralistic is the Horatian "An Elegy to an old Beauty," which contains a well-known couplet about an elderly coquette's pretty granddaughter: "And all that's madly wild or oddly gay, / We call it only pretty *Fanny's* way."

As the volume moves toward its close the morality becomes predominant and specifically Chris-

tian, first in Samuel Johnson's favorite among Parnell's poems, "An Allegory on Man," and then in the three best-known and most influential of his poems, "A Hymn on Contentment," "The Hermit," and "A Night Piece on Death." Elaborate claims for original nature poetry and "preromantic" qualities have been made for all three. In the first, Parnell's octosyllabic couplets preserve hints of a seventeenth-century religious lyricism about nature, and he carries over the mode of the inspired prophetic poet from his early exercises in the biblical sublime. These elements are blended with Newton's influence in the idea of God as the "great source of Nature." What is seen here, in other words, is a deft modernizing of earlier traditions, not a romantic anticipation, and the poem is entirely orthodox in suggesting the need for spiritual purgation before a life of contemplative contentment in God and nature becomes possible.

The same is true of "The Hermit." Parnell takes a crude old parable about the restoration of a hermit's faith in providence by the actions of an angel in disguise and turns it into a gracefully symmetrical narrative. His hermit has all the conventional trappings and greatly appealed to later poets, but he remains a Christian contemplative, not a romantic solitary, and the theodicy, though not without the complacency that characterizes many such attempts in the period, remains primary.

"A Night Piece" achieves an extraordinary measured felicity of statement:

How deep yon Azure dies the Sky!
Where Orbs of Gold unnumber'd lye,
While thro' their Ranks in silver pride
The nether Crescent seems to glide.
The slumb'ring Breeze forgets to breathe,
The Lake is smooth and clear beneath,
Where once again the spangled Show
Descends to meet our Eyes below.

Yet it would be wrong to take this beautifully allusive conventional description as innovative and original nature poetry. It would be even more misleading to overemphasize the "Gothic" aspects of the poem. It is true that these were taken up by Parnell's imitators, such as Robert Blair in *The Grave* (1743), and that they influenced Thomas Gray's *Elegy Written in a Country Churchyard* (1751). But in Parnell's poem such elements are checked and corrected, in a remarkable stroke of Christian wit, by Death himself: "Fools! if you less provok'd your Fears / No more my Spectre-

Form appears." The poem is carefully arranged to move from darkness to the light of Christian resurrection at the close. It is a well-crafted piece of Christian consolation, not primarily an indulgence in a graveyard frisson.

The many eighteenth-century admirers of Parnell as a poet of polished sentiment included David Hume and Oliver Goldsmith, but they had a shock with the appearance of a volume of his so-called *Posthumous Works* in 1758. Johnson was only one of those who refused to believe in the authenticity of the volume. Recent scholarship has made clear, however, that the book was created out of the great mass of biblical and other apprentice poems not included in Pope's edition. They can indeed add little to Parnell's reputation, but they are interesting in showing how the poet was able to develop toward classical restraint and polite wit in his later career without losing touch with elements of the religious sublime. "A Night Piece" even more than "The Hermit" is the crown of this achievement.

Edmund Gosse, in *A History of Eighteenth-Century Literature* (1889), was one of those whose keen enthusiasm for Parnell's best poems led them to attribute "preromantic" qualities to him and to present him as the possessor of considerable "imagination, in the purely Wordsworthian sense." Modern critics such as Donald Davie have come to see him not as the precursor of the Romantics but as the poet of his own distinctive moment. Parnell delicately refines Christian sentiment to suit the tastes of his age and blends it with classicism. He achieves at his best, in Davie's words, a "valuable urbanity, a civilised moderation and elegance."

Biography:
Oliver Goldsmith, "Life of Parnell," in *Poems on Several Occasions written by Dr. Thomas Parnell* (London: Printed for T. Davies, 1770).

References:
A. H. Cruikshank, "Thomas Parnell, or What was Wrong with the Eighteenth Century?," *Essays and Studies*, 7 (1927): 57-81;

Donald Davie, *Purity of Diction in English Verse* (New York: Oxford University Press, 1953), pp. 41, 49n, 67, 68, 139, 197-198;

Richard Dircks, "Parnell's 'Batrachomuomachia' and the Homer Translation Controversy," *Notes and Queries*, 201 (August 1956): 339-342;

Hoxie Neale Fairchild, *Religious Trends in English Poetry* (New York: Columbia University Press, 1939), I: 231-236;

Edmund Gosse, *A History of Eighteenth-Century Literature* (London: Macmillan, 1889), p. 136;

A. P. Hudson, "The Hermit and Divine Providence," *Studies in Philology*, 28 (October 1931): 218-234;

C. J. Rawson, "New Parnell Manuscripts," *Scriblerian*, 1 (Spring 1969): 1-2;

Rawson, "Swift's Certificate to Parnell's Posthumous Works," *Modern Language Review*, 57 (April 1962): 179-182;

Rawson and F. P. Lock, "Scriblerian Epitaphs by Thomas Parnell," *Review of English Studies*, 33 (May 1982): 148-157;

T. M. Woodman, "Parnell, Politeness and 'Pre-Romanticism,'" *Essays in Criticism*, 33 (July 1983): 205-219;

Woodman, "'Softest Manners, Gentlest Arts': The Polite Verse of Thomas Parnell," in his *Politeness and Poetry in the Age of Pope* (Rutherford, N.J.: Fairleigh Dickinson University Press / London & Toronto: Associated University Presses, 1989), pp. 55-69;

Woodman, *Thomas Parnell* (Boston: Twayne, 1985).

John Philips

(30 December 1676 - 15 February 1708)

Caroline L. McAlister

Emory University

BOOKS: *The Splendid Shilling. A Poem, In Imitation of Milton* [unauthorized] (London: Printed & sold by B. Bragg, 1705); authorized edition published as *The Splendid Shilling. An Imitation of Milton. Now First Correctly Published* (London: Printed for Tho. Bennet, 1705);

Bleinheim, a Poem, Inscrib'd to the Right Honourable Robert Harley, Esq. (London: Printed for Tho. Bennet, 1705);

Cerealia: An Imitation of Milton (London: Printed for Thomas Bennet, 1706);

Honoratissimo Viro, Henrico St.-John, Armigero, Ode (London: Printed for J. Bowyer, 1707);

Cyder. A Poem. In Two Books (London: Printed for Jacob Tonson, 1708);

The Works of Mr. John Philips . . . To which is prefix'd, His Life and Character (London: Printed & sold by E. Curll, 1712);

The Poems of John Philips, edited by M. G. Lloyd Thomas (Oxford: Blackwell, 1927).

As the first Miltonic imitator, John Philips is responsible for keeping blank verse alive at the beginning of the eighteenth century. In an era that favored the elegant rhymed poetry of Alexander Pope and Jonathan Swift and frowned on John Milton's harsh lines, Philips paved the way for later writers of blank verse, such as William Cowper and James Thomson. Philips was a parodist, whose attitude toward Milton was at once emulous and playful. With wit and humor he carried Milton beyond the narrow walls of the academy to clubs and coffeehouses. He also managed to overcome the stumbling block of Milton's radical politics, adapting the antimonarchist to the purposes of eighteenth-century nationalism and making him respectable and readable in an age that frowned on political dissent.

Philips was born at Bampton, Oxfordshire, where his father, Stephen Philips, was the vicar. He was the sixth of seven sons. His paternal grandfather was the canon-residentiary of Hereford Cathedral and a staunch royalist. Philips developed an affinity for Milton while a student at Winches-

John Philips (engraving based on a painting by Godfrey Kneller)

ter. The *Biographia Britannica* says that he would retire to his room and procure a person to comb his hair: "In this very singular recreation he felt an exquisite delight. . . . He would sit almost absolutely without motion for several hours together, enjoying the pleasure it gave him with the highest degree of sensibility. It was in these intervals chiefly that he read Milton." Philips, however, did not seek to imitate Milton's sober demeanor or style of life. At Oxford Philips gained a reputation for being good company when in his cups. His best friend was Edmund Smith, also a poet and a notorious rake, referred to popularly as "Captain Rag" and "the handsome sloven." Philips gained the patronage of Robert Harley and Henry St. John in 1704, when they engaged him to write a poem celebrating John Churchill, Duke of Marlborough's victories at Bleinheim. Philips remained at the university, making brief visits to patrons and friends in London, until he died of a lingering consumption and asthma at the age of thirty-two.

Philips was extremely shy about the publication of his verses, and his first extant poem, *The Splendid Shilling. A Poem, In Imitation of Milton* (separately published in 1705), appeared without his consent in *A Collection of Poems* published by Daniel Brown and Benjamin Tooke in 1701. In a light vein Philips applies high Miltonic language and conventions to the unheroic experiences of a young man fleeing the debt collector. The arrival of the Dunn and the Catchpole on the student's doorstep evokes the gruesome appearance of Sin and Death at the gates of hell in Milton's *Paradise Lost*, as Philips writes:

> His faded Brow
> Entrench'd with many a Frown, and *Conic* Beard,
> And spreading Band, admir'd by Modern Saints,
> Disastrous Acts forbode; . . .
>   Behind him stalks
> Another Monster, not unlike himself,
> Sullen of Aspect, by the Vulgar call'd
> A *Catchpole*, whose polluted hands the Gods
> With Force incredible, and Magick Charms
> Erst have indu'd. . . .

Philips skillfully deflates the horror of this moment by comparing in an extended heroic simile the Dunn's pursuit of the student to a "Grimalkin's" pursuit of "domestick Vermin." He playfully intermingles Miltonic words such as "transfix'd," "Nectareous," and "discontinuous" with slang for tobacco and loose breeches: "mundungus," and "galligaskins."

Samuel Johnson's comments on *The Splendid Shilling* accurately assess Philips's achievement. He notes that to "degrade the sounding words and stately construction of Milton, by an application to the lowest and most trivial things, gratifies the mind with a momentary triumph over that grandeur which hitherto held its captives in admiration; the words and things are presented with a new appearance, and novelty is always grateful where it gives no pain." To conquer the anxiety produced by Milton's excellence is no small feat. In diminishing Milton, Philips makes him more approachable. Joseph Addison's judgment in 1710 that *The Splendid Shilling* was "the finest bur-

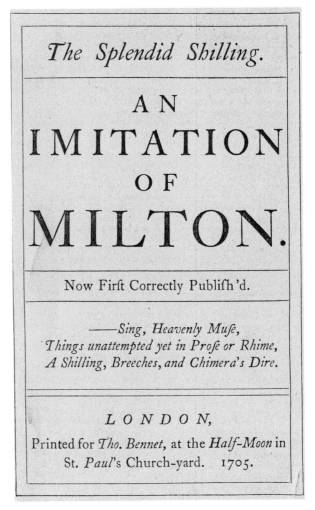

Title page for the authorized edition of Philips's first published poem, a light satire praised by Samuel Johnson and Joseph Addison among others

lesque poem in the British language" indicates the success and influence it had in the years immediately following its publication.

Philips imitates Milton in the progression of his poetic development as well as in the style of his verse. His second poem is in a more clearly heroic mode than "The Splendid Shilling," and, like Milton, he self-consciously announces his intentions to move on "From Low and abject Themes . . . to sing of Arms / Triumphant" in his invocation to the Muse. *Bleinheim, a Poem, Inscrib'd to the Right Honourable Robert Harley, Esq.,* was commissioned in 1705 by the Tories in response to Addison's *Campaign*. It thus properly belongs in the realm of polemic. Philips himself is reported to have been displeased with the artistic results of *Bleinheim*. His use of Miltonic conventions, borrowed from book VI of *Paradise Lost*, to depict a recent and actual battle are in some in-

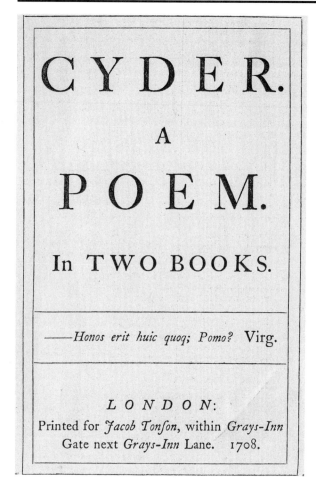

Title page for Philips's last poem, which celebrates English agriculture in the manner of Virgil's Georgics

heaven. The theme of national glory and the fulsome praise of the monarch in *Bleinheim*, however, could not be more unlike Milton. By invoking Milton in a nationalistic paean, Philips appropriates him for the mainstream of English poetry.

In his next work Philips returned happily to his earlier, mock-heroic vein to toast England's recent victories by singing the praises of English ale. He entitled the poem *Cerealia: An Imitation of Milton* (1706). Bacchus and Ceres hold a rousing debate over whether wine or beer is the better liquor for hailing the English heroes. While in *Bleinheim* Philips lauds the leadership and tactics of Churchill, in *Cerealia* he praises the spirit of the common fighting man, "Britain's hardy Sons, of Rustic Mould." Miltonic similes abound, and Philips satirizes the austere reformer when he compares the old soldier fired up with ale to a snake who has shed his old skin and rears "his crested head." Playfully he strips Milton's images of their serious moral connotations. *Cerealia* was one of the first of innumerable drinking poems that were popular in the eighteenth century.

Philips wrote one Latin ode, *Honoratissimo Viro* (1707), in honor of his patron, Henry St. John, later Viscount Bolingbroke, who was a renowned drinker, a rake, and a philanderer as well as a lover of letters and a political philosopher. Philips praises the generosity of St. John's cellars as well as his coffers. He offers St. John felicitations on his recent marriage (an unhappy match according to historians) and laments his own unrequited passion for a girl named Molly. A humorous celebration of friendship, liquor, and love, the Latin ode to St. John has the same light, jesting tone that characterizes Philips's English verse. Although in *The Reason of Church Government* Milton refers to poetry written in praise of patrons as "the trencher fury of a riming parasite," it is by the standards of the eighteenth century that Philips's ode should be judged. Philips's first biographer, John Sewell, wrote in 1712 that the ode is "certainly a Masterpiece: The style is pure and elegant, the Subject of a mixt Nature, resembling the sublime Spirit, and gay, facetious Humour of Horace." Johnson concurred in *Lives of the English Poets*, calling Philips's poem "gay and elegant." Indeed Philips works well within rigid conventions and within the blending constraints of patronage. He excels at elegance and wit rather than profundity or originality.

Philips's last poem, *Cyder* (1708), a celebration of England's agricultural achievements, is

stances infelicitous. Indeed, Johnson, in his *Lives of the English Poets* (volume 1), complains that *Bleinheim* is the poem "of a scholar, all inexpert of war; of a man who writes books from books, and studies the world in a college." Arnold Stein has argued that Milton's war in heaven has a comic-book quality and so, unfortunately, does Philips's description of cannon blasts that "Behead whole Troops at once; the hairy Scalps / Are whirl'd aloof, while numerous Trunks bestrow / Th'ensanguined Field." Other borrowings, however, work well: for example, in describing how Marlborough pushed the French troops into the Danube, Philips evokes Milton's depiction of the routed devils, pushed over the edge of heaven by Christ. To his credit, Philips sings of the glory of Marlborough's victory but not the glory of war. He concludes *Bleinheim* on an unusual pastoral note, perhaps suggested to him by Milton's placement of the pastoral Edenic portions of *Paradise Lost* directly after the battle in

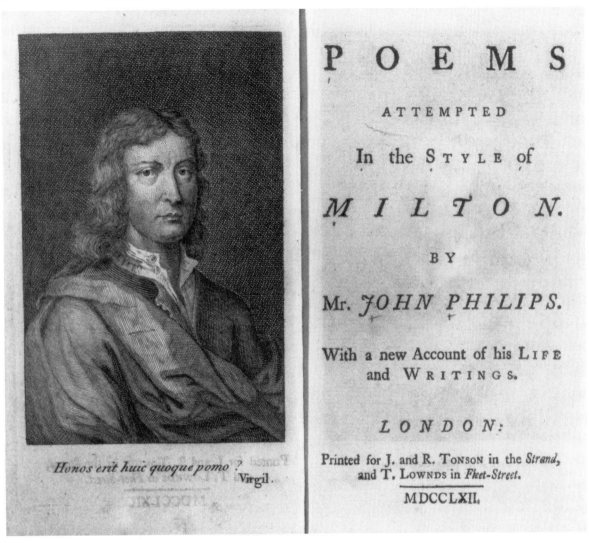

Frontispiece and title page for a 1762 collection of Philips's Miltonic poems (Special Collections, Thomas Cooper Library, University of South Carolina)

modeled after Virgil's *Georgics* as well as the Edenic portions of *Paradise Lost*. Like Virgil, Philips employs the georgic form for nationalistic and political purposes. He sings the praise of English crops and products, challenging the French and the Italians to produce wines of an equal caliber. Aware, like Virgil, of the destruction and horror of civil war, he hails the peace and prosperity England enjoys under Queen Anne. Philips is unlike Virgil, however, in his unabashed optimism. Virgil maintains a cautious tone throughout the four books of *The Georgics*. He emphasizes the hardships of the farmer's life and the tenuousness of his control over nature, advising the farmer to store up grain against future droughts. Virgil also reveals a certain political skepticism

when he predicts further outbreaks of civil war. Philips, by contrast, celebrates the regular production of an agricultural surplus and the concomitant economic boon for the English nation. He represents peace under Queen Anne as solid and secure, with a note of bravado in his poetic voice.

By invoking Milton's Eden as well as Virgil's countryside, Philips implies that the English countryside is a second Eden, surpassing Virgil's difficult, unstable georgic world. He is delightfully aware of the fact that Milton would have found such a suggestion of a second, secular paradise on earth blasphemous. Philips announces his debt to the English poet with a sly note of humorous impiety: "Thy gift, *Pomona,* in *Miltonian* Verse / Adventrous I presume to sing." By choosing to praise the apple, cause of Adam and Eve's fall, he wittily subverts Miltonic gravity. Although he writes in "Miltonian verse," his subject is the unqualified agricultural, economic, and political success of the English nation under Queen Anne, not sin and damnation. *Cyder* is undoubtedly Philips's cleverest transformation of Milton. He invokes him in order to overturn him, translating his paradise to the present and countering his revolutionary politics. In the conclusion to the first book he regrets that Milton had not "like his *Abdiel* been, / 'Mong many faithless, strictly faithful found." Yet he invokes Milton specifically for patriotic purposes, canonizing him as the English master of georgic verse.

Philips's themes in *Cyder* are of course less grand, less profound, less universal than Milton's in *Paradise Lost*. Philips was a master of the small

poem and the small subject, of wit and style rather than grand ideas. His achievement lies in accommodating the high Miltonic style to the elegant, neoclassical tastes of the eighteenth century. Although he is seldom studied today, Philips was widely read in his own time, his collected poems reaching a tenth edition by 1744. He thus exerted a considerable influence on the development of eighteenth-century poetic tastes.

References:

Dustin Griffin, *Regaining Paradise* (Cambridge: Cambridge University Press, 1986);

Raymond Dexter Havens, *The Influence of Milton on English Poetry* (Cambridge, Mass.: Harvard University Press, 1922);

Samuel Johnson, *Lives of the English Poets,* volume 1 (Oxford: Clarendon Press, 1905).

Alexander Pope

(21 May 1688 - 30 May 1744)

Aubrey L. Williams
University of Florida

SELECTED BOOKS: *An Essay On Criticism* (London: Printed for W. Lewis & sold by W. Taylor, T. Osborn & J. Graves, 1711);

Windsor-Forest. To the Right Honourable George Lord Lansdown (London: Printed for Bernard Lintott, 1713);

The Rape of the Lock. An Heroi-Comical Poem. In Five Canto's (London: Printed for Bernard Lintott, 1714; revised, 1718);

The Temple of Fame: A Vision (London: Printed for Bernard Lintott, 1715);

The Works of Mr. Alexander Pope (London: Printed by W. Bowyer for Bernard Lintot, 1717; enlarged edition, Dublin: Printed by & for George Grierson, 1727);

Eloisa to Abelard (London: Printed for Bernard Lintot, 1720 [i.e., 1719]);

The Dunciad. An Heroic Poem. In Three Books (London: Printed for A. Dodd, 1728); revised and enlarged as *The Dunciad, Variorum. With the Prolegomena of Scriblerus* (London: Printed for A. Dod [sic], 1729); revised and enlarged again as *The Dunciad, In Four Books. Printed according to the complete Copy found in the Year 1742. With the Prolegomena of Scriblerus, And Notes Variorum. To which are added, Several Notes now first publish'd, the Hypercritics of Aristarchus, and his Dissertation on the Hero of the Poem* (London: Printed for M. Cooper, 1743);

An Epistle To The Right Honourable Richard Earl of Burlington. Occasion'd by his Publishing Palladio's Designs of the Baths, Arches, Theatres, &c. of Ancient Rome (London: Printed for L. Gilliver, 1731); enlarged as *Of False Taste . . .* (London: Printed for L. Gilliver, 1731 [i.e., 1732]);

Of The Use of Riches, An Epistle To the Right Honorable Allen Lord Bathurst (London: Printed by J. Wright for Lawton Gilliver, 1732);

The First Satire Of The Second Book of Horace, Imitated in a Dialogue between Alexander Pope of Twickenham . . . and his Learned Council (Lon-

Alexander Pope in 1716 (painting by Godfrey Kneller; collection of Baron Barnard, Raby Castle, Durham)

don: Printed by L. G. & sold by A. Dodd, E. Nutt & the booksellers of London & Westminster, 1733);

An Essay On Man. In Epistles to a Friend, anonymous, 4 volumes (London: Printed for J. Wilford, 1733-1734); republished in one volume as *An Essay on Man, Being the First Book of Ethic Epistles to Henry St. John, L. Bolingbroke* (London: Printed by J. Wright for Lawton Gilliver, 1734; Philadelphia: Printed by William Bradford, 1747);

The Impertinent, Or A Visit to the Court. A Satyr (London: Printed for John Wileord [Wilford], 1733);

An Epistle To The Right Honourable Richard Lord Visct. Cobham (London: Printed for Lawton Gilliver, 1733 [i.e., 1734]);

The Second Satire Of The Second Book of Horace Paraphrased (London: Printed for L. G., 1734);

Sober Advice From Horace, To The Young Gentlemen about Town. As deliver'd in his Second Sermon (London: Printed for T. Boreman, 1734); republished as *A Sermon against Adultery* (London: Printed for T. Cooper, 1738);

An Epistle From Mr. Pope, To Dr. Arbuthnot (London: Printed for Lawton Gilliver, 1735);

The Works of Mr. Alexander Pope, Volume II (London: Printed for L. Gilliver, 1735);

Of The Characters of Women: An Epistle To A Lady (London: Printed for Lawton Gilliver, 1735);

The Second Epistle Of The Second Book of Horace, Imitated (London: Printed for R. Dodsley, 1737);

The First Epistle Of The Second Book of Horace, Imitated ["To Augustus"] (London: Printed for T. Cooper, 1737);

The Sixth Epistle Of The First Book of Horace Imitated (London: Printed for L. Gilliver, 1738);

The First Epistle Of The First Book Of Horace Imitated (London: Printed for R. Dodsley, 1738);

One Thousand Seven Hundred and Thirty Eight. A Dialogue Something like Horace (London: Printed for T. Cooper, 1738);

One Thousand Seven Hundred and Thirty Eight. Dialogue II (London: Printed for R. Dodsley, 1738);

The Works of Alexander Pope Esq. In Nine Volumes Complete. With His Last Corrections, Additions, And Improvements; As they were delivered to the Editor a little before his Death; Together With the Commentaries and Notes of Mr. Warburton (London: Printed for J. & P. Knapton, 1751).

Editions and Collections: *The Works of Alexander Pope*, edited by Whitwell Elwin and W. J. Courthope, 10 volumes (London: Murray, 1871-1889);

The Prose Works of Alexander Pope: The Earlier Works, 1711-1720, edited by Norman Ault (Oxford: Blackwell, 1936);

The Twickenham Edition of the Poems of Alexander Pope, edited by John Butt and others, 11 volumes (London: Methuen, 1938-1968);

The Prose Works of Alexander Pope: The Major Works, 1725-1744, edited by Rosemary Cowler (Hamden, Conn.: Archon, 1986).

THE

RAPE of the *LOCKE.*

AN

HEROI-COMICAL

POEM.

Nolueram, Belinda, *tuos violare capillos,*
Sed juvat hoc precibus me tribuiffe tuis.
MART. Lib. 12. Ep. 86.

Printed for BERNARD LINTOTT. 1712.

Title page for the first version of Pope's well-known satire, in Lintott's Miscellaneous Poems and Translations

OTHER: *Pastorals*, in *Poetical Miscellanies: The Sixth Part* (London: Printed for Jacob Tonson, 1709);

"The Rape of the Locke, An Heroi-Comical Poem" (original two-canto version) and other poems, in *Miscellaneous Poems and Translations. By Several Hands* (London: Printed for Bernard Lintott, 1712);

The Works of Shakespear, edited by Pope (London: Printed for Jacob Tonson, 1725);

"Peri Bathous, Or The Art of Sinking in Poetry" and other poems, in *Miscellanies. The Last Volume* (London: Printed for B. Motte, 1727).

TRANSLATIONS: *January and May; Or The Merchant's Tale: From Chaucer* and *The Episode of Sarpedon, Translated from the Twelfth and Sixteenth Books of Homer's Iliads*, in *Poetical Miscellanies: The Sixth Part* (London: Printed for Jacob Tonson, 1709);

Sappho to Phaon, in *Ovid's Epistles, Translated by Several Hands* (London: Printed for Jacob Tonson, 1712);

The First Book of Statius his Thebais in *Miscella-
neous Poems and Translations. By Several
Hands* (London: Printed for Bernard
Lintott, 1712);

The Iliad of Homer, 6 volumes (London: Printed
for Bernard Lintot, 1715-1720);

The Odyssey of Homer, 5 volumes (London: Printed
for Bernard Lintot, 1725-1726).

There was a time when scholars, and educated people in general, tended to think of the
first half of the eighteenth century as the "Age
of Pope." Now the period is more commonly
termed the "Augustan Age" or the "Neoclassical
Period." Yet the earlier denomination, no matter
its simplistic emphasis on the poetic art of one
man at the expense of great achievements by others in prose fiction, accurately reflects the fact
that Alexander Pope, both in his superbly crafted
verse and in his equally crafted public persona,
seemed, in the eyes of many gifted literary contemporaries if not of everyone else, to be the presiding artistic genius of his time.

Some degree of the esteem, and even awe,
aroused by his poetic powers and by his reputation for an exalted ethical rectitude is reflected in
the words of two of his most eminent contemporaries. Jonathan Swift, one of Pope's dearest
friends, in a fit of poetic petulance perhaps not altogether feigned, wrote, in *Verses on the Death of
Dr. Swift* (1739):

> In Pope, I cannot read a Line,
> But with a Sigh, I wish it mine:
> When he can in one Couplet fix
> More Sense than I can do in Six:
> It gives me such a jealous Fit,
> I cry, Pox take him, and his Wit.

The second testimony comes from David Garrick, the most esteemed actor of the eighteenth
century, who in later life recalled the occasion in
the winter of 1742 when Pope, who had less than
two years to live, attended a triumphant appearance of Garrick in the title role of Shakespeare's
Richard III. "When I was told . . . that POPE was
in the house," Garrick said (as quoted in *The Memoirs of the Life, and Writing of Percival Stockdale*, volume 2, 1809), "I instantaneously felt a palpitation
at my heart; a tumultuous, not a disagreeable emotion in my mind. I was then in the prime of
youth; and in the zenith of my theatrical ambition. It gave me a particular pleasure that RICH-
ARD was my character, when POPE was to see,
and hear me. As I opened my part; I saw our lit-

tle poetical hero; dressed in black; seated in a
side box, near the stage; and viewing me with a serious, and earnest attention. His look shot, and
thrilled, like lightning, through my frame; and I
had some hesitation in proceeding, from anxiety,
and from joy. As RICHARD gradually blazed
forth, the house was in a roar of applause; and
the conspiring hand of Pope shadowed me with
laurels." The character Garrick was playing before the diminutive hunchback Pope was ironically that of the legendary "crookback" Richard
III.

Tributes such as these, while serving to recall the genuine esteem in which Pope was regarded by some of the best talents of his time, obviously give a lopsided impression of the character
and art of a man whose actual existence, to use
his own words about the life of any so-called
"wit" (in the preface to the 1717 edition of his collected works), was for the most part "a warfare
upon earth." Throughout his life Pope struggled
not only with the extreme infirmities of a congeni-
tally frail constitution but also against various
establishments–religious, political, and critical–of
his time. And as much as it is possible to see him
as the very glass and mold of his age (master of a
shimmering poetic mode and self-conscious ava-
tar of certain traditional and putatively classical
values, private as well as public), it is well to keep
in mind that he was also a spokesman for values
and visions soon to be almost totally forsaken
and for which he was to suffer reprobation in
the oncoming Romantic and Victorian climates of
sensibility. Though he became, in the eyes of
many, *arbiter morum* as well as *arbiter elegantiarum*
to his own age, he himself was guilty of enough
bellicosity, petty intrigue, and self-aggrandize-
ment to forfeit, for many nineteenth-century readers, the high and special regard he received
through most of the eighteenth century. In the
twentieth century, with the publication of a definitive edition of all his works, a five-volume edition
of his letters, and a substantive and sympathetic biography, as well as the arrival of a critical sensibility willing to engage his art in more understanding and more historical terms, Pope once again,
with all his many personal shortcomings, seems securely positioned as the greatest English poet between John Milton and William Wordsworth.

The year of Pope's birth, 1688, was also the
year of the "Glorious Revolution," when the
Roman Catholic monarch James II, having alien-
ated most of the overwhelmingly Protestant population of England by his foolish endeavors to im-

Edith Turner Pope, the poet's mother (etching by C. Carter, based on a drawing by Jonathan Richardson)

pose Romish policies and appointees on church and state, was forced to abdicate his throne. Fleeing to France, James was replaced by William of Orange, a Protestant Dutch prince who had married James's Protestant daughter Mary and who had been invited to assume the throne by a coalition of Whigs and Tories, Anglicans (members of the Church of England), and Dissenters (Protestants who denied the authority of the Church of England in matters of doctrine and usage). The major group disadvantaged by this relatively peaceful revolution was the Roman Catholics; for repressive measures soon prohibited them from openly practicing their religion or holding public office, from inheriting and purchasing land or owning a horse valued at more than five pounds (an animal worth five pounds or less would presumably be of little military value), from living within ten miles of London, and from attending "public schools" (such as Eton, Rugby, and West-

minster) or the universities of Oxford and Cambridge. Such strictures, while not always rigorously enforced, necessarily circumscribed and influenced the daily life and upbringing of the young Pope, the child of Catholic parents, requiring that he be educated in private schools of uneven quality or tutored at home, determining to some extent how and where he lived, instilling in him and other Catholics even from childhood a sense that, no matter how patriotic and loyal they might feel as Englishmen, they were regarded by most of their fellow countrymen as alien, perhaps even subversive. Pope's own resentment at such status surfaces frequently in his mature verse, as in *The Second Epistle Of The Second Book of Horace, Imitated* (1737), when he writes of "certain Laws, by Suff'rers thought unjust," which not only deprived his own family of their "paternal Cell" but denied to any Roman Catholic "all Hopes of Profit or of Trust"; or when he alludes

Pope at age seven (anonymous portrait; collection of James M. Osborn, New Haven)

to the London Monument—erected in memory of the Great Fire of 1666 and bearing an inscription blaming Catholics for that catastrophe—as a "tall bully" who "lifts the head, and lyes" (*Of The Use of Riches,* 1732).

Pope's father, also named Alexander, was a London linen merchant; the poet was the only child of his second marriage, to Edith Turner, of a Yorkshire family. In an edition of Virgil he later possessed, Pope recorded the exact time of his birth as follows: "Natus Maji 21, 1688, Hora Post Merid. 6 3/4" (Born May 21, 1688, 6:45 p.m.). In his early childhood Pope lived in London or its environs, but in 1700 his father, who apparently retired from business about the time of his son's birth, moved his family, perhaps to comply with the ten-mile exclusionary law, to the village of Binfield, in the royal forest of Windsor. Before the move the young Pope had received some more or less formal schooling at two small Catho-

lic academies, at one of which he was "whipped and ill-used," according to Joseph Spence, for a "satire on his master, and taken from thence on that account." Until he was about twelve, therefore, Pope's educational experience was sporadic, frequently tutorial, certainly haphazard, and foreshortened, as is apparent when he speaks of his first teacher, a priest named Bannister who started him in "Latin and Greek together" (as quoted by Spence): "I was then about eight years old, had learnt to read of an old aunt, and to write by copying printed books. After having been under that priest about a year I was sent to the seminary at Twyford, and then to a school by Hyde Park Corner [in London]—and with the two latter masters lost what little I had got under my first. [When] about twelve, I went with my father into the Forest [i.e., to Binfield] and there learned for a few months under a fourth priest. This was all the teaching I ever had, and God

The house at Binfield in Windsor Forest, where Pope spent his boyhood. Windsor-Forest *and the* Pastorals *were inspired by this idyllic setting.*

knows, it extended a very little way." In effect, Pope's education was largely the result of his own intense energy and assiduity: "He set to learning Latin and Greek by himself [at] about twelve," reported a cousin (who was also a Catholic priest), "and when he was about fifteen would go up to London [by himself] and learn French and Italian. We in the family looked upon it as a wildish sort of resolution, for as his ill health would not let him travel we could not see any reason for it. He stuck to it, went thither, and mastered both those languages with a surprising dispatch. Almost everything of this kind was of his own acquiring. He had had masters indeed, but they were very indifferent ones, and what he got was almost wholly owing to his own unassisted industry" (as quoted in Spence). Irregular and autodidactic as it was, Pope's learning was eventually such that he could move at ease among many of the best and most formally trained minds of his age.

It was not only by a restrictive religious segregation and civil disfranchisement that Pope was early set apart. Although as a child he was described, according to Spence, as having a "particularly sweet temper" and a face that was "round, plump, pretty, and of a fresh complexion," at some time during his twelfth year, having already survived a trampling by a "wild cow" when he was about three, his outward form began to exhibit the ruinous consequences of Pott's disease (tuberculosis of the spine), which he must have contracted during infancy, possibly from his nurse's breast-feeding. For Pope the infection meant a crooking of chest and humping of back, along with a devastation of constitution so severe that for the rest of his life he seemed, in the solicitous words of one of his later friends, Allen, Lord Bathurst, "to have the headache four days in a week, and to be as sick as a breeding woman the other three" (in a 20 July 1732 letter to Pope). A description of Pope by the painter Sir Joshua Reynolds, who must have scrutinized him with an eye trained better than most, gives us a vivid image of his appearance in his early fifties. He stood, wrote Reynolds, (as quoted by James Prior in *Life of Edmond Malone*, 1860), "about four feet six high; very humpbacked and deformed; he wore a black coat; and according to the fashion of that time, had on a little sword; he had a large and very fine eye, and a long handsome nose; his mouth had those peculiar marks which always are found in the mouths of crooked persons; and the muscles which run across the cheek were so strongly marked as to appear like small cords. [Louis François] Roubilliac, the statuary [i.e., sculptor], who made a bust of him from life, observed that his countenance was that of a person who had been much afflicted with headache, and he should have known the fact from the contracted appearance of the skin between his eyebrows, though he had not otherwise been apprised of it."

While Pope's friends might have regarded his deformation and infirmities with fond and solicitous eyes, he early in life got a taste of how harsh and pitiless the gaze of others could be. In his precocious *Essay On Criticism* (1711), begun in his teens and published just before his twenty-third birthday, Pope was so rash and impudent as to deride the critical dicta, as well as the mien and mannerisms, of John Dennis, a leading critic but mediocre playwright, under the sobriquet of "Appius," who "reddens at each Word you speak, / And *stares, Tremendous!* with a *threatning Eye,* / Like some *fierce Tyrant* in *Old Tapestry!*" Dennis *had* written a failed tragedy entitled *Appius and Virginia*, his favorite adjective (as everyone knew) *was* "tremendous," and he *was* famed for his overbearing manner. But in return for the effrontery of this caricature, no matter its basic accuracy (or because of it), the youthful Pope was subjected not only to a savage attack on the content and style of *An Essay On Criticism*, his Roman Catholicism, and his supposed Jacobite sympathies for the exiled James II, but to the following brutal words (in *The Critical Works of John Dennis*, volume 1, 1939): "As there is no Creature in Nature so venomous, there is nothing so stupid and so impotent as a hunch-back'd Toad"; a "young, squab [i.e., pigeon-breasted], short Gentleman," marked by "the very Bow of the God of Love"; let his person "be never so contemptible, his inward Man is ten times more ridiculous; it being impossible that his outward Form, tho' it should be that of downright Monkey, should differ so much from

human Shape, as his immaterial unthinking part does from human Understanding."

Baptized, indeed drenched, so early by so wrathful and so caustic an assault on his personal figure, Pope acquired, outwardly at least, the fortitude and the witty and deprecatory regard of self that would enable him to face, with at least an appearance of sangfroid and nonchalance, a lifetime of personal abuse from hostile quarters. Only a year after Dennis's onslaught, in a letter to Sir Richard Steele printed in the *Guardian*, 12 August 1713, Pope wrote: "When a smart fit of sickness tells me this scurvy tenement of my body will fall in a little time, I am e'en as unconcern'd as was that honest *Hibernian* [i.e., Irishman], who being in bed in the great storm some years ago [the terrible "great storm" of 1703], and told the house would tumble over his head, made answer, What care I for the house? I am only a lodger." Years later this same cast of mind enabled him to regard with scornful amusement those who, in their efforts to flatter favors out of him, made attempts to transmute his obvious physical defects into the physiognomical traits and signs of genius. In his *Epistle . . . To Dr. Arbuthnot* (1735) he writes: "There are, who to my Person pay their court, / I cough like *Horace*, and tho' lean, am short, / *Ammon*'s great Son [Alexander the Great] one shoulder had too high, / Such *Ovid*'s nose, and 'Sir! you have an *Eye*'– / Go on, obliging Creatures, make me see / All that disgrac'd my Betters, met in me." A mind of such mettle may make itself the stuff of poetry, as when Pope reminds himself (and his readers) of his deportment in spite of a harrowing personal disfigurement: "What is't to me (a Passenger God wot) / Whether my Vessel be first-rate or not? / The Ship it self may make a better figure, / But I that sail, am neither less nor bigger" (*The Second Epistle Of The Second Book of Horace, Imitated*). As a twentieth-century writer has said about a twentieth-century poet: "If poems can teach one anything, [Philip] Larkin's teach that there is no desolation so bleak it cannot be made habitable by style. If we live inside a bad joke, it is up to us to learn, at best and worst, to tell it well" (Jonathan Raban, *Coasting*, 1987).

The move to Binfield was a propitious one for Pope, for there, among a circle of Roman Catholic neighbors, he established some of his most enduring friendships. Among others, he came to know John Caryll, through whom he probably met such notable literary figures as the playwright William Wycherley and the celebrated

SPRING.

Strephon.

Let rich Iberia Golden Fleeces boast,
Her Purple Wool the proud Assyrian Coast;
Thames's Shores the brightest Beauties yield,
Feed here my Lambs, I seek no distant Field.

Daphnis.

Celestial Venus haunts Idalia's Groves,
Diana Cynthus, Ceres Ætna loves;
If Windsor Shades delight the matchless Maid,
Cynthus and Ætna stoop to Windsor Shade.

Strephon.

Say Daphnis, say, what Region canst thou find,

The Prize, the Victor's Prize, shall be thy own.

Daphnis.

Nay tell me first, in what new Grove appears
A wondrous Tree that sacred Monarchs bears!

And

The First Pastoral.

And then a nobler Prize I will resign,
For Sylvia, charming Sylvia shall be thine.

Damon.

I've heard enough; and Daphnis, I decree
The Bowl to Strephon, and the Lamb to thee;
Ye gentle Swains, let this Exchange suffice,
That each may win, as each deserves the Prize.
Now haste, ye Shepherds, to my Beechen Bow'rs,
A safe Retreat from Suddain Vernal Show'rs;
The Turf with rural Dainties shall be spread,
And twining Trees with Branches shade y.r Head.
For see, the gath'ring Flocks to Shelter bend,
And from the Pleiads fruitfull Show'rs descend.

S U M-

S U M M E R :

The Second Pastoral,

OR

A L E X I S .

A Shepherd's Boy (he seeks no better Name)
Led forth his Flocks along the silver Thame;
There to the Winds he plain'd his hapless Love,
And Amaryllis fill'd the Vocal Grove.
For him, the Lambs a dumb Compassion show,
The list'ning Streams forget a while to flow;

Relenting

The Second Pastoral.

Relenting Naids wept in ev'ry Bow'r,
And Jove consented in a silent Show'r.

Ye shady Beeches, and ye cooling Streams,
Defence from Phœbus, not from Cupid's Beams;
To you I mourn; nor to the Deaf I sing,
The Woods shall answer, and their Echo ring.
The Hills and Rocks attend my doleful Lay,
Why art thou prouder and more hard than they!
And with my Cries the bleating Flocks agree,
They parch'd with Heat, & I inflam'd by thee.
The sultry Sirius burns the thirsty Plains,
But in thy Heart eternal Winter reigns!

Where are ye, Muses, in what Lawn or Grove,
While your Alexis pines in hopeless Love?
In those fair Fields, where Sacred Isis glides;
Or else where Cam his winding Banks divides?

Oft

Last two pages of "Spring" and first two pages of "Summer" in the earliest extant manuscript (circa 1704) for Pope's Pastorals, *in the hand Pope used to imitate printing (auctioned by Christie, Manson & Woods, Ltd., 11-12 June 1980)*

actor Thomas Betterton. He became friendly also with the two young sisters Martha and Teresa Blount, both of whom were later to appear in some of his finest verse, and one of whom, Martha, was to be his lifelong friend (supposed by some, who were probably mistaken, to be his mistress). The warm, and affectionate regard Pope received from this group was powerfully supplemented by the attention and favor he gained from Sir William Trumbull, a statesman who had served three English monarchs and who, now retired to his estate near Binfield, acted as verderer, or overseer, of the Windsor Forest district. With Trumbull, Pope was later to say, according to Spence, that he used "to take a ride" on horseback in the forest "three or four days in the week, and at last, almost every day." Trumbull's affection for Pope was intense. He wrote his nephew in 1707 that "the little creature is my darling more and more." It was he, furthermore, who urged Pope to write a poem on Windsor Forest and to attempt translations of Homer. By this time Pope also apparently had come to the attention of William Walsh, member of Parliament and a minor poet and critic, and William Congreve, the best dramatist of the late seventeenth century. The results of the encouragement and fostering given to Pope by such eminent early admirers are evident in the following letter which he, a lad of seventeen, received on 20 April 1706 from Jacob Tonson, the leading publisher of the time: "Sir,—I have lately seen a pastoral of yours in mr. Walsh's and mr. Congreves hands, which is extreamly ffine & is generally approv'd off by the best Judges in poetry. I Remember I have formerly seen you at my shop & am sorry I did not Improve my Acquaintance with you. If you design your Poem for the Press no person shall be more Carefull in the printing of it, nor no one can give you a greater Incouragment to it; than Sir Your Most Obedient Humble Servant."

The four poems of the *Pastorals*, along with Pope's *Episode of Sarpedon, Translated from the Twelfth and Sixteenth Books of Homer's Iliads*, and *January and May*, his redoing in modern English of Chaucer's *Merchant's Tale*, appeared in 1709 in Tonson's *Poetical Miscellanies: The Sixth Part*. "A Discourse on Pastoral Poetry," which later prefaced the *Pastorals* in other editions, was not published until 1717 (in the collected works), but Pope always maintained that both the poems and their introductory essay were substantially in shape by 1704. If this claim is true, the works are only slightly less remarkable for their precocity than

they are for their introduction of a couplet style more refined and musical than any before in English versification. In content the four poems, named after the four seasons, may appear today as rather bland and conventional, largely because Pope chose to write in a pastoral tradition that idealized shepherd life. According to this tradition, pastoral poetry should be an "imitation" of shepherd life in a putative golden age, reflective of a state of innocence and simplicity, and devoid of any such intrusions of real life as human venality and betrayal, much less war and homicide. Such a mode of pastoral, in contrast to Virgil's *Eclogues* (37 B.C.) or Spenser's *Shepheardes Calender* (1579), is drastically limited in depth, complexity, and imaginative range. Yet the judgment of Samuel Johnson, in his *Life of Pope* (1781), may be invoked in defense of these youthful poems: "To charge these Pastorals with want of invention, is to require what was never intended.... It is surely sufficient for an author of sixteen ... to have obtained sufficient power of language, and skill in metre, to exhibit a series of versification, which had in English poetry no precedent, nor has since had an imitation." Tame in subject though the *Pastorals* may be, they nevertheless augur truly that supple couplet instrument that later would so cunningly "Eye Nature's walks, shoot Folly as it flies, / And catch the Manners living as they rise" (*An Essay On Man*, 1733-1734). Even in themselves, as in the following lines later used in George Frideric Handel's oratorio *Semele* (1744), they have given a delicate pleasure to many who may never have known their source in Pope's "Summer": "Where-e'er you walk, cool Gales shall fan the Glade, / Trees, where you sit, shall crowd into a Shade, / Where-e'er you tread, the blushing Flow'rs shall rise, / And all things flourish where you turn your Eyes."

Prophetic, in their small way, as the *Pastorals* were of things to come, it was Pope's next publication, *An Essay On Criticism*, which established him, in spite of Dennis's wrathful onslaught, as a major poetic figure. The manuscript of the poem says it was "Written in the Year 1709," but the evidence for an exact date of composition is vague. In all probability the poem was assembled from fragments written when Pope was in what, according to Spence, he called his "great reading period," the time between his thirteenth and twentieth years, when he "went through all the best critics, almost all the English, French, and Latin poets of any name, the minor poets, Homer and some other of the greater Greek poets in the origi-

Pope with his friend Martha Blount, circa 1715-1720 (painting by Charles Jervas; National Portrait Gallery, London)

nal, and Tasso and Ariosto in translations"; to this he added: "I wrote the *Essay on Criticism* fast, for I had digested all the matter in prose before I began upon it in verse." In any event, the poem appeared, anonymously, in mid May 1711, only a week before Pope turned twenty-three, and the following December it received high praise from the reigning critic of the day, Joseph Addison, in the *Spectator*. Terming it a "Masterpiece in its Kind," Addison particularly praised Pope's demonstration of the ways "*Sound* must seem an *Eccho* to the *Sense*" (as Pope writes in line 365 of the poem). Addison also admired how Pope, like Longinus, the Greek philosopher and critic, "exemplified several of his Precepts in the very Precepts themselves." Johnson, in his biography of Pope, seconded Addison's estimation of the poem, declaring that if Pope "had written

nothing else," it "would have placed him among the first criticks and the first poets, as it exhibits every mode of excellence that can embellish or dignify didactick composition, selection of matter, novelty of arrangement, justness of precept, splendour of illustration, and propriety of digression."

An Essay On Criticism is in three parts, in a design reflective of a pattern to be discovered as far back as the Old Testament and pagan classics: successive stages representative of an Edenic or golden age; a fall or decay into sin and disorder; and finally a restoration to some semblance of the original state (though not the original purity itself). In another context, in his treatise *Of Education* (1644), John Milton had written that "The end then of learning is to repair the ruins of our first parents by regaining to know God aright," a proposition reaffirmed and transferred to the secular context of poetry by, ironically enough, John Dennis, who asserted that "The great Design of Arts is to restore the Decays that happen'd to human Nature by the Fall, by restoring Order" (*The Critical Works*, volume 1).

The relevance of this traditional scheme to Pope's poem can be seen when one considers how, in part one, he creates a vision of a golden era in art and criticism, when the ancients, in a kind of springtime of the world, and with a clearer and purer perception of reality, could better follow "Nature" and the "light of Nature," that "Unerring Nature," which, "still divinely bright, / One *clear, unchang'd,* and *Universal Light,* / Life, Force, and Beauty, must to all impart, / At once the *Source,* and *End* and *Test* of Art." Nature, while not quite divine herself, yet stands as a correlative entity to that Divine Being supposed to lie behind and within all other beings–order and the source of order within the creation, mysterious yet apprehensible. The ancients, the patriarchs (such as Homer), in the secularized terms of Pope's poem but rather like Adam in paradise, were able to see more clearly than their descendants this "Nature" and reflect it in their art, to the extent that modern writers may find, even as Virgil did, that "*Nature* and *Homer* were . . . the same." In celebration of such a glorious past state, the first part ends: "Still green with Bays each *ancient* Altar stands, / Above the reach of *Sacrilegious* Hands. . . . / Hail *Bards Triumphant*! born in *happier Days*; / *Immortal* Heirs of *Universal* Praise!"

The second part of the poem creates a vision of the decay and disorder into which literary criticism has fallen, specifically because of pride, the original sin and source of all other sin: "Of all the Causes which conspire to blind / Man's erring Judgment, and misguide the Mind, / What the weak Head with strongest Byass rules, / Is *Pride,* the *never-failing Vice of Fools.*" Other eyes than Pope's saw early-eighteenth-century literary criticism as having fallen into a degenerate state. Swift, for example, in *The Battle of the Books* (1704), describes a "malignant Deity, call'd *Criticism*": "At her right hand sat *Ignorance,* her Father and Husband, blind with Age; at her left, *Pride* her Mother, dressing her up in the Scraps of Paper herself had torn. . . . About her play'd her Children, *Noise* and *Impudence, Dullness* and *Vanity, Positiveness, Pedantry,* and *Ill-Manners.*" In agreement was Samuel Cobb, who in *A Discourse of Criticism* (1707) declared: "Criticism, which was

Arabella Fermor, on whom Pope based the character Belinda in his Rape of the Lock *(painting by W. Sykes, circa 1714; collection of the Roch family, Llanarth Court, Raglan)*

formerly the Art of Judging well, is now become the pure Effect of Spleen, Passion, and Self-conceit." In such a climate it was not difficult for Pope to parallel the enervating dissensions within literary criticism to those that had characterized the history of Christianity: "Some *foreign* Writers, some our *own* despise; / The *Ancients* only, or the *Moderns* prize; / (Thus *Wit,* like *Faith,* by each Man is apply'd / To *one small Sect,* and All are *damn'd beside*)."

Having documented the divisions, failings, and egoisms that pervaded the critical establishment, Pope in the third part of the poem turns to the means of reformation, reconciliation, and restoration, making clear in his opening lines that what is needed is not simply more learning or even more acumen, but rather more personal virtue: "Learn then what MORALS Criticks ought to show, / For 'tis but *half a Judge's Task,* to Know. / 'Tis not enough, Taste, Judgment, Learning, join; / In all you speak, let Truth and Candor shine." The hortatory tenor of these lines rounds off and makes more explicit an ethical dimension and intent present throughout the poem: a concern with matters of morality amidst matters of criticism; a concern with humility ("So *vast* is Art, so *narrow* Human Wit"; "A *little Learning* is a dang'rous Thing"); with charity ("In ev'ry Work regard the *Writer's End*"; "To Err is *Humane*; to Forgive, *Divine*"); and with prudence ("Let such teach others who themselves excell"; "*Fools* rush in where *Angels* fear to tread").

Within the poem's large, conciliatory, imaginative design and embrace, one finds Pope attempting also to accommodate apparently conflicting and even contradictory artistic principles and values. The accommodations are usually made in the most appropriate, albeit teasing, rhetorical terms, those of oxymoron and paradox. On the claims of authority and the rules versus individual freedom and spontaneity, he writes: "Great Wits sometimes may *gloriously offend*, / And *rise to Faults* true Criticks *dare not mend*; / From *vulgar Bounds* with *brave Disorder* part, / And *snatch* a Grace beyond the Reach of Art"; on the serendipitous stroke versus painstaking application: "Some Beauties yet, no Precepts can declare, / For there's a *Happiness* as well as *Care*"; on, most puzzling of all, the idea that unrestricted Nature is no more productive of the "natural" than unrestricted Liberty is productive of total "freedom": "*Nature*, like *Liberty*, is but restrain'd / By the same Laws which first *herself* ordain'd." If *An Essay On Criticism* is to be taken as a neoclassical critical "platform," that platform must be seen as an attempt to pull together an array of diverse, often almost mutually exclusive premises and precepts. It is certainly not expressive of a narrow rationalistic or highly prescribed literary ideal; for as the language of the poem repeatedly makes clear, the art it endorses is an art comprehending "*nameless Graces*," "*brave Disorder*," "*gen'rous Pleasure*," and an imaginative energy "Which, without passing thro' the *Judgment*, gains / The *Heart*, and all its End *at once* attains."

The next five or six years completed the first third of Pope's career, with the publication of a variety of works scarcely anticipatory of the preeminent satirist he was to become in the last phase of his life. In 1712, in *Miscellaneous Poems and Translations. By Several Hands*, there appeared the *Fable of Vertumnus and Pomona*, a translation from Ovid, and also Pope's translation of the first book of the *Thebais*, an epic poem by the Latin poet Statius. In 1712 Pope also published another, very loose, translation from Ovid, *Sapho to Phaon*, as well as his last experiment in the pasto-

Illustration of a scene in the fourth canto of The Rape of the Lock *(engraving, circa 1717, attributed by Horace Walpole to William Hogarth)*

ral mode, *Messiah: A Sacred Eclogue*, an adjustment of certain prophetic, Messianic passages of the Old Testament Book of Isaiah to Virgil's fourth Eclogue, the "Pollio," which had predicted the birth of an infant whose reign would inaugurate a new golden age. In 1713, with the appearance of *Windsor-Forest*, Pope exchanged the pastoral mode for the georgic, etymologically suggestive of farming and the rural life, which Virgil (in his *Georgics*) had employed to celebrate the blessings of peace brought to Italy by Caesar Augustus. In his poem, Pope draws upon a variety of resources–classical, continental, and English– to celebrate the peace and prosperity England seemed to be enjoying under Queen Anne, the last of the Stuart line. In particular the poem commemorates the Treaty of Utrecht (1713), which brought an end to the War of the Spanish Succession and which ceded to Great Britain both Gibraltar and Minorca, as well as Nova Scotia, Newfoundland, and the Hudson Bay region in North America. One of Pope's predecessors in the georgic mode had been Sir John Denham, whose *Cooper's Hill* (1642), in its versification and its topographical subject matter, became one of the most admired poems of the seventeenth century. In one of Pope's comments on this work may be seen his own intentions and strategies in *Windsor-Forest*. In a note to Book XVI in his later translation of the entire *Iliad*, he speaks of Homer's "indirect and oblique manner of introducing moral Sentences and Intentions ... even in Descriptions and poetical Parts, where one naturally expects only Painting and Amusement." Pope continues: "I must do a noble *English* Poet the justice to observe, that it is this particular Art that is the very distinguishing Excellence of *Cooper's-Hill*: throughout which, the Descriptions of Places, and Images rais'd by the Poet, are still tending to some Hint, or leading into some Reflection, upon moral Life or political Institution: Much in the same manner as the real Sight of such Scenes and Prospects is apt to give the Mind a compos'd Turn, and induce it to Thoughts and Contemplations that have a Relation to the Object."

During this period Pope produced his most celebrated work, *The Rape of the Lock*: "the most airy, the most ingenious, and the most delightful of all his compositions," in the opinion of Johnson *(Life of Pope)*. First published in 1712, in two cantos of only 334 lines, the poem appeared two years later in five cantos (comprising 794 lines) and included for the first time its brilliantly conceived "machinery" (the "supernatural" personages: sylphs and gnomes, nymphs and salamanders); the heroine's ominous prophetic dream; the card game of Ombre (literally, "man"); the Cave of Spleen episode; and much more. Pope's poem is supposedly based on a real-life incident: during a social occasion in 1711, a young peer, Robert Lord Petre (the "Baron" of the poem), snipped a lock of hair from the head of a young, beauteous, and distant relation, Arabella Fermor (the poem's "Belinda"); the poem was reportedly written at the request of Pope's friend John Caryll to heal a consequent estrangement between the two families. *The Rape of the Lock* fuses classical and Christian resources in a mock-heroic manner both satirical and playfully tender. The classical background is omnipresent, from the opening invocation through the descent into the "underworld" of Belinda's bowels to the closing grandiose battle of the sexes; but the main structural design of the poem seems to depend on its sequences of allusions and parallels to Milton's *Paradise Lost*: the "Morning-Dream" summoned to the sleeping Belinda by Ariel, her "Guardian Sylph," which not only warns her of some impending "dread Event" and encourages her to know her "own Importance," but also recalls the dream, similarly encouraging of excessive self-esteem, insinuated into Eve's mind by Milton's Satan; the scene at Belinda's dressing table, where she appears to worship her own image in her mirror, is reminiscent of the newly created Eve's narcissistic admiration of her self as reflected in the Edenic pool; and most crucially, just before the Baron's cutting of Belinda's lock, the moment when Ariel seeks out the "close Recesses of the Virgin's Thought" and finds an "Earthly Lover lurking at

her Heart" clearly recalls the scene in *Paradise Lost* when, after Adam's fall of his own free will, his angelic guardians, "mute and sad," depart from him, as powerless as Ariel finds himself to be before Belinda's own free choice of an earthly rather than a sylphic lover.

Belinda's fall, in one sense, appears merely to be part of the normal human process of "falling" in love, or a maiden's innermost and private decision not to spurn so attractive and eligible a suitor as the Baron. From this point of view the state of her heart at her moment of choice deserves sympathy more than censure: neither she nor the world in general would wish her to remain a virgin forever (as the poem later says, "she who scorns a Man, must die a Maid"). But if she secretly acquiesces to the Baron's courtship (leaving aside for the moment the incivility of his approach), she has no right to consider the cutting of her lock equivalent to a "rape" of her person: it is a desired rather than a forced "deflowering." In light of Belinda's apparent compliance in the Baron's act, her immediate response to the loss of a lock seems utterly prudish and hypocritical, particularly since her outraged and tearful denial of any complicity in the event is made in defense of an "Honour" at whose "unrival'd Shrine," in the words of her friend Thalestris, "Ease, Pleasure, Virtue, All, our Sex resign." Amidst this ugly situation, an alternative to Thalestris's viragolike indignation is offered by Clarissa (the "clarifier") in a passage added to the poem by Pope in 1717, in order, he says, *"to open more clearly the MORAL of the Poem."* Based on a Homeric speech by the Trojan warrior Sarpedon, which Pope had earlier translated and published, Clarissa's words offer Belinda a course of candor and equanimity in the face of her loss (however she may define that loss). But, as one might expect in a poem so reflective of moral disarray in a society's values and priorities (a disarray succinctly established by the articles on Belinda's dressing table: "Puffs, Powders, Patches, Bibles, Billet-doux"), Ariel's sylphic tutelage of Belinda is replaced by that of Umbriel, under whose gnomish influence she chooses the path of prudery (allied in the poem with *"Ill-nature"* and *"Affectation"*) and demands an impossible "restoration" of the virginity symbolized by her stolen curl. And though the lock is actually lost for good (as her virginity, if defined as a state of psychic chastity, has been), in the tumultuous melee of the sexes in the last canto, Pope assures the reader that it has been "translated" (in the theological sense) to

Belinda's Toilet *(circa 1795), a drawing by Benjamin West of a scene from* The Rape of the Lock *(from Edmund Gosse,* English Literature: An Illustrated Record, *1903)*

the heavens and metamorphosed into a star, "consecrate to Fame." The pattern of the poem, and of Belinda's day, resembles the tripartite pattern in *An Essay On Criticism*: a state of "innocence," its loss, and a kind of "restoration."

In 1717 *Eloisa to Abelard* was published in *The Works of Mr. Alexander Pope*, another poem of extraordinary warmth and empathy for female character. Sometimes described as an example of a "pre-Romantic" trend in English letters, the poem is more properly perceived as "post-Metaphysical" in character. Again based on an actual sexual relationship, though a far more illustrious one than that of a belle and a beau, the poem may have been inspired by the publication in 1713 of an English translation of letters exchanged between Pierre Abélard, the renowned French philosopher and theologian, and his most

famous pupil, Héloïse, who became celebrated as a nun, abbess, and thinker in her own right. Falling in love when he was thirty-eight and she was seventeen, they had a son and were subsequently married, though secretly. Héloïse's uncle, a canon at Notre Dame in Paris, outraged at Abélard's seduction of his niece and unaware of their marriage, hired a gang of thugs to trap and emasculate him. Héloïse retreated to a convent, and later, when Abélard became a Benedictine monk, she, at his desire, became a Benedictine nun. Some time later Abélard founded a monastic school, which he called the Paraclete (meaning the Comforter, or Holy Spirit), and which, after he had become abbot of a monastery in Brittany, he turned over to Héloïse and a group of sisters. Pope's poem, a kind of dramatic monologue in the form of a verse epistle from Eloisa to Abe-

Frontispiece for The Works of Mr. Alexander
Pope, *1717*

lard, was provided with a headnote by the poet
in which he recalls some of their history and
states the "Argument" of his own fictional recreation of it: "*It was many years after* [their] *separation, that a letter of* Abelard's *to a Friend which
contain'd the history of his misfortune, fell into the
hands of* Eloisa. *This awakening all her tenderness,
occasion'd those celebrated letters (out of which the following is partly abstracted) which give so lively a picture
of the struggles of grace and nature, virtue and passion.*"

Struggles of "grace and nature" are scarcely
Romantic or even pre-Romantic themes, so one
must look backward to understand the shape, content, and tone of Pope's poem. One relevant precursor is the Ovidian verse epistle, in Ovid's so-
called *Heroides*, whose common theme is female
love, frequently of a despairing kind. Pope, of
course, had translated and published in 1712 one
of these epistles, *Sappho to Phaon*. The Ovidian format and subject had also been acclimated to the
English scene by earlier poets (John Donne and

Michael Drayton among them), but *Eloisa to Abelard* derives special flavor from Pope's incorpora-
tion of specifically Roman Catholic devotional
practices and theological sanctions in a highly
charged erotic dilemma for Eloisa: love of God is
apparently opposed to love of man. The dilemma may be seen as resolved by the end of the
poem but probably only by understanding the
way Pope's epistle is shaped and slanted by such
specifically Catholic devotional usages as the "spiritual exercise" (a disciplined meditation on the
events in Christ's life, most especially when one is
saying the Rosary); by earlier devotional literature (the autobiography of St. Teresa, for example) that had vividly combined the mystical and
the erotic; and by the fact that ultimately, in the
Roman Catholic vision of the totality of human experience, there really need be no essential conflict between "grace" and "nature."

As noted, Pope, from boyhood, had tried
his hand at translating various classical writers,
but he seems to have been especially attracted to
Homer. Late in life he told Spence that the translation of Homer by John Ogilby was "one of the
first large poems" he read; "he still," Spence
added, "spoke of the pleasure it then gave him,
with a sort of rapture only on reflecting on it."
And more poetically, in one of his imitations of
Horace (*The Second Epistle*), Pope writes: "Bred
up at home, full early I begun / To read in
Greek, the Wrath of Peleus' Son [Achilles]." During his early years Pope must also have been meditating on William Trumbull's suggestion that he
translate the entire *Iliad*.

At any rate, in 1713, in his twenty-fifth
year, he announced a proposal to undertake, by
subscription, just such a staggering task, one that
would dominate his life for the next seven years
or so. This period, followed by the years from
1720 to 1725, when he was additionally busied
with the translation of Homer's *Odyssey*, may be
said to constitute the second phase of Pope's literary career, when little original work appeared.
Not that the *Iliad* translation should be depreci-
ated for not being "original" work, for as Johnson unequivocally asserted in his *Life of Pope*: "It
is certainly the noblest version [translation] of poetry which the world has ever seen; and its publication must therefore be considered as one of the
great events in the annals of Learning."

Some idea of the magnitude of the undertaking, at least Pope's idea of it, may be gathered
from his comments to Spence years later: "What
terrible moments does one feel after one has en-

Frontispiece for the 1719 edition of Pope's poem inspired by the love letters of French philosopher Pierre Abélard and his student Héloïse

gaged for a large work! In the beginning of my translating the *Iliad* I wished any body would hang me, a hundred times"; the *Iliad* "took me up six years, and during that time, and particularly the first part of it, I was often under great pain and apprehensions. Though I conquered the thoughts of it in the day, they would frighten me in the night. I dreamed often of being engaged in a long journey and that I should never get to the end of it. This made so strong an impression upon me that I sometimes [in 1743, thirty years later] dream of it still."

Pope's "pain and apprehensions" intensified when rumors began to circulate that Thomas Tickell, a minor poet, university trained, and a protégé of Joseph Addison, was being egged on by Addison (even as he feigned support for Pope's venture) and his coterie at Button's Coffee House to undertake a rival translation that supposedly would reveal, by contrast, just how deficient any effort by such an upstart as Pope must be. By now, however, Pope's standing was such that, whatever his personal trepidations may have been, he was able to attract as subscribers to his translation many of the most powerful and prestigious figures of his day. And when his first volume appeared in 1715, it not only completely overshadowed Tickell's effort (which had been timed to appear simultaneously) but immediately established him in the public consciousness as the predominant literary figure of his age. In a gesture declaring his independence from any personal patronage by the rich, aristocratic, or politically powerful, he dedicated his translation to a fellow writer, William Congreve. Proceeds from the undertaking, indeed, helped found the fortune that would make Pope the first English man of letters to become financially independent by means of his own work. Specifically, he received two hundred guineas for each of the edition's six volumes from the publisher, plus 750 sets printed in a noble and limited edition for which the subscribers each paid six guineas. Now, "thanks to *Homer*," he writes in *The Second Epistle*, he could "live and thrive, / Indebted to no Prince or Peer alive." As for Addison and the part he played in the scheme to denigrate and imperil Pope's arduous task, his reward would be Pope's masterly portrayal of him as "Atticus," "Willing to wound, and yet afraid to strike," and "so obliging that he ne'er oblig'd," in *An Epistle to Dr. Arbuthnot*.

The last of the *Iliad* volumes appeared in 1720. For a time afterward, Pope was preoccupied with editing the work of two deceased friends: a collection of poems by Thomas Parnell, and the writings of John Sheffield, Duke of Buckinghamshire. But he was also apparently contemplating, and even making progress on, a translation of the *Odyssey*. This time, however, he solicited, covertly, the collaboration of two friends: a cleric, William Broome, and Elijah Fenton, a minor poet. The arrangement was obviously muffled so as not to deter potential subscribers, who, if they had known that Pope was to be fully responsible for translating only twelve of the original's twenty-four books, might well have backed off; but such was the division of labor, with Fenton responsible for four books and Broome for eight others plus all of the prose commentary. And even though Pope rigorously supervised and re-

Godfrey Kneller's 1721 portrait of Pope, employing numismatic motifs (by permission of Lord Home of the Hirsel K.T. Coldstream, Berwickshire)

vised the work of his partners, when the duplicitous nature of the whole business leaked out, as it inevitably did, it not only gave Pope much personal embarrassment; it also gave ammunition of fairly heavy caliber to all those whose animosity he had stirred for whatever reasons.

The *Odyssey* translation, appearing in five volumes in 1725 and 1726, did turn out to be, in spite of the taint it gave to Pope's reputation, a financial success, for both him and his collaborators. But adding to Pope's discomfiture over the revelations that accompanied it were the consequences of two other projects undertaken during these years. The first, the editing of Sheffield's works, must have seemed innocent enough at the time, but when the two volumes of the duke's writings appeared in January 1723, they were almost immediately seized by the government under suspicion of containing Jacobite and therefore seditious leanings. The ban against the edition was soon enough lifted, but there can be little doubt that Pope suffered some alarm at the possible government mistrust of his own loyalties, as well as

some chagrin over scurrilous insinuations in the public press about his role in getting the edition published. The second project with an unpleasant sequel was his agreement, for a flat fee of one hundred pounds, to act as editor of a six-volume edition of Shakespeare, a task for which he cannot be said to have been even minimally qualified—though given the general state of textual scholarship at the time his performance is more understandable. Not that he failed to enable the educated public better to "appreciate" Shakespeare; that he did, not only by singling out passages that seemed to him especially admirable but also by providing an evaluative preface, which ends with this remarkable comment: "I will conclude by saying of *Shakespear*, that with all his faults, and with all the irregularity of his *Drama*, one may look upon his works, in comparison of those that are more finish'd and regular, as upon an ancient majestick piece of *Gothic* Architecture, compar'd with a neat Modern building: The latter is more elegant and glaring [i.e., bright, conspicuous], but the former is more

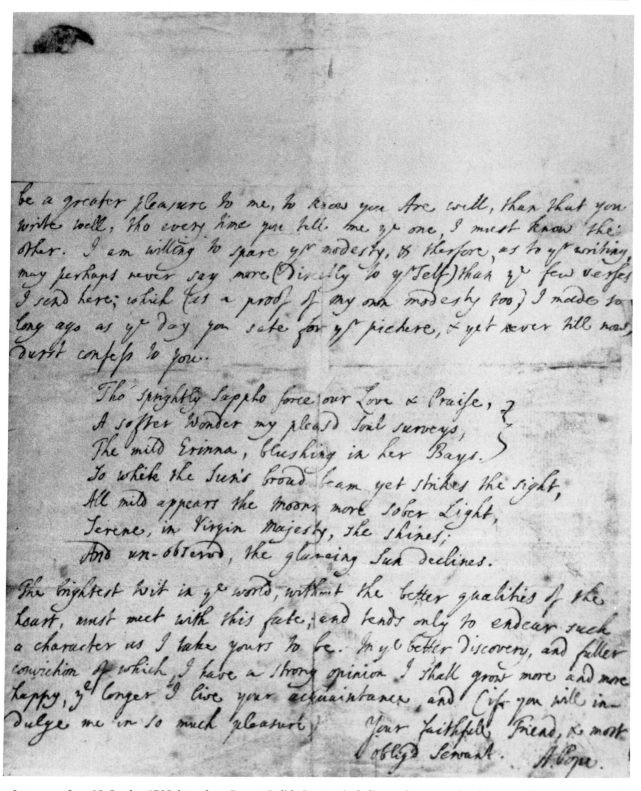

Last page of an 18 October 1722 letter from Pope to Judith Cowper, including a short poem that he eventually revised and published in Of The Characters of Women, *1735 (auctioned by Christie, Manson & Woods, Ltd., 11-12 June 1980)*

strong and solemn [i.e., distinguished]. It must be allow'd, that in one of these there are materials enough to make many of the other. It has much the greater variety, and much the nobler apartments; tho' we are often conducted to them by dark, odd, and uncouth passages."

But whatever virtues Pope's edition of Shakespeare may be said to have, its flagrant shortcomings were disdainfully exposed barely a year after its publication, when Lewis Theobald, an attorney and poetaster with pretensions to scholarship, in 1726 issued a work the title of which alone makes its animus apparent: "SHAKESPEARE restored: OR, A SPECIMEN OF THE Many ERRORS, AS WELL *Committed*, as *Unamended*, by Mr. POPE In his Late EDITION of this POET. DESIGNED Not only to correct the said EDITION, but to restore the True READING of SHAKESPEARE in all the Editions ever yet publish'd." Theobald's work, often heavy-handed, nit-pickingly pedantic, and self-glorifying, nonetheless scored many valid points against Pope's inadequacies and made some real contributions to Shakespearean interpretation as well. Coming when it did, when Pope had been smarting for some time from allegations of his deficiency in the Greek necessary to translate Homer, and more recently from rumors of his Jacobite sympathies and from public disapproval of his actual disingenuous dealings in the *Odyssey* translation, it must have rankled the more. Leaving aside the steady drumbeat of snide and brutal comment on his physical deformities, from 1711–with the attack on his person, character, and talent by Dennis–until 1727, over fifty printed assaults had appeared, in pamphlets, books, plays, novels, and miscellanies, most of them written by literary hacks or out of personal envy and spite. They charged Pope variously with blasphemy, obscenity, plagiarism, and libel, and damned him as venal, vain, seditious, malicious, and faithless as a friend.

· For two decades Pope held his peace amidst such calumnies. If he had died before his fortieth birthday there would be little, except for a few derisive squibs and pieces of mockery, to presage the preeminent satirist he was to become. But during this period he must have been meditating his revenge, and when it came it was on a scale as massive as it was devastating: in May 1728 appeared the first version of *The Dunciad*, in three books, with Pope's Shakespearean adversary Theobald (always spelled "Tibbald" by Pope, to belittle him and to rhyme with such words as

"ribald") crowned as king of duncery, supreme embodiment of everything tasteless, inept, and depraved in art and criticism–as well as in those who fostered and patronized such art. In Pope's usage, duncery is not so much mere stupidity of mind as it is a perverse misapplication of one's reason and talents; its implications may be somewhat better understood if we recall that etymologically the word stems from the name of Duns Scotus, the medieval theologian whose disciples, because of their specious and hairsplitting habits of reasoning, became known contemptuously as "duns men." The broad pejorative implications of duncery were such, moreover, that Pope could use the word to stigmatize a wide range of individual types and institutions, from obtuse royalty to hack writers, from degenerate theatrical performances to unscrupulous publishers, from the schools and universities to mendacious politicians and the current poet laureate, Laurence Eusden, a clergyman known at the time more for his drunkenness than for any other attributes, priestly or poetic. The poem's impact was instantaneous and explosive, if we may believe the contemporary account by Richard Savage of the immediate uproar and outrage among Pope's victims: "On the Day the Book was first vended, a Crowd of Authors besieg'd the Shop [of the publisher]; Entreaties, Advices, Threats of Law, and Battery, nay Cries of Treason were all employ'd to hinder the coming out of the *Dunciad*: On the other Side, the Booksellers and Hawkers made as great Efforts to procure it."

While *The Dunciad* certainly enabled Pope to settle personal scores, the poem is also formed on a larger template incised to convey breathtakingly larger alterations in Western culture. The opening lines–"The Mighty Mother, and her Son who brings / The Smithfield Muses to the ear of Kings"–suggest the upheavals and transformations Pope has in mind: the displacement of traditional classical and Christian values, ideally embodied in the crown, by the crass and debased tastes associated with the fairs and rabble of Smithfield–puppet shows, prizefights, bearbaitings, and so on. As Pope says through his editorial mouthpiece, the duncely pedant Martinus Scriblerus, the poem was written at a time when paper "became so cheap, and Printers so numerous, that a deluge of Authors covered the land." Before this authorial flood, swollen in part by a suddenly enlarged reading public with an apparently insatiable appetite for the most heterogeneous (as well as cheap and vulgar) reading

Pope's home at Twickenham, which he affectionately dubbed "Twit'nam" (engraving by J. Michael Rysbrach, based on a painting by Augustin Heckell)

A Perspective View of Mr. Pope's Grotto (*engraving based on a drawing by J. Serle*)

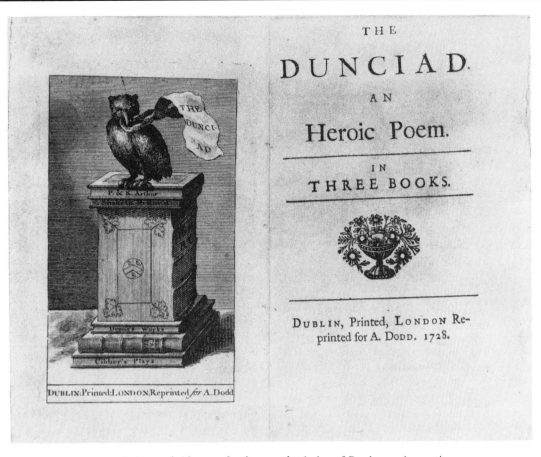

Frontispiece and title page for the second printing of Pope's notorious satire

matter, the more traditional (and aristocratic) strongholds of learning and literature might well have seemed, from one point of view, in danger of being totally swept away. That such a concern is at the heart of Pope's poem seems clearly indicated by alternative but reciprocal descriptions of its "*one, great,* and *remarkable action*": in 1729 that action is said by Scriblerus to be "the introduction of the lowest diversions of the rabble in *Smithfield* to be the entertainment of the court and town; or in other words, the Action of the Dunciad is the Removal of the Imperial seat of Dulness [the presiding deity or 'Mighty Mother' of the poem] from the City to the polite world"; in the revised version of 1743, the "action" has been redefined and given a cosmic range: it is "the restoration of the reign of Chaos and Night, by the ministry of Dulness their daughter, in the removal of her imperial seat from the City to the polite World."

Art, and taste in art, and even the topography of Greater London thus become metaphors expressive of the poem's import. When the god-dess Dulness, having "annointed" Theobald as her son and earthly "king," leads him and the rest of his fellow dunces, her "chosen," through the streets of London from the "City" (that part of London within the old Roman walls that had become associated with mercantile, "moneyed," values) on an invasion of the "polite world" (the West End of London with its cluster of aristocratic values), the cultural upheaval Pope aims to portray is apparent: the overrunning and smothering of traditional values by low, cheap, and modern substitutes. And since the poem is also a mock-epic, reminders of the gigantic figures and events of the past, in one parodic analogue after another, continuously make scornful and ridiculous all those who, in Pope's eyes, have contributed to the degrading of art and learning.

Publication of *The Dunciad* effectually confirmed Pope's posture as an antiestablishment figure. As early as 1713, although he apparently tried to avoid a partisan political stance in *Windsor-Forest*, he betrayed in that poem a deep sympathy for Queen Anne, last of the Stuarts. At about the

The Distressed Poet, *a 1736 engraving by Hogarth, with a quotation from* The Dunciad *as its caption*

same time, he became intimate with a select group of Anne's Tory ministers and adherents who were to become abiding friends: Robert Harley, Earl of Oxford, the lord treasurer and "prime" minister; Dr. John Arbuthnot, the queen's personal physician, himself an ingenious writer; Swift, at the time a polemical writer on behalf of the queen and her ministry; and the poets John Gay, later to write *The Beggar's Opera* (1728), and Parnell, mentioned earlier. This group established the famed Scriblerus Club, named after an imaginary blockhead of a pedant (the one Pope put to such comical use in *The Dunciad*), in whose name they met and planned to satirize abuses in learning and art wherever they might be found. The group met as an entity for only six months or so (the death of Queen Anne inevitably caused its disintegration), but in their association were planted the seeds that would later bear such fruit as *Gulliver's Travels* (1726) and Gay's opera, as well as the collaborative *Memoirs of the Extraordinary Life, Works, and Discoveries of Martinus Scriblerus* (1741) and Pope's own "Peri Bathous: Or, Of the Art of Sinking in Poetry" (1728), a hilarious prose satire on bad writers and bad writing. Pope's intimacy and empathy with this alliance almost certainly prohibited fraternal relationships with the writers and hangers-on at Button's, the circle around Addison, whose Whig ties and loyalties were such that he became secretary of state under Anne's successor, George I. For a variety of reasons, then (Pope's Roman Catholic background and the insults and prejudices it inspired, his membership in the Scriblerian group and the loyalties formed there, the envy and animosity shown him by Addison and his cronies in the matter of the Homer translation, and his growing sense that neither he nor his friends could expect royal or ministerial favor under the first two Georges and their powerful prime minister, Robert Walpole), Pope henceforth became an unrelenting hounder of the monarchy and its minions, a role enunciated when, in *The Dunciad*, glancing at George II's succession to his father's throne, he inquires: "Say from what cause, in vain decry'd and curst, / Still Dunce the second reigns like Dunce the first?"

Back in 1716, perhaps as a result of more stringent tax penalties recently enacted against Roman Catholics, Pope's father had disposed of his property at Binfield, and for a time the family had lived at Chiswick, nearer to London. There, in 1717, the elder Pope died. His life and his death were commemorated by his son in *An Epistle to Dr. Arbuthnot*:

> Born to no Pride, inheriting no Strife,
> Nor marrying Discord in a Noble Wife,
> Stranger to Civil and Religious Rage,
> The good Man walk'd innoxious thro' his Age.
> No Courts he saw, no Suits would ever try,
> Nor dar'd an Oath, nor hazarded a Lye:
> Un-learn'd, he knew no Schoolman's subtle Art,
> No Language, but the Language of the Heart.
> By Nature honest, by Experience wise,
> Healthy by Temp'rance and by Exercise:
> His Life, tho' long, to sickness past unknown,
> His Death was instant, and without a groan.
> Oh grant me thus to live, and thus to die!
> Who sprung from Kings shall know less joy than I.

A year or so after his father's death Pope leased a villa at Twickenham, which he was to make celebrated for the elegance of the house and the variegated pleasures and graces of its grounds. Twelve miles outside London (and therefore outside the ten-mile limit), and facing the Thames, the two-story edifice and its front lawn were separated from five acres in the rear by the London Road. Pope had a subterranean passageway made to connect the two areas, explaining to his friends that "What we cannot *overcome*, we must *undergo*." This underground passageway, with its various recesses, became the famous grotto in which he delighted to entertain his most intimate friends and

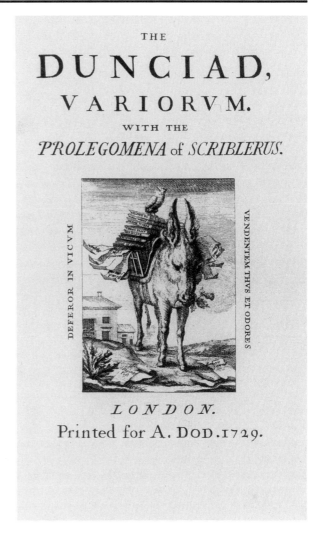

Title page for the revised and enlarged Dunciad, *which was to be expanded again in 1743*

which he once described in a 2 June 1725 letter to Edward Blunt: "it is finished with Shells interspersed with Pieces of Looking-glass in angular forms; and in the Ceiling is a Star of the same Material, at which when a Lamp (of an orbicular Figure of thin Alabaster) is hung in the Middle, a thousand pointed Rays glitter and are reflected over the Place."

At Twickenham (or "Twit' nam," as he affectionately dubbed it) Pope could indulge a passion he apparently inherited from his father–gardening. Small as the space was at his command, he managed to fill it with an astonishing variety of features: a bowling green and a kitchen garden, a shell temple and a vineyard, an orangery and, after his mother's death, an obelisk in her memory. In a facetious October 1725 letter to the earl of Stafford, he described his landscaping activities: "I am as busy in three inches of Gardening, as any man can be in threescore acres. I fancy myself like the fellow that spent his life in cutting the twelve apostles in one cherry-stone. I have a Theatre, an Arcade, a Bowling-Green, a Grove, & what not? in a bitt of ground that would have been but a plate of Sallet to Nebuchadnezzar, the first day he was turn'd to graze." He was fond of reminding his friends that, in Cicero's words, "*Agricultura proxima Sapientiae*" (agriculture is nearest to wisdom) and that gardening was a most "innocent Employment, & the same that God appointed for his First Man." A "true relish of the beauties of nature," he wrote, "is the most easy preparation and gentlest transition to an enjoyment of those of heaven; as on the contrary a true town life of hurry, confusion, noise, slander, and dissension, is a sort of apprenticeship to hell and its furies."

In his letters, Pope remarked several times that "*Mihi & Amicis* [for me and my friends] would be the proper Motto" over his garden gate; or "indeed, Plus Amicis quam Meipsi" (more for my friends than for myself). Several years later he referred to his "Grotto of Friendship & Liberty" and even mentioned a Latin version of this same phrase ("Libertati & Amicitiae"), which he was "putting over [his] Door at Twitnam." Friendship seems to have been the first of secular pieties for Pope, and whatever asperity of temper is exhibited in his published work finds its counterpoise in the warm affection he lavished privately on his remarkable number of friends from all ranks. During the 1730s especially, as his opposition to Walpole and the establishment stiffened, his villa and its grotto became a center in which "friendship" and its twin virtue "liberty" found a quiet and hospitable harbor; there, among a few cherished companions, including others also out of ministerial favor, he could share a "Feast of Reason" and a "Flow of Soul" (as he says in *The Second Satire*). There also he could enjoy alone a place of retreat and meditation, away from what he increasingly regarded as the corrupt, and corrupting, world of London, the world of what he called the "Money-headed & Mony-hearted Citizen" (the mercantile "Cits" within the old City walls). In the sanctuary provided by "Twit' nam," as he says in *The Second Epistle*, he could meet with and catechize his very heart:

> Soon as I enter at my Country door,
> My Mind resumes the thread it dropt before;

> Thoughts, which at Hyde-Park-Corner I forgot,
> Meet and rejoin me, in the pensive Grott.
> There all alone, and Compliments apart,
> I ask these sober questions of my Heart.
>   If, when the more you drink, the more you
>   crave,
> You tell the Doctor; when the more you have,
> The more you want, why not with equal ease
> Confess as well your Folly, as Disease?

Shortly before *The Dunciad* appeared, Pope too confidently wrote to Swift that the poem would "rid" him of "those insects," the "fools and scoundrels" who had pestered him for so many years. If anything, of course, the poem simply inflamed the dunces the more. And so they attempted a kind of revenge, of the shoddiest sort to be sure, in 1731 when the first of Pope's "Epistles to Several Persons" appeared. Entitled *An Epistle To The Right Honourable Richard Earl of Burlington. Occasion'd by his Publishing Palladio's Designs of the Baths, Arches, Theatres, &c. of Ancient Rome*, the poem is informed throughout by Pope's proficiency, empirical as well as conceptual, in landscape gardening, as well as in the ways the gardener's art may offer analogues to the art of poetry. In addition, the work is a withering satire on the vanity, false taste, and misuse of riches all too frequently exhibited by the wealthy in their creation of vast and opulent estates. There seems absolutely no reason to think Pope had any particular estate, or nobleman, in view; the particular example he gives of follies and monstrosities—the "Timon's Villa" of the poem—is obviously a fictional amalgam of common excesses and deficiencies. But the dunces, in a campaign as malicious as unjustified, spread rumor and gossip, in lampoon and pamphlets, that the poem was aimed mainly at the estate of one particular nobleman, James Brydges, Duke of Chandos, a person to whom Pope had reason to be grateful and who was, furthermore, a friend of the very earl to whom he had addressed the "Epistle."

During this period Pope had been planning a major poem on the human condition in general, a work more philosophical than satirical, as he told Spence, which would serve as both a "*general Map* of MAN" and as an introduction to a larger poetic scheme including the "Epistles to Several Persons" as well as other poems on such subjects as "knowledge and its limits," "government, both ecclesiastical and civil," and "morality, in eight or nine of the most concerning branches of it." Such a grand design was never to be realized, but with the furor raised by *The Dunciad* and the

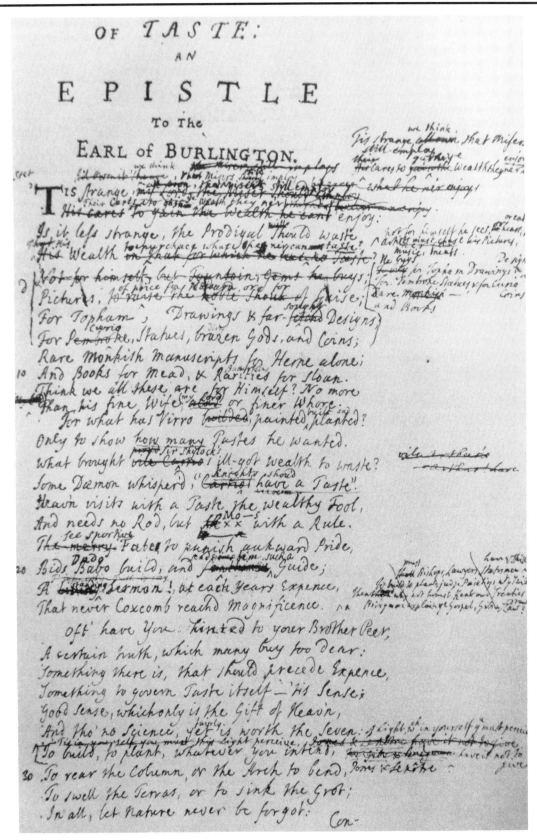

First page of an early draft for the poem Pope published as An Epistle To The Right Honourable Richard Earl of Burlington, *1731 (MA 352: by permission of the Pierpont Morgan Library)*

Epistle to . . . Burlington in mind, and to ensure an unbiased reception of the introductory poem, Pope devised an elaborate stratagem to persuade the public, including the dunces, that the *Essay* was the work of a new and unknown author. To this end he had his regular publisher issue, in early 1733, two poems under his own name: in January there appeared *Of The Use of Riches, An Epistle To the Right Honorable Allen Lord Bathurst* (dated 1732), followed in February by Pope's first "Imitation" of Horace, *The First Satire Of The Second Book of Horace.* Having thus signaled himself as busied with such satiric pieces, Pope in late February had a publisher previously unassociated with his work issue the first epistle of *An Essay On Man,* with the second and third epistles following in the next several weeks (a fourth and final epistle was published in early 1734).

The scheme was enormously successful, exceeding, one imagines, even Pope's wildest dreams, for not only did the general public hail the poem as the work of a newly risen genius, but some of his most inveterate detractors and traducers were hoodwinked into according it the most adulatory praise—and in print. As perhaps no protest or appeal could have done, the entrapment of his enemies in their own acclaiming words made it utterly clear how personally prejudiced their incessant hounding of him had been. In later editions of *The Dunciad* Pope, no doubt with considerable gleefulness of spirit, reprinted, among other "testimonies" to himself, some of the choicer specimens of praise the dunces of that very poem had accorded him, including these verses by Bezaleel Morris:

> Auspicious bard! while all admire thy strain,
> All but the selfish, ignorant, and vain;
> I, whom no bribe to servile flatt'ry drew,
> Must pay the tribute to thy merit due:
> Thy Muse, sublime, significant, and clear,
> Alike informs the Soul, and charms the Ear.

This was a gratifying salute indeed, especially considering its authorship.

As for the poem itself, *An Essay On Man* probably has an ancestry as ancient as Psalm 19, the opening lines of which are: "The heavens declare the glory of God; and the firmament sheweth his handiwork. Day unto day uttereth speech, and night unto night sheweth knowledge." The psalm is in two parts, the first six verses presenting the argument for God's creation of the universe in the very "talk" of the natural world itself, while the second half refers us to the testimony of the "law,"

that is, the revelations to man found in the Pentateuch, the first five books of the Old Testament. Pope follows the mode of the first half of the psalm in his poetic "theodicy"—his investigation, that is—of the evils and deficiencies to be found in the creation, and his "vindication" or "justification" of the "ways of God to Man" in man's earthly experience of such evils. Choosing to exclude from his poem any appeal to revelation, Old Testament or New, Pope proceeds by way of "physico-theology"—the examination of Nature (including, in Pope's case, "human" nature) for evidence of God's existence and purposes. Such a procedure can in part be understood and justified by Milton's view (in *Of Education*) that "our understanding cannot in this body found itself but on sensible things, nor arrive so clearly to the knowledge of God and things invisible, as by orderly conning over the visible and inferior creature." Pope's consonance with Milton may be seen in the second paragraph of *An Essay On Man:*

> Say first, of God above, or Man below,
> What can we reason, but from what we know?
> Of Man what see we, but his station here,
> From which to reason, or to which refer?
> Thro' worlds unnumber'd tho' the God be known,
> 'Tis ours to trace him only in our own.

Pope's deliberate eschewing of matters of faith and revelation in his argument (however ancient and honorable his method) was liable to misinterpretation from certain quarters, and it is not surprising that after several years of acclaim, both in England and on the Continent, the poem was suddenly attacked for supposedly unorthodox tendencies, particularly some of a fatalistic tenor, by a Swiss theologian, Jean-Pierre de Crousaz. Crousaz's attack was based primarily on two faulty French translations of *An Essay On Man,* one in prose and one in verse, the last a hopeless battering and hacking of both Pope's words and intentions. The charges nevertheless disturbed Pope deeply and once again provided his enemies with new opportunities for detraction. Amidst this commotion, the poet unexpectedly acquired a potent, even commanding, champion in Rev. William Warburton, an Anglican clergyman (later bishop of Gloucester) who took it upon himself to come to Pope's defense with a vigorous rebuttal to Crousaz's accusations. Pope's relief, and gratitude, were such that he immediately established a friendship with his new ally, one that would lead to Warburton's becoming a close literary confidant for the last four years of Pope's life

First page of the manuscript for Pope's 1732 poem to Lord Bathurst (HM 6007; by permission of the Henry E. Huntington Library and Art Gallery)

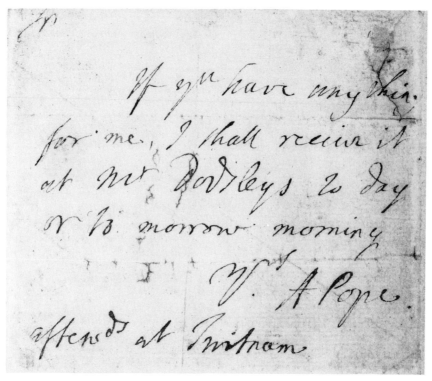

Note by Pope written in a copy of the first edition of his Essay on Man, *during a visit to Robert Dodsley (RB 106530; by permission of the Henry E. Huntington Library and Art Gallery)*

as well as one of his chief legatees after his death.

In *An Essay On Man* Pope expounds the premises of philosophic "optimism," not the optimism of a cheery or evolutionary view of things but rather the view that this world is the "best" or "optimum" world that God could create (to suppose that He could have done better but did not is to impugn His goodness and benevolence). Such a world has both physical and moral evil in it: "There deviates Nature, and here deviates Will." Nevertheless, there is a grand and general order in the cosmos, usually only dimly or incorrectly perceived by man, mainly because of a prideful disposition it is his duty to overcome: "From pride, from pride, our very reas'ning springs; / Account for moral as for nat'ral things: / Why charge we Heav'n in those, in these acquit? / In both, to reason right is to submit." Evoking the immensities of the universe, full of its multitudes of creatures with multiple claims and appetites of their own, Pope's "vindication" of what he calls the universe's "disposing Pow'r" is clear and unequivocal (and not lacking in reminiscences of the Book of Job, chapters 38-41):

> Cease then, nor ORDER Imperfection name:
> Our proper Bliss depends on what we blame.

Know thy own point: This kind, this due degree
Of blindness, weakness, Heav'n bestows on thee.
Submit–In this, or any other sphere,
Secure to be as blest as thou canst bear;
Safe in the hand of one disposing Pow'r,
Or in the natal, or the mortal hour.
All Nature is but Art, unknown to thee;
All Chance, Direction, which thou canst not see;
All Discord, Harmony, not understood;
All partial Evil, universal Good:
And, spite of Pride, in erring Reason's spite,
One truth is clear, "Whatever IS, is RIGHT."

Sometime in May 1730 Spence recorded that Pope had formed a "new hypothesis, that a prevailing passion in the mind is brought with it into the world, and continues till death (illustrated by the seeds of the illness that is at last to destroy us being planted in the body at our births"). This hypothesis of a "ruling Passion" found its poetic enunciation three years later in Epistle II of *An Essay On Man*:

> As Man, perhaps, the moment of his breath,
> Receives the lurking principle of death;
> The young disease, that must subdue at length,
> Grows with his growth, and strengthens with his strength:

The idea that a person's entire life and character (no matter how various, contradictory, and finally mysterious) might be explained by such a "passion" has appeared to most to be crude and simplistic, and possibly Pope himself came to such a realization, for there is scant appeal to it in the poems of the last decade of his life (1734-1744). For one thing, in the Christian view of life (and Pope, no matter how vague or free his religious beliefs, never seemed to write in opposition to Christian doctrine) the concept would seem an obvious encroachment on the doctrine of free will; for another it would seem to preclude any kind of conversionary experience.

The hypothesis of a ruling passion does appear as a significant element once more in one of Pope's best pieces, the last of his "Epistles to Several Persons," *Of The Characters of Women: An Epistle To A Lady* (1735). The lady of the title was Martha Blount, whom Pope had met early in life and who became his lifelong intimate companion. The imaginary setting for part of the poem is an art gallery, with the speaker a cicerone who conducts the reader past portraits of various female characters exemplifying the notion that, "good as well as ill, / Woman's at best a Contradiction still." There is the flirtatious Rufa (a redhead), who studies the philosopher John Locke; the timid Silia (snub-nosed?), who flies into a rage over a pimple; Papillia (butterfly), who longs for a country estate but cannot stand the "odious, odious Trees"; and Narcissa—"A very Heathen in the carnal Part, / Yet still a sad, good Christian at her heart." Five or six more portraits are also designed to enforce Pope's thesis that women in general, and in contrast to men, are governed by only two "Ruling Passions": the "Love of Pleasure, and the Love of Sway." The poem's conclusion, in contrast to the unflattering female characterizations and the highly suspect maxim just quoted, offers a tender, affectionate, admiring portrayal of Blount (never mentioned in the poem by name), to whom Phoebus Apollo, the god of poetry, has given "good Sense, Good-Humour, and a Poet."

In several poems written during the 1730s Pope conducts an on-and-off defense of his life and art, but *An Epistle . . . To Dr. Arbuthnot* provides the major apologia of these years. The poem appeared in January 1735, a month before the *Epistle To A Lady* and only a few weeks before the death of Arbuthnot, the witty physician who had been a kindly adviser to Pope since the days of Queen Anne and the Scriblerus Club. In a

Sepia drawing by Pope later engraved as the frontispiece for a 1745 edition of An Essay on Man *(collection of W. S. Lewis, Farmington, Connecticut)*

So, cast and mingled with his very frame,
The Mind's disease, its ruling Passion came;
Each vital humour [i.e., each of man's energizing spirits] which should feed the whole,
Soon flows to this, in body and in soul.

A year later, in the third of his "Epistles to Several Persons," addressed to Richard Temple, Viscount Cobham, Pope adverted to the same idea with the following injunction and comment:

Search then the Ruling Passion: There, alone,
The Wild are constant, and the Cunning known;
The Fool consistent, and the False sincere;
Priests, Princes, Women, no dissemblers here.
This clue once found, unravels all the rest. . . .

Time, that on all things lays his lenient hand,
Yet tames not this; it sticks to our last sand.
Consistent in our follies and our sins,
Here honest Nature ends as she begins.

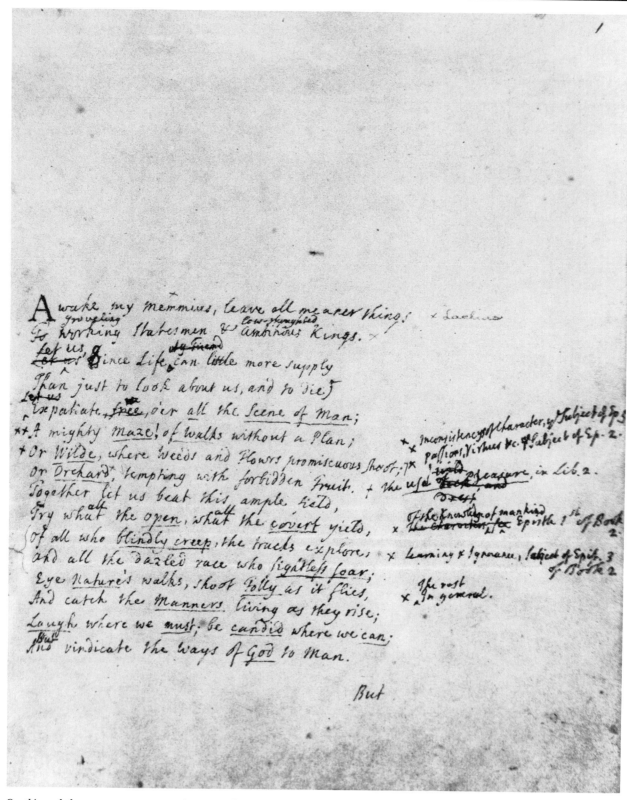

On this and the next two pages: opening pages from the earliest extant draft, written circa 1731, for Pope's Essay on Man *(MA 348; by permission of the Pierpont Morgan Library)*

Say
~~But~~ first, of God above, or Man below,
What can we reason but from what we know?
~~Thro endless worlds His endless works are known;~~
~~But sure to trace him only in our own.~~

not used

Of Man, what see we but his Station here,
From which to reason, or to which refer?
~~thro worlds unknown ad This is God, when this is try to trace him in~~
3 page. Of this vast Frame, the Bearings, & the Ties,
The close Connections, nice Dependencies,
× qu. And Centres just, has Thy pervading Soul
Look'd thro', or can a Part contain the Whole?
Is the strong Chain that draws all to agree,
And drawn supports, upheld by God, or thee?
He who can all th' flaming limits pierce
Of worlds on worlds, that form one Universe,
Observe, how System into System runs,
What other Planets, & what other Suns?
What ~~other~~ vary'd Being peoples ev'ry Star?
May tell, why Heav'n has made us as we are.

When the proud Steed shall know, why man now
His stubborn neck, now drives him o'er the plains,
Pag. 4ᵗʰ When the dull Oxe, why now he breaks the clod,
Now wears a Garland an Egyptian God;
Then shall Man's pride & dulness comprehend
His Action's, Passion's, Being's Use and End;
Why doing, suffring, check'd, impell'd, and why
This hour a Slave, the next a Deity?

Pre-

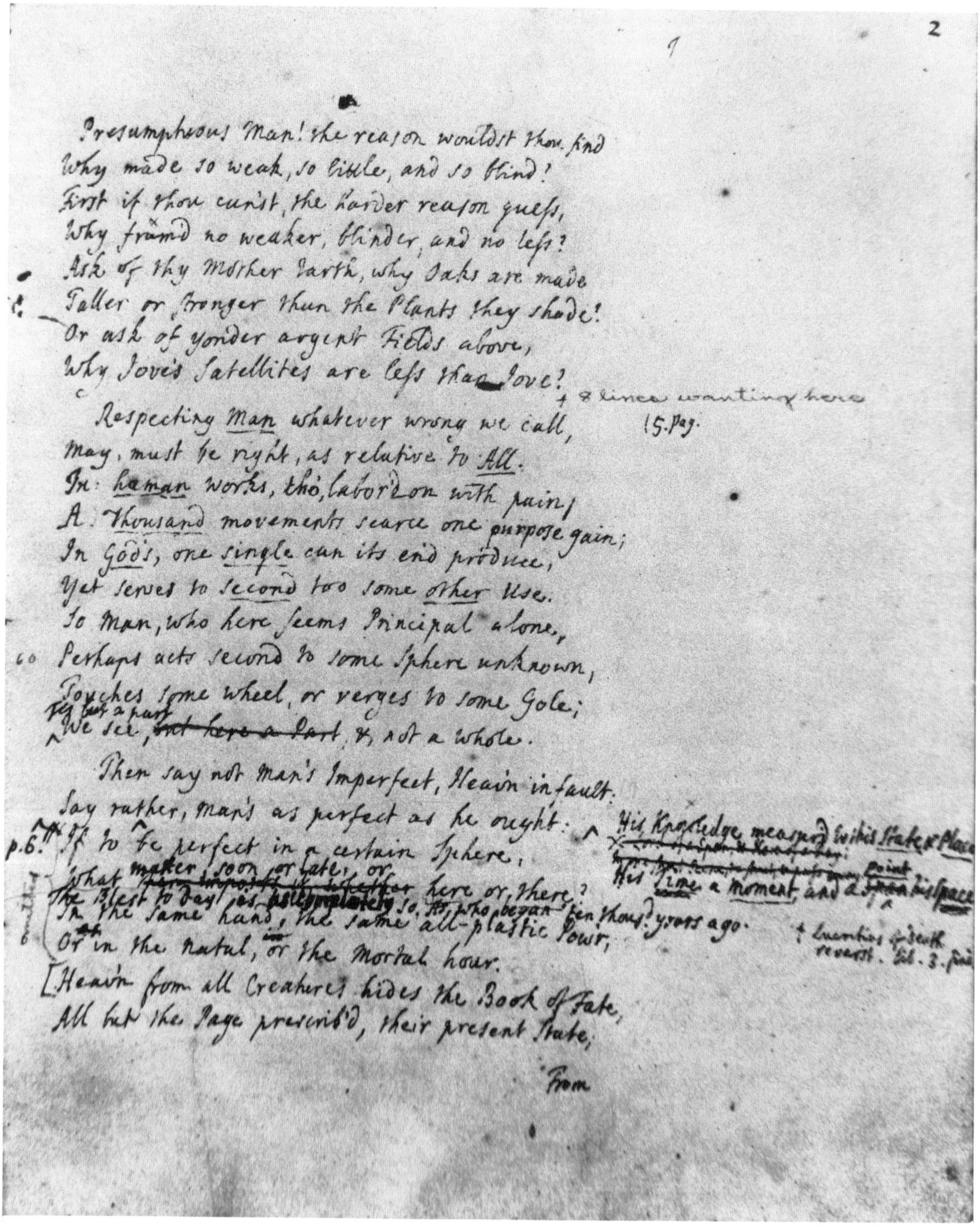

2

Presumptuous Man! the reason wouldst thou find
Why made so weak, so little, and so blind!
First if thou can'st, the harder reason guess,
Why fram'd no weaker, blinder, and no less?
Ask of thy Mother Earth, why Oaks are made
Taller or stronger than the Plants they shade?
Or ask of yonder argent Fields above,
Why Jove's Satellites are less than Jove?

Respecting Man whatever wrong we call,
May, must be right, as relative to All.
In human works, tho' labor'd on with pain,
A thousand movements scarce one purpose gain;
In Gods, one single can its end produce,
Yet serves to second too some other Use.
So Man, who here seems Principal alone,
Perhaps acts second to some Sphere unknown,
Touches some wheel, or verges to some Gole;
We see, but here a part, &, not a whole.

Then say not Man's Imperfect, Heav'n in fault.
Say rather, man's as perfect as he ought:
If to be perfect in a certain Sphere;
What maker, soon or later, or here or there,
The Blest to day is as completely so,
In the same hand, the same all-plastic Powr,
Or in the natal, or the Mortal hour.
[Heav'n from all Creatures hides the Book of Fate,
All but the Page prescrib'd, their present State;

From

† 8 lines wanting here
15. Pag.

His Knowledge measurd to his State & Place
His Time a moment, and a point his space
who began ten thous' years ago.
† lurnties of death reverse. fol. 3. pag.

headnote to the poem Pope explained that it was *"a Sort of Bill of Complaint, begun many years since, and drawn up by snatches, as the several Occasions offer'd,"* and that he had *"no thoughts of publishing it, till it pleas'd some Persons of Rank and Fortune [the Authors of* Verses to the Imitator of Horace, *and of an* Epistle to a Doctor of Divinity from a Nobleman at Hampton Court,] *to attack in a very extraordinary manner, not only my Writings (of which being publick the Publick judge) but my* Person, Morals, *and* Family, *whereof to those who know me not, a truer Information may be requisite."* The "Persons of Rank and Fortune," and authors of the two poems cited within Pope's brackets, were Lady Mary Wortley Montagu, a minor poet later famous for, among other things, her early advocacy of inoculations against smallpox, and John, Lord Hervey, a courtier and confidant of Caroline, George II's queen, notorious for his profligacy and effeminate manner. Miffed by what they took as slighting allusions to themselves in Pope's first "Imitation" of Horace, Montagu (with whom Pope had been deeply infatuated before they were estranged by some obscure quarrel) and Hervey joined such talents as they possessed, along with an inordinate supply of spleen, to produce *Verses addressed to the Imitator of Horace* (1733), one of the most malicious attacks ever directed at Pope— and the more disgraceful, considering the aristocratic status of the authors. An unpleasant taste of their addresses to Pope may be absorbed from lines that tell him that his "crabbed Numbers" (rough verses) are as "Hard as [his] Heart, and as [his] Birth obscure"; that question how he could "by Beauty's Force be mov'd, / No more for loving made, than to be lov'd"; and that conclude with this malediction:

> Like the first bold Assassin's be thy Lot,
> Ne'er be thy Fault forgiven, or forgot;
> But as thou hat'st, be hated by Mankind,
> And with the Emblem of thy crooked Mind,
> Mark'd on thy Back, like *Cain*, by God's own Hand;
> Wander like him, accursed through the Land.

The second of the two poems cited in Pope's headnote, *An Epistle to a Doctor of Divinity from a Nobleman at Hampton Court* (1733), apparently by Hervey alone (unlike the first, which Pope called his "Witty Fornication" with Montagu), was comparatively tame. But for their pains, both virulent and doggerel, the pair of attackers achieved a kind of surpassing notoriety, Montagu living on in Pope's verse as a venal and slovenly poetess called Sappho, and Hervey des-

Engraving based on a portrait of Pope by William Hoare

tined to endure in the Proteuslike shape-shifting nastiness of his portrayal in *An Epistle . . . To Dr. Arbuthnot* as Sporus, the name of the young catamite who was gelded and taken in "marriage" by the Emperor Nero:

>   this Bug with gilded wings,
> This painted Child of Dirt that stinks and stings;
> Whose Buzz the Witty and the Fair annoys,
> Yet Wit ne'er tastes, and Beauty ne'er enjoys,
> So well-bred Spaniels civilly delight
> In mumbling of the Game they dare not bite.
> Eternal Smiles his Emptiness betray,
> As shallow streams run dimpling all the way.
> Whether in florid Impotence he speaks,
> And, as the Prompter breathes, the
>   Puppet squeaks;
> Or at the Ear of *Eve*, familiar Toad,
> Half Froth, half Venom, spits himself abroad,
> In Puns, or Politicks, or Tales, or Lyes,
> Or Spite, or Smut, or Rymes, or Blasphemies.
> His Wit all see-saw, between *that* and *this*,
> Now high, now low, now Master up, now Miss,
> And he himself one vile Antithesis.
> Amphibious Thing! that acting either Part,
> The trifling Head, or the corrupted Heart!
> Fop at the Toilet, Flatt'rer at the Board,

Now trips a Lady, and now struts a Lord.
Eve's Tempter thus the Rabbins have exprest,
A Cherub's face, a Reptile all the rest;
Beauty that shocks you, Parts that none will trust,
Wit that can creep, and Pride that licks the dust.

In *An Epistle . . . To Dr. Arbuthnot* Pope so arranged and tinted autobiographical materials as to distinguish the motivations and values of his own poetic art from those of a dreary horde of scribblers and hirelings: the hacks of Grub Street with their prostitutions of self as well as the "witlings" of the beau monde with their tripping insipidities. Unquestionably, amidst the poem's carefully crafted defense of his own works and its equally artful construction of an authorial ethos favorable to Pope himself, the poet achieved retaliations for personal injuries, some new, as with Montagu and Hervey, some of an elder date, harking back to the Buttonian conspiracy against his Homer. Here Addison is transfigured into Atticus, a man "Blest with each Talent and each Art to please," but also a critic whose habit it was to "Damn with faint praise, assent with civil leer, / And without sneering, teach the rest to sneer." But above all, *An Epistle . . . To Dr. Arbuthnot*, along with the four "Epistles to Several Persons," may be seen as inaugurating, if not fully incorporating, the more introspective, even pensive and self-examining tone that characterizes Pope's work during what remained of the 1730s–in spite of his unremitting inveighings against King George II, his ministry, and their political and poetical spawnings.

It is the "Imitations of Horace," however, which appear to represent Pope, amidst his self-examining moments, at his most relaxed, assured, and mature, still pressing his embarrassing charges against royal and ministerial fatuity and corruption, but also seeking out, defining, and defending the qualities of mind and spirit essential to good poetry and the good life. Leaving aside some relatively minor pieces in this mode, there appeared during a five-year span seven major "imitations" of Horace, plus "versifyings" of two satires by John Donne. In order of appearance, these nine works are: *The First Satire Of The Second Book of Horace, Imitated* (1733); *The Impertinent, Or A Visit to the Court. A Satyr* (1733), the initially anonymous redoing of a Donne poem later given the title *The Fourth Satire of Dr. John Donne, Dean of St. Paul's, Versifyed*, and included in Pope's *Works* of 1735; *The Second Satire Of The Second Book of Horace Paraphrased* (1734); *Sober Advice*

From Horace, issued anonymously in 1734, then twice reissued in 1738 as, first, *A Sermon against Adultery*, and then as *The Second Satire of the First Book of Horace; The Second Satire of Dr. John Donne, Dean of St. Paul's, Versifyed* (1735); *The Second Epistle Of The Second Book of Horace, Imitated* (1737); *The First Epistle Of The Second Book of Horace, Imitated* (1737); *The Sixth Epistle Of The First Book of Horace Imitated* (1738); and *The First Epistle Of The First Book Of Horace Imitated* (1738).

The attraction of the Horatian originals, and the allusive advantages he gained in adapting them to his own time and situation, were given in part by Pope himself in two "Advertisements." In the 1735 *Works* version of *The First Satire* he wrote: "*The Occasion of publishing these* Imitations *was the Clamour raised on some of my* Epistles [to Several Persons]. *An Answer from* Horace *was both more full, and of more Dignity, than any I cou'd have made in my own person; and the Example of much greater Freedom in so eminent a Divine as Dr.* Donne, *seem'd a proof with what Indignation and Contempt a Christian may treat Vice or Folly, in ever so low, or ever so high, a Station.*" Then, in 1737, in the "Advertisement" to *The First Epistle Of The Second Book of Horace* (his ironic adaptation of Horace's complimentary address to Caesar Augustus to the character of his own English monarch, christened George Augustus), Pope says:

The Reflections of Horace, *and the Judgments past in his Epistle to* Augustus, *seem'd so seasonable to the present Times, that I could not help applying them to the use of my own Country. . . .*

We may farther learn from this Epistle, that Horace *made his Court to this Great Prince, by writing with a decent Freedom toward him, with a just Contempt of his low Flatterers, and with a manly Regard to his own Character.*

Although entitled "Imitations," and originally published with the Latin texts on facing pages, the Horatian poems (and the "versifications" of Donne as well) must be respected as poems having a new and distinct entity of their own, susceptible to interpretations quite at variance with their forebears. With Horace's and his own text printed side by side, Pope invited reference to the original so that both his adherence to and departure from it could be assessed: the accommodations of the Roman to the English scene leading to a new artifact, one whose paternal lineaments are everywhere evident but whose independence, filial though it be, is continually affirmed. With the possible exception of *Sober Advice from*

A copy of the only full-length portrait of Pope, drawn without his knowledge by William Hoare, as Pope was in conversation with Ralph Allen at Prior Park, Allen's estate (from Gosse, English Literature: An Illustrated Record, *1903)*

Horace, a bawdy "sermon" against adultery that argues that a "tight, neat Girl" will serve one's needs much more safely than "thy Neighbour's Wife," the "Imitations" have a variety and complexity not easily summarized. Nevertheless, one is steadily aware of three themes or emphases: corruptions in poetry as well as in politics; Pope's own intense preoccupation with satire and the role of the satirist in society; and his striving for a personal *ars vivendi*, an art of living, grounded in virtue of mind, engendering both strength and tranquillity of spirit.

These emphases are not easily distinguished one from the other. In *The First Satire*, for example, Pope early disavows any seeking of royal favor from George II (a monarch who despised poetry and indeed most learning but preened himself on his martial bent), refusing to cram his

verse with "ARMS, and GEORGE, and BRUNSWICK" (German origin of the Georges), in order to rend "with tremendous Sound your ears asunder, / With Guns, Drum, Trumpet, Blunderbuss & Thunder." The declaration not only distances Pope from the sycophancy so widespread among George's courtiers and hireling poets but asserts a sturdy independence of spirit, poetic as well as personal. And when, some lines later, he further declares that, while he lives, "no rich or noble knave / Shall walk the World, in credit to his grave," and that he will be "To VIRTUE ONLY and HER FRIENDS, A FRIEND," he stakes out the moral high ground from which he henceforth will challenge the establishment and its hangers-on.

The most daring of Pope's challenges to the crown as being itself the center and source of political corruption and cultural flaccidity is doubtless *The First Epistle Of The Second Book*, the poem so mockingly addressed to George Augustus, the first six lines of which are the sliest and most impertinent possible disclosure of the king's hollow monarchal pretentions:

> WHILE YOU, great Patron of Mankind, sustain
> The balanc'd World, and open all the Main;
> Your Country, chief, in Arms abroad defend,
> At home, with Morals, Arts, and Laws amend;
> How shall the Muse, from such a Monarch steal
> An hour, and not defraud the Publick Weal?

Any sophisticated reader of the day would have known that while George II, of the German House of Hanover, delighted in military affairs, much of his time in "Arms," whether at "home" or "abroad," was in the arms of one or another of his mistresses, and that any interest he had in "amending" the "Morals, Arts, and Laws" of his English subjects was negligible. The word "Patron," by which he is addressed in line one, is in all probability a pun. Sometimes pronounced in the period like "pattern," it may have been designed to recall an ancient Latin maxim: *qualis rex, talis grex* (like king, like people). The likelihood that Pope had such a concept in mind while composing his poem is further suggested by a later passage that centers on the line, "All, by the King's Example, liv'd and lov'd." In this passage the principal allusion is to the atmosphere of luxury and debauchery imparted to the English court by King Charles II on his restoration to the throne in 1660; but the passage at the same time reinforces the idea, pervasive in the *Epistle*, that kingdoms generally take on the distinguishing characteristics of their rulers, for good or bad. As Pope presents George II's reign, the throne, traditional embodiment of a nation's moral, intellectual, and artistic ideals, has become a contaminant of such ideals, much in accord with Swift's observation (in *A Project for the Advancement of Religion and the Reformation of Manners*, 1709) that "human nature seems to lie under this disadvantage, that the example alone of a vicious prince, will, in time, corrupt an age."

But *The First Epistle*, known as "To Augustus," was not merely a caustic attack on the monarchy and what it represented—difficult if not impossible legally to refute or chastise because of its ironies and ambiguities. It also offered an appraising survey of English literary history, from Chaucer and John Skelton, through Shakespeare,

Marble bust of Pope by L. F. Roubiliac, 1741 (by permission of the Shipley Art Gallery, Gateshead)

Philip Sidney, and Cowley, even up to Addison, to whom, in spite of their earlier antipathies, Pope pays a compliment: if we "excuse some Courtly stains," he says, "No whiter page than Addison remains. / He, from the taste obscene reclaims our Youth, / And sets the Passions on the side of Truth; / Forms the soft bosom with the gentlest art, / And pours each human Virtue in the heart." The history also extends to Colley Cibber, the buffoonish playwright and actor whom George II was to make poet laureate and who would succeed Theobald as king of the dunces in the revised 1743 edition of *The Dunciad*: Pope gives even him a mite of applause for at least one of his plays (*The Careless Husband*, 1704). Much of the point of Pope's evaluative literary history is that antiquity alone neither guarantees nor measures excellence: "I lose my patience, and I own it too, / When works are censur'd, not as bad, but new; / While if our Elders break all Reason's laws, / These Fools demand not Pardon, but Applause."

As he comes to the close of his critique of the English literary scene, past and present, Pope suddenly intrudes with a personal poetic manifesto, vibrant in its emotional surge, and utterly inconsistent with any view of him as the personification of a cold and formal "neoclassicism":

> Yet lest you think I railly more than teach,
> Or praise malignly Arts I cannot reach,
> Let me presume for once t'instruct the times,
> To know the Poet from the Man of Rymes:
> 'Tis He, who gives my breast a thousand pains,
> Can make me feel each Passion that he feigns,
> Inrage, compose, with more than magic Art,
> With Pity, and with Terror, tear my heart;
> And snatch me, o'er the earth, or thro' the air,
> To Thebes, to Athens, when he will, and where.

The last two lines, it is obvious, repudiate the so-called "classical" or "neoclassical" unities of time and place. But the preceding lines, with their insistence on the "magic" in art, and on the poet's capacity to arouse pain, even "a thousand pains," to re-create "Passion," to "Inrage, compose," to "tear" the heart with "Terror" or with "Pity," declare clearly the primacy of the passional (rather than the rational) in great art. From *An Essay On Criticism*—when as a mere youth he had praised those "Great Wits" who

> may *gloriously offend*,
> And *rise to Faults* true Criticks *dare not mend*;
> From *vulgar Bounds* with *brave Disorder* part,
> And *snatch a Grace* beyond the Reach of Art,
> Which, without passing thro' the *Judgment*, gains
> The *Heart*, and all its End *at once* attains—

to the Horatian imitations, Pope was never the advocate of a cold poetic "correctness." His verse may be honed to a fine edge and polish, coiled for lithe and ready strike, but the seeming ease and inevitability of his match of form and sense in his couplets is the product of a genius racked by the effort to discipline its own imaginative energies; as his epigraph to *The First Epistle* has it, *Ludentis speciem dabit & torquebatur* (He will give the appearance of playing, and yet be tortured with effort). The severity he believed practiced by great poets, the severity he imposed on himself, and the severity he would have all poets emulate, is the theme of this passage, also from *The First Epistle*:

> But how severely with themselves proceed
> The Men, who write such Verse as we can read?

> Their own strict Judges, not a word they spare
> That wants or Force, or Light, or Weight, or Care,
> ....
> Prune the luxuriant, the uncouth refine,
> But show no mercy to an empty line;
> Then polish all, with so much life and ease,
> You think 'tis Nature, and a knack to please.

These lines, from the poem of 1737, are then rounded off with lines only barely modified from a couplet of 1711 (in *An Essay On Criticism*): "But Ease in writing flows from Art, not Chance, / As those move easiest who have learn'd to dance." The severity Pope preached and practiced from the beginning to the end of his career prompted these words from Johnson in the *Life of Pope*: "he did not court the candour, but dared the judgement of his reader, and expecting no indulgence from others, he shewed none to himself. He examined lines and words with minute and punctilious observation, and retouched every part with indefatigable diligence, till he had left nothing to be forgiven."

These poems of the 1730s are not often far from an autumnal contemplative self-appraisal. In 1738, when Pope was forty-nine and in what he calls the "Sabbath" of his days (seven times seven), he wrote in *The First Epistle Of The First Book Of Horace*: "A Voice there is, that whispers in my ear, / ('Tis Reason's voice, which sometimes one can hear) / 'Friend Pope! be prudent, let your Muse take breath, / And never gallop Pegasus to death' "; and so he resolves:

> Farewell then Verse, and Love, and ev'ry Toy,
> The rhymes and rattles of the Man or Boy:
> What right, what true, what fit, we justly call,
> Let this be all my care—for this is All:
> To lay this harvest up, and hoard with haste
> What ev'ry day will want, and most, the last.

Though he is still unwavering in his determination to "Brand the bold Front of shameless, worthless Men" (*The First Satire*), he also yearns for "the Virtue and the Art / To live on little with a chearful heart" (*The Second Satire*). And (as a Catholic) unable legally to own his villa and grounds at Twickenham, he nonetheless recommends a freehold within anyone's power (in *The Second Satire*): "Let Lands and Houses have what Lords they will, / Let US be fix'd, and our own Masters still." Time's annual erosions, even those imperceptible ones of the self, are traced in these haunting lines from *The Second Epistle*:

Pope in 1742 (painting by J. B. Van Loo; collection of W. S. Lewis, Farmington, Connecticut)

Years foll'wing Years, steal something ev'ry day,
At last they steal us from our selves away;
In one our Frolicks, one Amusements end,
In one a Mistress drops, in one a Friend:
This subtle Thief of Life, this paltry Time,
What will it leave me, if it snatch my Rhime?
If ev'ry Wheel of that unweary'd Mill
That turn'd ten thousand Verses, now stands still.

There comes a time, however, when even the tuning of verses must give way to a tuning of self, for

Wisdom (curse on it) will come soon or late.
There is a time when Poets will grow dull:
I'll e'en leave Verses to the Boys at school:
To Rules of Poetry no more confin'd,
I learn to smooth and harmonize my Mind,
Teach ev'ry Thought within its bounds to roll,
And keep the equal Measure of the Soul.

As the 1730s drew to a close, Pope called attention to governmental corruption and mendacity with two final poems in the "manner," though not in "imitation," of Horace. Following upon passage of the Licensing Act of 1737, a measure designed to stifle criticism of the government in stage plays but perceived as threatening wider literary sanctions, and following also a steady stream of usually anonymous but also, at times, apparently government-sponsored attacks on Pope, the two poems were originally entitled *One Thousand Seven Hundred and Thirty Eight. A Dialogue Something like Horace*, and *One Thousand Seven Hundred and Thirty Eight. Dialogue II*. In 1740 the two poems were subsumed under the title *Epilogue to the Satires, Written in 1738, Dialogues I and II*. Some feel of the menacing climate in which they appeared may be gathered from a footnote to the last line of *Dialogue II*, presumably written by

Pope (though possibly by Warburton), but not printed until an edition (1751) after his death:

> This was the last poem of the kind printed by our author, with a resolution to publish no more; but to enter thus, in the most plain and solemn manner he could, a sort of PROTEST against that insuperable corruption and depravity of manners, which he had been so unhappy as to live to see. Could he have hoped to have amended any, he had continued those attacks; but bad men were grown so shameless and powerful, that Ridicule was become as unsafe as it was ineffectual. The Poem raised him, as he knew it would, some enemies; but he had reason to be satisfied with the approbation of good men, and the testimony of his own conscience.

The "dialogue" of the two poems is carried on between a "Friend" (identified as "Fr." or "F." in the texts) and a character identified only as "P." (either for "Pope" or the "Poet"). The friend's cautionary voice nervously urges P. to play it safe, as stated in the first poem, not to offend those in power, and, if he must "lash the Greatest," to do so only when they are "in Disgrace." The voice of P. is stubbornly, though deviously, recalcitrant, scoring points even while seeming to back off, and, at the close of the first dialogue, hardening to a scathing indictment of a divine "Vice" worshipped with a "reverential Awe" by all classes of English society, but particularly by those in positions of "Greatness." The indictment, and the poem, are concluded with this restrained but scornful couplet: "Yet may this Verse (if such a Verse remain) / Show there was one who held it ["Vice"] in disdain."

Dialogue II opens on a renewed note of urgency, with "P." declaring that "Vice with such Giant-strides comes on amain, / Invention strives to be before in vain; / Feign what I will, and paint it e'er so strong, / Some rising Genius sins up to my Song." The "Friend's" remonstrances continue, objecting when P.'s attacks become either too particular or too general, too "high" or too "low," and finally accusing P., because of his judgmental terms and attitudes, of being "strangely proud," provoking P. to this rejoinder:

> So proud, I am no Slave:
> So impudent, I own myself no Knave:
> So odd, my Country's Ruin makes me grave.
> Yes, I am proud; I must be proud to see
> Men not afraid of God, afraid of me:
> Safe from the Bar, the Pulpit, and the Throne,
> Yet touch'd and sham'd by *Ridicule* alone.

In the closing passages of *Dialogue II* Pope dramatizes, perhaps to the point of histrionics, the figurative stance of the lonely satirist, sole surviving and knightly champion of truth and freedom, beset on all sides by a host of fools, knaves, and coxcombs, but armed with the customary weapons, consecrate to virtue. First the lance:

> O sacred Weapon! left for Truth's defence,
> Sole Dread of Folly, Vice, and Insolence!
> To all but Heav'n-directed hands deny'd,
> The Muse may give thee, but the Gods must guide.

Then the sword: .

> Yes, the last Pen for Freedom let me draw,
> When Truth stands trembling on the Edge of
> Law. . . .

The sound of Roland's horn, however distant, is not without an echo in these lines.

One last great poetic enterprise emerges from the remaining three or four years of Pope's life. In 1743, over fourteen years after the original appearance of *The Dunciad*, with Theobald crowned king of the dunces, Pope published a fourth book in which the satiric targets are vastly multiplied, and Theobald is not even mentioned. A year later, after he had revised all four books in an attempt (not altogether successful) to give them new coherence, the "greater" *Dunciad* appeared, with Theobald deposed and Cibber, the bumptious but talented actor and playwright who had been created poet laureate by George II, crowned in his stead. To name Cibber monarch of duncery, however much a matter of personal animus on Pope's part, was inspired; for the king's choice of so vile a poet and so boorish and immodest a man as poet laureate itself glaringly indicted the royal grossness of taste and judgment imputed by Pope to George II in "To Augustus." The appointment also supported the other charges Pope had made about the contemporary state of letters and the hireling and sycophantic writers who "served" that state.

The fourth, and by far the longest, book of *The Dunciad* is something of a satiric avalanche, picking up and overwhelming in its path a multitude of human types and vocations not even hinted at in the original three-book version: logicians and rhetoricians, opera singers, schoolmasters and university professors, antiquarians and scientific dilettantes, clergy and philosophers. The scene is supposedly that of a royal levée, or formal court reception, where the Goddess Dulness (with her "Laureate son" in repose on her lap) "mounts the Throne." Before her appear all those other "sons" and suitors who will be blessed and encouraged in the great undertaking of making "ONE MIGHTY DUNCIAD OF THE LAND!" Grand, hilarious, sweeping as the progress of this new book is, it does not seem to be smoothly integrated into the "action" or vision of the original version. Yet complaining about the four-book version's congruity of parts ultimately seems, in the face of its satiric energy and scope, merely captious. And the magnificent close, seemingly testifying to the expiration of civilization (and indeed Pope did witness the close of one particular epoch of Western culture), elevates to apocalyptic intensity all of those threats, insidious as well as brutally overt, by which, as Pope saw it, his particular era of civilization was being undermined and overthrown. Here is Pope's dramatic evocation of the "black hole" into which he sees the "world" he inherited being sucked and out of which he sees another "world" being born:

> She comes! she comes! the sable Throne behold
> Of *Night* Primaeval, and of *Chaos* old!
> ....
>
> See skulking *Truth* to her old Cavern fled,
> Mountains of Casuistry heap'd o'er her head!
> *Philosophy*, that lean'd on Heav'n before,
> Shrinks to her second cause, and is no more.
> *Physic* of *Metaphysic* begs defence,
> And *Metaphysic* calls for aid on *Sense!*
> See *Mystery* [i.e., divine revelation] to *Mathematics*
> fly!
> In vain! they gaze, turn giddy, rave, and die.
> *Religion* blushing veils her sacred fires,
> And unawares *Morality* expires.
> Nor *public* Flame, nor *private*, dares to shine;
> Nor *human* Spark is left, nor *Glimpse* divine!
> Lo! thy dread Empire, CHAOS! is restor'd;
> Light dies before thy uncreating word;
> Thy hand, great Anarch! lets the curtain fall;
> And Universal Darkness buries All.

During the final months of 1743 and the early months of 1744, Pope's physical condition deteriorated rapidly, and he endured periods of amnesia and delusion. On 12 December 1743 his friend Spence "was asked to witness Pope's signature on his will," which specified among other things that he was to be buried near the monument to his "dear parents" in "Twit'nam" church, and that his body "be carried to the grave by six of the poorest men of the parish," for each of whom he ordered "a suit of grey coarse cloth, as mourning." On 10 May 1744 he said to Spence:

"One of the things I have always most wondered at is that there should be any such thing as human vanity. If I had any, I had enough to mortify it a few days ago, for I lost my mind for a whole day." And "on the fourteenth he complained of seeing false colours on objects." When "a friend asked him whether he would not die as his father and mother had done, and whether he should send for a priest," Pope replied: "I do not suppose that is essential, but it will be right, and I heartily thank you for putting me in mind of it." The next morning, "after the priest had given him the last sacraments," Pope commented: "There is nothing that is meritorious but virtue and friendship, and indeed friendship is only a part of virtue." His last hours were thus recorded by Spence: "Mr. Pope died the thirtieth of May, in the evening, but they [including Spence himself] did not know the exact time, for his departure was so easy that it was imperceptible to the standers-by. May our end be like his!"

Letters:

The Correspondence of Alexander Pope, 5 volumes, edited by George Sherburn (Oxford: Clarendon Press, 1956).

Bibliography:

R. H. Griffith, *Alexander Pope: A Bibliography*, 2 volumes (Austin: University of Texas Press, 1922, 1927).

Biographies:

Owen Ruffhead, *The Life of Alexander Pope* (London: Printed for C. Bathurst, 1769);

George Sherburn, *The Early Career of Alexander Pope* (Oxford: Clarendon Press, 1934);

Maynard Mack, *Alexander Pope: A Life* (New Haven: Yale University Press, 1985).

References:

John M. Aden, *Pope's Once and Future Kings: Satire and Politics in the Early Career* (Knoxville: University of Tennessee Press, 1978);

Aden, *Something Like Horace: Studies in the Art and Allusion of Pope's Horatian Satires* (Nashville: Vanderbilt University Press, 1969);

Emmett G. Bedford and Robert J. Dilligan, *A Concordance to the Poems of Alexander Pope* (Detroit: Gale, 1974);

Frederic V. Bogel, *Acts of Knowledge: Pope's Later Poems* (Lewisburg, Pa.: Bucknell University Press, 1981);

Benjamin Boyce, *The Character-Sketches in Pope's Poems* (Durham: Duke University Press, 1962);

Douglas Brooks-Davies, *Pope's Dunciad and the Queen of Night: A Study in Emotional Jacobitism* (Manchester: Manchester University Press, 1985);

Reuben Arthur Brower, *Alexander Pope: The Poetry of Allusion* (Oxford: Clarendon Press, 1959);

Laura Brown, *Alexander Pope* (Oxford: Blackwell, 1985);

Morris Brownell, *Alexander Pope and the Arts of Georgian England* (Oxford: Clarendon Press, 1978);

Leopold Damrosch, *The Imaginative World of Alexander Pope* (Berkeley: University of California Press, 1987);

Thomas R. Edwards, *This Dark Estate: A Reading of Pope* (Berkeley: University of California Press, 1963);

H. H. Erskine-Hill, *The Social Milieu of Alexander Pope* (New Haven: Yale University Press, 1975);

David Fairer, *Pope's Imagination* (Manchester: Manchester University Press, 1984);

Rebecca Ferguson, *The Unbalanced Mind: Pope and the Rule of Passion* (Philadelphia: University of Pennsylvania Press, 1986);

Dustin M. Griffin, *Alexander Pope: The Poet in the Poems* (Princeton: Princeton University Press, 1978);

Joseph V. Guerinot, *Pamphlet Attacks on Alexander Pope, 1711-1744* (New York: New York University Press, 1969);

Brean Hammond, *Pope and Bolingbroke: A Study of Friendship and Influence* (Columbia: University of Missouri Press, 1984);

Wallace Jackson, *Vision and Re-vision in Alexander Pope* (Detroit: Wayne State University Press, 1983);

John A. Jones, *Pope's Couplet Art* (Athens, Ohio: Ohio University Press, 1969);

Douglas M. Knight, *Pope and the Heroic Tradition: A Critical Study of His Iliad* (New Haven: Yale University Press, 1951);

Maynard Mack, *Collected in Himself: Essays Critical, Biographical, and Bibliographical on Pope and Some of His Contemporaries* (Newark: University of Delaware Press, 1982);

Mack, *The Garden and the City: Retirement and Politics in the Later Poetry of Pope, 1731-1743* (Toronto: University of Toronto Press, 1969);

Mack, *The Last and Greatest Art: Some Unpublished Poetical Manuscripts of Alexander Pope* (Newark: University of Delaware Press, 1984);

Mack, " 'Wit and Poetry and Pope': Some Observations on His Imagery," in *Pope and His Contemporaries*, edited by James L. Clifford and Louis A. Landa (Oxford: Clarendon Press, 1949);

Mack, ed., *Essential Articles for the Study of Alexander Pope* (Hamden, Conn.: Archon, 1968);

Mack and James A. Winn, eds., *Pope: Recent Essays* (Hamden, Conn.: Archon, 1980);

Thomas E. Maresca, *Pope's Horatian Poems* (Columbus: Ohio State University Press, 1966);

A. D. Nuttal, *Pope's Essay on Man* (London: Allen & Unwin, 1984);

Robert W. Rogers, *The Major Satires of Alexander Pope* (Urbana, Ill.: University of Illinois Press, 1955);

John Paul Russo, *Alexander Pope: Tradition and Identity* (Cambridge, Mass.: Harvard University Press, 1972);

Robert M. Schmitz, *Pope's Essay on Criticism: 1709: A Study of the Bodleian Manuscript Text with Facsimiles, Transcripts, and Variants* (St. Louis: Washington University Press, 1962);

Schmitz, *Pope's Windsor Forest: 1712: A Study of the Washington University Holograph* (St. Louis: Washington University Press, 1952);

John Sitter, *The Poetry of Pope's Dunciad* (Minneapolis: University of Minnesota Press, 1971);

Patricia Ann Spacks, *An Argument of Images: The Poetry of Alexander Pope* (Cambridge, Mass.: Harvard University Press, 1971);

Joseph Spence, *Observations, Anecdotes, and Characters of Books and Men*, edited by James M. Osborn, 2 volumes (Oxford: Clarendon Press, 1966);

Frank Stack, *Pope and Horace: Studies in Imitation* (Cambridge: Cambridge University Press, 1985);

Geoffrey Tillotson, *On the Poetry of Pope* (Oxford: Clarendon Press, 1950);

Tillotson, *Pope and Human Nature* (Oxford: Clarendon Press, 1958);

Joseph Warton, *An Essay on the Writings and Genius of Pope* (London: Printed for M. Cooper, 1756);

Earl R. Wasserman, *Pope's Epistle to Bathurst: A Critical Reading with an Edition of the Manuscripts* (Baltimore: Johns Hopkins University Press, 1960);

Howard Weinbrot, *Alexander Pope and the Traditions of Formal Verse Satire* (Princeton: Princeton University Press, 1982);

Douglas H. White, *Pope and the Context of Controversy: The Manipulation of Ideas in An Essay on Man* (Chicago: University of Chicago Press, 1970);

Aubrey L. Williams, *Pope's Dunciad: A Study of Its Meaning* (London: Methuen, 1955);

William K. Wimsatt, *The Portraits of Alexander Pope* (New Haven: Yale University Press, 1965).

Matthew Prior

(21 or 23 July 1664 - 18 September 1721)

Frances Mayhew Rippy
Ball State University

SELECTED BOOKS: *A Satyr on the modern Translators* (London, 1685);

Satyr on the Poets. In Imitation of the Seventh Satyr of Juvenal (London, 1687);

The Hind and the Panther Transvers'd to the Story of The Country Mouse and the City-Mouse, by Prior and Charles Montagu (London: Printed for W. Davis, 1687);

An Ode in Imitation of the Second Ode of the Third Book of Horace (London: Printed for Jacob Tonson, 1692);

An Ode. Presented to the King, on his Majesty's Arrival in Holland, After the Queen's Death. 1695 (London: Printed for Jacob Tonson, 1695);

An English Ballad: In Answer to Mr. Despreaux's Pindarique On the Taking of Namur by the King of Great Britain, 1695 (London: Printed for Jacob Tonson, 1695);

Carmen Sæculare, For the Year 1700. To the King (London: Printed for Jacob Tonson, 1700);

To a Young Gentleman in Love. A Tale (London: Printed for J. Tonson, 1702);

A Letter to Monsieur Boileau Despreaux; Occasion'd by the Victory at Blenheim, 1704 (London: Printed for Jacob Tonson, 1704);

An English Padlock (London: Printed for Jacob Tonson, 1705);

Pallas and Venus. An Epigram [single sheet] (London: Printed for John Nutt, 1706);

An Ode, Humbly Inscrib'd to the Queen. On the Late Glorious Success of Her Majesty's Arms. Written in Imitation of Spenser's Stile (London: Printed for Jacob Tonson, 1706);

Poems on Several Occasions: Consisting of Odes, Satyrs and Epistles; With Some Select Translations and Imitations [unauthorized edition] (London: Printed for R. Burrough, J. Baker & E. Curll, 1707);

Poems on Several Occasions [authorized edition] (London: Printed for Jacob Tonson, 1709 [i.e., 1708]; revised and enlarged edition, London: Printed for Jacob Tonson & John Barber, 1718);

Earl Robert's Mice. A Poem In Imitation of Chaucer, &c. [unauthorized edition] (London: Printed for A. Baldwin, 1712);

Erle Robert's Mice. A Tale, In Imitation of Chaucer, &c. [authorized edition] (London: Printed for John Morphew, 1712);

A Second Collection of Poems on Several Occasions (London: Printed for J. Roberts, 1716);

The Dove. A Poem (London: Printed for J. Roberts, 1717);

The Conversation. A Tale (London: Printed for Jacob Tonson, 1720);

Colin's Mistakes. Written in Imitation of Spenser's Style (London: Printed for Jacob Tonson, 1721);

A Supplement to Mr. Prior's Poems. Consisting Of such Pieces as are Omitted in the late Collection of his Works, and Others, now first Published, from his Original Manuscripts, in the Custody of

G. Adcock sc.

his Friends (London: Printed for E. Curll, 1722);

Some Memoirs of the Life and Publick Employments of Matthew Prior, Esq.; With a Copy of his Last Will and Testament. Drawn up by himself in the Year MDCCXXI (London: Printed for E. Curll, 1722);

The Turtle and the Sparrow. A Poem (London: Printed for J. Roberts, 1723);

Down-Hall: A Poem (London: Printed for J. Roberts, 1723);

A New Collection of Poems on Several Occasions. By Mr. Prior, and Others (London: Printed for Tho. Osborne, 1725); revised and enlarged as *Poems on Several Occasions, . . . Volume III. The Second Edition* (London, 1727); revised again as *Poems on Several Occasions . . . Volume the Third, and Last. The Third Edition. To Which is Prefixed The Life of Mr. Prior, By Sam-*

uel Humphreys, Esq. (London: Printed & sold by S. Birt & W. Feales, 1733); revised and enlarged again as *Poems on Several Occasions . . . The Fourth Edition. To which is Prefixed, The Life of Mr. Prior, By Samuel Humphreys, Esq.* (London: Printed for C. Hitch & J. Hodges, 1742);

Miscellaneous Works of His late Excellency Matthew Prior Esq.; Consisting of Poems on Several Occasions, Viz. Epistles, Tales, Satires, Epigrams, &c. With some Select Latin Performances. Now first published from His Original Manuscripts. Revised by Himself, and Copied fair for the Press By Mr. Adrian Drift, His Executor (Dublin: Printed by S. Powell, 1739); enlarged edition, edited by J. Bancks, 2 volumes (London: Printed for the editor & sold by C. Corbett, 1740 [i.e., 1739]);

The History of His Own Time. Compiled from the Original Manuscripts of His late Excellency Matthew Prior Esq.; Revised and Signed by Himself, and Copied fair for the Press by Mr. Adrian Drift, His Executor, edited by Bancks (London: Printed for the editor, 1740);

Lyric Poems; Being Twenty Four Songs (Never before Printed:) by the Late Matthew Prior Esqr.; Set to Music by Several Eminent Masters (London: Printed for & sold by Sam: Harding, 1741);

Eighteen Canzonets for Two, and three Voices; (The Words chiefly by Matthew Prior Esqr.) Set to Musick by John Travers (London: Printed by John Simpson for [Travers], 1745?);

Songs, Duets, Choruses, &c.: in The Speechless Wife . . . Performed at the Theatre Royal Covent-Garden (London: Printed by W. Woodfall, 1794).

Editions and Collections: *The Poetical Works of Matthew Prior. In Three Volumes. With the Life of the Author* (Edinburgh: At the Apollo Press by the Martins, 1777);

The Poetical Works of Matthew Prior: Now First Collected, With Explanatory Notes, And Memoirs of the Author, 2 volumes (London: Printed for W. Strahan, T. Payne, J. Rivington & Sons, J. Dodsley, T. Lowndes, T. Cadell, T. Caslon, J. Nichols & T. Evans, 1779); revised as *The Poetical Works of Matthew Prior: A New Edition Revised with Memoir by Reginald Brimley Johnson*, edited by Johnson, 2 volumes (London: Bell, 1892);

The Poetical Works of Matthew Prior. Collated with the Best Editions, edited by Thomas Park, 2 volumes (London: J. Sharpe, 1807);

Selected Poems of Matthew Prior, edited by Austin Dobson (London: Kegan Paul, Trench, 1889);

Poems on Several Occasions, edited by A. R. Waller (Cambridge: Cambridge University Press, 1905);

Matthew Prior: Dialogues of the Dead, and Other Works in Prose and Verse, edited by Waller (Cambridge: Cambridge University Press, 1907);

The Shorter Poems of Matthew Prior, edited by Francis Bickley (London: Chapman & Dodd, 1923);

The Literary Works of Matthew Prior, edited by H. Bunker Wright and Monroe K. Spears, 2 volumes (Oxford: Clarendon Press, 1959, 1971).

Matthew Prior was the most important poet writing in England between the death of John Dryden (1700) and the poetic maturity of Alexander Pope (about 1712). A significant influence on British and German poetry throughout the eighteenth century, Prior had an effect on several different forms: long philosophical poems either serious or half-mocking, Horatian imitations, psychologically realistic tales, and polished, metrical songs and lyrics. Though his influence was still plainly discernible in Britain, Germany, and the United States throughout the nineteenth century, it was felt almost exclusively, especially in the English-speaking countries, in the one genre of vers de société. He was particularly important in his own century in England for two accomplishments: he helped to keep alive as a lesser current, in the main current of polished Augustan couplets, the Restoration gifts of lyricism and levity in tone and of octosyllabics and anapests in metrical form; and the tremendous financial success of his 1718 *Poems on Several Occasions*, with its 1,446 subscribers paying half the price of the edition in advance, helped to teach his fellow poets a significant economic lesson—that it was possible to support oneself handsomely by relying on the reading public in general rather than on one titled patron.

Prior was born in the Westminster area of London on either 21 or 23 July 1664 to Elizabeth and George Prior, a London joiner (skilled carpenter). He was the fifth of their six children but the only one to survive infancy. George Prior had left his native Dorset to practice his carpenter's trade in London, where two of his brothers had already opened taverns. From early childhood the precocious Matthew wrote poetry, his first hero being Guy of Warwick, the hero of the popular Anglo-Norman verse romance. Noting his literary bent, his parents sent him, at the age of eight, to nearby Westminster School, ruled rigidly by Richard Busby, who emphasized strict discipline, the traditional classical curriculum, extemporaneous composition in prose and verse, and oratory. Before Prior had attended Westminster, it could boast of such distinguished alumni as Ben Jonson, Abraham Cowley, John Locke, Christopher Wren, and Dryden; Prior's own generation included Nicholas Rowe and Francis Atterbury. Prior later praised the training he had received at Westminster, particularly in the making of extemporaneous verses and the composing of declamations in a short length of time.

Three years later (about 1675), when Prior was about eleven, his father died. Unable to support Prior in Westminster, his mother withdrew him from school and put him to work keeping the books at his uncle Arthur Prior's Rhenish Tavern. A year later, Charles Sackville, Sixth Earl of Dorset and patron to Dryden, William Congreve, Thomas Shadwell, Nathaniel Lee, Thomas Otway, and George Etherege, came into the Rhenish Tavern and found the twelve-year-old Prior behind the bar reading Horace. Dorset asked him first to construe a passage or two, then asked him to turn an ode into English verse. Prior performed these tasks so well that, on later visits to the tavern, Dorset and his aristocratic friends often asked him to turn Horace or Ovid into English verse. Soon Dorset offered to pay Prior's tuition to return to Westminster School, if his uncle Arthur would continue to provide his clothing and other necessities. The family gratefully agreed, and Prior returned to Westminster in 1676. Five years later (in 1681) Prior was named a King's Scholar there—an important award based upon a distinguished command of classical languages—exempting him from tuition and residence fees, giving him a dress allowance and funds for luxuries like holidays and festivals, and conferring upon him a range of ceremonial and practical rights and privileges.

Most Westminster King's Scholars went to Christ Church, Oxford, but Prior chose instead to try to win one of the five scholarships just established by the duchess of Somerset at St. John's College, Cambridge. The scholarship he won paid all his tuition and gave him a living allowance, a shared bedroom, and a private study. During his four years at Cambridge, Prior pursued a curricu-

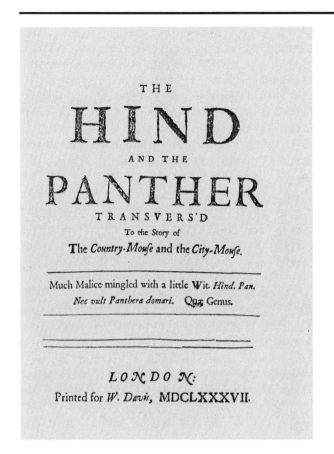

THE

HIND

AND THE

PANTHER

TRANSVERS'D

To the Story of

The *Country-Moufe* and the *City-Moufe*.

Much Malice mingled with a little Wit. *Hind. Pan.*

Nec vult Panthera domari. Qua; Genus.

LONDON:

Printed for *W. Davis,* MDCLXXXVII.

Title page for Prior and Charles Montagu's satire on John Dryden's Hind and the Panther, *published earlier in 1687*

lum still heavy in logic and divinity. During these years he wrote mainly occasional poetry; still extant from this period are over thirty Latin poems and a dozen English ones. The most interesting of these poems now is the English *A Satyr on the modern Translators* (1685), which Prior steadfastly refused to acknowledge as his in later life. The poem is a sort of *Dunciad* of translators, attacking mainly Dryden but also John Sheffield, Third Earl of Mulgrave, Aphra Behn, Thomas Rymer, and Thomas Creech. Witty but uneven, the poem is important in Prior's development for showing his close acquaintance with George Villiers, Second Duke of Buckingham's *Rehearsal* (1672) and his realization that its method would once again prove useful in satirizing Dryden–as Prior would again employ it in his first great public poetic success: *The Hind and the Panther Transvers'd* (1687).

Shortly after his 1687 graduation from St. John's College, Prior wrote *Satyr on the Poets. In Imitation of the Seventh Satyr of Juvenal,* adapting the first hundred lines of Juvenal's poem to attack contemporary poets. Prior shifts the emphasis, how-

ever; the main point of the poem is not the existence of bad poets but the fact that England would not support even its good ones. A recent college graduate, Prior did not forget this point.

In July of 1687 Prior published *The Hind and the Panther Transvers'd,* on which he collaborated with Charles Montagu, a mixed prose and verse attack upon Dryden's *Hind and the Panther,* which had appeared two months earlier. In their work Prior and Montagu, a school friend, gained literary fame, travestying and deflating Dryden's elegant beast-epic by approaching it with humdrum and unmetaphorical common sense. Prior objected to Dryden's poem in content as defending Roman Catholicism by a slanderous attack on Anglicans and Dissenters, and in style as taking the devices of a tradition beast-epic but changing the animals, with unconventional symbolism, into verbose and unrecognizable types.

Despite the great public acclaim *The Hind and the Panther Transvers'd* received, Prior found no clear professional direction for over a year after his graduation from St. John's. On 3 April 1688, however, he was entered as a Keyton Fellow at St. John's. In that same month he moved into the Fellows' quarters at St. John's and was assigned to one of the two medical fellowships. He was later required to lecture on Galen as Linacre Lecturer (1706-1710). About the middle of the year of his St. John's appointment, Prior accepted a position at Burleigh as tutor to the sons of the earl of Exeter. His poems written during the period are chiefly occasional, directed to William III, to members of the family of the earl of Exeter, to Lady Margaret Beaufort, mother of Henry VII and foundress of St. John's College, and (the most interesting of the lot) four times to Fleetwood Shepherd, the poet and wit who acted as intermediary between the earl of Dorset and the young men he sponsored. These poems to Shepherd are particularly important both in their content–sometimes asking Dorset to award Prior a political post–and in their evidence that Prior was becoming increasingly sure in his command of light verse.

On 1 November 1690 Prior's political hopes were realized when he was appointed secretary to Lord Dursley at The Hague, a city where Prior was to stay, with growing political power, for the next seven years. The Hague was an important outpost in the War of the Grand Alliance (The War of the League of Augsburg), which was already two years underway when Prior was appointed, and was to go on for almost another seven. The struggle for power between the Bourbons and the Hapsburgs pitted France against England, Spain, Savoy, the Netherlands, and the Holy Roman Empire. In his seven years at The Hague during this war, Prior performed the duties that Americans would expect of a cultural attaché or a vice consul in the modern foreign service.

Prior never married, but about the time of his appointment to The Hague he established the first of three intimate relationships with women who would successively become his mistresses for the remaining thirty years of his life. This first one was Jane Ansley, known as Flanders Jane, the widow who became his mistress and housekeeper for the next sixteen years and was to be the subject of one of his most popular poems, "Jinny the Just," not collected until 1907 (in *Dialogues of the Dead*).

Besides the diplomatic correspondence Prior carried on as a part of his appointment to The Hague, he wrote several poems there. Understandably many of these poems took on a distinctly patriotic and political tone. Others, however, were nonlaureate verse: love poems, religious poems, classical paraphrases, occasional poems called forth by his school, his noble patrons, or the royal family, and personal poems about his private life.

As to these panegyrics, Prior gained his greatest fame with the much celebrated and circulated *An English Ballad . . . On the Taking of Namur by the King of Great Britain* (1695). Three years earlier, Nicolas Boileau-Despréaux had written a mythologically ornate poem, "Ode Sur la Prise de Namur, Par les Armes du Roy, L' Année 1692," praising Louis XIV extravagantly for having taken Namur. Prior deflated Boileau's distended mythological rhetoric by printing the two poems side by side and parodying Boileau's encomia figure by figure, for William III had now retaken Namur. The poem's success was immediate.

In contrast, Prior's best personal poem of the period was a work never printed till two decades after his death, "Written in the Year 1696" (in *Miscellaneous Works*, 1740), often called "The Secretary"–but never called that by Prior. The poem is interesting both biographically and artistically. Describing the pleasures of a weekend (Saturday evening and Sunday), it also suggests Prior's professional activities during the rest of the week. In tone and approach, moreover, it strikes notes that would later prove most successful in Pri-

or's colloquial poems: a casual self-deprecatory use of classical learning, comic feminine rhymes, and an underplaying of his work that yet makes it seem important.

Despite his writing of these strong poems, however, Prior's activities at The Hague remained chiefly diplomatic. He went back to London briefly, returning to The Hague on 10 March 1697 as secretary of the embassy. The first meeting of the Congress at Ryswick took place on 9 May 1697; the peace treaties were signed on 20 and 21 September of that same year. Prior's duty was to check the Latin and French versions of these papers and to carry to London on 24 September, the official message that England, Holland, and Spain had signed the treaty with France, thus ending the War of the Grand Alliance. Earlier (on 17 May 1697) Prior had been named chief secretary to the Lords Justice of Ireland. More important to his later poetical career, he had met at the Congress of Ryswick, there in the service of the earl of Jersey, a fellow Londoner, Adrian Drift, who was to become Prior's friend, amanuensis, transcriber, and preserver of his manuscript poems after his death.

On 11 December 1697 it was announced that Prior was to serve as secretary to the reopened British Embassy in Paris. He left for Paris on 21 January 1698 and remained there for nineteen months. On 4 February 1698 he had his first audience with Louis XIV; in mid August of the same year he saw the exiled James II and his queen; still later he glimpsed the young Prince James. His primary duty in Paris seems to have been to report to his superiors in England anything he learned of the actions and designs of Jacobites and of those in power in France. While in Paris he was elected (on or about 23 March 1698) to membership in the Royal Society in England. Although these initial nineteen months in Paris were not successful for Prior in every sense (they were a financial disaster and a period in which he produced no poetry), they were important to him because of the strong ties he established: in literature, with Boileau, André Dacier, and Bernard Le Boviér de Fontenelle; in politics, with the Duc de Villeroi, the Marquis de Torcy, and Louis XIV.

Prior returned to London in late 1699 and was based there for the next two years, the last years of the life of William III. Prior served the king as a traveling diplomatic agent, going repeatedly to Paris and Marly to carry out secret negotia-

Prior in 1700 (painting by Godfrey Kneller; by permission of Trinity College, Cambridge)

tions with Louis XIV on the Second Partition Treaty. On 28 June 1700 he was also appointed a commissioner of the Board of Trade and Plantations, succeeding John Locke, who had been forced to resign because of ill health. This important board oversaw all the American colonies and all international English trade, including that of the mighty trading companies. By early 1700 Prior had also joined the Kit-Cats, Whig aristocrats and the young writers for whom they were patrons, meeting weekly in London in the Cat and the Fiddle under the sponsorship of the publisher Jacob Tonson. The Kit-Cats included Joseph Addison, Richard Steele, Congreve, and Rowe. For four months in 1701 (February to June) Prior also served as a member of Parliament, accepting the pocket borough of East Grinstead in Sussex from the earl of Dorset. Before the appointment Prior had already been mov-

ing to the right politically, advocating that a strong king such as William be unhindered by the majority opposition in Parliament; by the end of his four months in Parliament, he had openly become a Tory. He thus did not receive again his Whig pocket-borough seat, and his membership in the Kit-Cats was abruptly terminated. The money from his various positions came in erratically or not at all, but although sometimes short of funds, Prior managed in 1700 to buy for himself a London home he called "Matt's Palace" to be his chief place of residence during the twenty remaining years of his life. This Westminster house was on the west side of Duke Street, with its rear overlooking St. James Park. During all this period, Prior served William III in shaping the Grand Alliance between England, Austria, and Holland as a force for containing or defeating Louis XIV.

In these London years (1699-1702) Prior produced a significant part of his poetry. *Carmen Sæculare* (1700) is his most elegantly contrived Pindaric poem, a celebration almost six hundred lines long of the glorious future of England as it entered a new century under the rule of its patriot king. Three later and more private political poems, however, expressed the fear that William was losing his chance at greatness by dealing weakly with the political factions that beset him. His nonpolitical poems of this period show an impressive range and power. He wrote two polished love songs and his first ribald tale in verse, "Hans Carvel," a free adaptation of Jean La Fontaine, who in turn had taken his account from Rabelais. Filled with realistic details of Augustan life, lively and bawdy, "Hans Carvel" was later to be praised by Oliver Goldsmith. This same three-year period also produced the most famous of Prior's poems for and about children, "To a Child of Quality of Five Years Old, the Author suppos'd Forty." In this poem Miss Mary (Lady Mary Villiers, daughter of Edward Villiers, First Earl of Jersey) rolls up her hair and makes beds for her silkworms from the love poems Prior has written her. Prior adds four years to his real age to intensify his contention that their possible love affair is defeated by time: "For as our diff'rent Ages move, / 'Tis so ordain'd wou'd Fate but mend it, / That I shall be past making Love, / When she begins to comprehend it." During this same period Prior wrote two other poems advocating Horatian simple life: "Written at Paris, 1700. In the Beginning of Robe's Geography" (asking Rhea, the nature goddess, for a garden); and "Song. Sett by Mr: Abell" (praising friendship above learning, love, riches, or mere joviality).

This literary period brought Prior a growing literary reputation; however, it also brought him the strongest attack upon himself produced during his lifetime by a literary figure of some importance. Daniel Defoe, in the second part of *Reformation of Manners, A Satyr* (1702), spent over twenty lines attacking Prior, on the undeniable grounds that he had spent his early years in a tavern and that he had both praised and blamed William III.

Already in failing health, William was thrown from a horse on 21 February 1702 and died on 8 March. He was succeeded to the throne on 23 April 1702 by his sister-in-law Anne, who was to rule for the twelve years until her death. Under her reign Prior's political range was reduced; Anne disliked using him, because he was a person of "meane extraction" and was much influenced by the duchess of Marlborough, who disliked and distrusted Prior. In this first decade of the eighteenth century Prior was to find himself not so much a powerful political figure as an important poet. Dryden had died in 1700; Pope would not achieve his full poetic development until about 1712. For this one decade Prior became perhaps the most important practicing poet in England. Two collections of his poems came out during this decade. The fifth part of Tonson's *Miscellanies*, published early in 1704, contained eighteen of Prior's poems, as well as poems by Addison, Congreve, and Thomas Sackville, Earl of Dorset. In 1707 Edmund Curll published a pirated edition of Prior's *Poems on Several Occasions*; in 1709 Tonson printed an authorized edition, carefully prepared by Prior, with a second edition appearing in the same year and later editions in 1711, 1713, and 1717, attesting to the book's popularity.

The poems in Tonson's *Miscellanies* and in *Poems on Several Occasions* show Prior to be a poet with a wide range of topic, tone, approach, and metrical form, now writing with a sure and steady hand. Some of these poems resulted from his unsettled private affairs with women. For several months in 1703 and 1704 Prior casually courted Elizabeth Singer, a twenty-nine-year-old pastoral poet, to whom he wrote at least nine letters and two poems. Several years later, sometime between 1706 and 1708, Prior exchanged Jane Ansley, his mistress for sixteen years, for Anne Durham, in her mid teens at that time. She was to remain his mistress until about 1718 and became the subject of at least three of his poems and probably of nine others as well.

The best description of Prior during this decade was written by John Mackey in *Memoirs of the Secret Service of John Macky* [sic], *Esq. (1733)*: "one of the best Poets in *England*, but very factious in Conversation; a thin hollow-looked Man, turned of forty years old." Twelve or more years afterward, Jonathan Swift concurred with Mackey's description, writing under it in his copy: "This is near the truth."

The year 1709 was propitious for Prior, politically as well as poetically. Some of his implacable political enemies–the Sidney Godolphin ministry and the duchess of Marlborough–fell from power in that year. The new ministry was made up of Moderates and began, on 3 August 1710, to publish the Tory *Examiner*, a political newspaper. Prior's entry into journalism came through

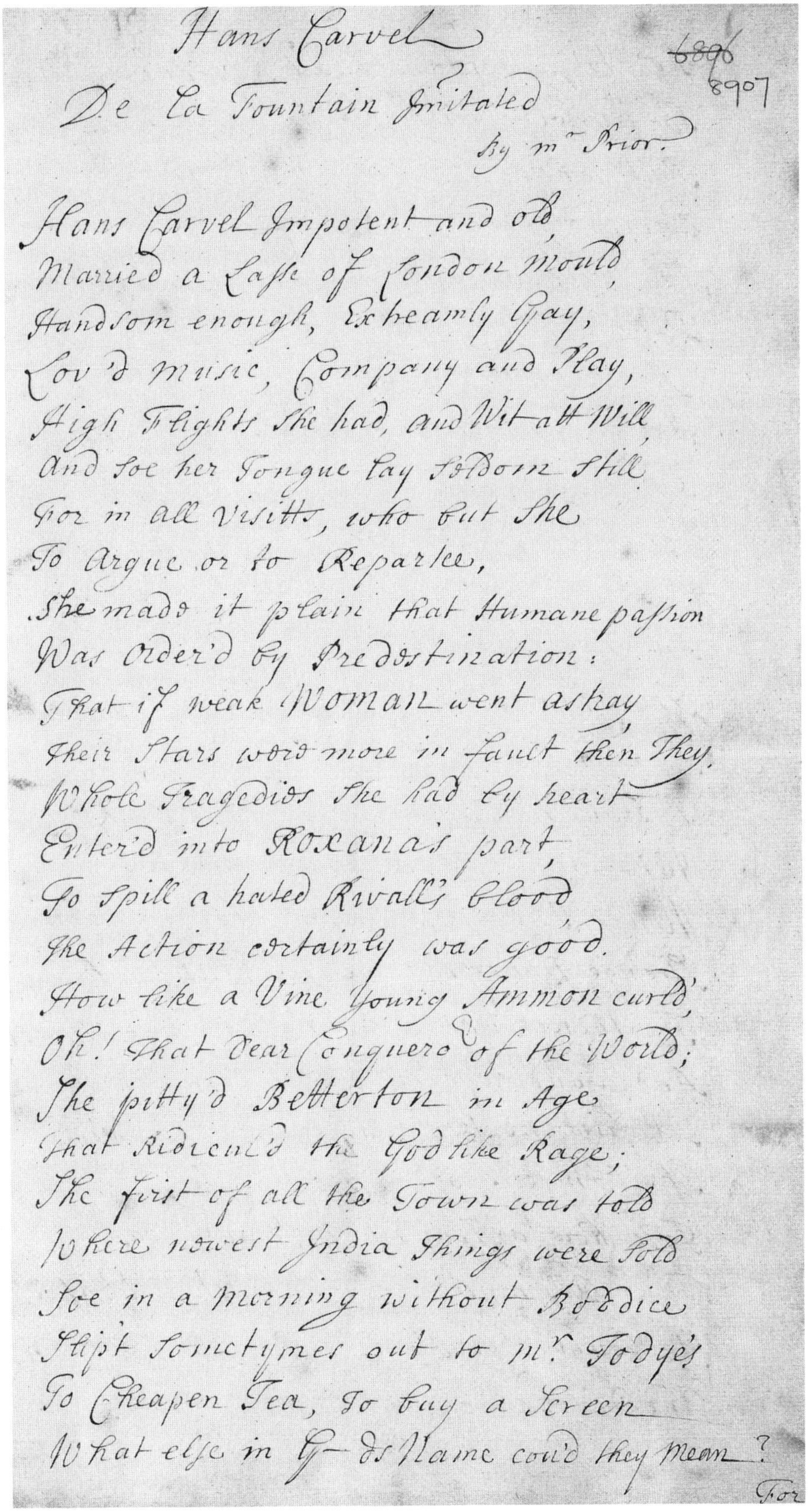

Hans Carvel

De La Fountain Imitated

by mr Prior.

Hans Carvel Impotent and old
Married a Lass of London mould,
Handsom enough, Exteamly Gay,
Lov'd music, Company and Play,
High Flights She had, and Wit att Will,
And soe her Tongue lay seldom still.
For in all visitts, who but She
To Argue or to Repartee,
She made it plain that Humane passion
Was Order'd by Predestination:
That if weak Woman went astray
Their Stars were more in fault then They.
Whole Tragedies She had by heart
Enter'd into Roxana's part,
To Spill a hated Rivall's blood
The Action certainly was good.
How like a Vine Young Ammon curld,
Oh! That dear Conquerod of the World;
She pitty'd Betterton in Age
That Ridicul'd the God like Rage;
She first of all the Town was told
Where newest India Things were Sold
Soe in a morning without Boddice
Slipt sometymes out to mr. Todye's
To Cheapen Tea, To buy a Screen
What else in G—ds Name coud they mean?

For

First page of a manuscript for Prior's poem, written in 1700, based on a tale by Jean de la Fontaine (EL 8907; by permission of the Henry E. Huntington Library and Art Gallery)

this newspaper, for which he wrote one poem and at least one entire issue (no. 6, 31 August 1710). On 30 November 1710 Swift, Rowe, and Prior collaborated on a letter to the *Tatler*, attacking the Whig-British chauvinism of Steele.

Prior ventured into Tory journalism at least partly because of his deepening friendship with Swift and the other members of the Brothers Club, a group of Tory friends ranging in number from seventeen to twenty-two and meeting weekly during the last few years of Queen Anne's reign. Swift's *Journal to Stella* (1710-1712) records at least thirteen occasions when Prior was dining with Swift, often with all the brothers, but sometimes with only two or three. Prior and Swift were close friends by 18 November 1710. By 1711 the two men were showing each other their manuscripts before they were published, exchanging gifts (Prior gave Swift a fine edition of Plautus), and walking together around St. James's Park. "This walking is a strange remedy," wrote Swift in the *Journal*. "Mr. Prior walks to make himself fat, and I to bring myself down; he has generally a cough, which he only calls a cold: we often round the Park together." On 21 April 1711 Swift wrote again of "Prior's lean carcase." The two men became so identified in the public mind that works by one were often attributed to the other, and as Swift wrote to Stella, a Whig newspaper in that year called Swift and Prior "the two Sosias," alluding to the doubling of Mercury and the slave in Plautus's *Amphitryon*.

In his preface to the 1709 edition of *Poems on Several Occasions*, Prior characterizes himself as a writer of "*Public Panegyrics, Amorous Odes, Serious Reflections, or idle Tales . . . .*" In considering his poems of this first decade of the century, it is useful to look at them in terms of these four categories.

The "Public Panegyrics" include several short poems and two longer state panegyrics: *A Letter to Monsieur Boileau Despreaux; Occasion'd by the Victory at Blenheim, 1704* and *An Ode, Humbly Inscrib'd to the Queen. On the Late Glorious Success of Her Majesty's Arms* (1706). For different reasons, each of these long pieces of laureate verse (the last that Prior wrote) are of special interest. *A Letter to Monsieur Boileau Despreaux* begins by jeering at Boileau as a hired eulogist who will have trouble finding anything encouraging to say on this occasion of an undeniable military defeat. But during Prior's prolonged stay in France he made an admiring friend of Boileau and sympathizes with Boileau's problem on this occasion. The poem

praises Marlborough's military prowess while never praising Louis XIV's, but it also praises Boileau's poetical powers as superior to Prior's, though applied to a less worthy object. An accident of fate has placed the two friendly poets on opposite military and national sides. Prior feels that he should write a Virgilian panegyric for Marlborough and the English victory, but it is too late in his life for him to do that:

> But We must change the Style.–Just now I said,
> I ne'er was Master of the tuneful Trade.
> Or the small Genius which my Youth could boast
> In Prose and Business lies extinct and lost.
> Bless'd, if I may some younger Muse excite;
> Point out the Game, and animate the Flight.

The poem is, in a sense, Prior's resignation at forty from the writing of laureate verse. He can no longer see the world (or military victories) in simple terms; that is a business better left to younger men, who have less knowledge of the world as it is.

The other long piece of laureate verse from this period, *An Ode, Humbly Inscrib'd to the Queen*, is less interesting in content than *A Letter to Monsieur Boileau Despreaux* but more interesting in metrical form. Like many of Prior's poems, it is in content strongest at its close, which mixes praise of Anne and Marlborough (whom the poem treats as William's successor), belittling of Prior's panegyric talents, and a wish for a lasting peace. It is in its stanzaic form, however, that the poem is distinctive. Prior chose for the poem–and defended in its preface–a modified form of the Spenserian stanza, with a less complicated rhyme scheme in the octave and a rhyming alexandrine couplet at the end. Prior hoped to instigate a Spenserian revival by using this stanzaic form and by sprinkling his language with occasional antiquated terms; there is considerable evidence that he did just that. Such a revival gained strength later in the eighteenth century.

Prior never again wrote the lengthy political poem, though this same period saw some short, informal poems on political topics. Perhaps the most memorable of these is his "True Statesmen," datable to the latter part of Queen Anne's reign. The poem draws a moral:

> Be not the Bully of the Nation
> Nor foam at mouth for Moderation.
> Take not thy Sentiments on trust
> Nor be by others Notions just.
> To Church and Queen and Laws be hearty

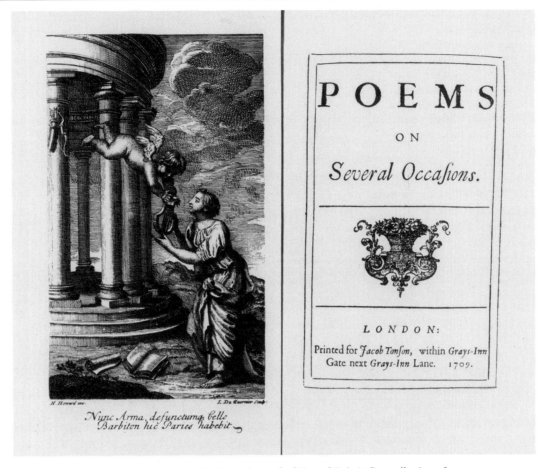

Frontispiece and title page for the authorized edition of Prior's first collection of poetry

But hate a Trick and scorn a Party. . . .
Vote Right tho certain to be blam'd
And rather Starve than be asham'd.

Eighteen of Prior's poems written during the period from 1702 to 1708 belong in his second category, "Amorous Odes." Eleven of these poems employ mythology or pastoral conventions as key elements; the others use an occasional pastoral name or term and maintain their tone of formal elegance. In this second less conventional grouping Prior sounds one of his most convincing notes: a wry recognition of the mutability of love. In "The Merchant, to secure his treasure," for example, Prior draws an uneasy triangle of persons: a new lover courting his mistress in the presence of the old one, which embarrasses all three.

The half-concealed cynicism of "The Merchant" becomes open in Prior's third category, "Idle Tales." Three of these were written and published between 1700 and 1710. *To a Young Gentleman in Love. A Tale* (1702) presents lovers, Celia

and Celadon, who speak to each other with hypocritically flowery language but whose thoughts are elsewhere. Each desires something else far more than his or her purported love. Celadon wants a place at court; Celia wants Thyrsis, who is hidden under the bed.

A year later, in 1703, Prior wrote "The Ladle," reworking Ovid's story of Baucis and Philemon. This second "Idle Tale" belongs to those folktales that relate three wishes, granted by the gods or other supernatural beings but wasted by the human beings on which they are bestowed. In these folktales the pattern is similar: a couple is granted the three wishes; one of them (usually the wife) wastes the first on a triviality. Enraged at the waste, the husband uses the second wish to punish his wife physically and then must use the last to reverse his cruelty. Prior follows Ovid in most of his recounting, but adds a moral distinctively his, a close unlike that in any other idle tale—but much like his position and concepts in the more serious poems. "The Ladle" ends:

Against our Peace We arm our Will:
Amidst our Plenty, *Something* still
For Horses, Houses, Pictures, Planting
To Thee, to Me, to Him is wanting.
That cruel *Something* unpossess'd
Corrodes, and levens all the rest.
That *Something*, if We could obtain,
Would soon create a future Pain:
And to the Coffin, from the Cradle
'Tis all a WISH, and all a LADLE.

The third of Prior's "Idle Tales" is "Paulo Purganti and His Wife: An Honest, but a Simple Pair" (1708). Like "Hans Carvel" earlier, the poem deals with a wife who demands more of her husband sexually than he can provide: "The Doctor understood the Call; / But had not always wherewithal." Perhaps its most interesting comment, however, is literary-critical, not domestic or sexual. Like "The Ladle," it contains a warning that tales must be brief: "Reduce, my Muse, the wand'ring Song: / A Tale should never be too long." When later eighteenth-century critics discussed the reputation of these "Idle Tales," the talk tended to center upon "Paulo Purganti and His Wife." Both Samuel Johnson and Oliver Goldsmith considered these tales to be moral and not shocking, but the two men were already facing opposition when they did so. As reported in his *Life of Johnson*, James Boswell reminded Johnson that David Dalrymple, Lord Hailes, had attacked Prior's "impure tales," but Johnson retorted, "There is nothing in Prior that will excite to lewdness. If Lord Hailes thinks there is, he must be more combustible than other people." When Boswell specifically referred to "Paulo Purganti and His Wife," Johnson responded, "Sir, there is nothing there, but that his wife wanted to be kissed, when poor Paulo was out of pocket. No, Sir, Prior is a lady's book. No lady is ashamed to have it standing in her library."

But in the matter of these "Idle Tales" the tastes of the time were running against Johnson and Goldsmith by the late eighteenth century. Goldsmith in 1767 edited *The Beauties of English Poesy*, intending it especially as an anthology for young people and including some of Prior's work. "To our youth, particularly," Goldsmith wrote in his preface, "a publication of this sort may be useful ... ; every poem here is well known, and possessed, or the public has been long mistaken, of peculiar merit. ..." The *Critical Review* (June 1767), however, attacked Goldsmith's choice of pieces, particularly his inclusion of "Hans Carvel"; the buying public apparently

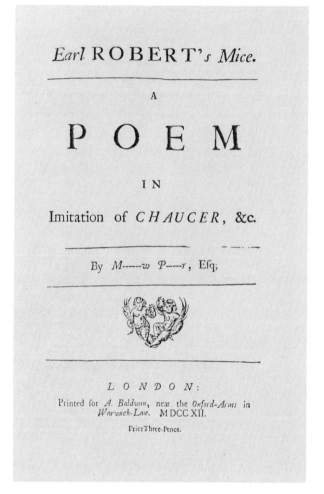

Earl ROBERT's *Mice.*

A

P O E M

I N

Imitation of *CHAUCER*, &c.

By *M-----w P---r*, Esq;

L O N D O N:

Printed for *A. Baldwin*, near the *Oxford-Arms* in *Warwick-Lane*. MDCCXII.

Price Three-Pence.

Title page for the unauthorized edition of Prior's poem that features Robert Harley, Earl of Oxford, and Charles Montague, Earl of Halifax, as two of the characters

agreed and objected also to "The Ladle," and Goldsmith's anthology had only a limited sale. It was this very Chaucerian quality in the tales that did Prior great harm in the nineteenth century when they were considered unacceptably bawdy.

Prior's fourth category was "Serious Reflections," though the seriousness is generally salted with bits of grim humor. In this category fall the first two of Prior's self-epitaphs, the 1702 "NOBLES, and Heralds by Your leave ...," and the 1703 "Adriani Morientis ad Animam Suam. Imitated." In 1703 Prior also wrote "Charity. A Paraphrase on the Thirteenth Chapter of the First Epistle to the Corinthians," a sixty-line elaboration upon the same New Testament passage that he had treated at equal length twelve years earlier in "Charity never faileth." Two of Prior's "Serious Reflections" from this first decade of the eighteenth century were classical translations, and two others were poems of unusual melancholy strength, including "An Ode. Inscribed to the Memory of the Honble Col. George Villiers, Drowned in the River Piava, in the Country of Fruili. 1703," a Horatian imitation in heroic couplets, especially strong in its expressions of man's predestined doom:

> In vain We think that free-will'd Man has Pow'r
> To hasten or protract th' appointed Hour.
> Our Term of Life depends not on our Deed:
> Before our Birth our Funeral was decreed.
> Nor aw'd by Foresight, nor mis-led by Chance,
> Imperious Death directs His Ebon Lance;
> Peoples great HENRY's Tombs, and leads up
>   HOLBEN's Dance.

Prior, who had won his way back into Westminster School by his precocious mastery of the art of turning Horace into English verse, had not lost his touch, as shown in this description of the imagined burial of Villiers: "And fragrant Mould upon his Body throw; / And plant the Warrior Lawrel o'er his Brow: / Light lye the Earth; and flourish green the Bough."

An equally powerful melancholy piece was Prior's "Written in the Beginning of Mezeray's History of France," in which he took six lines written a decade earlier and expanded them to four times that length. Over a century later, the aging Sir Walter Scott repeated the twenty-four line poem by memory, applying it to himself, for it points out how tenaciously men cling to life. No lame, blind beggar in the Invalides would trade his wretched life for the completed, distinguished ones of the dead Mezeray or of the dead kings whom Mezeray has described: "All covet Life, yet call it Pain: / All feel the Ill, yet shun the Cure: / Can Sense this Paradox endure?" Even the old are reluctant to leave the stage of life, long after their roles, whether tragic or comic, have been played out:

> The Man in graver Tragic known
> (Tho' his best Part long since was done)
>   Still on the Stage desires to tarry:
> And He who play'd the *Harlequin*,
> After the Jest still loads the Scene,
>   Unwilling to retire, tho' Weary.

Several important poems from this first decade of the eighteenth century do not fit neatly into any of Prior's four categories. There are wittily cynical reflections upon human nature; a reaction to a foreign book just read; an elaboration upon a foreign epigram; a comic epilogue to a

highly serious tragedy; and a Latin epitaph. More important, four of Prior's most highly regarded poems were written in this decade but do not fit clearly into any of Prior's categories: *Henry and Emma* (1708), *Solomon* (1718), *An English Padlock* (1705), and "Jinny the Just."

In one sense *Henry and Emma* is an "Amorous Ode," but its almost eight hundred lines are more narrative and dialogic than lyric. Prior modeled his poem on the anonymous late-Middle-English *Nut-brown Maid* (1503?) and printed the earlier poem immediately preceding his in the 1709 edition of *Poems on Several Occasions*. The *Nut-brown Maid* was a poem about a test in which a woman proved her fidelity in a manner suggested by the Franciscan defense of women; Prior recast the story along eighteenth-century lines in eighteenth-century phraseology. As in the original, Prior's Emma is confronted by her disguised lover, who challenges her to stay with him under a series of conditions increasingly painful to her. He tells her that he is a murderer who must flee into perpetual exile, that if she accompanies him, she will damage her reputation, live in danger, want, and discomfort, wear male garb, and associate with "a lewd abandon'd Pack." He suggests that her eagerness to accompany him to the woods is "loose Desire" not "constant Love," and that he has taken on a younger, fairer mistress. But when Emma insists that she will nevertheless accompany him into exile, even if only to serve him and his new mistress, Henry reveals that he has been testing the limits of her fidelity, that he is really a blameless young lord of high repute. In telling this story, Prior doubles the length of the original *Nut-brown Maid* and changes its meter to heroic couplets, with an alexandrine refrain for each lover. Henry's alexandrines ring changes upon "Condemn'd in lonely Woods a banish'd Man to rove," Emma's "That I, of all Mankind, will love but Thee alone." The lovers address each other in the elegantly stylized language of Augustan courtship. Prior also modifies the original poem by adding a specific setting ("South of the Castle, in a verdant Glade"), a personal prologue addressed to Cloe, an explanatory framework, and a closing section that uses mythology to eulogize Queen Anne and the duke of Marlborough.

Henry and Emma became an international success. By 1748 it had been translated into Latin, by 1753 into German, and by 1764 into French. Sections of it were set to music in 1749, other parts in 1774. Critics in England, even those as difficult to please as John Dennis, openly praised it. Lady Mary Wortley Montagu, as an early advocate of women's rights, objected to the test story in principle yet liked the poem itself so well that even at seventy-three she could still recite it all by memory.

In the late eighteenth century two key critics–Dr. Johnson and Thomas Warton the younger–raised objections to *Henry and Emma* (Johnson found it immoral and tedious), but William Cowper and John Wesley replied vigorously to Johnson in its defense, and Horace Walpole angrily responded to Warton. Lady Montagu's poem, "The Basset Table" (1716), resounds with echoes of Prior's poem. In 1739 William Shenstone went through his copy of *Poems on Several Occasions* (which he had purchased when an Oxford student four years earlier) "marking the Pieces I most admired with a proportionate Number of Crosses," as he wrote in his copy of the book. His highest commendation was seven crosses: "The Garland" and *Henry and Emma* received this award. Two contemporaries of Pope, James Ralph and Richard Savage, insisted that Pope wrote *Eloisa to Abelard* (1720) in a deliberate attempt to compete with Prior's *Henry and Emma* while taking advantage of its popularity. Surely *Eloisa to Abelard* resembles *Henry and Emma* in certain of its themes and approaches, and there are many verbal echoes. *Henry and Emma* also provided phrasing for some of Pope's other poems: *The Rape of the Lock* (1714), *Windsor-Forest* (1713), *The Dunciad* (1728), and *Of the Characters of Women: An Epistle to a Lady* (1735).

But the general admiration for *Henry and Emma* did not last beyond its own century. Of all Prior's poems it was the one most consistently attacked in the nineteenth century, and it has had only one detailed and friendly examination in the twentieth. James Sutherland, in his 1948 *Preface to Eighteenth Century Poetry*, treated the poem in detail, favorably interpreting it in the light of Prior's intentions: "What Prior has done is not so much to translate the poem into modern English as to inject it with some sort of poetical serum which completely alters the blood-content. He has treated it as a modern choreographer might treat sophisticated ballet."

Prior as modernizer had two motives and two audiences. For the unsophisticated reader, he was attempting to put the material into accessible form. For the sophisticated reader, he offered the pleasure of hearing a familiar old story retold in modern fashion and phrasing. All any mod-

ernizer can expect is what Prior received for *Henry and Emma*: spectacular success in his own poetic age and rejection and obscurity in the ages that follow, which need once more to do their own modernizations.

Prior was also writing another long poem in 1707 and 1708, one which he himself was to prize most highly–*Solomon on the Vanity of the World*. Although not printed until the 1718 *Poems on Several Occasions*, the poem was completed a decade earlier. The longest of Prior's poems (2,652 lines), *Solomon* is also the most serious of his major efforts, and Monroe K. Spears and H. Bunker Wright are surely correct in calling it "an important document in literary and intellectual history" (Introduction to *The Literary Works*, 1959). Its three books are Solomon's description of his unsuccessful attempts to find happiness and meaning in knowledge, in pleasure, or in power.

In the preface, of particular critical interest, Prior writes of his efforts to find the proper verse form for *Solomon* and of his eventual decision to choose a modified form of heroic couplets and include occasional triplets, because "He that writes in Rhimes, dances in Fetters: And as his Chain is more extended, he may certainly take larger Steps."

In book I Solomon looks for satisfaction in physical and metaphysical learning but is thwarted repeatedly. He finally concludes, Pyrrhonistically, that human reason is insufficient to give sure answers to material or spiritual questions.

In book II Solomon turns from seeking knowledge to seeking pleasure–in wealth, architecture, music, dance, drink, and love. He is most conspicuously unsuccessful in love. First he falls in love with but is spurned by an Egyptian beauty. Then he is sought out by Abra, a simple, low-born girl. He first falls into uxoriousness with her and corrupts his court and himself to please her; when he finally throws off her degrading power over him, she kills herself. In grief Solomon seeks satisfaction in "Tribes of Women," adopting their gods. Finally he rejects these as well, despairing of finding happiness in love.

By book III Solomon feels little hope ("For Hope is but the Dream of Those that wake") but turns to the only source of possible happiness left for him on earth: power. However, he has already observed the vicissitudes of fortune. Today's hero, already of questionable merit (his laurel "Wet with the Soldier's Blood, and Widow's

Prior, circa 1713-1714 (painting by A. S. Belle; by permission of the Master and Fellows of St. John's College, Cambridge)

Tears"), becomes tomorrow's scorned prisoner or dishonored corpse. It would be best never to have lived. All mankind is trapped between the past and the future:

> Amid Two Seas on One small Point of Land
> Weary'd, uncertain, and amaz'd We stand:
> On either Side our Thoughts incessant turn:
> Forward We dread; and looking back We mourn.
> Losing the Present in this dubious Hast:
> And lost Our selves betwixt the Future, and the
>   Past.

An angel appears in response to Solomon's lamentations and tells him to cease looking for relief from sorrow and trouble. The angel then foretells the history of Israel from Solomon's time to the coming of Christ, advising Solomon to "Stop Thy Enquiry then; and curb Thy Sense: / Nor let Dust argue with Omnipotence. / 'Tis GOD who must dispose, and Man sustain, / Born to endure,

forbidden to complain." Telling Solomon to "Be Humble, and be Just," the angel flies upward, and Solomon accepts its injunctions: "Benign Creator, let Thy plastic Hand / Dispose it's own Effect. Let Thy Command / Restore, Great Father, Thy Instructed Son; / And in My Act may THY great WILL BE DONE."

Hoxie Neale Fairchild, studying Prior as a melancholy skeptic influenced by his early Calvinist background and by later scientific determinism, quipped that "Set amidst all the *vers de société* and bawdy tales, *Solomon* looks like a parson in a night club." Yet *Solomon* is simply the longest expression of Prior's lifelong interest in religious questions, ranging from his "On Exodus iii. 14," written while he was still a student at St. John's College, to "Predestination," written during the last months of his life and left in fragments at the time of his death. In most of the religious poems written throughout his mature life Prior shows two consistent philosophical strains: Pyrrhonism (extreme skepticism about the efficacy of human reason) and fideism (accepting on faith matters that cannot be determined by this fallible reason). Prior cannot decide, however, whether it is better under these dubious circumstances to solace oneself with admittedly transitory pleasures. Most of his poems, like "Jinny the Just," suggest that it is; *Solomon* argues that it is not.

Though never as popular as *Henry and Emma, Solomon* was favorably received in its own day. By 1736 it had been translated into Latin; in 1743 book II received yet another Latin translation; in 1757 the whole poem was translated into German. Pope apparently preferred Prior's *Alma* to *Solomon,* yet Pope's *Essay on Man* (1733-1734) is heavily indebted to *Solomon.* Because Prior refuses to accept rational answers, *Solomon* is more consistent but less lively than is the *Essay on Man.* Johnson found this tedium fatal to *Solomon.* Damon in Prior's *The Conversation* (1720) pretends to be intimate with Prior and says of *Solomon*: "Indeed poor SOLOMON in Rhime / Was much too grave to be Sublime." Yet, though both Pope and Johnson found fault with the tedium of the poem as a whole, each learned much from its parts. The *Essay on Man* has forty verbal borrowings from *Solomon,* these almost always appearing in the parts of the *Essay on Man* that examine the moral and physical ills of the world, man's search for happiness, reason versus passions, and the animal kingdom. Both poets are similar in their treatment of the Great Chain of Being and of the Ages of Man. But when Pope endeavors in the *Essay on Man* to establish reasonably that those things that appear to man to be evil and unjust may not be so when viewed in the whole scheme of things, Prior can conclude in *Solomon* only that man must accept on faith evils that he cannot explain. While *Solomon* is less lively than the *Essay on Man,* it may ultimately have more philosophical depth. Thus, George Saintsbury maintained (in *The Peace of the Augustans,* 1916) that "If he had not Pope's intense craftsmanship, Prior . . . has something of the 'behind the veil' touch that Pope never even hints at." It is this quality of unresolved doubt in Prior that leads Spears to call him "a harbinger of future dissatisfactions." In a line that intrigued William Empson, Pope speaks of the world in the *Essay on Man* as "A mighty maze! but not without a plan . . . ." Prior had earlier found it without a discernible plan and himself "unable to explain / The secret Lab'rynths of Thy Ways to Man. . . ."

Like Pope, Johnson found *Solomon* unattractive as a whole yet learned much from it. Both *Rasselas* (1759) and *The Vanity of Human Wishes* (1749) show strong and direct influence from *Solomon.* Like *Solomon, Rasselas* is an elegant, serious narrative in which a young prince is attempting to make a choice in life, but finds himself frequently blocked from this choice. Ian Jack has pointed out that both works have a "remote, vague, and Oriental" setting, are heavily indebted to the Bible, and are basically "Christian satires on the lot of Man," standing squarely in the tradition of Christian pessimism. Likewise, Johnson's *Vanity of Human Wishes* reinforces specifically *Solomon's* categories of investigation. And Johnson's dictum that *Solomon* was tedious, partly vitiated by his heavy borrowings from Prior's poem, was answered directly by John Wesley, who called *Solomon* "one of the noblest poems in the English tongue" and replied specifically to Johnson's charge: "Did any one ever discern it before? . . . So far from it, that if I dip in any of the three books, I scarce know where to leave off." Furthermore, Wesley quotes forty-nine lines from *Solomon,* then asks "Now what has Mr. *Pope* in all his eleven volumes, which will bear any comparison with this?"

Most of the other critics at the end of the eighteenth century who talked or wrote of *Solomon* shared Wesley's high opinion of the poem as a whole, though a few shared Johnson's lower one. Most Victorian critics paid little attention to *Solomon,* but those who did were not entirely unfriendly, finding its high seriousness to their taste. In the twentieth century, critics have continued to mix praise and blame of *Solomon* in single pronouncements. *Solomon* has many strong lines, a number of memorable images, and a versification worthy of notice. It has moreover proved a particularly useful storehouse of Augustan attitudes–theological, ethical, and scientific–both those that it accepts and those that it ultimately rejects.

The third of Prior's poems from the period under discussion that fails to fit into his four categories is *An English Padlock.* Partly an amorous ode, partly a serious reflection, partly an idle tale, *An English Padlock* deals with the best way to keep a wife faithful. It begins by reminding its reader that "MISS DANAE" could not be shut away from Jove's embrace. How, then, can a modern English husband keep his wife? Every scheme that attempts to confine or isolate her physically can be circumvented. Therefore the answer must be to set her free to see the world. Then she may return of her own free will.

The fourth and last of these important uncategorizable poems is "Jinny the Just," not published until the twentieth century but highly regarded in manuscript form by Pope and Swift, who wished to include it in their 1728 *Miscellanies* but did not receive permission to do so. The poem is a long tribute, in anapestic triplets, probably to Jane Ansley, once Prior's housekeeper and mistress. Its subject is a warm-blooded, earthy, simple woman, unlearned yet shrewdly adaptable, moving comfortably and charitably through her domestic world:

> So Notions and modes she referr'd to the Scholes
> And in matters of Conscience adher'd to two rules
> To advise with no biggots and jeast with no
>   fools . . .
>
> While she read and accounted and pay'd and
>   abated
> Eat and drank, play'd and workt, laught and cry'd,
>   lov'd and hated
> As answer'd the End of her being created. . . .

This first decade of the eighteenth century thus remains of particular interest in Prior's life. In it he wrote many of his most important and highly valued poems, while he was then the most significant living English poet.

Prior matched the impressive gain in his poetical fortunes during the last few years of Queen Anne's reign by an equally impressive recovery of his political fortunes. The fall from power of the Godolphin ministry and of the duchess of Marlborough made it possible for Prior once more to be active in diplomatic negotiations. During the latter part of June 1711, Robert Harley, Earl of Oxford and Lord Treasurer, asked that Prior be sent to France to take part in the peace negotiations being worked out there with England. On 12 July 1711 Prior left for France for that purpose. The negotiations continued through August and September, often at Prior's house, and on 8 October three documents were signed as preliminary treaties between England and France. These documents eventually became the Treaty of Utrecht, but once again Prior almost missed the glory of being plenipotentiary when it was signed. Queen Anne acquiesced but objected to Prior's "meane extraction"; Thomas Wentworth, Earl of Strafford, at first refused to serve with one of such low birth. Perhaps by way of compensatory apology, Prior was on 25 Janu-

ary 1712 appointed commissioner of customs. (He complained in person to Swift that [as quoted in the *Journal to Stella*] the appointment was ruining his wit, that he now dreamed of nothing but "Cockets, & Dockets and Drawbacks, and other Jargon words of the Custom house.") By the end of September 1712 papers arrived in France naming Prior as minister plenipotentiary, and in November and December of that year he continued to travel back and forth between France and London, smoothing out disputed details in the treaty. On 8 November 1712 Swift wrote in his *Journal to Stella*: "Prior is just come over from France for a few days; I suppose, upon some important affair. I saw him last night, but had no private talk with him. Stocks rise upon his coming." Finally, on 11 April 1713, the Treaty of Utrecht was signed between England, Holland, Portugal, Prussia, Savoy, and France, ending the War of the Spanish Succession for these nations. The duke of Shrewsbury, ambassador to France, wrote on 8 March 1713 to the earl of Oxford about the large role Prior's "zeal, diligence and ability" had played in the successful drawing up of the Treaty.

Prior wrote only a few poems during this period of increasing political turmoil (1711-1714), but two of these deserve special notice. The unfinished "Frederic & ca.: From Boccace" is significant as a reworking of La Fontaine in blank verse. "For His Own Epitaph," the fullest and most detailed of his three self-epitaphs, sums up in eight quatrains his view of himself at fifty. Written in 1714, the poem begins with Prior confessing that he is writing his own epitaph for fear that his heir will fail to do so. (Actually, there was no heir.) He assures the reader that the sculptor of the monument has been paid but advises mistrusting its inscription, "For we flatter our Selves, and teach Marble to lye." Summing up his first half century, he writes:

> Yet counting as far as to Fifty his Years,
>   His Virtues and Vices were as other Mens are,
> High Hopes he conceiv'd, and he smother'd great
>   fears,
>   In a Life party-colour'd, half Pleasure half care.
>
> Nor to Business a Drudge, nor to Faction a Slave,
>   He strove to make Intrest and freedom agree.
> In public Employments industrous and grave,
>   And alone with his Friends, Lord, how merry was
>   He.
>
> Now in Equipage Stately, now humbly on foot,

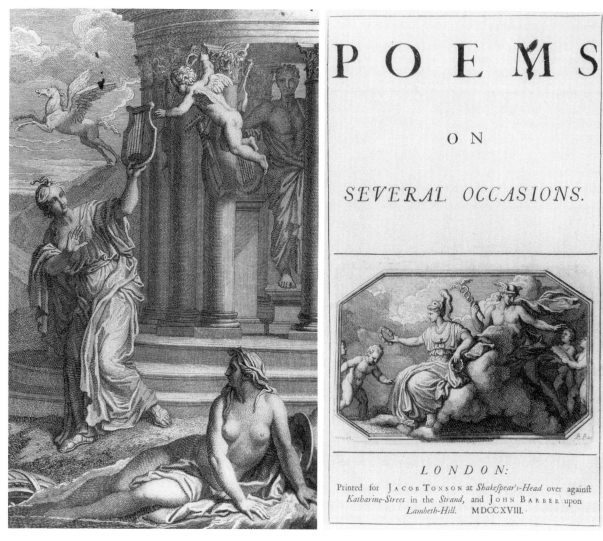

Frontispiece and title page for the revised and enlarged edition of Prior's first collection (Special Collections, Thomas Cooper Library, University of South Carolina)

Both Fortunes he Try'd but to neither wou'd
    Trust
And whirl'd in the round, as the Wheel turn'd
    about
    He found Riches had wings, and knew Man was
        but dust.

Prior recognizes the epitaph's tentative nature. In case of robbery, hanging, or drowning, there may not even be bones to put beneath the stone. The poem closes by asking its reader to give Prior "a Smile, or a Tear / He cares not—Yet prythee be kind to his Fame." The epitaph shows Prior's mixture of smiles and tears.

By 1714 a quarrel between Oxford and Bolingbroke threatened the Tory party and its individual members, among whom Prior was particu-

larly vulnerable because of his role in the secret negotiations for the Treaty of Utrecht, popularly known as "Matt's Peace." In *Henry Esmond* (1852), William Makepeace Thackeray describes Prior as "the earthen pot swimming with the pots of brass down the stream, and always and justly frightened lest he should break in the voyage . . . thinking about his plate and his place, and what on earth should become of him should his party go out." Prior's concern was more than that. Not only his plate and his place but his life might have hinged on the settling of the quarrel between Oxford and Bolingbroke before the imminent death of Queen Anne. Swift believed that Prior could have reconciled the two angry ministers if he had been in England at this critical time, but he had been sent back to France, and the quarrel climaxed by Oxford's being forced out of office on 30 July 1714. Two days later Queen Anne died, and the Stuarts no longer ruled England.

The Hanoverian succession to the throne found Prior still forced to act as ambassador in Paris without official appointment or sufficient funding, negotiating with Louis XIV about the destruction of Dunkirk while worrying about the five-thousand-pound debt he had incurred, but poorly funded and mistrusted by the new Whig government. Prior was removed from his post of commissioner of customs. The Whig ministry finally agreed to pay off his debts in Paris so that he could return home to be questioned and examined. On 9 June 1715 he was arrested and confined in his Duke Street home; a week later he was summoned to testify before the secret committee set up to investigate corruption and treason in the preceding Tory ministry, especially concerning the Treaty of Utrecht. As Prior later noted in his *History of His Own Time* (1740), the committee intended to support charges of treason against the earl of Oxford by having Prior verify that the earl had been present at a meeting at Prior's Duke Street house with the French negotiators. Prior replied, however, that either the duke of Shrewsbury or the earl of Oxford had been present, with the other absent, but that he could not recollect, four years later, which man had attended–an answer, Prior recorded in the *History*, that "had this Effect, that it was the same Thing as if they were both absent, since they could not determine which of them was present." Despite repeated questioning, Prior refused to implicate either man. He thus managed to protect his Tory friends at the risk of his own life. To punish him for his noncooperation, the Whig government confined him for more than a year in the home of the sergeant at arms of the House of Commons, not allowing him to receive guests except by permission of the speaker of the House (Robert Walpole) or to write or receive letters from friends. In response to Prior's letter protesting his imprisonment, Walpole replied that Prior had lied to the secret committee and was being held as a material witness against others. He was not released until 26 June 1716, when Parliament was prorogued. Even a year later his name was omitted from the list of those pardoned by the Royal Act of Grace in July 1717. The spitefulness in the whole episode rankled many Tories; Prior's name became synonymous with unde-

served ill-treatment. After Prior's death Swift wrote "To Charles Ford Esq. on his Birth-day January 31st for the Year 1722-3,"

> Your Foes, triumphant o'er the Laws,
> Who hate Your Person, and Your Cause,
> If once they get you on the Spot
> You must be guilty of the Plot,
> For, true or false, they'll ne'er enquire,
> But use You ten times worse than Pri'r.

Yet this troubled period, 1715 to 1716, in which Prior's life hung in the balance, produced three significant poems and a critical prose work, only one of which had any connection with contemporary politics. The poems were "The Viceroy. A Ballad," "Daphne and Apollo" (both date 1715), and *Alma: or, The Progress of the Mind* (*Poems*, 1718); the critical prose work was "Observations on Homer: A Letter" (written circa 1715).

"The Viceroy. A Ballad" was Prior's only political poem of this period. Spears and Wright consider this poem, of all Prior's ballads, to be "closest to the street-ballads in style." Prior instructed that it was to be sung "To the Tune of the Lady Isabella's Tragedy: Or: The Step-Mother's Cruelty." In the typical ballad fourteener meter, "The Viceroy" attacks Thomas Coningsby for his dishonesty, greed, maladministration, and cruelty in Ireland, particularly for having Gafney executed without a trial. Thirteen stanzas praise the late Queen Anne (against whom Coningsby is shown as satanically ungrateful), and the poem closes with the prediction that Coningsby will eventually be punished, either in hell or at the hands of the mob.

"Daphne and Apollo" is an entirely non-political poem and one of the best instances of Prior's domestication of myth. The poem is subtitled "Faithfully translated from Ovids Metamorp," but there is nothing faithful about this translation, loved by both Pope and Horace Walpole. Talking to Joseph Spence of Prior's collection of manuscripts, Pope said, "there are nine or ten copies of verses among them, which I thought much better than several things he . . . published. In particular, I remember there was a dialogue of about two hundred verses, between Apollo and Daphne, which pleased me as much as anything of his I ever read." In an October 1790 letter, Walpole called "Daphne and Apollo" one of Prior's "wittiest and genteelest poems." In the poem, Apollo may come from Ovid, but Daphne comes straight from Augustan England. Their worlds are ill fitted together: Apollo can offer Daphne nothing that interests her in her modern world. He boasts that he rules Claros Isle and Tenedos, but she replies, with sound English pride, "Thank you, I would not leave my Native Land." He can foretell the future, but so, she retorts, can Partridge. His beautiful locks do not interest her–they might be a Spanish Wig; she worries more about his bare chin. His healing arts are no use to her in her wholesome English climate. When he boasts that he composes fine verses, she replies that she is tired of versifiers: "So do your Brother Quacks and Brother Beaux / Memorials only and Reviews write Prose." She likewise has no use for his skill in archery–it would be dangerous to her in civil society, and has its place only in the thicket. When in despair Apollo surrenders to Daphne and begs, "Oh let me woo thee as thou wou'd'st be woo'd, " she has a list ready of Augustan rules for well-bred country courtship. He is to quiet down, coming at evening to her father's home to read the newspaper with him and discuss European politics; he is to inquire respectfully of the servants how Daphne is doing; he is to bring home gifts from all his journeys–"A Lacquer'd Cabinet some China Ware / You have them mighty cheap at Pekin fair"; he is never to philander as did his Father Jove; finally, he is to marry her, legally and properly. The Augustan world has met the classical world and demanded capitulation.

In three weeks, while under house arrest, Prior wrote one of his most successful long poems, again nonpolitical in nature, *Alma: or, The Progress of the Mind.* As reported by Owen Ruffhead, he did not initially think highly of the poem, "a loose and hasty scribble, to relieve the tedious hours of my imprisonment, while in the messenger's hand," but after it was highly praised by Pope, Bathurst, and Harley, he went to some pains to revise it extensively.

Prior divides *Alma* into three cantos, all written in Hudibrastic couplets and satirizing philosophers who construct physical and metaphysical systems. There was currently a conflict between philosophers at Oxford and those at Cambridge as to the placing of the human mind. Following Aristotle, those at Oxford argued that the mind or soul was to be found everywhere throughout the body; those at Cambridge followed Descartes and found it only in the brain. In a dialogue with his crabbed but *fidus Achates*, Richard Shelton, Prior jestingly proposes a compromise system. The mind passes from the feet to the head as the man grows older. (Prior can thus also provide a

comic tracing of the Ages of Man.) The serious implications of the comic treatment are sweeping. Prior is mocking those who build confident systems on flimsy evidence, and this particular mock-system deals directly with the existence of *alma* (more frequently translated as soul than mind), if it does exist, with its relationship to the body.

The first canto introduces the Oxonian and Cantabrigian systems, rejecting them both in favor of Prior's. Then it traces "Alma" from the feet (in infancy) to the waist (in young adults). Prior opens the second canto with a tribute to Samuel Butler, who provided him with the Hudibrastic metrical form, then produces some consequential inferences of his proposed new system. For example, he argues that the mind will return in age to wherever it resided most happily in youth (whether the leg or the tongue). He further maintains that the way the mind reacts is partly conditioned by its environment: "In ALMA's Manners You may read / The Place, where She was born and bred." Each of the consequential inferences provides Prior with wide-ranging opportunities to satirize individual and collective human folly. In the third canto Shelton, who has been dozing, objects that Prior has done just what he accused the Oxford and Cambridge philosophers of doing: he has created an elaborate system on unsubstantial evidence and then insisted that others join him in believing in it. When Prior ignores this objection and describes instead the mind's final progress in elderly persons, Shelton counters this new system with his own: the mind really seats itself in the belly. Prior retorts that Shelton's system lacks spontaneity and logic. The two friends can agree only that in the face of uncertain systems and of certain death, the mind does best to forget itself in harmless pastimes and entertainments.

Alma had a strong impact on eighteenth-century writing in England and on the Continent. When John Arbuthnot and the Scriblerus Club were writing the *Memoirs of . . . Martinus Scriblerus* in 1713 and immediately thereafter (not printed till its inclusion in the second volume of Pope's prose works in 1741–Pope had revised the *Memoirs* broadly), they found *Alma* congenial to their satiric attacks on pedantry and apparently incorporated parts of it into chapter 12. In France it influenced Denis Diderot's *Les Bijoux Indiscrets* (1748), and it was made more immediately available to non-English-speaking readers by its translation into Latin verse by Thomas Martin in 1763. Ruffhead reports that Pope called *Alma* a "master-

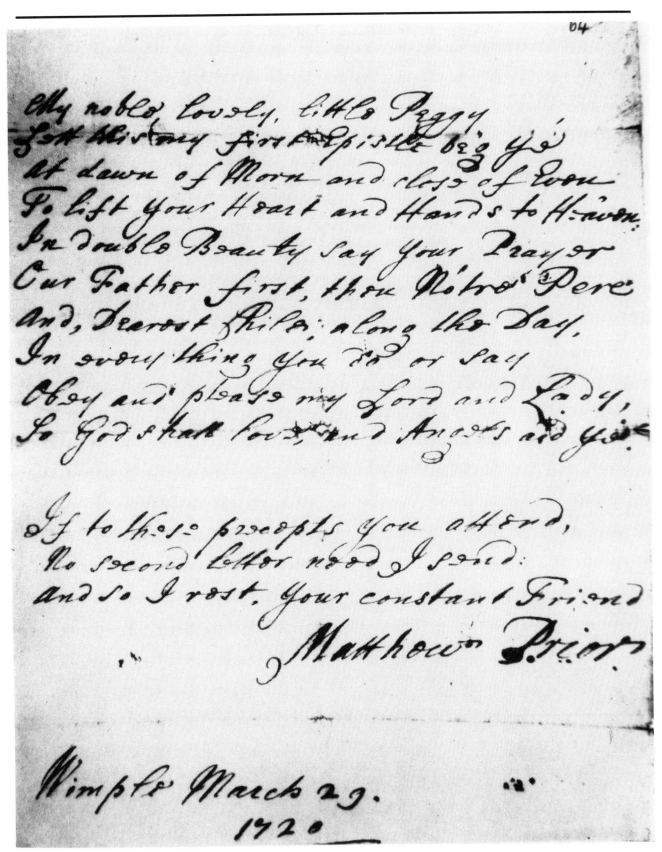

Last page from a letter including the poem that Prior wrote for Margaret Harley (later Holles), granddaughter of Robert Harley,
Earl of Oxford, on the occasion of her sixth birthday (Prior MSS. vol. i, fol. 64; Longleat Collection; by permission of the
Marquis of Bath, Longleat House, Warminster, Wiltshire, Great Britain)

piece" and said that it was the only poem of Prior's that he would like to have written, "abating its excessive scepticism." Studying *Hudibras in the Burlesque Tradition* (1937), E. A. Richards shows that when eighteenth-century readers wished to read polished Hudibrastic verse, they turned to Prior's *Alma* rather than to its source, Butler's *Hudibras*. Johnson raised a minority voice in the eighteenth century, in the "Life of Prior," when he admitted that "Alma has many admirers," but rejected it as without plan, drift, or design. Walpole wrote to Hannah More on 13 November 1784 that he found *Alma* far superior to *Solomon* and much more learned. Goldsmith's reactions to *Alma* in his "Introductory Criticisms," were mixed; he found "some parts of it very fine," others bad, but he was uncertain as to Prior's intention: "What Prior meant by this poem I cannot understand. . . ." William Cowper wrote to Lord Thurlow in August 1791 that *Alma* owed "all its neatness and smartness" to its use of "the agreeable effect of rhyme or euphony." Slightly earlier, Joseph Warton had spoken for many contemporary educated readers when he called *Alma* "elegant and witty" and later (1782), in his *Essay on the Genius and Writings of Pope*, wrote of it: "Enquiries into the Seat of the Soul are finely ridiculed in the first canto of Prior's Alma; an original work, and perhaps the very best of all his compositions, which abounds equally in wit, pleasantry, humour, and good sense, and is a perfect pattern of facility of versification."

John Wesley provided the most detailed explication of *Alma* for two centuries after its composition, responding to Johnson's charge that the poem was without plan, drift, or design. Wesley replied: "The drift and design of it is tolerably plain. It is a strong satire on that self-conceited tribe of men, who pretend to philosophize upon every thing, natural, or spiritual. It keenly exposes those who continually obtrude their own systems upon the world, and pretend to *account* for everything. His design is, if possible to make these men less wise to their own conceit, by showing them how plausibly a man may defend, the oddest system that can be conceived: and he intermixes many admirable reflexions, and closes with a very striking conclusion; which points out, where one would least expect it, that *all is vanity*."

Prior's wit in *Alma*, his learning, and his refusal to take himself seriously for long hold special appeal for the modern temperament. Louis I. Bredvold expresses a typical modern reaction calling *Alma* Prior's "only readable long poem." *Alma*

is especially interesting to moderns because of its unusual metrical form and because of its revelation of eighteenth-century attitudes toward science.

Prior's octasyllabic couplets in *Alma* make rhyming seem impossibly difficult, continually rhyming with tortuous pain, achieving a humorous effect. Two of the most important scholars of the Hudibrastic and the burlesque–Richards and Richmond P. Bond–agree that Prior took the Hudibrastic as far as it could be taken in polite verse and thereby virtually exhausted its possibilities.

Prior's mock-system may have had its source in Montaigne, but Prior added much from eighteenth-century schools of natural philosophy, so that almost every current study of eighteenth-century science has drawn heavily upon *Alma*. As a member of the Royal Society, as Linacre Lecturer on medicine at St. John's College, Cambridge, and as an omnivorous reader, Prior knew about the new science. He disliked it, but he knew what it taught. For one who would understand eighteenth-century scientific philosophy, there is no livelier introduction than its sprightly but unfriendly treatment in *Alma: or, The Progress of the Mind*.

One significant piece of Prior's critical prose, "Observations on Homer. A Letter," is undated but can have been composed no later than 1715, thus probably also dating from Prior's period of confinement. It is apparently a penultimate draft, restricting itself to the *Iliad* and consisting mainly of Prior's remarks upon specific passages, similes, and images. Prior begins by disclaiming any profound scholarship in Greek, saying that he has relied heavily upon French and Latin translations. James William Johnson in *The Formation of English Neo-Classical Thought* (1967), establishes, however, that Prior "was pervasively affected by his study of Greek. A highly proficient Latin scholar and writer, Prior nevertheless found the Greek idiom and attitude a constant stimulation." Johnson gives examples of Prior's particular interest in and knowledge of Greek metrics and prosody.

After he has modestly disclaimed expertise in Greek, Prior turns to general comments on the *Iliad*. He dismisses the theory that the poem is distinct songs collected after Homer's death, because he finds its parts too interwoven for separate origin. Does Homer have dull passages? Horace had thought so, writing that Homer sometimes nodded; the young Pope had rejected the charge in 1711 in the *Essay on Criticism*: "Nor is it

Homer Nods, but *We* that *Dream*." Prior takes an intermediate position: "if Homer as our Friend Horace confesses Does sometimes Sleep, he makes a very glorious Noise wherever he is thorowly awake." Prior cannot consider the *Iliad* to be the perfect epic poem in structure, however, because it ends too soon–Troy has not fallen; Helen has not been returned to Menelaus. Perhaps, Prior admits, Homer intended a more limited subject–"to Show how destructive the Disentions of the Great are to the Public." If so, then the poem is "more Perfect, but his Design not so great." Prior is made uneasy by the motivation of the epic. He sees the whole quarrel as having been caused by three harlots–Helena, Chryseis, and Briseis–and he feels that "the Sons and Grandsons of Gods and Goddesses" are too strongly roused by these harlots, expressing their emotions in low and inappropriate language. Prior also disapproves of certain incidents in the plot. Apollo should not have given the Trojans a wind (wind-giving is the province of Aeolos), and Jupiter should not have sent a lying spirit to seduce Ahab. "In these cases how can Heroic Virtue know how it is deceiv'd." Prior agrees with J. C. Scaliger's criticism that Homeric characters should not properly "make long Speeches in the heat of their Battles . . . ," and he dislikes what he sees as a universal epic device, the intervention of the deus ex machina, in human form, to save favorites: "This takes all merit and blame from human Action and is in a less degree the fault of all Epic Writers. . . ."

Having made these rather general observations, Prior spends most of the rest of the "Observations on Homer" in commenting upon particular events, speeches, and figures in the *Iliad*, calling some of these "very fine" but some not "very just," "silly," "rediculous" [*sic*], or "very childish." Prior ends the "Observations" by commenting again that he finds the *Iliad* flawed in structure. If centered upon the death of Hector, it goes on too long; if centered upon the fate of Troy and of Helen, it stops too soon. He particularly worries that Homer may have made of Hector a more sympathetic character than he intended. He may thus have detracted from Achilles's achievement in killing Hector and inadvertently provided his epic with two heroes (Hector and Achilles) on opposing sides of his narrative. Nor is Prior impressed by those who praise Homer for restricting the time of the *Iliad* to one year. The only real action it covers, according to Prior, is the quarrel and eventual reconciliation of Achilles and Agamemnon and the death of Hec-

tor, and these events could have occurred within a week.

Although Prior never brought the "Observations on Homer" into polished essay form, the piece is interesting as Prior's longest piece of purely literary criticism. Prior shows himself closely aware of the *Iliad* and its major critics. He esteems Homer but does not venerate him, and he does not hesitate to differ with him, amusingly and convincingly.

Released from arrest on 26 June 1717, Prior returned to his Duke Street residence. With the Whigs firmly ensconced in power, his political career was ended, and it had left him with little money with which to support himself. Bathurst and Lord Edward Harley therefore conceived the plan of bringing out a subscription edition of his poems. They met with Prior, Pope, John Gay, and Arbuthnot in January 1717 to work out details of the plan, which Erasmus Lewis on 23 January wrote to describe to Swift in Ireland: "Our friend, Prior, not having had the vicissitude of human things before his eyes, is likely to end his days in as forlorn a state as any poet before him if his friends do not take better care of him than he has done himself. Therefore to prevent the evil which we see is coming very fast, we have a project of printing his *Solomon*, and other poetical works by subscription; one guinea to be paid in hand and the other at the delivery of the book." Kathleen M. Lynch has called the resultant volume, which appeared as *Poems on Several Occasions* in 1718, a "de luxe edition" and has commented on "Prior's fastidious and constant supervision," which "contributed to making this perhaps the most attractive of Tonson's illustrated editions,. . . one of the handsomest and literally the weightiest volume that Tonson's press produced." It was a large, handsome folio, a foot across and a yard tall, five hundred pages long, with a list of 1,446 persons who had subscribed for 1,786 books. (It also appeared at the same time in two smaller and cheaper editions, for readers who could not afford the subscription edition.) The edition reprinted and rearranged (slightly) all fifty-seven of Prior's poems from the 1709 edition and added some poems not published there, notably *Alma* and *Solomon*.

This 1718 subscription edition made Prior's fortune; his own profit on it may have been close to four thousand guineas. When Henry Fielding's Mr. Wilson (in *Joseph Andrews*, 1742) is attempting to educate Parson Adams as to the intricacies of subscription publication, he cites Prior (along with Pope and Nicholas Rowe) as men of genius who have made their literary fortunes from the publication of subscription editions. The Prior edition is important not only as clear evidence that a writer could now make a fortune directly from his writings but also in indicating a much broader base for authorial support. An analysis of the 1,446 names of subscribers indicates a strong broadening of the base of support for the poet, particularly when coupled with the fact that many less affluent readers were buying the two cheaper editions. Some subscribers were aristocrats, but a large number were professional persons: clergymen, military officers, lawyers, doctors, and other intellectuals and academics. Many were from outside England: Ireland, France, Parma, Prussia, Tuscany, Genoa, and America; and many were persons whose names are still familiar. Among Prior's fellow writers were Swift, Gay, Pope, Steele, John Vanbrugh, Samuel Garth, and William Congreve; among painters, Charles Jervas and Godfrey Kneller; among scientists, Isaac Newton. Of the 1,446 persons who subscribed, 153 were women, and still others were persons who would not formerly have been thought of as patrons of the arts–two London aldermen and an apothecary, two dancing masters, a merchant, and two musicians. This subscription list represents an immense broadening of support from the single-patron system with which Prior had begun his artistic life. It was a striking instance of W. A. Speck's later description of the subscription edition as "a half-way house between dependance on a single patron to underwrite a book and reliance upon sales."

Thus, in the last three years of his life, Prior found himself retired, independently wealthy, and able to devote himself to the things which interested him most: women, friends, his country estate, book and art collecting, and writing.

By 1715 or 1716 Prior had met the last of his three mistresses, Elizabeth Cox, the wife of John Cox, a tavern keeper in Long Acre; by 1718 she had apparently supplanted Anne Durham as Prior's mistress. John Cox died a month before Prior did; Arbuthnot later wrote (on 30 September 1721) to Henry Watkins that "PRIOR has had a narrow escape by dying; for, if he had lived, he had married a brimstone bitch, one Bessy Cox. . . ." Indeed, Elizabeth Cox proved upon Prior's death to be greedy, boastful, ungrieved, suspicious, and very troublesome.

Lady Margaret Harley Holles, Duchess of Portland, at twenty-five (engraving by Joseph Brown based on a painting by C. F. Zincke)

Prior was perhaps a wiser selector of other items than of mistresses. He became a virtuoso with his new wealth, collecting so many treasures that his Duke Street house was rightly called "Matt's Palace." He collected prints, drawings, jewels and trinkets, coins and medals, antique bronzes. His greatest interest as a collector, however, lay in books, paintings, and sculpture. His drawing room and its adjacent "closet" boasted almost a hundred pictures; his library contained several thousand books.

In these last few years of his life (between 1716 and 1721), Prior expanded and deepened his friendships, by visits and by correspondence. With Swift, whom he would never see again, he maintained his closeness by letters. By the end of 1717, Adrian Drift had moved into Prior's Duke Street house, to serve him as amanuensis and as companion and friend. Drift wrote after Prior died that Prior had given him "Esteem and Affection full Five & Twenty Years, without One harsh word ever falling from his Tongue" (in a letter in the Welbeck manuscripts). Prior moreover established a bright new friendship with Edward Harley, son of the earl of Oxford, his wife, Lady Harriett, and daughter, Margaret. It was to young Margaret Harley in 1720 that Prior wrote one of his most appealing children's poems, "My noble, lovely, little Peggy," advice on the occasion of her sixth birthday. He also addressed the coda of his long poem *The Turtle and the Sparrow* (1723) to her, "O DEAREST Daughter of Two dearest Friends. . . ."

Another of Horace Walpole's favorites among Prior's poems, *The Turtle and the Sparrow* contrasts two irreconcilable attitudes toward love, courtship, and marriage. The turtledove mourns Columbo, its dead mate, in elegiac language, but the sparrow recounts multiple marriages with colloquial jollity and reports the death of its various spouses with wry relief, though expectations still triumph over experience, and his is looking forward to the end of this year of mourning so that he may marry again. The poem closes by urging the young Peggy to emulate the fidelity of the turtledove, but Prior has given the sparrow the livelier and more convincing side of the dialogue. Whatever Peggy made of her role as recipient of these poems, however, her affection for Prior never wavered. When she was old, then dowager-duchess of Portland, she still spoke of him with affection.

Edward Harley, Peggy's father, made it possible for Prior to realize one of his dreams, owning a country estate—Down Hall in Essex. Each man paid half the purchase price of the estate (a total of four thousand pounds). Prior was to have the use of the estate during his lifetime; then it was to revert to Harley after Prior's death. They purchased the estate sight unseen; when Prior did first view it, he wrote to Harley with mixed emotions: "It is impossible to tell you how beautiful a situation Down is, and how fine the wood may be made; but for the house, as all the cross unmathematical devils upon earth first put it together, all the thought and contrivance of man cannot make a window to be looked out of, or a door to be shut." The present house on the estate was "Plaister, and Lath," but Prior hired James Gibbes as architect for a new house and Charles Bridgeman as landscape architect for its projected gardens. Gibbes's plans still exist, in elaborate detail, though Prior died before the construction could begin.

The most important effect of Prior's purchase of Down Hall was his poem *Down-Hall* (written in 1721 and first printed in 1723). The poem describes the journey Prior makes with John Morley, the land jobber who had sold him the estate, to get Prior's first view of his purchase. Because ballads often employ the nonsense refrain of "hey derry down," Prior takes advantage of the name of the estate to recount his journey in ballad terms. In the early twentieth century, Oswald Doughty lauded Prior as "The Poet of the 'Familiar Style,' " using *Down-Hall* as a particularly rewarding example of Prior's use of that style. L. G. Wickham Legg, one of Prior's modern biographers, calls it Prior's best longer poem, realistic, mocking, and melancholy. The poem describes Prior's two-day journey from London to Essex to view his new purchase. Early in the poem he rejects the classical style, choosing colloquial English instead: "Hang HOMER and VIRGIL, their Meaning to seek, / A Man must go poke in the LATIN and GREEK; / They who love their own Tongue, we have reason to hope, / Have read them translated by DRYDEN and POPE." Throughout *Down-Hall* Prior juxtaposes the tedious isolation of the "chariot" journeys with Morley by day with the lively conviviality of the inns by evening–places where Prior had stopped eight years before. The trip is described in minute realistic detail, to which the inn stops add a sense of the accumulated joys and woes that have occurred in each place in the last eight years–some joys but more woes. On the third day, Prior, Morley, and a local guide approach Down Hall, but though they are in the right neighborhood, they cannot find the estate. The house proves to be so unimpressive that Prior takes it at first for a low, ruined white shed or barn. Realizing his error, he reproaches Morley, who answers him sharply: "I wish you cou'd tell what a Duce your head ails; / I show'd you DOWN-HALL, did you look for VERSAILLES?" Prior's grandiose plans for improving the estate lead Morley to warn him that he may expend his whole fortune in this effort: "If you have these Whims of Apartments and Gardens, / From twice Fifty Acres You'll n'er see Five Farthings. / And in Yours I shal find the true Gentlemans Fate, / E'er you finish your House, you'l have spent your Estate."

Harley is frequently regarded as Prior's benefactor and was certainly his friend, but in all their financial transactions Harley profited heavily from Prior's unexpectedly early death. Prior possessed Down Hall for a year, making numerous improvements upon it. With Prior's death at the end of the year, the estate reverted to Harley, who had in essence purchased it at half

Engraving of Prior and land jobber John Morley, assisted by a local guide, near Down Hall in Essex. Their journey is described in Prior's poem Down-Hall *(1723).*

price. Moreover, Prior had bought from Harley two annuities, paying large lump sums for them, with Harley then to pay him one-tenth of their initial amount each year that Prior lived. Prior would have had to live ten years after the purchase of each of these instruments to receive back the initial purchase price; he lived only four years after buying the first and two after buying the second. In the Welbeck manuscript, Drift writes that Harley "was a Gainer by Mr. Prior's Death by the sum of £2058. 6s. 8d."

The last year of Prior's life saw him write two other poems of significance. *The Conversation* Prior showed to the young Pope for his criticism. Written in tetrameter verse, the poem shows a self-important Damon, who begins by enjoining truth and modesty but practices neither one. He tells the assembled company that he often advised Matthew Prior, in politics and in poetry, and evalu-

ates Prior's achievements and shortcomings in both, not realizing until too late that "The Man You talk with is MAT. PRIOR." Damon's pompous self-assurance affords Prior a chance to mock shallow critics of his political and poetical career.

The other of these two significant late poems is the serious "Predestination, A Poem," written in 1721, in the last month before Prior's death, but not published until the A. R. Waller edition of *Dialogues of the Dead* in 1907. Consisting of almost three hundred lines or, as transcribed and numbered by Drift, ten "brouillons" in various stages of revision, "Predestination" returns to theological questions that had interested Prior recurrently for his whole adult career: free will versus predestination, God's mercy versus God's justice, and the concept of a loving and all-powerful God versus a painful and wicked world. Because Prior was a skeptic, he could not reach assertive conclusions in "Predestination"; he cannot, for example, choose between predestination and free will. In 1725, four years after Prior's death, Pope read the fragments of "Predestination," punctuated them, and worked toward publishing them (along with Prior's other works), but Harley withdrew permission, and Pope's collection was never published.

For all of his mature life, Prior had been subject to recurring bouts of cholera morbus, recurrent fits of vomiting. He went to visit the Harleys in August 1721 and fell violently ill of cholera morbus there on 11 September. He lived for only a week, dying on 18 September 1721. On the next day (Friday) his body was carried to Jerusalem Chapel, Westminster Abbey, where it lay in state for three days. The funeral, held on Monday, 25 September, was attended by both personal friends (Shelton, Arbuthnot, and Lewis) and by ceremonial figures (forty King's Scholars from Westminster School, carrying white tapers; seventy men in mourning with branch lights; and a dozen almsmen with torches). The friend who would grieve most for Prior, however, did not learn of his death until ten days after it occurred. Swift wrote to Archbishop King from Gaulstown on 28 September 1721, "I am just now told from some newspapers, that one of the King's enemies, and my excellent friend, Mr. Prior, is dead; I pray God deliver me from many such trials. I am neither old nor philosopher enough to be indifferent at so great a loss; and therefore I abruptly conclude. . . ." Gibbs, who had drawn up the plans for Prior's new country estate, turned instead to design his "stately Monument," the most impressive one in the Poets' Corner of Westminster Abbey.

Prior had invested a sizable share of his fortune in the South Sea Company and had thence suffered severe losses when the South Sea Bubble burst in 1720. (The Company, chartered in 1711 and given an extensive trade monopoly in exchange for assuming a considerable portion of the national debt, had boomed after the Treaty of Utrecht and particularly when a bill was passed in 1720 permitting persons to whom the government owed money to take payment in South Sea Company stock instead. Shares soared to ten times their value, panic ensued, and the Company failed. Prior lost heavily in his investments.) Despite these losses, funeral expenses, debts, appraisers' fees, and all other expenses of closing the estate, over £9,875 remained on 7 April 1722 to pay the legacies. Wright in "Matthew Prior: A Supplement to His Biography," calculates that another £15,000 had passed through Prior's hands, "Practically all of it—except for the Duke Street house and some indeterminable part of its furnishings—during the period which followed his confinement."

Throughout his life, Prior wrote skillfully in poetic forms as distinctly varied as the bawdy tale and the long philosophic disquisition, the formal ode and the epigram, the lyrical vers de société and the satirical street ballad. He wore his great classical learning lightly, yet found profundities in apparently trivial incidents. Although he could and did write well the heroic couplets that the Augustan age prized and the blank verse preferred by periods much earlier and later, he also excelled in the writing of octosyllabics and of anapests, two forms in which he remains one of the acknowledged masters, as he does of the mixing of tears and laughter in single poems—or single phrases. Nor is his effective writing limited to poetry. He left behind fragments for two plays, never completed: "Ladislaus" and "Britanicus and Junia." Much more important, he left in manuscript form at his death eight effective pieces of prose: two collections of critical observations ("Observations on Homer. A Letter" and "Observations on Ovid's Metamorphoses"), two epistemological essays ("Heads for a Treatise upon Learning" and "Opinion"), and four *Dialogues of the Dead*. Both the epistemological essays deal Pyrrhonistically with man's futile attempts to discover truth and with the factors that determine the opinions man substitutes for the certain knowl-

Engraving based on a portrait of Prior by Godfrey Kneller

edge he cannot gain. The *Dialogues of the Dead* were read by Pope in manuscript form and described by him to Spence as "four dialogues in prose, between persons of characters very strongly opposed to one another, which I thought very good." These dialogues pit Charles V, Holy Roman Emperor and King of Spain, against Nicolas Kleynaerts, a sixteenth-century priest-philologist; John Locke against Montaigne; Thomas More against the Vicar of Bray; and Oliver Cromwell against his mad porter. The tradition of the dialogues of the dead was an ancient and popular one; Prior is often called its best practitioner in English.

Because none of Prior's most important prose appeared in print until long after his death (not until 1907), it had no immediate influence, but his poetry had direct and widespread effects in the eighteenth century. To his friend Swift, Prior gave specific lines and, more significantly and pervasively, an elegant courtliness and ease of familiar verse that Swift had not hitherto mastered. Pope, Prior's friendly acquaintance, read in 1723, in print or in manuscript, almost everything extant of Prior's—an unusually full grouping, for Prior had, as Pope later told Spence, "kept every thing by him, even to all his school exercises." The young Pope made use of Prior as he did, on a larger scale, of Dryden. With each, he looked closely at a figure whose unusual merit both he and the public conceded without question. Pope analyzed the poetical virtues and limitations of each: his forte, his contributions, and the relative merits of his individual pieces. Then Pope set out first to emulate and then to surpass each one. Later, he merely borrowed phrases or ideas that were particularly apt for his own purposes. The influence of Prior upon the poetry of Pope is most apparent in Pope's two versions of the "Adriani Morientis" (1730), in *Eloisa to Abelard* (1720), *The Rape of the Lock*, the *Essay on Man*, and in two Horatian imitations (*An Imitation of the Sixth Satire of the Second Book of Horace*, 1738, and "The First Ode of the Fourth Book of Horace," 1737). Pope, setting out to become England's first "correct" poet, planned to use the writings of Prior as one of the "authorities for poetical language" in Pope's projected dictionary. Pope learned in part from Prior his mastery of the rococo and mock-heroic style, a delicate and easy tone, and (according to Robert Southey) improvements in the use of the heroic couplet.

A third prominent literary figure of the eighteenth century, Johnson, judged severely both Prior's private life and his philosophical speculations and damaged his contemporary reputation by the "Life of Prior," the most famous eighteenth-century biography of Prior. Johnson nevertheless showed the influence of Prior's *Solomon* in two works that shared its Christian pessimism: *The Vanity of Human Wishes* (1749) and *Rasselas* (1759).

Among lesser eighteenth-century writers influenced by the poetry of Prior were William Cowper, Anne Finch, Countess of Winchilsea, and John, Charles, and Samuel Wesley, the younger, in England; Allan Ramsay in Scotland; and Christoph Martin Wieland and Friedrich von Hagedorn in Germany.

In the nineteenth century the influence of Prior's lyrics was most conspicuous in Ireland upon Thomas Moore, in England upon Thackeray, W. M. Praed, Frederick Locker-Lampson, and William Johnson Cory, and in the United States upon Oliver Wendell Holmes. But by the nineteenth century the English influence had narrowed from the wide range of Prior's poetical attempts to his vers de société alone.

Finally, though, Prior's immediate impact upon his own century may have been more eco-

Prior's tomb in Poets' Corner, Westminster Abbey

nomic than literary. The immense financial success of the 1718 subscription edition of Prior's *Poems on Several Occasions* taught an important lesson: that a skillful practicing poet could support himself handsomely by a direct appeal to a broad-based reading public, rather than from the beneficence of a single titled patron. This lesson, taught chiefly by the success of the subscription volumes brought out by Prior, Dryden, and Pope, altered the circumstances of English book publication and hence the relationship of the poet to his audience.

Letters:

Prior's Papers, in *Calendar of the Manuscripts of the Marquis of Bath Preserved at Longleat, Wiltshire*, volume 3, includes letters (Hereford: Anthony, 1908);

The Correspondence of Jonathan Swift, edited by Harold Williams, 5 volumes, includes letters

by Prior (Oxford: Clarendon Press, 1963-
1965).

Bibliographies:

Charles Kenneth Eves, Bibliography, in his *Matthew Prior: Poet and Diplomatist* (New York: Columbia University Press, 1939), pp. 411-421;

H. Bunker Wright and Monroe K. Spears, eds., "Principal Collected Editions," in *The Literary Works of Matthew Prior*, 2 volumes (Oxford: Clarendon Press, 1959, 1971), I: xxxvii-xxxix;

Frances Mayhew Rippy, Bibliography, in her *Matthew Prior* (Boston: Twayne, 1986), pp. 154-161.

Biographies:

Samuel Johnson, "Life of Prior," in his *Lives of the English Poets*, 10 volumes (London: Printed by J. Nichols for C. Bathurst, 1779-1781), VI: 1-63;

Francis Bickley, *The Life of Matthew Prior* (London: Pitman, 1914);

L. G. Wickham Legg, *Matthew Prior: A Study of His Public Career and Correspondence* (Cambridge: Cambridge University Press, 1921);

H. Bunker Wright, "Matthew Prior: A Supplement to His Biography," Ph.D. dissertation, Northwestern University, 1937);

Charles Kenneth Eves, *Matthew Prior: Poet and Diplomatist* (New York: Columbia University Press, 1939).

References:

G. A. Aitken, "Matthew Prior," *Contemporary Review*, 57 (May 1890): 715-729;

John Arbuthnot, "Letter from Arbuthnot to Henry Watkins, 30 September 1721," *European Magazine and London Review*, 13 (January 1788): 8;

Wilfred Phillips Barrett, "Matthew Prior's *Alma*," *Modern Language Review*, 27 (October 1932): 454-458;

Veronica Bassil, "The Faces of Griselda: Chaucer, Prior, and Richardson," *Texas Studies in Literature and Language*, 26 (Summer 1984): 157-182;

Francis Bickley, "New Facts about Matthew Prior," *Quarterly Review*, 218 (January 1913): 91-117;

R. P. Blackmur, "Homo Ludens," *Kenyon Review*, 21 (Autumn 1959): 662-668;

Richmond P. Bond, *English Burlesque Poetry, 1700-1750*, Harvard Studies in English, no.

6 (Cambridge, Mass.: Harvard University Press, 1932);

Louis I. Bredvold, *The Intellectual Milieu of John Dryden: Studies in Some Aspects of Seventeenth-Century Thought* (Ann Arbor: University of Michigan Press, 1934);

Bredvold, "The Literature of the Restoration and the Eighteenth Century, 1660-1798," in *A History of English Literature*, edited by Hardin Craig (New York: Oxford University Press, 1950);

Edward L. Carroll, "A Memoir of Matthew Prior," *Union College Bulletin*, 26 (1932): 43-61;

Theophilus Cibber [and Robert Shiels], "Matthew Prior, Esq.," in *The Lives of the Poets of Great Britain and Ireland* (London: Printed for R. Griffiths, 1753), IV: 43-57;

William Cowper, *The Life and Letters of William Cowper, Esq.*, edited by William Hayley (London: Baldwin, Cradock, 1824);

Mary Elizabeth Cox, "Prior's Conversation Poems," *Bulletin of the West Virginia Association of College English Teachers*, 1 (Spring 1974): 20-27;

John Dennis, "Matthew Prior," in his *Studies in English Literature* (London: Edward Stanford, 1876), pp. 109-147;

Austin Dobson, "Matthew Prior," *New Princeton Review*, 6 (November 1888): 281-311;

Oswald Doughty, "Matthew Prior (1664-1721)," in his *The English Lyric in the Age of Reason* (London: O'Connor, 1922), pp. 46-56;

Doughty, "The Poet of the 'Familiar Style,'" *English Studies*, 7 (February 1925): 5-10;

Majl Ewing, "Musical Settings of Prior's Lyrics in the 18th Century," *ELH*, 10 (June 1943): 159-171;

Hoxie Neale Fairchild, *Religious Trends in English Poetry*, volume 1: *1700-1740. Protestantism and the Cult of Sentiment* (New York: Columbia University Press, 1939);

Henry Fielding, *The History of the Adventures of Joseph Andrews, and of His Friend Mr. Abraham Adams. Written in Imitation of the Manner of Cervantes, Author of Don Quixote* (London: A. Millar, 1742);

Caroline Goad, *Horace in the English Literature of the Eighteenth Century* (New Haven: Yale University Press, 1918);

Oliver Goldsmith, Introduction to *The Beauties of English Poesy*, volume 2, in *The Works of Oliver Goldsmith*, Turk's Head Edition, edited by Peter Cunningham (New York and London: G. P. Putnam's Sons, 1908);

John Higby, "Ideas and Art in Prior's *Dialogues of the Dead*," *Enlightenment Essays*, 5 (Summer 1974): 62-69;

Ian Jack, "The 'Choice of Life' in Johnson and Prior," *Journal of English and Germanic Philology*, 49 (October 1950): 523-30;

James William Johnson, *The Formation of English Neo-Classical Thought* (Princeton: Princeton University Press, 1967);

Johnson, "Rasselas and His Ancestors," *Notes and Queries*, 204 (May 1959): 185-188;

Frederick M. Keener, *English Dialogues of the Dead: A Critical History, Anthology, and a Check List* (New York: Columbia University Press, 1973);

R[obert] W[yndham] Ketton-Cremer, *Matthew Prior* (Cambridge: Cambridge University Press, 1957);

Kathleen M. Lynch, *Jacob Tonson: Kit-Cat Publisher* (Knoxville: University of Tennessee Press, 1971);

Maynard Mack, "Matthew Prior: et multa prior arte," *Sewanee Review*, 68 (Winter 1960): 165-176;

T. K. Meier, "Prior's Adaptation of 'The Nut-brown Maid,'" *Moderna Sprak* (Stockholm), 68 (1974): 331-336;

Richard Morton, "Matthew Prior's *Dialogues of the Dead*," *Ball State University Forum*, 8 (Summer 1967): 73-78;

Alexander Pope, and others, "Memoirs of Martinus Scriblerus," in *The Works of Mr. Alexander Pope, in Prose*, volume 2 (London: Printed for J. & P. Knapton, 1741);

Harry Ransom, "The Rewards of Authorship in the Eighteenth Century," *University of Texas Studies in English*, 18 (1938): 47-66;

E. A. Richards, *Hudibras in the Burlesque Tradition* (New York: Columbia University Press, 1937);

Frances Mayhew Rippy, *Matthew Prior* (Boston: Hall, 1986);

Rippy, "Matthew Prior as the Last Renaissance Man," in *Studies in Medieval, Renaissance, American Literature: A Festschrift* (Fort Worth: Texas Christian University Press, 1971), pp. 120-131, 203;

Ronald E. Rower, "Pastoral Wars: Matthew Prior's Poems to Cloe," *Ball State University Forum*, 19 (Spring 1978): 39-49;

Owen Ruffhead, *The Life of Alexander Pope, Esq. Compiled from Original Manuscripts: with a Criti-*

cal *Essay on His Writings and Genius* (London: C. Bathurst, 1769);

George Saintsbury, *A History of English Prosody from the Twelfth Century to the Present Day*, volume 2 (London: Macmillan, 1908);

Saintsbury, *The Peace of the Augustans: A Survey of Eighteenth Century Literature as a Place of Rest and Refreshment* (London: Bell, 1916);

T. B. Shepherd, "John Wesley and Matthew Prior," *London Quarterly and Holborn Review* (July 1937): 368-373;

Walter Sichel, "Matthew Prior," *Quarterly Review*, 190 (October 1899): 356-380;

Robert Southey, Preface to *Specimens of the Later English Poets*, volume 1 (London: Longman, Hurst, Rees, & Orme, 1807), pp. iii-xxxii;

Monroe K. Spears, "Matthew Prior's Attitude toward Natural Science," *PMLA*, 63 (June 1948): 485-507;

Spears, "Matthew Prior's Religion," *Philological Quarterly*, 27 (April 1948): 159-180;

Spears, "The Meaning of Matthew Prior's *Alma*," *ELH*, 13 (December 1946): 266-290;

Spears, "Some Ethical Aspects of Matthew Prior's Poetry," *Studies in Philology*, 45 (October 1948): 606-629;

W. A. Speck, "Politicians, peers, and publication by subscription 1700-1750," in Isabel Rivers, ed., *Books and their Readers in Eighteenth-Century England* (Leicester University Press, 1982), pp. 47-68;

Joseph Spence, *Observations, Anecdotes, and Characters of Books and Men Collected from Conversation* [1820]), edited by James M. Osborn, 2 volumes (Oxford: Clarendon Press, 1966);

William Stebbing, "Two Poet-Politicians: Abraham Cowley, Matthew Prior," in his *Some Verdicts of History Reviewed* (London: John Murray, 1887), pp. 82-121;

Louise Stuart, "Introductory Anecdotes" to *The Letters and Works of Lady Mary Wortley Montagu*, Lord Wharncliffe, ed. (New York: AMS Press, 1861, 1970), I: 49, 121;

James Sutherland, *A Preface to Eighteenth Century Poetry* (Oxford: Clarendon Press, 1948);

Jonathan Swift, *Prose Works of Jonathan Swift*, volumes 7 and 8, edited by Herbert Davis (Oxford: Blackwell, 1939);

William Makepeace Thackeray, "Prior, Gay, and Pope," in *The English Humourists of the Eighteenth Century*, edited by Derek Stanford (London: Grey Walls Press, 1949), pp. 110-146;

Harvey Waterman Thayer, "Matthew Prior, His Relation to English *Vers de Société*," *Sewanee Review*, 10 (April 1902): 181-198;

Thomas Tickell, *A Poem, to His Excellency the Lord Privy-Seal on the Prospect of Peace* (London: J. Tonson, 1713);

Horace Walpole, *Horace Walpole's Correspondence*, edited by W. S. Lewis and others (New Haven: Yale University Press, 1937-1983);

Thomas Warton, *The History of English Poetry, from the Close of the Eleventh to the Commencement of the Eighteenth Century*, volume 3 (London: J. Dodsley, et al., 1781).

John Harlan Welsh, "The Earthen Pot: Ups and Downs of Matthew Prior," Ph.D. dissertation, University of California at Berkeley, 1971;

John Wesley, "Thoughts on the Character and Writings of Mr. Prior," *Arminian Magazine*, 5 (November-December 1782): 600-603, 660-665;

H. Bunker Wright, "Ideal Copy and Authoritative Text: The Problem of Prior's *Poems on Several Occasions* (1718)," *Modern Philology*, 49 (1952): 234-241;

Wright, "Matthew Prior and Elizabeth Singer," *Philological Quarterly*, 24 (January 1945): 71-82;

Wright, "Matthew Prior's Cloe and Lisetta," *Modern Philology*, 36 (August 1938): 9-23;

Wright, "Matthew Prior's Funeral," *Modern Language Notes*, 57 (May 1942): 341-345;

Wright, "Matthew Prior's Last Manuscript: 'Predestination,'" *The British Library Journal*, 11 (Autumn 1985): 99-112;

Wright, "Matthew Prior's 'Welbeloved and Dear Cossen,'" *Review of English Studies*, 15 (July 1939): 318-323;

Wright, "William Jackson on Prior's Use of Montaigne," *Modern Language Review*, 31 (April 1936): 203-205;

Wright and Henry C. Montgomery, "The Art Collection of a Virtuoso in Eighteenth Century England," *Art Bulletin*, 27 (September 1945): 195-204.

Papers:

Over half of Prior's literary works are extant in manuscript form; often there are two or more manuscript versions. The two major English collections are at Welbeck Abbey, Worksop, Nottinghamshire, in the library of the duke of Portland (including manuscripts of rough drafts in Prior's hand, fair copies in Drift's hand, and Prior's emendations and expansions of Drift's copies, in both prose and verse); and at Longleat, Warminster, Wiltshire, in the library of the marquis of Bath (including manuscripts in Prior's hand, in Drift's cursive hand with emendations and additions in Prior's hand, fair copies in Drift's hand, fair copies in the hand of an anonymous copyist, insertions by Alexander Pope, the manuscript printing of a professional scribe, letters, records, and printed copies of poems). The British Library houses other Prior manuscripts and is the current repository of many of those under the titular control of Welbeck Abbey and of Longleat. Some copies of Prior manuscripts are also found in the Bodleian Library. In the United States, Prior manuscripts (fair copies) and Adrian Drift materials are housed at the Miami University Library, Oxford, Ohio.

Allan Ramsay

(1684 or 1685 - January 1758)

Allan H. MacLaine
University of Rhode Island

BOOKS: *A Poem to the Memory of the Famous Archbald Pitcairn, M.D.* (Edinburgh: Printed by Andro Hart for the members of the Easy Club, 1713);

The Battel: Or, Morning-Interview. An Heroi-Comical Poem (Edinburgh: Printed [by William Adams, Jr.] for George Stewart, 1716);

Edinburgh's Address to the Country (Edinburgh: Printed by William Adams, Jr., for the author, 1718);

Christ's Kirk on the Green in Two Canto's (Edinburgh: Printed by William Adams, Jr., for the author, 1718); enlarged as *Christ's-Kirk on the Green, in Three Cantos* (Edinburgh: Printed [by Thomas Ruddiman] for the author, 1718);

Elegies on Maggy Johnston, John Cowper, and Lucky Wood (Edinburgh: Printed [by William Adams, Jr.] for the author, 1718);

Tartana: Or, The Plaid (Edinburgh: Printed [by William Adams, Jr.] for the author, 1718; revised edition, Edinburgh: Printed by Thomas Ruddiman for the author, 1720);

The Scriblers Lash'd (Edinburgh: Printed for the author, 1718);

Scots Songs (Edinburgh: Printed [by William Adams, Jr.] for the author, 1718; enlarged edition, Edinburgh: Printed [by Thomas Ruddiman] for the author, 1719; enlarged again, 1720);

Lucky Spence's Last Advice (Edinburgh: Printed by William Adams, Jr., for the author, 1718);

Content. A Poem (Edinburgh: Printed [by Thomas Ruddiman] for the author, 1719);

Richy and Sandy, a Pastoral on the Death of Mr Joseph Addison (Edinburgh: Printed by Thomas Ruddiman for the author, 1719);

Familiar Epistles between W---- H---- and A---- R---- (Edinburgh: Printed by Thomas Ruddiman for Allan Ramsay, 1719; enlarged, 1719);

Patie and Roger: A Pastoral inscribed to Josiah Burchet, Esq., Secretary of the Admiralty (Edinburgh: Printed by Thomas Ruddiman for the author, 1720);

Allan Ramsay in 1723 (painting by William Aikman; by permission of the Scottish National Portrait Gallery, Edinburgh)

Poems by Allan Ramsay, 2 volumes (Edinburgh: Printed [by Thomas Ruddiman] for the author, 1720-1721, 1728);

The Prospect of Plenty: A Poem on the North Sea (Edinburgh: Printed by Thomas Ruddiman for the author, 1720);

Scots Songs, viz. Mary Scot. Wine and Musick. Oe'r Bogie. Oe'r the Moor to Maggy. I'll never leave thee. Polwart on the Green. John Hay's bonny Lassie. Genty Tibby, and sonsy Nelly. Up in the Air

(Edinburgh: Printed [by Thomas Ruddiman] for the author, 1720);

Robert, Richy, and Sandy, A Pastoral on the Death of Matthew Prior, Esq. (London: Printed by S. Palmer for Bernard Lintot, 1721);

Fables and Tales (Edinburgh: Printed for the author, 1722);

A Tale of Three Bonnets, anonymous (Edinburgh, 1722);

Jenny and Meggy, a Pastoral, Being a Sequel to Patie and Roger (Edinburgh: Printed for the author, 1723);

Mouldy-Mowdiwart: or the Last Speech of a Wretched Miser (Edinburgh, 1724);

The Monk and the Miller's Wife (Edinburgh, 1724);

The Gentle Shepherd (Edinburgh: Printed for the author by Tho. Ruddiman, 1725; revised edition, 1728; New York: Printed by James Parker, 1750);

Collection of Thirty Fables (Edinburgh: Printed for the author, 1730).

Editions and Collections: *The Poems of Allan Ramsay*, edited by George Chalmers, 2 volumes (London: Cadell & Davies, 1800); enlarged as *The Works of Allan Ramsay*, edited by Chalmers, 3 volumes (London: Cadell & Davies, 1848);

The Works of Allan Ramsay, 6 volumes: 1 and 2 edited by Burns Martin and John W. Oliver; 3-6 edited by Alexander M. Kinghorn and Alexander Law (Edinburgh: Blackwood, 1945-1974).

OTHER: *The Tea-Table Miscellany*, edited by Ramsay, 4 volumes (Edinburgh: Printed for the editor by Thomas Ruddiman, 1723-1737);

The Ever Green, edited by Ramsay, 2 volumes (Edinburgh: Printed for the editor by Thomas Ruddiman, 1724);

A Collection of Scots Proverbs, compiled and edited by Ramsay (Edinburgh: Printed for the editor, 1737).

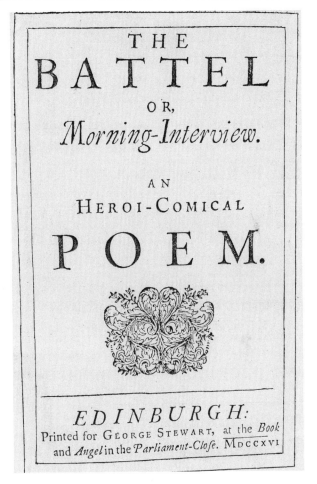

Title page for one of Ramsay's first poems, an imitation of Alexander Pope's Rape of the Lock

Allan Ramsay was an early-eighteenth-century Scots poet who has been generally undervalued in recent times, partly because his best work presents some language difficulties (not serious ones) for modern readers, and partly because he has been overshadowed by the towering figure of his successor, Robert Burns. Yet in his own right Ramsay is of considerable importance. In the historic evolution of Scottish poetry his is a crucial position, since he succeeded almost single-handedly in launching an impressive revival of the Scots poetic tradition–a movement that culminated in the supreme achievement of Burns at the end of the century. In the wider perspective of British literature Ramsay's position, though a modest one, is also secure: he was a pioneer in domesticating the ancient genre of pastoral poetry, and in his masterpiece, *The Gentle Shepherd* (1725), he produced one of the best pastoral dramas–a play that is still readable and surprisingly enjoyable. His work in other genres–especially in Scots songs, verse epistles, and satires–deserves solid respect.

Ramsay was born in the remote village of Leadhills in southwestern Lanarkshire, Scotland, in 1684 (or possibly 1685). His father, John Ramsay, who was superintendent of lead mines there, died when the poet was an infant; his mother, Alice Bowyer Ramsay, remarried, and Allan was raised as a shepherd boy in that wild, hilly countryside. His formal schooling must have been sporadic, most probably in the parish school of Crawfordmoor, six miles away.

About 1700, after the death of his mother, Ramsay was sent to Edinburgh, where in 1704 he was apprenticed to a wig maker. He succeeded in completing his six-year apprenticeship on 19 July 1710, when he was enrolled as a "burgess" of Edinburgh. He then presumably set up in business for himself. The first ten years of Ramsay's life in Edinburgh (1700-1710) are generally obscure, but after that the records of his career are fairly copious. On 14 December 1712 he married Christian Ross, an Edinburgh woman by whom he eventually had at least five children, including his eldest son, Allan Ramsay the Younger, who became a distinguished portrait painter. This marriage was a long and happy one.

Ramsay's business career is a story of gradual but steady success. He set up his first wigmaking shop probably in 1712 in the Grassmarket near the west end of Edinburgh. From there Ramsay moved his business three times, as he became increasingly prosperous and as he shifted his main occupation by degrees to bookselling and publishing. By 1718 he was established at the east end of the High Street, opposite the entrance to Niddry's Wynd (now Niddry Street). Thence, as his business continued to grow, he moved up the slope of the High Street (both physically and socially), first in 1722 to a shop opposite the Cross-Well, and finally in 1725 into the heart of the old city to a very desirable location in the east end of the Luckenbooths, next to the High Kirk of St. Giles. By then Ramsay had achieved commercial success as bookseller and publisher as well as celebrity as a national poet. His shop in the Luckenbooths had become, moreover, the chief focal point of Edinburgh's literary life.

The qualities of shrewdness, persistent energy, and versatile talent that characterized Ramsay's business life are also prevalent in his development as a poet. His creative career divides naturally into three periods: from the beginnings around 1712 until the appearance of his *Poems* in 1720-1721; from 1721 to the publication of the second volume of *Poems* in 1728; and from 1728 until his death in 1758.

Even in the first phase of his original work as a poet Ramsay shows a notable versatility. His earliest audience seems to have been fellow members of the Easy Club, a group of young Scots nationalists founded in May 1712. Like Ramsay, these bright young men were opposed to the par-

liamentary union with England of 1707, they shared literary interests, and they listened sympathetically to his early poems until the club disbanded in 1715. Throughout his life Ramsay wrote in fashionable neoclassical English as well as in vernacular Scots, and this dichotomy is apparent from the very beginning. One of his earliest major works, *The Battel: Or, Morning-Interview* (1716), is in genteel English couplets, a moderately skillful but insipid imitation of Alexander Pope's *The Rape of the Lock* (1714). Soon after this came two other long pieces in English heroic couplets, *Tartana: Or, The Plaid* (1718) and *Content* (1719), both of which are marred by pretentiousness and a straining for effects.

During these same years when Ramsay was producing these derivative English works, he was also writing far more effective poems in Scots. His first major success in the vernacular came in 1718 with his ambitious continuation of the fifteenth-century *Christis Kirk on the Green*. Ramsay reprinted the old poem as "Canto One," and then added his own original cantos 2 and 3, lengthy sequels that offer brilliant and vigorous vignettes of country life and customs in Scotland. It was natural that he began as a Scots poet in this humorous vein, since by Ramsay's time the Scots tongue had declined sadly as a literary vehicle and had come to be used only for comic sketches of low life. Ramsay himself was to change all that, but he began, inevitably, with the comic Muse. His sequels to *Christis Kirk* gave new life to the Middle Scots poem, and at the same time proved that the venerable, distinctively Scottish *Christis Kirk* tradition of the peasant brawl was an adaptable and viable genre for more modern poets. At about the same time Ramsay produced another long poem in broad Scots, *A Tale of Three Bonnets*, a trenchant satire on the parliamentary union of Scotland and England. This is his most politically radical work, unusual for a man who was habitually discreet about such matters. Wisely, he withheld it from publication until 1722, and even then had it printed anonymously. In the meantime, Ramsay moved into other Scots comic genres, publishing in 1718 the comic *Elegies on Maggy Johnston, John Cowper, and Lucky Wood*. These were all modeled on the prototype of this genre dating from the previous century, Robert Sempill's *Life and Death of Habbie Simson* (circa 1640), and, like Sempill's, all were written in the distinctive six-line stanza–later called the "Habbie stanza" or the "Burns stanza." In these elegies Ramsay is sometimes remarkably original, es-

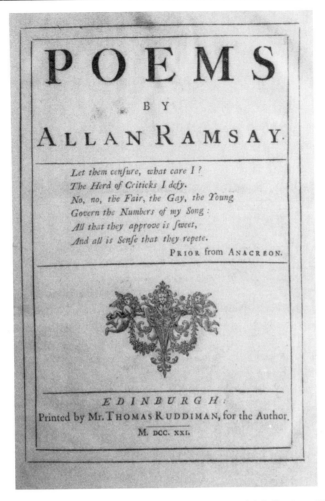

POEMS
BY
ALLAN RAMSAY.

Let them censure, what care I ?
The Herd of Criticks I defy.
No, no, the Fair, the Gay, the Young
Govern the Numbers of my Song :
All that they approve is sweet,
And all is Sense that they repete.

PRIOR from ANACREON.

EDINBURGH:
Printed by Mr. THOMAS RUDDIMAN, for the Author.
M. DCC. XXI.

*Title page for the deluxe edition of Ramsay's first poetry collection (Special Collections, Thomas Cooper Library,
University of South Carolina)*

pecially in the one on John Cowper, where he uses an ironic voice, a technique that he passed on to Burns. Ramsay's next major poem was *Lucky Spence's Last Advice* (1718), in the last-dying-words genre of *Bonny Heck* (circa 1715) by Ramsay's contemporary William Hamilton of Gilbertfield, another pioneer in Scots comic verse. Finally, also initiated by Hamilton, came in 1719 a series of "familiar" Horatian verse epistles by Ramsay in the "Habbie stanza," which launched a wholly new Scottish genre that later culminated in the great epistles of Burns.

Until 1719 all of Ramsay's work in the Scots tongue had been in more or less comic genres. However, in that year he began to use Scots for serious purposes, the first time since the sixteenth century it had been thus utilized. The earliest of these revolutionary experiments was *Richy and Sandy*, a fairly effective pastoral eclogue on the death of Joseph Addison. In 1720 Ramsay contin-

ued in this vein with a serious love pastoral in Scots, *Patie and Roger*, which eventually became the starting point for Ramsay's masterpiece, the fine pastoral play *The Gentle Shepherd*. A little earlier, in 1718, he had begun to work in yet another form, Scots songs, wherein he composed new or refurbished words for traditional tunes—an experiment that was to take hold with the public and ultimately lead to the supreme songwriting of Burns at the end of the century.

By 1720 Ramsay was firmly established and recognized in Edinburgh and beyond as a new Scots poet of real talent. He was, of course, also a bookseller and publisher, and that enabled him to have his poems printed in pamphlet form as soon as he composed them; he could then publish and distribute his work from his own shop. Thus his two professions reinforced one another: for his poetry he had easy access to publication, while at the same time his growing poetic fame

well as the names of several distinguished individuals from elsewhere in Scotland and even in England. Among those listed, for example, was "*Mr. Alexander Pope.*" Priced at a guinea per copy, the volume was expensive, impressive, and clearly a resounding success. By persistent effort combined with solid talent, Allan Ramsay had risen in ten short years from obscure wig maker to national poet.

During the years from 1721 to 1728, the second phase of his career, Ramsay flourished in business and expanded his range as a writer still further. In 1722 appeared the first edition of his *Fables and Tales*, chiefly witty and vigorous adaptations, very "free" translations of French fables by Antoine Houdart de La Motte and Jean de la Fontaine, but including two of his own invention. In the field of pastoral poetry Ramsay continued to write prolifically. His second pastoral elegy came out in 1721, *Robert, Richy, and Sandy*, lamenting the death of Matthew Prior; then in 1723 appeared *Jenny and Meggy*, a sequel to the earlier love eclogue *Patie and Roger*. These two pieces were joined together as act 1 of *The Gentle Shepherd*, a full-length pastoral play that is Ramsay's longest and best work as an original poet. Here he created a pleasing amalgam of Scottish setting (in the countryside near Edinburgh) and mostly Scottish dialogue with the literary conventions of ancient international pastoralism and of English sentimental comedy (such as Richard Steele's *Conscious Lovers*, 1722). The combination still makes enjoyable reading. In 1728, on the heels of the huge success in London of John Gay's *The Beggar's Opera*, Ramsay allowed his friends to persuade him to add some twenty songs to his play and so transform *The Gentle Shepherd* into a ballad opera. In this form the work enjoyed broad popularity with countless performances in Scotland well into the nineteenth century, ensuring Ramsay a secure, permanent place in British literary history.

In this same middle phase of his creative life Ramsay produced a good deal of miscellaneous poetry, in Scots and English, in a variety of genres. Two of the most original and skillful pieces of these years, both published in 1724 and later collected in the second volume of *Poems*, are *Mouldy-Mowdiwart: or the Last Speech of a Wretched Miser* and *The Monk and the Miller's Wife*, the latter being a free, earthy adaptation of the Middle Scots poem *The Freiris of Berwick* (early sixteenth century).

ALLAN RAMSAY.

From an Original Drawing by his Son the late Allan Ramsay Painter to His Majesty

Published June 4th 1800 by Cadell & Davies Strand.

Frontispiece for volume 1 of the first comprehensive collection of Ramsay's poetry, edited by George Chalmers in 1800

brought more business to his bookstore. Consequently, nearly all his early works were first issued as pamphlets or broadsides, so that by 1720 he was able to publish a preliminary volume of his *Poems*, consisting simply of unsold copies of individual pamphlets bound together. In the next year, however, by means of subscriptions he was able to put out a collected edition, freshly and handsomely printed, of *Poems by Allan Ramsay*, including all his significant work to date (except for the radical *Tale of Three Bonnets*). For many years Ramsay had been assiduously cultivating the goodwill of the more enlightened gentry and professional people in Edinburgh, and most of their names appeared in his list of subscribers, as

Illustration from a 1788 edition of Ramsay's Gentle Shepherd, *a pastoral drama (Special Collections, Thomas Cooper Library, University of South Carolina)*

During the 1720s much of Ramsay's energies were diverted into his extremely important work as an editor of Scots songs and of earlier Scots poetry. In 1723 he published *The Tea-Table Miscellany*, which was so successful that it grew over the years by popular demand from one to four volumes, the first important anthology of Scots songs. In it Ramsay printed some genuine old ballads and folk songs, a larger proportion of "modernized" lyrics (in English as well as Scots) set to traditional Scots tunes, and some wholly new songs (also to traditional tunes) by himself and by several younger poets whom he recruited for this purpose, including Robert Crawford and William Hamilton of Bangour. Thus the anthology fulfilled several aims at once: it preserved some of the lyric riches of the past, it provided acceptable lyrics for old tunes and so kept the tunes themselves alive, and (most important) it created an outlet for new songwriting. The *Miscellany* became the most successful and lucrative of all Ramsay's publishing ventures.

Immediately after the launching of the *Miscellany* came a two-volume anthology of Middle Scots poetry called *The Ever Green*, published in 1724. This ambitious collection was largely tran-

scribed from the priceless Bannatyne Manuscript of 1568, which Ramsay borrowed from a wealthy antiquarian friend. Naturally, this was not nearly as popular as the song collection, but it was nevertheless a notable patriotic achievement, wherein Ramsay made easily available for the first time the great Scottish poetry of the past.

About 1725, when Ramsay moved his business to its final location in the Luckenbooths, he established as a sideline a "circulating library" that was apparently the first of its kind in Great Britain—a library, that is, where people could take out books at a small fee per day or week. At first there was a storm of criticism by rigid moralists in Edinburgh who objected to some of the books, but Ramsay held on and the library was a conspicuous success; it flourished under Ramsay and his followers for generations. Then, in 1728, Ramsay published a second collected volume of *Poems by Allan Ramsay*, again by subscription, including *The Gentle Shepherd* (without the songs) and almost all the new poetry he had written since 1721. This volume was larger, with a longer and more impressive list of subscribers than the first. It decidedly established Allan Ramsay as the popular and acknowledged national poet of Scotland.

The final, third phase of Ramsay's life extended from 1728 until his death thirty years later in 1758. After 1728, having made his fortune, Ramsay published almost no new poetry, though he continued to write occasional, mostly informal poems for the private amusement of his friends to the very end of his long life. He remained busily employed with his booming bookshop in the Luckenbooths until 1740, when he could afford to retire from active commercial life. During the last dozen years of his business life, however, Ramsay became deeply involved in Edinburgh's civic affairs. In 1729 he helped to found the Academy of St. Luke, a school for drawing and painting in which his eldest son, Allan the Younger, was an early pupil. A little later he became centrally concerned in a courageous effort to start a theater in Edinburgh to improve the city's cultural side. Indeed, Ramsay himself opened a theater in Carrubber's Close in 1736 that enjoyed some success. In 1737, however, the Licensing Act was passed, forbidding commercial theaters in Britain outside London, and this measure created legal difficulties for Ramsay. Worse yet, Edinburgh's puritanical majority, opposed on moral grounds to any theaters at all, took advantage of the licensing law to close down the house in Carrubber's Close. The bigots prevailed and

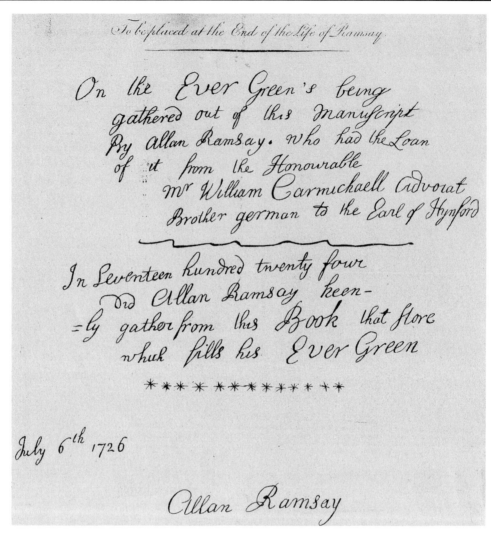

To be placed at the End of the Life of Ramsay

On the Ever Green's being
gathered out of this Manuscript
By Allan Ramsay. who had the Loan
of it from the Honourable
    Mr William Carmichaell Advorat
    Brother german to the Earl of Hynford

In Seventeen hundred twenty four
   Did Allan Ramsay keen-
=ly gather from this Book that store
  which fills his Ever Green

July 6th 1726

Allan Ramsay

Facsimile of a note Ramsay placed with the Bannatyne Manuscript of 1568, from which he drew most of the Middle Scots poetry contained in The Ever Green (*from volume 1 of* The Poems of Allan Ramsay, 1800, *edited by George Chalmers)*

after three years of hard struggle Ramsay was forced to disband his company of actors in the spring of 1739. For him this was a frustrating defeat in a worthwhile venture, though far from a catastrophic one.

In 1740, now rich enough to retire, Ramsay had built for himself a comfortable octagonal house perched on the edge of the Castlehill with a dramatic view of the Firth of Forth and of Fife beyond. This was the famous "Goose-Pie" house (still extant on the little street called Ramsay Gardens), and it was then in an almost rural spot though only a short walk from the busy High Street. In 1743 the death of his wife, Christian, was a severe blow; but the poet himself lived on for another fifteen years of pleasant literary leisure, relishing his status as a celebrity, visiting from time to time the fine country houses of his

wealthy friends, and frequently entertaining in his own cozy home. Ramsay remained active to the end—a cheerful, distinguished citizen of "Auld Reekie," the crowded, battered town of Edinburgh that he loved.

Though by no means a towering genius, Allan Ramsay made the most of his substantial talents, and his life, on the whole, was a large success. Starting with next to nothing, he built his prosperity gradually, by careful management, discretion, and determined effort, which, combined with solid, versatile ability, resulted in his final achievement of the Horatian dream of literary leisure in a cheerful old age. Ramsay worked hard and deserved his success. More important, as poet and editor he laid the essential foundations for the eighteenth-century revival of the Scots poetic tradition. Despite the tremendous pressure

Invitation to Ramsay's funeral, written by his nephew Thomas Young (from the G. Ross Roy Scottish Poetry Collection, Thomas Cooper Library, University of South Carolina)

of English influence, Ramsay dared to write in Scots, and he boldly extended the moribund native tradition to include serious as well as comic subject matters. In this, and in publicizing the older Scottish poetry, Ramsay was a genuine and selfless pioneer. The sheer vitality and skill of his best work in Scots verse demonstrated what could yet be done in this medium. By himself Ramsay invented or popularized almost all the genres of the Scots revival. He built bridges to the future and made possible the later triumphs of Robert Fergusson and Robert Burns.

Biographies:

George Chalmers, "Life of Ramsay," in *The Poems of Allan Ramsay*, volume 1, edited by Chalmers, two volumes (London: Cadell & Davies, 1800);

Burns Martin, *Allan Ramsay: A Study of His Life and Works* (Cambridge, Mass.: Harvard University Press, 1931);

Alexander M. Kinghorn, "Biographical and Critical Introduction," in volume 4 of *The Works of Allan Ramsay*, edited by Kinghorn and Alexander Law (Edinburgh: Blackwood, 1970), pp. 1-169.

References:

Thomas Crawford, "The Gentle Shepherd," in his *Society and the Lyric: A Study of the Song Culture in Eighteenth-Century Scotland* (Edinburgh: Scottish Academic Press, 1979), pp. 70-96;

Allan H. MacLaine, *Allan Ramsay* (Boston: Twayne, 1985);

MacLaine, "The *Christis Kirk* Tradition: Its Evolution in Scots Poetry to Burns," *Studies in Scottish Literature*, 2 (1964-1965): 3-18, 111-124, 163-182, 234-250;

Carol McGuirk, "Augustan Influences on Allan Ramsay," *Studies in Scottish Literature*, 16 (1981): 97-109;

John W. Oliver, "The Eighteenth Century Revival," in his *Edinburgh Essays on Literature* (Edinburgh: Edinburgh University Press, 1933), pp. 78-104;

Alexander Fraser Tyler, Lord Woodhouselee, Introduction to *The Poems of Allan Ramsay*, volume 1, edited by George Chalmers, 2 volumes (London: Cadell & Davies, 1800);

John C. Weston, "Robert Burns' Use of the Scots Verse-Epistle Form," *Philological Quarterly*, 49 (1970): 188-210;

Peter Zenzinger, *My Muse is British: Allan Ramsay und die Neubelebung der Schottischen Dichtkunst im 18. Jahrhundert* (Grossen-Linden, West Germany: Hoffman, 1977).

Elizabeth Singer Rowe

(11 September 1674 - 20 February 1737)

Madeleine Forell Marshall
Saint Olaf College

See also the Rowe entry in *DLB 39: British Novelists, 1660-1800.*

BOOKS: *Poems on Several Occasions*, as Philomela (London: Printed for John Dunton, 1696);

Friendship in Death, in Twenty Letters from the Dead to the Living. To which are added Thoughts on Death (London: Printed for T. Worrall, 1728; enlarged, 1736; Boston: Printed for R. Hodge, W. Green & J. Norman, 1782);

Letters Moral and Entertaining in Prose and Verse, 3 volumes (London: Printed for T. Worrall, 1728-1733);

The History of Joseph. A Poem (London: Printed for T. Worrall, 1736; enlarged edition, 1737; Philadelphia: Printed & sold by David Hall & William Sellers, 1767);

Philomela; or, Poems by Mrs. Elizabeth Singer (now Rowe) (London: Printed for Edmund Curll, 1736);

Devout Exercises of the Heart in Meditation and Soliloquy, Prayer and Praise, edited by Isaac Watts (Coventry: Printed & sold by M. Luckman, 1737; Boston: Printed by Rogers & Fowle for J. Blanchard, 1742).

Editions and Collections: *The Miscellaneous Works in Prose and Verse of Mrs. Elizabeth Rowe*, edited by Henry Grove and Theophilus Rowe, 2 volumes (London: Printed for R. Hett & R. Dodsley, 1739); enlarged as *The Works of*

Mrs. Elizabeth Rowe, including original poems and translations by Mr. Thomas Rowe. Life of the Author, 4 volumes (London: J. & A. Archy, 1796);

The Poetical Works of Mrs. Elizabeth Rowe, including the History of Joseph (London: Suttaby, Evance & Fox/Baldwin, Craddock & Joy, 1820);

Friendship in Death, Thoughts on Death translated from the Moral Essays of the Messieurs du Port Royal, Letters Moral and Entertaining (New York & London: Garland, 1972);

The Poetry of Elizabeth Singer Rowe (1674-1737), compiled by Madeleine Forell Marshall (Lewiston, N.Y./Queenston, Ont.: Mellen, 1987).

OTHER: *Divine Hymns and Poems on Several Occasions . . . by Philomela, and several other ingenious persons*, includes poems by Rowe (London: Printed by R. Janeway for Richard Burrough, 1704); revised as *A Collection of Divine Hymns and Poems on Several Occasions* (London: Printed for J. Baker, 1709);

"On the Death of Mr. Thomas Rowe," in *Poems on Several Occasions: by His Grace the Duke of Buckingham and other eminent hands* (London: Printed for Bernard Lintot, 1717);

Poems on Several Occasions, includes poems by Rowe (London: Printed for J. Tonson & J. Barber, 1718).

Elizabeth Rowe; engraving by George Vertue for Rowe's Miscellaneous Works in Prose and Verse, *posthumously published in 1739 (by permission of the National Portrait Gallery, London)*

Widely admired by distinguished contemporaries and popular with the reading public well into the nineteenth century, the poetry of Elizabeth Singer Rowe has, despite the resurgence of interest in women writers and new understandings of eighteenth-century poetry, come only slowly to modern critical attention. Rowe devised an elegant and credible poetic voice that spoke with eloquent female authority. Writing within the rich tradition of Christian verse, she shared the devotional and moral concerns of her age. She provided a model of piety and virtue that her contemporaries, male and female, understood and admired. Although important for the appreciation of eighteenth-century values and literary history, neither this tradition of Christian verse nor these concerns with piety and virtue are easily accessible for modern readers. Perhaps

this explains the general lack of critical recognition of Rowe's achievement.

Elizabeth Singer, who married Thomas Rowe in 1710, was the eldest daughter of Walter and Elizabeth Portnell Singer, and was born 11 September 1674 in Ilchester, Somersetshire. (One sister died in infancy, and a second only survived her teens.) Walter Singer was a prosperous clothier and a prominent Dissenter whose wealth provided his daughter with material comfort, books, a basic education, and access to important friends. His Christian commitments provided a model of kindly, educated sanctity.

Rowe's first published poems appeared from 1691 to 1695 in early issues of the *Athenian Mercury*, the popular literary periodical compiled by John Dunton, founder of the "Athenian Society" in 1691. Correspondents and contributors, writing under pen names, posed and answered questions on a wide range of subjects. Without revealing who she was, Rowe sent poems and literary queries to Dunton, using the names "Philomela" and "the Pindarick Lady." Samuel Wesley, Richard Sault, John Norris, William Temple, Jonathan Swift, and Daniel Defoe were also involved in the Athenian project. The Athenians provided both an appreciative audience and good counsel, in fact a writing workshop, by correspondence. In 1693, for example, in response to her request, they recommended a reading list for a young poet. More generally, they supported intellectual women, virtuous literature, and noncontroversial Christianity, the familiar agenda of Restoration reform.

In her contributions to the *Mercury* the young poet experimented with various roles. She played the obstinately learned ingenue, rejecting acceptable female pursuits of dance, song, and drawing, refusing to "forego the *charming Muses.*" Playing the shepherdess, in "To one that perswades me to leave the Muses," she embraced the pastoral life: "Now welcome all ye *peaceful Shades and Spring,* / And Welcome all the *inspiring* tender things; / That please my *genius,* suit my make and years, / Unburden'd yet with all but lovers cares." In a different voice, in "A Pindarick, to the Athenian Society," she credited those "matchless men" who have "unmaskt and *challeng'd*" the "abhorred crimes" of the age, with her own heroic inspiration: "So much was I by your *example* fir'd, / So much the *heavenly form* did win: / Which to my eyes *you'd painted virtue in.*" (Both these poems were collected in her first book, 1696.) In other poems she played the maiden, left by her lover, gone in search of glory, then the visionary dreamer, inspired by her love of Theron. She penned extravagant compliments, often remarkable for their female perspective. In 1694 the fifteenth volume of the *Mercury* was dedicated to the "Pindarical Lady," who had just turned twenty. The following year she identified herself to Dunton, and they began a remarkable, self-consciously platonic friendship.

In 1696 Dunton published her collected *Poems on Several Occasions*. These poems indicate the young poet's wide range of interests as she experimented with poetic roles and genres: she attempted heroic verse; she tested the voices of the earnest ingenue, the shepherdess, and the virtuous lady. Her devotional poems are most successful, however, particularly the paraphrases of Canticles (the Song of Songs) and John 21. The Spouse in the Song of Songs provided a dramatic model for the self-consciously female poet–a female voice that spoke with intense passion for all humanity. This persona is the most distinctive achievement of Rowe's early devotional poetry, which otherwise follows established seventeenth-century traditions and interest in the sublime.

Meanwhile, during the years of correspondence with the Athenians, Rowe's mother died. Walter Singer, with Rowe and her sister, moved, perhaps in 1692, to Eggford Farm in Frome. The teenaged administrator of a complex, middle-class household, Rowe fell seriously ill while she watched over her dying sister. However, in Frome, Rowe came into the social and cultural world of the Thynne family at Longleat, Somerset. Thomas Thynne, the first Viscount Weymouth of Longleat, became a family friend, and his son, Henry Thynne, tutored Rowe in French and Italian. The daughter of Henry Thynne, Frances, subsequently countess of Hertford and duchess of Somerset, became, as she grew in years, the poet's faithful friend, even follower, and the important copyist of her later correspondence. Thomas Ken, bishop of Bath and Wells, after losing his episcopate, lived with the Thynne family at Longleat. He became Rowe's intellectual mentor and friend and visited her regularly. The "Pindarick Lady" soon ended her platonic correspondence with Dunton and his Athenian colleagues in London.

While correspondence with her friends and seemingly autobiographical poetry provide some information about the middle period of the poet's life (1696-1719), modern readers are wise to recognize the conscious artificiality of these pub-

lished sources, signaled by the typical use of pen names and the flair for dramatic role-playing, a romantic convention that particularly misleads the biographer in search of lovers, at least three of whom have been proposed at various times.

Benjamin Colman, a young Bostonian clergyman, met the poet at Bath shortly after the publication of her first volume of poetry. Their friendship pleased Walter Singer, and Colman continued to visit the Singers until his return to America in 1699. Colman and Rowe maintained a correspondence until her death. He wrote a biography of her for the *Boston Weekly Newsletter* (28 April 1737), commending her great knowledge and achievement as philosopher, theologian, and poet.

Matthew Prior met Rowe when he visited Longleat in the autumn of 1703. His letters to her, including comments on her translations from Tasso and her poem "Despair," have been published (by H. Bunker Wright, *Philological Quarterly*, January 1945). Beginning in 1704 their work appeared together in several of Tonson's *Poetical Miscellanies* (including his *Poems on Several Occasions*, 1718). Rowe's "Love and Friendship," with Prior's reply, "To a Lady: She Refusing to Continue a Dispute with me, and Leaving me in the Argument. An Ode," and her subsequent verses "To Mr. Prior. On his Solomon" suggest the challenges of their complex friendship.

Isaac Watts was, more than Prior, a kindred spirit. While they may have met earlier, the first documented connection between Rowe and Watts is the Watts poem "To Mrs. Elizabeth Singer, On the Sight of some of her divine Poems, never printed," dated 19 July 1706. The poem ingeniously invokes the conventions of both pastoral and divine poetry, deploys the Philomela-nightingale mythology, and describes the desired reader response of rapt attention, of "divine delight." The title indicates that manuscript circulation of Rowe's poetry was not uncommon. She returned the compliment in the lines "To Mr. Watts, on his Poems sacred to Devotion." Her verses suggest that, having read Watts's *Horae Lyricae* (1706), she was no longer interested in secular poetry. Watts's verses, she says, stop pastoral streams in their course and bend worldly forests to devout attention. The exchange of compliments was printed in the second edition of the *Horae Lyricae* in 1709 and in Rowe's *Miscellaneous Works* (1739).

Watts provides useful critical guidance to the proper reading of Rowe's poetry, early and

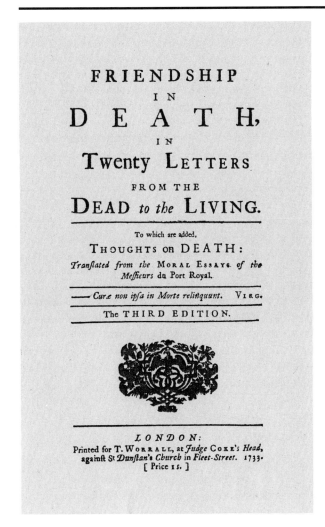

FRIENDSHIP
IN
D E A T H,
IN
Twenty Letters
FROM THE
DEAD to the LIVING.

To which are added,
THOUGHTS ON DEATH:
Translated from the MORAL ESSAYS *of the*
Messieurs du Port Royal.

Curæ non ipsa in Morte relinquunt. VIRG.

The THIRD EDITION.

LONDON:
Printed for T. WORRALL, at *Judge* COKE's *Head*,
against St *Dunstan's Church* in *Fleet-Street*. 1733.
[Price 1*s*.]

Title page for the third edition of Rowe's 1728 book, her most popular work. Praised by Samuel Johnson and others, it was republished many times in England and the United States.

The poet's Augustan transformation is evident in several of these contributions. While inappropriate as congregational songs, her eight hymns, for example, are remarkable for their astute theological understanding and bright, elegant imagery. Pastoral and divine love conventions are finely integrated in paraphrases of Canticles. Clearly by 1709 Rowe had studied Milton, Tasso, and much more. Drawn to the sublime, she mitigates its enthusiastic excesses by exemplary control. Her religious poems are no spontaneous, expressive rhapsodies. However passionate her devotion, she speaks with authority as a spiritual mentor, modeling correct religious sentiment, as she continued to do. Watts, in his preface to *Devout Exercises*, writes: "It should be remarkable also, there is nothing to be found here which rises above our ideas. Here are none of those absurd and incomprehensible phrases which amuse the ear with sounding vanity, and hold reason in sovereign contempt. Here are no visionary scenes of wild extravagance, no affections of the tumid and unmeaning style, which spreads a glaring confusion over the understanding; nothing that leads the reader into the region of those mystical shadows and darkness which abound in the Romish writers, under the pretence of refined light and sublime extasy." Her religious poetry, like her later devotions, was exemplary, the passions it expressed being approved and recommended by eminent divines.

The divine love tradition and her disciplined authority permit her to long for "Seraphick love," in a poem of the same name included in the 1709 collection:

How strongly thou my panting heart dost move
With all the holy ecstacies of love!
In these sweet flames let me expire, and see
Unveil'd the brightness of thy deity.

Oh! let me die! for there's no earthly bliss
My thoughts can ever relish after this;
No, dearest Lord, there's nothing here below,
Without thy smiles, to please, or satisfy me now.

Such otherworldly sensuality is steeped in convention and sanctioned by a long tradition.

The poet met her future husband, Thomas Rowe, in 1708 at Bath. A young scholar and libertarian in the best Nonconformist tradition, he had just returned from the University of Leyden. The letters of the couple indicate their devotion to one another as well as a certain literary self-consciousness. Written in 1710, Thomas Rowe's

late. After her death, having been requested by her to do so, he edited her meditations and published them as *Devout Exercises of the Heart in Meditation and Soliloquy, Prayer and Praise* (1737). His preface explains the conventions of devotional verse, including that of divine love, which he had used in his own early poetry, insisting on the inappropriateness of biographical readings.

Divine Hymns and Poems on Several Occasions . . . by Philomela, and several other ingenious persons appeared in 1704. Five years later a second edition, heavily revised, was issued as *A Collection of Divine Hymns and Poems on Several Occasions.* Rowe's reputation as Philomela earned her recognition, by name and in distinguished company, on the title pages of both editions. The collections contain both familiar and new devotional work by her.

"Epistle to Daphnis" and "An Epistle to a Friend" (included in *Miscellaneous Works*) suggest his lively combination of feminism and passion, all within the conventions of the pastoral. The couple married in 1710 and moved to Hampstead. It was there that Thomas died, after a long illness, on 13 May 1715. Mrs. Rowe returned to Frome to live with her father until his death four years later. She lived in Frome for the remainder of her life.

Rowe's elegy "On the Death of Mr. Thomas Rowe" is perhaps her most remarkable poem. Here the familiar conventions of pastoral elegy frame exemplary sentiments and heroic gesture, all loaded with clear, unconventionally autobiographical meaning. Most unconventional of all, the ideas of divine love, which had been basic to her poetry, are radically confused with earthly love. The "dear youth" whose death she mourns had been the devotional center of her life:

My prayers themselves were thine, and only where
Thou wast concern'd, my virtue was sincere.
Whene'er I begg'd for blessings on thy head,
Nothing was cold, or formal, that I said;
My warmest vows to Heav'n were made for thee,
And love still mingled with my piety.

The poem was first printed by Bernard Lintot in 1717 in his *Poems on Several Occasions*, the collection of verse that also included Alexander Pope's second version of *The Rape of the Lock*, and Pope doubtless saw the elegy. The personality and situation of the protagonist of his *Eloisa to Abelard*, as well as several passages of Eloisa's pathetic monologue, are strikingly similar to some of Rowe's lines. *Eloisa* and Rowe's elegy were published together by Pope in 1720 under the single title *Eloisa to Abelard*.

Over the course of time since her death, abetted by the elegy, a certain novelistic pathos has attached itself to Rowe's life. Indeed the grieving widow is one more in a series of the poet's public identities–as Philomela, as shepherdess, as spiritual mentor, and as the longing Spouse of the Canticles. These identities were roles she devised that facilitated her poetry, providing voices for a woman poet who had few appropriate female models to which she could turn. Thus the poet as widow collaborated in her contemporary literary characterization as a pious, world-weary ascetic, longing for death. Her vastly popular prose in *Friendship in Death, in Twenty Letters from the Dead to the Living* (1728) and the *Letters Moral and Entertaining* (1728-1733) depends for its authority

upon this romanticized persona. Dedicated to Edward Young, translated into French, reprinted again and again in England and America, and praised by Samuel Johnson, both volumes are important in the history of women's writing and the development of the epistolary novel.

Perhaps nothing presents more of an obstacle to the modern reader's appreciation of Rowe's writing than her seeming fixation on death. Mourning the agony of loss, longing for reunion with friends beyond the grave, imagining touching letters from the dead to the living–this is the graveyard world of Young's *Night Thoughts* (1742-1746). In defense of Rowe, however, it must be noted that she was the sole survivor of her family and a childless widow who had suffered the deaths of siblings, parents, and husband. Nor, given the mortality statistics of her day, was her experience unique. In her poetry and her correspondence with and her visits to Frances Thynne, Lady Hertford, one finds her offering eloquent consolation at the deaths of Frances's mother, and her sister Mary, Lady Brooke. The age required a spiritual mentor who would define, perhaps especially for women, the appropriate response to painful and frequent loss. Rowe was such a writer.

While Rowe's correspondence may be selected to support a withdrawn and morbid portrait of world-weariness and death-longing, modern readers should note that her activity as author of best-sellers, hundreds of pages of written devotions, as correspondent and friend, and as a devout and charitable lady would naturally preclude much travel or social engagement. In her highly sociable age, with all its demands, her advocacy of retreat often sounds rather more practical than misanthropic, defending a need for space and time to read, think, and write. Nor, except in contrast to Lady Hertford's life at court, was hers much of a retreat. Her visits to friends, her interest in American colonial settlements in Georgia, her financial support of a local school in Frome, and her active involvement in the affairs of the Rook Lane congregation indicate a lively engagement with the world. Even her isolation has often been misrepresented in the interest of heightening her persona. Evidence that she lived with the Rook Lane minister, John Bowden, and his family is generally ignored.

While in the absence of a critical edition one can only speculate, it is quite possible that the texts of Rowe's poetry have been as heavily edited as her biography. She did not review the

TO

Dr. YOUNG.

SIR,

 HAVE no Design in this Dedication, but to express my Gratitude, for the Pleasure and Advantage I have received from your Poem on the LAST JUDGMENT, and the *Paraphrase on Part of the Book of* JOB.

THE Author of these Letters is above any View of Interest, and can have no Prospect of Reputation, resolving to be concealed: But if they prove a serious
A 2   Enter-

DEDICATION.

Entertainment to Persons whose leisure Hours are not always innocently employed, the End is fully answered.

THE greatest Infidel must own, there is at least as much Probability in this Scheme, as in that of the FAIRY TALES, which however Visionary, are some of them Moral, and Entertaining.

I am,

SIR,

Your most humble

Servant, &c.

THE

THE

PREFACE.

 HE Drift of these Letters is, to impress the Notion of the Soul's Immortality; without which, all Virtue and Religion, with their Temporal and Eternal good Consequences, must fall to the Ground.

Some who pretend to have no Scruples about the Being of a GOD, have yet their Doubts about their own Eternal Existence, though valuable Authors abound in Christian, and Moral Proofs of it.

But since no Means should be left unattempted in a Point of such Importance, I hope

The PREFACE.

hope endeavouring to make the Mind familiar, with the Thoughts of our Future Existence, and contract, as it were, unawares, an Habitual Persuasion of it, by Writings built on that Foundation, and addressed to the Affections and Imagination, will not be thought improper, either as a Doctrine, or Amusement; Amusement, for which the World makes by far the largest Demand, and which generally speaking, is nothing but an Art of forgetting that Immortality, the firm Belief, and advantageous Contemplation of which, this Amusement would recommend.

LET-

Dedication to Edward Young and preface as they were printed in the third edition of Friendship in Death

proof sheets of *Poems on Several Occasions*; Edmund Curll's edition of her work (*Philomela*, 1736) was, as usual, unauthorized; and *The Miscellaneous Works* was compiled by Henry Grove and her brother-in-law, Theophilus Rowe, after her death. Watts, in his preface to *Devout Exercises*, admitted his meddling, how "here and there a too venturous flight is a little moderated." The selection and arrangement of poems, as well as the language, may or may not be as Rowe would have had it. Even dating her poems without topical references is difficult. Perhaps other poems of Rowe will come to light. (Indeed, among the most intriguing editorial puzzles is the attribution to Rowe of the anonymous 1720 *Expostulatory epistle to Sir Richard Steele upon the death of Mr. Addison. By a Lady*, bound with the sixth edition of Pope's *Essay on Criticism*.)

In the absence of exact dating, it has been tempting to view the secular as early and the religious as late poetry. Such a view conforms to the biographical construct, accurate or inaccurate, of the morbidly religious widowed recluse. Even in her early poems, however, Rowe had suggested that she had given up secular for religious verse, turned from mortal to divine love, a resolution she perhaps found difficult to maintain. Indeed, distinguishing the secular from the devotional poetry is often difficult: love poetry and meditative verse take on religious meaning and religious poetry draws heavily on secular experiences of love and nature.

The mature religious verse demonstrates a variety of genres, and influences. Biblical paraphrase was an established poetic mode, authoritative and serious yet allowing a great deal of imaginative freedom. In such "imitations" the scholarly requirements of Greek and Latin were replaced by the requirements of a biblical erudition and theological understanding that a woman like Rowe could acquire. Furthermore, a woman who was a sometime pastoral poet possessed an idiom appropriate to the Canticles, as seen in her "Cant. I. vii" from *Miscellaneous Works*: "O tell me in what verdant mead, / Or flow'ry vale, thy flocks are fed; / Or by what silver current's side, / Thou gently dost their footsteps guide?" The shepherdess of the pastorals searches out the Good Shepherd in the Song of Songs. Elsewhere, as a bride, she longs for the Lord in sensually charged verse sanctioned by scripture. The Psalms of David, the sometime shepherd, were also pastoral. Psalm paraphrase, at least since the work of Mary Sydney, Countess of Pembroke, had been available to

women, providing a paradigm and a voice for spiritual experience. Rowe accordingly paraphrased Psalms.

Not surprisingly, Milton's influence is occasionally felt in Rowe's verse. The verses "To Mrs. Arabella Marrow, in the Country" (in *Miscellaneous Works*) distinctly echo *L'Allegro* (1645): "May the charming visions rise, / That dance before the poet's eyes, / When the solitary muse / Does rural shades its subject chuse." Just so, "Despair" sounds more like *Il Penseroso* (1645) than like the cry for help of a young victim of depression. "A Dialogue between the Fallen Angels, and a Human Spirit just entered into the other world" is subtly Miltonic, while "A Description of Hell" is even subtitled "In imitation of Milton" and indeed illustrates the dangers of such attempts. All are collected in *Miscellaneous Works*.

Also in *Miscellaneous Works* are her sixty-four "Devout Soliloquies." As the name implies, this is a distinctive genre, at once personal and dramatic, and well suited to Rowe's established poetic persona. In "Soliloquy IV," Rowe shows how the shepherdess, with her humble reed, will convert the nymphs and swains to holy love:

The list'ning nymphs, instructed by my flame,
Shall teach their hearts to make a nobler claim;
The swains no more for mortal charms shall pine,
But to celestial worth their vows resign.
The fields and woods the chaste retreats shall prove
Of sacred joys, and pure, immortal love;
And angels leave their high abodes again,
To grace the rural seats, and talk with men.

In the following soliloquy, the poet faults slick love poetry: "By sighs, by gentle vows, and soft complaint, / Deluded lovers all their suff'rings paint; / Their joys in smooth similitudes they dress, / And all their griefs in flowing words express. . . ." High celestial ardors demand angelic skill:

           . . . for you alone can tell
What minds inflam'd with holy transports feel.
You feel them, when you touch the immortal
   strings,
And gaze, and love, and talk immortal things;
When ev'ry blissful shade, and happy grove
Repeat the sound, and softly breathe out love.

The raptures occasionally overflow in ecstasy:

      Fountain of love, in thy delightful streams
Let me for ever bathe my ravish'd soul,
Inebriated in the vast abyss,

The plentitude of joy; where all these wide,
These infinite desires shall die away
In endless plenty, and complete fruition.

It would be a mistake to deny the pleasures of Rowe's devotion. She was genuinely irritated by the limitations of secular love and secular poetry, an irritation that, in one soliloquy (XL), takes comic form:

I call not you that on Parnassus sit,
And by the flow'ry banks of Helicon,
Circle your brows with fading coronets;
While some romantic hero you adorn
With lying epithets, and airy praise:
Or some fantastic lover's fate rehearse
In notes that with a soft, inticing art,
A charming, but pernicious magic draw
The chastest minds from virtue's sacred paths.

Too long, in other words, she wrote love poetry in the rural shades, before invoking the much more important and interesting celestial muses.

As a tribute to these celestial muses, *The History of Joseph* (1736) stands supreme among Rowe's works. Variously considered a biblical romance, an epic, and a heroic poem, this narrative poem in ten books was widely popular and influential in Britain, America, and Germany. *Joseph* is at once Miltonic, moral, and sentimental. The subject struck Rowe as appropriate to her "virgin Muse":

Let others tell of ancient conquests won,
And mighty deeds by favour'd heroes done;
(Heroes enslav'd to pride, and wild desires)
A virgin Muse, a virgin theam requires;
Where vice and wanton beauty quit the field,
And guilty loves to stedfast virtue yield.

Like its biblical original, the story is, nevertheless, packed with crime and wild desires, all testing the virtuous young Joseph.

The vast biblical erudition behind *Joseph* is evident, however, and the Miltonic sweep of the invocation and the hellish descriptions have sure authority. At the same time, Rowe seizes every chance to touch the reader's heart. Joseph's brothers, after all, had failed to be touched by his piteous appeals, which resulted in the catastrophe, turned to good by a benevolent Deity: "Unmov'd we saw the anguish of his breast, / In mournful looks, and flowing tears express'd: / Unmov'd, and lost to nature, virtue, sence, / Unmov'd, we heard his tender eloquence."

Among the most subtle achievements of the poem is its parody of romance literature: in Book V, the maid of Potiphar's wife tells the story of Semiramis in cheap sensationalist poetry of the kind Rowe had criticized as drawing "The chastest minds from virtue's sacred paths" with its "pernicious magic." The seductive poem has the expected effect and Potiphar's wife confesses her love to Joseph. "Celestial virtue sparkling in his look," Joseph repulses her and ends up in prison.

The happy ending, the family reunion in Egypt, at once rewards Joseph's celestial virtue and demonstrates the benevolence of Providence. It is appropriately touching, as the hero's "heart expands with sympathetick joy" and he "flies to hide the swelling tears, / That melting love and soft surprise excite."

In *Joseph*, as in Rowe's other poetry, aspects of eighteenth-century literature usually regarded as distinct are revealed as compatible: piety and pastoral, poetry and prose, Miltonic influence and romance, venerable devotional genres and sentimentalism, virtue and scripture, female writing and male literature—each has its place. The popular and critical reception of Rowe's writing indicates that the combination appealed to her contemporaries. Her work was widely read and approved, reprinted well into the next century. Colleagues as different as Watts, Prior, and Johnson praised her efforts. German and French translations and admiration suggest international influence.

Modern scholarship, perhaps hampered by its own distinctions and categories, has generally ignored Rowe or dismissed her as a religious or neurotic curiosity. Her careful crafting of a sincere, authoritative, female poetic voice, her novel use of conventions, her rapport with contemporary sensibility, her probable influence on subsequent poetry: these suggest the injustice of such neglect. As feminist scholarship reviews and restores the literary tradition, it is possible that "this excellent woman," as Watts called her in his preface, "who has blessed and adorned our nation and our age" will find a place in the revised canon of eighteenth-century poetry.

Letters:

The Works of Mrs. Elizabeth Rowe, volume 4 (London: J. & A. Archy, 1796).

Bibliography:

Henry F. Stecher, Bibliography in *Elizabeth Singer Rowe, the Poetess of Frome: A Study in Eighteenth-*

Century English Pietism (Bern: Herbert Lang/Frankfurt am Main: Peter Lang, 1973), pp. 220-238; 259-264.

Biographies:

Benjamin Colman, Obituary, *Boston Weekly News-Letter*, 28 April 1737, p. 1;

Henry Grove and Theophilus Rowe, "The Life of Mrs. Elizabeth Rowe," in *The Miscellaneous Works in Prose and Verse of Mrs. Elizabeth Rowe*, edited by Grove and Rowe, 2 volumes (London: Printed for R. Hett & R. Dodsley, 1739);

Henry F. Stecher, *Elizabeth Singer Rowe, the Poetess of Frome: A Study in Eighteenth-Century English Pietism* (Bern: Herbert Lang/Frankfurt am Main: Peter Lang, 1973).

References:

Hoxie Neale Fairchild, *Religious Trends in English Poetry*, volume 1 (New York: Columbia University Press, 1939), pp. 134-140;

Helen Sard Hughes, "Elizabeth Rowe and the Countess of Hertford," *PMLA*, 59 (1944): 726-746;

Hughes, *The Gentle Hertford: Her Life and Letters* (New York: Macmillan, 1940);

Madeleine Forell Marshall, Introduction to *The Poetry of Elizabeth Singer Rowe (1674-1737)*, compiled by Marshall (Lewiston, N.Y./Queenston, Ont.: Mellen, 1987), pp. 1-94;

Gilbert D. McEwen, *The Oracle of the Coffee House: John Dunton's Athenian Mercury* (San Marino, Cal.: Huntington Library, 1972);

Isaac Watts, Preface to *Devout Exercises of the Heart in Meditation and Soliloquy, Prayer and Praise*, edited by Watts (Coventry: Printed for M. Luckman, 1737);

H. Bunker Wright, "Matthew Prior and Elizabeth Singer," *Philological Quarterly*, 24 (January 1945): 71-82.

Papers:

Rowe's papers, including some poems and Lady Hertford's transcriptions of letters she received from Rowe, are collected in Alnwick Manuscript no. 110 at Alnwick Castle; the British Museum and the Library of Congress hold microfilm copies. The University of Nottingham Library holds several translations by Rowe of Tasso.

Richard Savage

(16 January 1697? - 1 August 1743)

Harry Rusche
Emory University

SELECTED BOOKS: *The Convocation: or, a Battle of Pamphlets* (London: Printed for E. Young & sold by J. Morphew, 1717);

Love in a Veil: a Comedy (London: Printed for E. Curll, R. Francklin & W. Chetwood, 1719);

The Tragedy of Sir Thomas Overbury (London: Printed for Samuel Chapman, 1724);

The Authors of the Town; a Satire (London: Printed for J. Roberts, 1725);

A Poem, Sacred to the Glorious Memory of Our Late Most Gracious Sovereign Lord King George (London, 1727);

The Bastard. A Poem, Inscribed with All Due Reverence to Mrs. Bret, Once Countess of Macclesfield (London: Printed for T. Worrall, 1728);

The Wanderer: A Poem. In Five Canto's (London: Printed for J. Walthoe, 1729);

An Author to Be Lett, as Iscariot Hackney (London: Printed for Alexander Vint, 1729; modern edition, Augustan Reprint no. 84, Los Angeles: Clark Memorial Library, 1960);

Verses, Occasion'd by the Right Honourable the Lady Vicountess Tyrconnell's Recovery at Bath (London: Printed for A. Millar & sold by J. Roberts, 1730);

A Poem to the Memory of Mrs. Oldfield (London, 1730);

The Volunteer Laureat. A Poem. Most Humbly Address'd to Her Majesty on Her Birthday (London: Printed for John Watts, 1732);

The Genius of Liberty. A Poem. Occasion'd by the Departure of the Prince and Princess of Orange (London: Printed for Lawton Gilliver, 1734);

The Progress of a Divine. A Satire (London: Printed for the author, 1735);

Of Public Spirit in Regard to Public Works (London: Printed for R. Dodsley, 1737; revised, 1739);

London and Bristol Compared. A Satire: Written in Newgate, Bristol (London: Printed for M. Cooper, 1744).

Editions and Collections: *Various Poems . . . By the late Richard Savage, Esq.* (London: Printed for J. Turner, 1761);

The Works of Richard Savage, Esq. Son of the Earl Rivers. With an Account of the Life and Writings of the Author, by Samuel Johnson, LL.D., 2 volumes (London: Printed for T. Evans, 1775, 1777);

The Poetical Works of Richard Savage, edited by Clarence Tracy (Cambridge: Cambridge University Press, 1962).

PLAY PRODUCTIONS: *Woman's a Riddle*, doubtfully attributed to Savage, London, Lincoln's Inn Fields, 4 December 1716;

Love in a Veil, London, Theatre Royal in Drury Lane, 17 June 1718;

Sir Thomas Overbury, London, Theatre Royal in Drury Lane, 12 June 1723.

OTHER: *Miscellaneous Poems and Translations by Several Hands, Published by Savage*, includes poems by Savage (London, 1726);

Clarence Tracy, "More Poems by Richard Savage," includes previously unpublished poems, *Notes and Queries*, 210 (December 1965): 452-453.

The man who called himself Richard Savage officially appeared in London in November 1715 when he was arrested and charged with possession of a seditious, pro-Jacobite pamphlet. When he was brought before the justice, according to court records he gave his name as "Mr. Savage, natural son to the late Earl Rivers." Whether or not this young man with the inflammatory pamphlet, who had himself written several poems attacking the new monarch—among them "An Ironical panagyrick on his pretended Majesty G—" and "The Pretender" (not published until included in *The Poetical Works*, 1962)—was in fact Richard Savage is still conjectural. Thanks to Samuel Johnson, we know much of what happened to the man who called himself Savage after 1715, but his life from the time he claims he was christened on 18 January 1697 as Richard Smith until his ar-

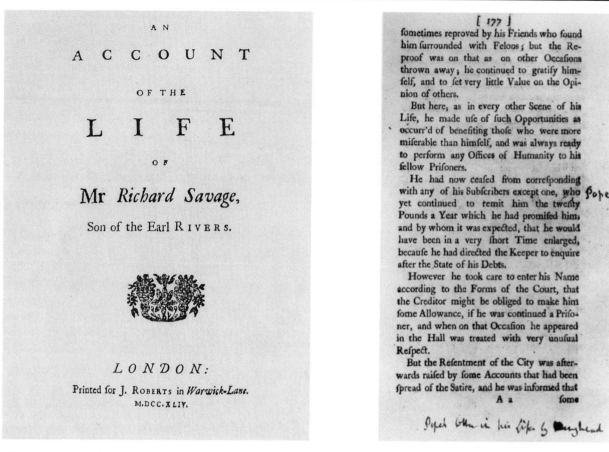

AN

ACCOUNT

OF THE

LIFE

OF

Mr *Richard Savage*,

Son of the Earl RIVERS.

LONDON:

Printed for J. ROBERTS in *Warwick-Lane*.
M.DCC.XLIV.

[177]

fometimes reproved by his Friends who found him furrounded with Felons; but the Reproof was on that as on other Occafions thrown away; he continued to gratify himfelf, and to fet very little Value on the Opinion of others.

But here, as in every other Scene of his Life, he made ufe of fuch Opportunities as occurr'd of benefiting thofe who were more miferable than himfelf, and was always ready to perform any Offices of Humanity to his fellow Prifoners.

He had now ceafed from corresponding with any of his Subfcribers except one, who yet continued to remit him the twenty Pounds a Year which he had promifed him, and by whom it was expected, that he would have been in a very fhort Time enlarged, becaufe he had directed the Keeper to enquire after the State of his Debts.

However he took care to enter his Name according to the Forms of the Court, that the Creditor might be obliged to make him fome Allowance, if he was continued a Prifoner, and when on that Occafion he appeared in the Hall was treated with very unufual Refpect.

But the Refentment of the City was afterwards raifed by fome Accounts that had been fpread of the Satire, and he was informed that

A a   fome

Title page for Samuel Johnson's first attempt at critical biography; and a page from his copy of the book with his notes for future revision. The life of his friend Savage later appeared in his Lives of the English Poets, 1779-1781 *(by permission of the Glasgow University Library)*

rest is a mystery, and the history of his early life is constructed from his own unverified accounts.

Savage's reputed mother, Anne Mason, married Charles Gerard, Viscount Brandon and the heir of the earl of Macclesfield, on 18 June 1683; the marriage was an unhappy one, and just two years later the couple began a long separation that ended in divorce in 1698. By then Brandon's father had died, so the couple were the countess and earl of Macclesfield. But before the divorce, Anne had begun an affair with Richard Savage (Earl Rivers), and the lovers had had two children, a daughter, Anne, who died in infancy, and a son, the boy christened Richard Smith in Fox Court, London, in 1697. So that Lord Macclesfield could not use the births and her obvious adultery against her in the divorce proceedings, Lady Macclesfield assumed a false identity, hid herself during her lying-in, and, wearing a mask so no one could identify her, delivered the baby boy. The boy was immediately sent into hiding to live with a series of foster families, and the subter-

fuge was so cleverly managed that it is impossible now to discover what happened to the child as he moved from nurse to nurse.

Lady Macclesfield, who after her divorce had married Col. Henry Brett in 1700, told Earl Rivers, who had planned a bequest of six thousand pounds for his illegitimate son, not to bother because his son was dead. Richard (Smith) Savage, of course, denied the report of his death, and if in fact the surviving son, then he had led a miserable childhood aggravated constantly by his mother's dislike for him and her unremitting neglect. He was passed from hand to hand, reportedly destined at one time for kidnapping and exile to the West Indies, and apprenticed finally to a shoemaker. But at about this time, when he says he was nine years old, his nurse died, and among her effects he found letters and documents disclosing his origins and his parentage. These papers, which were never produced by Savage and have eluded research, he used to press his claims against Anne Brett. The woman who

THE
BASTARD.
A
POEM,

Inscribed with all due Reverence to

Mrs. *BRET*, once *Countess* of
MACCLESFIELD.

By *RICHARD SAVAGE*,
Son of the late Earl RIVERS.

Decet, hæc dare dona Novercam.   Ov. Met.

L O N D O N:

Printed for T. WORRALL, at the *Judge's Head* against
St. *Dunstan's*-Church in *Fleet-Street.* 1728.

T H E
P R E F A C E.

THE *Reader will easily perceive these
Verses were begun, when my Heart was
Gayer, than it has been of late; and
finish'd in Hours of the deepest Melancholy.*

*I hope the World will do me the Justice to
believe, that no part of this flows from any real
Anger against the* Lady, *to whom it is inscrib'd.
Whatever undeserv'd Severities I may have receiv'd at her Hands, wou'd she deal so Candidly as
to acknowledge Truth, she very well knows, by
an Experience of many Years, that I have ever
behaved my self towards her, like one, who
thought it his Duty to support with Patience all
Afflictions from that Quarter. Indeed if I had
not been capable of forgiving a Mother, I must
have blush'd to receive Pardon my self at the
Hands of my* Sovereign.

*Neither to say Truth, were the manner of my
Birth All, shou'd I have any Reason for com-
plaint---- when I am a little disposed to a gay turn
of Thinking, I consider, as I was a De-relict*
B   *from*

The PREFACE.

*from my Cradle, I have the Honour of a lawful
Claim to the best Protection in* Europe. *For
being a* Spot of Earth, *to which no Body pretends
a Title, I devolve naturally upon the* KING, *as
one of the Rights of His Royalty.*

While I presume to Name his MAJESTY, *I look
back, with Confusion, upon the Mercy I have
lately experienc'd, because it is impossible to remember it, but with something I would fain forget; for the sake of my future Peace, and Alle-
viation of my past Misfortune.*

*I owe my Life to the Royal Pity; if a
Wretch can, with Propriety, be said to live, whose
Days are fewer than his Sorrows; and to whom
Death had been but a Redemption from Misery.*

*But I will Suffer my Pardon, as my Punish-
ment, till that Life, which has so graciously been
given me, shall become considerable enough not to
be useless in His Service, to Whom it was for-
feited.*

*Under Influence of these Sentiments, with
which his* MAJESTY'S *great Goodness has inspired
me, I consider my Loss of Fortune, and Dignity,
as my Happiness; to which, as I was born without Ambition, I am thrown from them without
Repining.----Possessing those Advantages, my Care
had been, perhaps, but how to enjoy Life; by the
want of them I am taught this nobler Lesson,
to study how to deserve it.*

R. Savage.

*Title page and preface for Savage's inflammatory autobio-
graphical poem, sarcastically dedicated to his mother*

AN

AUTHOR
To be LETT.
BEING

A PROPOSAL humbly addrefs'd to the Confideration of the Knights, Efquires, Gentlemen, and other worfhipful and weighty Members of the Solid and Ancient Society of the

BATHOS.

By their Affociate and Well wifher

ISCARIOT HACKNEY.

—*Evil be thou my Good.* SATAN.

NUMB. I, To be continued.

LONDON:

Printed for A. MOORE, near St. Paul's Church-Yard
1729

Title page for Savage's satire on literary practices of the day, which some saw as evidence that he provided Alexander Pope information used in his Dunciad *(1728)*

his first play on the boards was unfortunately diluted by charges of plagiarism and outright theft of the manuscript from another writer, Christopher Bullock. Although Savage's contemporaries seemed convinced he did write it, enough evidence exists to cast doubt on Savage's authorship. The second, *Love in a Veil,* was produced in 1718 and printed in 1719; the third, a tragedy entitled *Sir Thomas Overbury,* still did not bring Savage the fame he sought as a writer, although he did earn what for him was the great sum of one hundred pounds when his tragedy was printed in 1724, a year after it was acted. Prospects looked good for Savage, but in 1727 his affairs took a terrible reversal.

By this time Savage's story of his illegitimacy and his heartless mother seems to have been known to half of London, and many people sympathized with him in his claims against Brett. He had also begun to earn some money from his writing, and he was enlarging his circle of influential literary friends, among them the writer and publisher Aaron Hill and the poets James Thomson, Edward Young, Colley Cibber, John Dyer, and Alexander Pope, who was to show him uncommon consideration in the years to come. But on 20 November 1727 he killed a man named James Sinclair in an establishment called Robinson's Coffee-House. The argument was over a vacant room at the inn, and Savage, quick-tempered to the point of uncontrolled fury, stabbed the unarmed Sinclair, who named Savage as his assailant before he died. Savage and two friends also involved in the argument at Robinson's were arrested; Savage was found guilty of murder and condemned to death. His friends intervened on his behalf, however, and he was pardoned by the king and released on 4 or 5 March 1728. Savage says that he owed no thanks to Mrs. Brett in the matter of his pardon, for she had done everything she could to see to it that the death sentence would be carried out.

Brett might indeed have viewed execution as an unexpected but welcome means of disposing of a bumptious impostor, but surely Savage exaggerated the animus toward him by the woman he called mother. Whatever motive Brett might have furnished him when he was facing death, Savage intensified his attack and pressed his claims of his parentage after his release from prison. His story was already known from several sources. Edmund Curll first published it in his *Poetical Register* in 1719; Aaron Hill again related it in his periodical the *Plain Dealer* in 1724. A third

was the reputed mother of Savage declared that her illegitimate son, Richard, had died; Savage counterclaimed, on the strength of documents that he never chose to use as evidence, that she was his mother. Savage's two chief biographers, Johnson and Clarence Tracy, accept his claims of his parentage, but for reasons perhaps of faith rather than fact. Savage never proved his case, but on the other hand, Mrs. Brett never troubled to disprove it. As far as proof is concerned, there the matter rests, in the words of James Boswell (in his *Life of Johnson,* 1791), to "vibrate in a state of uncertainty."

Savage had failed in his attempts at reconciliation with his mother, but at first he did not press his claims too vigorously and seemed content to make his living, uncertain as it was, as a writer in the early years of his career. Aside from the occasional poem, he supposedly wrote three plays, none of them well received. The first, *Woman's a Riddle,* was produced in 1716; whatever pleasure Savage might have had in seeing

Queen Caroline, for whom Savage wrote seven "Volunteer Laureat" poems, the first of which earning him a pension of fifty pounds a year that continued until the queen's death in 1737 (painting by Charles Jervas; by permission of the National Portrait Gallery, London)

Blest be the *Bastard's* birth! through wondr'ous
    ways,
He shines eccentric like a Comet's blaze.
No sickly fruit of faint compliance he;
He! stampt in nature's mint of extasy!
He lives to build, not boast, a gen'rous race:
No tenth transmitter of a foolish face.
His daring hope, no sire's example bounds;
His first-born lights, no prejudice confounds.
He, kindling from within, requires no flame;
He glories in a *Bastard's* glowing name.

Unencumbered with a family name or a tradition to uphold, the bastard is his own man, free to roam the world, "His heart unbiass'd, and his mind his own."

The bastard owes these blessings in disguise to his mother, who defying both moral and social law, severs the bonds of maternity and pushes him from the shore, launching him "into life without an oar." Although he may be refused tradition, fortune, and even a name, "Far other blessings wait the *Bastard's* lot; / Conceiv'd in rapture, and with fire begot! / Strong, as necessity, he starts away, / Climbs against wrongs, and brightens into day." Fighting against adversity and neglect, he is privileged to make of himself what he will. The motives that prompted Savage to write *The Bastard* can fairly well be guessed, but the poem clearly rises above whatever sort of mean-spirited intentions that might have inspired it. Brett was made to suffer by the poem; people reportedly leered at her and maliciously quoted couplets from the poem within her hearing. That, however, is finally irrelevant to a critical appraisal of one of Savage's finer works.

A danger in considering Savage's rejection by the woman he claimed as his mother is that he can be romanticized, turned into the legend of a hero who fights and writes against all odds. To the contrary, Savage was, as A. D. McKillop says (in *English Literature from Dryden to Burns,* 1948), "a sturdy literary beggar" who lived by his wits and took help and money from anyone who offered it. Johnson says Savage was a man who "appeared to think himself born to be supported by others, and dispensed from all necessity of providing for himself." This, Johnson adds, contributed to his inability–perhaps "disinclination" better describes it–to make a living from his writing; Savage seemed content to avoid hard, productive work and to live totally dependent on patronage. But as in the past, something turned up, and Savage was invited to live in the home of John, Lord Tyrconnel, the nephew of Brett; he was given, in

account, an anonymous *Life of Mr. Richard Savage,* was published in 1727, the same year Savage gained notoriety through his trial and subsequent release. But the real blow, from which it is said Brett never recovered her reputation, was Savage's poem *The Bastard,* which was published in 1728 and went through five editions in several months.

The Bastard, heavy-handedly "Inscribed with All Due Reverence to Mrs. Bret, Once Countess of Macclesfield," is arguably Savage's finest poem. Here he celebrates illegitimacy, for, deprived of a family and a name, the bastard is by circumstance forced through his own endeavors to rise and create a life on his own. The poem opens with these lines, which are justly the most quoted from the poem:

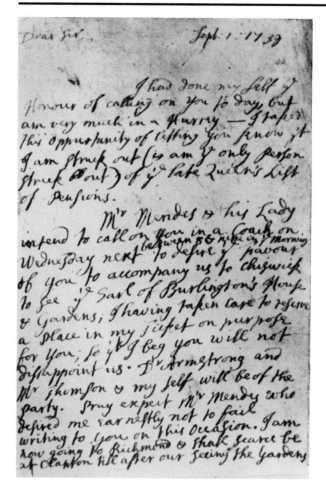
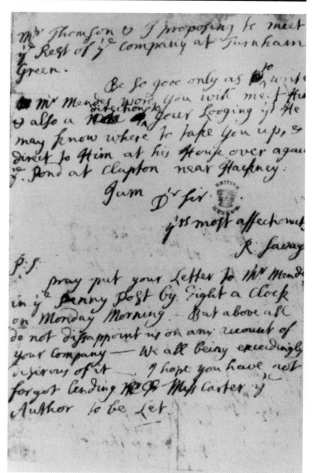

Letter from Savage to Thomas Birch, mentioning the fact that Savage had lost his royal pension (by permission of the British Library)

addition to lodging, an allowance of two hundred pounds. How Savage came to live in the house of a man related to the woman he had so severely harassed needs explanation.

Lord Tyrconnel's hospitality and patronage may at first look like a tacit acceptance of Savage's claims upon Brett; the truth of the situation may, however, be more sordid, involving an element of extortion. The first condition of Savage's improved situation at Tyrconnel's home in Arlington Street was that he publish no more attacks on Brett. *The Bastard* had indeed hit home, and this was not the first time that Savage had been paid off to stop his attacks. Earlier, around 1724, Savage had planned to publish an anthology of poems with works by himself and several other poets. When the work, *Miscellaneous Poems and Translations by Several Hands,* was published in February 1726, it was almost immediately withdrawn from circulation and did not reappear until Sep-

tember 1726, but without the dedication and preface that had originally been printed in the February edition of the book. Brett and Tyrconnel had, Johnson suggests, promised Savage an annuity of fifty pounds if he suppressed the volume's prefatory material, which they found offensive and defamatory. The preface is a frank attack on Brett, and Savage may have been less interested in the poetic merit of the volume than in its calculated effect on Brett and her family.

The preface is by any standard ugly and provocative; there are first of all several quotations from John Locke that deal with infanticide, and had Locke known of Brett's behavior, Savage adds, she no doubt would have figured in the philosopher's "Instances of Enormities." The preface of *Miscellaneous Poems* brims over with bitterness, made in a way all the worse because Savage affects a good humor about it all. Johnson's judgment that Savage, although basically "compassionate by nature and principle," was capable of prosecuting "his revenge with the utmost acrimony till his passion had subsided" is somewhat substantiated when one reads this preface. Pity is perhaps hard to elicit for this man who says, "Thus, while *legally* the Son of one Earl, and *naturally* of another, I am, *nominally*, No-body's Son at all: For the Lady, having given me *too much Father*, thought it but an equivalent Deduction, to leave me *no Mother*, by way of Ballance.–So I came sported into the World, a kind of Shuttlecock, between Law and Nature." Buying Savage's silence was possibly the best way to deal with him.

Although Savage's relationship with Tyrconnel was not to endure beyond 1735 and ended in an acrimonious quarrel, this time he spent in his benefactor's home was the most settled and prosperous period he ever enjoyed, and it gave him the security he needed to complete his most ambitious work, *The Wanderer* (1729). The poem, long, discursive, and contemplative, is made up of five cantos and more than two thousand lines of heroic couplets. Savage's friends were of various critical opinions about it. As quoted by Johnson, Pope admired it, finding himself "not displeased" with his first reading and "delighted" after he had read it the third time. Johnson was more reserved in his praise, and his comments aptly describe its sprawling structure and its sometimes striking imagery: "It has been generally objected to *The Wanderer*, that the disposition of the parts is irregular; that the design is obscure, and the plan perplexed; that the images, however beautiful, succeed each other without order; and that the whole performance is not so much a regular fabric, as a heap of shining materials thrown together by accident, which strikes rather with the solemn magnificence of a stupendous ruin, than the elegant grandeur of a finished pile." The poem was, however, as Johnson notes, considered by Savage as his masterpiece.

In Canto III of *The Wanderer*, Savage returns to the one subject he seems incapable of ignoring, his relationship with his unrelenting mother:

Ye *cruel Mothers*!–Soft! those Words command!
So near, shall *Cruelty*, and *Mother* stand?
Can the Dove's Bosom snaky Venom Draw?
Can its Foot sharpen, like the Vultur's Claw?
Can the fond Goat, or tender, fleecy Dam
Howl, like the Wolf, to tear the Kid, or Lamb?

The answer to Savage's unhappy question, as he says, is "Yes, there *are* Mothers–" who like Brett can act so unnaturally.

No poem after *The Wanderer* was so ambitious, but after leaving Tyrconnel's home Savage never again had the same kind of leisure, for again the hunt for patronage was on. In 1730 he had a chance for real success and security when he almost won the post of poet laureate. When Laurence Eusden died, Tyrconnel and other friends tried to win the appointment for Savage, but instead Cibber was made poet laureate. Never one to be put off, Savage wrote a poem celebrating Queen Caroline's birthday in 1732, and she liked it so much that she gave him a pension of fifty pounds and promised him something better when it came along. Savage presumptuously usurped a part of Cibber's duties as laureate and wrote seven poems in all for the queen's birthdays– from 1732 until 1738 (the last one a eulogy). Queen Caroline died in 1737, and the pension was discontinued, despite Savage's offering of "Volunteer Laureat, Number VII," an appeal for more help from her husband, George II. He was relieved at first to learn that King George had ordered all the queen's charitable bequests continued after her death; but then Savage discovered that one name had been struck from the list of pensioners: his own. Savage had lately been quite outspoken in his Tory sentiments and his opposition to the Whigs, and George and his advisers would not overlook Savage's offenses. Thus was another prop knocked from under Savage, and his affairs were deteriorating rapidly.

His association with Tyrconnel ended, and his hopes for a position and salary from the government were destroyed, so Savage now was literally out on the streets and living from day to day on the charity of his friends, who did what they could to help him. About this time in 1737 or 1738 Savage met Johnson, another writer recently arrived in London; Johnson could do nothing to mend Savage's fortunes, because he was just as poor as Savage. This meeting did, however, assure Savage's fame–probably beyond anything that his writing could do or even deserved– when Johnson published his *Account of the Life of Mr. Richard Savage* in 1744 and later included Savage's biography in his *Lives of the English Poets* in 1779. Thus Savage entered the company of those authors who are more often read about than read.

Johnson and Savage, who would wander the streets at night talking about literature and poli-

To His Most

SACRED MAJESTY,

This POEM is humbly In-scrib'd by His Majesty's most Obedient, Dutiful, and Loyal Subject to Command,

R. Savage.

DREAD SIR,

HAD I with *Plato's* Eloquence been fill'd,
    Sweet as the Honey from his Lips distill'd;
My great Attempt would even then be vain,
And Sing Your Glories in too low a strain.
The Muses all want Harmony to tell
The Noble Virtues that within you dwell.
The Musick of the Spheres can only sing
The Mind and Actions of so great a King.
Tho' many Princely Sufferings now you bear,
Yet Heav'n still shows, you're its peculiar Care;
It makes you most Illustriously shine,
Like to your Royal Dignity Divine.
    Then may Your Loyal Subjects hearty Prayer
Ascend, and reach to the Almighty's Ear:
May always You, in what You Wish, abound,
Your Expeditions with Success be Crown'd.
May the Almighty pour on You his Bliss,
And in the Temple we anoint You His.

An uncollected poem by Savage, addressed to King George II (by permission of the Bodleian Library, Oxford)

tics, shared more than their poverty, for both enjoyed company and good conversation. When one reads Johnson's account of Savage's vigorous and active mind, accurate judgment, quick apprehension, tenacious memory, and, above all, totally engaging conversation, one understands why Johnson, who himself possessed the same qualities, was drawn to the older, more sophisticated writer. Much of what is known about Savage is preserved in Johnson's biography; for example, no portrait of Savage exists, so what is known of his appearance as well as his personality and character is owed to Johnson. Savage was, Johnson says, "of a middle stature, of a thin habit of body, a long visage, coarse features, and melancholy aspect; of a grave and manly deportment, a solemn dignity of mien, but which, upon a nearer acquaintance, softened into an engaging easiness of manners. His walk was slow, and his voice tremulous and mournful. He was easily excited to smiles, but very seldom provoked to laughter."

Not long after the months spent in Johnson's company, Savage's creditors were hounding him in earnest, and London obviously was not the place for him to pursue his two most immediate projects, a revision of his earlier play *Sir Thomas Overbury* and an edition of his collected works. At this point in 1739 his friend Pope stepped in and devised a plan to raise for Savage a subscription of fifty pounds a year that would ease him into retirement and a quieter life somewhere outside London where he might live more cheaply and, without the distractions of the city's diversions, have more time to work. Pope's friendship with Savage went back at least to

A rare, uncollected song by Savage (by permission of the British Museum, Music Room)

1727, when Savage was in prison for the murder of Sinclair; at that time Pope had sent Savage some money and promised him more if he needed it. Circumstances suggest that the two may have been on intimate terms much earlier than this and that a long-standing friendship had prompted Pope to send the money to Savage while he was awaiting execution.

Savage may have known Pope in 1726 and 1727 while living in Richmond, which was within walking distance of Pope's home in Twickenham, but by 1729, when Pope published his *Dunciad Variorum*, all Savage's friends were convinced that it was Savage who had furnished the anecdotes and gossip with which Pope had reduced his literary enemies to laughingstocks. Their suspicions seemed justified when Savage's anonymous prose pamphlet, *An Author to Be Lett* (1729), a broad satire on literary practices of the day, appeared in 1731 in a volume entitled *A Collection of Pieces in Verse and Prose, Which have been publish'd on Occasion of the DUNCIAD*; the volume contained a preface signed by Savage. Savage's association with Pope must have been strong, for he indeed paid dearly for it with the loss of many friends from his earlier years in the theater when he was first establishing himself as a writer. The opinion of Savage's former associates is encapsulated in a single passage from an article in the *Hyp-Doctor*, published in April 1735: "*Richard Savage*, Esq; was the *Jack-all* of *that Ass* in a *Lyon's Skin* [Pope], he was his *Provider*: Like *Montmaur*, the *Parasite of Paris*, he rambled about to gather up *Scraps* of *Scandal*, as a Price for his *Twickenham Ordinary*; no Purchase no Pay; No Tittle-tattle, no Dinner: Hence arose those *Utopian Tales* of Persons, Characters and Things, that rais'd, by the *clean Hands* of this *Heliconian Scavenger*, the *Dunghil of the Dunciad*." How much of what Savage and Pope gossiped about ended up in *The Dunciad* we do not know, but the unassailable judgment of his friends was that Savage was a tattler and a traitor. However, when Savage truly needed a friend in 1739, Pope generously came to his aid.

The plan devised by Pope was that, after the fifty pounds was raised, Savage would retire to Swansea by way of Bristol. With money enough for the two-day journey to Bristol, Savage made his farewells. But in an almost amusingly typical fashion, the benefactors received a letter from Savage after two weeks, informing them that he was still on the road to Bristol and that he was broke. They sent him more money, and he arrived at Bristol without further trouble. But

it was still some months before he finally made his way to Swansea; he stayed there more than a year, finished his revisions on *Sir Thomas Overbury*, and wrote several occasional poems—despite the time he lost when he threw himself into Welsh society, courted a local widow, and cultivated the patronage of the literary gentry. He remained in Swansea until 1742, when he returned to Bristol with the intention of going on from there to London. He did not have the money to leave Bristol, however, and no one in London was willing to send him the amount he needed to get back home.

How Savage survived in Bristol is unclear; all his benefactors in London, with the exception of Pope, who felt personally responsible since he had urged Savage to get out of London, had withdrawn their aid. Pope sent an occasional bit of money—along with letters warning Savage to mend his ways—but it was usually spent on drink rather than the fare back to London. In January 1743 the ax fell for the last time; Savage was arrested for debt and put in Bristol's Newgate prison, where he remained because no one was willing to pay the debt of eight pounds that he owed. He railed against Pope, the only friend likely to help him, and after a series of nasty letters between them, Pope wrote to him for the last time in July 1743 and told him their association was over and that no more help would be forthcoming.

At the end of that month, on 25 July, Savage complained of pains in his back and side; a week later, on 1 August, he was dead. Dependent to the end on the charity of others, his burial expenses were paid by his jailer, a Mr. Dagge. He was buried in the churchyard of St. Peter's in Bristol, and, if we believe the story that he never proved, he would have been forty-six when he died. But the solution to that mystery went with him. Savage's story does not really end until a decade later, on 11 October 1753. On that day Mrs. Anne Brett, silent on the subject of her reputed son until the end, died and took with her the facts needed to finish the true account of Richard Savage's life.

Bibliographies:

Clarence Tracy, "Some Uncollected Authors, 36: Savage," *Book Collector*, 12 (Autumn 1963): 340-349;

P. F. Hinton, "Savage's Various Poems, 1761," *Book Collector*, 13 (Spring 1964): 66-67;

D. F. Foxon, *English Verse, 1701-1750* (London: Cambridge University Press, 1975), pp. 700-702.

Biographies:
Giles Jacob, *Poetical Register* (London: E. Curll, 1719), pp. 297-298;

Plain Dealer, edited by Aaron Hill, nos. 15, 28, and 73 (London, 1724);

Richard Savage, Preface to *Miscellaneous Poems and Translations by Several Hands* (London, 1726);

Anonymous, *The Life of Mr. Richard Savage* (London, 1727; modern edition, Augustan Reprint no. 247, Los Angeles: Clark Memorial Library, 1988);

Samuel Johnson, *Account of the Life of Mr. Richard Savage* (London: Printed for J. Roberts, 1744);

W. Moy Thomas, "Richard Savage," *Notes and Queries,* second series, 6 (November-December 1858): 361-365, 385-389, 425-428, 445-449;

Stanley V. Makower, *Richard Savage: A Mystery in Biography* (London: Hutchinson, 1909);

Clarence Tracy, *The Artificial Bastard* (Cambridge: Harvard University Press, 1953);

Bernard Lloyd, "Richard Savage in Swansea," *Anglo-Welsh Review,* 27 (1978): 98-104.

References:
W. H. D. Adams, *Wrecked Lives; or, Men Who Have Failed* (New York: Pott, Young, 1880), pp. 228-284;

Benjamin Boyce, "Johnson's *Life of Savage* and Its Literary Background," *Studies in Philology,* 53 (1956): 576-598;

Samuel Cunningham, "The Poetry of Richard Savage: A Critical Analysis," Ph.D. dissertation, Florida State University, 1973;

Gwyn Jones, *Richard Savage* (New York: Viking, 1935);

Thomas Kaminski, "Was Savage 'Thales'? Johnson's *London* and Biographical Speculation," *Bulletin of Research in the Humanities,* 85 (Autumn 1982): 322-335;

A. D. McKillop, *English Literature from Dryden to Burns* (New York: Appleton-Century-Crofts, 1948);

McKillop, "Letters from Aaron Hill to Savage," *Notes and Queries,* 199 (September 1954): 388-391;

Charles Whitehead, *Richard Savage: A Romance of Real Life* (London: Bentley, 1842).

William Shenstone
(18 November 1714 - 11 February 1763)

James E. Tierney
University of Missouri-St. Louis

BOOKS: *Poems Upon Various Occasions. Written for the Entertainment of the Author, and Printed for the Amusement of a Few Friends, Prejudic'd in his Favour* (Oxford: Printed by Leon. Lichfield, 1737);

The Judgment of Hercules, A Poem (London: Printed for R. Dodsley & sold by T. Cooper, 1741);

The School-Mistress, A Poem. In Imitation of Spenser (London: Printed for R. Dodsley & sold by T. Cooper, 1742; facisimile, Oxford: Clarendon Press, 1924);

The Works in Verse and Prose of William Shenstone, Esq., 3 volumes—comprises volume 1: *Poems,* 1764; volume 2: *Essays on Men, Manners, and Things,* 1764; volume 3: *Letters to Particular Friends,* 1769 (London: Printed for R. & J. Dodsley, 1764, 1769).

Editions and Collections: *Shenstone's Miscellany,* edited by Ian Gordon (Oxford: Clarendon Press, 1952);

"A Complete Edition of the Poetry of William Shenstone," edited by Richard Snyder, Ph.D. dissertation, University of Pittsburgh, 1955.

OTHER: *A Collection of Poems By Several Hands,* 6 volumes, includes poems by Shenstone in volumes 1, 4, 5, and 6 (London: Printed for R. & J. Dodsley, 1748-1758).

Engraving by an unknown artist (HM 44507; by permission of the Henry E. Huntington Library and Art Gallery)

Although a minor poet, William Shenstone was a significant presence in poetry during the last half of the eighteenth century. His much-respected burlesque *The School-Mistress* (1742) helped reawaken an interest in the style of Edmund Spenser. Shenstone's prominent position in the age's major poetic miscellany, Dodsley's *Collection of Poems By Several Hands* (1748-1758), implicitly acknowledged his status among the arbiters of taste in the metropolis of London. His continuing popularity long after his death is evident in the many editions of his poetry in the nineteenth century and in the commentary of such admirers as Robert Burns, Henry

McKenzie, William Hazlitt, and John Ruskin. Supporting this reputation were his accomplishments in landscape gardening at the refurbished family estate, Leasowes, in the West Midlands area, a multiyear project that not only influenced the departure from formal gardens but also brought a seasonal flow of noble and fashionable visitors to his *ferme ornée* (ornamented farm).

Shenstone was born in 1714 at what was then the family farm, Leasowes, in Halesowen,

268

Shropshire (now Worcestershire), the elder of two sons of Thomas Shenstone, an uneducated country gentleman, and of Ann Penn Shenstone, the eldest daughter of William Penn of Harborough Hall, a few miles to the southwest. Shenstone's father died when the boy was barely ten, and when his mother died eight years later (at the age of only thirty-nine), he was entrusted to the guardianship of his maternal uncle, Rev. Thomas Dolman, rector of Broom. His boyhood education began in the schoolhouse of the country dame, Sarah Lloyd, whom he identifies in a 1742 letter to Richard Jago (in the collection by Marjorie Williams, 1939) as the model for the main character in his *School-Mistress*. It appears he attended Halesowen Grammar School for a short while before being placed with a Rev. Crumpton, schoolmaster at Solihul (near Birmingham), where he met and began a lifelong friendship with Jago. In May 1732 Shenstone was admitted as a commoner to Pembroke College, Oxford, where he spent the happiest days of his life, writing poetry and conversing in the company of Jago, Anthony Whistler, and Richard Graves, who became his most intimate friend through life. Although he kept his name on the registers for ten years, Shenstone left the university without taking a degree.

In 1737 Shenstone published at Oxford his first volume, *Poems Upon Various Occasions*, a small miscellany of twenty-four poems in which the young poet tried his wings in several poetic forms, mostly imitative of the reigning Augustan tradition of Alexander Pope. The most notable of the group is the first version of *The School-Mistress*, a burlesque portrait of a day in the life of a birch-wielding but sensitive country dame and her hornbook charges. This lightly sketched twelve-stanza version in the Spenserian mode, as the poet later admitted, was not sufficiently appreciative of the true Spenser in that it had imitated his style via Pope's vulgar Spenserian burlesque, "The Alley" (published in *Miscellanies*, 1727). In contrast to Pope's scornful tone and coarse imagery, however, Shenstone's rural portrait is good-natured and poignantly nostalgic.

Residing intermittently at Harborough Hall, his maternal grandparents' estate, and Leasowes beginning in 1736, Shenstone made extended trips to London and Bath from 1740 to 1743, anxious to gain acceptance and patronage in the literary world. He attended the theater regularly, took part in the ongoing debate on the poetic nature of riddles in columns of the *Gentleman's Maga-*

zine (October 1740-March 1741), to which he contributed anonymous verses, and read newspapers avidly at George's Coffee House, where he kept up on the Parliamentary debates presaging Robert Walpole's resignation. Despite his eagerness for success, his shy nature–together with the probable undermining effect of a country estate awaiting him at Leasowes–makes one wonder just how full-fledged was his pursuit of Lady Fame. Support for such a doubt is found in a recurring theme in Shenstone's poetry that makes its first appearance in his second publication, *The Judgment of Hercules* (1741). Ostensibly the poem honors George Lyttelton, Prince Frederick's secretary and Shenstone's neighbor, through whom Shenstone hoped to gain patronage, as had the poet James Thomson in 1738. But the parallel to Shenstone's own circumstance is too obvious to be overlooked. The poem's hero, Alcides, when approached by two lustrous female figures offering diverse paths of life–passive retirement among country pleasures and the active Spartan pursuit of fame amidst the distant towers–is entranced by the former but then chooses the latter. However, the martial maid soon proved too elusive, and ensuing poetry, while projecting the same choice, will find the author opting for the easier pleasures of rural retirement.

Although Shenstone had hoped to make his mark with this piece, the poem had essentially nothing new to offer either in content or style. It was a rendering of the Hercules episode from Xenophon, somewhat dependent for detail on Anthony Cooper, Earl of Shaftesbury's essay, *A Notion of the Historical Draft . . . of the Judgment of Hercules* (1713), and conservative in its reliance upon a now tiring poetic diction. Supposedly his bookseller, Robert Dodsley, lost money on the work.

Undaunted, Shenstone spent much of the following winter revising *The School-Mistress*, elaborating the poem into twenty-eight stanzas (mostly concerned with a fuller picture of the dame, praise of Shropshire, and a concluding reflection on pride), and adding a ludicrous index to assure the poem's acceptance as burlesque. Most importantly, however, a new appreciation of Spenser led him to drop much of the archaic language and emphasize Spenser's "Simplicity, his manner of description, and a peculiar Tenderness of Sentiment," as he states in his "Advertisement" in *The School-Mistress*.

Much to Shenstone's disappointment, the new edition, published in the spring of 1742, made no great impression in London. This sec-

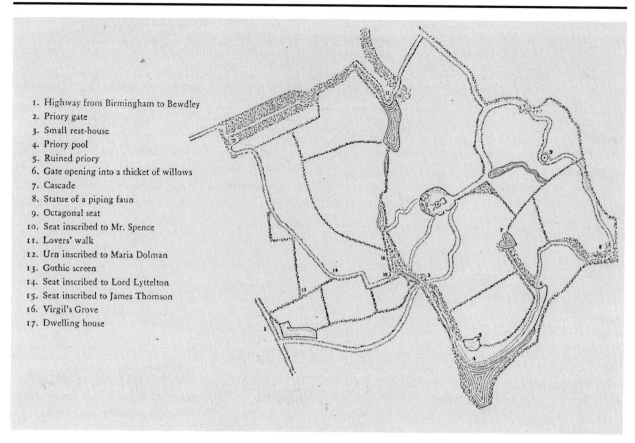

A map of Shenstone's estate, Leasowes, based on the map in his Works in Verse and Prose, *volume 2 (1764; from* Letters of William Shenstone, *edited by Duncan Mallam, 1939)*

1. Highway from Birmingham to Bewdley
2. Priory gate
3. Small rest-house
4. Priory pool
5. Ruined priory
6. Gate opening into a thicket of willows
7. Cascade
8. Statue of a piping faun
9. Octagonal seat
10. Seat inscribed to Mr. Spence
11. Lovers' walk
12. Urn inscribed to Maria Dolman
13. Gothic screen
14. Seat inscribed to Lord Lyttelton
15. Seat inscribed to James Thomson
16. Virgil's Grove
17. Dwelling house

ond tepid reception, not surprisingly, confirmed a growing disenchantment with the city. His attendance at plays dropped off, as did, it seems, his spirit for pursuing fame. The previous September he had written to Graves: "I absolutely despair of ever being introduced to the world . . . I wish indeed to be shewn into good company" (*Letters*, edited by Williams). Writing to Jago in June 1742, he said, "Here am I still, trifling away my time, my money, and, I think, my health" (*Letters*, edited by Williams). And so crept in a melancholy that permeated his life over the next few years and was perhaps responsible for his retirement to Leasowes in 1745.

The twenty-six elegies Shenstone had written by 1748 (published in his *Works*, volume 1, 1764) also reflect these early frustrations but in a suspiciously defensive manner. Emblematic of the group, the persona in the first elegy embraces rural retirement, disdains the insincerity of ambitious, flattering poets, and encourages lovers like himself to write from the heart and to scorn vulgar cares. Repeated again and again,

such recriminations against the vices of ambition, together with protestations of love for simple country pleasures—occasionally alternated with expressions of self-doubt—are, at best, literary clichés and, at worst, autobiographically transparent, seeming to be an attempt to make a virtue of necessity.

With few exceptions Shenstone's elegiac favorites are dull, affected performances in the Augustan mode without the vigor of Pope or Jonathan Swift. On the other hand, they do occasionally make an original contribution and show true emotion. For one thing, Shenstone deserves credit for expanding the elegy's traditional concerns, love or death, to include, as he says in his "Prefatory Essay on Elegy" (*Works*, volume 1), whatever subject bears "a tender and querulous idea . . . as its peculiar characteristic." So his elegies take up such topics as retirement, fame, disdain for wealth, estranged friendship, travel, the wool industry, and even grave robbers, and, by so doing, open the form to the varied concerns of the Romantics. Also, Shenstone's poetic concep-

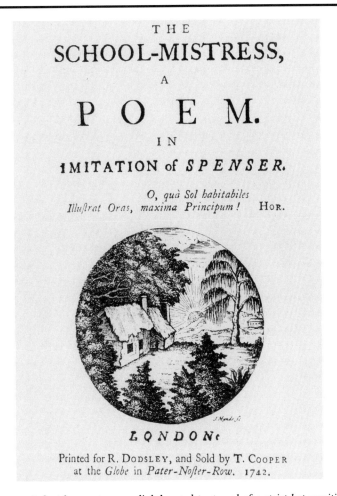

THE

SCHOOL-MISTRESS,

A

P O E M.

I N

IMITATION of SPENSER.

O, quà Sol habitabiles
Illustrat Oras, maxima Principum! HOR.

L O N D O N:

Printed for R. DODSLEY, and Sold by T. COOPER
at the *Globe* in *Pater-Noster-Row*. 1742.

Title page for Shenstone's best-known poem, a lighthearted portrayal of a strict but sensitive country teacher

tions and imaging capacity occasionally break through the affected Augustan poetic diction, as in "Elegy XXIII," to excite genuine emotion and to reveal his potential genius. Had Shenstone more often taken his own advice ("Write from thy bosom–let not art controul / The ready pen," he says in "Elegy I"), he might not have had to retire to Leasowes.

During the early 1740s Shenstone was quite prolific, experimenting with various kinds of poetry and prosody. In fact, most of what now forms his canon originated in these years. Rarely satisfied with his performance, however, Shenstone would temporarily abandon a poem and then later resurrect it for other purposes. One of these, "A Pastoral Ballad, in Four Parts. Written 1743"–which was to become one of his most popular poems after appearing in Dodsley's *Collection of Poems,* volume 4, in 1755–was begun upon parting from his first love, Mary Graves, his friend's sister, whom he had met on a trip to the Graves's

family home at Mickleton in 1736. In 1743 he revised the ballad, now in honor of another young lady, "Miss C----," who had stolen his heart while on a trip to Cheltenham in that year. Although thematically structured like so many similar predecessors–tales of despairing unrequited lovers–"A Pastoral Ballad" evokes more pity than sympathy for its fainthearted lover, Corydon (Shenstone), who has thoughtfully removed himself from his beloved's presence because he feels the diminutive size of his estate might not be acceptable to her. The poem has charm in its simple movement, economy, and stylized pastoral imagery, but more venturesome than Corydon is Shenstone's extensive use of anapest to effect the pace and rhythm of the ballad form.

From this period also stems a host of "songs" that later appeared either in the last three volumes of Dodsley's *Collection of Poems* or in the poet's collected *Works,* volume 1. None is especially remarkable, for each echoes typical love

271

Page from a 19 July 1758 letter written by Shenstone to engineer Matthew Boulton on behalf of John Scott Hylton
(by permission of the Matthew Boulton Trust and the Archives Department, Birmingham Library Services)

themes and language, although some reflect Shenstone's love interests treated above. Also mentioned in his correspondence of the time are the beginnings of three poems that would later develop into substantial pieces. His "favorite" among them, "Rural Elegance" (in *A Collection of Poems*, volume 5) is notable for both its espoused aesthetic principle and its verse form. After extolling the elegance of rural nature, Shenstone claims in the ode that art arranges nature to its best advantage: "Nature exalts the mound where art shall build; / Art shapes the gay alcove, while nature paints the field." Although by no means a new aesthetic, by applying it to his landscaping at Leasowes, Shenstone played a major role in shift-

ing contemporary taste from the geometrically formal gardens of the early eighteenth century to more natural shapings. The ode also shows Shenstone working with a rural theme in blank verse, after the mode of Thomson, an early visitor to Leasowes for whom Shenstone had much admiration.

The other two pieces he mentions in letters eventually appeared in *Works* as "Oeconomy, a Rhapsody" and "The Ruin'd Abbey; or the Effects of Superstition." Also in blank verse, they are overly long, dismal pieces that Robert Dodsley included in *Works* under the heading "Moral Pieces." Something of a hindsight piece, the first primarily admonishes young poets not to allow their poetic genius to be distracted by temporal ambition and pleasures and urges an attention to thrift that will allow them to endure in bad times. In the second, the sight of an abbey's moldering remnant wall prompts Shenstone, as rural bard, to review the corrupting effects of papal "superstition" on England from the time of Thomas à Becket and then to rejoice that once again peace reigns and the Muse has returned to her wooded haunts.

The year 1744 marked a turning point in Shenstone's career. Having finally given up hope of patronage, he capitulated and retired to Leasowes. "I have withdrawn all my views from court preferment," he told Jago in a 1744 letter (*Letters,* edited by Williams). But his failed efforts continued to haunt him amidst the distractions of landscaping the family farm. "The Progress of Taste" (in *Works*), a long autobiographical poem in octosyllabic couplets, records "Damon's" desperate attempts at fame, his present failure to attract the noble and the fair to his renovated estate, and his regret for thwarting the social passions by an early retirememt. Only the simple delights of gardening bear him up in his present poverty.

In 1748 Shenstone experienced a modest resurgence of poetic spirit. He wrote several verses, including "The Dying Kid" (*A Collection,* volume 5) and "Ode to Memory" (*A Collection,* volume 4), considered publishing his elegies, and although vexed with Robert Dodsley for printing the 1742 text of *The School-Mistress* in *A Collection of Poems* before it could be revised, he launched into a revision of it for the second edition of Dodsley's miscellany. For this new version, he dropped archaisms almost completely, rendered the sentence structure less quaint and the verse more graceful, and expanded the poem to thirty-five stanzas.

By the end of 1750 most of the poems on which Shenstone's reputation would stand had already been written. With a few exceptions, the thirteen poems to appear in volume 4 of Dodsley's *Collection of Poems* in 1755 and the thirty in volumes 5 and 6 in 1758 were revisions of earlier pieces. During these years in his "Castle of Indolence," as he called it in letters to his close friend Lady Luxborough, Shenstone had become more the host of Leasowes and less the poet. His efforts in the latter capacity were largely concerned with critical readings of his friends' pieces, jotting his *pensées* and letters, supplying Dodsley with various literary services (primarily revisions of the bookseller's tragedy *Cleone* [1758] and a translation of Lamotte-Houdar's

Shenstone in 1760 (painting by Edward Alcock; by permission of the National Portrait Gallery, London)

essay on fable [1719]), looking after John Baskerville's printing of Horace (1762), and assisting Thomas Percy in the selection and editing of his *Reliques* (1765).

In early 1763 Shenstone again had hopes of gaining a government pension through the influence of such noble friends as Lords Loughborough and Stamford; in fact, he thought a patent had actually been ordered. But before it could be awarded, he died on 11 February. He was buried beside his brother Joseph in Halesowen churchyard.

In his early years Shenstone had eagerly cultivated his modest share of poetic genius by imitating the standard poets of the time. In his middle years, perhaps sensing his limitations, he turned to experimenting with various poetic forms and verse styles–Miltonic blank verse, the Spenserian stanza, the quatrain stanza, octosyllabic couplets, and anapestic meter. His application of these modes of prosody to rural and moral themes significantly influenced the next generation of poets, particularly the Scots. His later verses became vehicles for personal reflections and moods, a subjectivity that helped pave the way for the Romantics.

Letters:

Select Letters between the Late Duchess of Somerset, Lady Luxborough, Mr. Whistler, Miss Dolman, Mr. R. Dodsley, William Shenstone, Esq., and Others, edited by Thomas Hull, 2 volumes (London: J. Dodsley, 1778);

Letters of William Shenstone, edited by Duncan Mallam (Minneapolis: University of Minnesota Press, 1939);

The Letters of William Shenstone, edited by Marjorie Williams (Oxford: Blackwell, 1939);

The Correspondence of Thomas Percy and William Shenstone, edited by Cleanth Brooks, volume 6 of *The Percy Letters* (New Haven: Yale University Press, 1977).

Biographies:

Richard Graves, *Recollections of Some Particulars in the Life of the Late William Shenstone, Esq.* (London: Printed for J. Dodsley, 1778);

Samuel Johnson, "The Life of Shenstone," in his *Lives of the English Poets,* 10 volumes (London: Printed by J. Nichols for C. Bathurst, 1779-1781); modern edition, edited by G. B. Hill, 3 volumes (Oxford: Oxford University Press, 1905);

J. F. Fullington, "Mr. William Shenstone," Ph.D. dissertation, Ohio State University, 1930;

E. Monro Purkis, *William Shenstone: Poet and Landscape Gardener* (Wolverhampton, U.K.: Whitehead, 1931);

Marjorie Williams, *William Shenstone and His Friends* (London: English Association, 1933);

Williams, *William Shenstone, A Chapter in Eighteenth Century Taste* (Birmingham, U.K.: Cornish, 1935);

A. R. Humphreys, *William Shenstone: An Eighteenth-Century Portrait* (Cambridge: Cambridge University Press, 1937);

Francis D. Burns, "William Shenstone: A Biographical and Critical Study," Ph.D. dissertation, University of Sheffield, 1970.

References:

Richmond P. Bond, "Shenstone's Heroi-Comical Poem," *Studies in Philology,* 28 (October 1931): 744-749;

F[rancis] D. A. Burns, "The First Published Version of Shenstone's 'Pastoral Ballad,'" *Review of English Studies,* 24 (May 1973): 182-185;

Randall Lee Calhoun, "William Shenstone's Aesthetic Theory and Poetry," Ph.D. dissertation, Ball State University, 1985;

Irving L. Churchill, "Shenstone's Billets," *Publications of the Modern Language Association,* 52 (March 1937): 114-121;

Churchill, "William Shenstone's Share in the Preparation of Percy's Reliques," *PMLA,* 51 (December 1936): 960-974;

A. J. Craig, "Shenstone and Burns," *Burns Chronicle,* 29 (1920): 86-89; 30 (1921): 67-80;

J. Fisher, "Shenstone, Gray, and the 'Moral Elegy,'" *Modern Philology,* 34 (1936-1937): 273-294;

Nicholas Gale, "The Work of William Shenstone," Ph.D. dissertation, Cornell University, 1944;

Alice I. Hazeltine, *A Study of William Shenstone and His Critics* (Menasha, Wis.: Collegiate Press, 1918);

Hans Hecht, *Thomas Percy und William Shenstone, ein Briefwechsel aus der Entstehungszeit der Reliques of Ancient English Poetry* (Strassburg: Trübner, 1909);

Charles Jarvis Hill, "Shenstone and Richard Graves's *Columella,*" *Publications of the Modern Language Association,* 49 (June 1934): 566-576;

Helen Sard Hughes, "Shenstone and the Countess of Hertford," *Publications of the Modern Language Association,* 44 (December 1931): 1113-1127;

Joe J. Keen, "William Shenstone and the English Dame School," Ph.D. dissertation, University of Colorado, 1966;

Edward Malins, *English Landscaping and Literature, 1660-1840* (London: Oxford University Press, 1966), pp. 65-79;

Duncan Mallam, "Some Inter-relationships of Shenstone's Essays, Letters, and Poems," *Philological Quarterly,* 28 (October 1949): 458-464;

Virginia F. Prettyman, "The Poetic Career of William Shenstone," Ph.D. dissertation, Yale University, 1943;

Prettyman, "Shenstone's Reading of Spenser," in *The Age of Johnson: Essays Presented to Chauncey Brewster Tinker,* edited by Frederick W. Hilles (New Haven & London: Yale University Press, 1949), pp. 227-237;

John C. Riely, "Shenstone's Walks: The Genesis of The Leasowes," *Apollo*, 110 (September 1979): 202-209;

James Sambrook, "Another Early Version of Shenstone's *Pastoral Ballad*," *Review of English Studies*, new series, 18 (May 1967): 169-173;

David Nichol Smith, "The Early Versions of Shenstone's *Pastoral Ballad*," *Review of English Studies*, 17 (January 1941): 47-54;

Ralph Straus, *Robert Dodsley: Poet, Publisher, & Playwright* (London: Lane, 1910), pp. 118-304;

James E. Tierney, *The Correspondence of Robert Dodsley 1733-1764* (Cambridge: Cambridge University Press, 1988);

Geoffrey Tillotson, "William Shenstone," in his *Essays in Criticism and Research* (Cambridge: Cambridge University Press, 1942), pp. 105-110;

James G. Turner, "The Sexual Politics of Landscape: Images of Venus in Eighteenth-Century English Poetry and Landscape Gardening," *Studies in Eighteenth-Century Culture*, 11 (1982): 343-366.

Jonathan Swift

(30 November 1667 - 19 October 1745)

Nora Crow Jaffe
Smith College

See also the Swift entry in *DLB 39: British Novelists, 1660-1800.*

SELECTED BOOKS: *A Discourse Of The Contests and Dissensions Between The Nobles and the Commons In Athens and Rome, With The Consequences they had upon both those States* (London: Printed for John Nutt, 1701; Boston, 1728);

A Tale Of A Tub, Written for the Universal Improvement of Mankind. Diu multumque desideratum. To which is added, An Account of a Battel Between the Antient and Modern Books in St. James's Library (London: Printed for John Nutt, 1704); enlarged as *A Tale of a Tub . . . The Fifth Edition: With the Author's Apology and Explanatory Notes* (London: Printed for John Nutt, 1710);

A Project For The Advancement of Religion, And the Reformation of Manners (London: Printed for Benj. Tooke, 1709);

Baucis and Philemon, Imitated from Ovid (N.p., 1709);

A Meditation Upon A Broom-Stick, and Somewhat Beside; Of The Same Author's (London: Printed for E. Curll & sold by J. Harding, 1710);

The Examiner, by Swift and others, 6 volumes (London: Printed for John Morphew, 1710-1714);

Miscellanies in Prose and Verse (London: Printed for John Morphew, 1711; enlarged edition, 5 volumes, London: Printed for Benjamin Motte, Lawton Gilliver & Charles Davis, 1727-1735);

The Conduct Of The Allies, And Of The Late Ministry, In Beginning and Carrying on The Present War (London: Printed for John Morphew, 1712 [i.e., 1711]);

The Fable of Midas (London: Printed for John Morphew, 1712);

A Proposal For Correcting, Improving and Ascertaining The English Tongue; In A Letter To the Most Honourable Robert Earl of Oxford and Mortimer, Lord High Treasurer of Great Britain (London: Printed for Benj. Tooke, 1712);

Part of the Seventh Epistle Of The First Book Of Horace Imitated: And Address'd to a Noble Peer (London: Printed for A. Dodd, 1713);

The First Ode Of The Second Book Of Horace Paraphras'd: And Address'd to Richard St—le, Esq (London: Printed for A. Dodd, 1713);

Jonathan Swift, circa 1718 (painting by Charles Jervas; by permission of the National Portrait Gallery, London)

The Lucubrations Of Isaac Bickerstaff Esq., 5 volumes (London: Printed for E. Nutt, A. Bell, J. Darby, A. Bettesworth, J. Pemberton, J. Hooke, C. Rivington, R. Cruttenden, T. Cox, J. Battley, F. Clay & E. Simon, 1720);

The Bubble: A Poem (London: Printed for Benj. Tooke & sold by J. Roberts, 1721);

Apollo's Edict (N.p., 1721);

Fraud Detected; Or, The Hibernian Patriot. Containing, All the Drapier's Letters to the People of Ireland, on Wood's Coinage, &c. (Dublin: Reprinted & sold by George Faulkner, 1725);

The Birth Of Manly Virtue From Callimachus (Dublin: Printed by & for George Grierson, 1725);

Cadenus and Vanessa. A Poem (Dublin, 1726);

Travels Into Several Remote Nations Of The World. In Four Parts. By Lemuel Gulliver, First a Surgeon, and then a Captain of several Ships, 2 volumes (London: Printed for Benj. Motte, 1726); enlarged as *Travels Into Several Remote Nations Of The World . . . To which are prefix'd, Several Copies of Verses Explanatory and Commendatory; never before printed*, 2 volumes (London: Printed for Benj. Motte, 1728);

The Intelligencer, by Swift and others (Dublin: Printed by S. Harding, 11 May 1728-7 May 1729; collected edition, London: Printed for Francis Cogan, 1730);

A Modest Proposal For preventing the Children Of Poor People From being a Burthen to their Parents, Or The Country, And For making them Ben-

eficial to the Publick (Dublin: Printed by S. Harding, 1729);

An Epistle Upon An Epistle From a certain Doctor To a certain great Lord: Being A Christmas-Box for D. D---y (Dublin, 1730);

An Epistle To His Excellency John Lord Carteret, Lord Lieutenant of Ireland (Dublin, 1730);

A Libel On D-------- D--------- And A Certain Great Lord (N.p., 1730);

Lady A–S–N Weary of the Dean [single sheet] (N.p., 1730);

A Panegyric On the Reverend Dean Swift (London: Printed for J. Roberts & N. Blandford, 1730);

An Apology To The Lady C–R–T (N.p., 1730);

Horace Book I. Ode XIV. O navis, referent, &c. Paraphrased and inscribed to Ir–d (N.p., 1730);

Traulus . . . In A Dialogue Between Tom and Robin, 2 volumes (N.p., 1730);

A Soldier And A Scholar: Or The Lady's Judgment Upon those two Characters In the Persons of Captain— and D–n S–T (London: Printed for J. Roberts, 1732); republished as *The Grand Question debated* (London: Printed by A. Moore, 1732);

An Elegy On Dicky and Dolly, With the Virgin: A Poem. To which is Added The Narrative of D. S. when he was in the North of Ireland (Dublin: Printed by James Hoey, 1732);

The Lady's Dressing Room (London: Printed for J. Roberts, 1732);

The Life And Genuine Character Of Doctor Swift, Written by Himself (London: Printed for J. Roberts, 1733);

An Epistle To A Lady, Who desired the Author to make Verses on Her, In The Heroick Stile. Also A Poem, Occasion'd by Reading Dr. Young's Satires, Called the Universal Passion (Dublin & London: Printed for J. Wilford, 1734 [i.e., 1733]);

On Poetry: A Rapsody (Dublin & London: Printed & sold by J. Huggonson, 1733);

A Beautiful Young Nymph Going to Bed. Written for the Honour of the Fair Sex. Pars minima est ipsa Puella sui. Ovid Remed. Amoris. To Which Are Added, Strephon and Chloe. And Cassinus and Peter (Dublin & London: Printed for J. Roberts, 1734);

The Works of J. S, D.D, D.S.P.D., 4 volumes (Dublin: Printed by & for George Faulkner, 1735; enlarged to 20 volumes, 1738-1772);

An Imitation Of The Sixth Satire Of The Second Book Of Horace, by Swift and Alexander Pope (London: Printed for B. Motte, C. Bathurst &

J. & P. Knapton, 1738);

The Beasts Confession To The Priest, On Observing how most Men mistake their own Talents. Written in the Year 1732 (Dublin: Printed by George Faulkner, 1738);

A Complete Collection Of Genteel and Ingenious Conversation, According to the Most Polite Mode and Method Now Used at Court, and in the Best Companies of England. In Three Dialogues, as Simon Wagstaff (London: Printed for B. Motte & C. Bathurst, 1738); also published as *A Treatise On Polite Conversation* (Dublin: Printed by & for George Faulkner, 1738); dramatized as *Tittle Tattle; Or, Taste A-la-Mode. A New Farce. Perform'd with Universal Applause by a Select Company Of Belles and Beaux, At The Lady Brilliant's Withdrawing-Room*, as Timothy Fribble (London: Printed for R. Griffiths, 1749);

Verses On The Death Of Dr. Swift. Written by Himself: Nov. 1731 (London: Printed for C. Bathurst, 1739);

Directions To Servants (Dublin: Printed by George Faulkner, 1745); enlarged as *Directions To Servants In General* (London: Printed for R. Dodsley & M. Cooper, 1745);

The Last Will And Testament Of Jonathan Swift, D.D. (Dublin & London: Printed & sold by M. Cooper, 1746);

D–n Sw–t's Medley (Dublin & London: Printed & sold by the booksellers, 1749);

The History of the Four Last Years of the Queen (London: Printed for A. Millar, 1758).

Editions and Collections: *The Works Of Dr. Jonathan Swift*, 14 volumes (London: Printed for C. Bathurst, 1751);

The Works Of D. Jonathan Swift . . . To which is prefixed, The Doctor's Life, with Remarks on his Writings, from the Earl of Orrery and others, not to be found in any former Edition of his Works, 9 volumes (Dublin & Edinburgh: Printed for G. Hamilton, J. Balfour & L. Hunter, 1752);

The Works of Dr. Jonathan Swift . . . With Some Account of the Author's Life, And Notes Historical and Explanatory, edited by John Hawkesworth, Deane Swift, and John Nichols, 27 volumes (London: Printed for C. Bathurst, 1754-1779);

The Sermons of the Reverend Dr. Jonathan Swift (Glasgow: Printed for Robert Urie, 1763);

The Works Of The Rev. Dr. Jonathan Swift . . . Arranged, Revised, And Corrected, With Notes, edited by Thomas Sheridan, 17 volumes (London: Printed for C. Bathurst, 1784); cor-

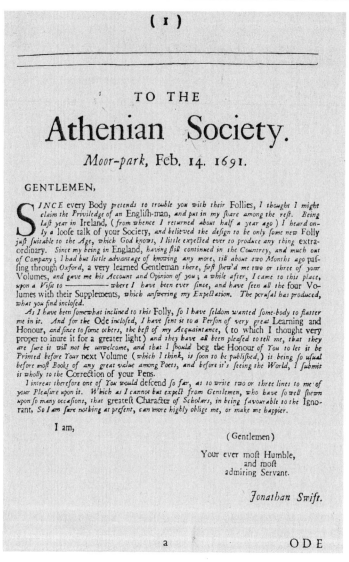

(I)

TO THE

Athenian Society.

Moor-park, Feb. 14. 1691.

GENTLEMEN,

SINCE every Body *pretends to trouble you with their* Follies, *I thought I might claim the Priviledge of an* Englifh-man, *and put in my fhare among the reft. Being laft year in* Ireland, (*from whence I returned about half a year ago*) *I heard only a* loose talk of your Society, *and believed the defign to be only fome new* Folly *juft fuitable to the* Age, *which God knows, I little expected ever to produce any thing* extraordinary. *Since my being in* England, *having ftill continued in the Countrey, and much out of Company ; I had but little advantage of knowing any more, till about two Months ago paffing through* Oxford, *a very learned Gentleman there, firft fhew'd me two or three of your* Volumes, *and gave me his Account and Opinion of you ; a while after, I came to this place, upon a Vifit to* ———— *where I have been ever fince, and have feen all the four Volumes with their* Supplements, *which anfwering my Expectation. The perufal has produced, what you find inclofed.*

As I have been fomewhat inclined to this Folly, fo I have feldom wanted fome-body to flatter me in it. And for the Ode *inclofed, I have fent it to a Perfon of very great* Learning *and* Honour, *and fince to fome others, the beft of my Acquaintance,* (*to which I thought very proper to inure it for a greater light*) *and they have all been pleafed to tell me, that they are fure it will not be unwelcome, and that I fhould* beg the Honour of You *to let it be* Printed *before Your* next Volume (*which I think, is foon to be publifhed,*) *it being fo ufual before moft Books of any great value among Poets, and before it's feeing the World, I fubmit it wholly to the* Correction of your Pens.

I intreat therefore one of You would defcend fo far, as to write two or three lines to me of your Pleafure upon it. Which as I cannot but expect from Gentlemen, who have fo well fhewn upon fo many occafions, that greateft Character of Scholars, *in being favourable to the* Ignorant, *So I am fure nothing at prefent, can more highly oblige me, or make me happier.*

I am,

(Gentlemen)

Your ever moft Humble,
and moft
admiring Servant.

Jonathan Swift.

a   O D E

The cover letter for Swift's "Ode to the Athenian Society," as it appeared before the poem in the Athenian Gazette, *no. 467 (1691)–his first publication*

rected and revised by Nichols, 24 volumes (London: Printed for J. Johnson, John Nichols & Son, 1803; New York: Durell, 1812);

The Poetical Works of Jonathan Swift, edited by Thomas Park, 4 volumes (London: Printed by Charles Whittingham for J. Sharpe & sold by W. Suttaby, 1806);

The Works Of Jonathan Swift . . . Containing Additional Letters, Tracts, And Poems, Not Hitherto Published; With Notes, And A Life Of The Author, edited by Sir Walter Scott, 19 volumes (Edinburgh: Printed for Archibald Constable & Co., 1814);

The Works of Jonathan Swift . . . Containing Interesting and Valuable Papers, Not Hitherto Published, edited by Thomas Roscoe, 2 volumes (London: Washbourne, 1841);

The Poems of Jonathan Swift, edited by Harold Williams, 3 volumes (Oxford: Clarendon Press, 1937; revised, 1958);

Collected Poems of Jonathan Swift, edited by Joseph Horrell, 2 volumes (London: Routledge & Kegan Paul / Cambridge, Mass.: Harvard University Press, 1958);

Swift: Poetical Works, edited by Herbert Davis (Oxford: Standard Authors; London: Oxford University Press, 1967);

Gulliver's Travels, edited by Robert A. Greenberg (New York: Norton, 1970);

Jonathan Swift: The Complete Poems, edited by Pat Rogers (London: Penguin Books / New Haven: Yale University Press, 1983).

OTHER: "Ode to the Athenian Society," in *The Supplement To The Fifth Volume Of The Athenian Gazette* (London: Printed for John Dunton, 1692);

Memoirs Of Capt. John Creichton. Written by Himself, edited by Swift (N.p., 1731);

"The Legion Club," in *S---t contra omnes. An Irish Miscellany* (Dublin & London: Sold by R. Amy & Mrs. Dodd, 1736).

(Editor's note: In a break from normal *DLB* procedure, the contributor has insisted that conjectural dates of composition, instead of dates of publication, be inserted after Swift's titles in the text.)

Jonathan Swift–author of *A Tale Of A Tub* (1704), *Gulliver's Travels* (1726), and *A Modest Proposal* (1729)–was the greatest prose satirist in the history of English literature. Since the recent publication of five monographs and a collection of essays on the subject of his poetry, he has also become recognized as a master of satiric verse. His poetry has a relationship either by interconnections with, or by reactions against, the poetry of his contemporaries and predecessors. He was probably influenced, in particular, by the Restoration writers John Wilmot, Earl of Rochester, and Samuel Butler (who shared Swift's penchant for octosyllabic verse). He may have picked up pointers from the Renaissance poets John Donne and Sir Philip Sidney (from whom he may have adopted the name "Stella" for his best friend, Esther Johnson). That is all, however, one can say with certainty. Beside the borrowings of his contemporaries, his debts are almost negligible. In the Augustan Age, of all periods, his poetic contribution was strikingly original.

In reading Swift's poems, one is first impressed with their apparent spareness of allusion and poetic device. Anyone can tell that a particular poem is powerful or tender or vital or fierce, but all the paraphernalia of criticism seems inadequate to explain why. A few recent critics have carefully studied his use of allusion and image, but with only partial success. Thus it still seems justified to conclude that Swift's prosody seldom calls for close analysis, his allusions seldom bring a whole literary past back to life, and his images

are not very interesting in themselves. In general, Swift's verses read faster than John Dryden's or Alexander Pope's. He apparently intends to sweep the reader along by the logic of the argument to the several conclusions he puts forth. He seems to expect that the reader will appreciate the implications of the argument as a whole, after one full and rapid reading. For Swift's readers, the couplet will not revolve slowly upon itself, exhibiting intricate patterns and fixing complex relationships between fictive worlds and contemporary life.

The poems are not always so spare in reality as Swift would have his readers believe. But he seems deliberately to induce in them an unwillingness to look closely at the poems for evidence of technical expertise. He does this in part by working rather obviously against some poetic conventions, in part by saying openly that he rejects poetic cant, and in part by presenting himself–in many of his poems–as a perfectly straightforward man, incapable of a poet's deviousness. By these strategies, he directs attention away from his handling of imagery and meter, even in those instances where he has been technically ingenious. For the most part, however, the impression of spareness is quite correct; and if judged by the sole criterion of technical density, then he would have to be judged an insignificant poet. But technical density is a poetic virtue only as it stimulates and accompanies subtlety of thought. One could argue that Swift's poems create a density of another kind: that "The Day of Judgement" (1731?), for example, initiates a subtle process of thought that takes place after, rather than during, the reading of the poem, at a time when the mind is more or less detached from the printed page. One could argue as well that Swift makes up in power what he lacks in density: that the strength of the impression created by his directness gives an impetus to prolonged meditation of a very high quality. On these grounds, valuing Swift for what he really is and does, one must judge him a major figure in poetry as well as prose.

Where does Swift obtain his power, if not from the formal devices of conventional poetry? He generates it in part from the sheer force of his personality, from what the critic Maurice Johnson has called his "biographical presence." When the reader's attention does not engage with the form, it engages more immediately with the nature of the poet. The effect of technical spareness is to throw emphasis not only on the subject

First page of the manuscript for one of Swift's poems about the house that John Vanbrugh, dramatist and architect, built for himself on the ruins of Whitehall Palace (by permission of the Pierpont Morgan Library)

matter, but on the mind of the man who treats it. That is why one can say with a certain justice that readers like some poems because they like *Swift*. Where he has not been so successful in controlling the impression he creates, one may dislike the poem because one dislikes a quality—coyness in *Cadenus and Vanessa* (1713), or sadism in "The Legion Club" (1736), or vanity in *Verses On The Death Of Dr. Swift* (1731)—that the poet projects. In reading the poems, where Swift allowed himself greater emotional latitude than in his prose, the audience comes face-to-face with a fascinating personality, one whose railing and coaxing can never simply be ignored.

Besides the force of the man himself, one can appreciate in the poetry the complex rhetorical strategies that Swift invented to persuade his readers. In his satirical poems, the primary interpretive challenge lies in distinguishing Swift's voice from those of the ironical speakers in which it is embedded. Along with others, this device operates in the prose works as well. By means of a persona in *A Modest Proposal*, for example, Swift first seduces the reader and then betrays him. His poem "The Day of Judgement" depends upon a more sophisticated version of the same maneuver. Both the minor prose works (like *A Meditation Upon A Broom-Stick*, 1710) and the major prose works (*Gulliver's Travels* and "A Digression concerning . . . Madness" from *A Tale Of A Tub*, for example) owe a great deal of their trenchancy to Swift's willingness to satirize himself, usually in the role of vindictive and ineffectual satirist, before he turns his weapon against his readers. His political poem *An Epistle To A Lady* (1733) derives some of its power from the same source.

The apparent spareness of Swift's verse closes off some common avenues of research. At the same time, his nearness to the surface of his poems and his rhetorical dexterity open other prospects for critical reading and evaluation. How well he uses his personality to shape the reader's response and how well his strategies work to break down the traditional alliance between satirist and reader and compel the audience to see its face in the glass of satire—these are legitimate subjects for critical inquiry. Whatever his lack of interest in the other aspects of poetry, or rather, however strong his disdain for them, his facility at what he does do proves him an indispensable poet. These poems are not expendable. Anyone who thinks so should try imitating them. By the force of his personality and the richness of his satiric experience, Swift does things with poetry that other poets simply cannot do.

Jonathan Swift was born in Dublin, of English parents, seven months after his father died. His mother, Abigail Erick, may have been born in Ireland; but his father, also named Jonathan, immigrated to Ireland in about 1660. Swift spent little of his childhood with his mother. As an infant, he was kidnapped by his nurse, who took him to her home in Whitehaven and kept him there for three years. Only a few years after his return to his mother, he was sent to grammar school in Kilkenny; and she and his sister Jane moved to England. In 1682 he entered Trinity College, Dublin, where he was to spend six years. Irvin Ehrenpreis has exploded the myth of Swift's deplorable academic record at T.C.D. He did passably well, very well in Greek and Latin, less well in metaphysics and rhetoric. Although he did take his B.A. degree *speciali gratia*, this fairly common dispensation was not a mark of disgrace. Upon leaving Trinity College, he went to England and visited his mother for a few months, then moved to the estate of Sir William Temple, whose father had been a family friend. At Moor Park and (later) Sheen, he served Temple as a kind of secretary. While living with Temple, he also experienced the first symptoms of what we now know was Ménière's syndrome, a disturbance of the inner ear that caused him vertigo and deafness for the rest of his life. He applied for and received the M.A. degree from Oxford University in 1692.

Swift wrote his early odes in part to please Temple, and he probably adopted some points of view that fit Temple better than himself. All but the last two of the poems are written in the Pindaric manner, which required from the poet irregularity, obscurity, and grandeur. He labored hard to fulfill these requirements. His lines are sometimes so irregular that the reader cannot say them aloud without pausing awkwardly or slurring words together. A couple of lines from his "Ode to the King. On his Irish Expedition. And The Success of his Arms in general" (1691; published in *Miscellanies*, volume 4, 1735) illustrate the difficulties: "And what I us'd to laugh at in *Romance* / And thought too great ev'n for effects of Chance. . . ." The same poem, though not the most obscure of the odes, is surely obscure enough. Swift writes a whole stanza about James II without identifying him by name. The only clues about the subject of the stanza are the phrase "Your fond *Enemy*" and the vague biographical facts of the description. Perhaps realizing how difficult his poetry could be, Swift studs his early odes with footnotes; yet many almost incomprehensible lines, like certain passages from the "Ode to the Athenian Society" (1691), he leaves unannotated. He seems to glory in his obscurity and take it as evidence of kinship with his models. He may have associated obscurity with grandeur, the third of the Pindaric requirements. The whole tenor of his poems shows his eagerness for epic dignity. Especially telling is the kind of writer (Homer, Virgil, Milton, Dryden) he chooses to imitate.

But Swift clearly thought Abraham Cowley the best of his models, and the degree to which the odes depend on Cowley testifies to this admiration. The "Ode to the Athenian Society" is an obvious reply to Cowley's "Ode to the Royal Society" (1667). The Platonism in the first and the assertion of faith–"I believe in much, I ne're can hope to see"–answer the scientific skepticism in the second. Ehrenpreis finds not only general parallels to Cowley, but also echoes of him in the details of the odes, especially in the "Ode to the King," the "Ode to the Honourable Sir William Temple" (1692), and the ode "To Mr. Congreve" (1693), the last two being collected in the 1711 *Miscellanies*.

Swift's borrowings throw light on his conception of himself in the 1690s, and that conception is quite pompous. The writers he imitates prove that he wanted to be a heroic poet. His use of the old poetic conceits shows that he thought of himself as a traditional writer, not as the poetic maverick he was to become. The odes reveal that for the young Swift poetry was a conventionally divine calling. In the ode "Occasioned by Sir William Temple's late Illness and Recovery" (1693; *Miscellanies*, 1711), he speaks of a poetic priesthood and includes himself among the initiated: "Unknown the forms we the high-priesthood use / At the divine appearance of the Muse, / Which to divulge might shake profane belief, / And tell the irreligion of my grief. . . ." In the "Ode to the Honourable Sir William Temple," he says that he owes his vocation to Nature's decree, that she has tied him to the muse's oar. And like Pope after him, he claims that he cannot help himself.

In later life Swift was to ridicule the ideas of the divinity and inevitability of the poetic calling, as well as a number of other high-flown notions about poets and poetry. At some points in the odes, a more familiar personality seems to break through. Swift occasionally puns, makes co-vert jokes, and bursts into invective. Usually in these passages, when he begins to write like the Swift of the satires, the meter becomes more regular and the poetry more coherent. The early odes are, nonetheless, failures. Swift seems to recognize as much when he bids farewell to his youthful style in "Sir William Temple's late Illness," the last of the odes. Speaking to his muse, he says: "There thy enchantment broke, and from this hour / I here renounce thy visionary pow'r; / And since thy essence on my breath depends, / Thus with a puff the whole delusion ends." He dismisses the muse of the odes because she has failed to provide him with the hope of success– probably in the eyes of Temple. A long silence of five years ensues before he begins to write for himself rather than for his mentor. The new poems have none of the pomposity of the early odes. Swift had begun to develop an animus against the complacencies and posturings of conventional poetry that was to last for the rest of his life.

In 1695 Swift was ordained in Ireland as an Anglican priest and appointed to the prebend of Kilroot, an impoverished stall in a bleak neighborhood offering few parishioners and a meager income of a hundred pounds a year. In this vicinity he met Jane Waring ("Varina"), to whom he proposed marriage. The relationship was to end under the pressure of Swift's curt demands that Varina rearrange her life and reform her character. In 1696 he returned to Moor Park. After Temple's death in 1699, he returned to Ireland as domestic chaplain to the earl of Berkeley. In 1700 he was appointed vicar of Laracor, in County Meath, and prebend of St. Patrick's Cathedral, Dublin. In 1702 he was granted the D.D. degree by Trinity College, Dublin.

Swift liked to claim that he was a Whig in the decade before 1710, and he was certainly friends with the Whig writers Joseph Addison and Richard Steele. He was not, however, sympathetic to the Whig Junto and expressed opposition to favorite Whig policies: the toleration of Dissenters, the repeal of the Sacramental Test, the Act of Union with Scotland. In 1710 he became firmly associated with the Tories. He had traveled to London in September on behalf of the Church of Ireland to seek remission of the First Fruits, a substantial tax imposed upon the clergy by Queen Anne. There he met Robert Harley, leader of the new Tory ministry, who recruited him as a propagandist by helping him obtain the remission he was seeking. Although J. A. Downie has recently argued that Swift never really be-

Swift's close friend Esther Johnson (Stella), whom he met in 1689, when she was eight years old (painting by James Latham; by permission of the National Gallery of Ireland)

came a Tory, the more conventional view of his politics focuses on his friendship with the Tory ministers and his support for the Tory causes in his famous *Examiner* papers (1710-1711). Ehrenpreis sees his poems "A Description of the Morning" (1709) and "A Description of a City Shower" (1710), both collected in *Miscellanies* (1711), as the last works associated with his Whiggish phase.

"A Description of the Morning" has as its governing principle the interplay of order and disorder. Whether lowly or exalted, the figures who appear in the poem have duties that should contribute to the ordering of their world. Betty, who flies from her master's bed like Aurora from the bed of Tithonus, is presumably a servant girl with responsibilities for keeping the household in order. The apprentice is supposed to be cleaning the dirt from around his master's door. Moll is caught with her mop in midair, just prepared to scrub. The youth should be using his broom to sweep, not merely to find old nails. Turnkeys and bailiffs have the job of seeing that society—like houses, stairs, streets, and chimneys—is kept clean. His Lordship, at the apex of his world, has the broadest duties of all.

Most of these figures charged with preserving order are actively engaged in disrupting it. The apprentice scatters the dirt as fast as he pares it away. The turnkey, a modern shepherd with a convict flock, promotes crime for his own profit. His Lordship, who should be supervising the work of social sanitation, is hiding from his creditors. Even the bailiffs do no more than stand in silence. But at the same time, with the breaking of dawn, as real order appears in its death throes, a false impression of order is coming alive. Betty is returning to her own bed, and the convicts are returning to prison. Swift's irony reaches the highest level of complexity in the case of the servant girl. Participating in an illicit relationship that reflects the general disorder, Betty preserves the illusion of order by disordering her bed to give the impression she has slept there.

Swift seems to be suggesting that radical disorder is the state of this world, and the best that can ever be attained is a frail and unstable impression of order. He emphasizes the sense of disorderly flux by catching all his characters at a transitional moment, when the reality is just coming into contact with the respectable illusion. The moment comes at dawn–the transition between night and day. Betty is between beds. The apprentice has hardly started on his real work. Moll is merely prepared to scrub; and interestingly enough, she is prepared only for the entry and the stairs–the most visible and public parts, the avenues into disorderly houses. The youth is just beginning to trace the kennel edge. Duns are beginning to gather at his Lordship's door. Moll has screamed through only half a street. The turnkeys, the bailiffs, and the schoolboys have as yet no idea of what the night has brought or the day will bring.

Why this interest in the beginnings of things– in the dynamics of a situation rather than in static pictures? Why this interest in a particular moment? In introducing Swift's poem in his *Tatler* (1709-1711), Steele said that the author was concerned with "incidents just as they really appear," not with fantastical descriptions cranked out by poets and steeped in classical clichés. Perhaps things as they are appear in their truest light when shown in contrast with what they are not. And they are not orderly, complete, static, or even necessarily moral.

Yet the lines themselves contain no notes of rancor or censure. The primary clue to the proper reception of this poem is simply the absence of any disparaging comment from Swift. The poem contains no focused objects of blame. Whom is one to accuse: Betty, or her master? The turnkey, or the prisoners? The whole city? For what? In speaking nostalgically of the lagging schoolboys, in a line reminiscent of Shakespeare's "Ages of Man" speech, Swift mixes the clearly innocent with the dubious. The whole listing procedure implies equality: screaming Moll is no more disgusting than a reluctant schoolboy. As for the screaming, it might well have been music to Swift's ears. London street cries interested him so

much that he wrote half a dozen delightful imitations of them. The cries of Brickdust Moll, the cadence of the Smallcoal-Man, and the shriller notes of the Chimney-Sweep make up the kind of urban symphony that Swift could find charming. Details like these, realized so vividly, work with the other evidence to prove this poem is not about hating London. One must assume that a man who listened so carefully and saw so clearly rather enjoyed things as they really were. Instead of invoking Virgil's *Georgics* (first century B.C.) in order to censure the city, Swift has adapted them to modern life.

Although Swift preferred "A Description of a City Shower," his mock-eclogue, to "A Description of the Morning," the later poem is the less coherent. Unless one assumes, like Brendan O Hehir, that the poem is a premonition of doom for a damned city, "A Description of a City Shower" appears a compilation of urban sights and sounds freshly perceived by a writer who has been tucked away for too long in the Irish countryside. As if conscious of his audience in Ireland, Swift flaunts his familiarity with the small drawbacks of London life. "Look what *we* Londoners have to put up with," he seems to say; and to emphasize the point, he includes a portrait of a bedraggled poet fleeing from the rain. A famous triplet ends the poem: "Sweepings from Butchers Stalls, Dung, Guts, and Blood, / Drown'd Puppies, stinking Sprats, all drench'd in Mud, / Dead Cats and Turnip-Tops come tumbling down the Flood." The final lines are indeed repulsive. They are meant in part to parody Dryden's triplets. But more than anything else, they reveal Swift's gruff sense of belonging among the eminent Englishmen he had come to know.

In 1689, at Moor Park, Swift had met "Stella" (Hester or Esther) Johnson, who was then a girl of eight, nearly fourteen years his junior. She was the daughter of Temple's late steward and Bridget Johnson, to whom Sir William made several annual payments. Some have cited Temple's generosity to Swift and Stella as evidence that the two were related by blood (and could therefore never marry); but the arguments are more ingenious than convincing. Ehrenpreis believes that Temple was drawn to Bridget Johnson's eldest child, and bequeathed her a lease of lands worth a thousand pounds, because his own beloved daughter had died shortly before Stella's birth. Swift befriended both Stella, whom he described in 1699 as "one of the most beautiful, graceful, and agreeable young women in Lon-

Apollo to the Dean

Right Trusty (and so forth) we let you to know,
We are very ill us'd by you Mortals below.
For, first, I have often by Chimists been told,
(Though I know nothing on't) it is I that make Gold,
Which when you have got, you so carefully hide it,
That since I was born, I hardly have spy'd it.
Then, it must be allow'd that whenever I shine
I forward the Grass, and I ripen the Vine;
To me the good Fellows apply for Relief
Without whom they could get neither Claret nor Beef;
Yet their Wine and their Vittels, those Curmudgeon Lubbards
Lock up from my Sight in Cellars and Cubbords:
That I have an ill eye they wickedly think,
And taint all their Meat, and sow'r all their Drink.
But thirdly, and lastly, it must be allow'd
I alone can inspire the Poeticall Croud;
This is gratefully own'd by each Boy in the Colledge,
Whom if I inspire, it is not to my Knoledge;
This ev'ry Pretender in Rime will admit,
Without troubling his Head about Judgment or Wit:
These Gentlemen use me with Kindness and Freedom,
And as for their Works, when I please I may read 'em;
They ly open on Purpose on Counters and Stalls,
And the Titles I view when I shine on the Walls.
    But a Comrade of yours, that Traitor Delany
Whom I for your sake have us'd better than any,
And of my meer Motion, and speciall good Grace,
Intended in time to succeed in your Place;
On Tuesday the tenth, seditiously came
With a certain false Traitress, one Stella by name,
To the Deanery House, and on the North Glass
Where for fear of the Cold, I never can pass,
Then and there, vi et armis, with a certain Utensill
Of value five shillings, in English a Pencill,
Did maliciously, falsly, and traitrously write,
While Stella aforesaid stood by with the Light;

First page of the manuscript for the poem Swift wrote about his friends Stella and Dr. Patrick Delany, circa 1720, after the two had written a poem on the window glass of Swift's deanery (MA 1207; by permission of the Pierpont Morgan Library)

don," and her older companion, Rebecca Dingley, Sir William's spinster cousin. In 1701 he persuaded the two women to come to live near him in Dublin; apart from a trip to England in 1708, they never left Ireland again.

Besides being beautiful, Stella endeared herself to Swift by being at once spirited and teachable. He directed her education and shaped her character on the model of his own. Although no evidence exists that the two were ever married, or ever had sex, or (for that matter) were ever alone together, Stella was always to be Swift's best friend and truest love. When in 1704 his acquaintance and fellow clergyman William Tisdall proposed to marry Stella, Swift dragged his feet and made his feelings just clear enough to cause her to break off the match. Ehrenpreis says that at her death, in 1728, Swift must have sensed that his real life was over.

Swift was interested in developing an original form of compliment for his best friend. "To Stella, Who Collected and Transcribed his Poems" (1720) provides the reasons that he despised the love poets of the Renaissance and the Restoration: they praised the wrong women, for the wrong motives, in the wrong way, and for the wrong things. Their heroines were degenerate, susceptible to seduction, hardly worthy of writing about in poetic style. The poets praised them in order to seduce them. The images these writers scratched their heads to summon up were trite, empty, and insincere. The womanly qualities they praised were beauty and "kindness," not virtue. Swift evokes the tradition of compliment to ladies and either dismisses it with ridicule or transforms it into something he can approve of. In his first birthday poem for Stella, written in 1719, her nickname sets up the ridicule, for "Stella" reminds the reader of Sidney and all those poetical goddesses, with names ending in *a*, who frequented England in the golden time. The references to nymphs and swains also recall the complimentary tradition and clash bathetically with the fact that Stella is fat and middle-aged. Swift proves to the reader that he can write a better compliment than his predecessors, because he takes actuality into account and still manages to indicate that Stella is twice as beautiful and twice as wise as any other woman. At the same time, he proves to Stella that he loves her, for the compliment absorbs so much of the insulting truth that it must be sincere. Besides, Stella would know that in the course of teasing, one veers so close to insult only with people one loves and trusts. The complimen-

tary strategy is raillery, Swift's primary rhetorical device for pleasing the women he loves. It credits the woman addressed with intelligence and humor sufficient to understand the poem.

Swift's ridicule extends to all the trappings of the complimentary tradition, even to the traditional claims about inspiration and originality. The first stanza of "Stella's Birth-Day. A great Bottle of Wine, long buried, being that Day dug up" (1723) presents the poet unable to write well because "Long-thinking" hinders the work of his imagination. The reader expects Swift's muse to intervene with advice that he look in his heart and write, but the idea of inspiration is too high-flown for his taste, and the claim to originality has been too much abused. He substitutes alcohol for the promptings of the muse and implies that the spring of inspiration is more a mechanical coil than a metaphysical fountain. The appearance of the muse is a hallucination common to rhyming drunkards, and the real motive for summoning the muse is not so much love as reputation.

He corrects the tradition by redefining its favorite terms, as well as by ridiculing it. "To Stella, Who Collected and Transcribed his Poems" begins with a traditional assertion that all the merit and the praise of the poetry should be Stella's. But where Shakespeare and Sidney claim that the immortal beauty and grace of their subjects make their poems immortal, Swift explicitly dissociates Stella and his poems from such qualities. Stella deserves the credit if his poetry endures, because it reflects her virtue—not because it reflects the accidentals of appearance. Stella may be an angel; in "Stella's Birth-day. Written A.D. 1720-21," she is alternately the sign and the hostess of the Angel-Inn. But she is not quite so ethereal as her counterparts in the Renaissance and Restoration. The poet endows her with all the humanity of a good-natured barmaid; and her face, though "An Angel's Face," is "a little crack't."

Swift redefines the idea of "honor" in his poem "To Stella, Visiting me in my Sickness" (1720). He deliberately leads the reader to believe that he is about to treat feminine honor in the traditional sense, for he says that Pallas, seeing Stella's beauty, must fix honor in her mind to prevent the disruption of the state. For the benefit of a stupid, vicious age, he explains that he has in mind neither the courtly female virtue nor the courtly male virtue, neither chastity nor the "Quarrels of a Rake." He means, instead, the kind of fair dealing characteristic of the Augustan good man. The idea includes chastity, but only by implication. He compliments Stella for asexual virtues. His emphasis falls on qualities usually associated with men. He comically suggests that the gods mistook Stella's sex when they allotted virtues to her. It is a strange suggestion, and one which recurs in *Cadenus and Vanessa*. Like Swift's comparisons of Lady Anne Acheson to a skeleton, devoid of any sexual characteristics, the "masculinity" of these women, his pupils and very much his junior, might have shored up the formal relationship between himself and them by helping him forget their sexual identity. Whatever its psychological function, the idea may be a necessary step away from usual kinds of poetic condescension. This emphasis on masculine qualities and the contrast he draws between Stella's patience and his own "unmanly" complaints neutralize any sexual possibilities. Instead of aiming at seduction, the poet is presenting a pattern for female behavior which is as much a pattern for all human behavior.

When Stella lay dying, Swift wrote for her "Stella's Birth-Day. March 13. 1726/7," the most moving of his poems and the one that best displays his capacity for tenderness, his honesty, and his strength of mind. He begins with a full concession to the seriousness of the situation. The phrase "whate'er the Fates decree," like the later "whatever Heav'n intends," implies his willingness to face the bitterest fact that he and Stella can confront. The voice of a man able to see reality in the worst of lights predominates throughout the poem and confirms that the offered comfort is realistic. But in the first fourteen lines Swift is mostly occupied with a different stance toward his friend and his own feelings. Despite his recognition of her imminent death, he wants to postpone mourning and worry over her sickness his old age and "mortifying Stuff" about "Spectacles and Pills." He does not wish to talk about death, but rather to celebrate the day.

This less serious style, however, proves inadequate to the moment. The long central passage that follows is not at all humorous, and the extended argument is clearly intended to comfort the two friends in the face of death. Though Swift has desired to put off the thought of death, he has not done so. His honesty appeals to certain universal emotions. His determination to argue from "Reason" and his recommendation of the virtues of courage, contentment, and patience reinforce the reader's admiration. He could have turned to Christian doctrine to palliate the evils of death. Instead, he chooses to persuade Stella on rational grounds that virtue can make her happy and makes a temporary concession to atheism that Heaven and Hell might not exist as recompense for goodness and vice.

In this middle section the love is only implicit, for Swift has suppressed everything personal. Abstract reasoning sets the tone. Stella herself becomes something of an abstraction, full of estimable qualities. As if realizing that this style will not suffice in the end, he turns to an open and personal declaration of love. The last lines of the poem define the human context by focusing on the relationship between the two friends:

> Me, surely me, you ought to spare,
> Who gladly would your Suff'rings share;
> Or give my Scrap of Life to you,
> And think it far beneath your Due;
> You, to whose Care so oft I owe,
> That I'm alive to tell you so.

The professions verge on the extreme, but they are expressed in simple, tonic phrases. Preceding them is a description of the kind of hard fact that requires Swiftian strength to face. Speaking of Stella and her friends, specifically himself, he says, "Nor let your Ills affect your Mind, / To fancy they can be unkind." The extraordinary tacit realizations and admissions of these lines suggest the most unsentimental kind of observation and analysis, but do nothing to undercut the impression of overwhelming love.

Though the prospect of Stella's death could drive Swift in the direction of open compliment, he seems to have been much more comfortable with obliquity. His mode of indirect compliment had its advantages. Stella would never think of him as a parrot of insincere and hackneyed phrases. She could always regard herself as one whom he loved and trusted enough to treat with "abusive" familiarity. She could value herself the more because he addressed her with raillery. But how well did such raillery wear? Stella must have felt, after a time, that Swift was withholding from her the commitment that other women enjoyed from their literary lovers. A declaration of commitment need not have been trite, like the love poems he hated, or even stilted, like *Cadenus and Vanessa*. He could have found an acceptable way of professing his love before, and not after, Stella reached the point of impending death. He did not make the declaration when it would have had its fullest practical value. That he did not suggests an inadequacy in the poet or in the relation-

Dean Swift at St. Patrick's Cathedral, Dublin, circa 1724 (painting by Francis Bindon; by permission of the National Gallery of Ireland)

ship that the woman who loved him would have sensed.

Raillery, however affectionate, is a form of suspended aggression. Stella must always have felt, in reading the poems, that Swift could hurt her if he wanted to. In one sense, he was dangling a carrot. In another, he was arresting the downward swing of an ax. These darker aspects do not obscure the genuine love that infuses the poems. They do reveal the complexity, and perhaps the ambivalence, of Swift's feelings in his most significant relationship with a woman.

Felicity A. Nussbaum has recently argued that Stella's death, in 1728, precipitated the writing of Swift's notorious excremental poems. While it is quite true that excrement became for Swift a symbol of life's disappointments and defeats and that Stella's death may have been the bitterest blow he ever sustained, Nussbaum's plausi-

ble suggestion needs qualifying. "The Progress of Beauty" (1719) precedes the other poems in this group by more than a decade, and Swift had more than one source of frustration and despair. In 1713 he was installed as dean of St. Patrick's Cathedral, Dublin. He had expected, in reward for his services to the Tory ministry, a bishopric in England. When Queen Anne died in 1714 and the Tory ministry dissolved, he reluctantly said goodbye to his friends in the Scriblerus Club (Pope, Harley, John Gay, Thomas Parnell, and John Arbuthnot) and returned to Ireland. He was to become an Irish national hero, particularly after 1724, with his successful attacks on William Wood's project for devaluing the Irish coinage (*The Drapier's Letters*, 1724); but he never ceased to view Ireland as a place of exile. The excremental poems may owe something to his continuing sense of being trapped, thwarted, and cast aside.

Like many of the poems to Stella, "The Progress of Beauty" plays with certain conventions of Renaissance and Restoration poetry. Swift does have an ethical point to make: his heroine here is a whore, and her syphilitic decay is a reflection and an effect of her moral deficiencies. But the reader is left not so much disturbed at the moral indictment as gleeful at the destruction of a foolish form of art. Swift names his "beauty" Celia to show her affinities with the swarm of pastoral goddesses. He proceeds to substitute dramatic insult for the usual romantic compliments. Rather than an inventory of female charms, he lists "Crackt Lips, foul Teeth, and gummy Eyes." Rather than the conventional floral tribute, one discovers that Celia's lily-colored tints have slipped down to her lips while her rose-colored tints highlight the nose. She is like Diana, goddess of the moon, not in her chastity, but in her frowsy looks as she rises from bed and in the "waning" of her syphilitic face. When the speaker cries out for new nymphs every month, one realizes that he is not Swift, but a caricature of the poetic gallant.

There are a few parodic elements in *A Beautiful Young Nymph Going to Bed* (1731)–the name Corinna, for example, and the loving particularity with which her body is described. But this poem comes much closer than "The Progress of Beauty" to pure invective against vice. The speaker doesn't scruple to call Corinna what she is: "Never did *Covent Garden* boast / So bright a batter'd, strolling Toast." With "gentlest touch," she explores the oozing sores of her syphilitic body. Swift dwells on her appalling decrepitude:

> Now, picking out a Crystal Eye,
> She wipes it clean, and lays it by.
> Her Eye-Brows from a Mouse's Hyde,
> Stuck on with Art on either Side,
> Pulls off with Care, and first displays 'em,
> Then in a Play-Book smoothly lays 'em.
> Now dextrously her Plumpers draws,
> That serve to fill her hollow Jaws.
> Untwists a Wire; and from her Gums
> A Set of Teeth completely comes.
> Pulls out the Rags contriv'd to prop
> Her flabby Dugs and down they drop.

Citing Swift's description of her "Anguish, Toil, and Pain," John M. Aden has argued that the poem is ultimately pathetic. It is more likely that the pity lies with the compassionate reader, and not Swift. Aden's conclusion ignores the obvious contempt of the last line: "Who sees, will spew; who smells, be poison'd." It rests on the very dubi-ous assumption that Swift could not realize so vividly the sordid details of Corinna's life without commiserating with her, and it neglects Swift's capacity for cruelty in the service of morals.

Cassinus and Peter. A Tragical Elegy (1731) takes issue with male romantic delusion, not merely with the forms of romantic compliment. The "obscenity" Cassinus sees in his Cælia exposes the folly of his notions about women. It does not, as in "A Beautiful Young Nymph," imply an indictment of her. Cassinus and Peter are young enough and foolish enough to believe in the grand illusions the poets have created for them–the illusion, for example, that women move on a high spiritual plane, exempt from physical needs. At the same time, Cassy himself is the embodiment of filth. Since he would have preferred that Cælia be dead, disfigured, or whorish to her being a real woman with real needs, his probity and judgment are not above question. As he speaks to his friend Peter, the most famous lines in all Swift's excremental poems explain, but do not excuse, his ridiculous dilemma: "Nor wonder how I lost my Wits; / Oh! Cælia, Cælia Cælia sh–."

In *Strephon and Chloe* (1731?), Swift continues his attack on romantic forms of expression; but his attitude toward the romantic delusion is highly ambiguous. The poem as a whole is a parodic epithalamium, Swift taking every occasion to deflate poetic clichés. Strephon is no poet, however; and Swift gives no evidence that the character admires poetic cant. He simply believes his lady is a goddess for him to worship and serve. Swift seems at first to laugh at him for his ridiculous ideas. But when Chloe brings the chamber pot to bed and Strephon's delusions are finally and completely routed, Swift seems to regret the effectiveness of his satiric maneuvers. He seems to look around at the wreckage of romantic thought and find "gross and filthy" everything that has survived:

> To see some radiant Nymph appear
> In all her glitt'ring Birth-day Gear,
> You think some Goddess from the Sky
> Descended, ready cut and dry:
> But, e'er you sell yourself to Laughter,
> Consider well what may come after;
> For fine Ideas vanish fast,
> While all the gross and filthy last.

The writer who turns from romantic ideas to satire makes a bargain with the devil. When he

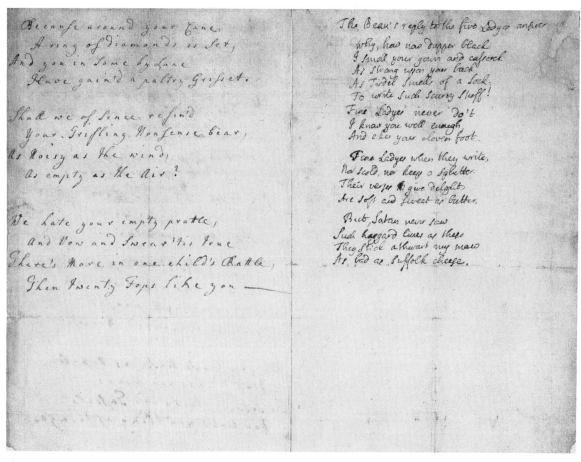

Swift's response (right) to Thomas Sheridan's "The five Ladies Answer to the Beau" (circa 1728). Swift wrote his lines at the end of a transcription, in an unknown hand, of Sheridan's poem (428: HM 14335; by permission of the Henry E. Huntington Library and Art Gallery).

"sells" himself to laughter, he relinquishes the blessing of being well deceived.

With the vanishing of fine ideas, Swift enters the poem himself to make a complaint on behalf of husbands of all ages. Women "take Possession of the Crown / And then throw all their Weapons down." He demands that wives hide "each Blemish" from their husbands. In *Strephon and Chloe*, the satire flies in all directions. Women are at fault for exposing their blemishes and destroying their husbands' illusions. Men are at fault for their ridiculous notions. Women are advised to maintain their "Beauty" by sustaining their husbands' wrong opinions. And men are advised not to build on beauty at all. Swift seems to have lost artistic distance here and introduced the inconsistencies of his personal attitudes into the piece. Perhaps the contentions of critics like Aldous Huxley and John Middleton Murry deserve a measure of credence: he may be excessively upset by the idea of excrement even

though he makes a joke of it, or his attitude may fluctuate between horror and attraction. But another possibility remains. The man whose whole life was devoted to the destruction of "fine Ideas" would find sufficiently disturbing the realization that "all the gross and filthy last." What the poem acknowledges, painfully, about satire may best account for its inconsistencies.

The reader might expect the same problems to arise in *The Lady's Dressing Room* (1730), in which Celia is damned for her violation of romantic forms, and Strephon, who finds her out, is damned for resenting it. Swift takes Celia to task with unprecedented violence:

Now listen while he next produces,
The various Combs for various Uses,
Fill'd up with Dirt so closely fixt,
No Brush could force a way betwixt.
A Paste of Composition rare,
Sweat, Dandriff, Powder, Lead and Hair;

A Forehead Cloth with Oyl upon't
To smooth the Wrinkles on her Front;
Here Allum Flower to stop the Steams,
Exhal'd from sour unsavoury Streams. . . .

But the narrator seems to excuse Celia and find Strephon at fault for holding his discoveries against her. Recommending indifference to the repulsive revelations, the narrator claims that *he* can accept the Queen of Love, despite her origin in "stinking Ooze," and that he feels only joyful amazement at a woman's ability to transform herself: "Such Order from Confusion sprung, / Such gaudy Tulips rais'd from Dung." Swift has here found a device that permits him to accomplish his two satiric purposes at the same time. The invective against Celia is not undermined by the satire on Strephon, because the narrator intervenes to make the second point in his own person. Swift's difference from the narrator is confirmed by the force and abruptness of the pejorative words, like "Dung" and "stinking Ooze." But Swift and Strephon, who is a kind of satirist-figure, would surely take his advice if they could.

The reader who thinks that excrement, even as a symbol of life's disappointments and defeats, should not provoke so strong a reaction might well try to imagine himself transported back to that time. Seeing what Swift was up against might change the mind of the hardiest modern. The eighteenth century considered Swift's sense of cleanliness odd, if not outright pathological. In habit, in personal delicacy and views of hygiene, twentieth-century readers are actually far closer to him than his own contemporaries were.

During his stay in London from 1707 to 1709, Swift had become intimate with the second-best-known woman in his life, "Vanessa" (Esther or Hester) Vanhomrigh. Her father had been a prominent revenue commissioner in Ireland; her mother, who inherited from him an ample fortune in 1703, brought her family to London four years after his death. Swift enjoyed dropping by the Vanhomrigh household and shared a standing joke with Vanessa about his delight in drinking coffee with her. Swift scolded her for sleeping late and for taking insufficient exercise, and he tried to regulate the books she read and the company she kept. In short, he adopted the same role of teacher, father, and quasi-lover that he had been acting with Stella. Meanwhile, the fatherless girl, who was twenty-one years younger than Swift, was falling in love. Ehrenpreis describes

the "shaky equilibrium" they established as composed of her "fearful ardour" and his "eager reluctance." Swift could not seem to keep himself from encouraging her: whenever he was in England, he visited the Vanhomrighs, and whenever he was in Ireland, he exchanged letters with them. After her mother died in 1721, Vanessa gave in to what she called her "inexpressible passion" and followed Swift to Ireland. He seems to have visited her there as little as he decently could. She died in 1723. Swift left Dublin and took a long journey on horseback through the south of Ireland.

Swift wrote *Cadenus and Vanessa* shortly before a return to Ireland that he hoped, no doubt, would forever end this troublesome relationship. Though some feminist critics have recently focused on the many excellencies the poem ascribes to the girl, they tend to forget that it is, at bottom, a brush-off. Vanessa was more desirable than desired. The poem attempts to persuade her that she is too good for Swift, with the further implication that she should leave him alone.

Cadenus and Vanessa opens with Venus holding court: the nymphs blame the shepherds for the failure of modern love, and the shepherds blame the nymphs. To help decide the case, Venus chooses an infant, Vanessa, and endows her with beauty, cleanliness, decency, and charm. She tricks Pallas into mistaking the infant for a boy and showering her with all the virtues conventionally associated with men (plus five thousand pounds). When Vanessa grows up, her virtues earn her few female friends and even fewer masculine admirers. To avenge his mother's failure, Cupid inspires Vanessa with love for her middle-aged tutor, Cadenus. (His name is an anagram of the Latin *decanus*, or "dean.") Using Cadenus's own lessons, Vanessa attempts to argue him into loving her. She scorns his offer of passionless friendship and offers to be his tutor in love. "But what Success *Vanessa* met, / Is to the World a Secret yet": Swift rather coyly declines to reveal the outcome of the negotiations. Meanwhile, Venus calls together the nymphs and shepherds and decides the case against the men: they have failed to love the perfect Vanessa. Swift failed, too, and that is why he desperately wanted to transform the explosive affair into a placid understanding.

When Swift got to know Lady Anne Acheson, in 1728, Vanessa was dead and Stella had just died. He spent extended periods with the lady and her husband, Sir Arthur, at their home at Market Hill in the county of Armagh. His first

Swift's friend Hester Vanhomrigh, whom he called Vanessa (portrait by Philip Hussey; by permission of the National Gallery of Ireland)

visit to Market Hill lasted from June 1728 to February 1729. His second visit, beginning in June 1729, lasted for four months. He spent another summer with the Achesons in 1730; but after this, problems with his health and the rift he may have perceived between the Achesons made such long stays difficult.

Latest and least known of Swift's most intimate female friends, Lady Acheson maintained the tradition that Stella and Vanessa had begun. Though the crotchets of his age (sixty-one, in 1728) and her actual differences from the others affected his attitude and tone, one might still say he created Lady Acheson in their image to fulfill his need for a tutorial relationship that offered

more than pedagogical satisfaction. She was probably about twenty-five years younger than Swift. (The interval between his age and the ages of his female friends was progressively greater.) The tutor vied with the father in Swift as he strove to inculcate in her, as in the other two, a love for walking or riding, a hatred for fops, an impeccable pronunciation in reading aloud, and a comprehensive acquaintance with writers in philosophy, religion, politics, and literature. She presented special problems as a pupil: for example, she liked to wear high-heeled shoes that impeded her walking. A mark of her ineluctable femininity, her shoes thwarted Swift's plan for her improvement through exercise. In "The Revolution at Market-Hill" (1730), he devised a scheme to incapacitate her while he stormed her husband's fortress: her maid tempts her with high-heeled shoes that cause her to stumble. But sometimes Swift saw in Lady Acheson the same problems that he had encountered in Stella or Vanessa, giving rise to the impression that he saw the women as much alike. In "To Stella, Who Collected and Transcribed his Poems," he criticized Stella for "Perverseness" in argument; and in "Daphne" (1730), he took Lady Acheson to task for the same error. Stella may have been more pliable, but even the recalcitrant Lady Acheson bent to the discipline of her teacher. In a letter, Swift wrote, referring to his first visit to Market Hill: "She was my pupil there, and severely chid when she read wrong."

The three Galateas not only looked like each other: they looked also like their Pygmalion. When Swift praises Stella and Vanessa, their learning, their opinions, and their tastes reflect the leanings of their tutor. Both, he claims, have been mistaken for boys and endowed with masculine qualities. He is unusually literal in accepting an old pedagogical principle: students are there to be transformed into wizened little replicas of their teachers. In this respect, Lady Acheson proved to be troublesome. With her cards, her vapors, and her high-heeled shoes, she could hardly be taken for a man. Swift occasionally tried to unsex her, as when, in 1732, he wrote in a letter, "She is an absolute Dublin rake, sits up late, loses her money, and goes to bed sick." But the strain of his frustrated efforts to make her more like himself shows up clearly in a poem like "Daphne."

He wanted all three pupils to resemble him, for reasons that become clear when one looks at the best of the Market Hill poems, "Death and Daphne. To an agreeable young Lady, but extremely lean" (1730). In the opening lines, Pluto deplores the dearth of dead men since the Peace of Utrecht and insists that Death seek a wife and beget young Deathlings to forward his work. A council of underworld coquettes rigs Death out like a beau, with the help of owls, ravens, bats, and snakes; and he goes to take up residence in Warwick Lane, among his fellow physicians. Hearing praise of Daphne (Lady Acheson), Death approaches her as she sits at cards. Because his skeletal frame pokes through the lawyer's parchment he wears as skin—because he looks like her—the extremely lean lady falls in love. She shows her wit. He advances to touch her. Finding her hand "as

dry and cold as Lead," he becomes frightened and runs away. The rule for Swift, it seems, is likeness begets love. Death is most probably a stand-in for Swift himself, and the poem is about the tutorial relationship he cultivated with Lady Acheson.

But Swift was sixty-three when he wrote this poem. Surely he realized how foolish a figure he would cut as a beau. He would look as grotesque, in fact, as Death coming to court a young and agreeable lady. "Death and Daphne" exaggerates the unnatural picture of an old man courting a woman very much his junior. It also draws out and distorts other implications of the tutorial relationship peculiar to Swift. A celibate scholar and clergyman, with a system of pedagogy that covers such matters as eating and walking, binds to himself, with injunctions that supersede the advice of family and friends, a young and agreeable woman who might be much better suited to other activities. It is Death courting Life in another sense.

The paradoxical union of Life and Death, with the immediate goal of procreation and the ultimate goal of annihilation, never takes place within the context of the poem. Death runs from the lady because he finds her touch "dry and cold." Swift ran from the lady because he found her young, agreeable, and married. He probably feared to find her warm and moist. This reason for the dean's "not Building at Drapier's Hill" serves us better than the strangely flimsy ones he provides in the poem of that name (1730). In attempting to distance himself from Lady Acheson, Swift teased her in a manner less kindly than that he had adopted for Stella. He focused almost exclusively on her leanness, not only in "Death and Daphne" but also in "My Lady's Lamentation and Complaint against the Dean" (1728); *Lady A–S–N Weary of the Dean* (1728?); *The Grand Question debated* (1729); and *A Panegyric On the Reverend Dean Swift* (1730). This focus, like his suggestions that Stella and Vanessa were mistaken for boys, denied his attraction and her attractiveness by denying her a sexual identity. The attraction remained, as Swift obliquely testified in *The Grand Question debated,* where he invented a quasi-sexual rivalry for her favor between a swashbuckling captain and a bedraggled scholar. But Swift and his poetic counterparts always lost the lady, by default and design.

Throughout Ovid's *Metamorphoses* (first century A.D.), the gods who lose their ladies gain a noble recompense, more glorious but still second

Portion of a letter from Swift to Benjamin Motte, who had published Gulliver's Travels *and was in the process of publishing volume four of the enlarged edition of Swift's* Miscellanies in Prose and Verse, *1727-1735 (auctioned by Christie, Manson & Woods, Ltd., 11-12 June 1980)*

best. The most pertinent story here is, of course, the one about Apollo and Daphne. Deprived of his Daphne, Apollo can embrace instead a laurel, seal and sign of all his talents and powers. By accident or intention, in "Death and Daphne," Swift has given his final pupil the most comprehensible name. It reminds us of a myth that might serve as model for what he was doing when he wrote the poem.

As his political poems show, nothing could make Swift angrier than the turn politics took after the death of Queen Anne and the end of the Tories' tenure of power. He had dedicated his talents and loyalties to the Tory ministers, Harley (Earl of Oxford) and Henry St. John (Viscount Bolingbroke). The prominent issue they had had to deal with was the War of the Spanish Succession, which began when the dying king of Spain willed his throne to the grandson of Louis

XIV. This combination of Spanish and French power would have been fatal to English interests, so England allied herself with Holland, Denmark, Austria, and Sweden and went to war with France. By 1713 Swift and the Tory ministers had concluded that the war had gone on too long, that it was enriching England's allies at the expense of England herself, and that Whiggish vindictiveness was prolonging the hostilities. The Tories proceeded to conclude with France the Peace of Utrecht. The secret negotiations took place under the supervision of Oxford and Bolingbroke and under the personal direction of Swift's friend, the poet-diplomat Matthew Prior. The Queen's death left the Tories at the mercy of the enraged Whigs, who believed that the treaty had offered France unsuitably lenient terms. Swift feared exile because of his involvement with the Tory cause. Bolingbroke did flee to exile in

France, and Oxford was tried and imprisoned on charges of treason. The succeeding monarchs, George I and George II, favored the Whigs. Their prime minister, Robert Walpole, assumed what must have seemed an interminable tenure of office (1715-1717; 1721-1742) and laughed off the satiric attacks on his corruption by Swift, Pope, Gay, and Henry Fielding. Swift poured his resentment into four fine poems: *Verses On The Death Of Dr. Swift, An Epistle To A Lady, On Poetry: A Rapsody* (1733), and "The Legion Club."

The *Verses* mingle the poet's doubts about friendship, his fears about the recognition due him, and his convictions about the political situation. The poem opens with François La Rochefoucauld's maxim that in the worst distresses of our friends we find something that does not displease us. Swift depicts his acquaintances, and even close friends like Pope and Gay, first congratulating themselves that they are not so near death as he is and then recovering quickly when he dies. His writings almost immediately lose their popularity and are displaced by the works of Whig hacks. Friendship succumbs to what Swift repeatedly calls "private Ends," especially self-love and envy. Ehrenpreis speculates that this part of the poem was motivated by Swift's fear that, after his death, "his friends would defend him less heartily than his enemies would attack." In expressing his doubts about friendship, however, Swift does not exempt himself from blame: "In Pope, I cannot read a Line, / But with a Sigh, I wish it mine." He, too, consults his "private ends." But in opposition to that phrase stands "publick Uses"–the object of his final bequest and, as the last part of the poem will show, the object of his life in general. His early insistence on his own culpability, in combination with the announcement of his bequest and the description of his disinterested public service, suggests that only those who recognize their weakness have the power to resist it.

The most controversial section of the poem is the last part, in which an "impartial" speaker at the Rose Tavern draws an extremely flattering portrait of Swift and his service to the state. Though some have argued that the self-praise is exaggerated, or even ironic, the evidence from Swift's other writings shows that he was not timid about acknowledging his efforts for friends, his patriotism, and his devotion to liberty. Swift really did feel, and rightly, that he had been of use to friends and countrymen. On the other hand, when he speaks of his satire, one might expect a

degree of irony. In almost all his works, he deprecates his role as satirist. And so he stole a line from John Denham's elegy on Cowley and gave it to the "impartial" speaker to use about himself. The line is "what he writ was all his own." So, too, he permitted the speaker to praise him incorrectly for sparing the name in his satires. These examples of irony suggest a spirit of play between author and reader, whose trust in Swift should by now be well established. The writer who can recognize his own self-love and yet rise above it for "publick Uses" is entitled to a few ironical sallies and a good measure of self-congratulation. His invincible dedication to the public is confirmed in the poem by his risky praise of Oxford, Bolingbroke, James Butler, Duke of Ormonde, and William Pulteney, and by his dangerous open attacks on Walpole.

Swift's *Epistle To A Lady*, written for Acheson, illustrates the way his strategies work to reach his private friends and public enemies. He did not invent raillery, the most important of his methods for pleasing and persuading the lady, but the pose he cultivates to explain the raillery is largely an original creation. He plays an old curmudgeon, whose friends are to understand that he has a heart of gold and a habit of having all his whims indulged–a role he enjoyed in real life as well. Only such a man could write such a poem and expect to insinuate his advice in the guise of affectionate ribbing: "Tho' you treat us with a Smile, / Clear your Looks, and smooth your Stile: / Load our Plates from ev'ry Dish: / This is not the Thing we wish." Nor did Swift discover invective, the most important of his strategies for blackening the ministry. What he did discover was the usefulness of convincing the reader that he, a loving and lovable man, could be pushed into invective frenzy only by the most atrocious of crimes: "Let me, tho' the Smell be Noisom, / Strip their Bums; let *Caleb* hoyse 'em; / Then, apply *Alecto's* Whip, / Till they wriggle, howl, and skip." Obviously, as the good-natured man who believes in lighthearted laughter is transformed into the ferocious satirist, the writer becomes almost comic. But the implied self-criticism does not weaken the point: Swift is not, like some of his fellow satirists, too proud to make fun of himself:

Safe within my little Wherry,
All their Madness makes me merry:
Like the Watermen of *Thames*,
I row by, and call them Names.

Like the ever-laughing Sage,
In a Jest I spend my Rage:
(Tho' it must be understood,
I would hang them if I cou'd. . . .)

Swift's several intentions–to compliment and teach the lady, to censure Walpole, and to comment comically on his art–merge perfectly to form one of the best and most significant of his poems.

In the verses *On Poetry*, Swift's intentions are again multiple: he wishes to describe the profession of poetry, particularly as practiced by political hacks, and he wishes to attack the court, this time by means of mock-eulogy. The subtitle, *A Rapsody*, should warn the reader that the poem is a satire, a "rapp" being a counterfeit coin as well as a blow to the head. It refers primarily, however, to the audience's expectations: the poet is expected to "rhapsodize." Instead of a rhapsody on poetry in the tradition of Milton and Dryden, the reader finds here a satire on poetry in the tradition of John Oldham and Rochester.

The first object of attack is clearly the society that favors the undeserving and mistreats the poet. But the opening stanzas imply as well that Swift feels contempt for the poet himself. The whole beginning of the poem explores this paradox: whereas every fool wants to write poetry, only a fool would want to be a poet. Not empire, nor lawmaking, nor science requires such enormous resources "As how to strike the *Muses Lyre*." And what is the poet's reward? In Swift's exaggerated terms, bastards are better qualified for advancement. The poet produces nothing anyone wants. The only way he can be useful, Swift implies, is through flattery or flunkyism. In a better world, the implication might be ironic. Under the circumstances, the poet is an impotent observer in a decadent age.

The end of *On Poetry* dramatizes Swift's advice to the poet about the flattery of kings and courts. He pretends to eulogize the royal family and the ministry, but the panegyric recoils on the objects of praise. There are scarcely any lapses into invective. The point is carried by the excess of praise. And yet that praise is almost indistinguishable from that loyally offered up to the court by Laurence Eusden and Colley Cibber. Queen Caroline apparently found it plausible enough to swallow it whole. Her advisers had to point out to her that the writer did not deserve a royal reward. Her feelings when she finally faced the truth can only be conjectured, but it is known

that several Dublin booksellers were taken into custody for printing and publishing Swift's poem. They would not betray the author's name.

The issue behind "The Legion Club" was the attempt of the Irish House of Commons to strip the clergy of some of their tithes–in particular the tithe of pasturage, or "agistment," a sum paid to the vicar or rector by the occupier of pasture lands. Both the Irish and the English courts had decided in favor of the clergy, but the members of the House, many of them landowners, continued to resist. In March 1736, the House was presented with a petition against the tithe of agistment, and on the 18th, it gave its opinion. One hundred ten members voted in support of the graziers who got up the petition, and fifty in support of the clergy. An enraged Swift struck back with "The Legion Club."

Whom Swift would destroy he first makes mad. His leisurely stroll through a madhouse (the House of Commons) is a much grimmer version of the cataloging technique used by Pope in his walk through a portrait gallery (*Epistle II. To a Lady: Of the Characters of Women*, 1735). Swift's development of an urbane, gentlemanly persona and his repeated displays of rhetorical control help distinguish him from the lunatics he observes soused in excrement and toasting "Old Glorious" in their urine. His addresses to his muse help define the impression he wants to give. She is "gentle," "obedient," and, most important, she is Clio, the muse of history. Through her he not only claims to be impartial, but also warns the Irish politicians of their reputation with posterity. And Clio introduces his second major metaphor. He appeals to her to "Shift the Scene," to alter "Time and Place"; and so he begins the Virgilian account of his descent to the Hell of Irish politics. Eventually, the two metaphors merge; and we see the honorable members suffering the consequences of both their impiety and their madness: "Tye them Keeper in a Tether, / Let them stare and stink together; / Both are apt to be unruly, / Lash them daily, lash them duly. . . ."

Written at the end of Swift's career, "The Legion Club," the most violent poem he ever wrote, is a testament to an old man's fire. His friend Patrick Delany thought it excelled all his other poems. That anyone could think so shows how well Swift has managed his fury. From a writer with feelings less intense, the devices used in "The Legion Club" might make up a masterpiece of artistic discipline; but Swift needed every bit of discipline he could muster merely to ensure

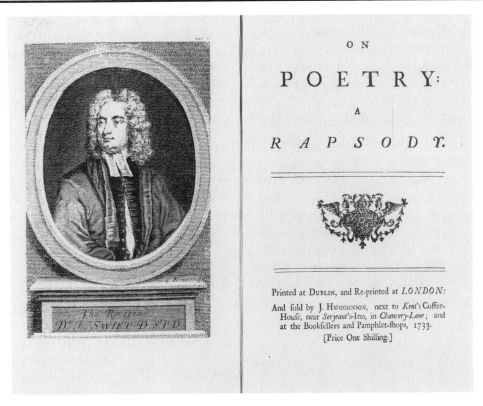

Frontispiece (engraved by George Vertue) and title page for Swift's satirical poem attacking hack writers who play up to royalty

that the reader would not fling the poem away. The facade of "The Legion Club" is like the architecture of New Bedlam in More Fields, the first building in England constructed specifically to house the mad. The splendid neoclassical structure, with perfectly balanced and symmetrical wings, with a graceful formal approach flanked by two mirror-image gardens, housed dark regions of unreason where sane and mad were confounded in common confusion and violence. On a larger scale, New Bedlam was the emblem of the age. On the smaller scale, it was like this poem, formal and rhetorical in its execution, full of underlying hatred and rage and fear.

In the verses on "The Day of Judgement," Swift shapes his material to ensnare mankind in general:

> WITH a Whirl of Thought oppress'd,
> I sink from Reverie to Rest.
> An horrid Vision seiz'd my Head,
> I saw the Graves give up their Dead.
> Jove arm'd with Terrors, burst the Skies,
> And Thunder roars, and Light'ning flies!
> Amaz'd, confus'd, its Fate unknown,
> The World stands trembling at his Throne.
> While each pale Sinner hangs his Head,

> Jove, nodding, shook the Heav'ns, and said,
> "Offending Race of Human Kind,
> By Nature, Reason, Learning, blind;
> You who thro' Frailty step'd aside,
> And you who never fell–*thro' Pride*;
> You who in different Sects have shamm'd,
> And come to see each other damn'd;
> (So some Folks told you, but they knew
> No more of Jove's Designs than you)
> The World's mad Business now is o'er,
> And I resent these Pranks no more.
> I to such Blockheads set my Wit!
> I damn such Fools!–Go, go, you're bit."

Only the cleverest, or blindest, of readers will find his way out of the satiric trap. "*SATYR is a sort of* Glass, *wherein Beholders do generally discover every body's Face but their Own,*" says Swift in his preface to the *Battel of the Books* (1710). At his best, however, he does not allow the reader to avoid self-knowledge. He is always seeking to break down the conventional satiric alliance, to discourage the reader from assuming a safe position at his shoulder. His methods are many, but "The Day of Judgement" relies on the most effective he ever found. First, he makes sure the reader sees that every single human being is involved in the satiric damnation. Second, he includes himself in that damnation and so destroys the reader's only hope for protection. When Swift "lashes first himself," as W. B. C. Watkins puts it, the reader can hardly claim exemption from the satire or dissociate himself from the satirist on grounds that he is prideful or partial. When Swift acknowledges his own reflection, the world must see itself in the mirror.

Whatever short-lived laughter "The Day of Judgement" may evoke can scarcely survive a second reading. Such laughter has its origin merely in the incongruity of low and lofty styles, as Swift adapts his language to the different aspects of his character Jove. The reader at first associates the dream vision with serious religious works and prepares to accept it seriously. He perceives Jove as a combination of traditional Christian and classically heroic elements, wielding his thunderbolt and shaking the heavens with his nod. The phrasing in the line "Amaz'd, confus'd, its Fate unknown" has even a Miltonic cast. Before Jove stand the pale sinners, appropriately terrified and appropriately ashamed. But Jove's first words detract from his dignity and change the heroic to the mock-heroic in the reader's retrospect.

As Jove departs from divine decorum to indulge in verbal games, his cleverness becomes cumulatively sinister, offensive, and unbecoming to a god. He is playing when he attributes "never falling" to the pride that caused, in part, the Fall. The whole joke involved in the equivalency of falling and never falling contributes to the reader's unease. Jove plays likewise with the idea that blindness, and not insight, proceeds from nature, reason, and learning. At the same time, he mocks the most cherished eighteenth-century ideals. The colloquial tone reaches its fullness when the god ceases to speak of himself as "Jove" and comes in his own person to damn, resent, and set his wit against the fools. The smug and colloquial parenthesis ("So some Folks told you") has prepared for the shift to "I resent" and "I damn." The use of the first person prepares in turn for the culmination of the witticisms: the execrable play on *damn.* The curse, on second reading, becomes the secularized swearing of a frustrated reformer. "God damn you," Jove is saying. "Go to hell." When the reader remembers that it was Swift who loved a "bite," or practical joke, more than any other form of humor, then Jove's announcement that he and the churches have

duped the poor sinners ("Go, go, you're bit") sounds like a satirist's crude dismissal.

The descent from the heroic to the colloquial and clever may provoke the reader's early laughter, but he will find in the cleverness of Jove grounds for Swift's real horror and, at the last, grounds for horror of his own. The god who sets his wit against mankind and speaks in Swift's own idiom is the satirist writ large. He dramatizes the problems of satire–the problems, in particular, which interested Swift himself. Jove-the-satirist fulfills the traditional desires of his human counterpart. From his omnipotence proceeds a measure of detachment, and he feels only resentment at the "Pranks" of men. From his omnipotence likewise proceeds his effectiveness in attack, and he may choose to annihilate man with the assurance that he can implement his choice. The human satirist longs to see the objects of his hatred as trivial. At the same time, he longs for the power to attack and obliterate.

But if Jove has successfully detached himself from human folly and spared himself the *saeva indignatio* that tortured Swift, he has little motive for annihilating man. Outside the scheme of the poem, the question may not occur. God may damn the fools because they deserve damnation, though he feels not even so much as resentment. Within the scheme of the poem, however, Jove refers not to the principles of justice and desert, but only to his own feelings. The race offends him personally, and personally he resents it. His resentment, as a motive, cannot satisfy the reader; but it is the only motive he offers.

The human satirist, on the other hand, finds his motive in the savage indignation that belies his conventional pretense to detachment. When the detached Jove damns all mankind, he raises questions about the motives of his counterpart–but only by implication, because his counterpart can never be detached. Jove raises questions, then, not about what the satirist is, but about what he would be if he could realize at once his desires for detachment and for effectiveness in attack.

Jove saves none, though presumably he might have exercised his omnipotence in the process of salvation. As a superhuman satirist, the character here suggests that Swift shares with his opponents real doubts about satire: it may be primarily destructive, and not reformative, in its motivation and effect. Swift's *Epistle To A Lady* contains the same suggestion. The poet pretends to Horatian calm until his anger asserts itself and

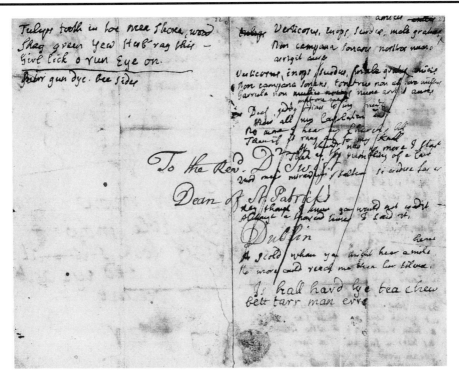

Draft for verses on his deafness, written by Swift on the back of a letter in 1734 (672: HM 14338; by permission of the Henry E. Huntington Library and Art Gallery)

he tells what he would really do if he only had the power: "I would hang them if I cou'd. . . ." In "The Day of Judgement," the satirist can laugh and hang them, too.

The reader cannot expect Swift-the-dreamer (the "I" of the poem) to perceive and decry the implications for satire that derive from the character of Jove. If the "I" were Swift-the-satirist, in fact, he might take pleasure in the vision because it fulfills his fondest wishes. The dreamer may perceive, however, the horror of his own predicament. When Jove damns all mankind without exception, the dreamer is drawn from his point of observation into the mass of the damned. He, too, has come to see his fellows damned, only to meet with damnation himself. He, too, in the course of the poem, has speculated on Jove's designs until he has come to the inevitable conclusion: the Swiftian Jove will damn the Swiftian dreamer. Swift in one of his aspects will pass judgment on Swift in another.

No less must the reader acknowledge his own presumption and self-delusion. He has expected from the first of the poem an apocalyptic vision–a sky rent in two and pale sinners before a godlike God. The "horrid Vision" humiliates the reader because it disappoints his literary and his religious expectations. The humiliation prepares him for another. The poem compels him to accept as his judge a god who cares nothing about his human dignity or his due process. Yet a third source of humiliation awaits those who ponder closely the last two lines. Since eighteenth-century typography was somewhat random, question marks can be substituted for either or both of the exclamation marks. Is it possible that Jove is too proud to send any of the sinners to Hell, but simply leaves them standing there, the victims of a cosmic joke?

Whatever the sinners' final fate, the arbitrary changes in tense throughout the poem extend the implications to the whole "Offending Race." They indicate, as well, the state of timelessness appropriate to Judgment Day. On that day the reader finds no exception made for anyone, whatever his time or place. His only hope would lie in alliance with the poet, but he cannot appeal to the poet because Swift has come from his point of vantage to join the pale sinners himself. The reader must submit, with Swift, to the judgment of an imperious Jove–a Jove who shares some characteristics with Swift as satirist and who emanates from the imagination of the Swift who dreams.

Marble bust of Swift by Louis François Roubiliac
(by permission of Trinity College, Dublin)

Because it handles the reader so expertly, "The Day of Judgement" is a study in rhetorical excellence. And yet, with all its perfections, the poem is not foolproof. The flaw is not one Swift could have remedied. He omits no ploy in his manipulation of the reader. The loophole is a function of the poet's expertise. It is this: the reader can deflect the satire, to some extent, by pure admiration of the skill. When his aesthetic interest in the poem outweighs his moral interest, the balance of his attention shifts from profit to pleasure. The better the poem, the more pleasure it gives him. That is why the clever reader, like the stupid one, runs the risk of learning little from Swift.

"The Day of Judgement" did not come to light until 1774, nearly thirty years after Swift's death. He certainly did not wish it published during his lifetime. In the last years of his life, he suffered from poor memory, arteriosclerosis, aphasia, orbital cellulitis, and the continuing effects of Ménière's disease. But he was never, as myth would have it, mad. He spoke on two different occasions just before he died. The first time he said, "I am what I am"–Jehovah's imperious an-

swer to those who would presume to penetrate his mystery. The second and final time he said, "I am a fool"–establishing an identity with the blockheads who were, after all, his fellow human beings.

Swift died in Dublin on 19 October 1745. He kept the promise he had made in *Verses On The Death Of Dr. Swift* by leaving money to found a hospital for madmen and fools.

Letters:

Letters Between Dr. Swift, Mr. Pope, &c. From the Year 1714 to 1736. Publish'd from a Copy Transmitted from Dublin (London: T. Cooper, 1741);

The Works of Mr. Alexander Pope, In Prose, volume 2, includes letters by Swift (London: J. & P. Knapton, C. Bathurst & R. Dodsley, 1741);

Letters To and From Dr. J. Swift, D.S.P.D. From The Year 1714, to 1738 (Dublin: George Faulkner, 1741);

The Correspondence of Jonathan Swift, D.D., edited by F. Elrington Ball, 6 volumes (London: Bell, 1910-1914);

The Correspondence of Jonathan Swift, edited by Harold Williams, 5 volumes (Oxford: Clarendon Press, 1963-1965).

Bibliographies:

Herman Teerink, *A Bibliography of the Writings in Prose and Verse of Jonathan Swift, D.D.* (The Hague: Martinus Nijhoff, 1937); revised and corrected by Teerink and edited by Arthur H. Scouten as *A Bibliography of the Writings of Jonathan Swift* (Philadelphia: University of Pennsylvania Press, 1963);

Louis A. Landa and James Edward Tobin, *Jonathan Swift: A List of Critical Studies Published from 1895 to 1945. To Which Is Added Remarks on Some Swift Manuscripts in the United States by Herbert Davis* (New York: Cosmopolitan Science and Art Service, 1945);

Ricardo Quintana, "A Modest Appraisal: Swift Scholarship and Criticism, 1945-65," in *Fair Liberty Was All His Cry: A Tercentenary Tribute to Jonathan Swift 1667-1745*, edited by A. Norman Jeffares (London: Macmillan / New York: St. Martin's, 1967), pp. 342-355;

James J. Stathis, *A Bibliography of Swift Studies 1945-1965* (Nashville: Vanderbilt University Press, 1967);

David M. Vieth, *Swift's Poetry 1900-1980: An Annotated Bibliography of Studies* (New York & London: Garland, 1982);

Richard H. Rodino, *Swift Studies, 1965-1980: An Annotated Bibliography* (New York & London: Garland, 1984).

Biographies:

Laetitia Pilkington, *Memoirs Of Mrs. Laetitia Pilkington, Written by Herself. With Anecdotes of Dean Swift* (Dublin & London: R. Griffiths & G. Woodfall, 1748);

John Boyle, Earl of Cork and Orrery, *Remarks On The Life and Writings Of Dr. Jonathan Swift, Dean of St. Patrick's, Dublin, In a Series of Letters from John Earl of Orrery To his Son, the Honourable Hamilton Boyle* (London: A. Millar, 1752);

Patrick Delany, *Observations Upon Lord Orrery's Remarks On The Life and Writings Of Dr. Jonathan Swift, &c. To which are added, Two Original Pieces never before publish'd* (London: W. Reeve, 1754);

John Hawkesworth, *The Life Of the Revd. Jonathan Swift, D.D. Dean of St. Patrick's, Dublin* (London & Dublin: S. Cotter, 1755);

Samuel Johnson, "Life of Swift," in his *Prefaces, Biographical and Critical, To The Works Of The English Poets*, 10 volumes (London: J. Nichols, 1779-1781), VIII: 1-112;

Thomas Sheridan, *The Life Of The Rev. Dr. Jonathan Swift, Dean Of St. Patrick's, Dublin* (London: C. Bathurst, 1784);

Sir Walter Scott, *Memoirs Of Jonathan Swift, D.D. Dean Of St. Patrick's, Dublin*, 2 volumes (Paris: Galignani, 1826);

John Middleton Murry, *Jonathan Swift: A Critical Biography* (London: Cape, 1954);

Irvin Ehrenpreis, *Swift: The Man, His Works, and the Age*, 3 volumes (Cambridge, Mass.: Harvard University Press, 1962-1983).

References:

John M. Aden, "Corinna and the Sterner Muse of Swift," *English Language Notes*, 4 (1966): 23-31;

F. Elrington Ball, *Swift's Verse: An Essay* (London: John Murray, 1929; New York: Octagon Books, 1970);

Louise K. Barnett, *Swift's Poetic Worlds* (Newark: University of Delaware Press / London & Toronto: Associated University Presses, 1981);

J. A. Downie, *Jonathan Swift: Political Writer* (London: Routledge & Kegan Paul, 1985);

A. B. England, *Energy and Order in the Poetry of Swift* (Lewisburg, Pa.: Bucknell University

Press / London & Toronto: Associated University Presses, 1980);

John Irwin Fischer, *On Swift's Poetry* (Gainesville: University Presses of Florida, 1978);

Fischer and Donald C. Mell, Jr., eds., *Contemporary Studies of Swift's Poetry* (Newark: University of Delaware Press / London & Toronto: Associated University Presses, 1980);

Aldous Huxley, "Swift," in his *Do What You Will* (Garden City, N.Y.: Doubleday, Doran, 1929), pp. 99-112;

Nora Crow Jaffe, *The Poet Swift* (Hanover, N.H.: University Press of New England, 1977);

Maurice Johnson, *The Sin of Wit: Jonathan Swift as a Poet* (Syracuse: Syracuse University Press, 1950);

Johnson, "Swift's Poetry Reconsidered," in *English Writers of the Eighteenth Century*, edited by John M. Middendorf (New York, 1971), pp. 233-248;

Timothy Leonard Keegan, "The Theory and Practice of Swift's Poetry," Ph.D. dissertation, University of Virginia, 1979;

Felicity A. Nussbaum, *The Brink of All We Hate: English Satires on Women 1660-1750* (Lexington: University Press of Kentucky, 1984);

Brendan O Hehir, "Meaning in Swift's Description of a City Shower," *ELH*, 27 (1960): 194-207;

Peter J. Schakel, *The Poetry of Jonathan Swift: Allusion and the Development of a Poetic Style* (Madison: University of Wisconsin Press, 1978);

Michael Shinagel, *A Concordance to the Poems of Jonathan Swift* (Ithaca, N.Y. & London: Cornell University Press, 1972);

W. B. C. Watkins, *Perilous Balance: The Tragic Genius of Swift, Johnson, & Sterne* (Princeton, N.J.: Princeton University Press, 1939).

Papers:

Cambridge University Library houses the great Rothschild collection of Swift materials. The Forster collection, at the Victoria and Albert Museum, was put together toward the end of the nineteenth century by John Forster, who intended to write a biography of Swift but died after publishing only one volume. The materials gathered by Swift's most famous bibliographer, Herman Teerink, are deposited at the University of Pennsylvania. Some of the items in Teerink's personal collection were destroyed during World War II and so were not available to his bibliographical successor, Arthur H. Scouten.

James Thomson

(11 September 1700 - 27 August 1748)

Eric Rothstein
University of Wisconsin-Madison

BOOKS: *Winter. A Poem* (London: Printed for J. Millan & sold by J. Roberts & N. Blandford, 1726);

Summer. A Poem (London: Printed for J. Millan, 1727);

A Poem Sacred to the Memory of Sir Isaac Newton (London: Printed for J. Millan, 1727);

Spring. A Poem (London: Printed & sold by A. Millar & G. Strahan, 1728);

Britannia. A Poem, anonymous (London: Printed for T. Warner, 1729);

The Tragedy of Sophonisba. Acted at the Theatre-Royal in Drury-Lane. By His Majesty's Servants (London: Printed for A. Millar, 1730);

The Seasons (London: Printed for the author, 1730; revised and enlarged edition, London: Printed by A. Millar, 1744; revised again, 1746; Philadelphia: Printed & sold by Robert Bell, 1777);

Autumn. A Poem . . . The Second edition (London: Printed by N. Blandford for J. Millan, 1730);

Antient [sic] *and Modern Italy Compared: being the First Part of Liberty, a Poem* (London: Printed for A. Millar, 1735);

Greece: being the Second Part of Liberty, a Poem (London: Printed for A. Millar, 1735);

Rome: being the Third Part of Liberty, a Poem (London: Printed for A. Millar, 1735);

Britain: being the Fourth Part of Liberty, a Poem (London: Printed for A. Millar, 1736);

The Prospect: being the Fifth Part of Liberty. A Poem (London: Printed for A. Millar, 1736);

A Poem to the Memory of the Right Honourable the Lord Talbot (London: Printed for A. Millar, 1737);

Agamemnon. A tragedy. Acted at the Theatre-Royal in Drury-Lane, by His Majesty's Servants (London: Printed for A. Millar, 1738);

The Works of Mr. Thomson, 2 volumes (London: Printed for A. Millar, 1738);

Edward and Eleonora. A tragedy. As it was to have been acted at the Theatre-Royal in Covent-

James Thomson, circa 1725-1726 (portrait by William Aikman; by permission of the Henry E. Huntington Library and Art Gallery)

Garden (London: Printed for the author & sold by A. Millar, 1739);

Alfred: a Masque. Represented before Their Royal Highnesses the Prince and Princess of Wales, at Clieffden, on the first of August, 1740, by Thomson and David Mallet (London: Printed for A. Millar, 1740);

Tancred and Sigismunda. A Tragedy. As it is acted at the Theatre-Royal in Drury-Lane (London: Printed for A. Millar, 1745);

The Castle of Indolence: an Allegorical Poem. Written in Imitation of Spenser (London: Printed for A. Millar, 1748);

Coriolanus. A tragedy. As it is acted at the Theatre-Royal in Covent-Garden (London: Printed for A. Millar, 1749).

Editions and Collections: *The Works of James Thomson*, 4 volumes, edited by George Lyttelton (London: Printed for A. Millar, 1750);

The Works of James Thomson, with his last corrections and improvements. To which is prefixed an account of his life and writings, edited by Patrick Murdoch (London: Printed for A. Millar, 1762; revised edition, 1768; Boston: Little, Brown, 1865);

The Castle of Indolence and Other Poems, edited by Alan Dugald McKillop (Lawrence, Kan.: University of Kansas Press, 1961);

The Seasons, edited by James Sambrook (Oxford: Clarendon Press, 1981);

Liberty, The Castle of Indolence, and Other Poems, edited by Sambrook (Oxford: Clarendon Press, 1986).

PLAY PRODUCTIONS: *Sophonisba,* London, Theatre Royal in Drury Lane, 28 February 1730;

Agamemnon, London, Theatre Royal in Drury Lane, 6 April 1738;

Alfred, by Thomson and David Mallet, Cliefden, 1 August 1740; London, Theatre Royal in Drury Lane, 20 March 1745;

Tancred and Sigismunda, London, Theatre Royal in Drury Lane, 18 March 1745;

Coriolanus, London, Theatre Royal in Covent Garden, 13 January 1749.

OTHER: "Of a Country Life," "Verses on Receiving a Flower from his Mistress," and "Upon Happiness," in *The Edinburgh Miscellany: consisting of Original Poems, Translations, etc. By Various Hands* (January 1720), I: 193-204;

"Hymn on Solitude," "A Paraphrase on the Latter Part of the Sixth Chapter of St. Matthew," "The Happy Man," and "The Incomparable Soporifick Doctor," in *Miscellaneous Poems by Several Hands, publish'd by Mr. Ralph* (London, 1729);

Preface to *Areopagitica: A speech for the liberty of unlicens'd printing, to the Parliament of England. First published in the year 1644,* by John Milton (London: Printed for A. Millar, 1738);

Prologue to *Mustapha,* by David Mallet (London, 1739).

Because the long, reflective landscape poem *The Seasons* (1730) commanded so much attention and affection for at least a hundred years after James Thomson wrote it, his achievement has

Title page for Robert Burns's copy of a 1769 edition of Thomson's most popular book, with Burns's signature (auctioned by Sotheby's, New York, on 24 April 1985)

been identified with it. Thomson, however, was also a political figure through other poems and through some of his plays, standing strongly for a kind of republican ideal against what he saw as the vulpine individualism and oligarchic government of Robert Walpole. As a Scot who spent his adult life in England, he embodied in his work a comity between the two lands and traditions. Partly with these sociopolitical interests in mind, partly to complement the sweep and poignancy of *The Seasons,* he wrote five tragedies and a patriotic masque of some distinction. Finally, his Spenserian allegory, *The Castle of Indolence* (1748), stands as the finest in English other than Spenser's own.

The son of the Scots clergyman Thomas Thomson and Beatrix Trotter Thomson of Berwickshire, Thomson was born on 11 September 1700 in Ednam, Scotland, a few miles north of the River Tweed, which marks the Scots-English boundary. On this poor, isolated, hilly territory, country people scratched out bare livings. Critics eager to spy out biographical influences on *The Seasons* have found the goads to Thomson's pictorial imagination in this border landscape, with its slopes and streams, skies heavy with clouds above the moors, and the constant play of light upon natural objects in such a changeable, assertive climate. Thomson's own family was large–he was the fourth of nine children–and, tucked away in barren country, he must have spent a great deal of time in familial games, tasks, and learning. His household, as one would expect from that of a clergyman father and a mother whose "devotional exercises," according to Patrick Murdoch, were raised by her warm imagination "to a pitch bordering on enthusiasm," gave him intimate knowledge of the Bible, that prime source of literary sublimity in the eighteenth century. Again, one can fancy that his early life was grist for *The Seasons*, in which love and family take on a rosy gleam and where God in His majesty pervades the text. As to his later life, as opposed to his poetry, he left the wild scenery of Scotland for London streets, never married or raised a family himself, and though he remained a profoundly religious man, lapsed from his Christian faith.

Beginning at the age of twelve, Thomson was sent to school, first for three years at Jedburgh, eight miles from home, and then, in 1715, at the College of Edinburgh, some fifty miles north. He was to be in Edinburgh for ten years. After a short time his family embosomed him again, for in February 1716 Thomas Thomson died, allegedly by being struck on the head by a ball of fire while exorcising a ghost at Woolie. Since Beatrix Thomson could, of course, no longer live in the manse, she chose to bring her family to the capital. Thomson may have once again enjoyed the comforts and suffered the constraints of home, but he now found himself in a culturally exciting environment. While at Jedburgh, his learning and writing had been fostered by interested neighborhood gentry, including Robert Riccaltoun and William Bennet, the latter a frequent host to the prolific, charming Scots songwriter, patriot, and poet Allan Ramsay, whom young Thomson may then have met. In Edinburgh he was exposed to new literature,

such as the periodical work of Joseph Addison and Richard Steele and the poetry of Alexander Pope, and to new doctrines, including those of Isaac Newton. Those with common interests formed clubs and societies in which they could discuss readings, debate one another, share the pleasures of the taverns in which they met, and exchange criticism and support for their own work as writers. Thomson became a member of the Grotesque Club. He had not been a stellar student and, according to his fellow club member and lifelong friend David Malloch, did not shine in the club either. Nonetheless, as a member in early January 1720 he did publish his first verse, three mediocre but not desperately weak poems in *The Edinburgh Miscellany*. All three are in couplets, and all bear the marks of a gentlemanly idleness, a refusal of focus and commitment.

In 1719 Thomson finished his arts course without taking a degree, a common procedure, and entered divinity studies as a scholarship student (in Scots terminology, a bursar); he held the bursary for four years. This new course of study was not very exacting; it certainly did not impede Thomson from continuing in his literary career. The annals of eighteenth-century poetry include a good deal of verse by clergymen, fancifully or earnestly whiling away their bucolic hours, and perhaps Thomson would have ended up in earned obscurity if he had been an Englishman. His talents were ill suited for casual verse. Fortunately for literature, however, the Scots church was hostile to poetic effusions. According to Murdoch, when Thomson performed an exercise in divinity class, the paraphrase of a psalm, in too florid a way, Professor William Hamilton at Edinburgh "told him, smiling, that if he thought of being useful in the ministry, he must keep a stricter rein on his imagination, and express himself in a language more intelligible to an ordinary congregation." In general the Scots at the time seem to have tended toward respect for the practical and snorted about the poetical. As he became less willing to give over his life and skills to the church, Thomson came progressively to realize that as a writer he would never revel in a large audience if he stayed in Scotland. By 1724, when a poem probably his, "The Works and Wonders of Almighty Power," appeared in Aaron Hill's London periodical *The Plain Dealer*, he seems to have made up his mind to go south, as his friend Malloch (by then anglicized to "Mallet") had done the year before. Armed with letters of introduction to well-placed Scots in London, Thomson sailed from Leith early in 1725, never again to set foot in Scotland.

After a few months of unhappy floundering, made more painful by his mother's death in mid May, his contacts found him a job as tutor to the son of the minor poet Charles, Lord Binning, who was himself the son of a minor poet, Thomas Hamilton, Earl of Haddington, and the son-in-law of the poet and songwriter Lady Grizel Baillie. At Lord Binning's country house at East Barnet, some ten miles north of London, Thomson set about teaching his pupil to read; he also taught himself to write a new, blank-verse poetry, as he worked on *Winter*. How much of this remarkable poem was written in Scotland and how much in England is not known, but at the end of the winter of 1725-1726 it was complete, and it appeared in April 1726. The second edition of *Winter* was published in July, and two further reimpressions came out the same year. To Thomson's eventual pleasure, his dedicatee Spencer Compton, speaker of the House of Commons, found that he could not continue to ignore the young Scot, and an interview between them ended with Thomson twenty guineas richer. Confident and on his way to being famous, Thomson began work on *Summer*, which appeared in February 1727, two years after his arrival in London. It confirmed the success of the poetic mode first deployed in *Winter*.

"Blank verse," wrote Raymond Dexter Havens, "seems to have been regarded in 1725 much as the telephone was in 1875, as a remarkable toy which it was interesting to experiment with but of which only a few enthusiasts expected to make any real use." Bell did not patent his phone until 1876, however, whereas by Havens's count, some 150 post-Miltonic blank-verse poems (some very short) preceded *Winter*. Unlike those 150, though, *Winter* is sustained, serious, and skillful. The earlier blank-verse corpus, which led Thomson to write and the public to accept this new poem, included Milton's epics *Paradise Lost* (1667) and *Paradise Regained* (1671) as its most distinguished nondramatic examples. It also included every tragedy current on the London stage, and Thomson couched *Winter* as a prolonged soliloquy or dialogue with oneself and one's surroundings. The speaker does often launch into imperatives that in some other poem, in another idiom, might address a reader directly: "See! Winter comes"; "Behold! the well-pois'd *Hornet*, hovering, hangs"; "Now . . . let me wander o'er the russet Mead"; "Oh! bear me

then to high, embowering, Shades." Here, though, they represent an inner urgency on the part of the speaker as his eye lights on the hornet or a keen wish strikes him. To some extent like soliloquists in drama, Thomson's speaker draws readers in to his inner state, but through indirect address. A combination of sympathy with the alert, urgent speaker and the resonance of the imperative form makes Thomson's reader a tacitly summoned participant in the speaker's excitement.

This roundabout way of talking to the audience makes apropos the analogy with blank-verse dramatic soliloquies, including those in *Paradise Lost*. Yet there is a difference. In Thomson, the effect is, by intention, psychologically shallow: whereas the self-absorbed Satan, the leading soliloquizer in Milton's poem, acts–busying himself making a hell of heaven–Thomson's speaker cultivates pure reaction. For example, he welcomes the "*Vapours*, and *Clouds*, and *Storms* . . . that exalt the Soul to solemn Thought" and become "kindred Glooms" and "wish'd, wint'ry, Horrors." As the scenes in *Winter* typify that season, so the speaker as onlooker must typify responses to it, and this interplay of what is common, open, broadly available in the world and in the speaker helps to express the sense of community that is central not only to this poem but to all Thomson's mature work. Nature in *Winter* is objective, "out there," and Thomson's speaker, through typification, becomes an analogue to this objectivity, though with a difference. Thomson typifies winter kaleidoscopically, by adding and mirroring new scenes one after the other; in contrast, his uniformly responsive speaker hardly develops a personality at all. Still, however standard the responses, *Winter* requires that they seem to emerge from experience. They could plausibly be framed in a blank verse that had strong generic associations with the drama. For Thomson himself, in whose mind the I, "nurs'd by careless *Solitude*," was probably not pure textual fiction, the use of dramatic monologue allowed him to accommodate his Scots experience to his new, English life: a young emigré author might be jarred in moving from Edinburgh to London, from a city of about thirty-five thousand people tightly nested in rural land to a city of about six hundred thousand, with room for urban sprawl. A dramatic self-projection, which is a self-reduction, allows him to be personal and at the same time to rise above the merely personal.

Illustration for Winter, *from the first edition of* The Seasons, *1730 (engraving by Nicolas Henri Tardieu, based on a drawing by William Kent)*

Winter presents itself as a retrospective poem of multiple estrangements and renewals, treating a nonurban milieu divinely created, fixed by natural rhythms. In recollecting his past for his dramatic monologue, Thomson needed at once to magnify these rhythms and to stand back from them, to come to terms with them, and to pen them in an ordering plan. He could do this best by setting the poem in the country, where nothing softens winter, and to organize it through balancing event with commentary, that which is in natural time with that which is not. *Winter*, therefore, has four movements in its 406 lines, in each of which the bleak, cruel season comes, and then the poem redresses its action. The "Sullen, and sad" winter of the opening produces "Philosophic Melancholy," which wakens sympathy, and its partner, aesthetic pleasure in nature; next, winter, "Striding the gloomy Blast,"

leads to reflections on the majesty of nature and, after more description, of God; then oncoming winter strands the poet at home with his books, a "Society divine" of the aesthetic and moral great; finally "the wintry Season" conquers all, producing an exhortation on vanities and a theodicy, when "*Time* swiftly fleets, / And wish'd *Eternity*, approaching, brings / Life undecaying." This clear pattern, doubled in each of the first two movements and more sustained in the last two, encompasses both the variety of the season as it moves toward uniformity ("*Horror* wide extends / His solitary Empire") and a single moral and aesthetic sense of life, variously prompted by winter but capable, as the other poems in *The Seasons* were to show, of equally being prompted by the world in other forms.

In May 1726 Thomson left Lord Binning's employ to live in London, again as a tutor, but

Illustration for Summer, *the second of Thomson's major poems, from the first edition of* The Seasons

now affiliated with a school well known for its Newtonian teachings, Watts's Academy. One of the teachers there, the mathematician James Stirling, knew Newton well, so well that Newton had even sent him money to return from Venice so that Newton might recommend him for a professorship. Perhaps in part through such colleagues, in part through his own teachers in Edinburgh, Thomson had learned enough about Newton to have placed passages in *Summer* about gravitation, optical refraction, and "the Man of *Philosophic* Eye" who looks for the physical causes of the aurora borealis rather than succumb to popular superstition about it. Both *Winter* and *Summer* are also rich with scientific explanation about such phenomena as bituminous vapors, lightning, ripening minerals, and fogs, all matters within the purview of the Royal Society over which Newton presided. Not only did Newton penetrate the order of nature and therefore, theologically,

some of nature's meaning as God's other Book, but he also was one of the chief glories of Britain, to which Thomson's deep loyalty never wavered. Unsurprisingly, then, Thomson was among the multitude who wrote commemorative verse after Newton's death on 20 March 1727. The result, dedicated to Prime Minister Walpole, was published in May 1727, *A Poem Sacred to the Memory of Sir Isaac Newton*.

Because Newton, like his contemporary John Locke, had long been deified in English patriotic myth, his soul's ascent would have seemed merely to confirm his proper place. Writers proclaimed that his grasp of the vast cosmic machine made him the modern counterpart of visionary prophets, and also better in combining imagination and reason. Indeed, his epic work spoke of what appeared to be the highest values of the true, the good, and the beautiful: the true because knowledge of God's world glorified Him,

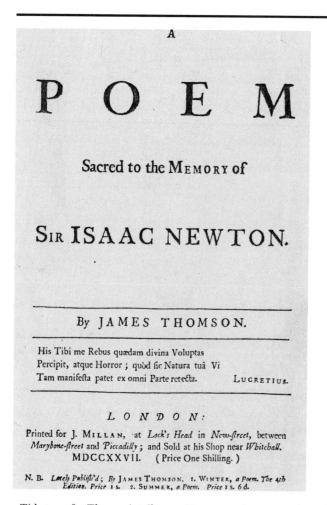

Title page for Thomson's tribute to Newton; and an engraving of the monument to Newton in Westminster Abbey, from the first edition of The Seasons

empowered His human creatures, and swept away old superstitions; the good because the Newtonian system typified a universe of cooperative motion like the balanced constitution of Britain itself (unlike French despotism); and the beautiful because the spectacle of nature offered unity in variety, with objects often beautiful in themselves and always so when considered within the great order in which they shared. The fifty years before Thomson's birth and the first quarter of the new century had seen the triunity of true, good, and beautiful split apart, to be studied within three different sciences: "natural philosophy"; ethics and a rationalized natural law; and the youngest branch of philosophy, aesthetics. Precisely on account of this splitting, Newton's harmonizing system was all the more gratifying, difficult, and therefore, in its triumphant absolutism, magnificent. It has turned out, as Thomson and his contemporaries could not guess, to be the last system

in the history of Western thought to provide society with an ontological guarantee of harmony. At the time, Newtonian thought as a guarantor of values was, if anything, more important than Newton the discoverer of natural, therefore divine, order. Of course a poet who was in the process of becoming the author of *The Seasons* saw and responded to the mythic power of such harmony in the 1720s, in appreciating Newton's work as in creating his own.

Others, most notably Pope in Epistle II of *An Essay on Man* (1733), moralized Newton as a genius still ignorant, as an emblem of limited human knowledge and so an a fortiori argument for humility. Thomson does not. His heroic Newton reunites Truth, Goodness, and Beauty by tracing "the secret Hand of Providence," by surpassing in scope and ethical merit the ancients' conquests won through "Violence unmanly, and sore Deeds / Of Cruelty and Blood," and by untwisting "all the shining Robe of Day," revealing a world of light, that "Infinite Source / Of Beauty, ever-flushing, ever-new!" Behind this achievement plays the rhetoric of temporality, since, after all, Thomson was writing a memorial poem. He therefore traces Newton's career through time, as "with heroic Patience Years on Years / Deep-searching," Newton "saw at last the System dawn, / And shine, of all his Race, on him alone." Thomson presents first the earthly, then the cosmic effects of gravitation; next, the plotting of orbits, even those of comets; the wonders of Newton's optics; and finally a brief tribute to the historical research–the recovery of human time itself–with which the great man occupied his later years. But for Newton a career in time mirrors a career after time. His progress on earth resembles that progress toward full and universal knowledge that some writers of the time saw as a promised delight of heaven: Newton's terrestrial life gave a foretaste of the hereafter to which he had now flown, to continue "comparing Things with Things, in Rapture lost, / And grateful Adoration" among "the whirling Orbs." Similarly, on earth he anticipated the very tone of mind that marks him on high, where he can sit "in dread Discourse" with angels or the other blessed; here among mortals he shared with his friends "the vast unborrow'd Treasures of his Mind," always "Fervent in doing well."

Thomson in his mid twenties had made a considerable reputation, and the humble Scots tutor felt confident enough to pitch himself into politics, at least in verse, with the poem *Britannia*. He now enjoyed the benefits of lofty friends, such as Algernon and Frances Seymour, the Earl and Countess of Hertford; the future bishop Thomas Rundle; the Oxford Professor of Poetry Joseph Spence; and George Bubb Dodington, Baron Melcombe, the dedicatee of *Summer*. In January 1729, perhaps influenced by Dodington's political advice, Thomson published anonymously his patriotic poem *Britannia*. When he had dedicated his lines on Newton to Walpole, Walpole and Dodington had been allies; now they were not. British indignation in the late 1720s was rising over Walpole's conciliatory–some thought cowardly–posture toward Spain, a nation that had besieged Gibraltar in February 1727 without calling forth a declaration of war from England. By the beginning of 1729, a process of peacemaking, begun in May 1727, was still incomplete, stalled after the congress of Soissons, and not to be given (temporary) fulfillment till the Treaty of

Seville in March 1729. Meanwhile, according to the patriot opposition, Spain continued to harm British interests on the high seas. *Britannia* appeared just in time for the opening of Parliament, with a Virgilian quotation from the indignant Neptune on its title page, and opening lines that presented a weeping Britannia, her garments rent and her laments flowing. "Unchastis'd, the insulting *Spaniard* dares / Infest the trading Flood" on which she gazes, while the weak, demoralized British slink. Peace, "first of human Blessings; and supreme!" is what Britannia desires, but sometimes war must keep the peace, "when Ruffian Force / Awakes the Fury of an injur'd State." Britannia invokes the glorious past of Britain, its special resources "By lavish Nature thrust into your Hand," its emptiness if deprived of trade, and the beauties of Liberty, "The Light of Life! the Sun of Human Kind! / Whence Heroes, Bards, and Patriots borrow Flame." At the conclusion she realizes that Parliament has convened–"my Sons, the Sons of Freedom! meet / In awful Senate"–and flies there to "Burn in the Patriot's Thought, flow from his Tongue / In fearless Truth."

Since both government and opposition seized on *Britannia*, it must have been thought successful. The opposition's use for it is plain, but the pro-Walpole faction also managed to turn it to advantage. The government newspaper, the *Daily Journal* (28 January 1729), quoted Britannia's paean to peace, insisting that the "charming . . . Description" would lead one "to extol and applaud the Pacific Measures that have hitherto been pursu'd by his Majesty and his Ministers, to preserve to us those invaluable Blessings" and to "give so just a Preference to those *Divine Men* . . . who study to cultivate the Arts of Peace." Despite this appropriation, other poets and pamphleteers hostile to Walpole's pacifism also took up Thomson's lead. The policy of war was eventually pursued unto disillusionment, and its heralds were forgotten. To the reader for whom the policy decisions of 1729 have lost their savor, *Britannia*, too, will have lost most of its.

Another public venue, besides political agitation, was the stage. Thomson's gift with blank verse and serious sentiments made tragedy a natural outlet for him, and the "Roman" genre, parented by John Dryden's *All for Love* (1677) and Addison's *Cato* (1713), was the mode of choice. In all he was to write five such plays, some more specifically "Roman" than others. The first of these, *The Tragedy of Sophonisba*, was performed

Illustration for Spring, *Thomson's 1728 poem, as it appeared in the first edition of* The Seasons

at Drury Lane on 28 February 1730. As reported by Grant, the painter William Aikman, one of Thomson's good friends, said it was praised on rehearsal so "extravagantly" by the actress "Mrs Oldfield and several of the [other] players" as to make him worry: "I wish they may not raise peoples' expectations to a height about it that cannot be satisfied." The cast and Thomson's lines, though, proved more than equal to the public's hopes. Anne Oldfield, a great Cleopatra and (in Nicholas Rowe's *The Fair Penitent*, 1703) Calista, played the title role; Thomson wrote in the preface to the published play that "she excelled what, even in the fondness of an author, I could either wish or imagine." The equally skilled Robert Wilks, impetuous and tender, was a fine Masinissa. Several of the royal family attended, and Thomson received permission to dedicate the play to the queen. Continuing the theme of *Britannia*, he did so by comparing the naval and commer-

cial power of Sophonisba's Carthage unfavorably with that of Caroline's England.

Thomson began with a much-used story, most familiar on the London stage in a version by Nathaniel Lee (1675) still occasionally revived. It comes from Livy's histories, where the beautiful Carthaginian Sophonisba, after the Romans' defeat of her nation, wins back the heart of her former betrothed, Prince Masinissa, now allied with the enemy. Scipio Africanus, fearful of her influence, successfully exhorts the blushing, groaning, and weeping prince to valor, not the weakness of love, and Masinissa presents his new bride with a bowl of poison so that she may save herself from the Roman slavery to which he otherwise would have to consign her. She drinks fearlessly and dies. By and large, Thomson (unlike Lee) keeps to this narrative, which he says in his preface attracted him by its "great simplicity": "It is one, regular, and uniform, not charged with a multiplicity of incidents, and yet affording several revolutions of fortune; by which the passions may be excited, varied, and driven to their full tumult of emotion." The passions here are love and honor, the staples of Restoration and early-eighteenth-century tragedy, sauced with militant patriotism, suitable for the author of *Britannia*. As might be expected from Thomson's description of his play, the conflicts are more emotional and moral than political, and he tries to make the group of characters embody these conflicts rather than to depict people with complex motives. *Sophonisba* presents not individuals but a system, the proper working of which generates a measure of disaster and a measure of triumph. In this it partly resembles *The Seasons*.

The action of the play consists of a series of dialogues: Sophonisba and her confidante Phoenissa; Masinissa and his confidante Narva; Masinissa and Sophonisba's vanquished, vengeful husband Syphax; Masinissa and Sophonisba; Sophonisba and Syphax; Masinissa and Scipio's lieutenant Lelius; Masinissa and Scipio—all have one or more dialogues in which each presents at least (and at most) a partially valid position in opposition to the other. Each of the main characters is compelled to a position that he or she also, in some respects, freely chooses. Masinissa alone has two such positions, the "Roman" and the lover's, that put him in a double bind, where each course of action has its powerful virtues and grave faults. Double-bind tragedy, which developed with those still-current favorites Dryden and Thomas Otway, suited an ethically passionate and interrogative mode of thought widespread in the eighteenth century. It also involved, from the 1670s on, a complicating of gender roles, with the hero torn between more "masculine" and softer, more "feminine" values. Perhaps George Lillo's tragedy *The London Merchant*, performed the year after *Sophonisba*, draws from this complication its fullest potential, but Thomson's play comes close. While Masinissa melts, Queen Sophonisba herself, far more militant a patriot than in Livy, thinks of love as a mere strategy for furthering the goals of Carthage. Her splendor is in being manly, as Masinissa's tragedy and the source of one's sympathy for him, is in his emotional androgyny.

Before Thomson gave the world *Britannia* and *Sophonisba*, he had published *Spring* in June 1728, dedicating it to Lady Hertford. Now two years later, in June 1730, *Autumn* appeared, first in a handsome one-guinea subscription edition of

the entire *Seasons*, together with "A Hymn on the Seasons" and the lines on Newton. The previously published poems on seasons were revised, especially *Winter*, in which Thomson nearly doubled the 405 lines of the first edition, and the volume was fitted with handsome plates drawn by the most important artist and designer of the day, William Kent. The dazzling list of subscribers, beginning with the queen and members of the peerage and including fellow writers such as Pope, Ramsay, William Somervile, John Arbuthnot, and Edward Young, indicates Thomson's stature as he approached the age of thirty. Keeping this intellectually and socially posh company had already affected the shape of *The Seasons*; so did the style of life into which Thomson now glided. With the sale of over 450 copies of this subscription edition, and the sale of his copyrights (from which he had been profiting quite amply) to his publishers, John Millan and Andrew Millar, he found himself nearly well-to-do. But, since he was feckless, he needed every shilling and in future years was to revise and enlarge *The Seasons* over and over in some measure for that reason. As he did so, he moved further from the sharp focus with which he had begun in 1726. Thomson progressively opened his poem to different poetic modes—the tale, homily, satire, poeticized science—so as to encompass the diverse voices that saturated the natural world of which he wrote. The four serial poems now presented a vast, mingled array of scenes, reflections, narratives, descriptions, and panegyrics. In its original form, *Winter* had among other things spoken to the experience of Thomson the emigré Scot; *The Seasons* spoke from the vantage of a modern Briton who knew the order and variety of the world through science, travel, and moral observation—a modern Briton was a cosmopolitan.

Some critics of *The Seasons* have drawn a post-Wordsworthian line between Thomson's fine, fresh depictions of nature and what they see as his woolly, worn homilies to man. As his poem went from version to version, their argument goes, he kept swathing and muffling the real merits of *The Seasons* in these pieties. Two issues are in play here, one of execution, the other of plan. As to execution, the critics may be right. Thomson's greatest talents lay in natural description, not moral comment, and the assured nods and amens for his moral observations may well have allowed him to be slipshod in working out his verse for them. During the eighteenth cen-

Illustration for Thomson's poem Autumn *from the first edition of* The Seasons. *The poem was revised and published separately later in 1730.*

tury, morality in verse could aim for elegance, if moral sensibility was supposed to be an effect of a refined and civilized spirit, or it could aim for a simple immediacy if it was to strike a universal chord in the human breast; but neither of these styles exercised much discipline over the poet. Thomson, therefore, does less well with commonplaces than with material where novelty, a specific imaginative vision, or an aphoristic energy prodded him to give precise shape to his lines. Besides, the vividness and evocative strength that distinguish much of *The Seasons* gave the homilies hard competition, made harder when later readers are supercilious about the homiletic mode itself.

As to the plan of *The Seasons*, however, opening his poem to greater diversity surely formed part of a design akin to the one that underlay his elegy for Newton: a weaving together of truth,

goodness, and beauty. The spatiotemporal world, imaged in the seasons, needed to be caught in a total mimesis, reflecting and reflected upon from the viewpoints Thomson might assume; or at least such a mimesis had to be successfully evoked. Whereas Newton himself could present nature in a regularized form, plotted out by the laws of physics, Thomson had to make do with a crowd of distracting particulars. No wonder he kept revising, and no wonder, too, that he produced some incoherences. Some earlier descriptive poems, such as John Denham's *Cooper's Hill* (1642) or Pope's *Windsor-Forest* (1713), had fitted together nicely in accord with a scheme of *discordia concors*, a harmony of heterogeneity. More than his predecessors, though, Thomson had to accommodate another complication–point of view. In *The Seasons* he had to bring together at least three incompatible, legitimate, and necessary perspectives: a sense of human beings as mere creatures within nature, of humans as moral and experiential centers within nature, and of human readers reflecting upon nature, including its human population. For this fidelity to nature as variously experienced, Thomson surrendered the sort of unity he achieved in the 1726 *Winter*, or he deferred it to an underlying divine order outside experience and to a conceptual or verbal order, the totalizing that the general term "Spring" or "Summer" implies. Different readers would have these orders in mind to different degrees when moving through the absorbing descriptions, sharp contrasts, and digressions of *The Seasons*, so that the interplay between a reader's sense of order and sense of untamable profusion becomes another significant effect in the poem. As Thomson lengthened *The Seasons*, the forest floor of profusion intertwined even more densely over the underlying order, so that he no doubt felt increasing need to proclaim how ordered his world was and how special the human condition within it.

The ultimate unifying truth of *The Seasons*, guarantor of beauty and goodness, was God's, such as could be intuited or named but known only as ground for all phenomena. The truths that testified to it were those of evoked experience, of course, but also those of science. From the regularity of scientific processes, Thomson could depict a nature of rich, indicative particulars that did not crumble into randomness or mere density. He could also place his readers as among a race of beings who were wise enough to rise above particulars precisely by passing through them, by observing them with a close eye. This double virtue for science–as witness to God's legible plan and as mediatrix between that plan and valuable, experienced details–Thomson drew from the mass of writing known as physicotheology, which stressed the wonderful fitness and economy of the natural world. Thus, for instance, in *Spring* he hails the "Source of Being! Universal Soul / Of Heaven and Earth! Essential Presence . . . !" whose "master-hand" makes plants nourish themselves; and in *Summer* he sings of the Sun, "in whom best seen shines out thy Maker," for " 'Tis by thy secret, strong, attractive force" that the solar "system rolls entire– from the far bourne / Of utmost Saturn . . . to Mercury." Other passages deal with insects, the percolation of subterranean waters, and the creation of fogs–all these, and some briefer references, betoken nature's complexity and yet ideal

legibility to someone who loves the world intellectually as well as emotionally. They remind the twentieth-century reader how thin much post-Thomsonian descriptive poetry was to become, limited to elaborating only two of Thomson's effects, verbal photography and reflection of the writer's own mind. There has been another loss, too, for the scientific passages can hardly strike one today as they did Thomson's audience, who knew gravitation, plant respiration, and microscopy as recent discoveries, not as ahistorical facts but as part of a new, surprising dominion of the mind. While Thomson would have thought– wrongly–of his homiletic passages as universal, free of history, he surely did mean in his scientific passages to allude to the historical momentum that his own age had given to finding the "timeless" truths of nature. Therefore, his Latinate diction not only harked back to his poetic ancestors, it drew from the language of the new science, so marking his readers both as heirs of the old philosophic poets, Lucretius or Virgil, and as voyagers in an age of nonclassical discovery, a British order of nature and humankind that transcended the Roman.

The blank verse of *The Seasons* is somewhat grander than that of the 1726 *Winter*: though Thomson continues to draw on dramatic and Miltonic blank verse, he refers more insistently to Virgil's *Georgics*, the last major classical poem to make the worlds of experienced nature and scientifically understood nature mesh. The example of the *Georgics*, language aside, surely prompted Thomson to produce as comprehensive, artfully disordered, and closely mimetic a poem as *The Seasons*, once the early *Winter* had started him presenting humans within a demanding, splendid nature. Scots education paid more homage to Latin than did English, and among Latin poems, the *Georgics* had a special place of honor, as what Addison called "the most complete, elaborate, and finished piece of all antiquity" ("Essay on Virgil's *Georgics*," 1697). Its vividness of description was thought to be such that, as Addison said, "we receive more strong and lively ideas of things from his words, than we could have done from the objects themselves." In addition, its majesty and grace of language ennobled the commonplace, allowing Virgil to move easily from the details of husbandry to moral precept, historical interlude, images of the natural order, and evocation of Roman majesty. Thomson's aims closely resembled those he saw modeled by Virgil, whose high rural patriotism and quick sense of the inter-

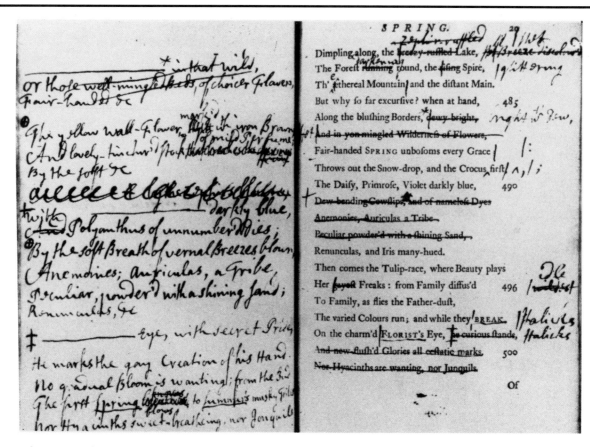

Pages from an interleaved copy of The Works of Mr. Thomson *(1738) with the poet's revisions for the 1744 edition of* The
Seasons *(by permission of the British Library)*

change between humans and nature generally inspired *The Seasons* and from whose work Thomson adapted or even, at times, paraphrased passages directly. In its language, then, *The Seasons* keeps returning to Latinate words, often ones with scientific force ("sublimed," "convolved," "efflux," "infracted," "ovarious," "flexile," "concoctive," and "constringent," for example), or, rarely, their etymological force ("the spreading beech, that o'er the stream / Incumbent hung"). Thomson also showed a fondness for compound words (such as "hollow-blustering," "new-creating," "mute-imploring," and "plume-dark") after the fashion of Latin ("res publica," "paterfamilias," "ignicolor," and "celeripes"). Latinate usages are also Miltonic, so that one might speculate that Thomson perhaps took the relation of the *Georgics* and the *Aeneid* in Latin as a model for that of his own poem, *The Seasons*, to *Paradise Lost* in English. However that may be, as the ambition and the lexicon of *The Seasons* make the Latin usages allude to Milton, the form, scope, and subject of the poem make them allude to Vir-

gil. One need not particularize further, for like several of his contemporaries, Thomson strives for a texture of broadly unified allusiveness that serves as a sign of emulation, an homage, an appropriation, and a going beyond.

Thomson placed *The Seasons* carefully, then, within poetic and cultural traditions, and located the objects he depicts within a variety of perspectives. In these concerns he resembled his contemporaries, as indeed he did in his moment-by-moment treatment of objects in his verse. Some lines from *Autumn* serve as an example:

Hence from the busy joy-resounding fields,
In cheerful error let us tread the maze
Of Autumn unconfined; and taste, revived,
The breath of orchard big with bending fruit.
Obedient to the breeze and beating ray,
From the deep-loaded bough a mellow shower
Incessant melts away. The juicy pear
Lies in a soft profusion scattered round.
A various sweetness swells the gentle race,
By Nature's all-refining hand prepared,
Of tempered sun, and water, earth, and air,

In ever-changing compositions mixed.
Such, falling frequent through the chiller night,
The fragrant stores, the wide-projected heaps
Of apples, which the lusty-handed year
Innumerous o'er the blushing orchard shakes.

In these lines are the compound words and terms used in Latin rather than English senses ("error" instead of "wandering," "wide-projected" meaning "thrown"); here is science, in the four elements of the "ever-changing composition"; here is also closely worked order, not only in Thomson's exquisite sense of sound, which a reading aloud will reveal, but also in the placement of objects. One moves from the openness of the field to a "maze" minus its usual negative connotation of baffled confinement, since instead one is "revived" along the mazy path one chooses among the trees in an orchard, while the notion of revival is emphasized by the personification and pregnancy of the orchard. The curvilinear movement of "error" now turns into the "big"-ness and "bending" of the boughs, the fully ripe "juicy pear," and the sweetness that "swells" the gentle race. The "breeze" (air), "beating ray" (sun/fire), water imagery in "shower" and "melts," and the earth on which the "soft profusion" of fruit lies are to reappear a few lines later as the "ever-changing composition." Thomson then steps back–with the comment about Nature's hand–from the sunny afternoon and juxtaposes it with the "chiller night" when apples fall; but, of course, both times offer delight and profusion (pears "scattered round" and "wide-projected heaps" of apples), just as the busy fields and the mazy orchard both offer joy. The leitmotif here, after all, is the ideal of cooperative compounding–difference as forms of the same–expressed in the mixing of the four elements. As this passage ends, the image of pregnancy returns when "the lusty-handed year" makes the orchard blush, responding to his shaken-down gifts but also simply red with apples. By such intertwining of analogy and contrast, Thomson constructs *The Seasons*, not as a unified poem but as a continuous experience.

Continuity on the level of the reading consciousness, a pointing toward a divine totality that one can suppose and believe in, and yet, between these wholes, only an unruly, fractured, and polyvalent world, represented by a succession of vivid, contrasting, and yet often analogous fragments–those are the forms of *The Seasons*. Thomson found much to do each time he

came to revise a poem the texture of which required such delicate, meticulous adjustments for continuity while the length and sequence of episodes remained so open. The public rewarded him well: in the fifty years after his death some 170 different editions of his *Works* or *The Seasons* appeared, including translations into French, German, and Dutch.

In early November 1730 Thomson set out for a tour of the Continent as companion to Charles Richard Talbot, the twenty-one-year-old son and heir of Solicitor-General Charles Talbot. The elder Talbot allotted Thomson two hundred pounds per annum, which must have been paid in 1731 and 1732, while the two travelers remained on the foreign side of the Channel. "Travelling," Thomson wrote to Dodington in October 1730, before setting off, "has long been my fondest wish.... The storing one's imagination with ideas of all-beautiful, all-great, and all-perfect Nature: these are the pure *Materia Poetica*, the light and colours, with which fancy kindles up her whole creation, paints a sentiment, and even embodies an abstracted thought. I long to see the fields where Virgil gathered his immortal honey, and tread the same ground where men have thought and acted so greatly." When he actually trod alien soil as a sturdy Briton, however, Thomson found the Virgilian fields bare of their mellifluous clover, and the grounds of past greatness overgrown with gorse. "That Enthusiasm I had upon me with regard to travelling goes off, I find, very fast," he informed Dodington from Rome a year later. In accord with the long-standing view that Italy was so badly governed, so priest-ridden, as he wrote to Dodington, that "human Arts and Industry" were nearly "extirpated" and "Nature herself" disfigured, he planned the first part of his long poem *Liberty* (1735-1736), moved by the evocative sight of Roman ruins. Because of his patriotism, his zeal for commerce, his successful Roman play (*Sophonisba*), his moral warmth, and his devotion to the pleasures of the imagination, he may also have seen himself as a successor to Addison, whose familiar poem *A Letter from Italy* (1704) and lengthy *Remarks on Several Parts of Italy* (1705) he drew upon quite heavily. Eventually *Liberty* was to have five parts, about thirty-four hundred lines in all, on which Thomson worked for two years after his return to England in January 1733: these were published over a little more than a year (January 1735-February 1736). But just as Europe disappointed him, so his Euro-

Damon (left background) discovers the nude Musidora bathing with two companions—a 1795 painting by Benjamin West based on a scene from Summer *(private collection; from* The Paintings of Benjamin West, *by Helmut von Erffa and Allen Staley, 1986)*

pean poem was to do. *Liberty* was Thomson's first critical failure: Millar had three thousand plain-paper copies of Part I printed, but only two thousand of Parts II and III, and a mere one thousand of Parts IV and V.

Liberty describes spatial and temporal denuding: land after land achieves magnificence through devotion to a republican ideal; land after land falls back into decay through selfishness, party politics, luxury, and despotism. In line with the dubious but widely believed principle that high culture flourishes most, if not exclusively, in free lands, the sojourns and flights of Liberty, here personified, also mark the points in history where the arts prospered or fell into ruin. Like *Britannia*, *Liberty* was an opposition poem, and its claim to state a universal principle of culture over a wide variety of nations represents opposition ideology, the rendering "natural" of a historically local set of nationalistic notions. The militancy of *Britannia* embodies part of this set, specified through British naval power and commerce: this is the language of empire, not (yet) for conquest at any cost but surely for peaceful conquest through the extension of

trade. *Liberty* embodies another two parts of the set. First it presents an ideal of the state as a res publica, a single and entire center of commitment. The rejected extremes here for Thomson are Continental despotism, in which the state is the king's instead of belonging to all citizens, and Walpole's individualism, in which the state is an arena for self-interest. Second, the poem presents a double lineage for Britain. One is a spiritualized version of the actual, in which monarchs succeed each other but in which freedom progresses, and the other is an actualized version of the spiritual, in which the ideal of liberty moves from one home to another till it settles, provisionally, in the Britain of the present day. Both the republican ideal and the double history erect in Britain a communal object of immeasurable value, thus magnifying any threat to it, thus justifying the union (in 1707) of England and Scotland, and thus interlocking the political and economic systems of free men and free merchants. The last section of *Liberty* depicts the arts and public works alike embellishing this happy land.

Obviously, though Thomson couches the poem as a dramatic narration of things seen, he himself did not see the events he narrates, and as a result *Liberty* is dense with borrowings from ancient and modern sources. Through these borrowings and the dramatic narration, Thomson tries to give the poem a context of authority, thence urgency. Eighteenth-century poets, of course, implicitly accepted a weak idea of intertextuality, that any poem is a weave of previous texts, although equally they placed far more weight on the writer's intentions than would late twentieth-century intertextual theorists. Thomson not only uses plain statements to make his intentions evident, he also invokes previous texts to attest to his opinions, and so he footnotes some claims. To show that the arts, exemplified by his own poem, traverse the same path as the movement of liberty, he reenacts these parallel movements with a double mimesis: the speech of Liberty, made in the 1730s, represents millennia of history; the poetry of Thomson, also made in the 1730s, merges history's realm of truth with the poet's realm of beauty and virtue. He wanted, finally, to bring the experiences of nations and ages into contemporary Britain, an appropriative commerce in ideas that Britain carries on by right. With the narrative voice of Liberty, Thomson hoped to give the poem the vividness that comes from personal witness, to justify his tropes with the suggestion that they arose from personal feeling, and to efface any impression of jingoism by making his speaker immune to mere national loyalties.

In doing all this, he had no more than mixed success. Samuel Johnson, writing his biography of Thomson for *The Lives of the Poets* forty years later, acidly remarks, "At this time a long course of opposition to Sir Robert Walpole had filled the nation with clamours for liberty, of which no man felt the want, and with care for liberty, which was not in danger." Yet, says Johnson, the poem remained unread, "condemned to harbour spiders, and to gather dust," and for a good reason, since "the recurrence of the same images must tire in time; an enumeration of examples to prove a position which nobody denied, as it was from the beginning superfluous, must quickly grow disgusting." Common experience shows, however, that people love to be told eloquently what they already know, and a fortiori so, one would think, for a populace who raise a cry for liberty even when (in Johnson's eyes) it was unendangered and ample. More likely than Johnson's reason is that *Liberty* did not meet the expectations of those whom *The Seasons* had delighted. As *Liberty* swept through time, gathering

Thomson, circa 1736 (portrait by Stephen Slaughter; by permission of the Leicester Museum)

dialectic speed, it offered little scope for Thomson's great descriptive powers. At such spots as he can exercise these, one realizes how much they have been missed, as in Part IV when "the snow-fed Torrent, in white Mazes tost" falls "to the clear Aetherial Lake below," while "high o'ertopping all the broken Scene" appears "The Mountain fading into Sky; where shines / On Winter Winter shivering, and whose Top / Licks from their cloudy Magazine the Snows." Much more often, *Liberty* is simply oratorical, well done in a style that would have brought some minor writer into a recognized place in literary history but that disappoints when coming from Thomson.

Thomson's idea of British liberty took party politics, luxury, and lust for personal gain as threats; and fresh from writing the dramatic verse of his poem, he turned once more to the theater, to show how self-interest defeats self-sacrificial public spirit. His new play was the tragedy *Agamemnon*, first performed in April 1738, with the reigning tragedian of the time, James Quin, in the title role and an excellent supporting cast. Thomson's version of the story reworks the structures of *Sophonisba*. Agamemnon himself takes on the moral positions of Masinissa and Scipio, in that virtue and (fallible) wisdom beam from him as king, that he loves deeply (Clytemnestra and Iphigeneia), but that he puts the public good before his own affections. Thus he has, for honor and duty's sake, spent ten years far from his beloved wife and has allowed his daughter to be sacrificed, an act that his other daughter, Electra, does not hold against him. The weakness and vacillation of Masinissa till the end here belong to Clytemnestra, guilt-racked for her adultery with Egisthus, rancorous about the sacrifice of Iphigeneia, and stung with jealousy over Agamemnon's supposed affair (he is wholly pure in this play) with Cassandra. *Sophonisba*, dedicated to Queen Caroline, depicted a patriot queen, but now a patriot king was in order, with the death of Caroline (an ally of Walpole's to the last) and the intensification of party politics around the figures of George II, the Prince of Wales, and the menacing prime minister. Thomson exhibits an Egisthus as spiteful and ill willed as Syphax, far stronger than Aeschylus's Aegisthus, and fit to stand in for the Patriots' archvillain, Walpole. This murderous underling in *Agamemnon* was a model of the "statesman" or wicked deputy, such as would in the political climate of the 1730s have been applied to Walpole even if Egisthus had not exiled the wise advisor Melisander in Thomson's play, just as Walpole had kept Bolingbroke, the opposition's *éminence grise*, in French exile for ten years. Pope, in May 1738 (the next month), was able to use "*Aegysthus*" as a name for Walpole in *Epilogue to the Satires . . . Dialogue I.*

Despite its Greek setting, *Agamemnon* fits the subgenre of the "Roman play," in which an admirable protagonist embodies virtue and patriotism, quelling personal desires in favor of serving his country's needs. The loftier the figure, the greater his benevolence in this intensified version of noblesse oblige. Some of Dryden's tragedies hint at this subgenre, and, as mentioned, Addison's *Cato* represents it fully. Still, Roman plays did not really thrive on the London stage till the opposition to Walpole grew in the 1730s. As in *Cato*, which also became more popular, the message of *Agamemnon* is intensified by the spectacle of its patriot king dead. He is a victim of his own rectitude, for Thomson's Agamemnon has to die partly to prevent his planned seizure of the villainous Egisthus: "The sleep of death alone shall seal these eyes," he proclaims, "While such a wretch holds power in my dominions." In this death, however, lies a serious weakness for Thomson's play. Unlike Cato, who commits suicide as he speaks noble soliloquies, Agamemnon could not very well die on stage—one cannot brave one's killer from one's bath—and the fact of his offstage murder could not keep the audience in suspense, since they knew the story in advance. As a result, the tension and tragedy mount as the patriot king's death impends, while Agamemnon himself stays unseen, unheard. The weight of the last two acts must therefore be borne largely by Clytemnestra, the most conflicted and psychologically most interesting (that is, least "Roman") of the characters, whose part Thomson wrote to good effect for the tragedienne Mary Porter. But this was to focus upon the politically least telling figure while making the patriot king wholly ineffective. Perhaps this misfiring explains why, star cast and all, *Agamemnon* played only nine times, twice at the command of the opposition's darling, the Prince of Wales, and then dropped from sight, never to return to the London stage in the eighteenth century. Its excellence as a reading tragedy, however, led Millar to be able to sell forty-five hundred copies of it.

The mid 1730s were years of change and consolidation in Thomson's life. In late 1733 he had lost his traveling companion Talbot to death, and he had gained a sinecure from the young man's father, for when the elder Talbot was made lord chancellor he appointed Thomson as secretary of the briefs. (When Thomson lost the post in 1737—at Lord Talbot's death the chancellorship passed to Lord Hardwicke, an ally of Walpole's—the Prince of Wales fully indemnified him with a pension of one hundred pounds a year.) After having lived for ten years in London or abroad, Thomson moved in 1736 from his old lodgings just off the Strand and took a cottage in Richmond, then a village about eight miles as the crow flies, a good bit longer as the roads ran, from Hyde Park Corner. This distance and his fear of horses gave glee to his two wig makers, for as the assistant of one later recalled (in William Hone's *Table Book*, 1827), "an excellent customer he was to both": Thomson had "a dozen [wigs] at a time, . . . and all of them so big that nobody else could wear them. I suppose his sweating to such a degree made him have so many; for I have known him spoil a new one only in walking from London," something he did "at all hours in the night." Despite the expense and bother, Thomson must have relished life in the near country, for in 1739 he moved to a larger cottage in Richmond, with seven rooms and a kitchen, where a housekeeper attended to his needs and he charitably attended to the needs of two nephews, whom he had employed as gardeners.

Lacking his own family, Thomson at Richmond gave himself over to a full social life, eating, drinking, and talking a great deal. His friend Andrew Mitchell told Boswell in 1764 (as reported in Boswell's *Journal*) "that notwithstanding of his fine imitation of Ovid on the Pythagorean system [of metempsychosis, in *Spring*], he was an egregious gormandizer of beefsteaks." As to his drinking, Lady Hertford, an early patron of Thomson's, wrote in 1742, that "He turns Day into Night, & Night into Day & is (as I am told) never awake till after Midnight & I doubt [that is, I suspect] has quite drown'd his Genius" (in Thomson's *Letters and Documents*, edited by Alan Dugald McKillop, 1958). He grew fat from his plate and punch bowl, and stoop-shouldered from, perhaps, his habit of writing late at night, peering dimly at his work by candlelight. His easygoing, sentimental temperament and disreputable hours might account for tales of his indolence. This ease of temper left Thomson often without money, with which he was quite negligent and generous, but it left him, too, with a great many friends, including Pope and Quin among the English, and numerous Scots. No harsh stories about him have ever appeared.

"Thomson used to sweat so much the first nights of his plays," said Mitchell, "that when he came and met his friends at a tavern in the [Covent Garden] Piazza, his wig was as if it had been dipped in an oil-pot." If so, his wig makers were disappointed in late March 1739 when the first night of Thomson's third tragedy, *Edward and Eleonora*, was cancelled by order of the lord chamberlain's office. Though this play is, by and large, politically innocuous, at least in its printed version, Thomson cannot have been amazed by the censorship. In January 1738, three months before *Agamemnon* with its Walpolean Egisthus, Thomson had responded to the Licensing Act for the stage (July 1737) by writing a preface to a new edition of Milton's *Areopagitica* (1644), and then having another of Milton's tracts, this time advocating war on Spain, printed together with his own *Britannia*. This second book appeared in the same month (March 1738) as Captain Robert Jenkins displayed his ear, severed by the Spanish, to Parliament, and the opposition was intensifying the cry for war. In February 1739 Thomson wrote the prologue to his friend Mallet's *Mustapha* in which an evil vizier and a vengeful queen slander a noble prince to his father, and so cause his death. *Mustapha* made the lord chamberlain's office deny a license a few weeks later to the next exercise in reading between the lines, Henry Brooke's *Gustavus Vasa, or, The Deliverer of His Country* (1739). Brooke, an Irish protegé of Swift's, enjoyed through Pope the friendship of opposition leaders, just as Thomson did. In *Gustavus Vasa*, the patriot king-to-be must contend with an evil "statesman," Trollio, to free his land from foreign domination by Christiern; George II, of course, often spent time in his Hanoverian realm. Given the battle between Prince Frederick and his father, the battle between Vasa and the older Christiern, who calls him "boy," may have seemed politically audacious, especially because it repeats the fatal conflict between father and son in *Mustapha*.

Brooke's play was the first to be forbidden under the Licensing Act, *Edward and Eleonora* the second. Brooke had immediately arranged for *Gustavus Vasa* to be printed by subscription, found the staunch defenders of liberty and opposition ready to buy, and profited handsomely. He also supervised a production of the play in Dublin, under the taunting name *The Patriot*. As to the printing, Thomson followed suit, selling a thousand fine royal copies of his play in addition to thirty-five hundred in ordinary paper. If the subscribers longed for political red meat, they were disappointed to find a tale of wifely sacrifice and manly honor. Eleonora surrenders her own life to save that of her husband, the future King Edward I of England, from whose envenomed wound she sucks the poison; the pagan sultan, Selim, accused of sending the assassin who stabs Edward, risks his life to save his honor by bringing the antidote to the poison; all ends happily as spouses are reunited, Christian and pagan rest at peace, and Edward returns to England as king. In the play's discussion of the prince's ascent to the throne lay the censor's objections, since Edward's royal father (as seen in act 1) needs to be saved "from his ministers, from those / Who hold him captive in the worst of chains," those "low corrupt insinuating traitors" who deny "the royal heir" his just claim "To share his father's inmost heart and counsels" while they "make / A property, a market of his honour." The death of Henry III, announced in act 4, again elicits comments about an English monarch "abus'd" and "deluded" by "smiling traitors." Mostly, though,

Manuscript (circa 1743) for one of the poems Thomson wrote to woo Elizabeth Young, referred to as Amanda in the published versions (MA 1575; by permission of the Pierpont Morgan Library)

Edward and Eleonora depicts virtue, strives for pathos, and preaches religious tolerance. This last matter was not entirely free of politics, however, since the Barbary states (Morocco, Algiers, Tunis, and Tripoli) served as Britain's natural allies against Spain in the Mediterranean near Gibraltar.

When Frederick, Prince of Wales's first child, Princess Augusta, had been born on 1 August 1737, Thomson had written an ode to the happy father, with expectable slurs on the *"selfish-Parties"* and "deep *Corruption*" that eat at Britain's soul, and praise of "the promis'd Glories of Thy Reign" and Frederick's prospective offspring, new Edwards, Henrys, Annas, and Elizas. For the Princess's third birthday, Frederick planned a gala masque at his estate Cliefden, for which the opposition's favorite playwrights, Thomson and Mallet, were to produce a script, with music by Thomas Arne. *Alfred* (1740) ended with what has become the most often-heard piece of eighteenth-century British music or poetry, "Rule Britannia," written by Thomson, set to music by Arne, and sung by Thomas Lowe, who, said Charles Burney, had the finest tenor voice he had ever heard in his life. In 1735, the prince had erected a statue of King Alfred in his gardens in Pall Mall, to endorse the patriot version of history, which assigned Saxon origins to the ideal of the free commonwealth. Since Alfred had been so declared the founder of English liberties, the plot of Thomson and Mallet's masque again presented the patriot myth, in which the true and meritorious king (like Mallet's Mustapha, Brooks's Gustavus

Vasa, and Thomson's Edward) waits to ascend the throne and right all wrongs. During the masque, King Alfred, briefly unseated by the Danes, whiles away his exile by watching a pageant of future British history, a lineage of virtue and freedom, before he receives news that a new battle has restored him. In keeping with the honor roll of monarchs to whom Thomson had paid homage three years earlier, the pageant presents an Edward and Eliza, Edward III and his son the Black Prince, together with Queen Philippa (since the Princess of Windsor was also to be honored), and Elizabeth I. Both these monarchs, Edward III and Elizabeth, had a special patriot status, as shown by the tribute they get in Bolingbroke's *Remarks on the History of England* (1754). Edward was "a glorious king," "fierce and terrible to his enemies [but] amiable and indulgent to his subjects," a man who "loved . . . the spirit of liberty in his people" and quashed the ministers who had ruled his unhappy father. Elizabeth "was neither deceived, like [her predecessors], by her ministers; nor betrayed by her passions, to serve any other interest at the expence of England," so that "she was supported by the spirit of liberty; and she overcame that of faction." (The Scots Thomson and Mallet both had so deep an investment in this patriot myth, through which the British nation-state had for many centuries been freeing itself from absolutism, that both were willing to worship Elizabeth, no friend to Scotland, just as Thomson had glorified Edward I, Scotland's foe, in his last play.) The final monarch in the pageant of *Alfred* is William III, who dethroned a bad king. No wonder that, despite managerial plans, *Alfred* did not appear on the London stage till 1745.

Edward and Eleonora and *Alfred* put forward the ideal of wedded love, the domestic expression of the social harmonies that Thomson preached. He himself had had no such bliss, unlike Mallet, who married his second wife in October 1742, only months after the death of his first. Shortly after that, Thomson fell in love with Elizabeth Young, the sister-in-law of his close friend James Robertson, a London neighbor who now was physician to the court at Kew. Thomson's first letter to Young, a quick, hard-headed Scot whose Border Scots burr must have resembled his own, dates from March 1743. He gets right to the point: "What shall I say but that I love you, love you with the utmost Ardor, the most perfect Esteem, and inexpressible Tenderness. Imagination, Reason and the Heart, all con-

spire to love you." Unfortunately, the letter goes on with what look suspiciously like posturings, as Thomson addresses himself to Young's "Compassion," imagines how he will hide in the country to "indulge the melancholy Pleasure of continually musing on those Charms that have undone me," and moralizes that "surely Nature is too just and benevolent to suffer a Passion like mine to be in vain, or to Purposes of Ruin." None of Young's letters survive, though she did not discourage Thomson actively, since he kept seeing her and writing to her; but one may assume that she kept her impecunious, awkward lover at some distance. He was a good bit older than she—she was to marry the naval officer John Campbell, twenty years Thomson's junior—and, set in his bachelor habits, he must have made her wary of what life with him would be like. Though this courtship continued for at least three years, he was never to marry. By late 1747, when George Lyttelton, another staunch patriot, proposed someone as a wife for Thomson, he replied in a letter by praising the lady's "good and worthy," "charming and piquant" qualities, but sadly concluded: "every Man has a singular and uncontroulable Imagination of his own: now, as I told you before, She does not pique mine." Less than a year later, still a "difficult old Batchelor," he was dead.

Thomson's unrequited pursuit of Young may have contributed to the theme and tone of his next tragedy, *Tancred and Sigismunda* (1745), which he wrote in 1744, following his publication of a revised edition of *The Seasons*. With David Garrick and Susannah Cibber as the young lovers, the new play appeared on 18 March 1745 and ran nine nights; Millar printed five thousand copies of the text and, this time, not because he counted on political fervor for sales. Walpole was no longer an issue: unhorsed as prime minister in 1742, he had become earl of Orford, giving up his seat in the Commons and with it, his power; coincidentally, on the first night of *Tancred and Sigismunda*, he died. The success of the play, rather, depended on Thomson's powers of eliciting pathos, for which he went back to the double-bind model of *Sophonisba*. Each character acts for the best in accord with his or her own understanding, and all end in disaster. In order to prevent civil war in Sicily, Matteo Siffredi forges a document by which Tancred, the rightful prince, agrees to ascend to the throne peacefully by marrying the rival pretender to it, Princess Constantia. Siffredi also urges his daughter

Hail to the Day! hail to the smiling Skies!
That first unseal'd my lov'd Amanda's Eyes.
Blest Day! thou still my annual Voice shalt hear,
Thou joyous Leader of the brightening year!
How dead to mine the Laureat's venal Lyre!
How faint his Ardor! and how forc'd his Fire!
While to the _sovereign of my Heart_ I pray,
At once, a _Natal_ and a _New-years_ Lay:
Dull sack and Pensions prompt his Muse to sing:
From Love and Beauty my glad Numbers spring.

Come, source of Joy! come from thy southern Goal,
O Phœbus come! and chear my drooping Soul!
Come, with the Loves and Graces in thy Train,
Whate'er inspires the Bard or charms the Swain:
The dancing Hours, the rosy-finger'd Dews,
The gentle Zephirs, and the vernal Muse.
Thou com'st! thou com'st! I see thee from afar,
Nearer and nearer, roll thy golden Car:
Each Day, still something, from oppressive Night
Thy Empire gains, some Minutes more of Light;
The lucid Sky, all Nature, feels thy Power,
And Spring smiles out in every brighter Hour.

First page of a birthday poem written by Thomson for "Amanda" Young in 1744 (collection of Lady Gordon Cumming of Altyre)

Sigismunda, Tancred's betrothed, to marry the chief of Constantia's faction, Osmond; horrified by the forged agreement that she mistakes for Tancred's betrayal, she obeys her father. Tancred himself can do nothing—enraged over Siffredi's trick and yet unable to revenge himself on his beloved's father; passionately in love with Sigismunda and yet denied her; trained to be a man of action and yet seeing himself a pawn of his own father's will (he can have the throne only if he marries Constantia), of Siffredi's judgment, and of his royal position, which requires him to keep the peace. In this predicament he comes to Osmond's home to protest his love for Sigismunda, kills Osmond when attacked by him, and witnesses Sigismunda's death at the sword of her dying husband, who hopes to protect his honor. This play, with its endogenous logic, focused action, and highly motivated plot comes the closest of any of Thomson's plays to the simplicity and inexorability of Jean Racine's, a writer he particularly admired. All Thomson's tragedies give evidence of great abilities, but not always wisely used; they are never better used than in *Tancred and Sigismunda*.

Though enriched by the success of this play and given some financial ease in 1744 by receiving another sinecure, this time via Lyttelton, Thomson found himself less able to enjoy his old life, maybe in the wake of his failed romance. He spent a good deal of time with Lyttelton, probably resisting that evangelical lord's urging to become a practicing Christian. A new tragedy, *Coriolanus* (1749), was finished by early 1747, but was kept from the Covent Garden stage by Garrick's refusal to play a supporting role to his rival Quin; or, as Thomson put it in a letter of April 1748 to William Paterson, "Coriolanus has not yet appeared upon the Stage, from the little dirty Jealousy of Tullus—I mean of him who was desired to act Tullus, towards him who alone can act Coriolanus." The part of Tullus, by far the more psychologically intriguing of the two, would perfectly have suited the lively, "realistic" acting style of Garrick, while Quin, with his majestic and ornate tragic manner, was ideal for Coriolanus. Since Tullus is gnawed by envy of Coriolanus, whom eventually he kills so as to assure his own preeminence, Garrick's decision probably kept the audience from gossiping about the play as an allegory of theatrical politics: Quin was appearing less and Garrick more while the two were at the same house. *Coriolanus* was not played till January 1749, when Garrick had left for the management

of Drury Lane and Thomson had died. Performances served as a benefit for the poet's sisters, Jean Thomson and Mary Thomson Craig.

Thomson's *Coriolanus*—following Livy rather than Plutarch, Shakespeare's source—is no more an adaptation of Shakespeare's than Thomson's *Sophonisba* is of Lee's or his *Agamemnon* is of Aeschylus's. Pared down to a simple action, in a more Racinian than Shakespearean manner, this tragedy passes over the battles within Rome between plebeians and patricians and the subterfuges by which Rome was drawn into war—political issues that would have piqued Thomson's interest in his patriot days. His play instead focuses on the last day of the noble-minded but somewhat overweening Coriolanus. When expelled from Rome, in act 1, for his fiery denunciation of the tribunes, "a victim yielded / by her weak nobles to the madd'ning rabble," he seeks out his old Volscian foe, Tullus. Tullus joyfully grants him half the Volscian command, but then finds himself outdone by the newcomer who by nature dominates the scene. The pride that led Tullus to his magnanimity, "to see my rival-warrior / . . . bend his soul / . . . to sue for my protection," now (in act 4) leads him to repent it, and at the same time to recognize his self-deceit, as "down I plunge, betray'd even by my virtue, / From gulph to gulph, from shame to deeper shame." Tullus's disillusionment with himself leads him to hate Coriolanus, its cause, still more. The play ends with Tullus's henchmen stabbing Coriolanus and the killers being led off to face "a full council of the states at Antium." Paradoxically, the two great generals suffer from the same vice, a subjection of patriotism to self-interest: Coriolanus, as the closing homily of the play announces, should not have "rais'd his vengeful arm against his country," and Tullus should not have sacrificed even a renegade on the altar of his own ego. Since in 1745 and 1746 many of Thomson's fellow Scots had rebelled with the Young Pretender and been savagely butchered by the English general, the duke of Cumberland, the treatment of these two Roman warriors must have imposed an exceptionally delicate task upon Thomson; he carried it off faultlessly.

Coriolanus complements its predecessor, *Tancred and Sigismunda*, another play in which self and society are set opposite one another. In *Tancred and Sigismunda*, love is the victim of what one might call social honor, not internalized but understood as an inexorable and estranging burden handed down by the fathers who arrange the

Sigismunda, heroine of Thomson's 1745 tragedy Tancred and Sigismunda *(engraving by James Basire based on a painting by William Hogarth)*

"wise" political matches. In *Coriolanus* honor is the victim of a self-love that proves deeper than the love and honor it takes as masks. Now that the war fever of the late 1730s had abated, too, Thomson could give the clearest, least selfish voices to those of peace, reminding one that sublimated pride and envy, which mark the successful warrior in the form of glorious and noble emulation, are necessary but treacherous virtues. They turn magnanimity into a form of rationalized retreat, altruism into a self-annulment, command into a habit of domination. As in some of the earlier plays, like *Tancred and Sigismunda*, Thomson pitches his moral battleground less between virtues and vices than between varieties of the ethically defensible, or at least the ethically respected.

Similar conflicts reappear in *The Castle of Indolence* (1748), wherein the active life routs contemplative inaction. In form *The Castle* differs strikingly from anything he had published before.

This Spenserian imitation had been hatching since Thomson's return from the grand tour in the early 1730s. As he settled into his comfortable life, he wrote stanzas mocking himself and his friends. Since at the time he was enlarging on Britain as a great and ancient nation-state in the Miltonic poem *Liberty*, he plausibly adapted another father of British verse for this teasing verse. Thomson was at first aiming for a kind of mock-heroic, what the poet William Julius Mickle was to call "the ludicrous of which the antique phraseology and manner of Spenser are so happily and peculiarly susceptible" (introduction to *Sir Martyn*, 1767). Nonetheless, the idiom of *The Faerie Queene* also led Thomson to imbue *The Castle* with strong moral and allegorical force, especially given *Liberty*'s censure of idle luxury. Thomson's lazy friends appear in *The Castle* as victims of a wizard whose malign enchantments make them still more passive than their predilections had. Beneath them in their indolent retreat

Thomson, circa 1746 (painting based on a portrait by John Patoun; by permission of the National Portrait Gallery, London)

lies a "dark Den" that harbors half-dead Lethargy, "Soft-swoln and pale" Hydropsy, moping Hypochondria, Gout, and Apoplexy. In the second canto, the Knight of Arts and Industry, son of Selvaggio and Dame Poverty, repeats the journey that Liberty had taken in Thomson's earlier poem: he passes through the once-golden nations, more recently gray, "to slavish Sloth and Tyranny a Prey," except of course for Britain. Called from retirement like a British Cincinnatus, the Knight disenchants the Castle and frees its denizens. The preachier and more militant parts of *The Castle*, like comparable episodes in *The Faerie Queene*, tend to sit less well with modern readers than parts that rely for their effect on complexity rather than righteousness, but for Thomson the lack of complexity, the simplicity of truth, itself effected a moral understanding.

As with much of Thomson's earlier work, the fault line between virtue and vice here divides republican from individualist principles. Rural retirement, soft arts, imagination, and convivial distractions are true goods when they can be turned to aid the community, but tainted goods when, as in the Castle, the "One great Rule for All" is "That each should work his own Desire," when "every Man [has] stroll'd off his own glad Way." The enclosed castle acts as a metaphor for the "indolent" state of easy, friendly alienation, where real pleasure levitates over an unseen chasm, here allegorized as the "dark Den" of solitary, self-absorbed illness at the end of the first canto. The castle dwellers "eat, drink, study, sleep, ... melt the Time in Love, or wake the Lyre" as they choose, while the world appears only reflected or imagined, therefore only as the stuff of poetic reverie or a satire on vanity. Of course these views of the world are right, friendship and ease and pleasure are right, though inadequate, and Thomson presents them at their most appealing. Those whom he affectionately portrays as inhabiting the castle, his companions, are also appealing. Because indolence sequesters the poets, the satirist, the bon vivant, and the great actor from their proper field, the res publica; however, the castle dwellers take these right ideas and behaviors as fully sufficient, in which they are self-deceived. The individualist ethic, for Thomson, cuts people off from themselves and from the possible scope of their understanding as well as from their society. Hence that ethic "dull[s] the Sense" of private as well as public virtue.

Part of the brilliance behind Thomson's use of Spenser, then, is his thereby casting his poem in a doubly communitarian mode, first that of allegory, with its responsibility to an order that lies outside the poem itself, and second that of British history, of which the modern but often archaized language keeps reminding one. The stylistic temporality of *The Castle of Indolence* itself shows up the sham atemporality of Indolence's castle. In the narration of the first canto Thomson mostly lets his hybrid style run in counterpoint to effects of suspended time, such as the pastoral setting of the castle, the Epicurean "Syren Melody," of Indolence himself, and descriptions of habitual action. Through masterful use of sound and "romantic" imagery, he plays on the visionary quality in Spenser and brings one into real time only—and then obliquely—with the satire and the genial depictions à clef starting in stanza 49.

Canto 2, though, represents time in the life history of the Knight and in a portrait of modern British liberty, a once "great Plan" rapidly fragmenting into personal license: "Mind, mind yourselves! Why should the vulgar Man, / The Lacquey be more virtuous than his Lord?" The Knight sets off to the castle with the bard Philomelus, a "Druid-Wight" whose name relates him to the nightingale, hence to nature, but who, as Joseph Warton claimed, probably represents Thomson's great patriot ally Pope, who had died in 1744. Playing his "*British* Harp," the bard sings of history and temporal processes, thus converting "the better Sort" of person. The balky, on the other hand, stubbornly doting on "the harmless Sabbath of [their] Time," end up driven by Beggary and Scorn in "a ceaseless Round" like swine goaded without rest or mercy through

the filthy market town of eighteenth-century Brentford. Thomson devotes the first canto, then, to the calm inhabitants of the castle who gaze amusedly at a representation of restless worldlings "bustling to and fro with foolish Haste, / In search of Pleasures vain." He devotes the second to reinterpreting this image for the gazers themselves, as time takes over from their delusory dream.

Time took over too fast for Thomson in 1748. The first edition of *The Castle of Indolence* appeared in early May 1748 and the second edition in late September. In between these dates, at four in the morning of 27 August, Thomson died, quite unexpectedly, of what his friend and fellow poet Dr. John Armstrong called a "low nervous malignant" fever. Thomson's death, Armstrong went on (in a letter to Murdoch), "makes a hideous gap; and the loss of such an agreeable Friend turns some of the sweetest scenes in England into a something waste and desolate." Thomson appears to have died without enemies, was mourned widely, and, through William Collins's superb "Ode Occasioned by the Death of Mr. Thomson" (1749), given a tribute comparable to his own art. One cannot say the same for the attentions of his friend Lyttelton. Having striven during Thomson's life to convert him to Christianity, Lyttelton strove after Thomson's death to convert his poetry to decorum, and so produced a liberally revised and generally ignored version of Thomson's work in 1750. An edition of what Thomson himself wrote appeared in 1762, edited by Murdoch, one of the friends teased in *The Castle of Indolence*. In the same year a monument to Thomson was erected next to Shakespeare's in Westminster Abbey. His sculptured attributes are a laurel wreath, a tragic mask, an ancient harp, a book, and the cap of Liberty.

Letters:

James Thomson (1700-1748), Letters and Documents, edited by Alan Dugald McKillop (Lawrence, Kan.: University of Kansas Press, 1958);

McKillop, "Two More Thomson Letters," *Modern Philology*, 60 (November 1962): 128-130.

Bibliography:

Hilbert H. Campbell, *James Thomson (1700-1748): An Annotated Bibliography of Selected Editions and the Important Criticism* (New York: Garland, 1976).

Biographies:

Patrick Murdoch, "An account of his life and writings," in *The Works of James Thomson*, edited by Murdoch (London: Printed for A. Millar, 1762);

Douglas Grant, *James Thomson: Poet of "The Seasons,"* (London: Cresset, 1951).

References:

Percy G. Adams, *Graces of Harmony: Alliteration, Assonance, and Consonance in Eighteenth-Century British Poetry* (Athens, Ga: University of Georgia Press, 1977);

R. R. Agrawal, *Tradition and Experiment in the Poetry of James Thomson (1700-1748)* (Salzburg: Universität Salzburg, 1981);

David R. Anderson, "Emotive Theodicy in 'The Seasons,' " in *Studies in Eighteenth-Century Culture*, volume 12, edited by Harry C. Payne (Madison, Wis.: University of Wisconsin Press, 1983), pp. 59-76;

John Arthos, *The Language of Natural Description in Eighteenth-Century Poetry* (Ann Arbor: University of Michigan Press, 1949);

James Boswell, *Boswell on the Grand Tour: Germany and Switzerland, 1764*, edited by Frederick A. Pottle (London: Heinemann, 1953), p. 37;

John Chalker, *The English Georgic; a Study in the Development of a Form* (London: Routledge & Kegan Paul, 1969);

Ralph Cohen, *The Art of Discrimination: Thomson's "The Seasons" and the Language of Criticism* (Berkeley & Los Angeles: University of California Press, 1964)–includes a checklist of the editions of *The Seasons (1726-1929)*;

Cohen, *The Unfolding of "The Seasons"* (Baltimore: Johns Hopkins Press, 1970);

Dwight L. Durling, *The Georgic Tradition in English Poetry* (New York: Columbia University Press, 1935);

Donald J. Greene, "From Accidie to Neurosis: *The Castle of Indolence* Revisited," in *English Literature in the Age of Disguise*, edited by Maximillian E. Novak (Berkeley & Los Angeles: University of California Press, 1977), pp. 131-156;

Dustin Griffin, *Regaining Paradise: Milton and the Eighteenth Century* (Cambridge: Cambridge University Press, 1986);

Jean H. Hagstrum, *The Sister Arts: The Tradition of Literary Pictorialism and English Poetry from Dryden to Gray* (Chicago: University of Chicago Press, 1958), pp. 243-267;

Raymond Dexter Havens, *The Influence of Milton on English Poetry* (Cambridge, Mass.: Harvard University Press, 1922);

William Hone, *The Table Book, of Daily Recreation and Information* (1827), in *Hone's Works*, 4 volumes (London: William Tegg, 1878), pp. 468-470, 603-604, 708-710;

D. W. Jefferson, "The Place of James Thomson," *Proceedings of the British Academy*, 64 (1978): 233-258;

William Powell Jones, *The Rhetoric of Science: A Study of Scientific Ideas and Imagery in Eighteenth-Century Poetry* (Berkeley & Los Angeles: University of California Press, 1966);

Michael G. Ketcham, "Scientific and Poetic Imagination in James Thomson's 'Poem Sacred to the Memory of Sir Isaac Newton,' " *Philological Quarterly*, 61 (Winter 1982): 33-50;

John Loftis, *The Politics of Drama in Augustan England* (Oxford: Oxford University Press, 1963);

Loftis, "Thomson's *Tancred and Sigismunda* and the Demise of the Drama of Political Opposition," in *The Stage and the Page: London's "Whole Show" in the Eighteenth-Century Theatre*, edited by George Winchester Stone, Jr. (Berkeley & Los Angeles: University of California Press, 1981), pp. 34-54;

Alan Dugald McKillop, *The Background of Thomson's "Liberty"* (Houston: Rice Institute, 1951);

McKillop, *The Background of Thomson's "Seasons"* (Minneapolis: University of Minnesota Press, 1942);

Marjorie Hope Nicolson, *Mountain Gloom and Mountain Glory: The Development of the Aesthetics of the Infinite* (Ithaca, N.Y.: Cornell University Press, 1959);

Nicolson, *Newton Demands the Muse* (Princeton: Princeton University Press, 1946);

Eric Rothstein, *Restoration and Eighteenth-Century Poetry, 1600-1780*, Routledge History of English Poetry, volume 3 (London: Routledge & Kegan Paul, 1981);

Mary Jane W. Scott, *James Thomson, Anglo-Scot* (Athens, Ga.: University of Georgia Press, 1988);

John Sitter, *Literary Loneliness in Mid-Eighteenth-Century England* (Ithaca, N.Y.: Cornell University Press, 1982);

Patricia Meyer Spacks, *The Poetry of Vision: Five Eighteenth-Century Poets* (Cambridge, Mass.: Harvard University Press, 1967), pp. 13-65;

Spacks, *The Varied God: A Critical Study of Thomson's "The Seasons"* (Berkeley & Los Angeles: University of California Press, 1959).

Papers:

There are manuscripts of Thomson's poems in the Newberry Library (Chicago), The University of Texas (Austin) Library, the Beineke Library (Yale), the J. Pierpont Morgan Library, Amherst College Library, Edinburgh University Library, and the University of Leeds Library.

Elizabeth Tollet
(1694 - 1 February 1754)

Deborah Baker Wyrick
North Carolina State University

BOOK: *Poems on Several Occasions. With Anne Boleyn to King Henry VIII. An Epistle*, anonymous (London: Printed for John Clarke, 1724; enlarged and printed under author's name, 1755).

Confinement in the Tower of London has produced a variety of literary responses. Many prisoners have inscribed their names into the stone walls, often adding coats of arms or moral sentiments, as if the power of the written sign could vanquish "the miseri of this house" (an inscription by Thomas Clarke in 1576). Other inhabitants freed the word from the incarcerating stone: Sir Walter Raleigh's *History of the World* was composed during imprisonment in the tower, as was Thomas More's *Dialogue of Comfort against Tribulation*, William Penn's *No Cross, No Crown*, and poetry by Robert Southwell, Chidiock Tichborne, and Charles, Duke of Orleans. To this list of "tower literature" should be added Elizabeth Tollet's *Poems on Several Occasions* (1724).

Tollet was not sent to the tower for political crimes or religious heresy; she lived there with her family. Her father, George Tollet, was appointed extra commissioner of the navy in 1701 and apparently was stationed at the Tower of London until after the death of Queen Anne in 1714. Elizabeth Tollet thus resided at the tower from the age of seven or eight until at least her early twenties. Educated there, she grew into womanhood in one of England's most solemn and severe historical environments. That her poetry is heavily informed by history, by the effects and imagery of confinement, by pride in intellectual curiosity, and by the belief that writing "outlasts the firmest Stone" ("In Memory of the Countess of Winchilsea") is, in part, a function of living in the tower. And so may be her courage, or her compulsion, to attempt the pen in an age inimical to serious writing by women.

Her pen produced one volume of poetry, finally published with her name on the title page in 1755, a year after her death. An unassuming duodecimal book, *Poems on Several Occasions* contains well over two hundred pages of verse. Tollet wrote dramatic epistles, panegyrics, pastoral elegies, philosophical meditations, musical dramas, religious verse, classical translations, lyrics, and occasional poems. Although individual poems are not frequently dated, the rough chronological arrangement of the book indicates that most of the work (excluding the psalms) was composed during the 1710s and 1720s. The heroic couplet is the dominant verse form; in addition, Tollet demonstrates great metrical virtuosity in various odal and lyric modes.

Poems on Several Occasions includes a short, unsigned biographical preface. It tells us that George Tollet gave his daughter "so excellent an Education, that besides great Skill in Music, and Drawing, she spoke fluently and correctly the *Latin, Italian* and *French* Languages; and well understood History, Poetry, and the Mathematicks." He also left her "a handsome Fortune," one that enabled her to live comfortably in Stratford and,

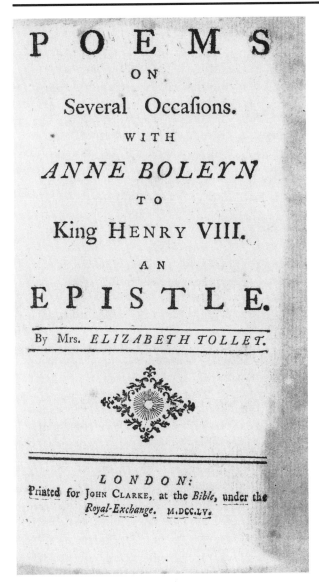

POEMS

ON

Several Occaſions.

WITH

ANNE BOLEYN

T O

King HENRY VIII.

A N

EPISTLE.

By Mrs. *ELIZABETH TOLLET*.

LONDON:
Printed for JOHN CLARKE, at the *Bible*, under the
Royal-Exchange. M.DCC.LV.

Title page for the enlarged edition of Tollet's only book. The original version was published anonymously in 1724 (Henry E. Huntington Library and Art Gallery).

later, in Westham. The introduction praises her "unfeigned Piety, and the moral Virtues, which she possessed, and practiced in an eminent Degree." Finally it reports that she died on 1 February 1754, at the age of sixty, and was buried in Westham. Apparently she never married.

These few facts and assessments comprise most of the biographical information available concerning Tollet. Janet Todd's *Dictionary of British and American Women Writers 1660-1800* adds that Tollet knew Isaac Newton personally (a circumstance also deducible from her poem "On the Death of Sir Isaac Newton," as well as the location of the Royal Mint, which Newton headed from 1696 to 1727, in the Tower of London). New-

ton liked her poetry and (as reported by Todd) characterized Tollet as a "little, crooked woman but a sharp wit." The rest of her life–more important, her inner life, her poetic life–must be reconstructed from her posthumous book.

Certainly *Poems on Several Occasions* bears out its introduction's assertion of Tollet's learning and intelligence. The volume is inaugurated by a series of translations and imitations of Ovid, Claudian, Virgil, and Horace that are marked by prosodic variety and pleasing diction. These pieces immediately establish her authority as a serious poet, prepare the reader for the classical allusions that punctuate subsequent poems and for the poems written in Latin, and create a pedigree for her supple handling of verse forms. Further, long poems such as "The Microcosm" and "Hypatia" contain informed references to the sciences as well as to the humanities. Tollet's "Piety, and the moral Virtues" are attested to by occasional religious poems and by the long series of psalms that closes the volume. The implicit chronology of *Poems on Several Occasions* indicates that Tollet's psalms were the primary output of her final decades, a proper and respectable poetic enterprise for an aging spinster.

The book also reveals aspects of Tollet's life not covered in its introduction. That she had at least one brother is made clear by "To my Brother at St. John's College in Cambridge"; she urges him to write poetry in praise of Robert Harley, Earl of Oxford and Henry St. John, Viscount Bolingbroke, thus disclosing her Tory sympathies. That she had a dear friend–a musical young woman who also lived in the tower, probably in circumstances similar to the Tollets', and who died there in 1717–is made evident by the panegyric and the pastoral elegy dedicated to one Elizabeth Blackler. That Tollet was not a dissenter is indicated by a poem that may adapt Jonathan Swift's narrative metaphor in *A Tale of a Tub* (1704); it is a quatrain that she entitled "Per Nobile Fratrem":

> Two Youngsters, with the same Preciseness taught,
> When rip'ning Time to due Perfection brought,
> Observe how well their Principels [*sic*] agree;
> An *Atheist* This, and an *Enthusiast* He.

Because of her father's position in the navy bureaucracy, one assumes that the family was centrist Anglican. Nonetheless, some of the religious poems exhibit a sort of Anglo-Catholic meditational mysticism reminiscent of Henry Vaughan,

George Herbert, or—more strikingly—Richard Crashaw (whom Tollet may have encountered through her reading of Alexander Pope). "Ecce Homo. An Ode," for example, composes a fairly gruesome picture of "how the sanguine Streams run down / And bath his heav'nly Face with Gore" as it lingers on dripping blood and livid stripes. "Hymn to the *Paraclete*. At Whitsontide, 1723" elaborates the trope that "thine the Temple of my Breast shall be, / If purify'd and consecrate by Thee," and in the poem dedicatory to her psalms she calls them an offering to be brought to the Lord's altar.

Tollet's literary tastes are also disclosed by her poems. She did not think highly of current novels (nor, perhaps, did she enjoy dancing) because she found them predictable, derivative, and, one suspects, déclassé:

Methinks that reading these Romances
Is just like dancing Country Dances:
All in the same dull Measures move,
Adventures brave and constant Love;
Each Pair in formal Order tread
The Steps their Predecessors led.

Her highest praise is reserved for serious poetry and poetic drama. In "The Triumvirate of Poets" she lauds her favorite contemporaries by pairing them with their classical counterparts:

Britain with *Greece* and *Rome* contended long
For lofty Genius and poetic Song:
Till this *Augustan* Age with Three was blest
To fix the Prize and finish the Contest.
In *Addison* immortal *Virgil* reigns;
So pure his Numbers, so refin'd his Strains;
Of Nature full, with more impetuous Heat,
In *Prior Horace* shines, sublimely great.
Thy Country, *Homer*, we dispute no more,
For *Pope* has fix'd it to his native Shore.

Imitation also reveals appreciation: although one cannot discern a great deal of Joseph Addison's influence in Tollet's work, her short lyrics resemble Matthew Prior's, and her philosophical poems and dramatic epistles resemble Pope's. If one were to create a triumvirate of the poets who most clearly helped shape Tollet's work, one might replace Addison with John Dryden, as even a cursory comparison of Dryden's "St. Cecilia's Day Ode" with Tollet's "To Mrs. Elizabeth Blackler, playing on the Harpsicord" will suggest. Tollet's literary panegyrics also include one to William Congreve ("the justest Glory of our Age! / The whole *Menander* of our British Stage") and one to William Shakespeare.

Although Tollet most frequently celebrates the achievements of male writers, she is not unaware of the female literary tradition. A poem by Lady Mary Wortley Montagu in John Hammond's *Miscellany* inspired a panegyric presenting the British Muse (in the person of the well-traveled Montagu) extending her domain into Mediterranean countries; Tollet ends with a claim that the wonders of the ancient world are "all reviv'd in thee." Tollet's elegy "In Memory of the Countess of Winchilsea" uses tetrameter quatrains (chosen, perhaps, in homage to the deceased lyric poet) to praise Anne Finch's wit and virtue. The mourners all seem to be female, and the final stanza cedes back to Finch responsibility for her own poetic immortality: "No Verse can speak her but her own, / The Spleen must be her fun'ral Song."

The women who seem to have influenced Tollet the most, however, are not poets but historical figures—specifically, women who were actually confined in the Tower of London or women who suffered similar persecutions in other countries. In "Mary, Queen of Scots, Farewel to Buxton," Tollet has the condemned queen write her own epitaph; Mary denies the signifying power of a stony tomb, concentrating instead on the physical and metaphysical decay that will disperse her atoms and elements into oblivion. Less serious in tone is "Written by Lady Jane Grey, when Prisoner in the Tower, with her Pin on her Chamber Wall." Jaunty Hudibrastics create a Renaissance noblewoman who not surprisingly reminds one of eighteenth-century literary ladies protesting against being stereotyped as vain, materialistic, and meddlesome:

On what wou'd I my Wishes fix?
'Tis not upon a Coach and Six:
'Tis not your rich Brocade to wear;
'Tis not on Brilliants in my Ear.
....
A lazy Life I first wou'd choose,
A lazy Life best Suits the Muse:
A few choice Books of ev'ry Sort;
But none that meddle with the Court.

Corollary sentiments occur in "the *Coquette* and *Prude*," Tollet's most successful piece of light verse. Sounding somewhat like Richard Steele in *The Tatler*, no. 126 or like Swift in his less vitriolic moments, Tollet recites the litany of female fopperies: mimicking airs, concern with dress, promiscuous flirting, card parties, and opera tickets. The beau who gains the coquette's heart "dresses alamode de *France*; / And bows—with perfect Complaisance." In contrast, the Prude shuns "odious Man," "gives herself excessive Airs / Of edifying Zeal at Pray'rs," yet is "slave to mercenary Ends." Both extremes, Tollet concludes, annihilate wit and virtue. Even in this comic poem, however, the language of compulsion—"fears," "drug . . . from," "suffer," "slave," "submit," "compell"—hints at the ways in which women are confined by "the censorious World."

The impact that female confinement had on Tollet's imagination is nowhere more apparent than in "*Anne Boleyn* to King *Henry* VIII. An EPISTLE." Knowledge of the tower allows not only historical accuracy but also a realistically presented setting. Boleyn, like Tollet, is "inmur'd in these relentless Tow'rs," visited by ghosts of murdered royalty; she watches the "subject" Thames flowing freely while she is the disturbing "Object" confined by male power: "A Band of Goalers, not a Guard of State, / With surley Aspect here observes the Gate: / Where in its Fall the massive Barrier clangs, / And threat'ning Ruin the *Portcullis* hangs." The combined forces of the state, history, architecture, and popular opinion ranged against her, Boleyn pleads not for freedom but for restoration of her good name. In doing so, she distinguishes between male honor, gained by "martial Toils," and the "diff'rent Dress" of female honor, which requires one to guard frailty, suppress pain, act cautiously, and regulate "the Motions of the Mind." Such a definition, occurring in the middle of a turbulent poem, is actually an admission of how Boleyn herself has wounded her own honor. She may not have committed adultery, but she has imperiled herself by failing to protect from suspicion all "that Woman has to boast."

Tollet obviously knew and admired Pope's *Eloisa to Abelard*, which in true Ovidian manner presents the agonies of physical passion and the difficulties of making choices when no choice is a happy one. But in "*Anne Boleyn* to King *Henry* VIII" sexuality is suppressed and choice is nonexistent. Tollet focuses instead on how a male cultural system will not listen to a woman's self-assessment; the issue for her heroine is respect, not sympathy. Boleyn demands to be interpreted properly, either through her epistle or through her daughter, in whom she hopes that Henry VIII can "read" the truth of her mother's conscience. Unlike Eloisa, who cedes her future to a

poet and to readers who can "feel" her turmoil and seal communion with tears of pity, Boleyn will write herself into history in search of the justice that follows rationally from accurate knowledge.

Similar in intent is Tollet's elaborate musical drama, "Susanna: or Innocence Preserv'd." Based on the Apocryphal book of Susanna, it presents thwarted desire, false accusations, and prophetic detective work through airs, recitatives, lyric songs, duets, and trios. Tollet follows her deuterocanonical source quite closely, except that she gives greater emphasis to the role of Susanna than to that of Daniel. Whereas in the Apocrypha Susanna has only two short speeches, Tollet's heroine talks to her maids, mourns the condition of her country, sings with the lascivious elders, calls to God, rues her fate, and tries to accept death. Tollet makes Susanna a symbol not only of God's fairness to his people but also of the plight of women in general. As a chorus of female captives laments:

> What alas! shall Woman trust?
> Youth and Beauty are but Dust:
> If to noble Blood ally'd,
> All is transitory Pride.
> Honour, and a spotless Name,
> Bubbles of uncertain Fame. . . .

Susanna, like Boleyn, is secure in her innocence and in her heavenly vindication; therefore, restoration of honor is ultimately a matter of using the "Force of Truth" to conform human justice to divine justice. If Susanna, as well as Sion, has been "in Bondage," truth sets her free and puts falsehood "in solid Fetters." But Susanna's freedom leads to reconsecration of "connubial Love," and another of Tollet's major works clearly calls marriage yet one more version of female imprisonment.

In the remarkable poem "Hypatia" (circa 1723), the eponymous heroine argues against the "cruel Laws [that] depress the female Kind"; the most cruel of these is "the domestic chain," the "Servitude" that forces woman's will to be "resign'd to an imperious Lord, / Or Slave to Avarice." Although the way in which patriarchal culture re-signs women is a major theme, "Hypatia" transcends other Restoration and Augustan poems dealing with women's unhappy lot. Tollet's poem is not an antimale or antimarriage polemic. Instead it is a stirring plea for fair treatment and equal opportunity.

A fifth-century leader of the Neoplatonic school at Alexandria known for her beauty and wisdom, Hypatia was captured by a Christian mob that stripped her naked and pelted her to death with shells. From this historical event Tollet has fashioned a dramatic monologue in which the shade of Hypatia addresses her "just Appeal" to the present age so that her virtue and intelligence are once again acknowledged (evidently, she was being used as an object lesson by various eighteenth-century divines–preached against by traditionalists, and self-servingly praised by freethinkers). Although Hypatia begins by criticizing the strictures of marriage, she soon moves to an examination of women's mental endowments. Wit unrefined by reason, she states, "Luxuriates," "degen'rates," or "becomes a dang'rous Thing," yet women are cursed if they cultivate their minds. The last half of the poem is organized around the rhetorical question, "Is this a Crime?" *This* signifies education for women in various disciplines: mathematics, chemistry, geology, history, botany, the nature of man, astronomy, and ontology.

Hypatia invokes the trope of the scale of being as a parallel for the scale of knowledge that she believes women should be allowed to ascend. Further, she suggests that in all people the "Heav'n-born Mind" is female; "she" must explore her powers and leave earth for the realms of metaphysical speculation. In a clever reversal of Pope's Belinda (in *The Rape of the Lock*, 1714), whose hair becomes a star, Tollet's Hypatia speaks of the female mind's apotheosis:

> She sees where Comets trail their fiery Hair,
> Terrific Lustre! thro' the shining Air:
> Nor Vapours they, whose Levity aspires
> At *Phoebus'* Car to catch *Promethean* fires;
> But real Stars, which unextinguish'd burn,
> Thro' larger Periods of a just Return.

Throughout, Hypatia appeals for the triumph of justice and reason over "Tyrant Custom." Her eloquent argument in defense of women's right to knowledge and meaningful virtue is its own best proof.

"Hypatia" seems to have spearheaded the rediscovery of Tollet; for instance, selections from it are included in the 1984 edition of the *New Oxford Book of Eighteenth-Century Poetry*. By fitting neatly with works by writers such as Sarah Fyge Egerton and Lady Mary Chudleigh, it helps place Tollet in the manageable–and relatively small–category of eighteenth-century feminist poets.

Yet Tollet's work is more ambitious and substantial than that. She was a serious philosophical poet, an imaginative historical poet, an accomplished lyric poet, and a devout religious poet. If her work were printed without attribution, it would stand by itself as a strong example of mainstream Augustan verse. Knowing that this work was written by a woman adds to its interest, as readers are alert to language and imagery indicating an intelligent woman's careful maneuvering within a male literary tradition.

The fact that Tollet wrote within this tradition, rather than stridently confronting it from without, may account for the tepid reception her work has received. Although her book was popular enough to be reprinted in 1760, it has been out of print ever since. The *Monthly Review* in 1755 would not place Tollet "in the first class" of poets but gave her dutiful praise for versifying skills and solemn temperament. In 1780 John Nichols decorously termed her a "worthy author" who promoted "Good-manners, Virtue, and Religion" (in his *Poems*, volume 6), but Robert Southey, according to Todd, was content to marginalize her into the realm of the mediocre. Until recently, Tollet's name has been completely erased from the pages of literary history.

Her reinscription will raise interesting issues of imitation, aesthetics, ideology, and canon formation as well as of feminism. For Tollet is not only a female poet. She is also an Augustan poet who, like others, had to grapple with the covering cherub of Pope; who, like others, used diction, figures, and modes that have fallen out of favor; and who, like others, could sing the imperial sublime in ways that grate against postcolonial ears. Reassessing Tollet's place within the canon thus should involve a broad range of considerations. If historical and literary contexts as well as feminist perspectives are not brought into account, Tollet and her work risk being confined once again. Her poetry deserves the open-minded scrutiny that Hypatia asked for herself: "Yet to th' Unbyas'd, the distinguish'd Few, / Whose clearer Judgment makes a just Review, / She turns undaunted, and submits her Cause: / Nor shrinks from Censure, nor demands Applause."

Biography:

Anonymous, Introduction to Tollet's *Poems on Several Occasions. With Anne Boleyn to King Henry VIII. An Epistle* (London: Printed for John Clarke, 1755).

Isaac Watts

(17 July 1674 - 25 November 1748)

Madeleine Forell Marshall
Saint Olaf College

SELECTED BOOKS: *Horae Lyricae. Poems, Chiefly of the Lyric kind. In Two Books* (London: Printed by S. & D. Bridge for John Lawrence, 1706); enlarged as *Horae Lyricae. Poems, Chiefly of the Lyric kind. In Three Books* (London: Printed for J. Humfreys for N. Cliff, 1709; Boston: Printed & sold by Rogers & Fowle, 1748);

A Sermon Preached at Salters-Hall (London: Printed by J. Humfreys for John Lawrence, 1707);

Hymns and Spiritual Songs. In Three Books (London: Printed by J. Humfreys for John Lawrence, 1707; revised and enlarged edition, 1709; Philadelphia: B. Franklin, 1741);

A Guide to Prayer: or, a Free and Rational Account of the Gift, Grace and Spirit of Prayer; with Plain Directions how every Christian may attain them (London: Printed for Emanuel Matthews & Sarah Cliff, 1715; Boston: Printed by J. Draper for D. Henchman, 1739);

Divine Songs Attempted in Easy Language for the Use of Children (London: Printed for M. Lawrence, 1715; Philadelphia: Reprinted & sold by B. Franklin & D. Hall, 1750); facsimile, London: Oxford University Press, 1971);

The Psalms of David Imitated in the Language of the New Testament, And apply'd to the Christian State and Worship (London: Printed for J. Clark, R. Ford & R. Cruttenden, 1719; Hartford, Conn.: Printed by N. Patten, 1785);

The Art of Reading and Writing English: or, the chief Principles and Rules of Pronouncing our Mother-Tongue, both in Prose and Verse; with a Variety of Instructions for True Spelling. Written first for Private Use, and now published for the Benefit of all Persons who desire a better acquaintance with their Native Language (London: Printed for John Clark, Em. Matthews & Richard Ford, 1721);

Sermons on Various Subjects (London: Printed for John Clark, E. M. Matthews & Richard Ford, 1721; Boston: Printed & sold by Rogers & Fowle, 1746);

An Elegy on the much lamented Death of Mrs. Elizabeth Bury (Bristol, 1722?);

Logic: or the Right Use of Reason in the Enquiry after Truth with a Variety of Rules to guard against error in the Affairs of Religion and Human Life, as well as in the Sciences (London: Milner & Co., 1724; Boston: Thomas & Andrews, 1796);

Prayers Composed for the Use and Imitation of Children, suited to their different Ages and their various Occasions: together with Instructions to Youth in the Duty of Prayer, drawn up by way of Ques-

tion and Answer. And a Serious Address to them on that Subject (London: Printed for John Clark, Richard Hett, Emanuel Matthews & Richard Ford, 1728);

An Essay towards the Encouragement of Charity-Schools, particularly those which are supported by Protestant Dissenters, for teaching the Children of the Poor to Read and Work (London: J. Clark, 1728);

The Doctrine of the Passions Explained and Improved; or, a brief and comprehensive Scheme of the Natural Affections of Mankind, and an Account of their Names, Nature, Appearances, Effects, and different Uses in Human Life; to which are subjoined Moral and divine Rules for the Regulation or Government of them (London, 1729; New York: Printed for Robert Hodge, 1795);

Discourses of the Love of God and the Use and Abuse of the Passions in Religion, with a Devout Meditation suited to each Discourse (London: Printed for J. Clark & R. Hett, 1729);

Catechisms; or, Instructions in the Principles of the Christian Religion, and the History of Scripture, composed for Children and Youth, according to their different Ages (London: Printed for E. Matthews, R. Ford & R. Hett, 1730; Boston: Reprinted by Rogers & Fowle for J. Blanchard, 1747);

An Humble Attempt toward the Revival of Practical Religion among Christians, and particularly the Protestant Dissenters (London: Printed for E. Matthews, 1731);

The Strength and Weakness of Human Reason: or, the Important Question about the Sufficiency of Reason to Conduct Mankind to Religion and Future Happiness, Argued between An Inquiring Deist and a Christian Divine: and The Debate Compromis'd and Determin'd to the Satisfaction of both, by an Impartial Moderator (London: Printed for J. Pemberton & R. Hett, 1731);

Reliquiae Juveniles: Miscellaneous Thoughts in Prose and Verse, on Natural, Moral and Divine Subjects; Written chiefly in Younger Years (London: Printed for Richard Ford & Richard Hett, 1734; Boston: Printed for William P. Blake, 1796; facsimile, Gainesville, Fla.: Scholars' Facsimiles & Reprints, 1968);

Self-Love and Virtue Reconciled only by Religion; or, an Essay to prove that the only Effectual Obligation of Mankind to practice Virtue depends on the Existence and Will of God; together with an occasional Proof of the Necessity of Revelation (London, 1739);

RELIQVIÆ JVVENILES:

MISCELLANEOUS

THOUGHTS

IN

PROSE and VERSE,

ON

Natural, Moral, and *Divine*

SUBJECTS;

Written chiefly in Younger Years.

By *I. WATTS,* D. D.

Et jucunda simul & idonea dicere Vitæ. HOR.

LONDON:

Printed for RICHARD FORD at the *Angel,* and RICHARD HETT at the *Bible* and *Crown,* both in the *Poultry,* MDCCXXXIV.

Title page for the book in which Watts collected, in Watts's words, "Gleanings of Verse, *and occasional* Thoughts *on* Miscellaneous Subjects, *which have been growing under my Hands for Thirty Years"*

The Improvement of the Mind: or, a Supplement to the Art of Logick: containing a Variety of Remarks and Rules for the Attainment and Communication of useful Knowledge in Religion, in the Sciences, and in Common Life (London: Printed for J. Brackstone, 1741; enlarged edition, 1751; Boston: Printed for David West, 1793).

Editions and Collections: *The Works of the late Reverend and Learned Isaac Watts, D.D. Published by himself, and now Collected into Six Volumes,* edited by D. Jennings and P. Doddridge (London: Printed for T. & T. Longman, 1753);

The Posthumous Works of the late Learned and Reverend Isaac Watts, D.D., In Two Volumes. Compiled from Papers in Possession of his immediate

Successors: Adjusted and Published by a Gentleman of the University of Cambridge (London, 1779);

The Poetical Works of Isaac Watts, D.D., 7 volumes (Edinburgh, 1782);

Devout Meditations from Dr. Watts (N.p., 1791).

OTHER: "An Elegiac Ode written in the form of a Soliloquy or Mourning Meditation at the Death of Sir Thomas Abney, Knt. and Alderman of London," in *The Magistrate and the Christian*, by Jeremiah Smith (N.p., 1722);

Preface to *Devout Exercises of the Heart, in Meditation and Soliloquy, Prayer and Praise*, by Elizabeth Rowe (Coventry: Printed for M. Luckman, 1737);

"His occasional Poems during his Studies, or very soon after his closing them," chapter 3 of *Memoirs of the Rev. Isaac Watts, D.D.*, by Thomas Gibbons (London: Printed for James Buckland & Thomas Gibbons, 1780), pp. 64-83.

Isaac Watts was a scion of seventeenth-century Independent Dissent, a religious culture distinguished by its attention to local congregational authority, the education of preachers and people, and the cultivation of individual piety. The politics, pedagogy, and piety of Independency are all in evidence in Watts's early life and throughout his long career. He was at once a churchman, an educator, and an important minor poet. Watts's poetry is, however, more than an expression of this particular religious culture. His writing, poetry and prose, was widely read and used for at least 150 years by believers and educators of all convictions in both Britain and America. Indeed Watts's model of congregational song, the hymn, remains in current use throughout the English-speaking world. It is arguably the most lively vestige of the eighteenth-century understanding of what poetry can and ought to do.

Born in Southampton on 17 July 1674, the first of eight children of Isaac Watts and Elizabeth Taunton, the infant Isaac was nursed on the steps of the Southampton jail where his father was imprisoned as a Dissenter. The father began tutoring his son in Latin when the boy was four. The poet's first biographer, Thomas Gibbons, records a specimen of the seven-year-old Isaac's early poetry:

I am a vile polluted lump of earth,
S o I've continued ever since my birth,

A lthough Jehovah grace does daily give me,
A s sure this monster Satan will deceive me,
C ome therefore, Lord from Satan's claws relieve
   me.

W ash me in thy blood, O Christ,
A nd grace divine impart,
T hen search and try the corners of my heart,
T hat I in all things may be fit to do
S ervice to thee, and sing thy praises too.

Somber religious conviction and precocity in versification both inform this acrostic.

Watts continued his education at the Free-School in Southampton, learning Greek, French, and Hebrew. In 1690 he refused a university scholarship with its requisite allegiance to the articles of the Church of England and went instead to London to study at the Newington Green Academy of Thomas Rowe, a leading liberal academic light among the Dissenters. Friends at the academy included the poet John Hughes and the critic Samuel Say. Here Watts wrote his first serious poetry and essays on theological subjects in Latin and English, samples of which are reproduced in Watts's *Horae Lyricae* (1706) and in Gibbons's *Memoirs of the Rev. Isaac Watts, D.D.* (1780). His studies in London concluded, Watts, then twenty years old, returned to his father's house in Southampton, where he spent two years in further reading, writing, and contemplation. Five years' residence in Stoke Newington, at the home of Sir John and Lady Hartopp, followed. Watts continued his studies, tutored the Hartopps' son, and in 1698 began preaching as assistant pastor at the prominent Mark Lane Meeting in London.

This education is of more than simply biographical interest. Watts was to become a prominent educator whose textbooks and educational theory were republished in Britain and America for more than a century. He wrote a basic text on English usage, *The Art of Reading and Writing English* (1721), and a guide called *Logic: or the Right Use of Reason* (1724) later supplemented with *The Improvement of the Mind* (1741). He wrote on psychology in *The Doctrine of the Passions Explained and Improved* (1729) and promoted popular education in *An Essay towards the Encouragement of Charity-Schools* (1728). His interest in the colonial American universities and liberal if nonclassical education for girls was particularly marked. This commitment to education was basic to Watts's understanding of devotional lyrics, congregational hymns and psalms, and songs for children.

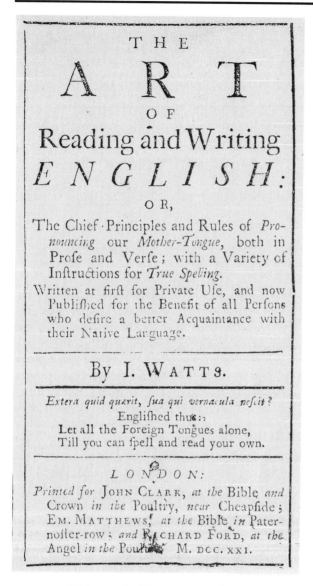

THE

ART

OF

Reading and Writing

ENGLISH:

OR,

The Chief·Principles and Rules of *Pro-
nouncing* our *Mother-Tongue*, both in
Profe and Verfe; with a Variety of
Inftructions for *True Spelling.*

Written at firft for Private Ufe, and now
Publifhed for the Benefit of all Perfons
who defire a better Acquaintance with
their Native Language.

By I. WATTS.

Extera quid quærit, fua qui vernacula nefcit?
Englifhed thus:
Let all the Foreign Tongues alone,
Till you can fpell and read your own.

LONDON:

Printed for JOHN CLARK, *at the* Bible *and*
Crown *in the* Poultry, *near* Cheapfide;
EM. MATTHEWS, *at the* Bible *in* Pater-
nofter-row; *and* RICHARD FORD, *at the*
Angel *in the* Poultry. M. DCC. XXI.

Title page for Watts's grammar book

King William died 8 March 1702, a frighten-
ing event for the Dissenters who feared the return of the Stuarts. On the same day, Watts accepted the invitation to serve as pastor of the
Mark Lane Meeting. Here Watts preached the
thousands of sermons, published in scores of volumes, that have perforce been left out of consideration here. His congregation and its world of prosperous, powerful, urbane Dissent provided the
social and political context of all Watts's writing.
Often incapacitated by long months and years of
fevers and nervous illness, he lived in the homes
of prominent Mark Lane families, first with the
Hartopps, then eight years with Thomas Hollis,
then, from 1712 until his death thirty-six years
later, with Sir Thomas and Lady Mary Abney.

Watts published four volumes of poetry:
Horae Lyricae; *Hymns and Spiritual Songs* (1707); *Divine Songs Attempted in Easy Language for the Use of
Children* (1715); and *The Psalms of David Imitated
in the Language of the New Testament* (1719). The
many reprintings of each of these works indicate
the poet's remarkable contribution to the traditions of devotional verse, congregational hymnody, children's literature, and psalmody. The
later collection of poetry and prose *Reliquiae Juveniles* (1734) demonstrates Watts's continued popularity and interest in poetry. Watts's poetry and
the critical writing of his prefaces provide an intriguing view of a lively, influential, eighteenth-
century literary counterculture. Literary history
that includes this culture discovers new perspectives on piety, morality, the affective aesthetics of
sentimentalism, graveyard poetry, congregational
hymnody as a distinctive poetic genre, and the Augustan reputation of John Milton. Seventeenth-
century Latin and French influences are apparent, as well as the critical context of much neglected writing by eighteenth-century women.

Watts's short critical essay introducing *Horae
Lyricae* claims poetry for the cause of religion
and virtue, rejecting the common secular debase-
ment of the heavenly genre. Invoking the sublimity and power of biblical poetry, he praises Jean
Racine and Pierre Corneille for their use of scriptural material. He wonders at the potential poetic
impact of the Incarnation and the Passion of
Christ and the evangelical power of Christian poetry to transform readers' lives. This line of argument at once recalls the criticism of John Dennis
and anticipates the achievements in Christian musical drama of George Frideric Handel and Johann Sebastian Bach. The poems that follow the
essay are arranged in three books (in the enlarged 1709 edition). The first contains poetry "Sacred to Devotion and Piety," including a section
called "On Divine Love"; the second, poems "Sacred to Virtue, Honor, and Friendship"; the
third, those "Sacred to the Memory of the Dead."

In "The Law Given at Sinai," something of
a biblical spectacular, Watts warns of the dangers
of frivolous poetry:

> Forbear, young muse, forbear;
> The flow'ry things that poets say,
> The little arts of simile
> Are vain and useless here;
> Nor shall the burning hills of old
> With Sinai be compar'd,
> Not all that lying Greece has told,
> Or learned Rome has heard. . . .

The alternative to poetic games and classical lies is profound poetry and Christian truth.

In "True Learning," aspects of the intellectual prehistory of the eighteenth-century idea of enlightenment come clear: sacred truth, the cheating senses, "the dust that fierce disputers raise," and "the vain opinions of the schools (that pageantry of knowing fools)," are superseded by divine light. In "True Wisdom," the psychology of the passions anticipates both ideas and imagery most familiar in the poetry of Alexander Pope. Watts writes: "Our headstrong lusts, like a young fiery horse, / Start, and flee raging in a violent course; / He tames and breaks them, manages and rides them, / Checks their career, and turns and guides them, / And bids his reason bridle their licentious force." Hard discipline is relieved by sublime visions of heavenly flight. Indeed Watts's version of sublimity is extraordinary. "The Day of Judgment: an ode attempted in the English Sapphic," is one instance of the poet's experimental energy, while "Launching into Eternity" provides a heroic, explorer's role for the soul. Carefully controlled by psychological understanding and conveyed in clear metaphors, rapture avoids the sort of rhapsody modern readers often find annoying.

Horae Lyricae, particularly Book II, brings into easy relationship trends and tendencies that literary history has kept separate: continental baroque taste, Miltonic grandeur, the rewards of piety, and profound sensibility. Watts's fondness for the Latin poetry of the Polish Jesuit Matthew Casimir Sarbiewski suggests unusual seventeenth-century, continental, baroque antecedents to English verse. The divine-love metaphor for the soul's relation to God, otherworldliness, and accounts of martyrdom each has its place. In "The Adventurous Muse" the heroic excitement of Christian poetry comes clear as "Urania takes her morning flight / With an illimitable wing. . . . / Touch'd with an empyreal ray / She springs, unerring, upward to eternal day, / Spreads her white sails aloft, and steers, / With bold and safe attempt, to the celestial land." In contrast, the little mortal skiffs of the worldly poets cling to the shores, as the "poor labourers sweat to be correctly dull."

In good classical fashion the exemplary protagonist of "The Happy Man" resists all honors, wealth, and pleasures: "He saw the tedious round, and, with a sigh, / Pronounc'd the world but vanity." In an interesting twist on the old theme of vain human wishes, he favors and is suit-

Frontispiece for a 1722 edition of Watts's Horae Lyricae

ably rewarded for his virtue by "social bliss . . . a blessing fit to match my mind, / A kindred-soul to double and to share my joys." Myrrha, a suitably wonderful wife, is his reward.

"The Mourning-Piece" is perhaps the strangest of Watts's lyrics. Addressed "To Mitio, My Friend," it opens with the familiar conceit that "Life's a long tragedy: the globe the stage." Demonic antagonists sit on the clouds of life "with fatal purpose," armed with "ten thousand arrows / perpetual and unseen." These are the arrows of "sorrow, infamy, disease, and death." Dianthe, like William Blake's Thel, moves across this mortal stage, by choice unmarried, unwilling to expose herself to the likely sorrows of her sister, Marilla, who is married and a mother. Children, "those tend'rest pieces / Of your own flesh . . . soften every fibre to improve / The mother's sad capacity for pain!" Fidelio, her husband, is no less vulnerable, pierced "to his inmost soul" by every harm to his family. Dianthe cries out: "Strange is thy power, O love! what numerous veins, / And arteries, and arms, and hands, and eyes / Are link'd and fasten'd to a lover's heart, / By strong but secret strings!" Dianthe is understandably "fearful to try / The bold experiment" of marriage and family. Watts has opened a window on the commonplace domestic sorrows of death and disease, a window frequently shuttered by exemplary piety and Christian stoicism.

Readers have often dismissed *Horae Lyricae* as the work of a young man, perhaps sowing the wild oats of his imagination before settling down to the serious business of inventing the English congregational hymn. Watts, in something of a pious version of Renaissance *sprezzatura*, encouraged this idea when he wrote, in a 1734 letter cited by Gibbons, "Though I have sported with rhyme as an amusement in younger life, and published some religious composures to assist the worship of God, yet I never set myself up among the numerous competitors for a poet of the age, much less have I presumed to become their judge." This view misrepresents the author, who in 1706 was no longer young, who revised and amplified the collection in 1709, and who supervised frequent reprintings. It improperly discredits the power and importance of many of the poems. As an old man Watts continued to argue (in a May 1735 letter in Gibbons's *Memoirs*) that "The christian scheme has glories and beauties in it, which have superior power to touch the soul beyond all the gods and heroes of the heathen heaven or elysium." His attitude toward sacred poetry remained much the same.

Watts's triple achievement in his second volume of poetry, *Hymns and Spiritual Songs*, is difficult to overestimate. First, as the progenitor of the English congregational hymn, guided by the affective poetics of his day, Watts designed a new public genre of poetry that combined metrical psalmody and the devotional lyric. The new genre flourished and tens of thousands of hymns—good, bad, and indifferent as poetry—were written in the following centuries. Hymns, especially the hymns of Watts, became the best known of all poetic kinds in English, psalmody excepted. Second, as author of several widely sung hymns in the tradition, Watts influenced later poets, particularly Blake and Emily Dickinson. And when Percy Bysshe Shelley's poetic goal was evangelical—albeit politically evangelical, as in his "Song for the Men of England"—he used the hymn genre. Third, Watts's hymns and those he inspired re-

Title page for the collection that marked Watts's introduction of the congregational hymn genre, its style and meter influencing such poets as William Blake and Emily Dickinson

main virtually the only extant eighteenth-century poetic texts that are read with pleasure and conviction outside the classroom or the library—if rarely, indeed, inside the classroom or the library. While the literary originality, excellence, and permanence of Watts's work is remarkable, hymnody traditionally has been studied apart from eighteenth-century poetry.

Hymns of original composition marked a departure from the English tradition of congregational psalm singing, a tradition originating with John Calvin's insistence on scriptural song. In the preface to his *Hymns and Spiritual Songs*, Watts defines the English congregational hymn as a poetic genre and defends its usefulness. Hymns, he writes, exhibit less "boldness" and "fancy" than lyrics do. Lyrics can be dangerous in the hands of common believers. Hymns, nonetheless, must be pleasurable and "should elevate us to the most delightful and divine Sensations." Such sensations, refined and disciplined, become devotion. The means to this end, precedented in psalm-singing practice and in Ignatian meditation, are exemplary: Watts's hymns provide expressions of perfect piety, a piety learned as it is articulated by worshippers. Spectacles of sacred events, heaven, or hell are interspersed with exemplary responses, defining appropriate devotional attitudes. Baroque tableaux of the Crucifixion and divine love scenes modeled on the Song of Solomon are typical.

As congregational song, hymns were an extraordinary kind of poetry. As texts for amateur public performance, loaded with evangelical importance and theological authority, they were severely limited to the three meters of psalmody and to common Christian language and understanding. It is no coincidence that Watts, as their originator, was both an accomplished poet and a recognized religious leader and teacher. His admiration of dramatic effects and familiarity with devotional imagery served him particularly well. Indeed, hymns depended for their success on real pleasures, on their value as entertainment. Insipid or obtuse poetry would fail to provoke the desired response. Singers, quite ordinary singers, perhaps distracted by worldly concerns, were to be caught up in the "divine delight" of a poetry that far surpassed secular enjoyments. This essential delight took highly visual, even dramatic, form akin to the stained-glass windows and liturgical drama of non-Calvinist traditions. Watts's description of God the Thunderer, in *Hymns and Spiritual Songs*, possesses this kind of entertainment value: "His Nostrils breathe out fiery Streams, / And from his awful Tongue / A Sovereign Voice divides the Flames, / And Thunder roars along." Watts's visions of heaven and hell, his Bible stories, and his domestic scenes of mortal life all show such an appreciation of dramatic effect.

Entertainment or delight was, however, only a means to a proper end. Hymns had to provoke but also to control response. The precise direction of devotion along approved lines was the whole point. Watts's hymns, as they direct and formulate response, are didactic literature, albeit of

a special sort. No expressive cries of the heart, the emotions of Watts's hymns are correct and salutary. This is the difference of exemplary literature, of model perfection. "When I survey the wond'rous Cross," also from *Hymns and Spiritual Songs*, provides one example. The hymn is a script for the believer, defining the appropriate response to the Crucifixion. In the first two stanzas, the believer, the "I," asserts that the Cross reorders all values and cancels all vanities:

> When I survey the wond'rous Cross
> On which the Prince of Glory dy'd,
> My richest Gain I count but Loss,
> And pour Contempt on all my Pride.
>
> Forbid it, Lord, that I should boast
> Save in the Death of *Christ* my God;
> All the vain things that charm me most,
> I sacrifice them to his Blood.

Properly prepared, the "I" then details the baroque tableau, the questions it raises, and the obliteration of the self it provokes:

> See from his Head, his Hands, his Feet,
> Sorrow and Love flow mingled down;
> Did e'er such Love and Sorrow meet?
> Or Thorns compose so rich a Crown?
>
> His dying Crimson like a Robe
> Spreads o're his Body on the Tree,
> Then am I dead to all the Globe,
> And all the Globe is dead to me.

The experience culminates in a lesson learned and a rededication of the self: "Were the whole Realm of Nature mine, / That were a Present far too small; / Love so amazing, so divine / Demands my Soul, my Life, my All." Watts has turned the constraints of public performance, didactic purpose, and psalm meter into healthy poetic discipline. As long as the language remained perfectly clear, the form permitted a wealth of theological understanding and Christian imagery. Watts's concept of the genre has stood the test of time.

Watts's *Divine Songs Attempted in Easy Language for the Use of Children* belongs to the history of children's literature. Less forthright than John Bunyan's *Book for Boys and Girls* (1686) and less fierce than James Janeway's *A Token for Children: being an exact account of the conversion, holy and exemplary lives, and joyful deaths of several young children* (1671?), the verses reflect common eighteenth-century views of childhood. The songs are no sim-

Rev.ᵈ & Dear Sir London. Sept.ʳ 6. 1733.

Yours of May 1ˢᵗ came to hand
about a month ago. I am ashamed of such extravag.ᵗ
Praises as y.ᵉ Youthfull Gratitude of a Poet offers to my
Name. Is not y.ᵉ word Divinest much too strong to be
coupled with so unequall a Name as mine? I acknow
ledge y.ᵉ Beauty of y.ᵉ Poem in severall parts of it &
in some of y.ᵉ happy Simile's. Yet I will not be
so much out of humor as not to accept his present,
& I make him a return of my Poems by your
hand. The other 2 books have not my Name, &
for want of y.ᵗ y.ᵉ Booksellers will not give me Copies enough to oblige my friends: Yet I thought
it not improper to let them stand in Yale College
as my Present, without acknowledging my self
the Author. I am Surpriz'd that Dean Berk
ley who is here esteem'd a high-church-man sh.ᵈ favor
your College with such a Beneficence. May all h.ᵃp-
piness & Success attend y.ᵉ Guides & y.ᵉ Scholars, by y.ᵉ
influences of Light & Grace from our Exalted Savior.
To him I commend you, & desire your recommenda
tions to y.ᵉ same Divine Patron when you think of
Your humble Servant & Bro:
my service to Mr Arnold. I Watts.

Letter from Watts to Yale Rector Elisha Williams, referring to New Haven poet John Hubbard's lavish praise for Watts's Psalms of David; *also mentioned are two of the many books Watts donated to Yale (by permission of Yale University Library).*

ple historical curiosity, however. Reprinted again and again, they held their place in British and American nurseries for close to two hundred years. By the middle of the nineteenth century Watts's songs were so widely known and at once sufficiently old-fashioned that Lewis Carroll could expect an appreciative audience for his *Alice in Wonderland* (1865) parodies of Watts in " 'Tis the Voice of the lobster, I heard him declare" and "How doth the little crocodile." Modern readers are generally repelled by the politics of the *Divine Songs*, the chauvinism of "Praise for birth and education in a Christian land," and the view of the hungry, half-naked, homeless poverty of other children as a spur to praise God "for mercies spiritual and temporal." Blake's songs and his politics are both more suited to modern taste, but one must remember that he, like Carroll, wrote for adults who had sung Watts's songs as children.

Watts's preface "To all that are concerned in the Education of Children" advocates Christian educational poetry as pleasurable, memorable, substantial, and devotionally useful. He declares the nonsectarian content of the songs, in which "the Children of high and low Degree, of the Church of England or Dissenters, baptized in Infancy or not, may all join together." He has "endeavoured to sink the Language to the Level of a Child's Understanding, and yet to keep it (if possible) above Contempt." To facilitate singing, the verse forms are those of the metrical psalter. Given these constraints, the songs in themselves are hardly remarkable as lyric poetry. Simple and straightforward in form and content, they range from little songs of praise to a concise scheme of redemption, Adam through the Judgment, in eight stanzas. Cautionary songs warn against lying, quarrelling, scoffing, swearing, idleness, mischief, keeping evil company, and having pride in clothes. In others, love between brothers and sisters and filial obedience are recommended.

Perhaps the *Divine Songs* compensates for what it lacks as adult poetry by the insight it provides into the history of childhood. Along with their record of childhood temptations, the songs remind readers of the important circumstance of infant and child mortality that added urgency to Christian education. Half of all children, often fewer, survived childhood. Accordingly, responsible Christian parents taught their children to sing:

There is an Hour when I must die,
Nor do I know how soon 'twill come;
A thousand Children young as I
Are call'd by Death to hear their Doom.

Let me improve the Hours I have
Before the Day of Grace is fled;
There's no Repentance in the Grave,
Nor Pardons offer'd to the Dead.

Just as a Tree cut down, that fell
To North, or Southward, there it lies:
So Man departs to Heaven or Hell,
Fix'd in the State wherein he dies.

The realities of heaven and hell, the danger of delay, the examples of early piety–these subjects take on added poignancy in historical context.

The Psalms of David Imitated in the Language of the New Testament required all Watts's tact and genius as a churchman and all his understanding of the place of poetry in worship. Since Calvin, the metrical psalms had been the only approved texts for English congregational song. The hardy and archaic "Old Version" of Thomas Sternhold and John Hopkins had been, until shortly before Watts's book was published in 1719, routinely bound with the *Book of Common Prayer*. The flowery and indirect "New Version" of Nahum Tate and Nicholas Brady, however "modern," was less than acceptable. Political, poetic, philological, and theological controversy swirled around the psalter. These were no texts to be trifled with: Watts's contemporaries knew the Psalms by heart and were conscious of every innovation. He worked long and hard on his Psalms, and his work was rewarded with broad acceptance. In the fifty years following the first publication, Watts's *Psalms of David* was issued in thirty-one editions in Britain, and scores of reprints followed until the mid nineteenth century. In addition, in the *National Index of American Imprints*, Clifford K. Shipton and James E. Mooney list ninety-nine eighteenth-century American reprints of the book.

Modern readers can easily underestimate the imaginative freedom allowed under the rubric of "Imitation" and ignore Watts's Psalms as original poetry. In fact the Christian recasting of Psalms for worship was a venerable tradition, a counterpart to the "imitation" of Greek and Latin poetry. Psalm imitations connected the original texts with New Testament experience and with the lives of modern believers. Imitations like Watts's, intended as congregational song, worked within the limits of the traditional tunes, the limits of short, long, and common meter. While Watts's complete *Psalms of David* is unavailable in any critical edition, several of his Psalms are among the best-known poems in the English-speaking world. "Joy to the World," for example, is Watts's rendering of the second part of Psalm 98 in common meter. A simple comparison of the hymn with the original Psalm reveals the rich possibilities of "Imitation." "Man frail, and God eternal," better known as "O, God, Our Help in Ages Past" (Psalm 90), is no less familiar and original. Watts's versions of Psalm 72 ("Jesus Shall Reign"), Psalm 100, Psalm 117 ("From all that Dwell Below the Skies"), and several others continue in common use.

For almost thirty years, following the publication of his *Psalms of David*, Watts lived in the Abney home, preaching and writing. Sermons, prayers, educational works, and theological essays flowed from his pen. It was Samuel Johnson's judgment, in his biography of Watts, that "their number and their variety shew the intenseness of his industry, and the extent of his capacity." In 1728 Watts received his Doctor of Divinity diploma from Edinburgh and Aberdeen, an award that pleased Johnson, who commented that "Academical honours would have more value if they were always bestowed with equal judgement." Watts continued to write poetry and to encourage the critical appreciation of the Christian poetry of his contemporaries. *Reliquiae Juveniles: Miscellaneous Thoughts in Prose and Verse* appeared in 1734, dedicated to Frances Thynne, the Countess of Hertford. In his preface, Watts once more defends sacred poetry and his own inclination to write. He praises Pope's *Messiah* (1712) and his imitations of Isaiah and Virgil; he admires Edward Young's *Job* (1719) and Elizabeth Rowe's "admirable Representations of Human Nature and Passion." Interspersed with short essays and prose meditations, the most notable verse in this miscellany is autobiographical or elegiac. The series of blank verse "Thoughts and Meditations in a long Sickness, 1712 and 1713" is particularly striking, while the elegies on Sophronia (1711), Elizabeth Bury (1720), and Thomas Abney (1721) suggest that the older Watts remained the laureate of Dissent.

Watts and his work have always represented a tradition apart from the Augustan mainstream, a tradition that nevertheless insists on recognition. Johnson praised Watts's pious intellect, ignored the hymns and psalms, and grudgingly admitted that, as a devotional poet, "It is sufficient for Watts to have done better than others what no man has done well." To some members of a Romantic generation in revolt against the purported artifice of neoclassical diction and concerns, Watts stood for emotional immediacy, the child's sensibility, and simplicity itself. To later readers, well into the twentieth century, convinced of the immoral, irreligious depravity of the eighteenth century, Watts represented a heroic Puritan resistance. More secular moderns, drawn to the century for its satiric wit and skepticism, have disregarded or dismissed the pious doctor as an aberration. Most recently, scholars reconsidering the wealth and diversity of Augustan poetry and its historical connections have undertaken the review of Watts's proper place in his age.

Letters:

The Posthumous Works of the late Learned and Reverend Isaac Watts, D.D., volume 2 (London, 1779).

Bibliographies:

Arthur Paul Davis, *Isaac Watts: His Life and Works* (New York: Dryden, 1943), pp. 271-295;

Harry Escott, *Isaac Watts: Hymnographer* (London: Independent, 1962), pp. 285-296.

Biographies:

Thomas Gibbons, *Memoirs of I. Watts* (London, 1750); revised and enlarged as *Memoirs of the Rev. Isaac Watts, D.D.* (London: Printed for James Buckland & Thomas Gibbons, 1780);

Samuel Johnson, "Watts," in his *Prefaces, Biographical and Critical, to the Works of the English Poets*, 10 volumes (London: Printed by J. Nichols for C. Bathurst, 1779-1781); modern edition published as *Lives of the English Poets*, edited by George Birkbeck Hill, 3 volumes (New York: Octagon, 1967);

Thomas Milner, *The Life, Times and Correspondence of the Rev. Isaac Watts, D.D.* (London: Simpkin & Marshall, 1834);

Edwin Paxton Hood, *Isaac Watts; His Life and Writings, His Homes and Friends* (London: Religious Tract Society, 1875);

Arthur Paul Davis, *Isaac Watts: His Life and Works* (New York: Dryden, 1943).

References:

Margaret Anne Doody, *The Daring Muse: Augustan Poetry Reconsidered* (Cambridge: Cambridge University Press, 1985);

Martha Winburn England and John Sparrow, *Hymns Unbidden: Donne, Herbert, Blake, Emily Dickinson and the Hymnographers* (New York: New York Public Library, 1966), pp. 113-147;

Harry Escott, *Isaac Watts: Hymnographer* (London: Independent, 1962);

John Hoyles, *The Waning of the Renaissance, 1640-1740: Studies in the Thought and Poetry of Henry More, John Norris, and Isaac Watts* (The Hague: Nijhoff, 1971);

Madeleine Forell Marshall and Janet Todd, "Isaac Watts's Divine Delight," in their *English Congregational Hymns in the Eighteenth Century* (Lexington: University Press of Kentucky, 1982), pp. 28-59 and passim.

Charles Wesley

(18 December 1707 - 29 March 1788)

Madeleine Forell Marshall
Saint Olaf College

SELECTED BOOKS: *A Collection of Psalms and Hymns* (Charles-town, S.C.: Lewis Timothy, 1737);

Hymns and Sacred Poems (London: Printed by William Strahan & sold by James Hutton, 1739);

Hymns for Times of Trouble and Persecution (London: Printed [by William Strahan], 1744);

Hymns on the Lord's Supper (Bristol: Printed by Felix Farley, 1745);

Hymns on the Great Festivals, and other occasions (London: Printed for M. Cooper, 1746);

Funeral Hymns (London: Printed [by William Strahan], 1746; revised, London: Printed by Henry Cock, 1753);

Hymns and Sacred Poems. In Two Volumes (Bristol: Printed & sold by Felix Farley, 1749);

An Epistle to the Reverend Mr. John Wesley (London: Printed for J. Robinson, 1755);

Hymns of Intercession for all Mankind (Bristol: Printed by E. Farley, 1758);

Hymns on the Expected Invasion, with Hymns to be used on the Thanks-Giving Day, Nov. 29, 1759. And after it, 2 volumes (London: Printed [by William Strahan], 1759);

Short Hymns on Select Passages of the Holy Scripture, 2 volumes (Bristol: Printed by E. Farley, 1762);

Hymns for the Use of Families (Bristol: Printed by William Pine, 1767);

An Epistle to the Reverend Mr. George Whitefield, written in the year 1755 (London: Printed by J. & W. Oliver, 1771; Baltimore, 1790);

A Collection of Hymns, for the use of the People called Methodists (London: Printed by J. Paramore, 1780);

The Journal of the Rev. Charles Wesley, M.A., Sometime Student of Christ Church, Oxford. To which are appended Selections from his Correspondence and Poetry, edited by Thomas Jackson, 2 volumes (London: Wesleyan Methodist Bookroom, 1849).

Editions and Collections: *The Poetical Works of John and Charles Wesley; reprinted from the originals, with the last corrections of the authors; together with the poems of Charles Wesley not before published,* edited by G. Osborn, 13 volumes (London: Wesleyan-Methodist Conference Office, 1868-1872);

Representative Verse of Charles Wesley, edited by Frank Baker (London: Epworth, 1962).

OTHER: "The Whole Armour of God," in *Character of a Methodist,* by John Wesley (London, 1742).

Charles Wesley (anonymous portrait; by permission of the Methodist Publishing House, London)

Charles Wesley as poet is a problematic figure. Exalted to the heavens by his advocates, credited with supreme genius, the man and his immense work find scant mention in standard eighteenth-century literary history. Scholarly advocates tend to be sympathetic to Methodism and inappreciative of canonical authors of the day. True believers look to the forthcoming relief of Romanticism and tout Wesley as its herald. Wesley's detractors have simply dismissed him without much interest or consideration, presumably as an enthusiastic historical aberration. The immense quantity of his poetry, its uneven quality, and its doctrinaire conviction and evangelical purpose compound the difficulty of editing, evaluating, and interpreting Wesley's work. Wesley's poetry nevertheless provides invaluable insight into the important international phenomenon of the eighteenth-century Christian revival, its theology, psychology, and understanding of the efficacy of useful verse.

Wesley was the eighteenth of Samuel and Susanna Wesley's nineteen children, ten of whom survived childhood. Born prematurely on 18 December 1707 in Epworth, he lay silent, wrapped in soft wool, for his first two months of life. When he was a toddler, the parsonage burned and the Wesleys narrowly escaped. Samuel Wesley divided his time between literary London and the parishes of Epworth and Wroot. In London he collaborated with his brother-in-law John Dunton on the "Athenian" projects and published long biblical works in Latin and English. Familiar with disasters and debt, in Epworth he relied heavily on the management and spirit of his wife. Susanna Wesley provided her many children with their early education and her absent husband's parishioners with spiritual guidance. Competent in Latin, she presided over the schoolroom for six hours each day and led Bible study and prayer meetings in the kitchen. The scholarship and piety of her children are to her credit.

When Charles Wesley was nine he was sent to Westminster School, where he lived with his eldest brother, Samuel. In 1721 he became a King's Scholar and, in 1725, captain of the school. The following year he joined his brother John at Christ Church, Oxford, placing first among the Westminster candidates and earning a studentship. Charles was a brilliant student, held in high regard by his contemporaries. He was, as well, the first Methodist, so called for his extraordinary attendance at the weekly sacrament and his following the recommended method of study outlined in the Oxford statutes, and he persuaded several others to join him. When John Wesley, Fellow of Lincoln, Greek Lecturer, and Moderator of the Classes, returned to Oxford from a year at Epworth, he assumed leadership of the growing group, the Methodist "Holy Club." The agenda expanded to include early rising, Bible study, and visiting condemned prisoners, as well as scholarship and sacramental observance.

When his father died in 1735, John, who had resisted pressure to succeed him at Epworth, fell under the spell of the remarkable General James Oglethorpe, prison reformer, founding father and governor of Georgia, and advocate for the cause of the Salzburg refugees. John agreed to go to Georgia as a missionary and persuaded Charles to be ordained and follow as Oglethorpe's personal secretary. Amidst the terrors of five months of transatlantic travel, John and Charles befriended their fascinating fellow travelers the Moravian Brethren, learned German, and sang hymns, which would prove a lasting influence. Despite the unpleasantness of colonial Georgia, the brothers published their first hymnbook, a collection of seventy hymns, culled from various sources. In Frederica, Oglethorpe's new town, Charles began his *Journal* (published in 1849).

The journal covers the twenty years from 9 March 1736 to November 1756, the years of Wesley's prime. As the account of a prolific poet's creative struggles, the journal is disappointing. Snatches of hymns and other bits of poetry aside, its pages provide little insight into the literary imagination or experience of the author. As an account of the revival and of one man's experience of it, however, the book is a remarkable document. The wealth of Wesley's experience is astonishing, encompassing high life and low, transatlantic travel and scholarship. At thirty he had seen more of life and the world than Henry Fielding, Alexander Pope, Jonathan Swift, or Samuel Johnson. One reads of the struggles in Georgia, the horror of slavery, and the perilous trip home by way of Boston; then of Wesley's life as a celebrity, returned from America. Most important to the poetry are tales of his conversion and the conversions of hundreds of fellow believers, of countless sermons in countless places, of persecution, acclaim, and endless travel through rain and snow. He was often ill and treated gratis by sympathetic doctors by means of bleedings, purgings, and vomits. He got lost at one point, fell off his horse, and slept poorly. He was an evangelical picaro, an ordained Church of England clergyman with an Oxford M.A., composing thousands of hymns and sermons on the road.

Wesley's hymns are indisputably his most important poetry. Like all hymns, they were written for public musical declamation and they are at the same time richly personal but not private, designed to engage and direct each singer's Christian devotional response toward a theologically appropriate end. As was customary, they were metrically limited to available tunes and imaginatively restricted by popular understanding. Wesley's hymns are new and different from the hymns of Isaac Watts to the extent that Methodist theological ends were distinct, that Methodists—who remained in the Church of England throughout Wesley's life—sang no hymns in church worship, and that Methodist hymns as tools of revival and means of discipline bore a heavy weight of didactic responsibility.

The hymns of Wesley convey the grand adventure of the revival, the dangers and delights, the heroic struggles against Satan, and the ecstasy of love, as in "Christ the Friend of Sinners,"

Medallion of Charles Wesley (left) and his brother John in Westminister Abbey

in *Hymns and Sacred Poems* (1739):

> Outcasts of Men, to You I call,
>   Harlots and Publicans, and Thieves!
> He spreads his Arms t'embrace you all;
>   Sinners alone his Grace receives:
> No Need of Him the Righteous have,
> He came the Lost to seek and save!

When Wesley sang these lines with prisoners in Cardiff (on 14 July 1741, as he reports in his *Journal*), twenty of them condemned felons, "many tears were shed." While this is clearly not normative eighteenth-century verse, the precise rhetorical purpose and the tears of joy are familiar from moral-sentimental literature.

The Bible's prodigal son was the model for conversion from sin, return home, and celebration. Methodists, like Saint Paul, lived with reference to the moment of complete conviction of personal salvation, as Wesley shows in "Free Grace" (in the 1739 *Hymns and Sacred Poems*):

> Long my imprison'd Spirit lay,
>   Fast bound in Sin and Nature's Night:
> Thine Eye diffus'd a quick'ning Ray;
>   I woke; the Dungeon flam'd with Light;
> My Chains fell off, my Heart was free,
> I rose, went forth, and follow'd Thee.

As "Lover of my Soul," Jesus then becomes the protector through the storm of life. The convinced Christian is Saint Paul's soldier, armed with God's strength for heroic encounter: "From Strength to Strength go on, / Wrestle, and fight, and pray, / Tread all the powers of Darkness down, / And win the well-fought Day ..." ("The Whole Armour of God," 1742). Indeed, as the title *Hymns for Times of Trouble and Persecution* (1744) suggests, the battles were not always metaphorical, and the well-known hymn "Ye Servants of God, Your Master proclaim," included in that book, is "To be sung in a tumult."

While the revival flourished, external threats and internal troubles multiplied. Parish pastors often refused their pulpits to the Wesleys, despite the brothers' credentials, forcing them out of doors. Parish authorities sometimes resented the revived masses who came to church to worship and receive the sacrament. While high-church critics rejected the Methodists as fanatics, dissenting critics associated them with the Jacobites. (To be fair, the Wesleys invoked Thomas à Kempis in Ireland, preached an apparently Puritan piety to a seeming mob, despised predestination, and quoted Martin Luther on grace, all while insisting on the Anglican ordinances.) The Methodist Societies, organized across the kingdom, suffered a lack of stable leadership when Charles or John moved on. Simple people, full of new enthusiasm, were left to sectarian winds: Moravian, Calvinist, Quietist, or prophetic.

Wesley's hymns, in this context, were supremely functional. In John's preface to the definitive *Collection of Hymns, for the use of the People called Methodists* (1780), he describes his brother's songs as versified divinity. The hymns prescribed and defined conversion, insisted on the free availability of grace, and rejected predestination. They invoked powerful images of Nativity, Crucifixion, Resurrection, and Second Coming, articulated appropriate responses, and insisted on the importance of Holy Communion.

The usefulness of hymns depends upon their accessibility, in word and idea, to common singers. They must also provide popular, albeit devotional, entertainment. Many of Wesley's hymns anticipate cinematic effects, as in "Thy Kingdom Come" (in *Hymns of Intercession*, 1758):

CWesley

> Lo! He comes with clouds descending,
>   Once for favour'd sinners slain!
> Thousand, thousand saints attending,
>   Swell the triumph of his train:
>   Hallelujah,
> GOD appears, on earth to reign!

The theatrical appeal was enhanced by new hymn tunes available to the Methodists. While Watts had been bound to the tunes of the metrical psalter, Wesley enjoyed access to the varied German tunes and the skills of contemporary musicians, including J. F. Lampe of Covent Garden.

The spectacular, noisy effect of some of Wesley's hymns is very different from that of Watts's controlled, baroque tableaux. Just so, the traditional love-longing of the Song of Songs is transformed by new metrical energy, for example, in Wesley's poem "That Happiest Place" (*Short Hymns*, 1762):

> Thou Shepherd of *Israel*, and mine,
>   The joy and desire of my heart,
> For closer communion I pine,
>   I long to reside where thou art;
> The pasture I languish to find
>   Where all who their Shepherd obey,
> Are fed, on thy bosom reclin'd,
>   Are skreen'd from the heat of the day.

The new energy permitted a rush of metaphor.

Hymns also instructed believers in the Christian preparation for and response to death. In no other hymns is the conscious, manipulative artificiality of the genre so evident. Wesley insisted that since salvation was assured, death was devoutly to be wished. As he shows in "On the Corpse of a Believer" (*Hymns on the Great Festivals*, 1746), death was beautiful and corpses were to be envied:

> Ah! lovely Appearance of Death!
>   No Sight upon Earth is so fair:
> Not all the gay Pageants that breathe
>   Can with a dead Body compare.
> With solemn Delight I survey
>   The Corpse, when the Spirit is fled,
> In love with the beautiful Clay,
>   And longing to lie in its stead.

Wesley, in his journal entry for 5 February 1746, records how he visited "our sister Webb, dying in childbed: prayed with earnest faith for her. At hearing the child cry, she had broke out into vehement thanksgiving, and soon after fell into convulsions, which set her soul at liberty from all pain and suffering." The next day "we sang that hymn over her corpse, 'Ah, lovely appearance of death,' and shed a few tears of joy and envy." The hymn continues, instructing the singers in such envy:

> To mourn and to suffer is mine,
>   While bound in a Prison I breathe,
> And still for Deliverance pine,
>   And press to the Issues of Death:
> What now with my Tears I bedew,
>   O might I this Moment become,
> My Spirit created anew,
>   My Flesh be consign'd to the Tomb!

The tears of the faithful are incidental to their experience of death.

Wesley's funeral hymns display one limitation of the hymn genre: an image of what perhaps should be in one's mind if one were perfect in the faith, but it is in fact repellent. Other generic limitations include the lock-step metrical patterning, the demand for doctrinal correctness, the insistence on perfectly clear language, and simple, traditional thought. Given such limitations, it is not surprising that some of Wesley's unsuccessful hymns are good poems, or that verses he wrote without reference to singers better meet one's expectations of lyric poetry.

"Dear, Expiring Love" (*Hymns on the Lord's Supper*, 1745) failed as a hymn because it ignored the rules: its sentiments are not at all exemplary, its ideas are difficult, and its verse is metrically mixed. It belongs, nevertheless, to the fine devotional lyric tradition:

> With Pity, LORD, a Sinner see
>   Weary of thy Ways and Thee:
>   Forgive my fond Despair
> A Blessing in the Means to find,
> My Struggling to throw off the care
>   And cast them all behind.

In April 1749 Wesley married Sarah ("Sally") Gwynne, the twenty-two-year-old daughter of a wealthy, well-established family of Garth, Brecon. The cautious financial arrangements included securing for the couple Wesley's share in the profits of the Wesleyan publications. They established their home in Bristol.

The poetry that Charles wrote as lover, husband, and father deserves consideration apart from his hymnody. Although many of these poems were eventually adapted and transformed into hymns, their differences are instructive. "Jesus, with Kindest Pity," for example, was published in volume 2 of the 1749 *Hymns and Sacred Poems*. Wesley prays in the four stanzas for an earthly devotion that proves "the noblest Joys of Heavenly Love." In the poem "Thou God of Truth and Love" (in volume 1) the lovers see their marriage as a providential means of their attendance on the Marriage of the Lamb. In "Two are Better Far than One" (volume 2) the poet celebrates the spiritual strength that comes from marriage:

> Woe to Him, whose Spirits droop,
>   To Him, who falls alone!
> He has none to lift him up,
>   And help his Weakness on;
> Happier We Each other keep,
>   We Each other's Burthen bear;
> Never *need* our Footsteps slip,
>   Upheld by Mutual Prayer.

These poems effortlessly combine romantic love and Methodist piety.

Wesley's "Hymn for April 8, 1750" (collected in *Representative Verse*, 1962) was an anniversary present, sent from London to Bristol. He begins with the opening lines of George Herbert's "Virtue" (1633), immediately transforming them: "Sweet Day, so cool, so calm, so bright / The

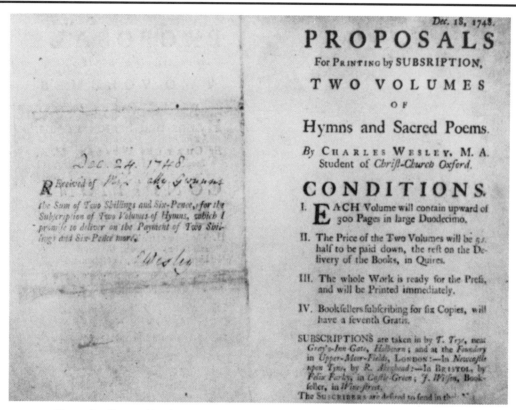

Wesley's prospectus seeking subscribers to his 1749 collection, with his annotation indicating that his fiancée, Sally Gwynne, was his first subscriber (by permission of the Methodist Bookroom, London).

Bridal of the earth & sky! / I see with joy thy chearing light, / And lift my heart to things on high." Sally is a guardian angel, sent by God, a heavenly gift, a bosom-friend: " 'Twas GOD alone who join'd our hands, / Who join'd us first in mind & heart, / In Love's indissoluble bands / Which neither life nor death can part." He will offer back the divine gift when he is summoned to live with God. "On the Birth-day of a Friend," written for Sally Wesley, was published in *Hymns for the Use of Families* (1767). It uses the Song of Songs as a springboard:

> Come away to the skies,
> My beloved arise,
> And rejoice on the day thou wast born,
>   On the festival day
>   Come exulting away,
> To thy heavenly country return.

The birthday poem anticipates the joyful heavenly reunion of husband and wife after death.

    Three of the eight children born to the Wesleys survived. His poems expressing paternal anxiety and grief are remarkable as poems and as documents in the history of the family. They are also noteworthy, as personal rather than exemplary poetry, for their generic difference from Wesley's hymns. A prayer for his then-unborn first child took lyric form, and when the son (Isaac) and his mother later contracted smallpox, Wesley turned again to verse: "God of love, incline thine ear, / Hear a cry of grief and fear, / Hear an anxious Parent's cry, / Help, before my Isaac die."

    The subsequent loss of his son provoked more poems, eight of them published as songs in the 1753 edition of *Funeral Hymns*. In "On the Death of a Child" Wesley tries unsuccessfully to force grief into otherwordly piety:

> Those waving hands no more shall move,
>   Those laughing eyes shall smile no more:
> He cannot now engage our love,
>   With sweet insinuating power
> Our weak unguarded hearts insnare,
> And rival his Creator there.

This is, clearly, a different grief from the hymn grief of "Ah, Lovely Appearance of Death." *Hymns for the Use of Families* includes prayer poems for pregnant women and an elegy on the death of his second child, the infant daughter Martha Maria, in 1755. The baby had been distressed, "gaul'd and burthen'd from the birth, / Only born to cry and grieve." The parents are left aching after the "balm of love."

Also in 1755, distressed at doctrinal politics that were moving the Methodists closer to an open breach with the Church of England, Wesley wrote a series of eight carefully considered "Epistles" in heroic couplets. The poet's brother John and their Calvinist friend and collaborator George Whitefield were among the intended recipients. Only the *Epistle to the Reverend Mr. John Wesley* was published that same year. In these lines Wesley undertook the delicate task of warning his brother, publicly and in print, of the dangers of separation. As it examines sectarian positions and advocates conservatism, the poem bears an almost unavoidable resemblance to John Dryden's *Religio Laici* (1682). The poem was widely published and republished. *An Epistle to the Reverend Mr. George Whitefield* remained in manuscript until after Whitefield's death in 1771. The poem is a testimonial to restored friendship and common goals:

> Our hands, and hearts, and counsels let us join
> In mutual league, t'advance the work Divine,
> Our one contention now, our single aim,
> To pluck poor souls as brands out of the flame;
> To spread the victory of that bloody cross,
> And gasp our latest breath in the Redeemer's
>   cause.

Wesley handles heroic measure comfortably and with rhetorical finesse. This poem and Wesley's "Elegy on the Late Reverend George Whitefield" (*The Poetical Works*, volume 6) were widely published in America.

The year 1758 saw the publication of *Hymns of Intercession for all Mankind*, concerned particularly with national and international politics. Frederick the Great was for Wesley "the Champion of Religion pure," for whom the faithful prayed that he might avoid the Faustian dangers of pride and power:

> Far from his generous bosom chase
>   That cruel insolence of power,
> Which tramples on the human race,
>   Restless to have, and conquer more,
> While bold above the clouds t'ascend,
> The Hero sinks into a Fiend.

Wesley in 1786 (engraving by Jonathan Spilsbury from his own painting)

Hymns on the Expected Invasion, with Hymns to be used on the Thanks-giving Day followed in 1759. In 1762 Wesley published *Short Hymns on Select Passages of the Holy Scripture*, including five thousand selections, a project that had kept him occupied during a long year's illness.

The sheer quantity of Wesley's hymns, published and republished in dozens of collections, has tended to obscure the breadth of his interests and the diversity of his achievement as poet. He wrote political, doctrinal, occasional, and personal poetry. Verses on riots and revolution, nursery rhymes, light satire, and elegies flowed from Wesley's pen. Many remain in manuscript. His later poetry conveys his disgust at the loss of the American colonies, his profound disappointment in his son Samuel's conversion to Roman Catholicism in 1784, and his bitterness at his brother John's ordination of lay preachers, a move that ultimately led to the Methodist break with the Church of England. Wesley died on 29 March 1788. He was survived by his brother,

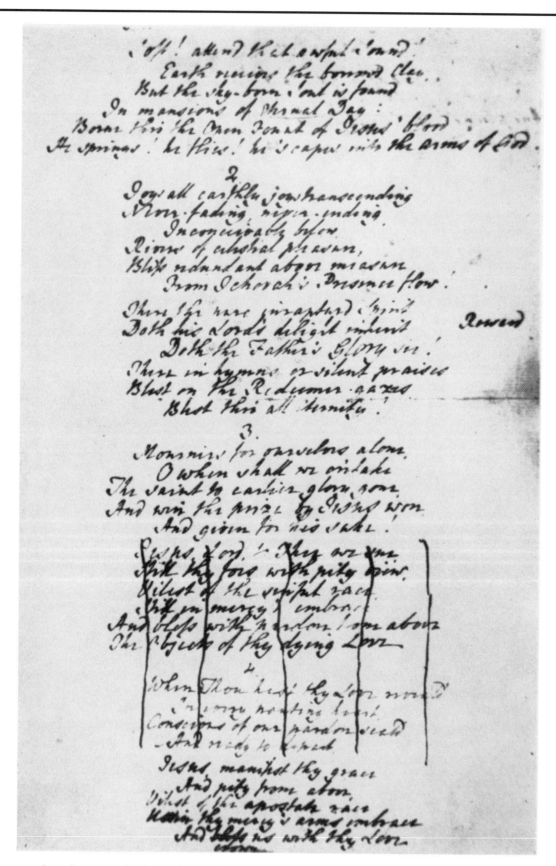

The first page from the manuscript for an elegiac ode by Wesley, not published until Frank Baker included it in Representative
Verse of Charles Wesley, *1962 (E. R. Hendrix Papers, Manuscript Department, Duke University Library)*

his wife, and three children.

Three related sets of difficulties in appraising Wesley's poetry may be collected under bibliographic, ideological, and literary historical headings. The bibliographic problems compromise any responsible interpretation of Wesley and his contribution to the literary tradition. There is no definitive collection of Wesley's work, nor is such an edition likely to appear. The quantity of material is one problem: Frank Baker has counted 180,000 lines of Wesley's poetry, contained in more than one hundred collections of verse and prose. The state of the material presents further difficulties: work by Charles and his famous brother is sometimes indistinguishable. Alterations, recombinations, new series, and new editions frequently frustrate researchers. Finally, there is the nature of the material itself, the ultimate challenge: these are not 180,000 lines of epic, satire, or tragedy, but, for the most part, vast quantities of evangelical verse, communicating a specific vision of Christian experience.

Indeed, Wesley and his poetry are practically indistinguishable from the phenomenon of the Methodist evangelical revival, which brings up the second set of difficulties, the ideological. The revival, by nature, does not and never did permit indifference. The preachers and poets worked hard to provoke responses from their contemporary audiences. The responses ranged from eggs, stones, and angry rejection to swooning conversion, joyful enthusiasm, and transformed lives. Moderns react similarly to the provocations of evangelical discourse, either being repelled or engaged by the affective power of the movement. Many readers resist such manipulation and its seeming transcendence of critical intellect. Enthusiasts for Wesley's verse, on the other hand, have invested it with extraordinary importance, studying the rhetoric, the diction, and the theology of his poetry, especially the hymns, in close detail.

A certain redundancy characterizes such doctrinally committed literary scholarship, and conviction can predetermine critical judgment. Bernard Lord Manning, for example, wrote of how the 1780 *Collection of Hymns* "ranks in Christian literature with the Psalms, the Book of Common Prayer, the Canon of the Mass. In its own way, it is perfect, unapproachable, elemental in its perfection . . . a work of supreme devotional art by a religious genius." Most literary historians are unaccustomed to comparing scriptural and liturgical texts to poetry and rebel at the idea of perfec-

tion. However, Martha Winburn England has refused to "compare Blake to Wesley as a religious poet" since "Blake cannot stand the comparison." Somewhat unusual literary values inform such a judgment, not least of which is the perception of Blake as a religious poet. Wesley's staunchest advocates often seem to frustrate their own campaign to treat his poetry within the literary tradition.

The Methodist revival was nevertheless an undeniably important historical phenomenon in both Great Britain and the United States. Through its poetry one comes to understand this importance. Very possibly one can also come to appreciate the poetry as significant itself, as a real contribution to the literary tradition. This is the third challenge, that of identifying a literary historical context for the poetry of Wesley. This work has begun: as a hymn writer, Wesley has repeatedly been compared to Watts. Martha England has argued for Wesley's influence on Blake's *Songs, Milton,* and *Jerusalem.* More generally, Richard E. Brantley has traced interesting connections between John Locke, John Wesley, and the empirical method of English Romanticism. These efforts all look for connections beyond the Wesleys' immediate era.

Very possibly Charles Wesley's poetic world will only come clear as scholars review and reinterpret the literature of the mid eighteenth century. Certainly biography, associated so closely with James Boswell and Samuel Johnson, was no less a concern of contemporaneous Methodist piety. A religious understanding that located a moment of conversion in each believer's personal history would lead to recording and interpreting biographical detail as a matter of serious consequence. Just so, poetry written with a clearly persuasive, even extraliterary purpose was fitting in Wesley's day. One might expect that a literary history concerned with the larger social world of ordinary, suffering men and women would come to recognize the wealth of information and insight that Wesley's poetry provides.

Letters:

The Journal of the Rev. Charles Wesley, M.A., Sometime Student of Christ Church, Oxford. To which are appended Selections from his Correspondence and Poetry, edited by Thomas Jackson, 2 volumes (London: Wesleyan Methodist Bookroom, 1849);

C. Ryder Smith, "The Richmond Letters of Charles Wesley," *Proceedings of the Wesley His-*

torical Society, 22 (1940): 150-154, 183-188; 23 (1941): 7-14.

Bibliographies:

Frank Baker, *A Union Catalogue of the Publications of John and Charles Wesley* (Durham, N.C.: Divinity School, Duke University, 1966);

Betty M. Jarboe, *John and Charles Wesley: A Bibliography* (Metuchen, N.J. & London: American Theological Library Association/Scarecrow Press, 1987).

Biographies:

John Whitehead, M.D., *The Life of the Rev. Charles Wesley, M.A., Collected from his Private Journal, and Never Before Published. The whole forming a history of Methodism, in which the principles and economy of the Methodists are unfolded* (London & Boston: Couchman & McLeish, 1844);

Wesley F. Swift, "Portraits and Biographies of Charles Wesley," *Proceedings of the Wesley Historical Society*, 31 (1957): 86-92;

Frederick G. Gill, *Charles Wesley: The First Methodist* (New York & Nashville: Abingdon, 1964).

References:

Frank Baker, *Charles Wesley's Verse, an Introduction* (London: Epworth, 1964);

Baker, Introduction and headnotes, in *Representative Verse of Charles Wesley*, edited by Baker (London: Epworth, 1962);

Baker, "Principal Sources of Charles Wesley's Verse," in *Representative Verse of Charles Wesley*, pp. 379-395;

Richard E. Brantley, *Locke, Wesley, and the Method of English Romanticism* (Gainesville, Fla.: University of Florida Press, 1984);

Donald Davie, "The Classicism of Charles Wesley," in his *Purity of Diction in English Verse* (London: Chatto & Windus, 1952), pp. 70-81;

Martha Winburn England, "Blake and the Hymns of Charles Wesley," in her *Hymns Unbidden: Donne, Herbert, Blake, Emily Dickinson, and the Hymnographers* (New York: New York Public Library, 1966), pp. 43-112;

John Lawson, "The Poetry of Charles Wesley," *Emory University Quarterly*, 15 (1959): 31-47;

Bernard Lord Manning, *The Hymns of Wesley and Watts: Five Informal Papers* (London: Epworth, 1942);

Madeleine Forell Marshall, "Self, Sense, and the Revival," in her *English Congregational Hymns in the Eighteenth Century* (Lexington: University Press of Kentucky, 1982), pp. 60-88.

Papers:

Wesley's papers and manuscripts are scattered among the following: the Methodist Bookroom, London; Cheshunt College, Cambridge; Richmond College, Surrey; Emory University, Atlanta; and Wesley's Chapel, London.

Edward Young

(circa 1 July 1683 - 5 April 1765)

Stephen N. Brown
Rhode Island College

BOOKS: *An Epistle to the Right Honourable the Lord Lansdown[e]* (London: Printed for Bernard Lintott, 1713);

A Poem on the Last Day (Oxford: Printed for Edw. Whistler, 1713; Boston: Printed & sold by D. Fowle, 1753);

The Force of Religion; or, Vanquished Love. A Poem. In Two Books (London: Printed for E. Curll & J. Pemberton, 1714; Burlington, N.J.: Printed by D. Allison for the Lexicon Press, 1815);

On the Late Queen's Death, and His Majesty's Accession to the Throne (London: Printed for J. Tonson, 1714);

Orationes duae Codringtono sacrae In Collegio Omnium Animarum nuper habitae. Una a Digbeo Cotes, Oratore Publico, Altera ab Edvardo Young, LL.B (Oxford: E Theatro Sheldoniano, Impensis Ant. Peisley, 1716);

A Paraphrase on Part of the Book of Job (London: Printed for Jacob Tonson, 1719);

Busiris, King of Egypt. A Tragedy. As it is acted at the Theatre Royal in Drury Lane (London: Printed for J. Tonson, 1719);

A Letter to Mr. Tickell Occasioned by the Death of the Right Hon. Joseph Addison Esq. (London: Printed for Jacob Tonson, 1719);

The Revenge. A Tragedy. As it is acted at the Theatre Royal in Drury Lane (London: Printed for W. Chetwood & S. Chapman, 1721; New York: Printed by Hugh Gaine, 1761);

The Universal Passion [Satires], anonymous, 7 volumes (London: Printed for J. Roberts, 1725-1728); revised and published in 1 volume as *Love of Fame, the Universal Passion. In Seven Characteristical Satires* (London: Printed for J. Tonson, 1728);

The Instalment. To the Right Honourable Sir Robert Walpole, Knight of the Most Noble Order of the Garter (London: Printed for J. Roberts, 1726);

Cynthio, anonymous (London: Printed for J. Roberts, 1727);

A Vindication of Providence: or, a True Estimate of Human Life, In which the Passions are considered in a new light (London: Printed for Thos. Worrall, 1728 [i.e., 1727]);

Ocean. An ode occas'd by His Majesty's late Royal Encouragement of the Sea-Service, anonymous (London: Printed for Thos. Worrall, 1728);

An Apology for Princes: or, The Reverence due to Government. A Sermon (London: Printed for T. Worrall, 1729);

Two Epistles to Mr Pope, concerning the Authors of the Age, anonymous (London: Printed for Lawton Gilliver, 1730);

Imperium Pelagi. A Naval Lyrick: Written in Imitation of Pindar's Spirit. Occas'd by His Majesty's Return, Sept. 1729, and the succeeding Peace, anonymous (London: Printed for Lawton Gilliver, 1730);

The Foreign Address: or, The Best Argument for Peace, anonymous (London: Printed for Lawton Gilliver, 1735); republished in part as *The Sailor's Song to the South* (London: Printed for R. & J. Dodsley, 1755); revised and enlarged as *A Sea-Piece* (London: Printed for R. & J. Dodsley & Sold by M. Cooper, 1755);

The Poetical Works of the Rev. Edw. Young, LL.D., 2 volumes (London: Printed for Messieurs Curll, Tonson, Walthoe, Hitch, Gilliver, Browne, Jackson, Corbett, Lintot & Pemberton, 1741);

The Complaint; or, Night-Thoughts on Life, Death, & Immortality—Nights I-VI (London: Printed for R. Dodsley, 1742-1744); *Nights VII-IX* (London: Printed for G. Hawkins & sold by M. Cooper, 1744-1746); collected in 1 volume (London: Printed for A. Millar & R. Dodsley, 1750; Philadelphia: Printed & sold by R. Bell, 1777);

The Brothers. A Tragedy. Acted at the Theatre Royal in Drury Lane (London: Printed for R. Dodsley, 1753);

The Centaur Not Fabulous: in Five Letters to a Friend, on the Life in Vogue, anonymous (London: Printed for A. Millar & R. & J. Dodsley, 1755; Philadelphia: Printed for T. Stephens & W. W. Woodward, 1795);

The Works of the Author of the Night-Thoughts. In Four Volumes. Revised and Corrected by Himself (London: Printed for D. Browne, C. Hitch & L. Hawes, J. Hodges, H. Lintot, A. Millar, J. & R. Tonson, J. Rivington, C. Corbett, J. Fletcher, J. Jackson & R. & J. Dodsley, 1757; Philadelphia: B., J. & R. Johnson, 1805);

An Argument, drawn from the Circumstances of Christ's Death, for the Truth of His Religion (London: Printed for R. & J. Dodsley, 1758);

Conjectures on Original Composition In a Letter to the Author of Sir Charles Grandison, anonymous (London: Printed for A. Millar & R. & J. Dodsley, 1759);

Resignation. In Two Parts, and a Postscript. To Mrs. B*******, anonymous (London: Printed for William Owen, 1762; Philadelphia: Reprinted by W. Bradford, 1764).

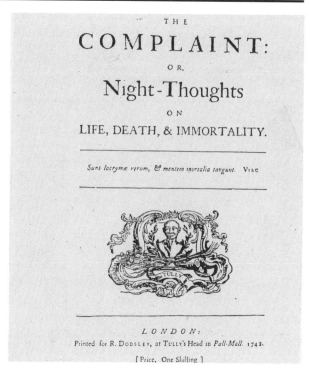

THE
COMPLAINT:
OR,
Night-Thoughts
ON
LIFE, DEATH, & IMMORTALITY.

Sunt lacrymæ rerum, & mentem mortalia tangunt. VIRG

LONDON:
Printed for R. DODSLEY, at TULLY's Head in Pall-Mall. 1742.
[Price, One Shilling]

Title page for the first volume of Young's Night Thoughts, *his best-known work*

Editions and Collections: *The Complete Works, Poetry and Prose, of the Rev. Edward Young, LL.D.*, 2 volumes (London: William Tegg, 1854);

Edward Young [anthology of selected writings], edited by Brian Hepworth (Cheadle, U.K.: Carcanet, 1974);

Night Thoughts, edited by Stephen Cornford (Cambridge: Cambridge University Press, 1989).

PLAY PRODUCTIONS: *Busiris, King of Egypt*, London, Theatre-Royal in Drury Lane, 7 March 1719;

The Revenge, London, Theatre-Royal in Drury Lane, 18 April 1721;

The Brothers, London, Theatre-Royal in Drury Lane, 3 March 1753.

OTHER: "To Mr Addison on The Tragedy of Cato," in *Cato, a Tragedy as it is acted at the Theatre-Royal in Drury Lane*, by Joseph Addison (London: Printed for J. Tonson, 1713);

"On Michael Angelo's Famous Piece of the Crucifixion, who is said to have stabbed a person that he might draw it more naturally," in *Poetical Miscellanies, Consisting of Original Poems and Translations. By the Best Hands. Publish'd by Mr. Steele* (London: Printed for Jacob Tonson, 1714).

Although celebrated as "the learned, pious and incomparable Dr. Young" (as reported by biographer Harold Forster) by generations of British, Continental, and American readers of his *Complaint; or, Night-Thoughts* (1742-1746), Edward Young has been little enough regarded by scholars and general readers of the last 130 years that Robert Birley could enshrine him among other neglected worthies in the 1962 volume *Sunk without Trace*. Few even of his late-eighteenth- and early-nineteenth-century admirers were aware of the extraordinary range of Young's achievement in a literary career that spanned half a century. His work in occasional verse, tragedy, verse satire, the lyric ode, meditative blank verse, and the prose essay at times reflected, but more often anticipated, his century's much-noted shifts in literary taste.

Young was baptized on 3 July 1683 at Upham near Winchester, the son of Edward and Judith Young. At that time rector of the parish, his father would in later years serve as chaplain in ordinary, first to William and Mary and then to Anne, and was, at his death in 1705, dean of Salisbury. The son progressed slowly through the stages of his education, more than once needing his father's influence to effect the transitions. Superannuated at Winchester College, where his father was a fellow, Young twice failed to win a fellowship himself at New College, Oxford, only to be admitted there in 1702 as a gentleman commoner by the warden, a friend of his father. Circumstances over the years twice forced transfers to other colleges, but Young eventually graduated with a Bachelor of Laws degree from All Souls in 1714. Five years later Young took his Doctor of Laws degree, also at All Souls, where as a fellow he resided irregularly until 1730, when he accepted a clerical living from the college.

With the example of Joseph Addison before him, Young had meanwhile set out to secure patronage and a career of public service through poetry. Addison had himself initiated such a career with the publication of his poem *The Campaign* in 1704, rising swiftly thereafter in Whig party ranks, eventually serving as secretary of state. Addison's dual achievement in literary and political realms was extraordinary, but the ambition to imitate him was conventional enough, and Young's first published poem, *An Epistle to the Right Honourable the Lord Lansdown[e]* (1713), had the clear objective of attracting patronage from a newly created peer, to whom Alexander Pope had dedicated *Windsor-Forest* (1713). In praising Lansdowne's association with the Peace of Utrecht as well as his eminence as a playwright, Young was also quite conventional, and in return he received a conventional response: Lansdowne ignored the poem. But a literary career had been launched, and within little more than a year Young had published four more poems.

Of these next productions, each was in some measure a bid for recognition within circles of power—two were addressed to Addison himself—and each can be seen retrospectively to reflect Young's aspirations as a dramatist. "To Mr Addison on The Tragedy of Cato" was published along with Addison's play in June 1713; only weeks later, *A Poem on the Last Day* appeared with a dedication to Queen Anne. An exercise in the genre of the religious sublime, the poem includes shockingly vivid imagery of bodily fragments reuniting at the last trumpet's sound. More often, however, the sublime is rendered in descriptions of a vast, nearly unimaginable setting, which Young curiously renders through a theatrical metaphor: "Lo! the wide theatre, whose ample space / Must entertain the whole of human race." Contemporary readers responded well to the poem, which by 1725 had gone through four editions.

The Force of Religion; or, Vanquished Love, which appeared in May 1714, was less successful, though Young's publisher seems to have hoped to capitalize on political tension by bringing out a second edition in August 1714. This narrative poem, which sets forth the last hours of the Protestant heroine Lady Jane Grey, no doubt confirmed Young's Hanoverian loyalties at a time when Queen Anne's death and subsequent threats to the Protestant succession seemed imminent. But the political purpose here may have been secondary to a more literary one: the immediacy of the poem comes less from its topicality than from the dramatic force of its present-tense narration, ample dialogue, and heavy pathos. Again, one sees the hand, if an unsubtle one, of the aspiring dramatist.

In *On the Late Queen's Death, and His Majesty's Accession to the Throne* (September 1714), Young returned to overtly political poetry. The poem was inscribed to Addison, recently appointed secretary to the lords justices, and surely to receive swift promotion in the new Hanoverian government. Young had by now established himself as a man of some literary talent in an age that still recognized such talent as a credential for public service; moreover, he was at the least a peripheral figure in the circle around Addison at

Four of Thomas Stothard's illustrations for an 1802 edition of Young's Night Thoughts

Button's Coffee-House. Thus, with the great man again in position to distribute patronage, Young was ready for his reward. Letters to his friend Thomas Tickell, who served Addison as undersecretary from April 1717, show that Young's expectations never flagged; but with Addison's death in 1719, they remained only expectations. Young's credentials may well have been lacking in only one area–but that was a crucial one. Echoing assessments made by other of Young's friends throughout his life, Pope once remarked (as recorded by Owen Ruffhead, in *The Life of Alexander Pope*, 1769) that "Young had much of a sublime genius, though without common sense. This made him pass a foolish youth, the sport of peers and poets, but his having a very good heart enabled him to support the clerical character when he assumed it, first with decency, and afterwards with honour." The lack of common sense was no doubt apparent as well to Addison and Tickell when Young first settled on his professional aspirations.

After his initial spate, Young did not publish another poem until 1719, when he produced three quite different works. His *Paraphrase on Part of the Book of Job* was another poem in the tradition of the primitive religious sublime, rendering expansively a single chapter of what the poet, in a note on the text, called "by much the finest part of the noblest and most ancient poem in the world." In *A Letter to Mr. Tickell Occasioned by the Death of the Right Hon. Joseph Addison Esq.*, Young offered the first of his several tributes to Addison, whose example most influenced his career, only mildly overstating Addison's more general influence: "The various labors of his easy page, / A chance amusement, polish'd half an age."

Before Addison's death, however, Young had made his entrance upon the stage. His tragedy *Busiris, King of Egypt* (1719), one of only three new plays produced at Drury Lane during the 1718-1719 season, had a healthy March run of nine nights, netting Young three benefit nights. In *An Epistle to . . . Lansdown[e]*, Young had defined the strength of British drama as the ability to "make the great plain action shine." In *Busiris*, grandeur abounds in setting, character, and action, but any moderating "plainness," such as simplicity of motivation or of plot, is missing. Young was encouraged enough, though, to hazard a second attempt in Augustan tragedy, and in April 1721 *The Revenge* was produced (and published later that year). Less of an immediate success than *Busiris* had been–it ran three fewer

nights–*The Revenge* is a more complicated literary work. It offers greater subtlety of motivation and characterization, especially in the Iago-like character of Zanga; its dramatic intensity, moreover, is concentrated in human passion, not diffused in grand action. Thirty years after it was first produced, *The Revenge* was declared by David Garrick in a 17 August 1751 letter to be "much the best modern play we have" (*The Letters of David Garrick*, 1963); revived many times in the eighteenth century, it remained in the repertoires of English companies well into the nineteenth.

Yet by the time Young's third tragedy went into rehearsal in early 1724, the author, now over forty years old, had begun to doubt that a comfortable living could be made in the theater. Struggling to decide the proper course of life, he twice withdrew *The Brothers* from rehearsal, ultimately giving up the stage in October, shortly to take deacon's orders in the Anglican Church. Some months before, Young had resumed correspondence with Tickell, now first secretary to the lord lieutenant of Ireland. For many of the English clergy of the time, the Irish church represented the best opportunity for preferment, and Young, finally realizing that his best interest, if not yet his heart, lay in his father's profession, appealed to Tickell for help. Having received promises of advancement from the lord lieutenant, Young nevertheless delayed taking orders, probably because he still hoped to have *The Brothers* produced. (Not until 1753, after the extraordinary success of *Night-Thoughts*, would Young see the play staged.) The correspondence with Tickell over the next four years is a remarkable record of Young's candor, persistence, and political naiveté. At one point in the midst of his frustration, Young confessed in a March 1726 letter to Tickell: "I shd not be thus perpetually troublesome, but that the real truth is, that my prudential motive for taking orders was my expectation from my Lord, & but for that motive it had not been prudent in me." But he was never preferred by John Carteret, the lord lieutenant.

It is possible, however, to overestimate Young's political naiveté. While he was campaigning with Tickell and Carteret, he was also gaining the attention of another influential old friend, George Bubb Dodington, and Dodington's political patron, Robert Walpole, the king's first minister–and a political rival of Carteret's. In this court of opinion Young was more fortunate. Beginning in January 1725, he published a series of satires with the title *The Universal Passion*, eventually totaling seven and collected in March 1728 as *Love of Fame*. Dedications to Dodington of the third satire (April 1725) and to Walpole of the fifth (January 1726) resulted in a royal pension of two hundred pounds per annum being awarded to Young in May 1726. He went on to publish a celebratory poem of fulsome praise, *The Instalment*, on the occasion of Walpole's knighthood in July 1726, as well as a sermon, *A Vindication of Providence: or, a True Estimate of Human Life*, dedicated to Queen Caroline, in November 1727. In April 1728 he was appointed chaplain in ordinary to the king, an honorary position, but one promising more substantial preferment.

By now a clear pattern had developed in his attempts to establish himself in the world. Whatever purer literary motives may have alloyed his earlier "prudential" ones, Young had begun to write with the hope that patronage would follow. And yet by 1729, nothing commensurate with his aspiration or his achievement had been offered. As would be the case during another thirty years of literary production, Young's substantial qualifications in the world of letters were largely ignored by those in power. His best attempts in any one genre, however hopeful he might be of their literary immortality, were never satisfactorily validated by the good opinion of those who mattered most in a hierarchical society. His habitual response was to shift genres, to experiment with style, to pursue originality almost obsessively—all in an attempt to validate himself. And so, despite the obvious formal and thematic connections to be found among his many works, the discontinuities among them are far more significant in an assessment of his career—of the works in the context of his life and of literary history.

The satires of the 1720s mark just such a discontinuity. Nothing in his literary production up to this time helps to explain the shift; nothing in his letters indicates budding interest in satire. These poems, then, though they ended as some of the finest of their kind, began as one more attempt on the part of their author to qualify himself for the very world that was his satiric target. Samuel Johnson (in *Lives of the English Poets*, 1781) called *Love of Fame* "indeed a very great performance." Joseph Warton (in his *Essay on . . . Pope*, 1756-1782) remarked that they were "the first *characteristical* satires in our language, and are written with . . . ease and familiarity of style." Jonathan Swift, with less admiration, found the satires *too* easy, their attacks on generic types finally toothless, their praise of peers, ministers, and the

king unconvincing ("On Reading Dr. Young's Satires," 1734). And indeed, by the standards set by Pope, Young lacked a consistent satiric vision. But Young, as a satirist who built poems out of loosely connected portraits of "characters," or types, was less concerned than Pope with an integrated vision. Pope wrote more compelling characteristical satires in his *Epistles to Several Persons* (1731-1735), but he also wrote them after Young's had been published.

Swift's judgment of the satires did not, however, make him shun their author. From the publication of *Love of Fame* in 1728 until Young moved to his clerical living in Welwyn, Hertfordshire, in 1730, he seems to have been an intimate of the circle around Pope and Swift. After a significant period of silence, he even entered into the "War of the Dunces," on Pope's side, of course, with *Two Epistles to Mr. Pope, concerning the Authors of the Age* (1730).

If, after his appointment as chaplain, Young expected more solid recognition of his worth and service to the king, he likely felt even more sure of good fortune when the House of Commons voted him their thanks and ordered his sermon, *An Apology for Princes: or, The Reverence due to Government*, delivered before them in early 1729, to be printed. He had the year before set forth into another new generic realm, that of the lyric, with *Ocean. An ode*, dedicated to the king and to the support of Walpole's foreign policy. Another ode, *Imperium Pelagi* (1730), offered a similar message, though in a greatly expanded form; indeed, Young's preface to this poem indicates that he sought nothing less than to perfect the venerable (but even by 1730 thoroughly outworn) tradition of the Pindaric ode in English.

Despite Young's substantial achievement in letters, despite his faithful service to the king and ministry at a time when both were under sharp attack by a formidable parliamentary and literary opposition, and despite even his extraordinary appeal to the king's mistress, Henrietta Howard, for intercession on his behalf, the poet and clergyman was without a regular living until he was finally given the rectory of Welwyn, Hertfordshire, in July 1730. Nor was this appointment clearly owing to any efforts of his own in the previous two decades to qualify himself for service in government or the church: the living was under the administration of his college, All Souls. A month after the appointment, Young, now forty-seven, married Lady Elizabeth Lee, a granddaughter of Charles II and a recent widow with three chil-

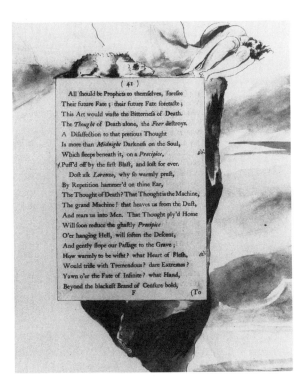

Four of William Blake's 537 watercolor designs, painted circa 1795-1797, for a deluxe edition of Young's Night Thoughts *published in 1797. Blake mounted pages from a 1745 edition of the poems on individual sheets and painted around the texts. Shown here are the title page for "Night" VIII and illustrations for "Nights" IV, V, and IX (by permission of the British Library).*

dren, and soon retired to his country living to begin a life wholly unlike any he had known. For more than a decade after these sudden events, Young was virtually silent as a poet, publishing only one more ode in his old mode: *The Foreign Address: or, The Best Argument for Peace* (1735). He seems to have settled quietly into clerical and family life, having one son, Frederick, born in 1732; one relative reported (according to Forster) that Young and Lady Betty "lived in great friendship and harmony."

Nor during that quiet decade did Young's circumstances appreciably change, though a stepdaughter, Elizabeth, died in 1736 while the family traveled in France. Not a single letter of Young's survives from the period 1730 to 1739. But in early 1740, Lady Betty herself died, and Young's circumstances changed enough to provoke from him a new kind of poetry—and new not only to himself. *The Complaint; or, Night-Thoughts on Life, Death, & Immortality*, published in separate "Nights" between May 1742 and January 1746, and totaling in the end ten thousand lines of blank verse, struck the reading public with extraordinary force. By the time its popularity died out in the mid 1800s, the poem had gone through hundreds of editions and reprints, had been illustrated by William Blake, and had been translated into virtually every language of Europe.

As the poem took shape over the years of piecemeal publication, certain persistent features became defining characteristics. A basic plot emerged in the poet's ongoing exhortation to the faceless, bloodless, silent antagonist Lorenzo to change his hedonistic, atheistic ways. In the process of engaging Lorenzo over many "Nights," the poet worked endless variations on the predominant themes of life, death, and immortality. As a result, modern critics have seen the poem as an exercise in orthodox Christian apologetics, or, more specifically, as a species of theodicy provoked by the earth-centered vision of Pope's *Essay on Man* (1733-1734). (Young had invited the comparison at the end of "Night I," referring explicitly to Pope: "Man too he sung: immortal man I sing.") And certainly the poem did function in these ways. But the feature perhaps most responsible for the vast popularity of the poem, for making it, as Johnson's friend John Hawkins complained (as quoted by Forster), "a favourite with the vulgar," was its intense focus on the poet himself, on his private character. *The Complaint; or, Night-Thoughts* was indeed, as subsequent legend would

hold, motivated mainly by Young's abiding grief over the recent losses of his stepdaughter, wife, and friend Henry Temple; readers were fascinated by the "confessional" quality of the poet's complaint. Such personal poetry was new in 1742, for not since George Herbert's religious lyrics of the previous century had a poet's sustained concentration on his private self informed so consistently a large body of verse.

When in 1756 Joseph Warton published the first part of his revisionist *Essay on Pope*, he dedicated it to Young, largely because he had found in *The Complaint; or, Night-Thoughts* a powerful expression of the new spirit—that of "pure poetry"—he was seeking. Warton was writing at a time when a major revaluation in poetics was under way, and in the work of his contemporaries—Thomas Gray, William Collins, Mark Akenside, and Warton's brother Thomas—as well as himself, the lyrical impulse is strong, even definitive. Young's poem is no lyric, but much of its energy, originating in the poet's passionate, often pained utterance, is essentially lyrical. The poem is simply too large, though, and too diffuse to be embraced as a model for lyric poetry; and though Samuel Taylor Coleridge and William Wordsworth, from the distance of a half century, could safely declare their admiration for Young's achievement, it was upon the German Romantics Friedrich Klopstock, Gotthold Lessing, and Johann Wolfgang von Goethe that Young's poem was most immediately and powerfully influential.

Although Young turned sixty early in the decade, the 1740s saw him form two new and significant friendships. Shortly after his wife's death he began a correspondence with the young Margaret Bentinck, Duchess of Portland, that would continue until his death. Young gloried in the esteem of the duchess and her polite circle, who in turn regarded the aging poet with reverence. It was the duchess, in fact, who would for years lead a campaign to win belated preferment for Young—even to the extent of demanding repeatedly from her cousin Thomas Pelham-Holles, Duke of Newcastle, a promotion for the poet to the first vacant prebendary in the duke's control. All of her efforts, as well as her orchestration of Young's own energies toward this elusive goal, were in vain, however, ending embarrassingly for Young when in 1758, at the age of seventy-five, he was reproved for his aspirations by Thomas Secker, Archbishop of Canterbury, who wrote to him: "Your fortune and your reputation set you above the need of advancement."

Young's home at Welwyn, Hertfordshire, where he lived from 1730 until his death in 1765

However personally gratifying Young found the acquaintance of the duchess, then, his more productive friendship was with the novelist Samuel Richardson, whom he met in 1744. Almost immediately Young was offering advice on the composition of *Clarissa* (1747-1748). The novelist would later more than repay the debt, making suggestions and even substantial contributions to Young's prose works *The Centaur Not Fabulous* (1755) and *Conjectures on Original Composition* (1759).

Sending along an early draft of *The Centaur Not Fabulous*, Young had in a 7 August 1751 letter begged Richardson for "your honest critique. . . . For I write to the heart, and you are master of the heart. . . . Pray let me be the better pastor for being acquainted with you; I fear I am not enough popularly plain." The expansion of that draft resulted in a moralistic satire (provoked in part, it seems, by the profligate habits of the poet's own son, Frederick) upon "the Life in Vogue," a sermon mixing the pleasing incident of fiction with direct exhortation, the goal being to reform the "congregation" of centaurs.

Young's last major work, *Conjectures on Original Composition*, is today often read as a represen-

tative piece of mid-century literary theory, at once reflecting central neoclassical tenets and anticipating revolutionary Romantic formulations. Young's contemporaries, however, were impressed less by the thought of the essay than by its energy. While Johnson, as reported by Boswell, "was surprized to find Young receive as novelties what he thought very common maxims," Richardson, with his friendly enthusiasm, actually gave the more representative contemporary response when he declared in a May 1757 letter to Young that the book was "the most spirited and original of all your truly spirited and original works! . . . With all the experience of years, it has all the fire . . . of youth." Young's essay is, in fact, as Joel Weinsheimer has observed, "blank at the center," leaving originality itself undefined and hence all "conjectures" on the subject unfounded. But Young's purpose was not argument in a discursive sense—it was argument in a homiletic sense. For *Conjectures* is not primarily prescriptive: it gives few rules; it offers inadequate definitions. It is primarily exhortative—at moments exhilaratingly so—another secular sermon, addressed this time to the "congregation" of English writers.

Edward Young at age seventy-one (painting by Joseph Highmore; by permission of All Souls College, Oxford)

Young published his last poem, *Resignation*, in 1762, but *Conjectures* represents the capstone of his career. For in the persistent exhortation to writers to "Know thyself" and to "Reverence thyself" and in the conviction that the poet's "genius is from heaven," Young was reconciling the dual roles that he had for so long and at times so awkwardly played: man of letters and minister of God. *Conjectures* closes with Young's account of the death, forty years before, of Addison. As Young reports it, having called a young relation to his deathbed, Addison calmly directed, "See in what peace a Christian can die." Young's own aspiration (he was now seventy-six) is plain here. As Addison had been his model in early life, so would he be, Young hoped, in death: "His compositions are a noble preface, the grand work is his death: that is a work which is read in heaven."

But Young's own death was less peaceful than he might have wished. After a long decline and much pain, he died in Welwyn on 5 April, Good Friday, 1765. There have been many assessments of the man both more and less generous than that of Johnson, but perhaps none fairer: "With all his defects, he was a man of genius and a poet."

Letters:
The Correspondence of Edward Young 1683-1765, ed-

ited by Henry Pettit (Oxford: Clarendon Press, 1971).

Bibliographies:
Walter Thomas, Bibliography, in his *Le Poète Edward Young* (Paris: Hachette, 1901), pp. 627-655;

Henry Pettit, *A Bibliography of Young's "Night Thoughts"* (Boulder: University of Colorado Press, 1954).

Biographies:
Samuel Johnson [and Herbert Croft], "Life of Young," in *Prefaces, Biographical and Critical, to the Works of the English Poets*, volume 10 (London: Printed by J. Nichols for C. Bathurst, 1781);

Walter Thomas, *Le Poète Edward Young* (Paris: Hachette, 1901);

Henry C. Shelley, *The Life and Letters of Edward Young* (Boston: Little, Brown, 1914);

Harold Forster, *Edward Young: The Poet of the Night Thoughts 1683-1765* (Alburgh Harleston, U.K.: Erskine, 1986).

References:
Robert Birley, *Sunk without Trace* (London: Hart-Davis/New York: Harcourt, Brace, & World, 1962);

Isabel St. John Bliss, *Edward Young* (New York: Twayne, 1969);

Bliss, "Young's *Night Thoughts* in Relation to Contemporary Christian Apologetics," *Publications of the Modern Language Association*, 49 (March 1934): 37-70;

Robert Chibka, "The Stranger Within Young's *Conjectures*," *ELH: A Journal of English Literary History*, 53 (Fall 1986): 541-563;

Stephen D. Cox, *"The Stranger Within Thee": Concepts of the Self in Later Eighteenth-Century Literature* (Pittsburgh: University of Pittsburgh Press, 1980);

George Eliot, "Worldliness and Other-Worldliness: The Poet Young," in *Essays of George Eliot*, edited by Thomas Pinney (New York: Columbia University Press, 1963), pp. 335-385;

John E. Grant, Edward J. Rose, and Michael Tolley, *William Blake's Designs for Edward Young's "Night Thoughts": A Complete Edition*, edited by David Erdman, 2 volumes (Oxford: Clarendon Press, 1980);

Leon Guilhamet, *The Sincere Ideal: Studies in Sincerity in Eighteenth-Century English Literature* (Montreal & London: McGill-Queen's University Press, 1974), pp. 171-187;

Alan D. McKillop, "Richardson, Young and the *Conjectures*," *Modern Philology*, 22 (May 1925): 391-404;

David B. Morris, *The Religious Sublime: Christian Poetry and Critical Tradition in Eighteenth-Century England* (Lexington: University of Kentucky Press, 1972), pp. 145-154;

Felicity Nussbaum, *The Brink of All We Hate: English Satires on Women, 1660-1750* (Lexington: University of Kentucky Press, 1984), pp. 129-136;

Daniel W. Odell, "The Argument of Young's *Conjectures on Original Composition*," *Studies in Philology*, 78 (Winter 1981): 87-106;

Odell, "Young's *Night Thoughts* as an Answer to Pope's *Essay on Man*," *Studies in English Literature*, 12 (Summer 1972): 481-501;

John Sitter, *Literary Loneliness in Mid-Eighteenth-Century England* (Ithaca, N.Y.: Cornell University Press, 1982), pp. 158-179;

Howard Weinbrot, *The Formal Strain: Studies in Augustan Imitation and Satire* (Chicago: University of Chicago Press, 1969), pp. 95-128;

Joel Weinsheimer, "Conjectures on Unoriginal Composition," *The Eighteenth Century: Theory and Interpretation*, 22 (Winter 1981): 58-73;

Merrill Whitburn, "The Rhetoric of Otherworldliness in *Night Thoughts*," *Essays in Literature*, 5 (Fall 1978): 163-174;

Cecil V. Wicker, *Edward Young and the Fear of Death: A Study of Romantic Melancholy* (Albuquerque: University of New Mexico Press, 1952).

Contributors

David R. Anderson...*Texas A&M University*
Carol Barash...*Rutgers University*
Stephen N. Brown ....*Rhode Island College*
Martine Watson Brownley...*Emory University*
Richard I. Cook...*Kent State University*
Paul Jacob...*University of Western Ontario*
Nora Crow Jaffe ....*Smith College*
Gregory G. Kelley ....*Emory University*
Donna Landry..*Wayne State University*
Allan H. MacLaine...*University of Rhode Island*
Madeleine Forell Marshall...*Saint Olaf College*
Caroline L. McAlister...*Emory University*
Anne McWhir...*University of Calgary*
Spiro Peterson ....*Miami University*
Frances Mayhew Rippy ....*Ball State University*
Eric Rothstein...*University of Wisconsin-Madison*
Harry Rusche ....*Emory University*
Harry M. Solomon ....*Auburn University*
Jamie Stanesa...*Emory University*
James E. Tierney ....*University of Missouri-St. Louis*
Aubrey L. Williams...*University of Florida*
Thomas M. Woodman..*University of Reading*
Deborah Baker Wyrick.............................*North Carolina State University*

Cumulative Index

Dictionary of Literary Biography, Volumes 1-95
Dictionary of Literary Biography Yearbook, 1980-1989
Dictionary of Literary Biography Documentary Series, Volumes 1-7

Cumulative Index

DLB before number: *Dictionary of Literary Biography,* Volumes 1-95
Y before number: *Dictionary of Literary Biography Yearbook,* 1980-1989
DS before number: *Dictionary of Literary Biography Documentary Series,* Volumes 1-7

B

C

H

I

J

K

M

N

P

T

Z

71: *American Literary Critics and Scholars, 1880-1900,* edited by John W. Rathbun and Monica M. Grecu (1988)

72: *French Novelists, 1930-1960,* edited by Catharine Savage Brosman (1988)

73: *American Magazine Journalists, 1741-1850,* edited by Sam G. Riley (1988)

74: *American Short-Story Writers Before 1880,* edited by Bobby Ellen Kimbel, with the assistance of William E. Grant (1988)

75: *Contemporary German Fiction Writers,* Second Series, edited by Wolfgang D. Elfe and James Hardin (1988)

76: *Afro-American Writers, 1940-1955,* edited by Trudier Harris (1988)

77: *British Mystery Writers, 1920-1939,* edited by Bernard Benstock and Thomas F. Staley (1988)

78: *American Short-Story Writers, 1880-1910,* edited by Bobby Ellen Kimbel, with the assistance of William E. Grant (1988)

79: *American Magazine Journalists, 1850-1900,* edited by Sam G. Riley (1988)

80: *Restoration and Eighteenth-Century Dramatists,* First Series, edited by Paula R. Backscheider (1989)

81: *Austrian Fiction Writers, 1875-1913,* edited by James Hardin and Donald G. Daviau (1989)

82: *Chicano Writers,* First Series, edited by Francisco A. Lomelí and Carl R. Shirley (1989)

83: *French Novelists Since 1960,* edited by Catharine Savage Brosman (1989)

84: *Restoration and Eighteenth-Century Dramatists,* Second Series, edited by Paula R. Backscheider (1989)

85: *Austrian Fiction Writers After 1914,* edited by James Hardin and Donald G. Daviau (1989)

86: *American Short-Story Writers, 1910-1945,* First Series, edited by Bobby Ellen Kimbel (1989)

87: *British Mystery and Thriller Writers Since 1940,* First Series, edited by Bernard Benstock and Thomas F. Staley (1989)

88: *Canadian Writers, 1920-1959,* Second Series, edited by W. H. New (1989)

89: *Restoration and Eighteenth-Century Dramatists,* Third Series, edited by Paula R. Backscheider (1989)

90: *German Writers in the Age of Goethe, 1789-1832,* edited by James Hardin and Christoph E. Schweitzer (1989)

91: *American Magazine Journalists, 1900-1960,* First Series, edited by Sam G. Riley (1990)

92: *Canadian Writers, 1890-1920,* edited by W. H. New (1990)

93: *British Romantic Poets, 1789-1832,* First Series, edited by John R. Greenfield (1990)

94: *German Writers in the Age of Goethe: Sturm und Drang to Classicism,* edited by James Hardin and Christoph E. Schweitzer (1990)

95: *Eighteenth-Century British Poets,* First Series, edited by John Sitter (1990)

Documentary Series

1: *Sherwood Anderson, Willa Cather, John Dos Passos, Theodore Dreiser, F. Scott Fitzgerald, Ernest Hemingway, Sinclair Lewis,* edited by Margaret A. Van Antwerp (1982)

2: *James Gould Cozzens, James T. Farrell, William Faulkner, John O'Hara, John Steinbeck, Thomas Wolfe, Richard Wright,* edited by Margaret A. Van Antwerp (1982)

3: *Saul Bellow, Jack Kerouac, Norman Mailer, Vladimir Nabokov, John Updike, Kurt Vonnegut,* edited by Mary Bruccoli (1983)